Advanced Intelligence Methods for Data Science and Optimization

Advanced Intelligence Methods for Data Science and Optimization

Edited by

Amir H. Gandomi
University of Technology Sydney, Australia
Obuda University, Budapest, Hungary

Seyedali Mirjalili
Centre for Artificial Intelligence Research and Optimization,
Torrens University Australia, Ultimo,
NSW, Australia

Levente Kovacs
Óbuda University, Budapest, Hungary

ELSEVIER

MK
MORGAN KAUFMANN PUBLISHERS
AN IMPRINT OF ELSEVIER

Morgan Kaufmann is an imprint of Elsevier
50 Hampshire Street, 5th Floor, Cambridge, MA 02139, United States

ISBN: 978-0-443-28940-8

For information on all Morgan Kaufmann publications visit our website at
https://www.elsevier.com/books-and-journals

Publisher: Mara Conner
Acquisitions Editor: Chris Katsaropoulos
Editorial Project Manager: Bhaviya Koul
Production Project Manager: M. Balakrishnan
Cover Designer: Miles Hitchen

Typeset by TNQ Tech

Contents

Contributors

Aabdulhady A. Abdullah, Artificial Intelligence and Innovations Centre, University of Kurdistan Hewler, Erbil, Iraq

Hamed Aboutorab, School of Business, UNSW Canberra, Campbell, ACT, Australia

Aram M. Ahmed, Computer Science and Engineering Department, University of Kurdistan Hewler, Erbil, Iraq

Ghazi Al-Rawas, College of Engineering, Department of Civil and Architectural Engineering, Sultan Qaboos University, Muscat, Oman

Naouel Arab, Faculty of Electrical Engineering, Laboratoire d'Ingénierie des Systèmes Intelligents et Communicants (LISIC), University of Sciences and Technology Houari Boumediene (USTHB), Algiers, Algeria

Mohsen Azimi, Department of Civil Engineering, The University of British Columbia, Vancouver, BC, Canada

Amin Beheshti, School of Computing, Macquarie University, Sydney, NSW, Australia

Diptendu Bhattacharya, National Institute of Technology, Agartala, Tripura, India

Mohamed Lamine Bouibed, Faculty of Electrical Engineering, Laboratoire d'Ingénierie des Systèmes Intelligents et Communicants (LISIC), University of Sciences and Technology Houari Boumediene (USTHB), Algiers, Algeria

Melissa Chan, Institute for Sustainable Industries and Liveable Cities (ISILC), Victoria University, Melbourne, VIC, Australia

Fang Chen, Data Science Institute, Faculty of Engineering & Information Technology, University of Technology Sydney, Ultimo, NSW, Australia

Youcef Chibani, Faculty of Electrical Engineering, Laboratoire d'Ingénierie des Systèmes Intelligents et Communicants (LISIC), University of Sciences and Technology Houari Boumediene (USTHB), Algiers, Algeria

Francisco De Caso, Department of Civil and Architectural Engineering, University of Miami, Coral Gables, FL, United States

El-Sayed M. El-Kenawy, Jadara Research Center, Jadara University, Irbid, Jordan

Armin Dadras Eslamlou, School of Civil Engineering and Transportation, South China University of Technology, Guangzhou, China

Yihai Fang, Department of Civil and Environmental Engineering, Monash University, Clayton, VIC, Australia

Salar Farahmand-Tabar, Department of Civil Engineering, Faculty of Engineering, University of Zanjan, Zanjan, Iran

Mohammad Fathian, School of Industrial Engineering, Iran University of Science and Technology, Tehran, Iran

Amir H. Gandomi, University Research and Innovation Center (EKIK), Óbuda University, Budapest, Hungary; Department of Computer Science, Khazar University, Baku, Azerbaijan; Data Science Institute, Faculty of Engineering & Information Technology, University of Technology Sydney, Ultimo, NSW, Australia

Harish Garg, Department of Mathematics, Thapar Institute of Engineering & Technology (Deemed University), Patiala, Punjab, India

Hassan Gharoun, Faculty of Engineering & Information Technology, University of Technology Sydney, Ultimo, NSW, Australia

Kia Ghods, Department of Computer Science, Princeton University, Princeton, NJ, United States

Ehsan Harati, Department of Civil and Architectural Engineering, University of Miami, Coral Gables, FL, United States

Bryar A. Hassan, Computer Science and Engineering Department, University of Kurdistan Hewler, Erbil, Iraq; Department of Computer Science, College of Science, Charmo University Sulaimani, KRI, Iraq

Alla A. Hassan, Department of Database Technology, Computer Science Institute, Sulaimani Polytechnic University, Sulaimani, KRI, Iraq

Amer A. Hijazi, Centre for Smart Modern Construction, School of Built Environment and Design, Western Sydney University, Parramatta, NSW, Australia

Mohammad Mehdi Hoseini Karani, College of Engineering, School of Civil Engineering, University of Tehran, Tehran, Iran

Juuso Itkonen, Macquarie University, Sydney, NSW, Australia; Cyber Intelligence House (CIH), Singapore, Singapore

Nima Khodadadi, Department of Civil and Environmental Engineering, Pacific Earthquake Engineering Research (PEER) Center, University of California, Berkeley, CA, United States

Ehsan Khodadadi, Department of Chemistry and Biochemistry, University of Arkansas, Fayetteville, AR, United States

Ehsaneh Khodadadi, Department of Pathology, Stanford University School of Medicine, Stanford, CA, United States

Mohammad Sadegh Khorshidi, Data Science Institute, Faculty of Engineering & Information Technology, University of Technology Sydney, Ultimo, NSW, Australia

Mohamed Rayane Lakehal, Faculty of Electrical Engineering, Laboratoire d'Ingénierie des Systèmes Intelligents et Communicants (LISIC), University of Sciences and Technology Houari Boumediene (USTHB), Algiers, Algeria

Parijata Majumdar, Dept. of IT, Tripura University, Agartala, Tripura, India

Pezhman Mardanpour, Department of Mechanical & Material Engineering, Florida International University, Miami, FL, United States

Sanjoy Mitra, Tripura Institute of Technology, Agartala, Tripura, India

Robert C. Moehler, Department of Infrastructure Engineering, The University of Melbourne, Carlton, VIC, Australia

Khalid M. Mosalam, Department of Civil and Environmental Engineering, Pacific Earthquake Engineering Research (PEER) Center, University of California, Berkeley, CA, United States

Mohammad H. Nadimi-Shahraki, International Graduate School of Artificial Intelligence, National Yunlin University of Science and Technology, Yunlin, Taiwan

Antonio Nanni, Department of Civil and Architectural Engineering, University of Miami, Coral Gables, FL, United States

M.Z. Naser, Glenn Department of Civil Engineering, Clemson University, Clemson, SC, United States

Atousa Nasertork, Department of Civil & Environmental Engineering, Amirkabir University of Technology (Tehran Polytechnic), Tehran, Iran

Hassiba Nemmour, Faculty of Electrical Engineering, Laboratoire d'Ingénierie des Systèmes Intelligents et Communicants (LISIC), University of Sciences and Technology Houari Boumediene (USTHB), Algiers, Algeria

Mikko S. Niemelä, Cyber Intelligence House (CIH), Singapore, Singapore

Mohammad Reza Nikoo, College of Engineering, Department of Civil and Architectural Engineering, Sultan Qaboos University, Muscat, Oman

Behnaz Nouhi, Data Science Institute, Faculty of Engineering & Information Technology, University of Technology Sydney, Ultimo, NSW, Australia

Moharram Dolatshahi Pirooz, College of Engineering, School of Civil Engineering, University of Tehran, Tehran, Iran

Morteza Rakhshaninejad, School of Industrial Engineering, Iran University of Science and Technology, Tehran, Iran; Department of Data Analysis and Mathematical Modeling, Ghent University, Ghent, Belgium; Institute for Computational Systems Biology, University of Hamburg, Hamburg, Germany

Tarik A. Rashid, Artificial Intelligence and Innovations Centre, University of Kurdistan Hewler, Erbil, Iraq

Hossein Roghani, Department of Civil and Architectural Engineering, University of Miami, Coral Gables, FL, United States

Alireza Shadmani, Faculty of Engineering & Information Technology, University of Technology Sydney, Ultimo, NSW, Australia

Sina Shirgir, Department of Structural Engineering, Faculty of Civil Engineering, University of Tabriz, Tabriz, Iran

Milad Baghalzadeh Shishehgarkhaneh, Department of Civil and Environmental Engineering, Monash University, Clayton, VIC, Australia

Siamak Talatahari, Data Science Institute, Faculty of Engineering & Information Technology, University of Technology Sydney, Ultimo, NSW, Australia; School of Computing, Macquarie University, Sydney, NSW, Australia; Department of Computer Science, Khazar University, Baku, Azerbaijan

Aliakbar Yaghoubzadeh, Department of Infrastructure Engineering, University of Melbourne, Parkville, VIC, Australia

T.Y. Yang, Department of Civil Engineering, The University of British Columbia, Vancouver, BC, Canada

Navid Yazdanjue, Data Science Institute, Faculty of Engineering & Information Technology, University of Technology Sydney, Ultimo, NSW, Australia

Mohammad Yazdi, Faculty of Science and Engineering, Macquarie University, Sydney, NSW, Australia

Ali Riza Yildiz, Department of Mechanical Engineering, Bursa Uludag University, Bursa, Turkey

Weiguo Zhao, School of Water Conservancy and Hydropower, Hebei University of Engineering, Handan, Hebei, China

Chapter 1

Evaluating hyper-parameter optimization techniques for SpanBERT-based named entity recognition in construction supply chain risk management

Milad Baghalzadeh Shishehgarkhaneh[1], Robert C. Moehler[2], Yihai Fang[1], Amer A. Hijazi[3], Melissa Chan[4] and Hamed Aboutorab[5]

[1]*Department of Civil and Environmental Engineering, Monash University, Clayton, VIC, Australia;* [2]*Department of Infrastructure Engineering, The University of Melbourne, Carlton, VIC, Australia;* [3]*Centre for Smart Modern Construction, School of Built Environment and Design, Western Sydney University, Parramatta, NSW, Australia;* [4]*Institute for Sustainable Industries and Liveable Cities (ISILC), Victoria University, Melbourne, VIC, Australia;* [5]*School of Business, UNSW Canberra, Campbell, ACT, Australia*

1. Introduction

The construction supply chain has become increasingly complex and dynamic, necessitating strategies that can handle a considerable number of risks to sustain continuity and efficiency in operations [1]. On the other hand, proper identification and management of the entities involved from the vast unstructured data that comes into play in this process is a significant concern, and where NER comes in. Some recent advancements in NLP, particularly regarding models such as SpanBERT, have greatly improved the capabilities of NER systems. However, model optimization for such performance remains a challenging task primarily due to the complex nature of hyperparameter tuning.

The construction supply chain is complete of several risks, ranging from material shortages and delays to regulatory compliance issues and financial constraints. Effective risk management in this domain requires a meticulous understanding of the various entities involved, such as suppliers, materials, regulatory bodies, and financial instruments. Traditional entity recognition methods have often failed to work on the diverse and context-rich data typically found in this field. This shortcoming highlights the necessity of more advanced methodologies in NLP, particularly those in which NER can, as best as possible, automatically extract and classify any relevant entities from large datasets. NER has undergone a massive evolution over the last few decades, from the rule-based and statistical models to the currently complex machine learning approaches. With the introduction of transformer-based models, such as BERT (Bidirectional Encoder Representations from Transformers) [2], and its variants, like SpanBERT [3], a new era in NER has been marked, with the state-of-the-art performance across different datasets and languages. SpanBERT is tailored to be superior in handling span-based nature entity extraction tasks compared to vanilla BERT models, with improved performance.

However, SpanBERT is an extension of BERT that has been specifically fine-tuned for span-based tasks, which makes it a highly suitable architecture for NER applications. The architecture includes span boundary representations that enhance the capabilities of the model to capture the context of entity spans, making it more effective in recognizing entities [3]. Such functionality is indeed essential in construction supply chain areas because the proper identification of entities such as project phases, materials, and stakeholders will facilitate risk management. The integration process of SpanBERT in construction supply chain management comprises data preprocessing, model training, and evaluation. Data preprocessing includes extracting and annotating relevant entities from unstructured text sources and a conversion to a format in which training of SpanBERT can be done. Fine-tuning with several hyper-parameters for the optimal performance of the model is required by the training procedure. This is quite a tedious task because of the high dimensionality of

Advanced Intelligence Methods for Data Science and Optimization. https://doi.org/10.1016/B978-0-443-28940-8.00023-3

the hyper-parameter space and usually requires considerable computational resources. Optimization of hyper-parameters is such a crucial part of developing machine learning models since it has a very strong influence on the model performance and generalization. In NLP and NER applications, for instance, learning rates, batch sizes, dropout rates, and the number of layers are some hyperparameters that can play a pivotal role in determining the outcome. The traditional optimization methods commonly used are grid search and random search, but most of these procedures show inefficiency and limitations, particularly in high-dimensional spaces [4–6]. Recent advances in hyperparameter optimization techniques, such as Bayesian optimization, evolutionary algorithms, and multiobjective optimization, hold promise in overcoming these challenges [7–9]. For example, Bayesian optimization uses a probabilistic model to predict the performance of hyper-parameter settings and selects the most promising ones for evaluation [10]. Similarly, it harnesses the power of evolutionary algorithms such as Particle Swarm Optimization (PSO) or Genetic Algorithms (GA) to explore the hyperparameter space more efficiently by imitating natural selection [11].

2. Background and literature review

2.1 Named entity recognition in CSCRM

Many recent developments in NLP, with the development of transformer-based models like BERT and SpenBERT, have brought some inspiring results toward NER. The models are developed by pretraining over large corpora and fine-tuning for the task at hand, with one such task being the detection of risk-related entities in the construction supply chain. This advancement allows for improved contextual understanding and enhanced precision in entity recognition, even when dealing with highly specific domain language [12]. For instance, in Australia, transformer models were applied to identify and classify specific risk-related entities from news articles on the construction industry. The process extracts the associated entities and insights related to particular risk taxonomies that are unique to the Australian construction landscape, hence providing detailed insight into supply chain vulnerabilities [5]. Furthermore, such models can adapt to geographical variations in supply chain risk factors, making them particularly useful in global construction projects [13]. Risk identification and analysis in the construction supply chain could be eased with the adaptation of NER. Thus, the most common 13 risk factors corresponding to the construction supply chain have been recognized and accordingly, the research also highlighted the importance of the project planning phase and the responsibility of the main contractor, who is the key proponent of the supply chain practice [14,15]. This just highlights the fact that there is a big call for a better NER system that will extract and categorize such risk factors from sources of text to provide more effective strategies for risk management.

In addition, NER can assist in analyzing and evaluating the risks. There have been several studies that prove how extracting clauses related to risk from contract documents can significantly benefit the risk assessment and mitigation strategy of construction companies. By focusing on context-aware entity extraction, NER applications are increasingly helping to isolate critical contractual clauses that directly impact project risk profiles [16]. For instance, in Engineering Procurement Construction (EPC) projects, software development using the NER technique has been exploited to automatically extract risk-involved clauses to enhance accuracy and efficiency in the process of identification and management of risks [17]. Additionally, NER applications facilitate contract compliance by ensuring that project stakeholders are alerted to any potential contract risks, which is essential in managing complex project deliverables effectively. This, therefore, underscores the transformational ability of NER in the contemporary practice of risk management with better precision and timeliness of information. Integrating NER with other advanced technologies, such as digital twins and IoT, will further improve the overall framework for supply chain risk management. For example, a construction system with digital twin capabilities attached to real-time can take in supply chain network monitoring for visibility over potential risks. This system uses NER for the extraction and analysis of the risk-related data obtained from different sources to support decision-making and reduce possible disruptions for the stakeholders [18]. Table 1.1 shows a comparison between the functions of NER in the management of risk in the construction supply chain.

A notable research gap lies in the application of hyper-parameter optimization (HPO) methods for enhancing NER systems tailored to construction supply chain risk management (CSCRM). Although transformer-based models like SpanBERT show significant potential in NER tasks, particularly in identifying domain-specific entities, current literature lacks a focused exploration on optimizing these models specifically for CSCRM applications. This study addresses this gap by implementing Genetic Algorithms (GA) to fine-tune SpanBERT's hyperparameters, allowing the model to improve its accuracy and robustness when extracting risk-related entities from unstructured text sources in construction contexts. Through detailed experimentation with GA-driven optimization, the research offers insights into achieving higher precision and recall in risk entity identification, marking an essential step toward integrating advanced NER capabilities within practical risk management frameworks for construction supply chains.

TABLE 1.1 Comparative analysis of NER models and techniques.

References	Model/Technique	Key findings	Impact
Shishehgarkhaneh et al. [5]	Transformer-based NER (BERT, RoBERTa)	Identified specific risk-associated entities in Australian construction news articles	Detailed insights into supply chain vulnerabilities
Aloini et al. [14]	Literature review and risk classification	Identified 13 common risk factors in the construction supply chain	Highlight the importance of the project planning phase and the main contractor's role
Choi et al. [17]	Digital tools with NER for EPC projects	Enhanced accuracy and efficiency in extracting risk-related clauses from contracts	Significantly improved risk assessment and mitigation strategies
Shojaei and Haeri [19]	Comprehensive risk management approach	Combined gray relational analysis with expert-based modeling	Informed selection of optimal risk mitigation strategies
Zhang et al. [18]	Digital-twin-enabled system with NER	Improved real-time risk monitoring and decision-making using a digital twin and NER	Enhanced visibility of risks and timely mitigation
Tang and Xu [13]	Risk analysis methods	Focus on information sharing and communication to mitigate risks	Enhanced interorganizational cooperation in risk management

2.2 Transformer models and optimization methods in NER

Hyper-parameter optimization is critical for the performance improvement of NER systems, especially when advanced models, such as SpanBERT, are used. This section highlights the recent developments and techniques of hyperparameter optimization in NER tasks.

Peng et al. [20] proposed a machine learning-guided model that integrates PSO with BERT and CRF for automatically tuning the hyperparameters in the NER task. This joint computing paradigm does enhance the computational performance and alleviate local optima issues, showing much improvement in NER accuracy and robustness. Zhang and Ma [21] researched the impact of hyperparameter settings for Bi-LSTM-CRF models with Chinese NER. They underlined that systematic tuning of parameters, including the dropout rate and learning rate, among others, must be achieved to make an accurate and robust model. This has shown that proper hyper-parameter settings can vastly improve NER performances on Chinese text datasets. Bhatia et al. [22] proposed Dynamic Transfer Networks for solving the NER issues in low-resource scenarios. The mechanism involves the sharing of hyperparameters between the source and target tasks; therefore, a lot less hyperparameter tuning is done. Such a DTN framework significantly boosts the NER performance through effective knowledge transfer from well-annotated datasets to ones that are not exceptionally resourced. The novelty in the work by Žukov-Gregorič et al. [23] comprises architecture for NER with multiple independent bidirectional LSTM units and soft and hard intermodel regularization. This spreads computation over small LSTMs, decreasing the total parameters and yielding state-of-the-art performance on the CoNLL 2003 NER dataset.

Yan et al. [24] developed the LHBN to improve nested NER by constructing several smaller, simpler local hypergraphs rather than a full-sized one. As a result, this method effectively captures shared boundaries and enhances the boundary information, and it attains state-of-the-art performance on a few nested NER datasets. Lebret and Collobert [25] researched hyperparameter settings in word embedding dimensions for the performance and training time of Bi-LSTM-CRF models for NER. They applied PCA to reduce dimensionality to demonstrate that optimized dimensional settings may maintain or enhance performance but with a reduced training time. Shibuya and Hovy [26] presented a technique to identify both outermost and inner nested entities with the help of a second-best sequence learning approach. This technique, not requiring more hyperparameters than the standard CRF-based models, brought up a significant improvement in *F1* on all nested NER datasets. An improved Cuckoo Search algorithm was proposed by Tong and Yu [27] for the optimization of continuous and mixed hyperparameters in activity recognition algorithms, which also led to significant performance improvements. The technique is relevant for NER models that require tuned hyperparameters. Monaikul et al. [28] dealt with continual learning for updatable NER models to support new entities without forgetting old ones. They used a Knowledge Distillation framework, in which the model was incrementally learned with new entities, and old ones were retained. Lu [29] proposed a combined neural network model for software named entity recognition based on character and word feature extraction with the support vector machine classifier. This method yielded high *F1* and KS performance, which could have improved the named entity label prediction accuracy. Li et al. [30] gave a comprehensive overview of deep learning techniques for NER, while existing methods were categorized using input representations, context encoders, and tag decoders. They emphasized that fundamental advances are in employing continuous real-valued vector representations and semantic composition through nonlinear processing to achieve state-of-the-art NER performance. In this regard, to address the problem, Xu et al. [31] developed the Synergized-LSTM (Syn-LSTM) model through which long-distance structured information from the dependency trees is synergized with contextual information from the linear sequences. This model achieved much better performance in NER, significantly improving the scores in multiple datasets but using fewer parameters.

In another work, Bokaei and Mahmoudi [32] benchmarked NER performance on a low-resource language, Persian. Recurrent and convolutional neural networks were used to extract feature vectors, which were then fed into a fully connected network and a CRF layer. The results showed significant improvements over existing methods. Ma and Ding [33] proposed T-NER: a new multi-model fusion architecture using transfer learning for NER. This combines BiLSTM and BiGRU sequence learning models and uses parameter sharing to transfer knowledge from well-labeled source domains to target domains with fewer labeled corpora. Their model showed the best performance both in small-sample and extensive sample experiments. Wang et al. [34] proposed a document-level optimization approach for domain-specific NER, using Long-Short-Term Memory (LSTM) networks and Integer Linear Programming (ILP) for global optimization. It uses many constraints for better identification of entities that are specific to domains, and it attains much higher precision. Xue et al. [35] proposed the coarse-to-fine pretraining framework, which injects entity-specific knowledge into the pretrained model. This method uses Wikipedia anchors and gazetteer-based distant supervision to improve span identification of entities and fine-grained recognition of entities. The framework performs well on state-of-the-art benchmarks without the need for human-labeled training data. Murugathas and Thayasivam [36] developed a domain-specific Tamil NER system through Conditional Random Fields (CRF) and tuning of hyperparameters using the random search algorithm. Evidently, from the competitive performance this system exhibits in the domain of the morphologically rich Tamil language, feature extraction that is specific to the domain of the problem and optimization of the hyperparameters are of prime importance. Nie et al. [37] enhanced the power of NER through an attentive ensemble approach that uses different types of syntactic information. The key-value memory networks, together with syntax attention and gate mechanisms, encode, weigh, and aggregate syntactic information into the overall model to enhance performance on NER across multiple datasets.

3. Methodology

3.1 Datasets

This research initiated the detailed examination of risk management in the Australian construction supply chain, starting with an elaboration in a structured way on the categorization of risks based on the Cambridge Taxonomy of Business Risks and proceeding with an extensive literature review. To do so, the team collected data from about 2000 articles obtained from significant news sources by using a specialized News API under proper ethical standards. This rich dataset allowed risks in the CSCRM domain to be analyzed in detail using NER. The process was based on the widely acknowledged "BIO" labeling schema and annotated the text corpus, exposing a significant count of 39,500 entities across six categories. This structured approach allows for the practical application of several Transformer-based NER models, including SpanBERT, to analyze the data in extracting meaningful insights in the context of construction supply chain risk. The methodology presents a highly detailed process—from data collection and annotation to model evaluation—that will guarantee an equally systematic approach toward understanding and managing risks in this sector. Figure 1.1 shows the entities considered in this study.

3.2 Transformer models

Transformer models are one of the significant developments in machine learning, especially in NLP. Vaswani et al. [38] introduced this new architecture in 2017, where transformers use self-attention mechanisms for the parallel analysis of sequential data, contrasting with the sequential nature of recurrent neural networks. This makes them much better at handling long-range dependencies. A great deal of research has followed this and has led to more recent and current applications, such as machine translation, text generation, and beyond. The key building blocks of the transformer

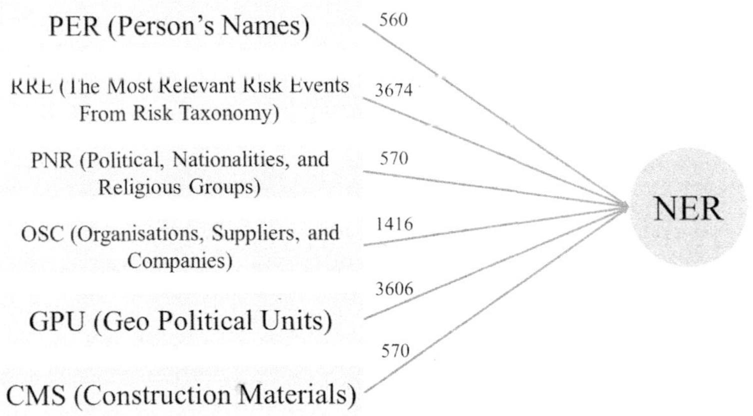

FIGURE 1.1 Annotated c''s entities information.

architecture are the encoder and decoder stacks. Each stack is formed by assembling several layers, and a layer comprises two sublayers: a multi-head self-attention mechanism and a positionwise fully connected feed-forward network. This allows the model to weigh the importance of different words in a sentence independently of their positions. The underlying equation governing the mechanism of self attention is defined as:

$$Attention\,(Q,K,V) = softmax\left(\frac{QK^T}{\sqrt{d_k}}\right)V \tag{1.1}$$

where Q, K, and V correspond to queries, keys, and values, respectively, while d_k represents the dimensionality of the keys. Training transformer models involves optimizing many parameters to bring out the best possible performance while maintaining stability. Standard training techniques include layer normalization, dropout, and gradient clipping. Additionally, transformers can be trained with increased parallel processing ability through multiple GPUs. A primary concern in training deep transformers is stability, which can be overcome with careful initialization and regularization. For instance, a deep transformer architecture with 60 encoding layers performs better with the correct initialization approaches [39]. Transformers have proven to be very versatile beyond NLP in many areas. In machine translation, they have set state-of-the-art benchmarks in both accuracy and efficiency. For example, deep transformer models have outperformed traditional models in language translation tasks with extensive pretraining/fine-tuning data [40]. Furthermore, applications of transformers have extended to several other areas besides, for instance, chemistry, where they are applied to predict molecular properties and reactions [41]. Such advancements only underscore the strength of the model in adapting and performing well in various complicated tasks, pushing machine learning to a new level.

3.3 SpanBERT

Pretraining methods like BERT have significantly advanced the state-of-the-art on numerous NLP tasks using self-supervised training objectives and masking individual words or subword units. Still, many NLP tasks require reasoning about relations between multiple text spans. For example, in extractive question answering [42], one must understand that "Denver Bronco" is a type of "NFL tea" to respond correctly to the question "Which NFL team won Super Bowl 50″ Predicting whole spans, such as "Denver Bronco", is much harder than predicting single tokens "Denve" given the next word is "Bronco". A new model of pretraining known as SpanBERT has been developed to enhance the representation and prediction of text spans. One of the key areas in which this technique differs from BERT is its approach to masking and training goals. While in the BERT model, we mask individual tokens, in SpanBERT we mask random contiguous spans of tokens within the same sentence at once, so that they can be seen as one together. The Span-Boundary Objective (SBO) is also introduced to predict the masked span entirely with respect to the tokens observed at its edge. Thus far, the model has consistently performed superior performance wise [3].

Mathematically, let $\boldsymbol{X} = \{x_1, x_2, \ldots, x_n\}$ represent a sequence of tokens, and $\boldsymbol{M} = \{m_1, m_2, \ldots, m_k$ denote the masked tokens where $\boldsymbol{M} \subseteq \boldsymbol{X}$. In SpanBERT, contiguous spans $\boldsymbol{S} = \{s_1, s_2, \ldots, s_l\}$ are masked such that $\boldsymbol{S} \subseteq \boldsymbol{X}$. The model is trained to predict the span $\boldsymbol{S}$ using the boundary tokens $B = \{b_1, b_2\}$, where b_1 and b_2 are the tokens immediately before and after the span $\boldsymbol{S}$, respectively. The SBO can be mathematically formulated as:

$$\mathcal{L}_{SBO} = -\sum_{i=1}^{|S|} \log P(s_i|\boldsymbol{B}) \tag{1.2}$$

3.4 Genetic Algorithms

Genetic Algorithms (GAs) are heuristic search and optimization methods inspired by the principles of natural selection. They include a population of candidate solutions, a fitness function for evaluating these solutions, and mechanisms for selection, crossover, and mutation. These components collaborate to evolve optimal solutions over successive generations. For hyper-parameter tuning in a transformer model for NER, it is essential to formalize the GA components mathematically. The following discussion details the mathematical representations of the objective function, selection, crossover, and mutation functions:

- ***Objective (Fitness) Function:*** The objective function f, known as the fitness function, assesses the performance of a set of hyper-parameters (an individual in the GA population). In the context of NER, performance is measured using precision P, recall R, and the F1 score. The F1 score is crucial as it balances precision and recall:

$$F1 = 2 \times \frac{P \times R}{P + R} \tag{1.3}$$

For an individual i with hyper-parameters θ_i, the fitness function $f(\theta_i)$ is defined as the F1 score achieved by the model when trained and evaluated with those hyper-parameters:

$$f(\theta_i) = F1(\theta_i) \tag{1.4}$$

- ***Selection Function:*** The selection function in GA picks individuals from the current population for reproduction. In tournament selection, k individuals are randomly chosen, and the one with the highest F1 score (*fitness*) is selected as a parent. This process is repeated to choose a set of parents for the next generation. Mathematically, for a population P with fitness scores f, the probability P_{select} *(i)* of selecting an individual i is:

$$P_{select}(i) = \frac{1}{k} \sum_{j=1}^{k} \mathbb{1}[f(i) \geq f(i_j)] \tag{1.5}$$

where $\mathbb{1}$ is the indicator function that equals 1 if the condition is true, and i_1, i_2, ..., i_k are the individuals in the tournament.

- ***Crossover Function:*** The crossover function merges hyperparameters from two parent individuals to generate a child. For parents i_1 and i_2 with hyperparameters θ_{i_1} and θ_{i_2}, the child's hyperparameters θ_c are determined as follows:

$$\theta_{c_j} = \begin{cases} \theta_{i_1} & if\ rand(a) < 0.5 \\ \theta_{i_2} & otherwise \end{cases} \tag{1.6}$$

where θ_{c_j} is the jth hyperparameter of the child, and *rand(a)* generates a random number between 0 and 1.

- ***Mutation Function:*** The mutation function introduces random changes to an individual's hyperparameters to maintain genetic diversity. For an individual i with hyperparameters θ_i, the mutated hyperparameters θ_{i}' are defined as:

$$\theta_{i_j}' = \begin{cases} \theta_{i_j} & if\ rand(a) > \mu \\ \theta_{new} & otherwise \end{cases} \tag{1.7}$$

where θ_{i_j}' is the mutated jth hyperparameter of individual i. Here, μ denotes the mutation rate, and θ_{new} is a new hyper-parameter value selected randomly from the predefined range for that specific hyperparameter. This ensures that the mutation results in a valid parameter within the allowed hyperparameter space.

In this fine-tuning setup, a variety of hyperparameters are systematically explored to optimize the mode's performance, providing a reproducible foundation for similar experiments. The learning rate is tested across a refined range from 1×10^{-5} to 5×10^{-5}, offering flexibility to accommodate models with different convergence requirements; smaller learning rates can ensure gradual convergence to avoid overshooting minima, while slightly higher rates can accelerate training in earlier stages. The epsilon parameter, tested between 1×10^{-7} and 1×10^{-9}, acts as a stabilizing term to prevent division by zero in the optimizer's calculations, especially valuable in handling very small gradient values that might otherwise destabilize training. The batch size parameter, explored at values of 16, 32, and 64, balances computational resources and training efficiency, where smaller batch sizes allow for nuanced updates but can be computationally expensive, while larger batches enhance gradient stability but demand more memory. For optimizer choice, both *torch.optim.AdamW* and *torch.optim.Adam* is considered; AdamW is particularly well-suited for transformer-based models as it directly incorporates weight decay for regularization, reducing the need for additional decay parameters and leading to more consistent performance improvements in NLP tasks. Together, these hyper-parameter ranges and choices allow a structured approach to model optimization, enhancing reproducibility by specifying the exact configuration used and offering deeper insights into how these parameters interact to impact convergence, stability, and overall performance.

4. Results and discussion

Figure 1.2 shows the normalized confusion matrix providing a detailed overview of the performance of the model, trained using SpanBERT with specific hyperparameters: the AdamW optimizer with a learning rate of 3×10^{-5}, epsilon of 1×10^{-8}, a batch size of 32, and 20 epochs. The matrix indicates the mode''s ability to correctly classify various classes, with high diagonal values for classes such as 'GPU', 'PNR', 'RRE', and 'CMS', which have values of 0.98, 1.00, 0.99, and 1.00, respectively. This reflects the mode's proficiency in identifying these classes with high accuracy. However, the 'PER' class shows a lower accuracy of 0.64, with significant misclassifications to the 'OSC' class (0.26). This suggests that the model struggles to distinguish between 'PER' and 'OSC', likely due to overlapping features. Similarly, the 'OSC' class, despite having a relatively high accuracy of 0.79, shows notable misclassifications to 'PER', further indicating potential feature overlap or class imbalance issues.

The mode's overall performance suggests that while it performs exceptionally well for certain classes, there is room for improvement in distinguishing more challenging or similar classes. The AdamW optimizer's efficiency in handling sparse gradients and weight decay, combined with the specified learning rate and epsilon settings, seems to have positively contributed to the model's convergence and generalization capabilities. The batch size of 32 and the choice of 20 epochs provided a balanced approach between training time and model performance, ensuring adequate learning without overfitting. To address the misclassification issues, particularly between 'PER' and 'OSC', further hyperparameter tuning, data augmentation, or advanced techniques such as class weighting, or ensemble methods could enhance the model's discriminatory power. These adjustments could lead to more balanced performance across all classes, reducing the misclassification rates observed in the current model. To provide a more granular view of the model's performance, evaluation metrics such as precision, recall, and F_1 *score* for each class are presented in Table 1.2. These metrics offer a deeper understanding of the model's effectiveness in classification tasks. For instance, 'PER' has a high precision of 1.0000 but a lower recall of 0.4902, resulting in an F_1 *score* of 0.6579. This indicates that while the model is highly precise in predicting 'PER', it fails to recall many true instances, suggesting potential underfitting or data sparsity issues. Conversely, 'GPU' shows balanced precision (0.9745) and recall (0.9479), leading to a high F_1 *score* (0.9610), indicating robust overall performance. The 'PNR' and 'OSC' classes exhibit lower recall values, impacting their F_1 *score* of 0.7529 and 0.6980, respectively, highlighting the need for improved recall mechanisms. 'RRE' and 'CMS' demonstrate high precision, recall, and F_1 *score*, reaffirming their strong performance as observed in the confusion matrix.

This study considers GAs for hyper-parameter fine-tuning of the SpanBERT model. GAs' parameters for the current study are presented in Table 1.3. A population size of 10 and 5 generations was chosen to ensure convergence without excessive computation, while a crossover rate of 0.7 and a mutation rate of 0.1 introduce genetic diversity, preventing premature convergence and exploring a broader solution space. The tournament size of three strikes a balance in selection pressure, allowing the survival of high-performing solutions while maintaining diversity. These choices optimize SpanBERT's hyperparameters effectively for the construction supply chain domain.

Figure 1.3 shows distinct patterns that differentiate the performance of the Adam and AdamW optimizers. The orange lines representing AdamW tend to show a more consistent clustering, especially in the higher ranges of the F_1 score, suggesting that AdamW might generally be more stable and reliable in achieving higher F_1 scores across varied parameter configurations. In contrast, the blue lines for Adam exhibit a wider spread, indicating more variability and a potential for both higher peaks and lower troughs in F_1 performance. This implies that while Adam might occasionally outperform

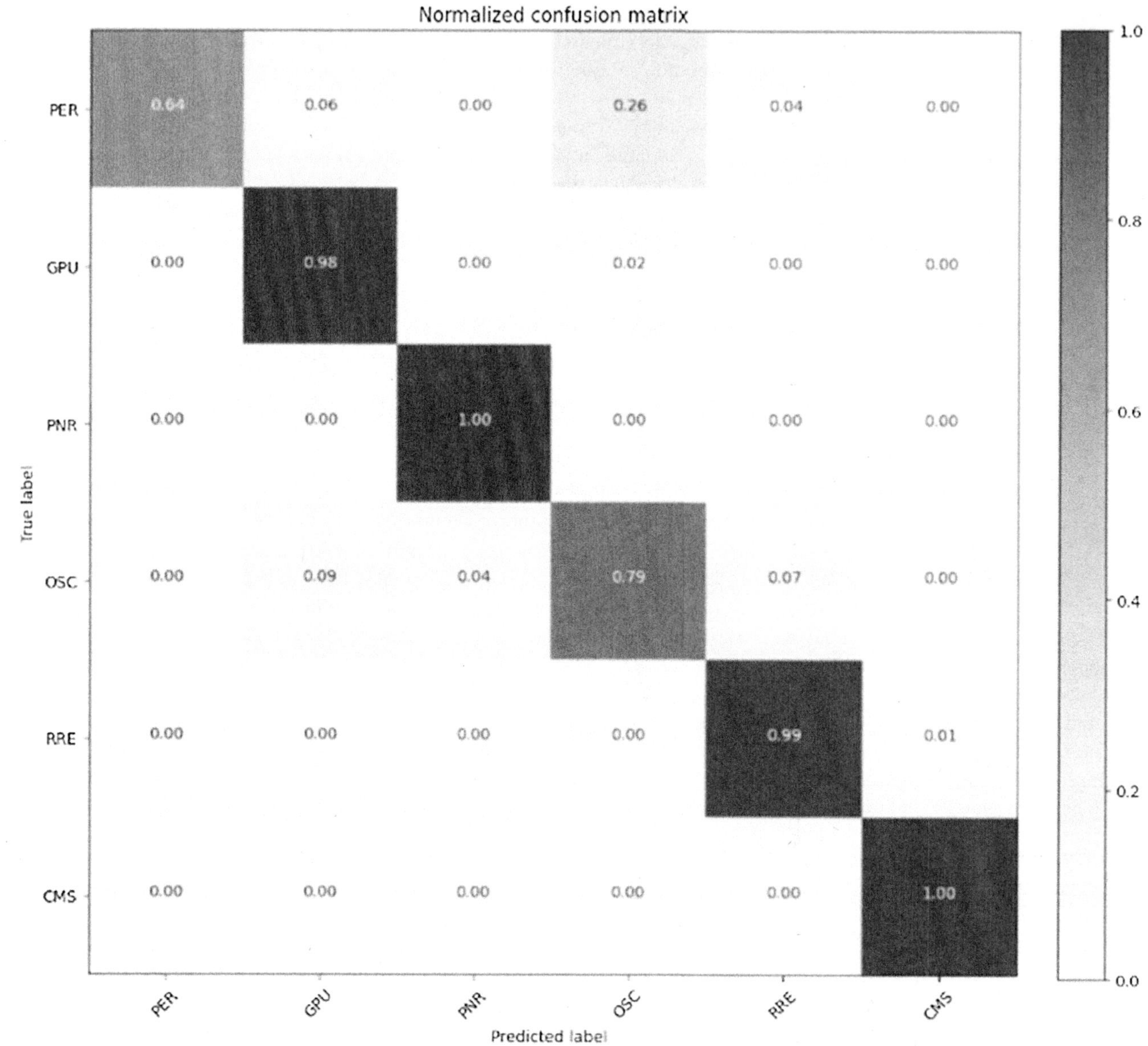

FIGURE 1.2 Normalized confusion matrix for SpanBERT model performance.

TABLE 1.2 Precision, recall, and F1-Score for each class.

Tag	Precision	Recall	F1-score
PER	1.0000	0.4902	0.6579
GPU	0.9745	0.9479	0.9610
PNR	0.8889	0.6531	0.7529
OSC	0.6667	0.7324	0.6980
RRE	0.9728	0.8834	0.9259
CMS	0.9388	0.9200	0.9293

TABLE 1.3 Genetic algorithm parameters and their values.

Parameter	Value(s)
Population size	10
Generations	5
Crossover rate	0.7
Mutation rate	0.1
Tournament size	3

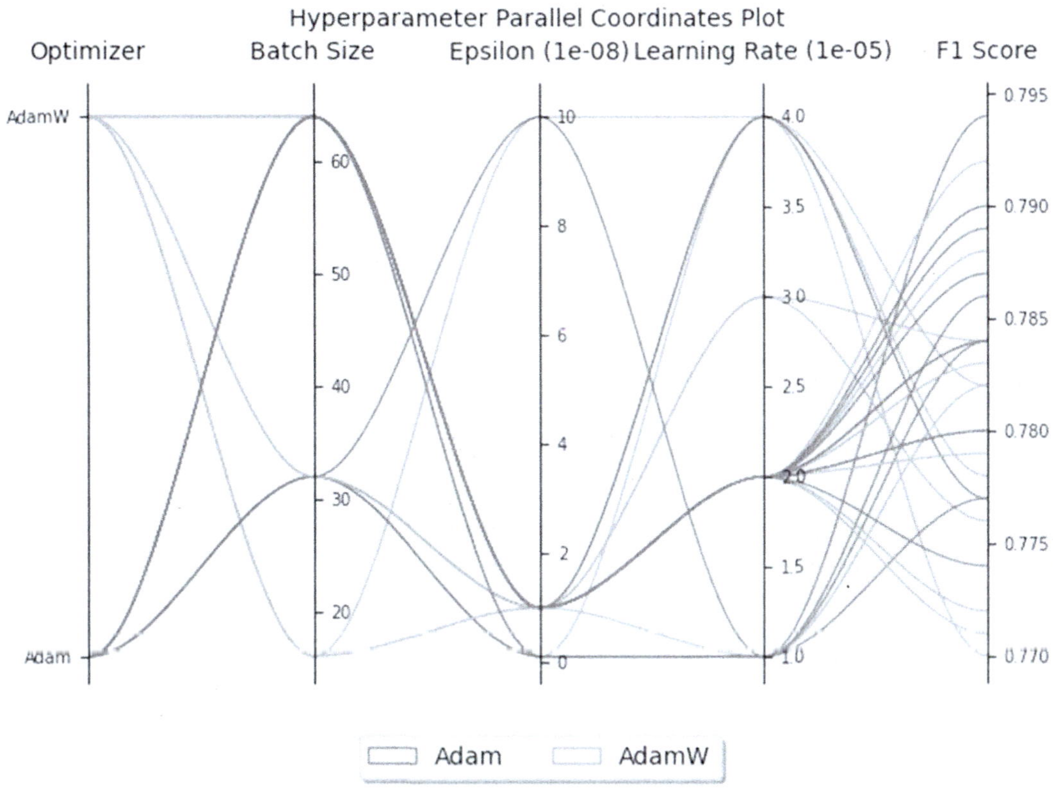

FIGURE 1.3 Hyperparameter parallel coordinates plot for SpanBERT model using GA.

AdamW under specific configurations, it is less predictable and more sensitive to parameter changes. Furthermore, analyzing the influence of batch size on performance, it is evident that larger batch sizes tend to correlate with better F_1 scores, particularly for the AdamW optimizer. This could be attributed to the enhanced stability and gradient estimates that larger batch sizes provide, which in turn support the optimizer in converging more effectively. For Adam, while larger batch sizes also show better performance, the correlation is less pronounced, indicating that Adam's performance is less dependent on this parameter. The plot reveals that some configurations with smaller batch sizes still achieve competitive F_1 scores, highlighting a flexibility that might be beneficial in resource-constrained environments.

Additionally, examining the axes for Epsilon and Learning Rate, these hyperparameters play critical roles in the optimization process. The lines indicate that both optimizers perform well within a specific range of these parameters. For instance, AdamW shows a propensity for higher F_1 scores when Epsilon values are lower, and the learning rate is moderately high. This suggests that AdamW benefits from precise adjustments in gradient updates, likely due to its weight decay properties. Conversely, Adam demonstrates varied performance across different Epsilon and Learning Rate values, reflecting its adaptability but also its susceptibility to tuning. The plot underscores the necessity for careful hyperparameter tuning to optimize performance, with specific combinations leading to significant improvements in the F_1 score.

Hence, the parallel coordinates plot effectively illustrates the interplay between hyperparameters and their impact on model performance for Adam and AdamW optimizers. AdamW appears more stable and generally superior in achieving higher F_1 scores, especially with larger batch sizes and finely tuned Epsilon and Learning Rate parameters. Adam, while more variable, can achieve competitive performance with precise tuning. These insights underscore the importance of systematic hyperparameter optimization in leveraging the strengths of each optimizer to achieve optimal model performance.

Comparing GA and Grid Search (GS) for hyper-parameter optimization in NER within CSCRM provides critical insights into each method's strengths and limitations. GA's evolutionary approach, which employs selection, crossover, and mutation, allows it to explore a broader and more diverse solution space, making it suitable for high-dimensional tasks such as optimizing SpanBERT for risk-related entity extraction. This adaptability is essential in NER, where capturing complex entities specific to the construction industry risks demands flexible, precise tuning. In contrast, GS systematically evaluates all possible hyper-parameter combinations within a defined grid, ensuring thorough exploration. Although GS offers reliable parameter selection for transformer-based models like BERT and RoBERTa, it often requires more computational resources and time than GA, as noted in NER studies focusing on Australian construction supply chain contexts, where GS was applied to evaluate BERT, RoBERTa, and ELECTRA across various configurations for NER tasks [5]. In practical terms, GA demonstrated superior precision and recall for SpanBERT in your study, likely due to its iterative approach that converges on optimal solutions without exhaustive computation, which can be resource-intensive with GS. The Australian NER study also observed that while GS produced high precision and recall values for BERT and RoBERTa, GA's flexibility in navigating hyper-parameter diversity positioned it as more efficient in reaching optimal results with fewer evaluations. This suggests that GA's adaptive mechanisms may be more suited to dynamic and complex hyper-parameter spaces like those found in CSCRM, where risk factors vary significantly. Thus, while both methods are valuable, GA's adaptability in evolving hyperparameters aligns well with the diverse entity recognition needs in CSCRM, providing an efficient alternative to the exhaustive, grid-based exploration of GS [43].

4.1 Practical integration of optimized NER in construction risk management

Expanding on the practical implications of integrating optimized NER models into construction risk management frameworks could significantly enhance real-world applications and operational efficiency. An optimized NER model, fine-tuned for identifying risk-related entities, can assist practitioners by rapidly processing and classifying extensive data from construction projects, including contractual documents, supplier information, and regulatory compliance records. Such models streamline the identification of critical risk factors, thus enabling more efficient allocation of resources for risk mitigation in high-stakes areas such as safety and regulatory compliance. This approach aligns with the broader goals of digital transformation in the industry, where construction firms increasingly seek to implement data-driven methods to optimize workflows and support predictive risk management, as demonstrated in frameworks like the Intelligent Risk Management System [44].

Integrating optimized NER models within construction-specific risk management frameworks offers a proactive layer of risk identification by enabling predictive analysis capabilities, which help identify potential disruptions in real-time. By coupling NER with machine learning algorithms, practitioners can create comprehensive models that evaluate risk factors across various stages of a project. For example, the RISCONA system, which unifies constructability and risk analysis using machine learning, exemplifies how NER and data-driven models can predict high-risk scenarios before they escalate [45]. This model allows project managers to dynamically adjust resource allocation and prioritize preventive actions based on entity extraction insights, fostering a risk-aware culture that improves decision-making under uncertain project conditions. Furthermore, optimized NER models further enhance Construction 4.0 initiatives by integrating with emerging technologies like digital twins, which offer real-time monitoring and simulation capabilities for construction projects. For instance, digital twins combined with NER allow practitioners to monitor ongoing activities and detect discrepancies between planned and actual construction processes, facilitating rapid response to emerging risks [46]. This integration supports continuous improvement and risk reduction, as the NER model's extraction of real-time risk factors from digital twin data helps refine predictive maintenance schedules and improve the overall project lifecycle management. Ultimately, NER-powered frameworks with digital twins reinforce a data-centric approach, aligning with the increasing adoption of AI in construction.

The application of optimized NER models not only aids in real-time risk assessment but also enhances compliance management, particularly in complex multi-stakeholder environments. Using machine learning to process and monitor compliance-related entities across jurisdictions, as demonstrated in studies on automated risk assessment tools, enables the model to quickly identify noncompliant practices and regulatory risks [47]. This rapid identification of compliance risks empowers managers to preemptively address regulatory concerns, ensuring project adherence to legal standards and minimizing potential penalties. Expanding such applications, this NER-based approach can significantly impact how compliance and risk data are integrated into strategic planning and operational management in construction projects, transforming risk management from a reactive to a proactive, data-informed process.

5. Conclusions and future directions

This study demonstrates the significant potential of advanced hyper-parameter optimization techniques, specifically Genetic Algorithms (GA), in enhancing the performance of SpanBERT-based Named Entity Recognition (NER) for managing risks in construction supply chains. By fine-tuning SpanBERT's hyperparameters, we achieved high precision and recall in identifying risk-related entities, thereby facilitating more effective risk management strategies. The results underscore the importance of systematic hyper-parameter optimization in leveraging advanced NLP models for practical applications in complex domains like construction supply chain management.

In preparing this study, it is essential to acknowledge potential limitations that could impact the scope and generalizability of the findings. One significant constraint is the reliance on a single dataset of 2000 Australian construction news articles. While this dataset provides valuable, context-specific insights, it may limit the generalizability of the model's performance and risk identification capabilities to other regions or sectors, where the language, terminology, and risk factors may differ. Additionally, the choice of SpanBERT as the primary model, though fine-tuned using Genetic Algorithms to optimize performance, introduces its own set of limitations. SpanBERT is specifically tailored for span-based tasks, which may differ in adaptability compared to other NER frameworks that could potentially handle contextual variations or nested entities differently.

Future research should explore integrating NER with emerging technologies such as digital twins and the Internet of Things (IoT). This integration could provide real-time monitoring and comprehensive risk assessment, enabling more proactive decision-making. Additionally, further refinement of optimization techniques, including hybrid approaches combining GA with other methods like Particle Swarm Optimization (PSO) or Bayesian optimization, could yield even better performance. Investigating the scalability of these techniques across different languages and datasets will also be essential to ensure their robustness and applicability in various contexts. Finally, expanding the scope of entity categories and improving the handling of nested and overlapping entities will enhance the overall effectiveness and accuracy of NER systems in construction supply chain risk management.

References

[1] S. Matarneh, A.Z. Piprani, R.M. Ellahi, D.N. Nguyen, T.M. Le, S. Nazir, Industry 4.0 technologies and circular economy synergies: Enhancing corporate sustainability through sustainable supply chain integration and flexibility, Environ. Technol. Innovat. 35 (2024) 103723.

[2] J. Devlin, M.-W. Chang, K. Lee, K. Toutanova, Bert: Pre-training of Deep Bidirectional Transformers for Language Understanding, arXiv preprint arXiv:1810.04805, 2018.

[3] M. Joshi, D. Chen, Y. Liu, D.S. Weld, L. Zettlemoyer, O. Levy, Spanbert: Improving pre-training by representing and predicting spans, Trans. Assoc. Comput. Linguist. 8 (2020) 64–77.

[4] J. Bergstra, Y. Bengio, Random search for hyper-parameter optimization, J. Mach. Learn. Res. 13 (2) (2012).

[5] M.B. Shishehgarkhaneh, R.C. Moehler, Y. Fang, A.A. Hijazi, H. Aboutorab, Transformer-based named entity recognition in construction supply chain risk management in Australia, IEEE Access 12 (2024) 41829–41851.

[6] L. Gharaibeh, S. Matarneh, B. Lantz, K. Eriksson, Quantifying the influence of BIM adoption: An in-depth methodology and practical case studies in construction, Results Eng. 23 (2024) 102555.

[7] M. Baghalzadeh Shishehgarkhaneh, S.F. Moradinia, A. Keivani, M. Azizi, Application of classic and novel metaheuristic algorithms in a BIM-Based resource tradeoff in dam projects, Smart Cities 5 (4) (2022) 1441–1464.

[8] M. Azizi, A.W. Mohamed, M.B. Shishehgarkhaneh, Optimum design of truss structures with atomic orbital search considering discrete design variables, in: Handbook of Nature-Inspired Optimization Algorithms: The State of the Art: Volume II: Solving Constrained Single Objective Real-Parameter Optimization Problems, Springer, 2022, pp. 189–214.

[9] M.B. Shishehgarkhaneh, M. Azizi, M. Basiri, R.C. Moehler, BIM-Based resource tradeoff in project scheduling using fire hawk optimizer (FHO), Buildings 12 (9) (2022) 1472.

[10] J. Snoek, H. Larochelle, R.P. Adams, Practical bayesian optimization of machine learning algorithms, Adv. Neural Inf. Process. Syst. 25 (2012).

[11] J. Kennedy, R. Eberhart, Particle swarm optimization, in: Proceedings of ICNN'95-international Conference on Neural Networks 4, IEEE, 1995, pp. 1942–1948.

[12] H.T. Pham, T. Pham, H. Truong Quang, C.N. Dang, Supply chain risk management research in construction: A systematic review, Int. J. Constr. Manag. 23 (11) (2023) 1945–1955.

[13] C. Tang, H. Xu, Risk analysis and research of construction supply chain, High. Bus. 11 (2023) 155–160.

[14] D. Aloini, R. Dulmin, V. Mininno, S. Ponticelli, Supply chain management: A review of implementation risks in the construction industry, Bus. Process Manag. J. 18 (5) (2012) 735–761, https://doi.org/10.1108/14637151211270135.

[15] M. Baghalzadeh Shishehgarkhaneh, R.C. Moehler, Y. Fang, A.A. Hijazi, H. Aboutorab, A comprehensive taxonomy of supply chain risks in construction project management: A systematic literature review, J. Leg. Aff. Dispute Resolut. Eng. Constr. 17 (4) (2025) 03125002.

[16] P.O. Achard, A. Nucciarelli, R. Rosato, G. Svensson, Risk identification in the infrastructure construction industry: A supply chain case study, Int. J. Logist. Econ. Glob. 1 (3–4) (2008) 343–356.

[17] S.J. Choi, S.W. Choi, J.H. Kim, E.-B. Lee, AI and text-mining applications for analyzing contractor's risk in invitation to bid (ITB) and contracts for engineering procurement and construction (EPC) projects, Energies 14 (15) (2021) 4632.

[18] W. Zhang, C. Yu, J. Xiao, D.C.H. Kin, R.Y. Zhong, Digital-Twin enabled construction system for supply chain risk management, in: 2023 IEEE 19th International Conference on Automation Science and Engineering (CASE), IEEE, 2023, pp. 1–6.

[19] P. Shojaei, S.A.S. Haeri, Development of supply chain risk management approaches for construction projects: A grounded theory approach, Comput. Ind. Eng. 128 (2019) 837–850.

[20] Q. Peng, X. Luo, H. Shen, Z. Huang, M. Chen, Collaborative optimization with PSO for named entity recognition-based applications, Intell. Data Anal. 27 (1) (2023) 103 120.

[21] T. Zhang, P. Ma, Effects of hyper-parameters setting in Bi-LSTM-CRF on Chinese named entity recognition, in: Fourteenth International Conference on Graphics and Image Processing (ICGIP 2022) 12705, 2023, pp. 1129–1137. SPIE.

[22] P. Bhatia, K. Arumae, E. Busra Celikkaya, Dynamic transfer learning for named entity recognition, in: Precision Health and Medicine: A Digital Revolution in Healthcare, 2020, pp. 69–81.

[23] A. Žukov-Gregorič, Y. Bachrach, S. Coope, Named entity recognition with parallel recurrent neural networks, in: Proceedings of the 56th Annual Meeting of the Association for Computational Linguistics (Volume 2: Short Papers), 2018, pp. 69–74.

[24] Y. Yan, B. Cai, S. Song, Nested named entity recognition as building local hypergraphs, Proc. AAAI Conf. Artif. Intell. 37 (11) (2023) 13878–13886.

[25] R. Lebret and R. Collobert, Word emdeddings through hellinger pca, arXiv preprint arXiv:1312.5542, 2013.

[26] T. Shibuya, E. Hovy, Nested Named Entity Recognition via Second-Best Sequence Learning and Decoding, 8, Transactions of the Association for Computational Linguistics, 2020, pp. 605–620.

[27] Y. Tong, B. Yu, Research on hyper-parameter optimization of activity recognition algorithm based on improved cuckoo search, Entropy 24 (6) (2022) 845.

[28] N. Monaikul, G. Castellucci, S. Filice, O. Rokhlenko, Continual learning for named entity recognition, Proc. AAAI Conf. Artif. Intell. 35 (15) (2021) 13570–13577.

[29] Q. Lu, Simulation of named entity label prediction based on combined neural network, in: 2022 2nd International Conference on Frontiers of Electronics, Information and Computation Technologies (ICFEICT), IEEE, 2022, pp. 623–626.

[30] J. Li, A. Sun, J. Han, C. Li, A survey on deep learning for named entity recognition, IEEE Trans. Knowl. Data Eng. 34 (1) (2020) 50–70.

[31] L. Xu, Z. Jie, W. Lu, L. Bing, Better Feature Integration for Named Entity Recognition, arXiv preprint arXiv:2104.05316, 2021.

[32] M.H. Bokaei, M. Mahmoudi, Improved deep persian named entity recognition, in: 2018 9th International Symposium on Telecommunications (IST), IEEE, 2018, pp. 381–386.

[33] H. Ma, Z. Ding, Research on multi-model fusion for named entity recognition based on loop parameter sharing transfer learning, in: 2022 7th IEEE International Conference on Data Science in Cyberspace (DSC), IEEE, 2022, pp. 564–569.

[34] L. Wang, S. Li, Q. Yan, G. Zhou, Domain-specific named entity recognition with document-level optimization, ACM Trans. Asian Low-Resour. Lang. Inf. Process. 17 (4) (2018) 1–15.

[35] M. Xue, B. Yu, Z. Zhang, T. Liu, Y. Zhang, B. Wang, Coarse-to-fine Pre-training for Named Entity Recognition, arXiv preprint arXiv:2010.08210, 2020.

[36] R. Murugathas, U. Thayasivam, Domain specific named entity recognition in tamil, in: 2022 Moratuwa Engineering Research Conference (MERCon), IEEE, 2022, pp. 1–6.

[37] Y. Nie, Y. Tian, Y. Song, X. Ao, X. Wan, Improving Named Entity Recognition with Attentive Ensemble of Syntactic Information, arXiv preprint arXiv:2010.15466, 2020.

[38] A. Vaswani, et al., Attention is all you need, Adv. Neural Inf. Process. Syst. 30 (2017).

[39] X. Liu, K. Duh, L. Liu, J. Gao, Very Deep Transformers for Neural Machine Translation, arXiv preprint arXiv:2008.07772, 2020.

[40] Q. Wang, et al., Learning Deep Transformer Models for Machine Translation, arXiv preprint arXiv:1906.01787, 2019.

[41] H. Abdel-Aty, I.R. Gould, Large-scale distributed training of transformers for chemical fingerprinting, J. Chem. Inf. Model. 62 (20) (2022) 4852–4862.

[42] P. Rajpurkar, J. Zhang, K. Lopyrev, P. Liang, Squad: 100,000+ Questions for Machine Comprehension of Text, arXiv preprint arXiv:1606.05250, 2016.

[43] M.B. Shishehgarkhaneh, M. Chan, R.C. Moehler, Y. Fang, A.A. Hijazi, H. Aboutorab, Named entity recognition in construction supply chain risk management using transformer-based models and genetic algorithm-driven hyperparameter tuning, in: International Conference on Electrical, Computer and Energy Technologies (ICECET, 2024, IEEE, 2024, pp. 1–7.

[44] L. Chenya, E. Aminudin, S. Mohd, L.S. Yap, Intelligent risk management in construction projects: Systematic literature review, IEEE Access 10 (2022) 72936–72954.

[45] D. Kifokeris, Y. Xenidis, The RISCONA system: Constructability appraisal through the identification and assessment of technical project risks sources, in: IABSE Symposium Guimarães 2019 Report 114, 2019, pp. 1696–1703.

[46] M. Kor, I. Yitmen, S. Alizadehsalehi, An investigation for integration of deep learning and digital twins towards construction 4.0, Smart Sustain. Built Environ. 12 (3) (2023) 461–487.

[47] G. Ma, Z. Wu, J. Jia, S. Shang, Safety risk factors comprehensive analysis for construction project: Combined cascading effect and machine learning approach, Saf. Sci. 143 (2021) 105410.

Chapter 2

Improving damage detection accuracy through wavelet analysis and hybrid machine learning models

Mohsen Azimi[1], Armin Dadras Eslamlou[2], Aliakbar Yaghoubzadeh[3] and T.Y. Yang[1]

[1]*Department of Civil Engineering, The University of British Columbia, Vancouver, BC, Canada;* [2]*School of Civil Engineering and Transportation, South China University of Technology, Guangzhou, China;* [3]*Department of Infrastructure Engineering, University of Melbourne, Parkville, VIC, Australia*

1. Introduction

Civil infrastructures are vulnerable to damage due to ambient conditions, which can influence their life-cycle performance and may lead to changes in dynamic characteristics, including stiffness as well as stability. The primary purpose of early damage detection in structural health monitoring (SHM) is to ensure the integrity of the system [1–4]. The response data from system observables lie at the center of SHM methods, which may be acquired using sensors, derived, or simulated. With recent technological advancements, it is now possible to deploy a large network of sensors. The acquired data may not always yield sufficient information using the conventional SHM methods, and researchers have proposed several machine learning-based techniques to efficiently and accurately estimate the global health condition of structures [5–7]. Among several advantages of these techniques are their adaptability and ability to deal with large data sets. These techniques mainly consist of two steps: feature (specific characteristics) extraction from the acquired data and classification that maps input to output classes. The data-driven methods attempt to identify perturbations in the measured responses for different damage states. Pattern recognition problems can leverage data-driven anomaly detection through neural networks [8]. An approach for extracting damage-sensitive features is to use signal processing tools with the acquired time-domain response data to detect changes in the response characteristics [9,10]. Other alternative methods effectively exploit the characteristics of the transformed signals using wavelet coefficients [4,11] and wavelet packet transform (WPT) [12,13].

Recently, several limitations of traditional neural networks have been addressed through deep learning for feature extraction and classifying tasks, particularly in damage detection problems without hand-designed features [14,15]. Convolutional neural networks (CNNs) are at the core of modern deep learning techniques. They have been extensively used in SHM applications [5,16,17], image-based anomaly detection [16,18], concrete crack detection [19], pavement crack detection [20], and overall system condition assessment [21].

Recent studies showed that support vector machine (SVM) for damage detection and localization are very effective [22–24]. The present study proposes a wavelet-based 2D-CNN model for damage detection, where the model utilizes vibration response data. A pretrained CNN is used as the feature extraction tool to improve the performance, while the SVM is used for classification. Instead of using the raw original acceleration responses, the transformed data are used to improve the accuracy of the technique using WPT [25]. A finite element model of a cable-stayed bridge was created using SAP2000 software to generate acceleration response data for the considered damage cases. The data is preprocessed in MATLAB before importing to Python, which provides powerful and advanced libraries in machine learning. The framework for implementation of the wavelet-based health monitoring method using deep learning is briefly illustrated in Fig. 2.1. In summary, the response data of the bridge under the sine-sweep excitations is transmitted to cloud-based

Advanced Intelligence Methods for Data Science and Optimization. https://doi.org/10.1016/B978-0-443-28940-8.00015-4

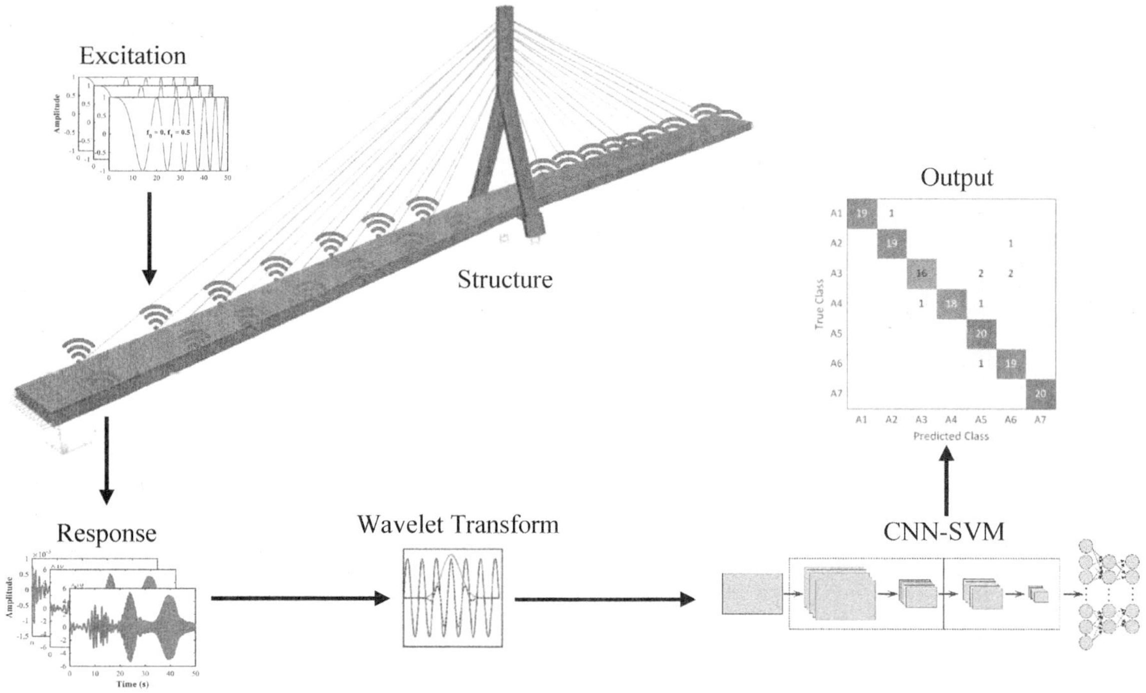

FIGURE 2.1 Workflow of the wavelet-based SHM of cable-stayed bridges using CNN.

storage and the computer. Then, the raw responses are transformed using WPT and fed into the deep learning models. The final outputs show the possibility of the damage location based on prior training data.

2. Wavelet analysis

The time-frequency decomposition methods, such as the wavelet transform, are gaining popularity in SHM. The continuous wavelet transformation (CWT) is described as [26]:

$$Wx(a,b) = x \otimes \psi_{b,a}(t) = \frac{1}{\sqrt{a}} \int_{-\infty}^{+\infty} x(t)\psi^* \left(\frac{t-b}{a}\right) dt, \tag{2.1}$$

where, ψ^* is the complex conjugate of ψ, a is a scale factor, and b is the translation coefficient. Therefore, the original time-domain series, $x(t)$, can be decomposed into the mother wavelet, or the basic function $\psi\left(\frac{t-b}{a}\right)$. With a scale factor of $a = 2$, the spectrum of the wavelet stretches by 2. Thus, for a discrete wavelet transformation (DWT):

$$Wx(j,k) = \int_{-\infty}^{+\infty} x(t)2^{\frac{j}{2}}\psi^*\left(2^j t - k\right)dt \tag{2.2}$$

Unlike CWT or DWT, the wavelet packet decomposition (WPD) uses different time-frequency windows for the decomposition of the original signal that are perhaps hard to perform using CWT or DWT alone. The wavelet pocket function is defined as:

$$\psi^i_{j,k}(t) = 2^{\frac{j}{2}}\psi^i\left(2^j t - k\right) \quad i = 1, 2, \ldots \tag{2.3}$$

where j is the scale factor, and k is the transition factor. Eqs. (2.4) and (2.5) show the recursive procedure to obtain ψ^i.

$$\psi^{2i}(t) = \sqrt{2} \sum_{k=-\infty}^{\infty} h(k)\psi^i(2t - k) \tag{2.4}$$

$$\psi^{2i+1}(t) = \sqrt{2}\sum_{k=-\infty}^{\infty} g(k)\psi^{i}(2t-k) \quad (2.5)$$

The quadrature mirror filters, $h(k)$ and $g(k)$, are defined based on the mother wavelet, ψ^1. This relation is visually illustrated in Fig. 2.2, where the frequency resolution is higher for the lower levels, while the time resolution is higher for the top levels. The wavelet transforms, and WPT is shown with thick and thick-dashed boxes. The letter H indicates high-pass filtering and the letter L indicates low-pass filtering. A is the approximation, and D is the details coefficient. In this study, the fifth-level WPT serves as the input for the 2D-CNN.

3. Convolution neural network

Convolutional Neural Networks (CNN) recently gained significant attention in SHM applications. The architecture of a CNN model is presented in Fig. 2.3. The following paragraphs describe each component in detail.

CNN layers: convolution layers are the essential parts of a CNN, which is followed by a pooling layer. Fig. 2.4 illustrates the 2D convolution process. The max-pooling layers reduce the convolution outputs. The stride parameter is set to 1 for the convolution layers and 2 for the pooling layers.

The fully connected layers are the last components of a CNN model. To map the n-dimensional outputs of the convolution layers to the FC layers, all the data is transformed into a vector called "flatten". FC layers do the classification tasks based on the features extracted by the convolution layers. Eventually, the final SoftMax layer maps the classification layers to the output labels.

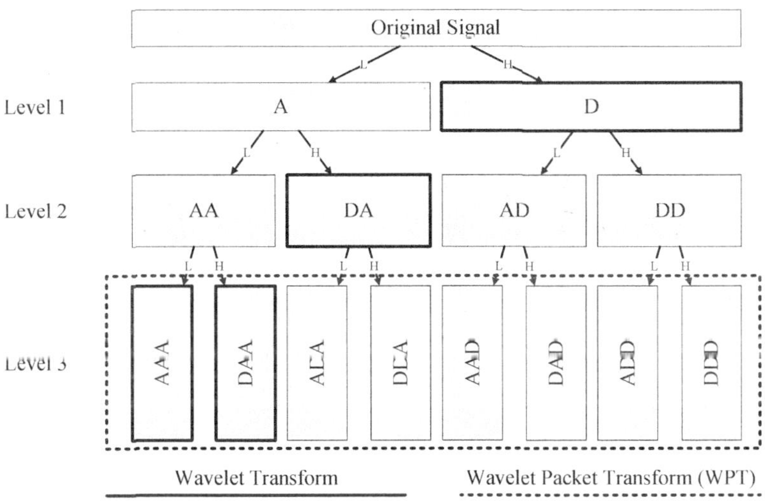

FIGURE 2.2 The wavelet transform and wavelet packet transform.

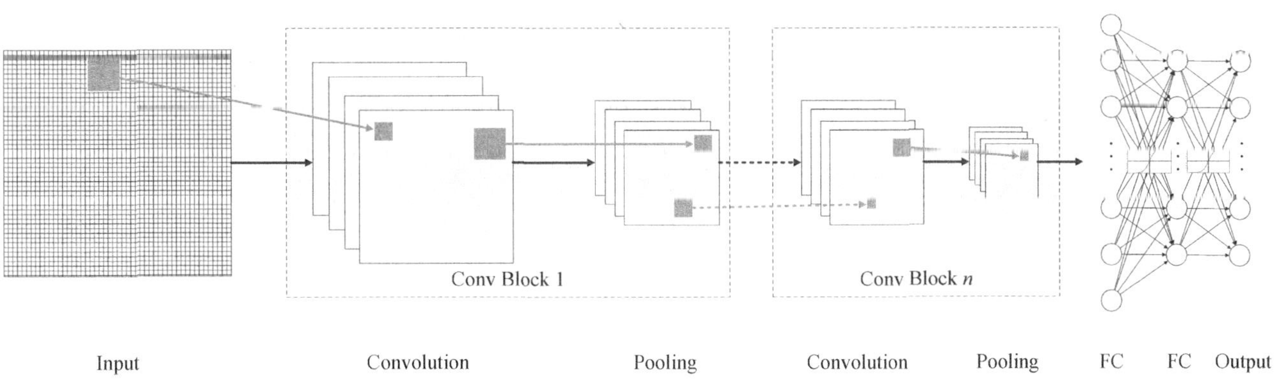

FIGURE 2.3 A typical CNN with n convolution blocks.

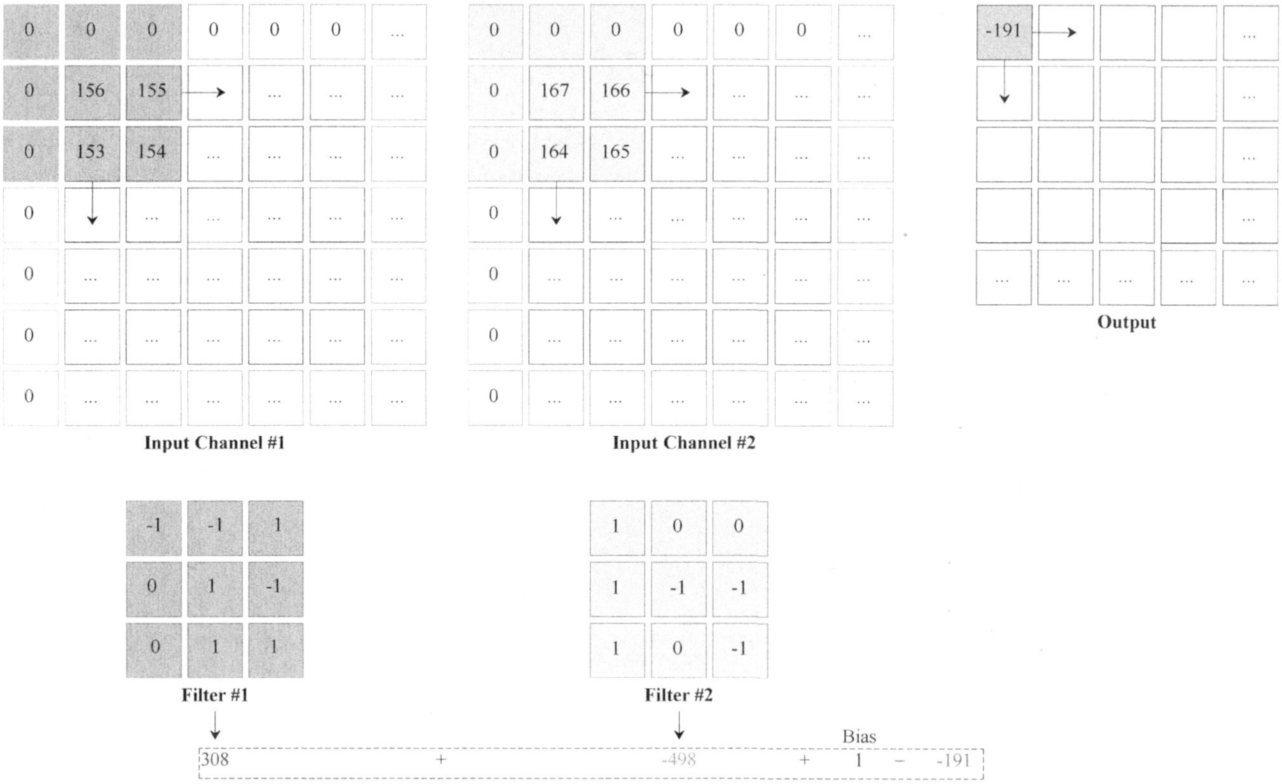

FIGURE 2.4 Illustration of 2D convolution for two-channel input data.

Activation functions: They are used in CNN architecture to implement a nonlinear mapping between each layer and block of a network. The most frequently used activation functions in the literature are the rectified linear units (ReLU) and the sigmoidal function, while the former has proven to have superior performance in deeper networks [27,28]. However, the ReLU may deactivate some of the weights in the negative region. This issue can be solved using the leaky ReLU function [29]. In this study, both ReLU and leaky ReLU are used.

Regularization: One of the major problems in training a model is overfitting. Therefore, a generalization method needs to be considered. Adding dropout layers after FC layers can solve this problem. Another issue with training a network is the vanishing gradient, known as the internal covariate shift. By normalizing the mini-batch data at each iteration, the outputs can have a similar distribution, and thus, easier for the next training batch to be trained with a higher learning rate. This method is called batch normalization (BN), which was developed by Google researchers, and is defined as follows:

$$\mu_B = \frac{1}{m}\sum_{i=1}^{m} x_i \tag{2.6}$$

$$\sigma_B^2 = \frac{1}{m}\sum_{i=1}^{m} (x_i - \mu_B)^2 \tag{2.7}$$

$$\widehat{x}_i = \frac{x_i - \mu_B}{\sqrt{(\sigma_B^2 + \epsilon)}} \tag{2.8}$$

$$y_i = \gamma\widehat{x}_i + \beta \tag{2.9}$$

where, μ_B and σ_B^2 denote the means variance values of the mini batch, respectively. $\widehat{x}_i$ is the normalized data that is scaled and shifted as y_i. γ and β are the parameters to be learned during the training stages. BN is introduced to several deep learning algorithms, and it is well-documented in the literature. More details can be obtained from the original paper by Ioffe and Szegedy [30]. By using BN, there will be no need for a dropout, especially for a small amount of data.

In addition to regularization, it is necessary to validate the trained network to avoid possible under- and overfitting. In this study, the *k*-fold cross-validation technique is used, which splits the whole shuffled data into *k* folds. One of the folds is selected for validation with each complete run. The final accuracy is the average of the accuracies from each run. This method is shown in Fig. 2.5.

Fig. 2.6 illustrates the flowchart and architecture of the 2D-CNN used in this study. As shown in the figure, the 2D-CNN is used to detect damage location, for which the 1D input acceleration data is transformed into 2D input data using the WPT. Within each convolutional block, the ReLU activation function is used for each convolutional layer. After a BN layer, the leaky ReLU activation layer is added. This block is repeated three times, and the outputs are reshaped into a vector using the flattening layer. The SoftMax layer has an output dimension equal to the number of damage scenarios. For the training purpose, the Adam optimization, with a learning rate of $lr = 0.000005$, is selected to minimize the categorical cross-entropy loss [31]. The training batch size for all the CNN models is set to be equal to 64 per epoch.

4. HYBRID CNN–SVM

A support vector machine (SVM) is a type of supervised classifier that identifies an optimal hyperplane using the labeled datasets [25,32]. As shown in Fig. 2.7 for a 2D space, the hyperplane is a line that has the maximum distance from the nearest data point on either side (class). For a nonlinear classification problem, the SVM can be used by selecting a proper

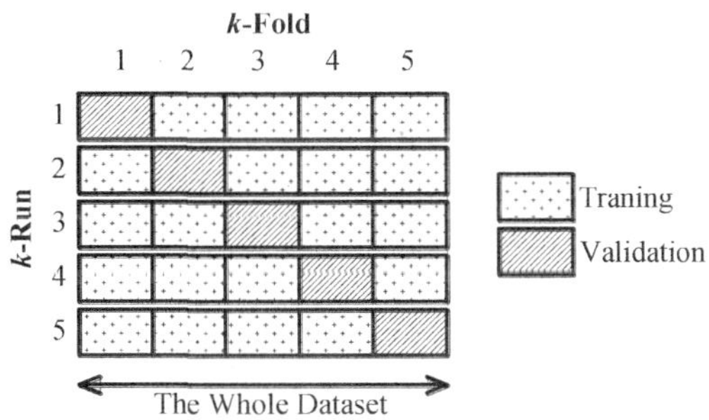

FIGURE 2.5 The *k*-Fold cross-validation.

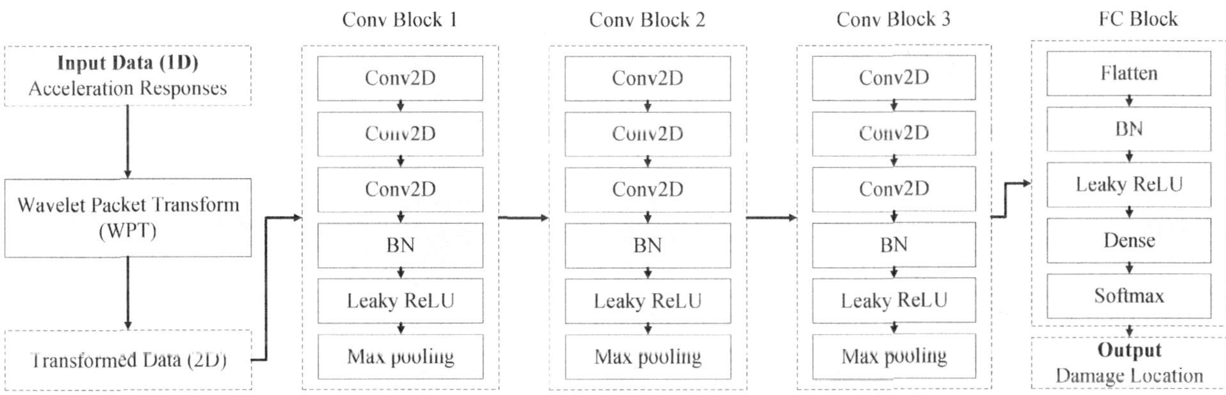

FIGURE 2.6 Overview of the 2D-CNN.

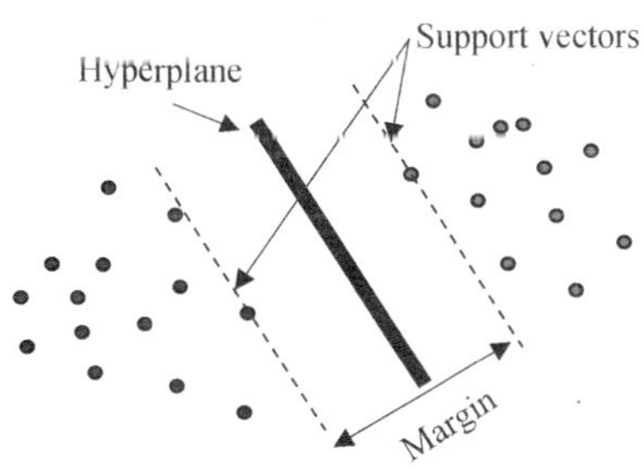

FIGURE 2.7 Support vector machine in 2D space.

kernel function, which is a set of mathematical functions to transform the input data into the feature space. The proposed method incorporates the WPT as a core component, which improves effective feature extraction for damage detection applications. Using WPT, decompose the original vibration signal and isolate sensitive features. The resultant transformed signal coefficients are fed into the CNN model to extract the spatial features, while the SVM layer classifies these features.

Inspired by similar studies [25,32–35], a hybrid CNN-SVM model is proposed, where the last layer of the initially designed CNN models is replaced with an SVM classifier. The architecture of the proposed model is presented in Fig. 2.8. Once the CNN is trained, the outputs of the last layer are extracted as the features for the SVM classifier. After training the SVM, the hybrid model can be used for automatic feature extraction and classification tasks for the testing dataset. In this study, different kernel functions are compared, and the optimal results are obtained using the RBF kernel. The same Conv blocks are used for the hybrid model, as well. In the hybrid CNN-SVM, the CNN autonomously extracts the features. However, the feature extraction method can be designed to select the most relevant information. In addition, with the superior generalization ability of the SVM, the overall classification performance of the hybrid model is enhanced.

5. Numerical simulations

The Manavgat bridge in Turkey was selected to demonstrate the effectiveness of the proposed hybrid method. The 202 m long and 13.7 m wide deck is supported by 28 cables that are connected to a 42 m high λ-shape steel pylon [25]. As shown in Fig. 2.9, a pair of continuous steel girders supports the 35 cm thick deck slab, including the 10 cm pavement.

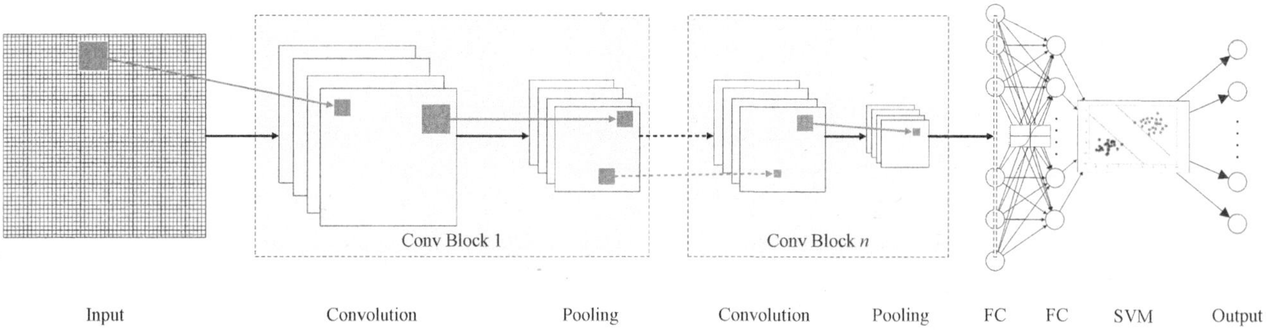

FIGURE 2.8 Overview of the hybrid CNN-SVM.

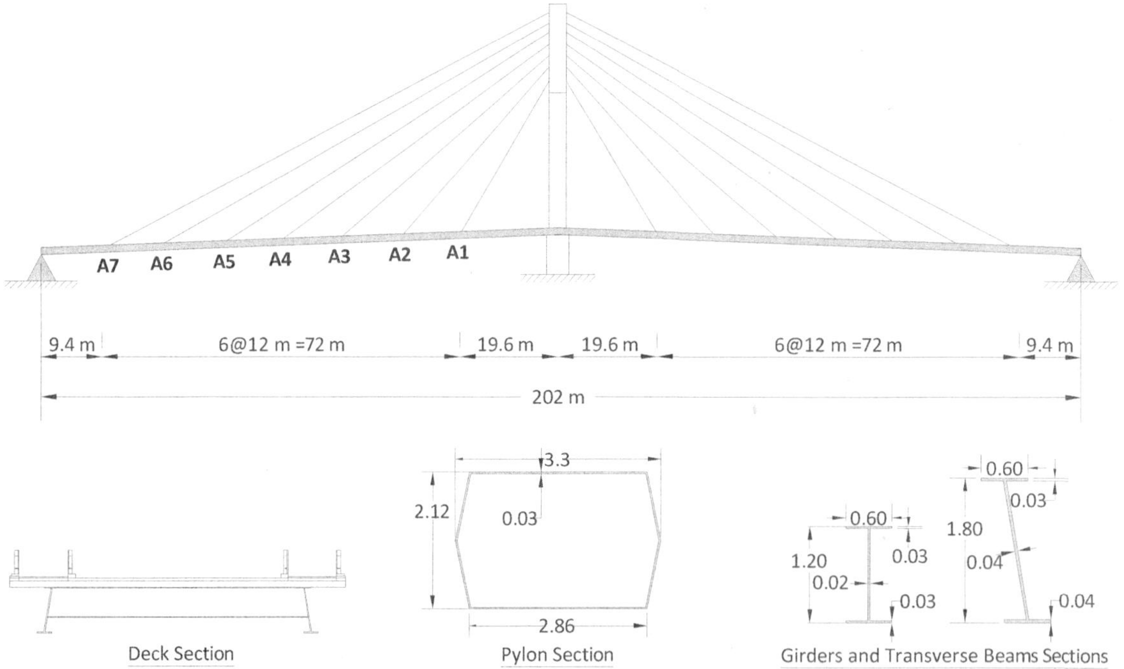

FIGURE 2.9 Manavgat bridge, layout, and cross-sections [25,36].

The first pairs of cables on each side are placed at a 19.6 m distance from the center of the pylon. For the other pairs, the distance is 12 m, except for the last cables that are 9.4 away from the end supports. The mechanical properties of the cables are provided in the literature [25,36]. The finite element models are generated using the CSI SAP2000 software. Further, it is assumed that the deck section is continuous through the bridge, and cables do not carry any loads except the axial loads. The soil-structure interactions and nonstructural components are not considered in the simulations. Comparison of the natural periods with the results from the previous studies [25,36] would indicate the sufficient accuracy of numerical models (Fig. 2.10). Understanding the vibration modes of the model and the participation factors would help to minimize the number of sensors and optimize the placement. Since the natural frequencies of the bridge are not easily separable, several chirp excitations are applied instead of impact loads. The load is vertically applied at the center of the left span. To ensure sufficient data, the linearly sweeping signals had different time-dependent frequencies. The sampling frequency is 100 Hz. Three sample excitations are shown in Fig. 2.11 with different rates for linearly time-variant frequency.

In this study, different damage levels are introduced as the axial stiffness reduction of the cables by 10%, 20%, 30%, 40%, and 50%. Therefore, there are 35 damage states in total, which are defined for the seven cables, A1–A7, on one side of the west span. Using 40 chirp-type sine-sweep excitations with different rates, 35×40 samples corresponding to the different damage states are collected. The identification of damage in a cable-stayed bridge has been investigated in previous studies [25], and the main goal of this study is to identify the location of the damage using the proposed hybrid CNN-SVM models.

A set of 28 accelerometers is placed at the end of each cable to record the nonlinear vertical responses; the response data has a size of (number of samples × signal length × number of sensors), which is (1400 × 5000 × 28) in this study. Various measurement noise levels are assumed in the response, which is transformed using WPT. Fig. 2.11 shows the vibration recordings from one sensor corresponding to different chirp excitations for two different damage states. Based on [25], the measured signals are given noise with signal-to-noise ratios (SNR) of 30, 40, and 50 dB. The SNR is defined as,

$$SNR = 10\ log_{10}\left(\frac{P_{signal}}{P_{noise}}\right) \tag{2.10}$$

where, P_{signal} and P_{noise} are, respectively, the power of the signal and white Gaussian noise.

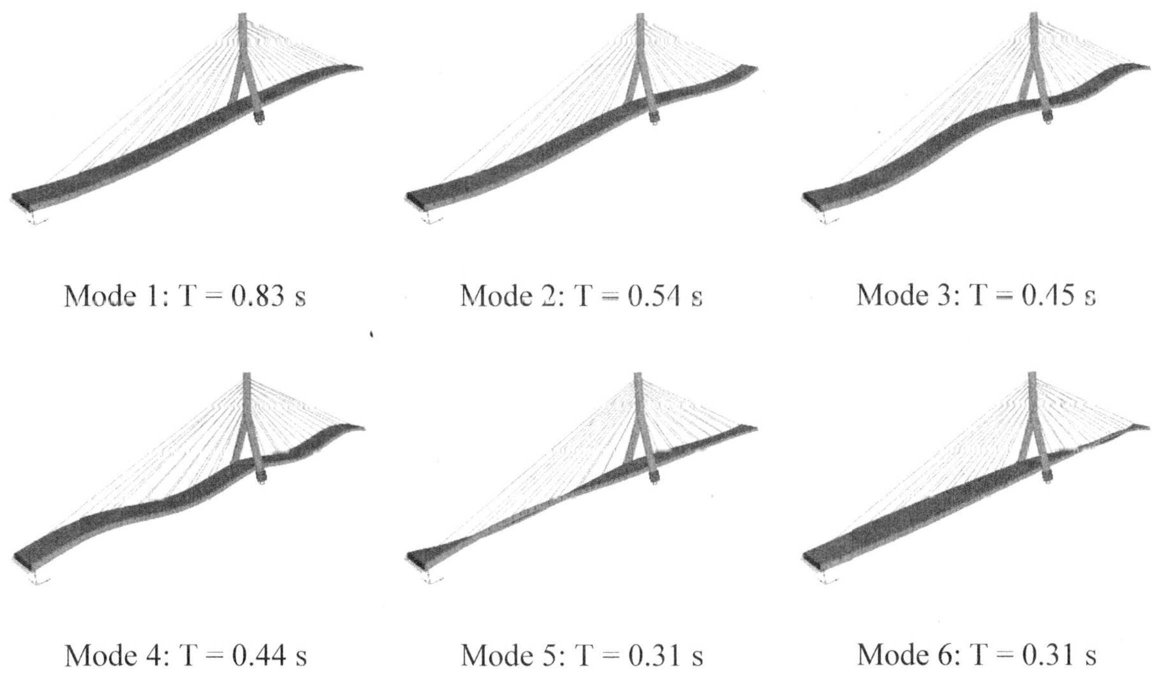

FIGURE 2.10 First six vibration mode shapes and periods for the Manavgat bridge.

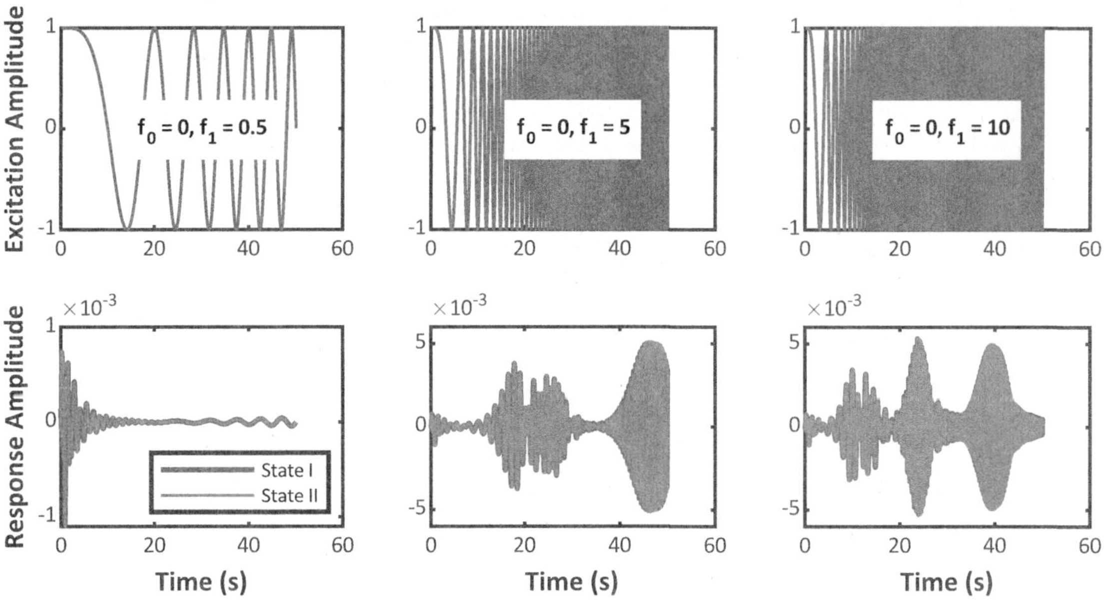

FIGURE 2.11 Time-history of the Manavgat bridge responses for two damage states under the same chirp excitations with different rates.

6. Results of the CNN models

The results of this study are presented in two sections. In the following subsections, the train and test results, as well as the performance curves, are presented.

6.1 Train and test results

This study utilizes k-fold cross-validation, and the results of this approach are summarized in Fig. 2.12. The best results can be achieved if the noise level is eliminated from the measured data. There are different techniques to remove noise from a signal. However, there is no guarantee of reaching a zero-percent noise level for practical cases. Therefore, four noise levels are considered in this study, and the experiment is repeated for each case. Fig. 2.12 shows the mean validation accuracies per fold for each noise level. For the SNR of 30 dB, the accuracy is nearly 75%; however, for the higher SNRs,

FIGURE 2.12 Performance of the 2D-CNN model for each fold considering different noise levels.

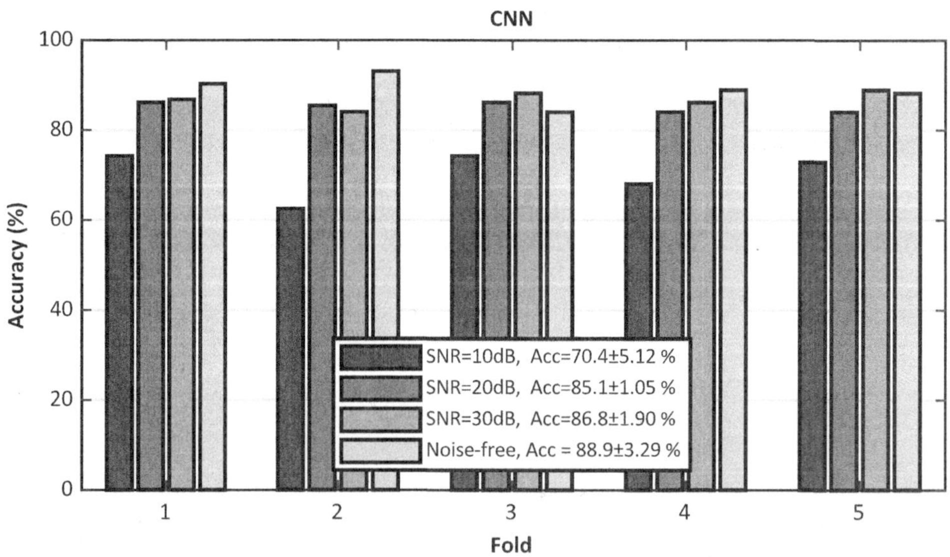

the performance of the base CNN model is improved. Therefore, it is necessary to redesign the architecture of the model with more robust classifiers, such as SVM.

The training accuracy and loss histories using the 2D-CNN model are shown in Figs. 2.13 and 2.14. The smoothed curves are plotted to show the overall trend. By comparing the performance of the model, it can be said that for the lower noise levels, the training is slower compared to the datasets with a higher noise ratio. The confusion charts show that the quick convergence for the noisy signals does not result in better classification. A closer look reveals that the damage in the middle cables has a significant impact on the responses that can be intensified using the WPT, which results in more accurate localization.

6.2 Receiver operating characteristic curves

One of the efficient ways of comparing the performance of a classification method is using receiver operating characteristic (ROC) curves [25]. Further, the area under each curve (AUC) provides a better picture to compare the complexity of each class during the specific classification and within the combination of patterns. When AUC $\geq$0.75, the performance of a classifier is considered to be acceptable, for which the maximum value is equal to the unit, indicating a perfect classification with 100% accuracy [25,32]. In Fig. 2.15, the effect of noise level on model performance is illustrated for each case. As the SNR increases, the accuracy of the model increases.

7. Results of the hybrid models

Different hybrid models are discussed in this section. Therefore, seven types of classifiers are considered to add on top of the trained 2D-CNN model. The details of each model, as well as the parameters, are provided in Table 2.1. SVM classifiers are used with three different configurations depending on the kernel functions. By replacing the SVM with the other models, the efficiency of the hybrid CNN-SVM is verified. From Table 2.1, the hybrid CNN-SVM results in the highest mean accuracy of 96.63% when the kernel is an RBF, and the decision function shape is one-vs-one. For a linear SVM classifier, approximately the same accuracy can be achieved. An SVM with a polynomial kernel function, however, results in slightly less accurate performance. Similarly, a hybrid CNN-MLP model results in 94.9% accuracy, which is

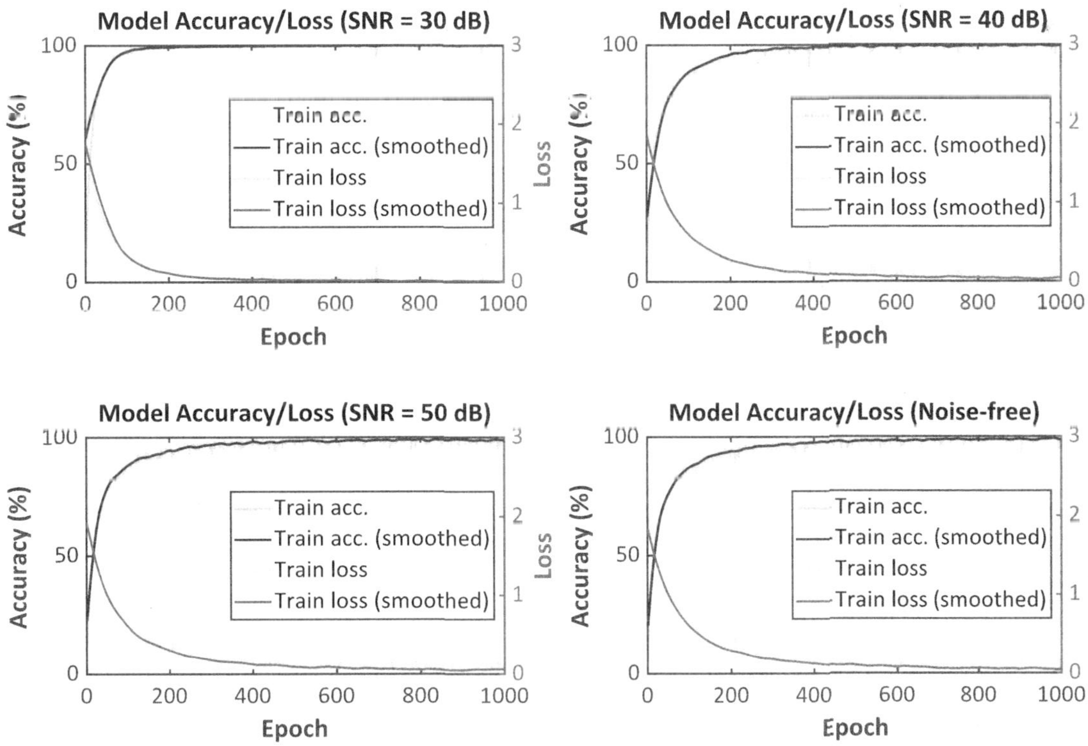

FIGURE 2.13 Train accuracy/loss histories using the 2D-CNN model.

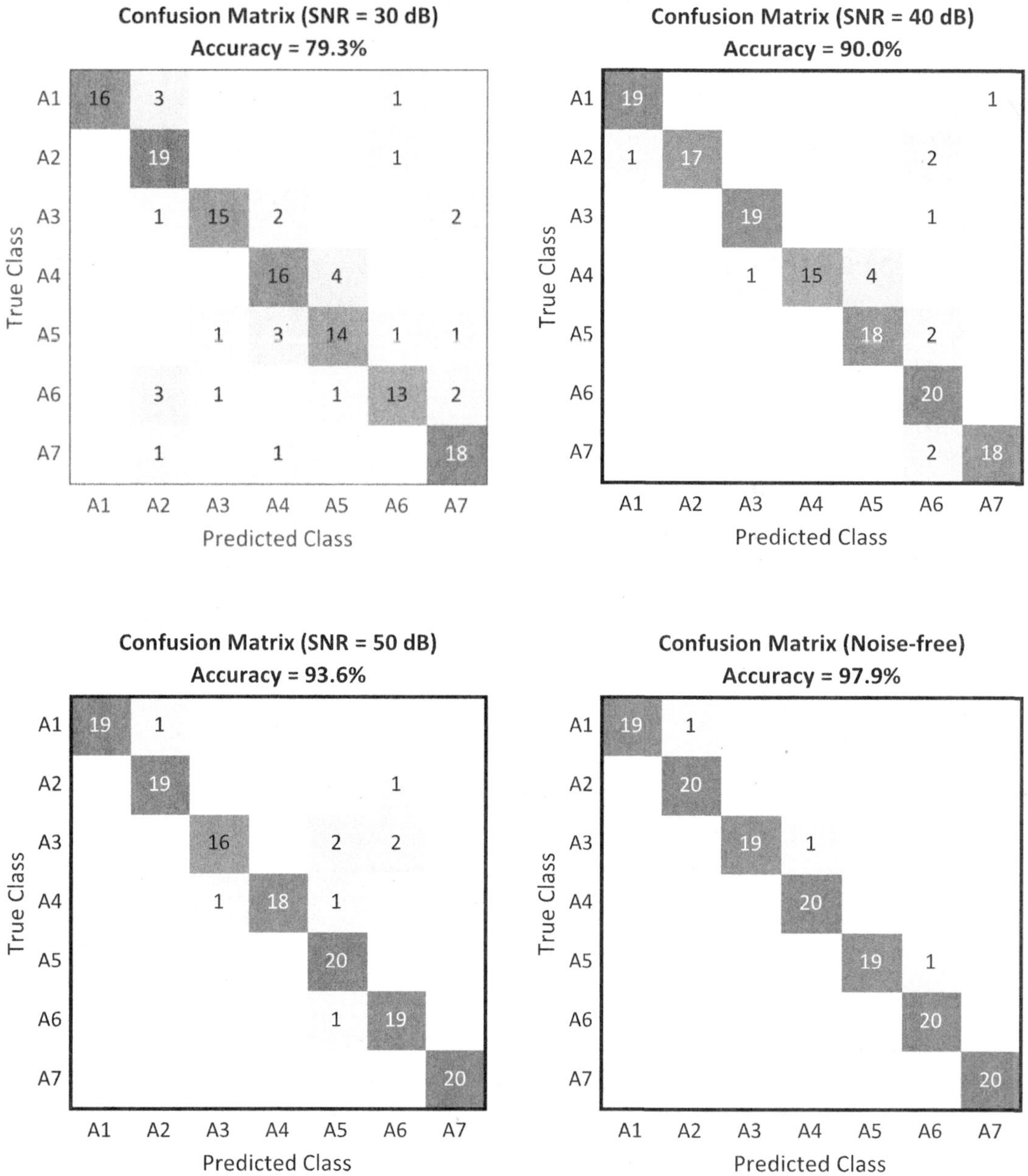

FIGURE 2.14 Confusion matrices (test) using the 2D-CNN model.

relatively high compared to the rest of the hybrid models that have the best mean accuracy of less than 90%. The hybrid CNN-AdaBoost model fails to satisfy the accuracy requirements, with the best mean accuracy of 43.91%.

Detailed results of the hybrid models considered are shown in Fig. 2.16, which considers the different SNRs. Other numerical parameters are optimized to get the best overall results. All three hybrid CNN-SVM models result in high classification accuracies. The minimum best mean accuracy is for the SVM classifier with a polynomial kernel function when SNR = 30 dB. Each fold results in approximately the same accuracy level, which indicates that the dataset is shuffled and stratified well and regularization and mapping techniques for the CNN and SVM are effective. For the k-nearest-neighbors algorithm, which is a nonparametric classifier, the selection of the best k depends on the data. A KNN algorithm is sensitive to noise, and the performance may degrade if the features are not scaled. Using different values of k indicates that an evolutionary algorithm may be used to optimize the feature scaling and enhance the hybrid model performance. Among the rest of the hybrid models, the performance of the multi-layer perceptron (MLP) classifier is

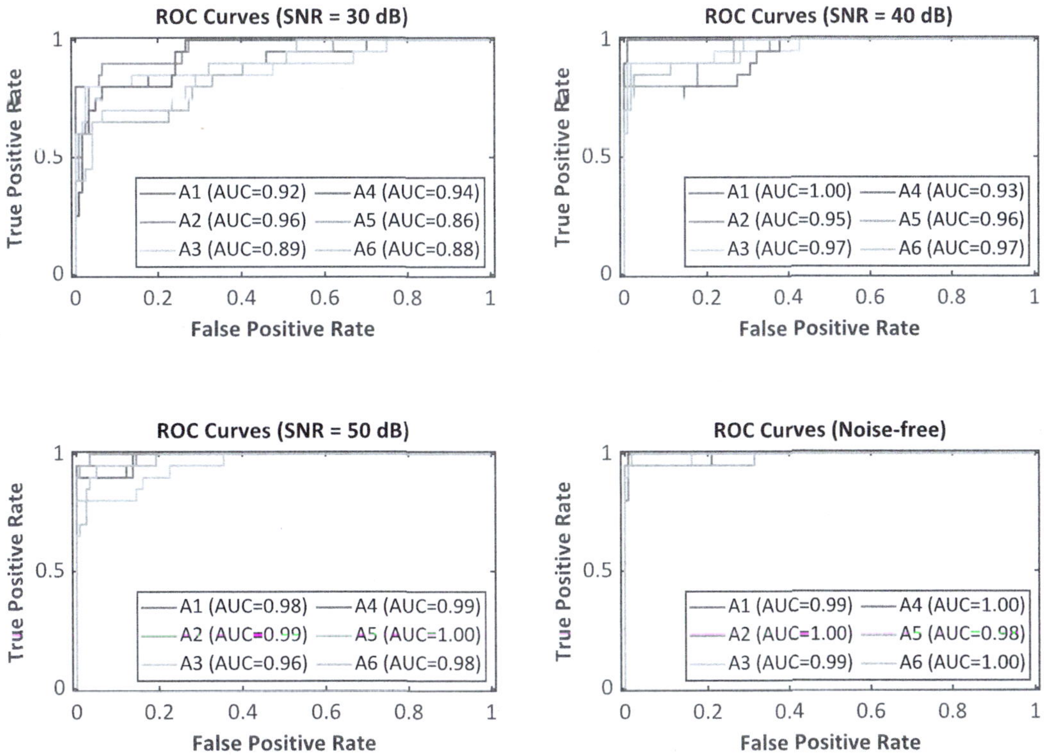

FIGURE 2.15 Receiver operating characteristic curves using the base 2D-CNN model.

TABLE 2.1 Different configurations of hybrid models.

Structure	Classifier	Parameters	Mean accuracy (%)
CNN-SVM	Support vector machine (SVM)	Kernel = linear C = 0.025	96.34
		Kernel = RBF, Decision function shape = *One-vs-one*	**96.63**
		Kernel = polynomial, degree = 3, Decision function shape = *One-vs-one*	92.15
CNN–KNN	*k*-Nearest neighbors (*KNN*)	k = 5	86.23
		k = 15	83.77
CNN-GP	Gaussian Process (GP)	Kernel = RBF	85.94
CNN-DT	Decision Tree (DT)	Max. Depth = 10	79.01
CNN-RF	Random forest	Max. Depth = 5, Number of estimators = 10, Max. Number of features = 8	88.4
CNN-MLP	Multi-layer perceptron (*MLP*)	$\alpha = 1$	94.9
CNN-AdaBoost	Adaptive boosting	–	43.91

more sensitive to higher noise levels, while the best mean accuracy is significantly higher for the noise-free datasets. The Adaptive Boosting classifier has the least accuracy. Similarly, the decision tree (DT) classifier does not show superior performance compared to the aforementioned SVM, MLP, and KNN algorithms. The Gaussian process (GP) and random forest (RF) perform similarly; however, considering the accuracy of the earlier CNN model, there are no

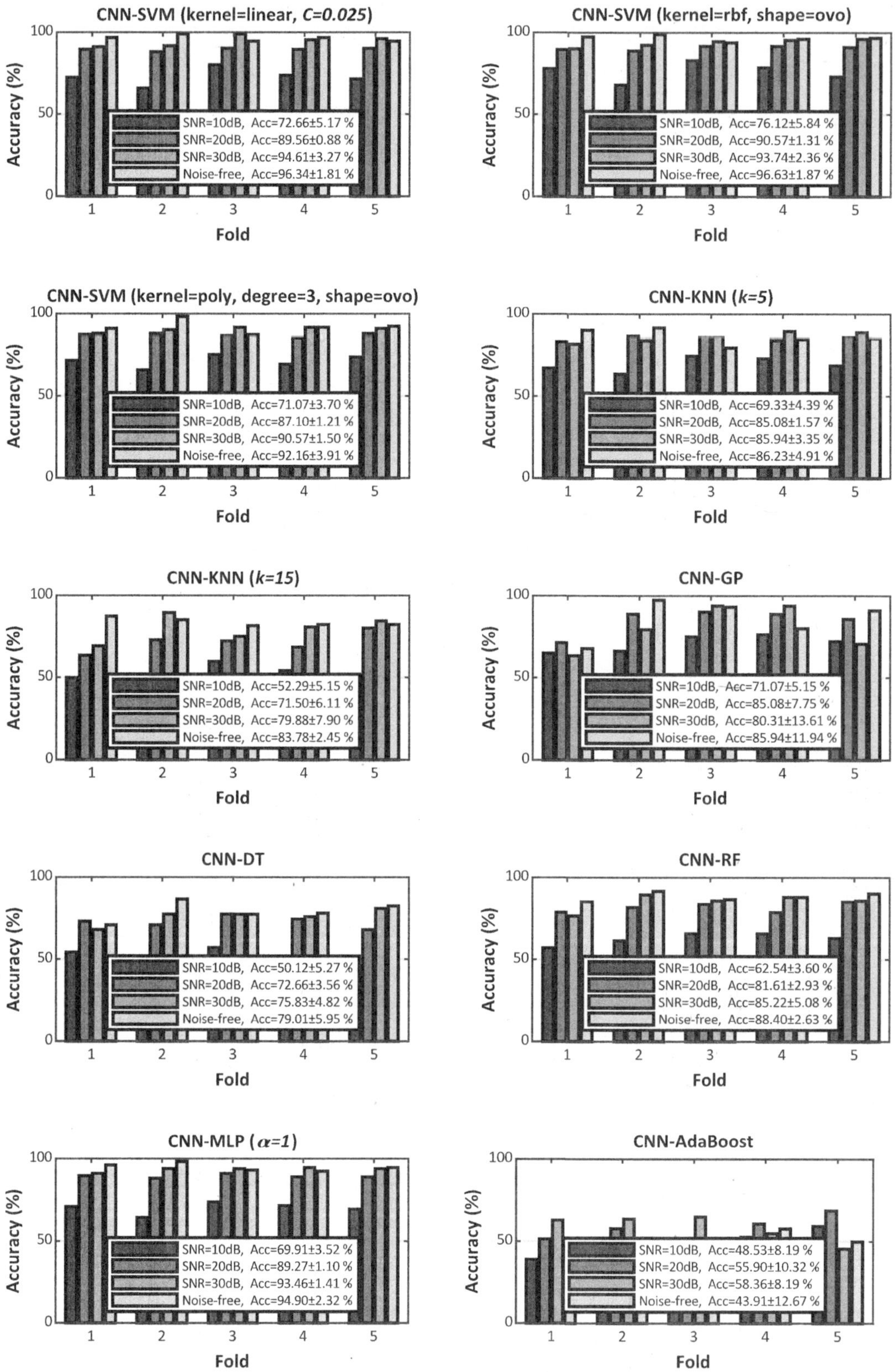

FIGURE 2.16 Performance of different hybrid models for each fold with different noise levels.

significant improvements in the overall behavior of the hybrid model. In summary, the best performance is achieved using the SVM classifiers that have been proven to be the best classifier when the bridge responses are transformed using wavelet analysis [25].

8. Conclusions

A vibration-based damage localization strategy that employs deep learning methods is introduced, and its implementation is demonstrated numerically for damage localization in a bridge structure. The proposed approach uses vibration response and WPT to prepare the 2D input data for the CNN. The performance of the base CNN model is further improved using the hybrid CNN-SVM framework.

The primary objective of the present study is damage detection and localization, which are defined as cross-sectional reduction in each cable of the bridge. Vibration response data is acquired using 28 accelerometers, which are used to train the CNN models by considering different noise levels in the measurements. The performance of the hybrid model is evaluated against six other well-known classifiers. The results demonstrate the effectiveness of the hybrid method in achieving accurate identification. It is noted that some of the aspects and limitations of the proposed approach require further attention and investigation. The sensitivity of the damage identification and localization is due to components that have a relatively negligible effect on the vibration response, combination, or copresence of different types of damage and extent, including the presence of cracks in the deck and pylon.

References

[1] X. Kong, C.-S. Cai, J. Hu, The state-of-the-art on framework of vibration-based structural damage identification for decision making, Appl. Sci. 7 (5) (2017) 497.

[2] P. Arafin, A.M. Billah, A. Issa, Deep learning-based concrete defects classification and detection using semantic segmentation, Struct. Health Monit. 0 (0) (2023) 14759217231168212, https://doi.org/10.1177/14759217231168212.

[3] D. Hu, S. Li, J. Du, J. Cai, Automating building damage reconnaissance to optimize drone mission planning for disaster response, J. Comput. Civ. Eng. 37 (3) (2023) 04023006.

[4] A. Mosleh, A. Meixedo, D. Ribeiro, P. Montenegro, R. Calçada, Early wheel flat detection: An automatic data-driven wavelet-based approach for railways, Veh. Syst. Dyn. 61 (6) (2023) 1644–1673.

[5] M. Azimi, A.D. Eslamlou, G. Pekcan, Data-driven structural health monitoring and damage detection through deep learning: state-of-the-art review, Sensors 20 (10) (2020) 2778.

[6] A. Kaveh, P. Rahmani, A.D. Eslamlou, Guided water strider algorithm for structural damage detection using incomplete modal data, Iran. J. Sci. Technol. Trans. Civil Eng. (2021) 1–18.

[7] A. Lenjani, et al., Towards fully automated post-event data collection and analysis: Pre-event and post-event information fusion, Eng. Struct. 208 (2020) 109884, https://doi.org/10.1016/j.engstruct.2019.109884.

[8] A. Ellenberg, A. Kontsos, F. Moon, I. Bartoli, Bridge related damage quantification using unmanned aerial vehicle imagery, Struct. Control Health Monit. 23 (9) (2016) 1168–1179, https://doi.org/10.1002/stc.1831.

[9] J. Amezquita-Sanchez, H. Adeli, Feature extraction and classification techniques for health monitoring of structures, Sci. Iran. Trans. A: Civ. Eng. 22 (6) (2015) 1931.

[10] J.P. Amezquita-Sanchez, H. Adeli, Signal processing techniques for vibration-based health monitoring of smart structures, Arch. Comput. Methods Eng. 23 (1) (2016) 1–15.

[11] A. Bagheri, S. Kourehli, Damage Detection of Structures under Earthquake Excitation Using Discrete Wavelet Analysis, 2013.

[12] S. Law, X. Li, X. Zhu, S. Chan, Structural damage detection from wavelet packet sensitivity, Eng. Struct. 27 (9) (2005) 1339–1348.

[13] Y. Xin, H. Hao, J. Li, Time-varying system identification by enhanced empirical wavelet transform based on synchroextracting transform, Eng. Struct. 196 (2019) 109313, https://doi.org/10.1016/j.engstruct.2019.109313.

[14] Z. Tang, Z. Chen, Y. Bao, H. Li, Convolutional neural network-based data anomaly detection method using multiple information for structural health monitoring, Struct. Control Health Monit. 26 (1) (2019) e2296.

[15] S.F. Ahmed, et al., Deep learning modelling techniques: Current progress, applications, advantages, and challenges, Artif. Intell. Rev. 56 (11) (2023) 13521–13617.

[16] M. Azimi, T. Yang, Transformer-based framework for accurate segmentation of high-resolution images in structural health monitoring, Comput. Aided Civ. Infrastruct. Eng. 39 (2024) 3670–3684, https://doi.org/10.1111/mice.13211.

[17] M. Azimi, G. Pekcan, Structural health monitoring using extremely compressed data through deep learning, Comput. Aided Civ. Infrastruct. Eng. 35 (6) (2020) 597–614.

[18] D. Soukup, R. Huber-Mörk, Convolutional neural networks for steel surface defect detection from photometric stereo images, in: International Symposium on Visual Computing, Springer, 2014, pp. 668–677.

[19] H.-L. Minh, T. Sang-To, S. Khatir, M.A. Wahab, A.H. Gandomi, T. Cuong-Le, Augmented deep neural network architecture for assessing damage severity in 3D concrete buildings under temperature fluctuations based on K-means optimization, in: Structures, vol 57, Elsevier, 2023 105278.

[20] A. Zhang, et al., Automated pixel-level pavement crack detection on 3D asphalt surfaces using a deep-learning network, Comput. Aided Civ. Infrastruct. Eng. 32 (10) (2017) 805–819.
[21] H. Khodabandehlou, G. Pekcan, M.S. Fadali, Vibration-based structural condition assessment using convolution neural networks, Struct. Control Health Monit. 26 (2) (2019) e2308, https://doi.org/10.1002/stc.2308.
[22] Y. Diao, D. Jia, G. Liu, Z. Sun, J. Xu, Structural damage identification using modified hilbert–huang transform and support vector machine, J. Civ. Struct. Health Monit. 11 (4) (2021/09/01 2021) 1155–1174, https://doi.org/10.1007/s13349-021-00509-5.
[23] K. Chaiyasarn, W. Khan, L. Ali, M. Sharma, D. Brackenbury, M. Dejong, Crack Detection in Masonry Structures Using Convolutional Neural Networks and Support Vector Machines, 2018.
[24] G. Gui, H. Pan, Z. Lin, Y. Li, Z. Yuan, Data-driven support vector machine with optimization techniques for structural health monitoring and damage detection, KSCE J. Civ. Eng. 21 (2) (2017) 523–534.
[25] H. Pan, M. Azimi, F. Yan, Z. Lin, Time-frequency-based data-driven structural diagnosis and damage detection for cable-stayed bridges, J. Bridge Eng. 23 (6) (2018).
[26] M. Azimi, Design of Structural Vibration Control Using Smart Materials and Devices for Earthquake-Resistant and Resilient Buildings, North Dakota State University, 2017.
[27] X. Glorot, A. Bordes, Y. Bengio, Deep sparse rectifier neural networks, in: Proceedings of the Fourteenth International Conference on Artificial Intelligence and Statistics, 2011, pp. 315–323.
[28] V. Nair, G.E. Hinton, Rectified linear units improve restricted boltzmann machines, in: Proceedings of the 27th International Conference on Machine Learning, ICML-10, 2010, pp. 807–814.
[29] A.L. Maas, A.Y. Hannun, A.Y. Ng, Rectifier nonlinearities improve neural network acoustic models, in: Proc. Icml, vol 30, 2013, p. 3.
[30] S. Ioffe, C. Szegedy, Batch Normalization: Accelerating Deep Network Training by Reducing Internal Covariate Shift, arXiv preprint arXiv, 2015, 1502.03167.
[31] D.P. Kingma, J. Ba, Adam: A Method for Stochastic Optimization, arXiv preprint arXiv, 2014, 1412.6980.
[32] H. Pan, M. Azimi, G. Gui, F. Yan, Z. Lin, Vibration-based support vector machine for structural health monitoring, in: International Conference on Experimental Vibration Analysis for Civil Engineering Structures, Springer, 2017, pp. 167–178.
[33] X.-X. Niu, C.Y. Suen, A novel hybrid CNN–SVM classifier for recognizing handwritten digits, Pattern Recogn. 45 (4) (2012) 1318–1325.
[34] M. Elleuch, R. Maalej, M. Kherallah, A new design based-SVM of the CNN classifier architecture with dropout for offline Arabic handwritten recognition, Procedia Comput. Sci. 80 (2016) 1712–1723.
[35] J. Nagi, G.A. Di Caro, A. Giusti, F. Nagi, L.M. Gambardella, Convolutional neural support vector machines: Hybrid visual pattern classifiers for multi-robot systems, in: ICMLA, vol 1, 2012, pp. 27–32.
[36] B. Atmaca, M. Yurdakul, Ş. Ateş, Nonlinear dynamic analysis of base isolated cable-stayed bridge under earthquake excitations, Soil Dynam. Earthq. Eng. 66 (2014) 314–318.

Chapter 3

A multiobjective Artificial Gorilla Troops Optimizer for engineering problems

Nima Khodadadi[1], Ehsaneh Khodadadi[2], Ehsan Khodadadi[3], El-Sayed M. El-Kenawy[4], Pezhman Mardanpour[5], Francisco De Caso[6], Antonio Nanni[6] and Khalid M. Mosalam[1]

[1]Department of Civil and Environmental Engineering, Pacific Earthquake Engineering Research (PEER) Center, University of California, Berkeley, CA, United States; [2]Department of Pathology, Stanford University School of Medicine, Stanford, CA, United States; [3]Department of Chemistry and Biochemistry, University of Arkansas, Fayetteville, AR, United States; [4]Jadara Research Center, Jadara University, Irbid, Jordan; [5]Department of Mechanical & Material Engineering, Florida International University, Miami, FL, United States; [6]Department of Civil and Architectural Engineering, University of Miami, Coral Gables, FL, United States

1. Introduction

One of the significant challenges of computer science and evolutionary computation is optimization, characterized by great application potential in capital sectors [1]. Optimization is choosing the best variable from a set of variables to obtain an objective function [2]. But behind optimization, there are meta-heuristic algorithms (MAs), which work with a chain of solutions, randomly chosen and refined using predefined processes to achieve better results for any optimization challenge. Faced with the fact that there are various optimization problems, over the last decade, meta-heuristics have become one of the favorite methods to be used by a researcher or professional who aims to develop the best possible solution to a problem, whether economic, geographic, or physical. The use of algorithms in optimization is favored based on their independence of derivatives and randomness [4], which is the stochastic parameter. The term stochastic is very closely related to the word random and defines behavior based on random mechanisms and operators in meta-heuristics. Usually, these algorithms start with a set of random solutions and improve this set using different mechanisms, some inspired by natural processes, leading to the desired valuable precision. The methods are extremely useful when faced with optimization problems that contain a large search space where it is impossible to explore all the possible solutions [3].

Examples of meta-heuristic algorithms include the Genetic Algorithm (GA) [4], Particle Swarm Optimization (PSO) [5], Circle Search Algorithm (CSO) [6], Imperialist Competitive Algorithm (ICA) [7] and Moth Search Algorithm (MSA) [8]. These methods have been applied to solve a range of optimization problems, including those related to truss structures [9], frame structures [10], machine learning application [11] and data mining [12].

While most of the optimization methods are developed for single-objective problems, optimization can be divided into two categories: single-objective (SO) and multiobjective (MO). Introducing MO problems will require an external archive and a target selection strategy for the optimization algorithm to account for multiple objectives in going from a single objective to MO problems.

That said, in multiobjective optimization (MOO), most solutions compete with each other. So, there is no such optimal (global) solution, but instead, the output is the set of Pareto Optimal (PO) [13] solutions within the same search domain. Optimization algorithms have been typically applied to intrinsic problems, particularly for the design of logistics network systems in urgent circumstances, so that the optimum infrastructure allocation algorithm can be developed to redesign the best transport routes for intrinsic substances with the lowest cost and highest disaster response rate [14] and the tracking problems [15,16].

MAs have been proven more effective than humans in finding a solution for MOO problems that work in the shortest period, that is, in a fixed number of evaluations. In the last decade, various nature-inspired metaheuristic algorithms have been proposed as a solution for MOO problems, including the Multiobjective Sine-Cosine Algorithm (MO-SCA) [17],

Advanced Intelligence Methods for Data Science and Optimization. https://doi.org/10.1016/B978-0-443-28940-8.00003-8

multiobjective Artificial Sheep Algorithm (MOASA) [18], multiobjective Harris Hawks Optimizer (MOHHO) [19], multiobjective Ant Colony Optimization (MOACO) [20], Archive-based Multiobjective Arithmetic Optimization Algorithm (MAOA) [21], and Multiobjective Marine Predator Algorithm (MOMPA) [22].

This previously mentioned set is called the Pareto optimal solutions (Pareto set). Users need to select one of the best solutions based on their preferences and user needs. If we don't have such data, all solutions of the Pareto set are equal to each other to a certain extent. Fig. 3.1. The Pareto concept for a biobjective optimization problem. The feasible objective space is shown in green, and the Pareto set is shown in black.

A priori, a posteriori, and interactive solutions in the literature for MO problems using MAs: Firstly, the a priori MO problems are solved by aggregating or merging multiobjective functions into an SO problem. Then, decision-making takes place prior to the optimization process [23]. Therefore, in an a priori approach, the SO objective function serves as one single solution that accounts for the global optimum. Secondly, the a posteriori approach is the other method, conserving the multiobjective design. It involves finding a set of representative solutions that can best exhibit the trade-offs of the MO problem [24]. In this approach, decision-making (DM) takes place post optimization process, where the DM is presented with a set of nondominated solutions on the Pareto front and chooses the suitable one depending on their preferences. Lastly, interactive or human-in-the-loop optimization approaches involve DM deciding on the optimization process, which guarantees the evolution of the process toward convergent Pareto optimal alternatives based on the feedback received from the DM [25]. The optimization process is continued until the DM chooses among the Pareto optimal alternatives that emerge from the optimization process. Then, the DM is also allowed to select the Pareto optimal alternatives that emerge from the optimization process [26].

The No Free Lunch (NFL) [27] hypothesis has become a standard reference in the field and has inspired many researchers to design novel optimization methods. Any optimization algorithm can solve every optimization problem if it is coupled with sufficient evaluation effort. If a search has an infinite number of attempts, it can always solve the problem by trying all points when optimizing for any cost function. One important consequence of the NFL is that it prevents researchers from finding one good optimization method that can solve any optimization problem. They need to continue proposing and improving new optimization methods in order to beat previous ones.

Abdollahzadeh et al. [28] introduced the Artificial Gorilla Troops Optimizer (AGTO) to solve SO optimization problems. AGTO is recognized as one of the most effective algorithms for global searchability. A limited review of related literature indicates that AGTO is beneficial in addressing complex optimization challenges across various fields. Motivated by this, the authors propose an MO version of AGTO, named MAAGTO, to tackle MOO problems. To summarize, this study offers the following contributions:

- An archive was implemented in AGTO to retain the optimal solutions obtained from Pareto.
- A leader function was embedded to expedite the algorithm's navigation of the multiobjective search space through Pareto optimality.
- A technique to distribute Pareto fronts was added, improving the spread and diversity of solutions.
- MAAGTO was evaluated on eight well-known engineering problems.
- Four performance metrics were used to assess the method's efficiency.
- The significant advantages of GTO led to the development of a multiobjective edition, MAAGTO, whose results were compared with established multiobjective optimization techniques.
- The Pareto solutions and fronts obtained by MAAGTO are illustrated through graphical analysis.
- The proposed MAAGTO demonstrated superiority in both descriptive and analytical results.

The rest of the chapter is organized as follows: Section 2 discusses the original version of AGTO. In Section 3, we present a general discussion on the multiobjective extension of the AGTO algorithm, namely, MAAGTO. In Section 4, we present the findings of our experiments, and Section 5 presents the conclusions.

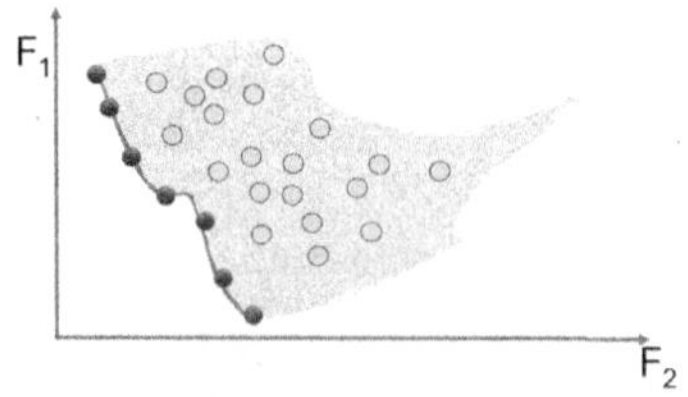

FIGURE 3.1 Concept of Pareto for MO problems.

2. Single-objective Artificial Gorilla Troops Optimizer

AGTO is a contemporary metaheuristic model inspired by the social intelligence of gorilla troops in the wild (See Fig. 3.2). The algorithm employs five unique operators to execute exploration and exploitation, known as optimization operations, that mimic gorilla behaviors.

2.1 Exploration phase

During the exploration phase, three operators that search different kinds of optimization spaces are added to enhance the diversification ability of AGTO: one operator that stochastically navigates to an unknown location, one operator that controls the movement of the gorillas to the landscape to enable a better balance between exploration and exploitation; and a third operator that manages migrations to a known location to reduce possible getting stuck in local optima.

2.2 Exploitation phase

During this phase, locating a target or food resources occurs, and all search agents converge toward the silverback. This phase includes two behaviors: pursuing the silverback, which is denoted as the optimal solution identified at this stage, and competing for mature females.

The following outlines the steps involved in the optimization process of the AGTO algorithm:

Step 1. The space of solutions in the AGTO algorithm includes three types of solutions – X represents the position vector of the gorillas, GX represents the gorilla candidate position vectors generated in each phase and used if they are better than the current one, and silverback stands for the best one found in each iteration.

Step 2. The entire population has only one silverback, irrespective of the number of search agents selected for optimization operations.

Step 3. The use of three types of solutions—X, GX, and silverback—are designed to accurately simulate the social life of gorillas in nature.

Step 4. Gorillas can enhance their strength by finding better food sources or positioning themselves within a strong group. In AGTO, solutions generated in each iteration are known as GX. If a new solution (GX) is found, it replaces the current solution (X); otherwise, it remains in memory (GX).

Step 5. Gorillas' tendency toward collective living prevents them from living individually. They search for food as a group and live under the leadership of a silverback, who makes all group decisions. In our formulation, the worst solution in the population is considered the weakest member of the gorilla group. The gorillas aim to move away from the worst solution and toward the best solution (silverback), thereby improving the positions of all gorillas.

Given the fundamental principles of gorilla group dynamics in finding food and their collective lifestyle, along with the distinctive characteristics of the AGTO algorithm used in various optimization problems, this algorithm has broad applicability.

FIGURE 3.2 Gorilla troops.

3. Multiobjective Archive-based Artificial Gorilla Troops Optimizer

As mentioned above, a fourth dimension has been added to the algorithm by tweaking three different components of the AGTO algorithm adapted from the one used in MOPSO [29]. The NFL [27] theorem says that these techniques cannot solve all optimization problems and that an algorithm that performs well on one benchmark problem in one domain can perform poorly on another benchmark problem in the same domain. A finding due to poor performance on one of the benchmarks is not proof of incompetence. Comparative studies across many different areas are needed, and they have begun to provide previously unknown insight into the efficacy of meta-heuristics. The MAAGTO is an algorithm that has yet to be introduced and applied to eight different engineering problems.

The Multiobjective Archive-based Artificial Gorilla Troops Optimizer (MAAGTO) employs the aforementioned key features to find near-optimal solutions. The archive mechanism represents all nondominated Pareto optimal solutions found so far, which assists in dealing with concave, convex, and disconnected Pareto fronts. Each population member is uniformly distributed along the Pareto front as the archive controller checks whether a given solution should be saved in the repository. The grid mechanism estimates the distribution of a Pareto front through the even division of the objective function space into different regions. When a new member is added to the population, a new grid dimension is generated for the entire population space, and the location of every population member is recalculated, with all population members distributed through the space using hypercubes to even out solution dispersion across the Pareto optimal set.

Furthermore, the leader mechanism directs search agents to promising new areas of the search space that carry a better chance of finding solutions close to the global or, at least, a near-optimal solution. Comparing results can be challenging, thanks to Pareto optimality in a multiobjective search space. To ensure the effectiveness of the search process, the leader selection mechanism chooses leaders from the sparsest regions in the search space based on the most effective nondominant solutions collected so far from the archive.

The probability for each hypercube is determined using the following equation [30]:

$$P_i = \frac{C}{N_i} \tag{3.1}$$

According to Eq. (3.1), hypercubes with fewer members are more likely to nominate new leaders. The probability of selecting a hypercube as a source for leader selection increases as the diversity of solutions obtained from that hypercube decreases. The MAAGTO algorithm is an enhanced version of the AGTO procedure. Improved consistency is expected when a solution is selected from the archive using the MAAGTO algorithm. Identifying Pareto-optimal responses can be difficult when there are numerous options. To address this issue, three mechanisms were applied as follows:

Archive Mechanism: A fixed-size external archive stores a nondominated Pareto-optimal solution. It uses a special controller to determine which solutions are admitted. If any existing archive member dominates a new solution, it is not added to the archive. It may be included if the new solution is superior to at least one existing solution. The new solution is added to the archive if neither dominates the other.

Grid Mechanism: This mechanism enhances the diversity of nondominated solutions in the full archive by reorganizing the objective space segmentation. It identifies the most congested areas to remove a solution, thus making room for new ones in less crowded areas, which improves the diversity of the Pareto-optimal front.

Leader Selection Mechanism: This mechanism guides search agents toward promising areas of the search space to find solutions near the global optimum. The leader selection process selects one of the archived nondominated solutions and positions it in the least congested regions of the search space to maintain diversity.

4. Simulation and results

In this section, the MAAGTO will be evaluated using a total of eight engineering multiobjective problems, and the results will be analyzed and compared with those of other methodologies. MAAGTO are compared to three state-of-art MO algorithms: MO Ant Lion Optimizer (MOALO) [31], MO Gray Wolf Optimizer (MOGWO) [30], MO Whale Optimization Algorithm (MOWOA) [32]. A comparison to state-of-the-art algorithms further demonstrates the MAAGTO 's efficacy. The optimization setup features a population size of 100 particles $\left(N_{pop}\right)$ and 30 adaptive grids $\left(N_{grid}\right)$ .The archive size is fixed at 100 $\left(N_{rep}\right)$ .The problem has two objectives ($M = 2$), with (D) representing the total number of decision variables. A maximum of 1000 function evaluations is allowed, and the procedures are executed 30 times.

The IGD and GD performance metrics results for eight engineering design challenges are presented in Tables 3.1 and 3.2, respectively. The MAAGTO method outperformed other algorithms across all eight instances according to the IGD metric. For the GD metric, MAAGTO excelled in all benchmarks except for the WELDED BEAM, the 4-BAR TRUSS,

TABLE 3.1 The IGD metric for different algorithms.

Functions		Algorithm			
		MOWOA	*MOGWO*	*MOALO*	*MAAGTO*
Eng 1: BNH	Ave	1.089E-03	3.346E-03	1.304E-02	**8.778E-04**
	SD	1.450E-04	1.598E-03	3.524E-03	**6.687E-05**
Eng 2: CONSTR	Ave	2.984E-03	6.859E-04	2.533E-03	**5.016E-04**
	SD	1.771E-03	1.305E-04	9.149E-04	**4.296E-05**
Eng 3: DISK BRAKE	Ave	6.534E-04	6.327E-04	1.863E-03	**5.657E-04**
	SD	9.120E-05	1.045E-04	7.088E-04	**6.789E-05**
Eng 4: 4 BAR-TURSS	Ave	2.022E-02	2.136E-02	2.218E-02	**1.994E-02**
	SD	2.657E-04	1.200E-04	8.200E-04	**2.465E-05**
Eng 5: WELDED BEAM	Ave	1.099E-03	1.341E-03	6.638E-03	**7.364E-04**
	SD	2.576E-04	6.085E-04	2.702E-03	**5.682E-05**
Eng 6: OSY	Ave	9.195E-03	9.265E-03	8.049E-03	**7.023E-03**
	SD	2.846E-03	3.198E-03	**1.408E-03**	1.538E-03
Eng 7: SPEED REDUCER	Ave	1.373E-02	1.424E-02	1.910E-02	**6.332E-03**
	SD	9.171E-03	3.203E-03	3.476E-03	**1.981E-04**
Eng 8: SRN	Ave	6.496E-04	2.482E-03	6.137E-03	**2.851E-04**
	SD	2.393E-04	1.061E-03	1.776E-03	**2.736E-05**

TABLE 3.2 The GD metric for different algorithms.

Functions		Algorithm			
		MOWOA	*MOGWO*	*MOALO*	*MAAGTO*
Eng 1: BNH	Ave	4.057E-02	6.631E-02	6.284E-02	**3.089E-02**
	SD	1.000E-02	1.663E-02	1.488E-02	**1.895E-03**
Eng 2: CONSTR	Ave	6.141E-04	8.214E-04	1.739E-03	**7.990E-04**
	SD	1.128E-04	**8.977E-05**	9.333E-04	1.069E-04
Eng 3: DISK BRAKE	Ave	3.284E-03	3.181E-03	3.651E-03	**2.194E-03**
	SD	9.604E-04	6.901E-04	5.901E-03	**2.195E-04**
Eng 4: 4 BAR TURSS	Ave	1.266E+01	1.082E+01	**3.198E+00**	1.259E+01
	SD	1.653E+00	1.553E+00	3.800E+00	**1.517E+00**
Eng 5: WELDED BEAM	Ave	3.364E-02	3.345E-02	**3.999E-03**	1.792E-02
	SD	2.767E-02	2.360E-02	**8.572E-04**	3.237E-03
Eng 6: OSY	Ave	2.281E+00	1.095E+00	9.196E-01	**9.009E-01**
	SD	5.942E-01	4.227E-01	6.665E-01	**8.218E-02**
Eng 7: SPEED REDUCER	Ave	8.519E+00	8.289E+00	**6.611E+00**	1.142E+01
	SD	3.415E+00	1.613E+00	1.998E+00	**7.642E-01**
Eng 8: SRN	Ave	5.348E-02	1.674E-02	1.861E-02	**1.065E-02**
	SD	7.203E-02	**3.992E-03**	1.803E-02	9.530E-03

and the SPEED REDUCER. Comparing MAAGTO's results to the SD values, it achieved superior performance in seven of eight IGD metrics and five of eight GD metrics. Compared with MOALO, MOGWO, and MOWOA, the proposed MAAGTO consistently demonstrated better performance on IGD and GD metrics. Both metrics' standard deviation (SD) values indicate that MAAGTO delivers reliable and consistent results across multiple experiments.

These findings confirm the method's effectiveness in solving complex multiobjective optimization problems in a mathematical context. For the engineering design problems considered, Fig. 3.3 and 3.4 illustrate the algorithm's ability to generate superior solutions that closely approach the Pareto front. This demonstrates that the proposed MAAGTO converges accurately to all real Pareto-optimal fronts.

Table 3.3 presents the S metric results for different algorithms across eight engineering design functions, focusing on the spread or distribution of solutions along the Pareto front. The algorithms compared include MOWOA, MOGWO,

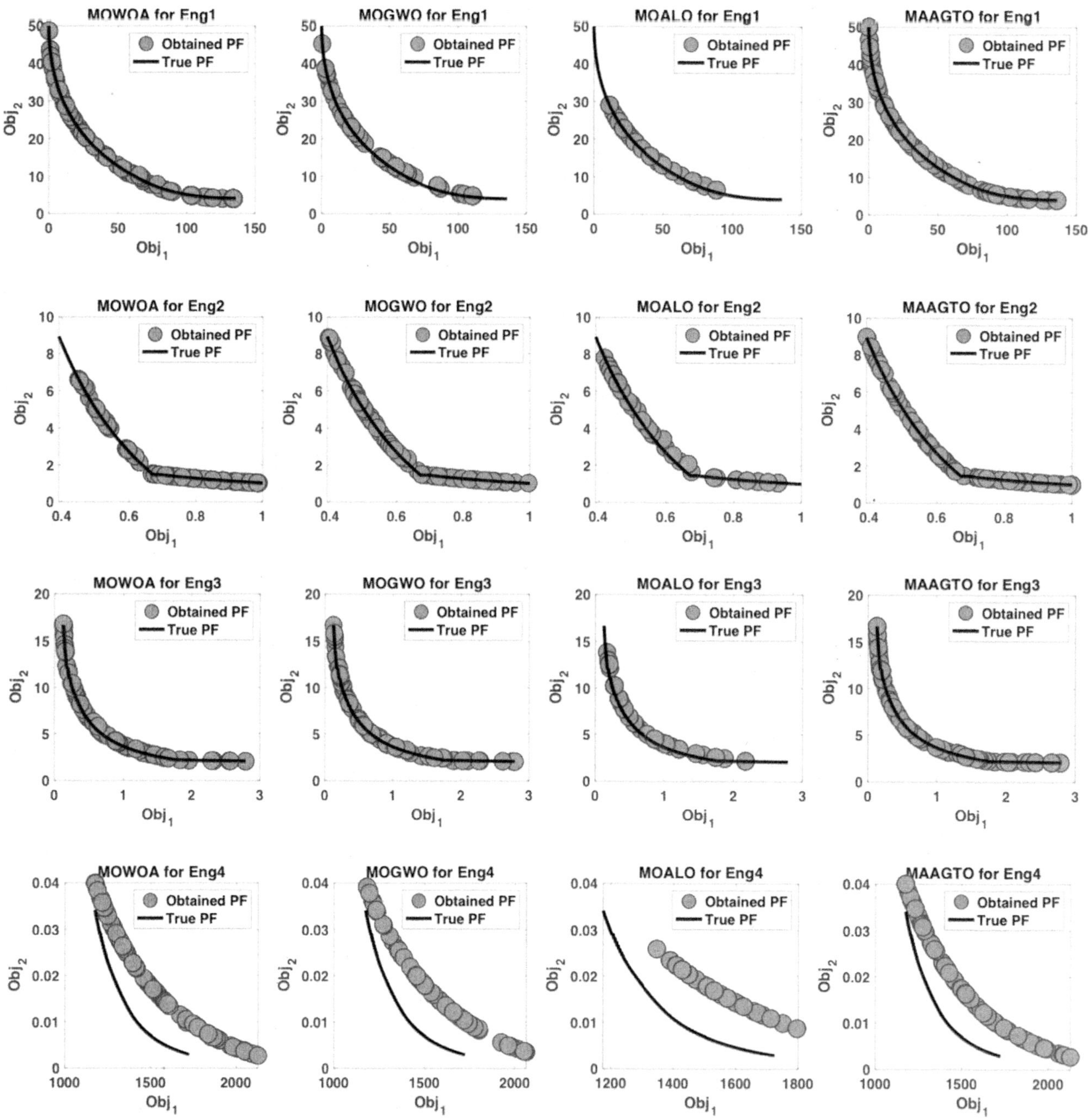

FIGURE 3.3 Results of different algorithms for Eng 1 to Eng 4.

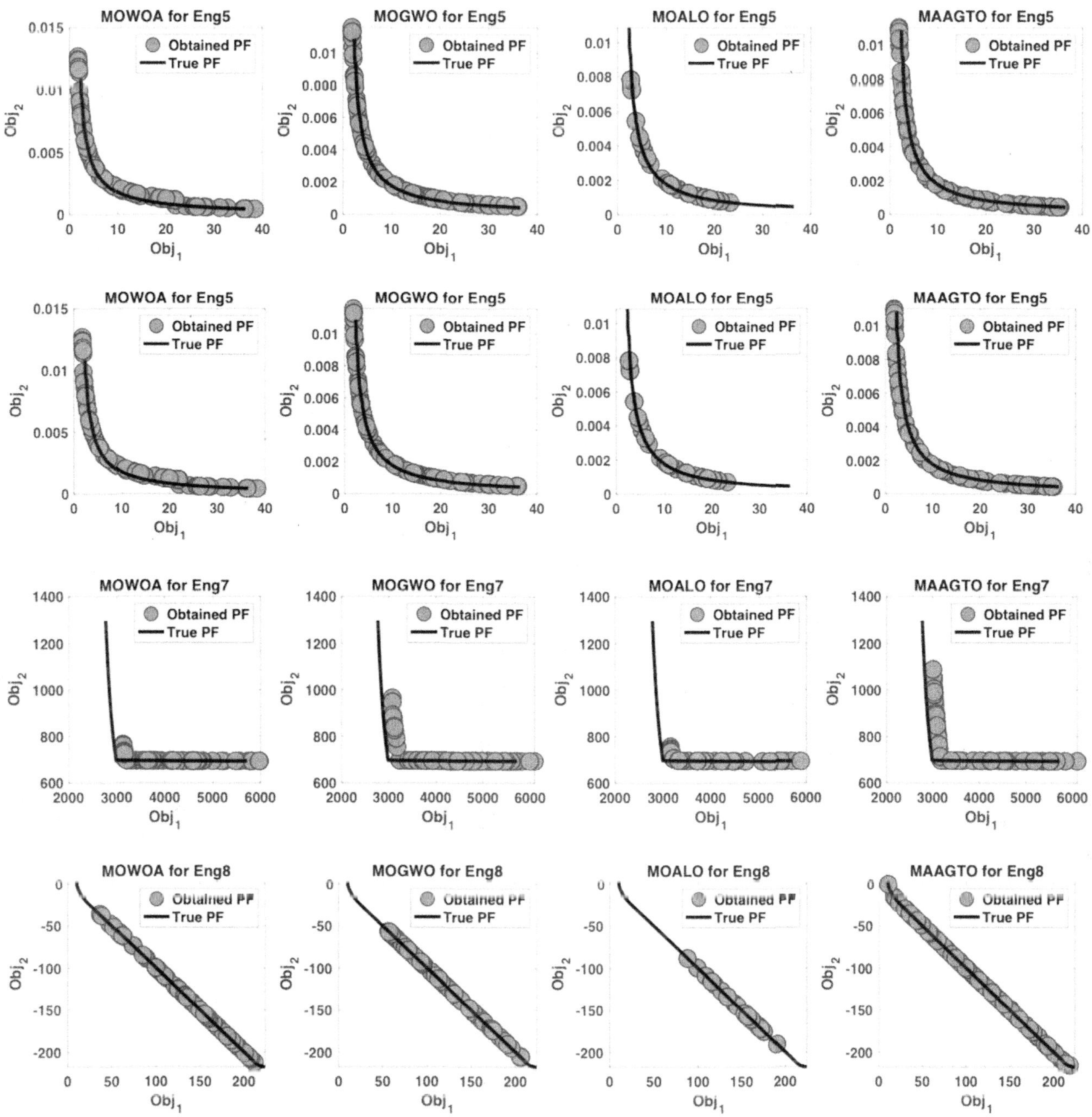

FIGURE 3.4 Results of different algorithms for Eng 5 to Eng 8.

MOALO, and MAAGTO. MAAGTO consistently shows competitive performance, achieving the lowest average S metric in four out of eight functions (BNH, CONSTR, DISK BRAKE, and SRN), indicating better solutions spread. MAAGTO's performance remains close to the best for the remaining functions, with notably low standard deviation values, demonstrating the algorithm's stability and reliability in maintaining a diverse set of high-quality solutions. These results confirm MAAGTO's effectiveness in providing a well-distributed set of solutions across the Pareto front, making it a robust choice for complex multiobjective optimization problems.

Table 3.4 presents the MS metric results for different algorithms across eight engineering design functions, evaluating the maximum spread of the solutions. The algorithms compared include MOWOA, MOGWO, MOALO, and MAAGTO. The MS metric measures how well the solutions cover the objective space. MAAGTO performs superior by achieving the average MS values in eight functions (Eng 1 to Eng 8). This indicates that MAAGTO effectively maximizes the spread of

TABLE 3.3 The S metric for different algorithms.

Functions		Algorithm			
		MOWOA	*MOGWO*	*MOALO*	*MAAGTO*
Eng 1: BNH	Ave	1.176E+00	1.825E+00	1.050E+00	**9.788E-01**
	SD	2.209E-01	6.005E-01	6.778E-01	**1.312E-01**
Eng 2: CONSTR	Ave	4.339E-02	5.939E-02	6.179E-02	**5.477E-02**
	SD	1.749E-02	9.437E-03	2.391E-02	**9.281E-03**
Eng 3: DISK BRAKE	Ave	1.235E-01	1.345E-01	1.634E-01	**1.029E-01**
	SD	2.088E-02	3.198E-02	3.457E-02	**1.091E-02**
Eng 4: 4 BAR-TURSS	Ave	5.706E+00	5.157E+00	**4.489E+00**	5.157E+00
	SD	7.018E-01	9.891E-01	2.042E+00	**6.283E-01**
Eng 5: WELDED BEAM	Ave	3.812E-01	3.455E-01	**2.341E-01**	2.389E-01
	SD	1.393E-01	1.214E-01	1.159E-01	**3.097E-02**
Eng 6: OSY	Ave	**1.211E+00**	1.506E+00	1.589E+00	1.310E+00
	SD	3.766E-01	1.236E+00	6.512E-01	**2.079E-01**
Eng 7: SPEED REDUCER	Ave	2.480E+01	**2.062E+01**	3.551E+01	2.304E+01
	SD	5.407E+00	**3.186E+00**	1.245E+01	5.883E+00
Eng 8: SRN	Ave	1.176E+00	1.825E+00	1.050E+00	**9.788E-01**
	SD	2.209E-01	6.005E-01	6.778E-01	**1.312E-01**

TABLE 3.4 The MS metric for different algorithms.

Functions		Algorithm			
		MOWOA	*MOGWO*	*MOALO*	*MAAGTO*
Eng 1: BNH	Ave	9.833E-01	8.837E-01	5.139E-01	**1.000E+00**
	SD	1.406E-02	7.761E-02	9.334E-02	**0.000E+00**
Eng 2: CONSTR	Ave	7.796E-01	9.868E-01	7.903E-01	**9.932E-01**
	SD	8.596E-02	**7.976E-03**	7.238E-02	1.357E-02
Eng 3: DISK BRAKE	Ave	9.939E-01	9.846E-01	8.501E-01	**9.991E-01**
	SD	1.385E-02	1.739E-02	1.123E-01	**1.244E-03**
Eng 4: 4 BAR-TURSS	Ave	1.479E+00	1.352E+00	8.348E-01	**1.487E+00**
	SD	9.578E-03	3.395E-02	1.669E-01	**2.341E-16**
Eng 5: WELDED BEAM	Ave	1.077E+00	1.084E+00	6.149E-01	**1.122E+00**
	SD	6.287E-02	1.046E-01	1.385E-01	**5.012E-02**
Eng 6: OSY	Ave	6.649E-01	5.744E-01	5.910E-01	**6.784E-01**
	SD	1.795E-01	1.610E-01	1.124E-01	**5.834E-02**
Eng 7: SPEED REDUCER	Ave	7.856E-01	7.671E-01	6.926E-01	**8.553E-01**
	SD	8.233E-02	2.418E-02	4.967E-02	**1.828E-02**
Eng 8: SRN	Ave	8.643E-01	7.001E-01	3.995E-01	**9.608E-01**
	SD	5.570E-02	8.018E-02	8.570E-02	**3.088E-02**

solutions across the Pareto front. Additionally, MAAGTO consistently achieves low standard deviation values, indicating its stability and consistency in delivering a wide range of diverse solutions. These findings underscore MAAGTO's effectiveness in providing comprehensive coverage of the solution space, making it a robust and reliable choice for solving complex multiobjective optimization problems in engineering design.

Figs. 3.3 and 3.4 show the Pareto front approximations by eight engineering design problems (Eng 1 to Eng 8) designed with four algorithms: (MOWOA, MOGWO, MOALO, and MAAGTO). Each figure shows eight problems with two objectives. Each Pareto front approximated by all algorithms obtained was compared to the true Pareto front. Overall, the MAAGTO algorithm provides the best solution. In general, each algorithm converges well with the True Pareto front. In addition, MAAGTO provides better coverage, logical distributions, and better approximations of the True Pareto front than the other algorithms. This is demonstrated by all problems. Therefore, it can be concluded that the proposed multiobjective algorithm MAAGTO is reliable, effective, and can solve multiobjective optimization problems.

5. Conclusion

In this chapter, we developed Multiobjective Archived-based Artificial Gorilla Troops (MAAGTO), an effective optimization solution for multiple objective problems, by integrating three components: leader selection, a grid mechanism, and an archive mechanism, into the original algorithm, which was able to deal with multiobjective problems. The algorithm's performance was illustrated with benchmark tests on eight standard problems in engineering. The results indicated that MAAGTO does better than the existing multiobjective algorithms of MOALO, MOGWO, and MOWOA. It does two particularly well: not only can MAAGTO deal with multiple constraints well, but the statistical analysis shows that MAAGTO has better performance than current standard optimizers for finding the optimal solutions. From a computational point of view, MAAGTO seems to be more effective than similar algorithms of its kind. Going forward, this strategy can be adopted in other data clustering methods that were initially developed to be used for multiobjective problems in bioinformatics.

References

[1] A. Charles, G. Parks, Application of differential evolution algorithms to multi-objective optimization problems in mixed-oxide fuel assembly design, Ann. Nucl. Energy 127 (2019) 165–177.

[2] C.A.C. Coello, Theoretical and numerical constraint-handling techniques used with evolutionary algorithms: A survey of the state of the art, Comput. Methods Appl. Mech. Eng. 191 (2002) 1245–1287.

[3] A. Kaveh, S. Talatahari, N. Khodadadi, Stochastic paint optimizer: Theory and application in civil engineering, Eng. Comput. 38 (2022) 1921–1952, https://doi.org/10.1007/s00366-020-01179-5.

[4] J.H. Holland, Genetic algorithms, Sci. Am. 267 (1992) 66–73.

[5] J. Kennedy, R. Eberhart, Particle swarm optimization, in: Proceedings of ICNN'95-International Conference on Neural Networks, IEEE, 1995, pp. 1942–1948.

[6] M.H. Qais, H.M. Hasanien, R.A. Turky, S. Alghuwainem, M. Tostado-Véliz, F. Jurado, Circle search algorithm: A geometry-based metaheuristic optimization algorithm, Mathematics 10 (2022) 1626.

[7] E. Atashpaz-Gargari, C. Lucas, Imperialist Competitive Algorithm: An Algorithm for Optimization Inspired by Imperialistic Competition, IEEE Congress on Evolutionary Computation, Ieee, 2007, pp. 4661–4667.

[8] G.-G. Wang, Moth search algorithm: A bio-inspired metaheuristic algorithm for global optimization problems, Memet. Comput. 10 (2018) 151–164.

[9] N. Khodadadi, S. Vaclav, S. Mirjalili, Dynamic arithmetic optimization algorithm for truss optimization under natural frequency constraints, IEEE Access 10 (2022) 16188–16208.

[10] Y. Yuan, L. Lv, X. Wang, X. Song, Optimization of a frame structure using the Coulomb force search strategy-based dragonfly algorithm, Eng. Optim. 52 (2020) 915–931.

[11] N. Khodadadi, H. Roghani, F. De Caso, E.-S.M. El-kenawy, Y. Yesha, A. Nanni, Data-driven PSO-CatBoost machine learning model to predict the compressive strength of CFRP-confined circular concrete specimens, Thin-Walled Struct. (2024) 111763.

[12] R.S. Parpinelli, H.S. Lopes, A.A. Freitas, Data mining with an ant colony optimization algorithm, IEEE Trans. Evol. Comput. 6 (2002) 321–332.

[13] A. Tharwat, E.H. Houssein, M.M. Ahmed, A.E. Hassanien, T. Gabel, MOGOA algorithm for constrained and unconstrained multi-objective optimization problems, Appl. Intell. 48 (2018) 2268–2283.

[14] Y. Wang, X. Ma, Z. Li, Y. Liu, M. Xu, Y. Wang, Profit distribution in collaborative multiple centers vehicle routing problem, J. Clean. Prod. 144 (2017) 203–219.

[15] Y. Wang, S. Peng, M. Xu, Emergency logistics network design based on space–time resource configuration, Knowl. Base Syst. 223 (2021) 107041.

[16] N. Khodadadi, S.Z. Mirjalili, S.M. Mirjalili, M.H. Nadim-Shahraki, S. Mirjalili, Multi-objective archived-based whale optimization algorithm, in: Handbook of Whale Optimization Algorithm, Elsevier, 2024, pp. 169–177.

[17] M.A. Tawhid, V. Savsani, Multi-objective sine-cosine algorithm (MO-SCA) for multi-objective engineering design problems, Neural Comput. Appl. 31 (2019) 915–929.
[18] X. Lai, C. Li, N. Zhang, J. Zhou, A multi-objective artificial sheep algorithm, Neural Comput. Appl. 31 (2019) 4049–4083.
[19] U. Yüzgeç, M. Kusoglu, Multi-objective Harris hawks optimizer for multiobjective optimization problems, BSEU, Journal of Engineering Research and Technology 1 (2020) 31–41.
[20] D. Angus, C. Woodward, Multiple objective ant colony optimisation, Swarm Intelligence 3 (2009) 69–85.
[21] N. Khodadadi, L. Abualigh, E.-S.M. Ei-Kenawy, V. Snasel, S. Mirjalili, An archive-based multi-objective arithmetic optimization algorithm for solving industrial engineering problems, IEEE Access 10 (2022) 106673–106698.
[22] K. Zhong, G. Zhou, W. Deng, Y. Zhou, Q. Luo, MOMPA: Multi-objective marine predator algorithm, Comput. Methods Appl. Mech. Eng. 385 (2021) 114029.
[23] Y. Jin, M. Olhofer, B. Sendhoff, Dynamic weighted aggregation for evolutionary multi-objective optimization: Why does it work and how, in: Proceedings of the Genetic and Evolutionary Computation Conference, 2001, pp. 1042–1049.
[24] J. Branke, K. Deb, H. Dierolf, M. Osswald, Finding knees in multi-objective optimization, in: Parallel Problem Solving from Nature-PPSN VIII: 8th International Conference, Birmingham, UK, September 18–22, 2004. Proceedings 8, Springer, 2004, pp. 722–731.
[25] J.B. Kollat, P. Reed, A framework for visually interactive decision-making and design using evolutionary multi-objective optimization (VIDEO), Environ. Model. Software 22 (2007) 1691–1704.
[26] M.T.M. Emmerich, A.H. Deutz, A tutorial on multiobjective optimization: Fundamentals and evolutionary methods, Nat. Comput. 17 (2018) 585–609.
[27] D.H. Wolpert, W.G. Macready, No free lunch theorems for optimization, IEEE Trans. Evol. Comput. 1 (1997) 67–82.
[28] B. Abdollahzadeh, F. Soleimanian Gharehchopogh, S. Mirjalili, Artificial gorilla troops optimizer: A new nature-inspired metaheuristic algorithm for global optimization problems, Int. J. Intell. Syst. 36 (10) (2021) 5887–5958.
[29] C.A.C. Coello, M.S. Lechuga, MOPSO: A proposal for multiple objective particle swarm optimization, in: Proceedings of the 2002 Congress on Evolutionary Computation. CEC'02 (Cat. No. 02TH8600), IEEE, 2002, pp. 1051–1056.
[30] A. Sahoo, S. Chandra, Multi-objective grey wolf optimizer for improved cervix lesion classification, Appl. Soft Comput. 52 (2017) 64–80.
[31] S. Mirjalili, P. Jangir, S. Saremi, Multi-objective ant lion optimizer: A multi-objective optimization algorithm for solving engineering problems, Appl. Intell. 46 (2017) 79–95.
[32] I.R. Kumawat, S.J. Nanda, R.K. Maddila, Multi-objective whale optimization, in: Tencon 2017-2017 Ieee Region 10 Conference, IEEE, 2017, pp. 2747–2752.

Chapter 4

SPO-ANN for predicting the compressive strength of concrete confined with CFRP using tube and wrap confinement types

Nima Khodadadi[1], M.Z. Naser[2], Ali Riza Yildiz[3], El-Sayed M. El-Kenawy[4], Francisco De Caso[5], Mohammad H. Nadimi-Shahraki[6], Antonio Nanni[5] and Khalid M. Mosalam[1]

[1]*Department of Civil and Environmental Engineering, Pacific Earthquake Engineering Research (PEER) Center, University of California, Berkeley, CA, United States;* [2]*Glenn Department of Civil Engineering, Clemson University, Clemson, SC, United States;* [3]*Department of Mechanical Engineering, Bursa Uludag University, Bursa, Turkey;* [4]*Jadara Research Center, Jadara University, Irbid, Jordan;* [5]*Department of Civil and Architectural Engineering, University of Miami, Coral Gables, FL, United States;* [6]*International Graduate School of Artificial Intelligence, National Yunlin University of Science and Technology, Yunlin, Taiwan*

1. Introduction

Fiber-reinforced polymer (FRP) materials have garnered significant attention in the construction industry due to their unique properties, including a high strength-to-weight ratio, corrosion resistance, and electromagnetic transparency [1]. These attributes make FRP suitable for internal and external applications in new construction and repair works. In new construction, FRP can be used as tubes that serve as formwork for freshly poured concrete or as wraps to reinforce and strengthen existing concrete structures. The combination of concrete and FRP leverages the advantages of both materials: concrete offers mass, stiffness, damping, and cost-efficiency, while FRP contributes to rapid construction, high strength-to-weight ratio, and environmental durability. The orthotropic characteristics of FRP make it particularly effective for encasing concrete columns [2,3].

Numerous studies have explored the behavior and efficacy of FRP-confined concrete systems. These investigations are typically categorized into two primary types: experimental and analytical. Experimental investigations involve tests conducted under various conditions to examine the material's performance. Analytical studies, on the other hand, focus on developing models to aid the design of FRP-confined concrete elements. Mirmiran et al. [4] investigated the effect of various parameters on the confinement efficiency of FRP jackets for concrete columns, including shape, length, and bond. A modified confinement ratio was introduced to evaluate confinement effectiveness as a function of FRP hoop strength and corner radius. The study showed that square-shaped jackets are less effective than circular jackets. The effect of the length parameter in columns with a maximum ratio of 5:1 was similar to that of tied columns, as stated in the American Concrete Institute (ACI) provisions. It was reported that confinement efficiency is not affected by the chemical adhesive bond; however, the load-carrying capacity of the concrete column can be improved using mechanical shear connectors. Various researchers have developed analytical models to predict the compressive strength (CS) of FRP-confined columns. These analytical studies can be classified into developing analytical equations and machine learning (ML) models.

For instance, the model introduced by Samann et al. [5] is based on the relationship between the concrete dilatation rate and the hoop stiffness of FRP, developed to predict the stress-strain behavior of FRP-confined concrete. The stress-strain response captured by the model agrees with the experimental results. Lam and Teng [6] also proposed a model to predict the stress-strain behavior of FRP-confined concrete. The model addressed issues such as FRP hoop strain at rupture, confinement sufficiency, and the impact of FRP stiffness on ultimate strain. Another model was developed by Jian and Teng [7] using a total of 48 test results to predict the stress-strain response of FRP-confined concrete elements. This model is capable of providing highly precise predictions.

Advanced Intelligence Methods for Data Science and Optimization. https://doi.org/10.1016/B978-0-443-28940-8.00010-5

Recent advancements in ML methods have also found applications in predicting the strength and behavior of construction materials and structural elements. These methods are able to predict target values if a sufficient amount of data is provided. Hu et al. [8] used six different prediction methods to predict the behavior and strength of FRP-CC (confined concrete) elements. This study utilized linear regression, ridge regression, decision tree, random forest, and extreme gradient boosting (XGBoost). Among these methods, XGBoost demonstrated the best results. It was reported that concrete strength, elastic modulus, and thickness of FRP are the most influential parameters affecting the results. It was also revealed that the relationship between FRP thickness and elastic modulus with concrete strength is logarithmic; however, the relationship between the CS of the section and concrete strength is nearly linear.

Cui et al. [9] gathered 366 data points on FRP-confined concrete and developed a machine-learning model to predict its compressive strength. The results from the proposed model were compared with the codes and models provided by other researchers. Among the models studied in this paper, XGBoost yielded the highest accuracy. FRP thickness, elastic modulus, and concrete compressive strength are the parameters that most influence the performance of FRP-confined concrete systems. In this work, the conditional tabular generative adversarial network (CTGAN) algorithm was also applied to the analysis, which is an algorithm that generates synthetic data due to limited experimental data. This led to the development of 3508 synthetic data points. The considered model yielded a high coefficient of determination statistic ($R^2 = 0.972$), demonstrating superior performance compared with other methods [10].

Metaheuristic algorithms are the most powerful practicable computational methods and refer to advanced computing strategies designed for solving complex problems that are difficult to tackle with conventional or exact algorithms [11,12]. Metaheuristic algorithms are computional methods that mimic natural phenomena to explore and exploit the search space efficiently. Examples include optimization algorithms such as Genetic Algorithm (GA) [11], Particle Swarm Optimization (PSO) [12], Harmony search (HS) [13], Flower Pollination Algorithm (FPA) [14], Butterfly Optimization Algorithm (BOA) [15], Pathfinder Algorithm (PA) [16], Search Group Algorithm (SGA) [17], Black Widow Optimization (BWO) [18] Lion Optimization Algorithm (LOA) [19], Chimp Optimization Algorithm (COA) [20] and Ebola Optimization Search Algorithm (EOSA) [21]. Because they use descriptions of biological evolution processes, animal social behaviors, etc., these algorithms efficiently explore and exploit the complex, multimodal, multivector search space while respecting the requested set of constraints. Exact optimization approaches are inefficient (computationally expensive) when the search space becomes very large and rugged. Important real-world problems with high dimensionality (thus complex) and vast search spaces that cannot be explicitly described include many nonconvex optimization problems with or without convex constraints.

One indispensable component in optimizing ANNs is metaheuristic algorithms, whose main function is fine-tuning network hyperparameters to improve the actual ANN's performance [22]. One of the main reasons for using metaheuristic algorithms is their ability to balance the options between exploration and exploitation during the search process for the best solution. Exploration is concerned with searching and exploring different areas in the search space and to keep away from unnecessarily early converging to poor solutions [23], while exploitation refers to the process of improving the best solution found thus far—that is, achieving a better and better solution according to the given criterion. Applying metaheuristic algorithms may optimize the hyperparameters of an ANN and how to initialize the network weights and design the network architecture to satisfy additional constraints. For instance, by using such algorithms in the training process, the predictive accuracy and robustness of ANNs could potentially be improved for their applied use in almost any discipline. Here, we introduce another novel approach for training ANNs through the application of SPO [24] to predict the CS of CFRP-CC under axial compression, using data collected from 916 experimental tests published in the literature.

Numerous studies have extensively explored experimental data on circular concrete specimens, forming the cornerstone of this research. CFRP is widely applied in civil engineering to repair and reinforce concrete structures. Existing equations for CFRP-confined circular concrete columns have been derived through regression analysis on limited datasets. Researchers have proposed various optimal design equations, but these models often rely on small data samples and employ basic linear or nonlinear regressions or algorithms, restricting their broader applicability. Researchers have compiled comprehensive concrete confinement data to validate these models. Consequently, there is an urgent need for a more precise and robust predictive model that can accurately reflect the intricate behavior of CFRP-confined circular concrete specimens. Extensive investigations have been conducted on concrete reinforced with FRP jackets to develop reliable and precise numerical models to predict its behavior. Nevertheless, most of these studies have focused on developing analytical models based on a limited range of experimental data. This chapter aims to advance the field by addressing the following key points:

- Although the SPO algorithm has demonstrated outstanding performance in various engineering applications, additional research is necessary to specifically evaluate its efficacy when combined with an ANN for predicting the CS of CFRP-CC under axial compression.

- This study evaluates the proposed model's prediction accuracy and computational costs for the CS of CFRP-CC.

The remainder of this chapter is structured as follows: Section 2 presents a comprehensive and updated compilation of experimental data from published research. Section 3 outlines the performance metrics used in the study. Section 4 describes the proposed model. Section 5 discusses the outcomes of the model. Finally, Section 6 concludes the study, summarizing the findings and implications.

2. Database

The experimental database [25] comprises 916 test data points derived from 116 studies on FRP-CC specimens. For modeling purposes, the key parameters include the diameter (D) and height (H) of the compression member, the compressive strength of unconfined concrete (f'_{co}), the FRP reinforcement ratio (ρf), the tensile modulus of elasticity (E_f), the ultimate tensile strength of FRP (f_f), the nominal thickness of FRP reinforcement (t_f), and the number of FRP layers. The compressive strength of confined concrete (f'_{ucc}) is the target value, with fiber orientation excluded from consideration in the dataset. Fig. 4.1 illustrates the statistical range of these parameters in the database.

Normalization is vital to address scale sensitivity in machine learning, particularly for algorithms that use distance measures or gradient descent methods. Normalization improves training speed, optimizes convergence, features significance comprehension, and improves numerical stability. All variables in the database are normalized to a range between −1 and 1 using the formula:

$$x_{i,\text{normal}} = 2 \times \left[\frac{x_i - \text{Min}(x)}{\text{Max}(x) - \text{Min}(x)} \right] - 1 \tag{4.1}$$

The database focuses on circular concrete specimens with FRP wraps or tubes, no other internal or external reinforcement, a height-to-diameter ratio of 5 or less, subjected to monotonic concentric compressive loads, with FRP rupture as the failure mode. Fig. 4.2 shows the classification of the database. The database contains 800 data points on concrete specimens wrapped with CFRP and 116 data points on concrete tubes filled with CFRP. Terms used in Fig. 4.2 include HM (High Modulus), UHM (Ultra-High Modulus), and C-Type (Concrete Type: Low, Normal, High).

3. Performance metrics

To evaluate the accuracy of the constructed model, several statistical indices were employed, including the coefficient of determination (R^2), mean squared error (MSE), root mean squared error (RMSE), and mean absolute error (MAE).

Coefficient of Determination

The coefficient of determination (R^2) assesses how accurately the model predicts outcomes, with possible values spanning from 0 to 1. This value is calculated as shown in Eq. (4.2).

$$R^2 = 1 - \frac{\sum_{i=1}^{N} \left(x_{\text{exp},i} - x_{\text{pre},i}\right)^2}{\sum_{i=1}^{N} \left(x_{\text{exp},i} - \underline{x}\right)^2} \tag{4.2}$$

Mean Squared Error

The mean squared error (MSE) is calculated as the average of the squared differences between the observed and predicted experimental values. It can be determined using Eq. (4.3).

$$MSE = \frac{1}{N} \sum_{i=1}^{N} \left(x_{\text{exp},i} - x_{\text{pre},i}\right)^2 \tag{4.3}$$

Root Mean Squared Error

The root mean squared error (RMSE) is another statistical metric used to evaluate a model's accuracy. The calculation of RMSE is outlined in Eq. (4.4).

$$RMSE = \sqrt{\frac{\sum_{i=1}^{N} \left(x_{\text{exp},i} - x_{\text{pre},i}\right)^2}{N}} \tag{4.4}$$

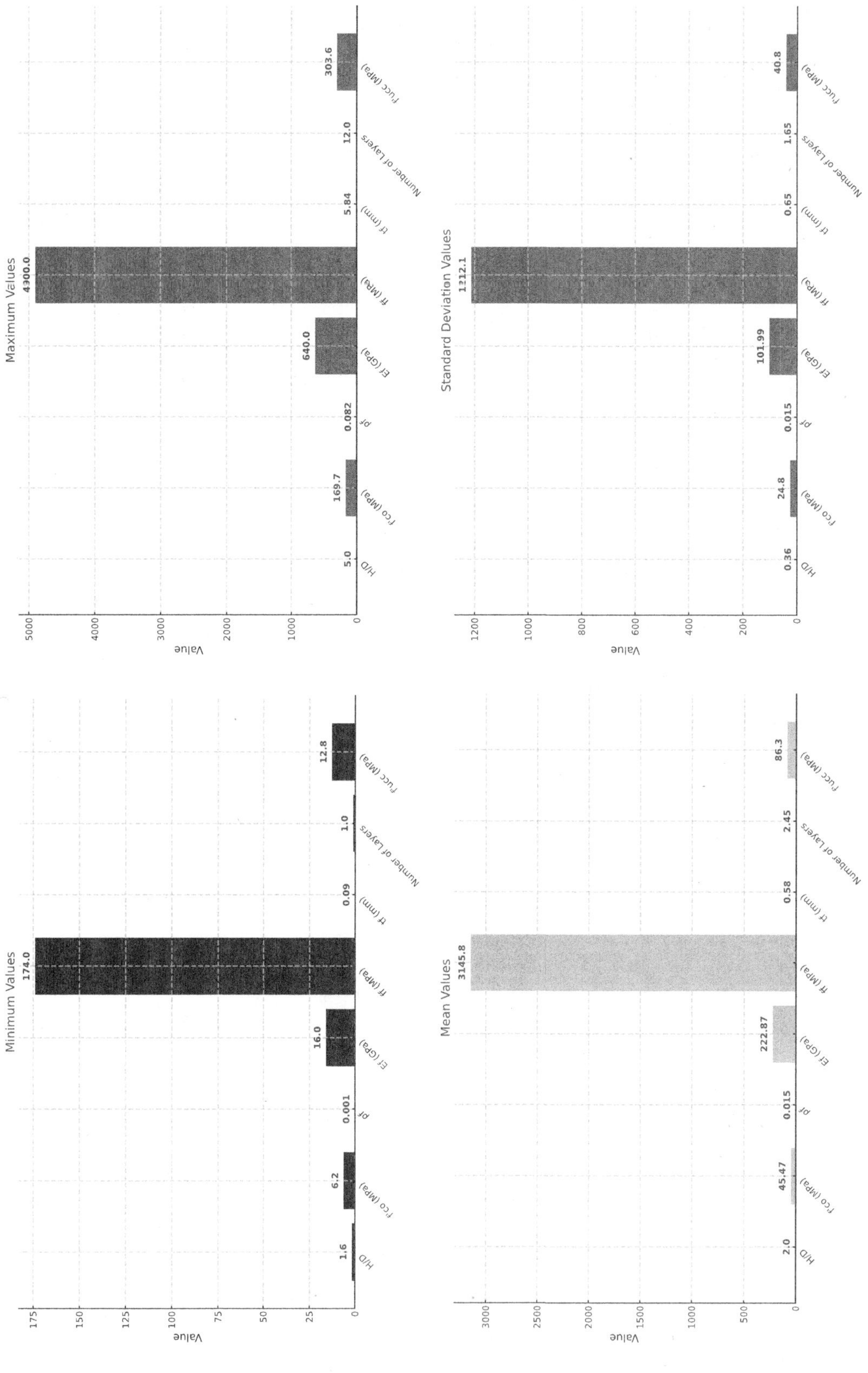

FIGURE 4.1 Statistical range of the database.

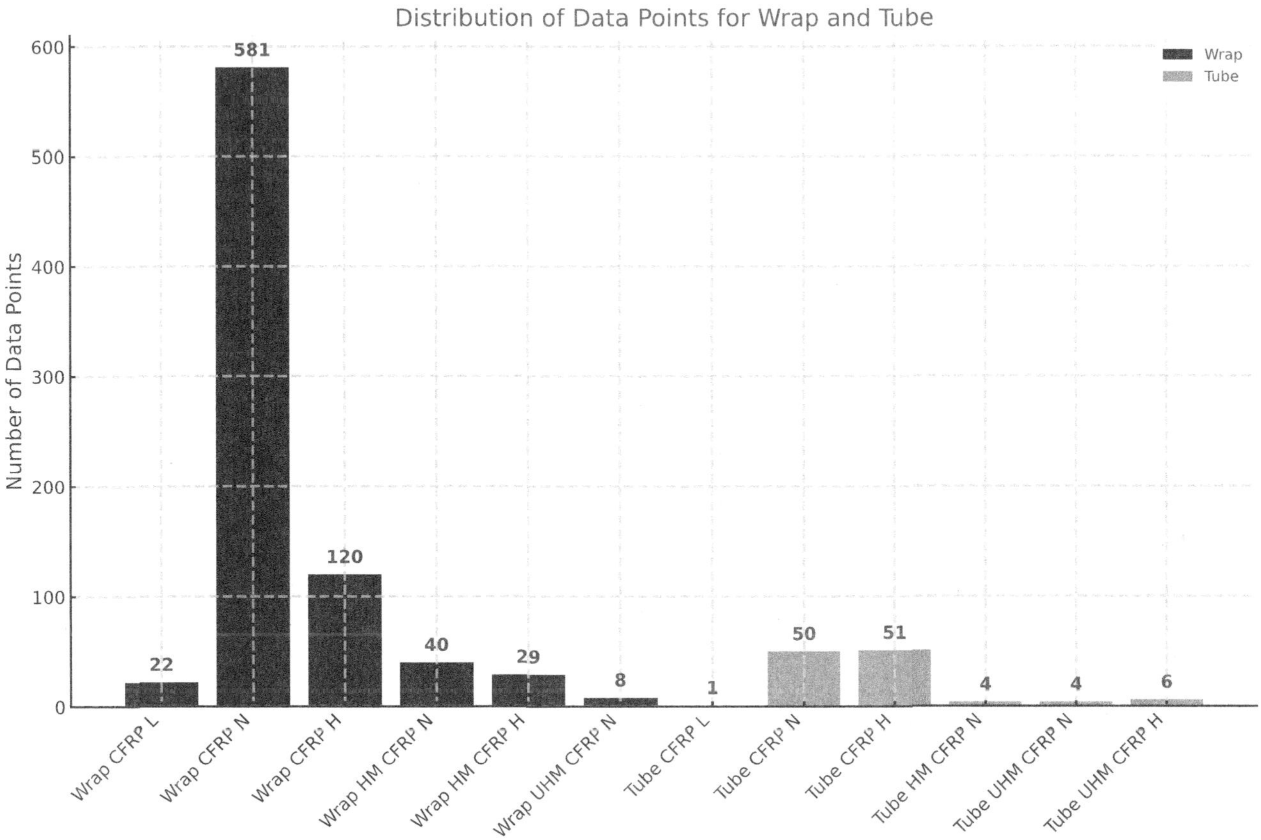

FIGURE 4.2 Classification of the database.

Mean Absolute Error

The mean absolute error (MAE) is calculated as the average of the absolute differences between the observed and predicted experimental values. This can be determined using Eq. (4.5).

$$MAE = \frac{1}{N}\sum_{i=1}^{N}\left|x_{\exp,i} - x_{\mathrm{mod},i}\right| \tag{4.5}$$

In all the above equations, $x_{\exp}$ represents the experimentally observed value, x_{pre} denotes the value predicted by the model, $\underline{x}$ is the mean of the observed values, and N indicates the total number of data points.

4. Construction of the model

This section provides an overview of artificial neural networks and the stochastic paint optimizer (SPO) [24]. Following this, the proposed model will be detailed.

4.1 Artificial neural network

ANN is a computational model that mimics the structure and function of the human brain, consisting of many interconnected artificial neurons, and it is capable of processing input data and delivering approximate solutions rather than a precise mathematical solution for a given problem. Thanks to advantageous features such as universal approximation capability, learning and generalization, and robust and fault-tolerant performance, ANNs have been extensively employed for many applications, including complex nonlinear function mapping, image processing, association memory, pattern recognition and classification, time-series prediction, and data mining, and they provide a fundamental example of computational intelligence. Training and ANN are of essential importance, and having a proper learning rule (algorithm) for this purpose is vital. Undoubtedly, the most commonly used learning rule is the backpropagation (BP) algorithm, with a number of variations, especially for training feed-forward networks, as exemplified by multilayer perceptron (MLPs), a typical ANN consisting of input, hidden, and output layers. Each node in one layer is connected to some nodes in the adjacent layers, and each node connection has an associated weight. Proper adjustment of these weights during network training is crucial. Network training is generally implemented by training instances (data samples) for many iterations.

However, any learning sample can be employed; splitting the entire dataset into a training set to tune network parameters and a validation set for network performance assessment is more straightforward and more common. In addition, it is also desirable to reserve a test set for external predictions after network training to ensure that the predictions are real and not introduced by the training process as an artifact.

In training networks with feed-forward backpropagation, arbitrarily assigned weights are often the beginning of the process. In each iteration for each parameter set, input data is fed through the network, where its output values are compared against target values using an error value. Weights are then modified in the following iterations to minimize this error, hence the name backpropagation for the backward weight adjustment from the output layer back to the input layer. The iterative process continues until the error is minimized to some acceptable level. In addition, a correlation coefficient is calculated to indicate the correlation-like relationship between the actual and predicted values produced by the network.

But feed-forward backpropagation Networks are not free from drawbacks. The use of too many adjustable weights can lead to the occurrence of overfitting and excessive network training iterations to overfitting. Risk must be neutralized during neuron weight adjustment to optimize the training model. The risk is controlled by finding the best network structure that bridges the risks of overfitting and overtraining. The number of adjustable weights significantly impacts the predictive models of artificial neural networks. A metaheuristic algorithm can be tailored to optimize loss functions and secure the network's best performance to nullify these drawbacks.

4.2 Stochastic paint optimizer

The Stochastic Paint Optimizer (SPO) [24] is a recent metaheuristic algorithm inspired by color theory, which merges solutions in a similar way that colors are mixed to create new physical shades. Four important fundamental color mixing techniques helped us to propose the SPO, including Analogous Combination, Color Complement Combination, Triadic Combination, and Tetradic Combination (See Fig. 4.3). Analogous Combination: In this color mixing technique, two adjacent colors are mixed, creating a new shade. Color Complement Combination: Two complementary colors of the same hue are mixed to produce a new color. Triadic Combination: This color mixing technique defines a regular triad composed of three evenly spaced hues. Then, the three grade colors are mixed in equal amounts to obtain a new color. Tetradic Combination: In this color mixing technique, a rectangular arrangement is formed by four colors. The colors associated with the solutions in the population depend on their objective values. In this manner, new solutions can be generated by the random selection of colors from the color wheel, which cannot arise from the normally implemented

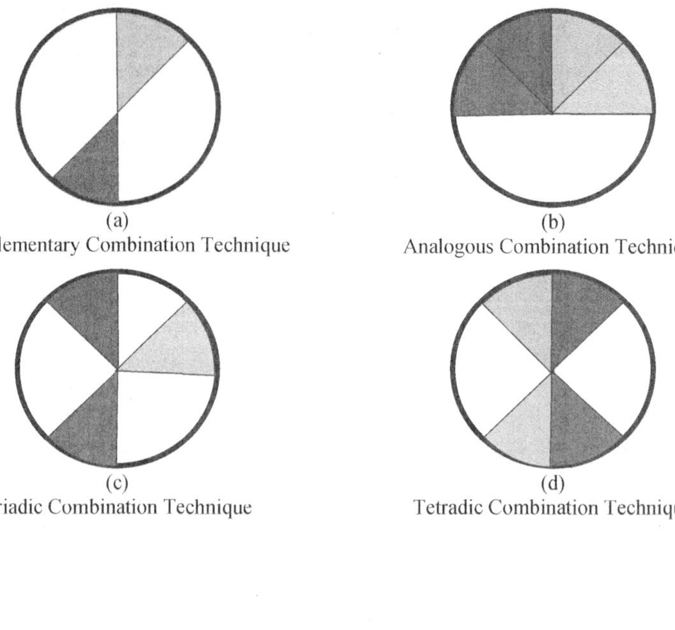

(a) Complementary Combination Technique
(b) Analogous Combination Technique
(c) Triadic Combination Technique
(d) Tetradic Combination Technique

FIGURE 4.3 Different combination of colors technique. (a) Complementary combination technique. (b) Analogous combination technique. (c) Triadic combination technique. (d) tetradic combination technique.

evolutionary. This color wheel helps to improve the algorithm's exploration and exploitation capabilities. It has recently attracted increasing attention from engineering optimization.

4.3 SPO-ANN

The dataset was divided into training and testing groups to predict the CS of CFRP-CC. Consistent with previous research recommendations, an 80/20 split was used. Consequently, 80% of the data, totaling 733 experimental datasets, were randomly selected for model development, while the remaining 20%, consisting of 183 datasets, was used to evaluate the performance of the SPO-ANN model.

An ANN model was constructed to predict the CS of CFRP-CC using the SPO-ANN model. SPO was then employed to optimize this model by fine-tuning the weights and biases. The ANN model featured one hidden layer with 1–20 neurons and utilized a sigmoid activation function. To prevent overfitting, min-max scaling was applied to normalize values within the range of [-1, 1]. The optimal ANN configuration for predicting the CS of CFRP-CC with SPO-ANN was identified as 8-10-1. Subsequently, the SPO was used to further optimize the weights and biases of the ANN model with the 8-10-1 architecture. The ANN architecture is illustrated in Fig. 4.4. The optimization technique's efficiency was assessed using MSE as the fitness function, described in Eq. (4.3). A thorough investigation involving 600 iterations was conducted to determine the optimal weights and biases for the chosen ANN model.

5. Discussion and results

The section begins with analyzing the results obtained from the SPO-ANN model. This is followed by obtaining and examining the specific formula crafted for this engineering problem. To tackle the issue, a termination criterion was set based on the total number of function evaluations. This process was conducted independently, with 20 runs carried out. Algorithm parameters were selected after reviewing the current literature and implemented using MATLAB 2023a. The runs were executed on a computer featuring an Apple with CPU M2 Max, 96 GB of RAM, running the Macintosh Ventura OS. The optimization goal was to minimize the MSE. The most successful model emerged during the 10th run, with R^2 values of 0.93 for training and 0.88 for testing. Model selection focused on achieving a high R-squared value and low MSE to balance model accuracy and prediction error. Fig. 4.5 shows the convergence curves, displaying the best and average convergence results achieved using SPO for the dataset.

Fig. 4.5 shows that the optimization process reduces the MSE; the best and average convergence lines decline substantially in MSE values over the first 100 iterations. After the rapid decrease, MSE values start to level off, gradually approaching a peak as the model performance stabilizes toward an optimal solution. The close spacing of the best and average convergence lines indicates that the optimization algorithm was largely successful each time it was run, with the algorithm tending to reduce error similarly at each iteration. The consistent accuracy of the optimization process indicates that it could be relied on to improve the model's accuracy.

Fig. 4.6 shows a heatmap based on the MSE scores for the training data set using the SPO algorithm. It visualizes the influence of the number of neurons in a hidden neural net layer and how these results change among different initialization seeds when the MSE score is acquired over 20 runs. The X-axis represents the number of runs and the number of varying initialization conditions. With each new run, a different initialization seed will be used to train the model. The value of the number of runs is measured from left to right and varies from 1 to 20. Each concentrated unit in the heatmap corresponds with the activation of the single run number to the MSE score. The Y-axis is the number of neurons in a hidden layer. As before, each graph extends from the smallest value at the bottom and lighter shade of the graph to the maximum value at the top and darker shade. The number of neurons in a hidden layer is measured from bottom to top with steps of single

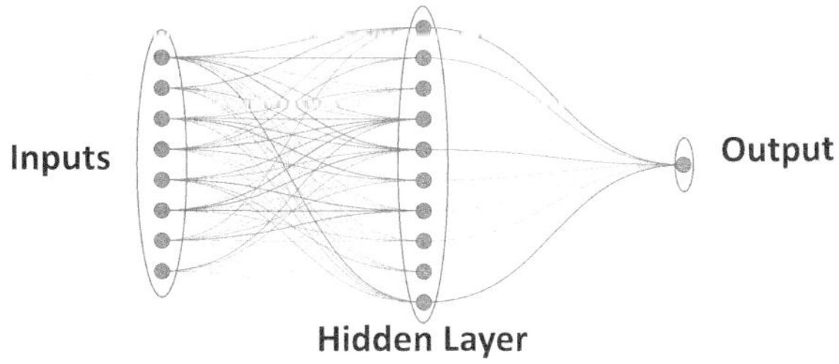

FIGURE 4.4 Architectural of ANN for SPO-ANN model.

FIGURE 4.5 The best and average convergence.

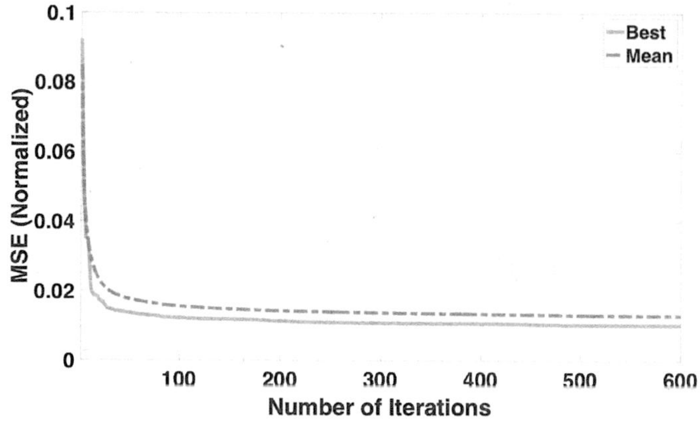

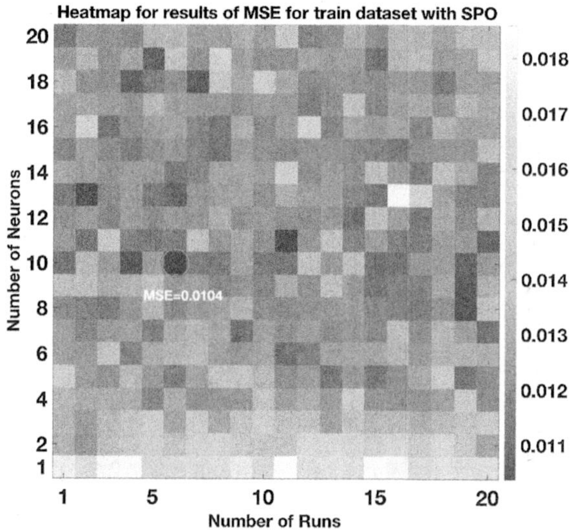

FIGURE 4.6 Heatmap results of MSE for 20 runs.

neurons from 1 to 20. It's seen that the number of neurons significantly impacts the model's performance by altering the MSE score. The lower the MSE score is, the better the model would perform (darker blue color). Conversely, the higher the MSE score, the worse the model would perform (lighter shade toward yellow color). This gradient facilitates quick visual identification of configurations yielding the best and worst performance. A specific cell, highlighted with a red circle, denotes the configuration that achieved the lowest MSE value of 0.0104. This optimal performance was observed with a neural network of 10 neurons in the hidden layer during the sixth run. The heatmap suggests that configurations with 10 neurons consistently perform better across various runs, highlighting this network structure as favorable for the given optimization problem.

Fig. 4.7 illustrates the predictive accuracy of the SPO algorithm by comparing experimental and predicted CS values across test, train, and all datasets. Fig. 4.7(a) compares the test dataset's experimental and predicted CS values, showing a close alignment over 183 data points. Fig. 4.7(b) extends this comparison to the training dataset, with experimental and predicted values plotted over 733 data points, again demonstrating a strong correlation.

Fig. 4.7(c) combines the test and train datasets, presenting the experimental and predicted values for a comprehensive dataset of 916 points. The consistent alignment between experimental and predicted values across all figures indicates the SPO algorithm's robust performance in accurately forecasting CS, thereby validating its effectiveness for this engineering application.

Fig. 4.8 provides a visual comparison of the R^2 values for the test, train, and all datasets, showcasing the predictive performance of the SPO algorithm. Fig. 4.8(a) displays the scatter plot of experimental versus predicted CS for the test dataset, with an R^2 value of 0.8855. The diagonal line represents the ideal fit where predicted values match the

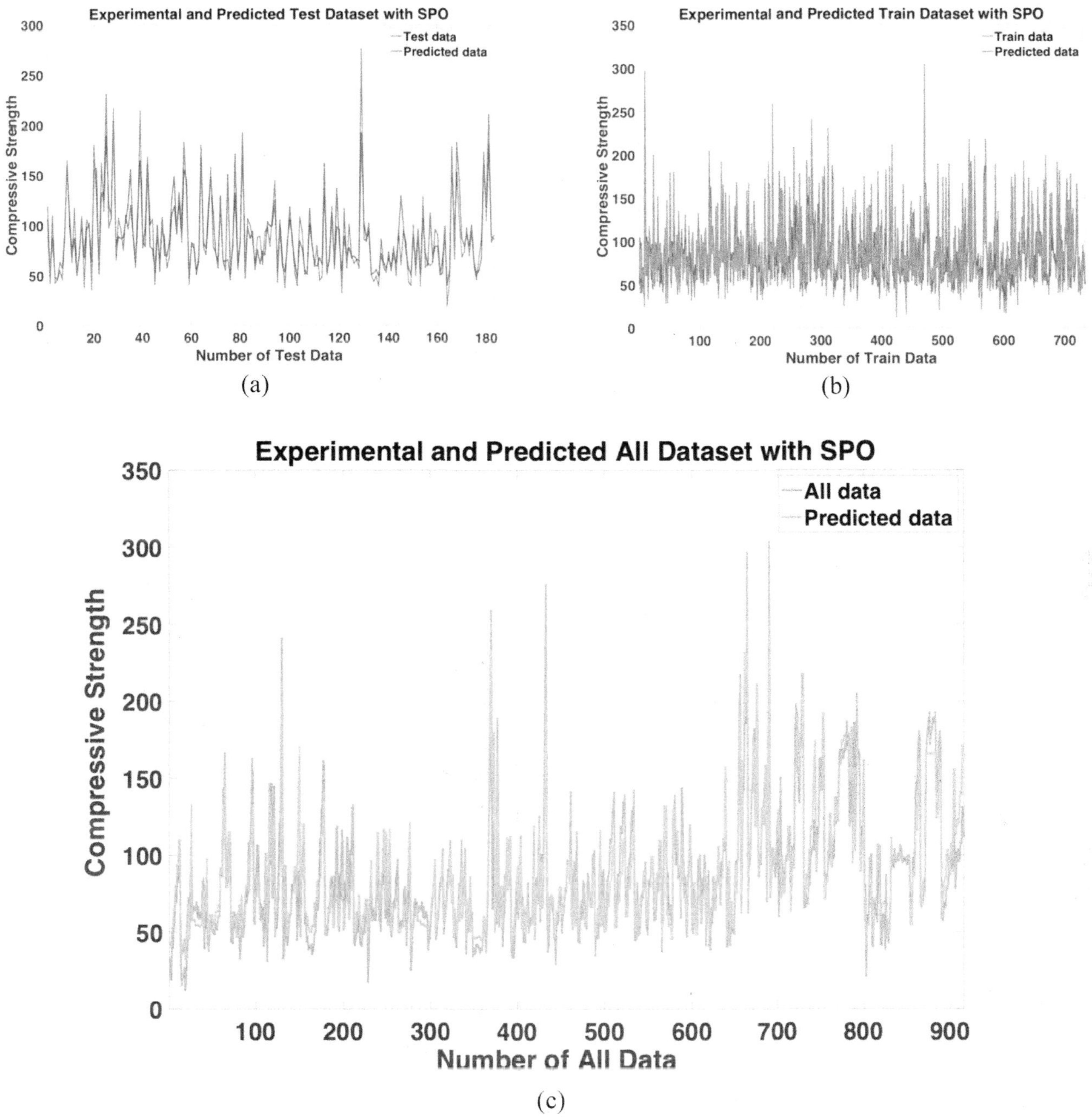

FIGURE 4.7 Comparing experimental and predicted for testing (a), training (b), and all data (c).

experimental data perfectly. The tight clustering of data points around this line indicates a strong correlation and high predictive accuracy for the test data.

Fig. 4.8(b) illustrates the comparison made for the training dataset for which we obtained an R^2 value of 0.9330. The points in the figure seem to have an even tighter fit to the diagonal line than the test dataset. Hopefully, this provides enough evidence to claim that the model performs well during training.

Fig. 4.8(c) illustrates the combination of test and train datasets to obtain an R^2 value of 0.9232. The scatter plot obtained in Fig. 4.8(c) for all the data has a close fit to the diagonal line, thereby providing evidence for the fact that our model is robust to all data points.

Overall, we can conclude that the SPO algorithm is well-predicted with very good R^2 values of 93.30% and 88.55% for the test and train set, respectively, and values of 92.32% for all dataset, which proves that the model is capable of finding out a relationship from experimental and predicted CS to be applied in real life applications.

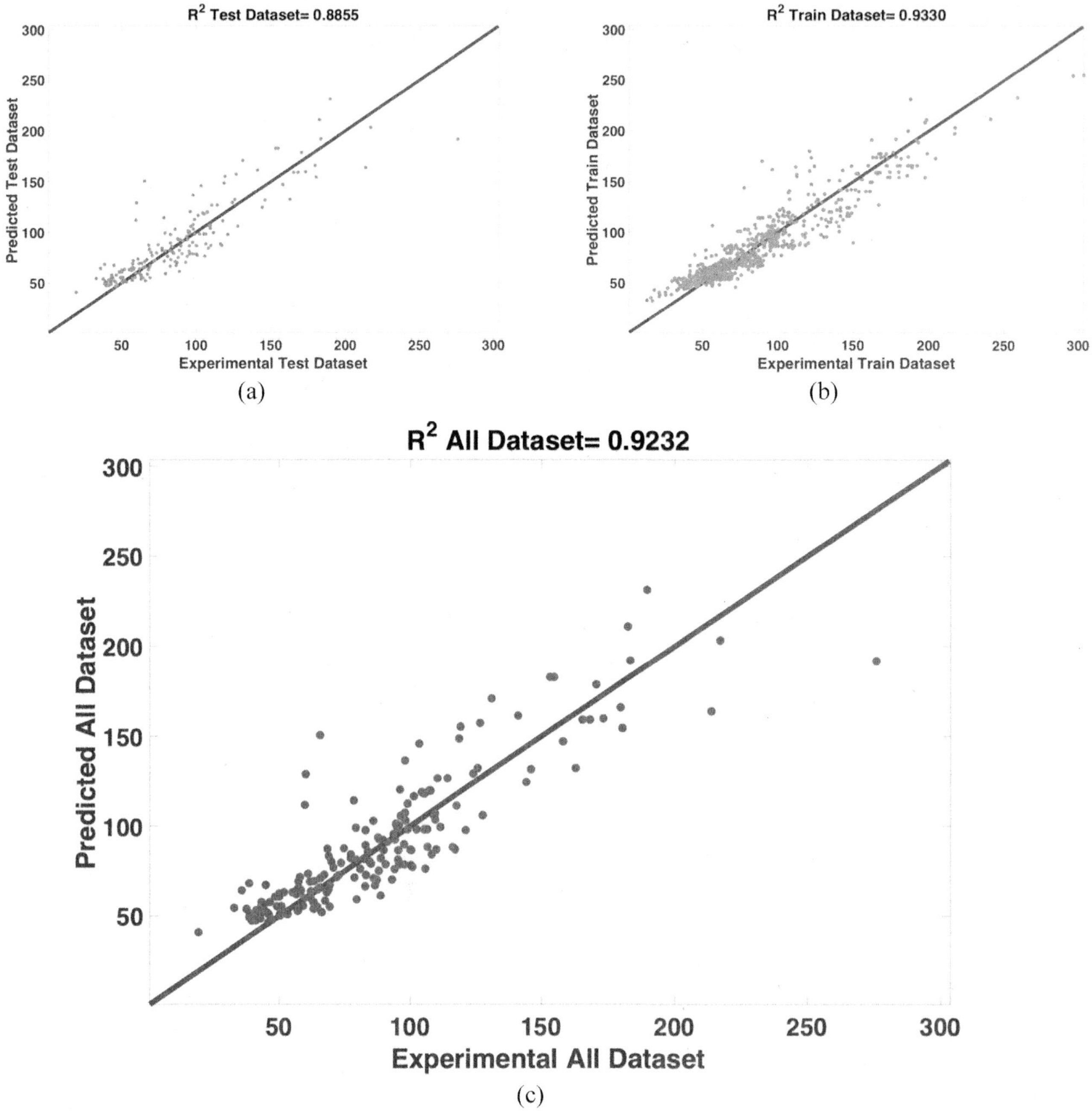

FIGURE 4.8 Comparing R-squared for test (a), train (b), and all data (c).

6. Conclusion

This chapter focused on developing sophisticated predictive models utilizing cutting-edge metaheuristic algorithms to improve the accuracy of compressive strength (CS) predictions for carbon fiber-reinforced polymer-confined concrete (CFRP-CC) samples. A dataset of 916 samples was used to train artificial neural networks (ANN) with the Stochastic Paint Optimizer (SPO) algorithm, forming the SPO-ANN model. Integrating SPO into the ANN significantly enhanced the model's predictive performance. The SPO-ANN model achieved a high coefficient of determination of 0.92 and demonstrated substantial reductions in MSE and RMSE compared with experimental benchmarks. The model's performance was thoroughly evaluated using several metrics, including R^2, MSE, RMSE, and mean MAE. These findings highlight the potential of incorporating metaheuristic algorithms such as SPO into machine learning models to enhance significantly their predictive capabilities. The improved accuracy and reliability of the SPO-ANN model underscore its practical applicability in structural engineering, especially for predicting the CS of CFRP-CC. This research validates advanced metaheuristic approaches in refining predictive models, paving the way for more precise and reliable engineering solutions.

References

[1] N. Khodadadi, H. Roghani, E. Harati, M. Mirdarsoltany, F. De Caso, A. Nanni, Fiber-reinforced polymer (FRP) in concrete: A comprehensive survey, Constr. Build. Mater. 432 (2024) 136634.

[2] A. Mirmiran, M. Shahawy, Behavior of concrete columns confined by fiber composites, J. Struct. Eng. 123 (1997) 583–590.

[3] S.M.P. Rashid, A. Bahrami, Structural performance of infilled steel–concrete composite thin-walled columns combined with FRP and CFRP: A comprehensive review, Materials 16 (2023) 1564.

[4] A. Mirmiran, M. Shahawy, M. Samaan, H.E.L. Echary, J.C. Mastrapa, O. Pico, Effect of column parameters on FRP-Confined concrete, J. Compos. Construct. 2 (1998) 175–185.

[5] M. Samaan, A. Mirmiran, M. Shahawy, Model of concrete confined by fiber composites, J. Struct. Eng. 124 (1998) 1025–1031.

[6] L. Lam, J.G. Teng, Design-oriented stress–strain model for FRP-Confined concrete, Constr. Build. Mater. 17 (2003) 471–489.

[7] T. Jiang, J.G. Teng, Analysis-oriented stress–strain models for FRP–Confined concrete, Eng. Struct. 29 (2007) 2968–2986.

[8] T. Hu, H. Zhang, C. Cheng, H. Li, J. Zhou, Explainable machine learning: Compressive strength prediction of FRP-Confined concrete column, Mater. Today Commun. 39 (2024) 108883.

[9] R. Cui, H. Yang, J. Li, Y. Xiao, G. Yao, Y. Yu, Machine learning-based prediction of compressive strength in circular FRP-Confined concrete columns, Front. Mater. 11 (2024) 1408670.

[10] S. Zeng, X. Wang, L. Hua, M. Altayeb, Z. Wu, F. Niu, Prediction of compressive strength of FRP-Confined concrete using machine learning: A novel synthetic data driven framework, J. Build. Eng. 94 (2024) 109918.

[11] J.H. Holland, Genetic algorithms, Sci. Am. 267 (1992) 66–73.

[12] J. Kennedy, R. Eberhart, Particle swarm optimization, in: Proceedings of ICNN'95-International Conference on Neural Networks, IEEE, 1995, pp. 1942–1948.

[13] Z.W. Geem, J.H. Kim, G.V. Loganathan, A new heuristic optimization algorithm: Harmony search, Simulation 76 (2001) 60–68.

[14] X.-S. Yang, M. Karamanoglu, X. He, Flower pollination algorithm: A novel approach for multiobjective optimization, Eng. Optim. 46 (2014) 1222–1237.

[15] S. Arora, S. Singh, Butterfly optimization algorithm: A novel approach for global optimization, Soft Comput. 23 (2019) 715–734.

[16] H. Yapici, N. Cetinkaya, A new meta-heuristic optimizer: Pathfinder algorithm, Appl. Soft Comput. 78 (2019) 545–568.

[17] M.S. Gonçalves, R.H. Lopez, L.F.F. Miguel, Search group algorithm: A new metaheuristic method for the optimization of truss structures, Comput. Struct. 153 (2015) 165–184.

[18] V. Hayyolalam, A.A.P. Kazem, Black widow optimization algorithm: A novel meta-heuristic approach for solving engineering optimization problems, Eng. Appl. Artif. Intell. 87 (2020) 103249.

[19] M. Yazdani, F. Jolai, Lion optimization algorithm (LOA): A nature-inspired metaheuristic algorithm, J. Comput. Des. Eng. 3 (2016) 24–36.

[20] M. Khishe, M.R. Mosavi, Chimp optimization algorithm, Expert Syst. Appl. 149 (2020) 113338.

[21] O.N. Oyelade, A.E. Ezugwu, T.I. Mohamed, L. Abualigah, Ebola optimization search algorithm: a new nature-inspired metaheuristic optimization algorithm, IEEE Access 10 (2021) 16150–16177.

[22] N. Khodadadi, S. Talatahari, A.H. Gandomi, ANNA: Advanced neural network algorithm for optimisation of structures, Proc. Inst. Civ. Eng. Struct. Build. (2023) 1–23, https://doi.org/10.1680/jstbu.22.00083.

[23] N. Khodadadi, E. Khodadadi, B. Abdollahzadeh, E.-S.M. Ei-Kenawy, P. Mardanpour, W. Zhao, F.S. Gharehchopogh, S. Mirjalili, Multi-objective generalized normal distribution optimization: A novel algorithm for multi-objective problems, Clust. Comput. (2024) 1–43.

[24] A. Kaveh, S. Talatahari, N. Khodadadi, Stochastic paint optimizer: Theory and application in civil engineering, Eng. Comput. 38 (2022) 1921–1952, https://doi.org/10.1007/s00366-020-01179-5.

[25] N. Khodadadi, H. Roghani, F. De Caso, E.-S.M. El-kenawy, Y. Yesha, A. Nanni, Data-driven PSO-CatBoost machine learning model to predict the compressive strength of CFRP-confined circular concrete specimens, Thin-Walled Struct. (2024) 111763.

Chapter 5

Quadratic interpolation optimization for optimizing truss structures using composite materials under natural frequency constraints

Nima Khodadadi[1], Weiguo Zhao[2], Ehsan Harati[3], El-Sayed M. El-Kenawy[4], Khalid M. Mosalam[1] and Antonio Nanni[3]

[1]*Department of Civil and Environmental Engineering, Pacific Earthquake Engineering Research (PEER) Center, University of California, Berkeley, CA, United States;* [2]*School of Water Conservancy and Hydropower, Hebei University of Engineering, Handan, Hebei, China;* [3]*Department of Civil and Architectural Engineering, University of Miami, Coral Gables, FL, United States;* [4]*Jadara Research Center, Jadara University, Irbid, Jordan*

1. Introduction

Engineering designs based on trusses of various configurations are highly popular since they are versatile and efficient for large-span (airplane hangars and industrial buildings) and lightweight construction (especially of telecommunication and power transmission towers), where towers can usually be built in large numbers. Optimization of these structures is an issue for engineering designers because of their lightweight, ease of fabrication, and rapid assembly. While minimizing weight is usually the goal for a structure subjected to dynamic loads, including earthquakes and storms, the natural frequencies of such structures are also important, particularly for limiting them to prevent destructive resonance with dynamic loads surrounding construction sites. The natural frequencies of truss structures are related to their vibration: the shape and value of the vibration depend on the natural frequencies of the structures, and information about the dynamic behavior is thus highly nonlinear and nonconvex.

Furthermore, dynamic equations with implicit variables make it difficult to derive their limits, and solving complicated, implicit-form dynamic equations affects the convergence of gradients. Many discrete models can represent the structural parameters of trusses well, and optimization of such structures is performed based on these models. However, all of these models are nonlinear, nonconvex, and time-consuming for traditional mathematical and gradient-based optimization methods to find their global optima, and often it is difficult to understand the relation between the objective function ($f(x)$) and its partial derivatives ($\nabla f(x)$) [1].

Consequently, in the last decades, there has been a rapid expansion of optimization methods called meta-heuristic algorithms, where fundamental decisions have been made based on probabilistic/random search principles. In this way, they could surpass the complexities of many traditional methods. Metaheuristic algorithms find near-global or global solutions by leveraging intelligence based on many natural phenomena. Over the years, various metaheuristic algorithms have been proposed for optimization of truss structures: Stochastic Paint Optimizer (SPO) [2], Particle Swarm Optimization (PSO) [3] Ant Colony Optimization (ACO) [4], Big Bang–Big Crunch Optimization (BB–BCO) [5], Genetic Algorithm (GA) [6], Teaching-Learning-Based Optimization (TLBO) [7], Flower Pollination Algorithm (FPA) [8], Chicken Swarm Optimization (CSO) [9] Political Optimizer (PO) [10] and Ray Optimization (RO) [11] Many of these researchers applied these algorithms to different structural optimization problems. These algorithms showed that they are useful for optimizing the geometry of engineering structures.Beam, truss, and plane frame problems are some of the problems in structures where the accuracy and capability of metaheuristic algorithms for solving these problems can be remarkably observed. Numerous studies claim that these algorithms successfully, and with acceptable computation time

Advanced Intelligence Methods for Data Science and Optimization. https://doi.org/10.1016/B978-0-443-28940-8.00005-1

compared to analytical solutions, reach the objective function. These algorithms have a few distinct advantages over analytical methods, which include implementation simplicity, generalized algorithm, good accuracy, and acceptable computing time. Consequently, many research studies are focusing on enhancing these algorithms. These studies may relate to optimizing engineering structures [12] and many other useful practical applications research. Enhancement of these algorithms leads to a continuous improvement in the applicability of the metaheuristic algorithms to truss structures.

Designing lightweight and high-performance truss structures is crucial to aerospace, automotive, and civil engineering, and recently, pultruded fiber-reinforced polymer (FRP) materials have attracted increasing attention due to their outstanding mechanical properties, such as superior strength-to-weight ratio, excellent corrosion resistance, and long-term durability [13]. Designing an optimal FRP truss that meets multiple design constraints, such as natural frequency requirements, is a new and challenging task.

The key contributions of this chapter are outlined below:

- This chapter identifies the absence of standardized methods to optimize truss structures for specific natural frequencies through Quadratic Interpolation Optimization (QIO) techniques.
- This research presents a QIO application for Fiber-Reinforced Polymer (FRP) trusses operating under natural frequency constraints.
- Carbon FRP truss structures exhibit a much lower weight than their steel counterparts, demonstrating their suitability for lightweight construction applications.

In aerospace engineering, for instance, minimizing structural weight while maintaining vibration control is critical for fuel efficiency and structural stability—making CFRP-optimized trusses ideal for aircraft components and satellite structures. In civil engineering, such designs can be employed in pedestrian bridges, roof systems, and modular structures where weight reduction can simplify construction and reduce costs without compromising safety.

2. Fiber-Reinforced Polymer Composites

The origins of FRP composites can be traced back to World War II, specifically within the aerospace sector for developing British bombers equipped with radar technology. The necessity for a radar-transparent material with sufficient strength and stiffness led to the creation of the first modern composite material, combining glass fibers with polyester resin [14,15].

Regarding the advantages of FRP, its utilization spans various sectors of modern society for critical applications. Initially embraced by the aerospace industry, it soon found applications in defense, the yacht industry, sporting goods, and the automotive sector (See Fig. 5.1). However, civil engineering had not significantly adopted FRPs for load-bearing structures, with limited use in nonstructural items like flowerpots and facade cladding. This realization sparked the notion that the infrastructure sector needed to explore FRPs' potential. Given their successful application in demanding fields such as space technology, aircraft, defense, wind turbines, boats, cars, and sporting equipment, it was proposed that constructing simple structural frames or bridges using FRPs should be a viable option.

Typically, in civil engineering, the development of a product follows a structured path, beginning with established rules and regulations. Trained engineers and architects utilize these guidelines to conceptualize a project. They then refine this concept into a detailed design, which is subsequently handed over to contractors for construction, such as building a

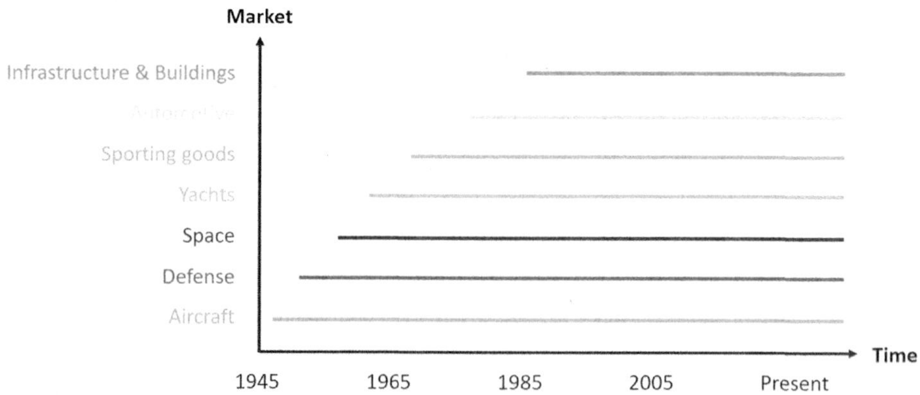

FIGURE 5.1 Market penetration of composite.

bridge for clients. The final product is often the result of a manufacturer's work. Pultruded structural profiles, also known as pultrusions, pultruded shapes, or pultruded members, have seen extensive use in various structures. These include pedestrian and building frames, vehicular bridges, cooling towers, stair towers, walkways, and platforms [16]. These profiles are frequently chosen for structures with a high demand for corrosion and chemical resistance, such as food and chemical processing facilities, cooling towers, and offshore platforms. They are also preferred in situations requiring electromagnetic transparency, such as in electronics manufacturing plants. Additionally, pultruded profiles are ideal for locations where accessibility is restricted, and lightweight skeletal structures need to be assembled onsite, like pedestrian bridges in park areas [17].

FRP pultruded truss bridge components are made from resin-infused strands, typically fiberglass, with tensile and bending strengths similar to steel or concrete. These FRP materials are both lightweight and long-lasting. They are available in standard profiles corresponding to the rolled steel shapes used in trail bridge construction, including tubes, channels, W shapes, and angles. The reduced weight of FRP structural elements facilitates transportation to remote sites, making them more convenient than traditional materials like steel or timber. Furthermore, their lightness enhances ease and safety during assembly.

The primary advantage of FRP composites lies in their unique combination of low weight, high strength, and significant stiffness. To substantiate these claims, it is essential to analyze and compare the mechanical properties of FRPs with conventional building materials like concrete, steel, and lightweight metal alloys such as aluminum and titanium [18]. For a comprehensive understanding, delve into the stiffness of these materials. Stiffness will be plotted against density in a log-log space graph, facilitating a broad range of comparisons between stiffness magnitudes. Fig. 5.2 shows the ideal material in the upper-left quadrant, indicating low weight and high stiffness. Steel, for example, has a density of about 7500 kg/m^3 and a stiffness of 210 GPa.

In contrast, concrete's stiffness ranges between 30 and 40 GPa with a density of 2400 kg/m^3. Aluminum alloys, while nearly matching concrete's density, offer double its stiffness. Titanium presents an intermediate stiffness between aluminum and steel.

Focusing on FRP constituents, glass fibers exhibit a density similar to concrete and aluminum but possess slightly greater stiffness, with Young's modulus between 70 and 80 GPa. Carbon fibers stand out due to their lower density (around 1800 kg/m^3) and superior stiffness, ranging from 230 to 350 GPa. It is noteworthy, however, that these stiffness values pertain predominantly to the axial direction of the fibers, which is also the most crucial orientation. Carbon fibers, being stiffer than steel and lighter than aluminum, have ideal material characteristics, while glass fibers also have promising properties. It is crucial to remember that these are standalone fiber properties. In FRPs, fibers are combined with a polymer matrix, commonly using epoxy, polyester, or thermoplastics such as PEEK. These polymers are notably

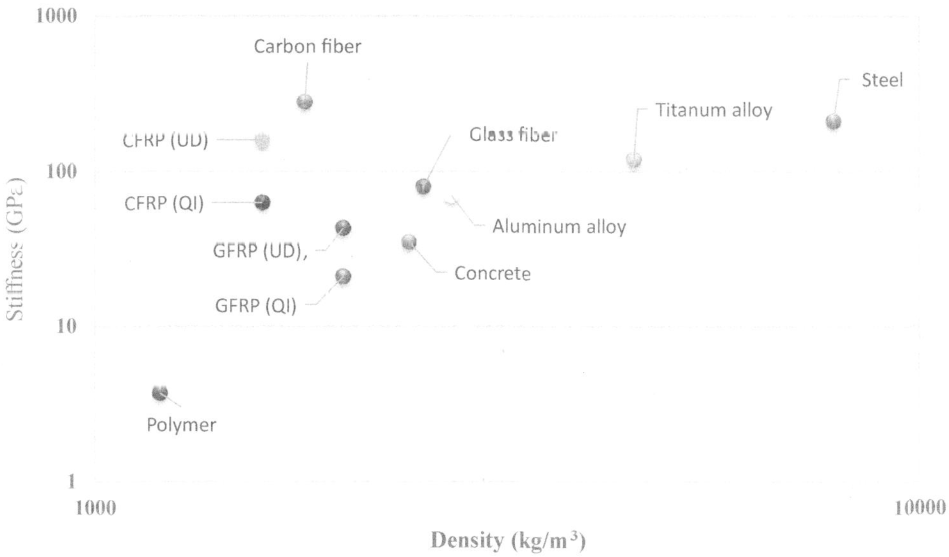

FIGURE 5.2 Stiffness to the density of all materials.

light, with densities between 1100 and 1280 kg/m^3, but their stiffness significantly trails behind other materials in the comparison.

To achieve desirable stiffness in FRPs, a high fiber content is essential. The overall stiffness of the composite will inevitably be lower than that of the fibers alone, but the weight will also decrease, particularly in GFRP, due to the heavier glass fibers. However, this analysis is not exhaustive. These properties are characteristic of unidirectional FRP composites, which exhibit lower stiffness and strength perpendicular to the fiber direction. Laminates are created with layered structures with fibers oriented in various directions to counteract this. Depending on the application, these can range from Unidirectional (UD) dominated to having uniform properties in all directions, achieved through quasi-isotropic layups. Although quasi-isotropic layups result in less impressive performance metrics, they are vital for attaining balanced properties. In practical FRP design, stiffness in the primary load direction will fall between the UD and quasi-isotropic values. However, higher stiffness in one direction can adversely affect stiffness in other directions, possibly dropping below quasi-isotropic values. Additionally, it's important to note that the out-of-plane shear stiffness in laminates remains low, regardless of the fiber orientation in the layers. Thus, while FRPs offer significant advantages, their application necessitates careful consideration of these multifaceted mechanical properties.

When examining the strength characteristics of various materials as outlined in Table 5.1, metals, notably steel and aluminum, exhibit considerable strength, with steel ranging from 370 to 770 MPa and aluminum between 200 and 414 MP a. Concrete, though strong in compression (up to 90 MPa), falls significantly short of these metals in terms of overall strength. The polymer matrices used in FRPs, while having lower strength values in the 40 to 80 MPa, are still noteworthy given their low weight.

Fibers, however, are the standout performers in FRP composites, offering exceptionally high strength. Glass and carbon fibers demonstrate strengths significantly surpassing classical engineering materials, ranging from 2700 to 5000 MPa. When these fibers are integrated with polymers to form UD FRP composites, the resultant material can exceed the strength of steel, achieving strengths between 1000 and 3000 MPa. This comparison suggests that when FRP composites have an advantage over natural materials, it is more likely to be strength rather than stiffness. It should be noted, though, that the strength of FRP composites is strongly directional. While UD composites have robustness parallel to the fiber direction, their strength in the transverse direction is much less than their through-thickness strength. The same limitation applies to multidirectional laminates, where strength is generally lower than that of UD composites. In addition, interlaminar strength in all types of FRP is low. A critically important variable is that, unlike the high tensile strength, compressive strength for FRP composites is often lower, leading to a range of strength values. Ductility is an additional important variable when comparing the failure characteristics of FRP composites with those of natural materials. FRP composites often have poor ductility, which means that even though their high strength is often available, their full benefits cannot be exploited.

TABLE 5.1 Properties of all materials.

	Density		Stiffness		Strength	
Material	*please explian*	lb/ft^3	*GPa*	*msi*	*MPa*	*ksi*
Steel	7850	491	207	30.0	360–770	52–112
Concrete	2400	150	35	5.1	25–90	3.6–13
Aluminum alloy	2700	170	70	10.2	200–415	29–60
Titanium alloy	4500	281	120	17.4	240–1400	35–203
Glass fiber	2500	156	80	11.6	2700–4500	390–653
Carbon fiber	1800	112	280	40.6	3100–5170	450–750
Polymer	1200	75	3.7	0.5	40–80	5.8–11.6
GFRP (UD)	1550	97	55	8	1140–1725	165–250
CFRP (UD)	1750	109	160	23.0	2240–3250	325–470
GFRP (QI)	1550	97	21	3.0	380–575	55–83
CFRP (QI)	1750	109	63	9.1	750–1080	109–157

Overall, the lesson from this summary is that GFRP and other FRP composites are attractive substitutes for materials such as steel and concrete. They are much lighter than steel and as stiff as concrete, if not more so, depending on the design. Most importantly, selecting an appropriate fiber orientation can optimize both stiffness and strength. When doing so, the performance in other directions is typically more compromised, as explained above. Out-of-plane performance, irrespective of laminate design, is always primarily controlled by the matrix. This development shows the complexity and constraints of the application road to reach an optimum solution when applying FRP composites in engineering and design.

3. Quadratic Interpolation Optimization

QIO has been presented [19] as an advanced technique based on the Generalized Quadratic Interpolation (GQI) method. This method considered the minimum of quadratic functions defined by any three points as the main drawback of the standard quadratic interpolation methods, and was able to overcome it. The QIO method combines two successful search strategies: exploration and exploitation.

3.1 Exploration strategy

- Selection of Points: For each dimension, two points are randomly selected from the population, and their positions are concatenated with the individual's current position.
- GQI Method: With these three points, we can form the quadratic interpolation function and find the minimum using the GQI method.
- Global Search: The minimum found is then combined with the position of another randomly selected individual to produce a new position for a global search.

3.2 Exploitation strategy

- Selection of Points: In each dimension, two individuals are chosen at random and the best individual at that point in the search to date.
- GQI Method: The GQI method forms a quadratic interpolation function from these three points and finds its minimum.
- Local Search: The minimum found is combined with the position of the best individual to produce a new position for a local search.

That is to say, by using these methods, QIO searches for the global minimum of a quadratic function with a much greater efficiency than corresponding quadratic interpolations. It utilizes the advantages of the GQI method in global and local searches.

4. Definition of problems

In this section, Fig. 5.3 outlines the optimization process of the truss structures within specific constraints of their natural frequencies using a detailed formulation. Three different truss structure examples are then also defined and studied below [20–25].

Optimizing truss structures involves determining the optimal cross-sectional areas (A_i) to minimize the structure's weight (A_i). The optimal cross-sectional areas must satisfy further constraints on the final design.

$$\text{Find } \left[a_1, a_2, \ldots, a_{ng}\right] \tag{5.1}$$

$$\text{Minimize } \quad W(\{a\}) = \sum_{i=1}^{nm} \gamma_i \,.\, A_i \,.\, L_i(a) \tag{5.2}$$

$$\text{Subjected to } \quad \begin{cases} A_{\min} \leq a_i \leq A_{\max} \\ \omega_j \leq \omega_j^* \\ \omega_k \geq \omega_k^* \end{cases} \tag{5.3}$$

In this context, $\{a\}$ denotes the set of design variables, ng indicates the number of these variables, and nm represents the range of structural members. The weight of the structure is expressed as $W(\{a\})$, while γ_i, L_i and a_i denote the

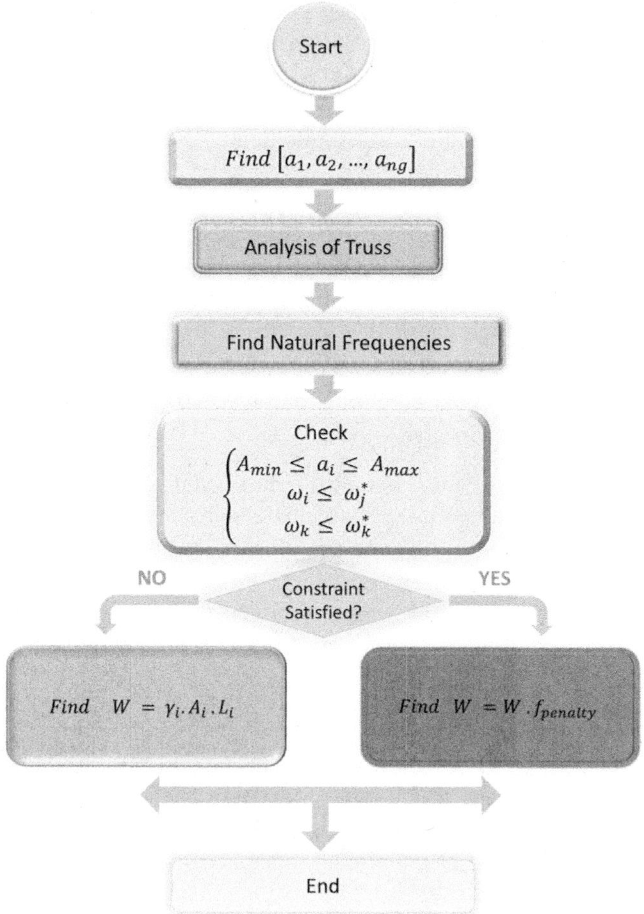

FIGURE 5.3 Flowchart of truss structures with frequency constraints.

members' material density, length, and cross-sectional area, respectively. The natural frequencies of the truss, ω_j and ω_k, have an upper bound of ω_j^* and a lower bound of ω_k^*. Weight is critical in reducing material costs and improving overall structural efficiency, especially in aerospace and civil applications. On the other hand, natural frequency constraints are essential to avoid resonance and ensure safe dynamic performance.

5. Truss structures examples and results

This section presents some of the usual structural optimization problems that demonstrate the benefit of using FRPs over steel in terms of QIO. Natural frequency is an important objective in truss structure optimization, and it is the frequency at which a structural system or physical system exhibits oscillations when disturbed. Thus, we can include natural frequency constraints in structural optimization to ensure the designed structure remains stable and can survive dynamic loads or vibrations throughout its life. A fair comparison is achieved using a termination criterion for the maximum number of function evaluations. Each problem is addressed individually, with 20 runs conducted for each. The analysis employs QIO with comparable function evaluations and representatives to ensure fair competition. The natural frequency constraints are applied to four truss designs: a 37-member planar bridge, a 72-member space truss, and a 120-member dome truss. These constraints, material properties, and cross-sectional area limitations are critical parameters that must be considered during optimization to create a design that meets performance requirements while minimizing weight. The constraints for these problems are as follows:

- **The 37-member planer truss:**

  Cross-sectional area constraint (**cm^2**): $1 \le A$.
  Natural frequency constraints (**Hz**): $f_1 \ge 20, f_2 \ge 40, f_3 \ge 60$.

- **The 72-member space truss:**

  Cross-sectional area constraint (***cm*²**): $0.645 \leq A$.
  Natural frequency constraints (***Hz***): $f_1 = 4, f_3 \geq 6$.

- **The 120-member dome truss:**

  Cross-sectional area constraint (***cm*²**): $1 \leq A \leq 129.3$.
  Natural frequency constraints (***Hz***): $f_1 \geq 9, f_2 \geq 11$.

The density and modulus of elasticity for GFRP, CFRP, and steel, as adopted in this study, are shown in Table 5.2.

The algorithm was implemented using MATLAB 2022b, with the truss problems solved using SAP2000 v14.1. The optimization process involved the application programming interface (API). The calculations were performed on a Macintosh machine running MacOS Big Sur, equipped with an Intel Core i9 processor at 2.3 GHz, 16 GB of 2400 MHz DDR4 RAM, and the specified software.

5.1 The 37-member planer truss

The initial example discussed in this subsection is the weight reduction of a planar truss structure consisting of 37 members, as illustrated in Fig. 5.4. The material properties relevant to this problem are outlined in previous sections. The design includes 14 size options and five variables. Additionally, a lumped mass of 10 kg is applied to the bottom nodes of the truss.

Table 5.3 provides a comprehensive overview of the performance metrics for different materials used in a 37-member truss. GFRP exhibits the lightest best weight at 76.473 kg, with an average weight of 76.861 kg and a standard deviation of 0.246 kg. CFRP demonstrates a slightly heavier best weight of 76.947 kg, accompanied by an average weight of 77.061 kg and a lower standard deviation of 0.073 kg, indicating minimal variation. In contrast, steel shows a substantially higher best weight of 363.817 kg, with an average weight of 364.325 kg and a standard deviation of 0.390 kg, reflecting greater variability. These findings highlight that, compared to steel, both GFRP and CFRP are more effective in maintaining lighter and more consistent weight distributions in truss structures.

Table 5.4 presents the natural frequencies (Hz) for the optimal design of a 37-member truss using GFRP, CFRP, and steel, considering the constraints $f_1 \geq 20, f_2 \geq 40, f_3 \geq 60$. The first natural frequency f_1 All materials meet the constraint, with GFRP at 20.0076 Hz, CFRP at 20.0061 Hz, and steel at 20.0004 Hz. For the second natural frequency f_2, CFRP exceeds the minimum requirement, achieving 43.4087 Hz, while GFRP and steel also meet the constraint with values of

TABLE 5.2 Material properties for this study.

	Density		Modulus of elasticity	
Material	lb/ft^3	Kg/m^3	GPa	Ksi
GFRP	97	1550	55	8000
CFRP	109	1750	160	23,000
Steel	490	7850	207	30,000

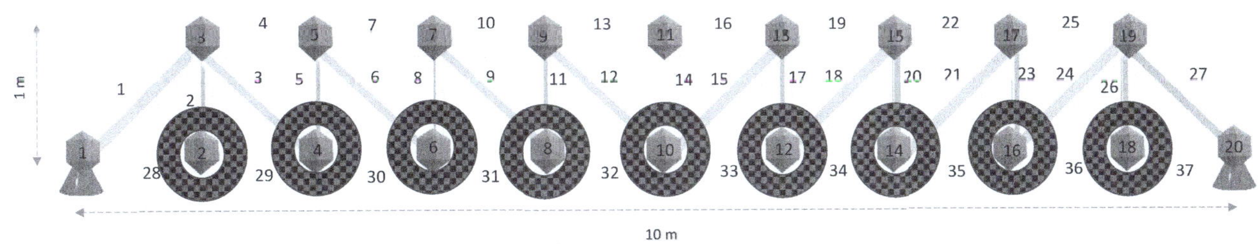

FIGURE 5.4 A 37-member planer truss.

TABLE 5.3 The best results of different materials for a 37-member truss.

Member Group	*GFRP*	*CFRP*	*Steel*
(Y_3–Y_{19}) *m*	1.012	1.002	1.052
(Y_5–Y_{17}) *m*	1.401	1.296	1.444
(Y_7–Y_{15}) *m*	1.556	1.509	1.625
(Y_9–Y_{13}) *m*	1.757	1.641	1.770
(Y_{11}) *m*	1.811	1.701	1.854
(A_1–A_{27}) cm^2	4.028	1.033	2.711
(A_2–A_{26}) cm^2	1.776	1.000	1.096
(A_3–A_{24}) cm^2	1.199	1.002	1.019
(A_4–A_{25}) cm^2	3.634	1.126	2.385
(A_5–A_{23}) cm^2	2.079	1.002	1.156
(A_6–A_{21}) cm^2	1.808	1.001	1.415
(A_7–A_{22}) cm^2	3.547	1.472	2.527
(A_8–A_{20}) cm^2	2.374	1.000	1.381
(A_9–A_{18}) cm^2	2.100	1.003	1.604
(A_{10}–A_{19}) cm^2	3.594	1.244	2.123
(A_{11}–A_{17}) cm^2	1.789	1.003	1.431
(A_{12}–A_{15}) cm^2	2.414	1.001	1.314
(A_{13}–A_{16}) cm^2	3.749	1.342	2.262
(A_{14}–A_{16}) cm^2	1.014	1.006	1.025
***Best weight* (*kg*)**	76.473	76.947	363.817
***Average weight* (*kg*)**	76.861	77.061	364.325
Standard deviation	0.246	0.073	0.390

TABLE 5.4 Natural frequencies (Hz) for the best design of a 37-member truss.

No. Frequency	*GFRP*	*CFRP*	Steel
f_1	20.0076	20.0061	20.0004
f_2	40.0141	43.4087	40.0009
f_3	60.0015	66.7583	60.0000

40.0141 Hz and 40.0009 Hz, respectively. The third natural frequency f_3 meets CFRP significantly surpassing the constraint at 66.7583 Hz, with GFRP and steel meeting the threshold at 60.0015 Hz and 60.0000 Hz, respectively. These results indicate that while all three materials satisfy the frequency constraints, CFRP offers superior performance in the second and third natural frequencies, suggesting enhanced dynamic characteristics.

Figs. 5.5 and 5.6 illustrate the convergence behavior of different materials (GFRP, CFRP, and steel) for a 37-member truss design over 20 runs. Fig. 5.5 shows the average convergence curve, depicting each material's mean weight reduction across iterations. Initially, all materials start with high weights but rapidly converge to lower weights as iterations progress. GFRP and CFRP demonstrate a significantly steeper decline than steel, achieving convergence much earlier and stabilizing. In contrast, steel converges more slowly, stabilizing. This highlights the superior efficiency of GFRP and CFRP in reaching optimal designs with lower weights more quickly.

Fig. 5.6 presents the best convergence curves for the same materials, showing the optimal weight reduction achieved in the best run out of the 20. Similar to the average convergence, GFRP and CFRP again outperform steel, with rapid

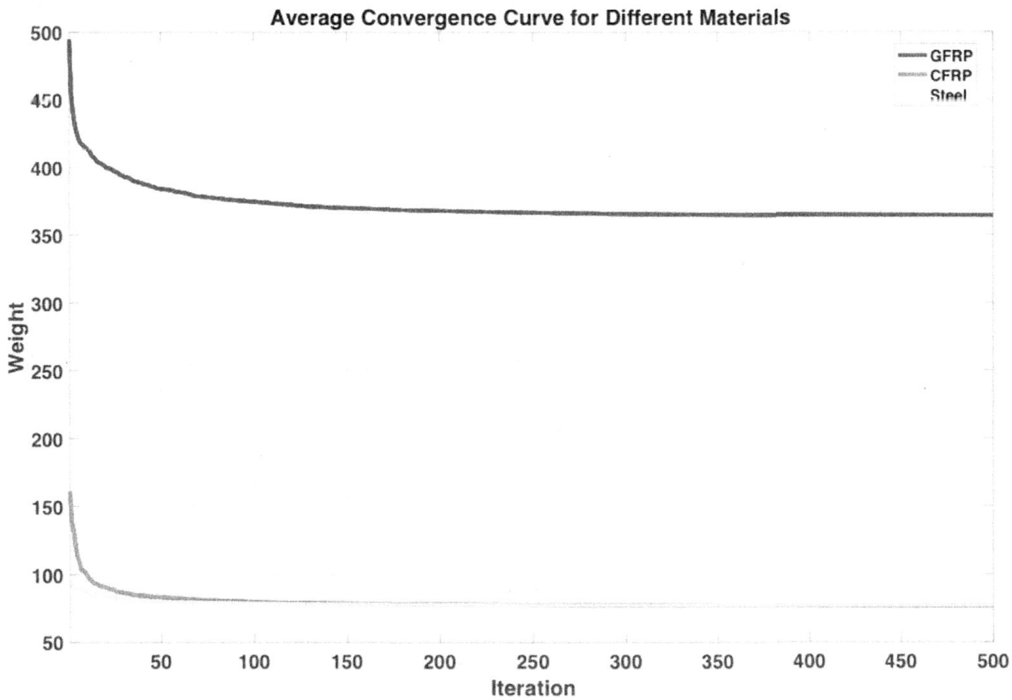

FIGURE 5.5 Average convergence curve of 20 runs for a 37-member truss.

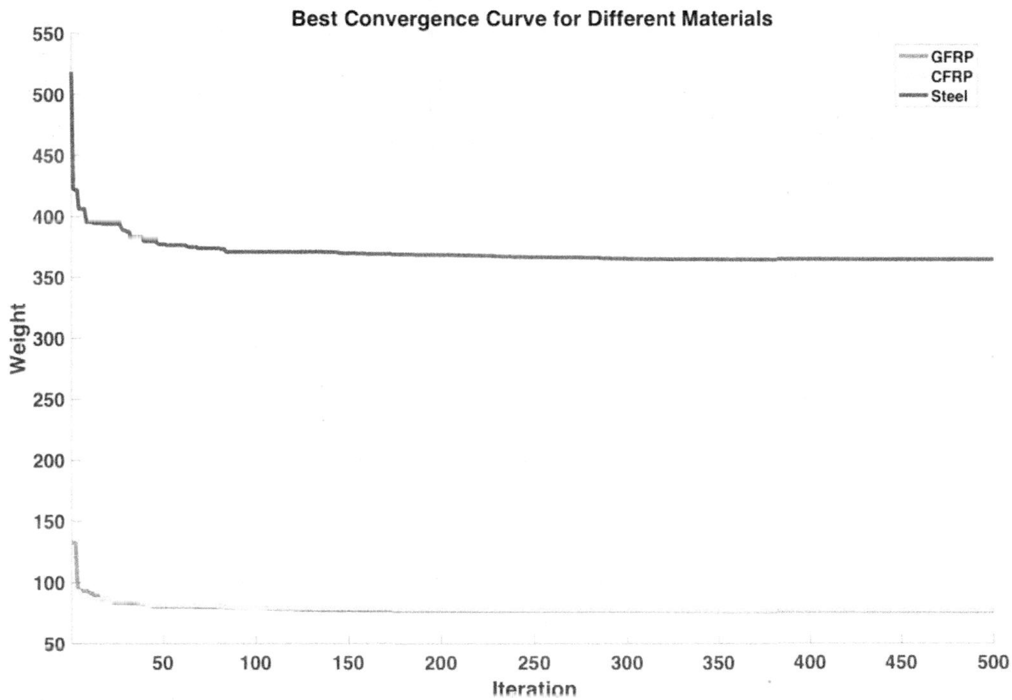

FIGURE 5.6 The best convergence curve of 20 runs for a 37-member truss.

declines and stabilization. Steel, however, maintains a higher final weight, approximately 363 kg. These results indicate that while all materials eventually converge, GFRP and CFRP achieve better and more efficient weight reductions than steel, underscoring their potential advantages in optimizing truss designs.

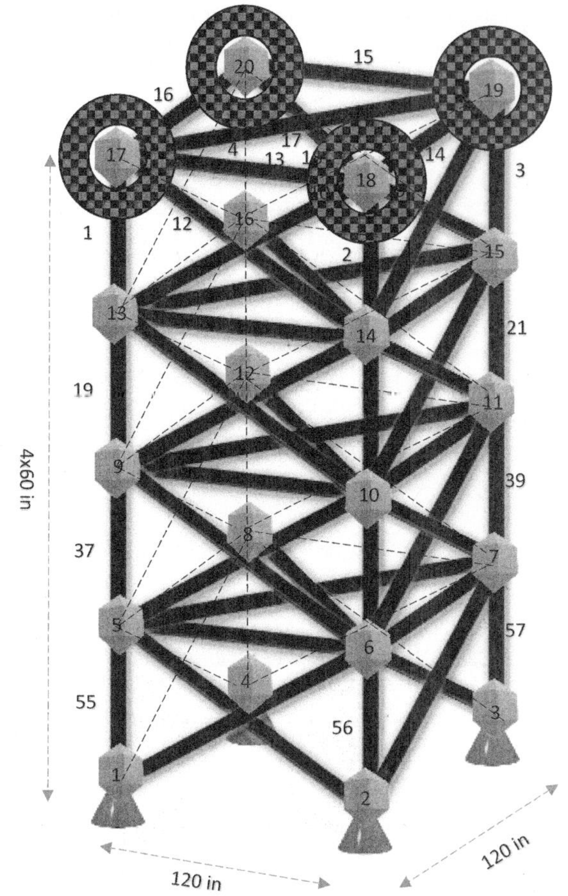

FIGURE 5.7 A 120-member truss.

5.2 The 72-member space truss

The second example presented in this section focuses on reducing the weight of a 72-member spatial truss, as shown in Fig. 5.7. Due to the symmetry of the structure, there are 16 sizing variables. The material properties and constraints for this case are detailed in the previous section. Additionally, nonstructural masses of 10 kg each are attached to nodes 17 through 19. The QIO algorithm is tested on this problem while incorporating natural frequency constraints.

Table 5.5 provides the optimal cross-sectional areas for various member groups in a 72-member truss using GFRP, CFRP, and steel materials. Additionally, the table summarizes the weight performance metrics for each material. GFRP exhibits the highest best weight at 227.821 kg and an average weight of 228.488 kg, with a standard deviation of 0.523 kg. In contrast, CFRP achieves the lowest best and average weights at 95.134 kg and 95.706 kg, respectively, with a standard deviation of 0.633 kg, indicating greater consistency. Steel, while having the best weight of 338.009 kg and an average weight of 339.365 kg, displays the highest variability with a standard deviation of 0.777 kg. These findings suggest that CFRP offers the most efficient weight performance, whereas GFRP and steel provide larger cross-sectional areas, potentially enhancing structural stability and strength.

Table 5.6 displays the natural frequencies (Hz) for the optimal design of a 72-member truss using GFRP, CFRP, and steel materials. The table highlights the first f_1, second f_2, and third f_3 natural frequencies for each material. All three materials exhibit identical values for \(f_1\) and f_2, both at 4.0000 Hz and 4.0003 Hz, respectively, meeting the constraint for f_1 set at 4 Hz. The third natural frequency f_3 is slightly above the constraint of 6 Hz for all materials, with GFRP, CFRP, and steel showing values of 6.0006 Hz, 6.0004 Hz, and 6.0006 Hz, respectively. These results indicate that each material satisfies the required natural frequency constraints, ensuring adequate dynamic performance for the truss design.

TABLE 5.5 The best results of different materials for a 72-member truss.

Member Group	*GFRP*	*CFRP*	*Steel*
1 (A_1–A_4) cm^2	4.836	1.911	1.050
2 (A_5–A_{12}) cm^2	10.620	3.485	2.706
3 (A_{13}–A_{16}) cm^2	0.652	0.646	0.646
4 (A_{17}–A_{18}) cm^2	0.720	0.662	0.646
5 (A_{19}–A_{22}) cm^2	10.837	3.398	2.700
6 (A_{23}–A_{30}) cm^2	10.124	3.500	2.673
7 (A_{31}–A_{34}) cm^2	0.649	0.650	0.647
8 (A_{35}–A_{36}) cm^2	0.692	0.655	0.647
9 (A_{37}–A_{40}) cm^2	16.637	5.127	4.505
10 (A_{41}–A_{48}) cm^2	9.639	3.598	2.633
11 (A_{49}–A_{52}) cm^2	0.683	0.652	0.646
12 (A_{53}–A_{54}) cm^2	0.655	0.650	0.646
13 (A_{55}–A_{58}) cm^2	19.988	7.624	5.581
14 (A_{59}–A_{66}) cm^2	9.793	3.330	2.713
15 (A_{67}-A_{70}) cm^2	0.653	0.646	0.648
16 (A_{71}-A_{72}) cm^2	0.665	0.655	0.647
***Best weight* (kg)**	227.821	95.134	338.009
***Average weight* (kg)**	228.488	95.706	339.365
Standard deviation	0.523	0.633	0.777

TABLE 5.6 Natural frequencies (Hz) for the best design of a 72-member truss.

No. Frequency	*GFRP*	*CFRP*	Steel
f_1	4.0000	4.0000	4.0000
f_2	4.0003	4.0003	4.0003
f_3	6.0006	6.0004	6.0006

Figs. 5.8 and 5.9 provide insights into GFRP, CFRP, and steel convergence performance for a 72-member truss design across 500 iterations, highlighting which material performs best in weight optimization. In Fig. 5.8, the average convergence curves indicate that GFRP and CFRP exhibit significantly faster convergence to lower weights than steel. This trend is consistent, with GFRP and CFRP stabilizing at much lower weights, demonstrating their efficiency and effectiveness in reducing overall truss weight.

Fig. 5.9 reinforces this finding by showcasing the best convergence curves for each material. GFRP and CFRP again outperform steel, rapidly achieving optimal weight reductions and stabilizing at considerably lower weights. Among these materials, CFRP shows the lowest final weight, followed closely by GFRP, making them the best choices for applications where minimizing weight is crucial.

Overall, CFRP emerges as the top-performing material due to its ability to consistently achieve the lowest weights, followed by GFRP. While useful in some contexts, steel does not match the weight optimization capabilities of GFRP and CFRP, making it less ideal for scenarios where weight reduction is a primary goal.

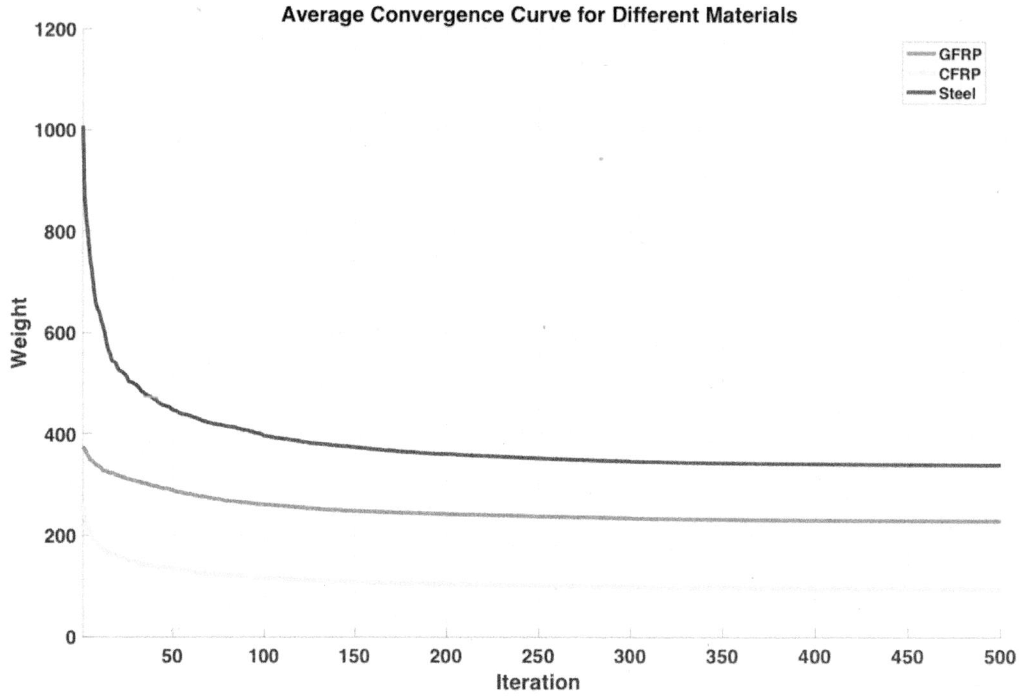

FIGURE 5.8 Average convergence curve of 20 runs for a 72-member truss.

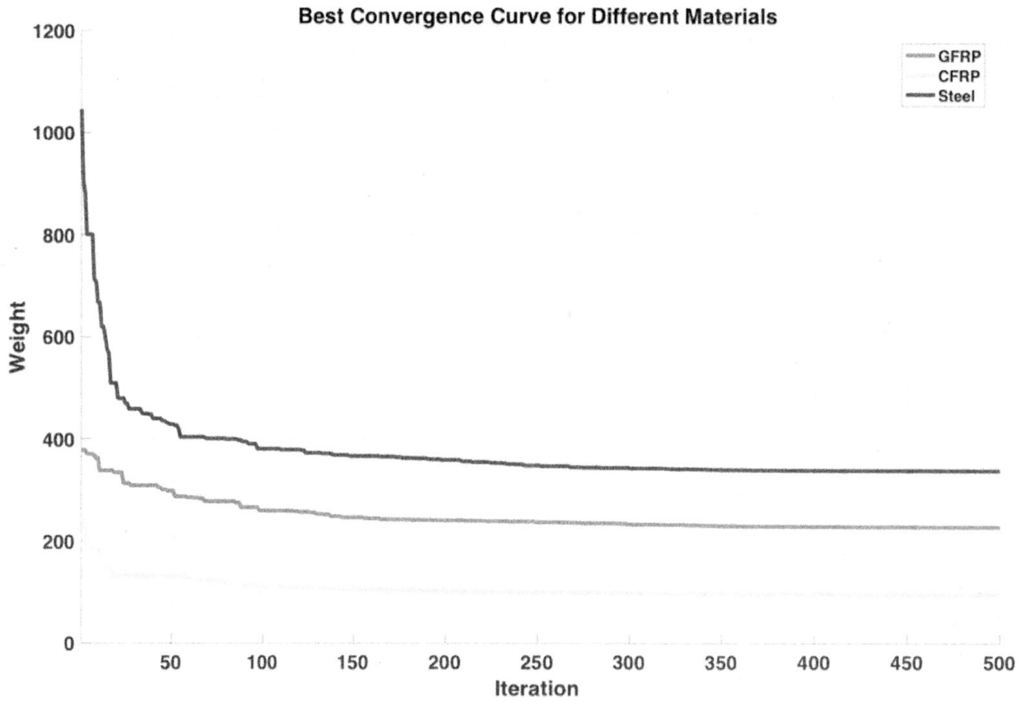

FIGURE 5.9 The best convergence curve of 20 runs for a 72-member truss.

5.3 The 120-member dome truss

The third benchmark problem, depicted in Fig. 5.10, focuses on optimizing the size of a 120-member 3-D dome truss. Nonstructural masses are distributed as follows: 3000 kg at node 1,500 kg at nodes 2–13, and 100 kg at the remaining free

FIGURE 5.10 A 120-member truss.

TABLE 5.7 The best results of different materials for a 120-member truss.

No. Group	GFRP	CFRP	Steel
G1 cm^2	80.223	24.694	20.051
G2 (cm^2)	129.293	46.199	41.479
G3 cm^2	37.419	11.501	11.389
G4 cm^2	74.997	21.057	21.702
G5 cm^2	33.235	9.241	10.014
G6 cm^2	42.637	12.198	12.957
G7 cm^2	47.986	12.000	15.365
***Best weight* (*kg*)**	5940.294	1965.564	8885.662
***Average weight* (*kg*)**	5942.355	1966.686	8890.904
Standard deviation	1.928	2.480	6.855

nodes. The elements are divided into seven groups, assuming symmetry around both the x-axis and y-axis. The cross-sectional areas range from 1 to 129.3 cm^2.

Table 5.7 presents the optimal cross-sectional areas and weight performance metrics for a 120-member truss made from GFRP, CFRP, and steel materials. Regarding weight performance, GFRP has a best weight of 5940.294 kg and an average weight of 5942.355 kg, with a standard deviation of 1.928 kg. CFRP shows superior efficiency, featuring a significantly lower best weight of 1965.564 kg and an average weight of 1966.868 kg. However, it has a slightly higher standard deviation of 2.480 kg, indicating some variability. Despite having the smallest cross-sectional areas, steel exhibits the highest best weight at 8885.662 kg and an average weight of 8890.904 kg, with a standard deviation of 6.855 kg, reflecting greater inconsistency.

TABLE 5.8 Natural frequencies (Hz) for the best design of a 120-member truss.

No. Frequency	GFRP	CFRP	Steel
f_1	9.0000	9.0001	9.0001
f_2	11.0000	11.0000	11.0000
f_3	11.0000	11.0001	11.0000

These findings suggest that while GFRP provides larger cross-sectional areas, CFRP achieves the most efficient weight performance, making it the preferred material for applications focused on weight minimization. Although offering compact cross-sectional areas, steel is the least efficient in terms of weight, highlighting its conventional use in scenarios where weight is not a primary concern.

Table 5.8 summarizes the natural frequencies for the optimal design of a 120-member truss using GFRP, CFRP, and steel materials. The first natural frequency f_1 is approximately 9 Hz for all materials. Both the second f_2 and third f_3 natural frequencies are around 11 Hz for each material. This consistency in natural frequencies across GFRP, CFRP, and steel indicates similar dynamic performance for the truss design, ensuring that all materials' frequency constraints are met.

Figs. 5.11 and 5.12 illustrate the convergence behavior of GFRP, CFRP, and steel materials for a 120-member truss over 500 iterations. Fig. 5.11 shows the average convergence curves, where GFRP and CFRP quickly reduce weight within the first 50 iterations and stabilize at lower weights than steel. Steel, on the other hand, converges more slowly and stabilizes at a significantly higher weight.

Fig. 5.12 presents the best convergence curves for the materials. The GFRP and CFRP demonstrate superior performance by rapidly achieving and maintaining lower weights throughout the iterations. steel's convergence curve shows it stabilizing at a higher weight than both GFRP and CFRP. These results indicate that GFRP and CFRP are more efficient in optimizing the truss design for weight reduction, with CFRP achieving the best overall performance, followed by GFRP and steel being the least efficient.

CFRP exhibits superior mechanical properties, such as a high strength-to-weight ratio and elevated stiffness, which directly contribute to its effectiveness in achieving weight reduction while satisfying natural frequency constraints. These characteristics enable CFRP trusses to maintain structural rigidity with significantly less mass than steel and GFRP.

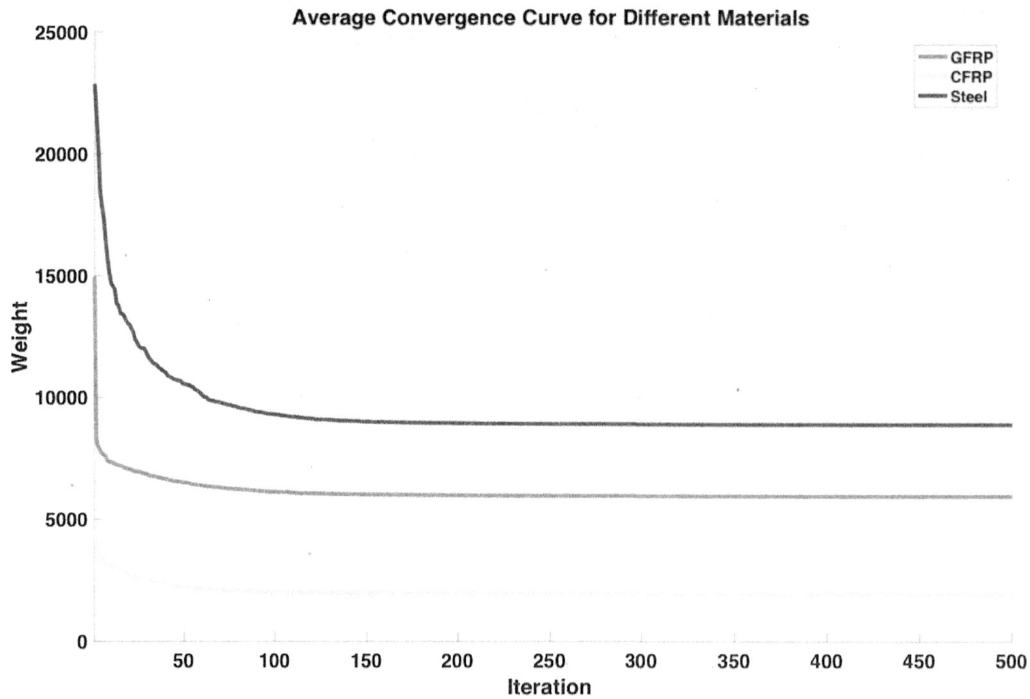

FIGURE 5.11 Average convergence curve of 20 runs for a 120-member truss.

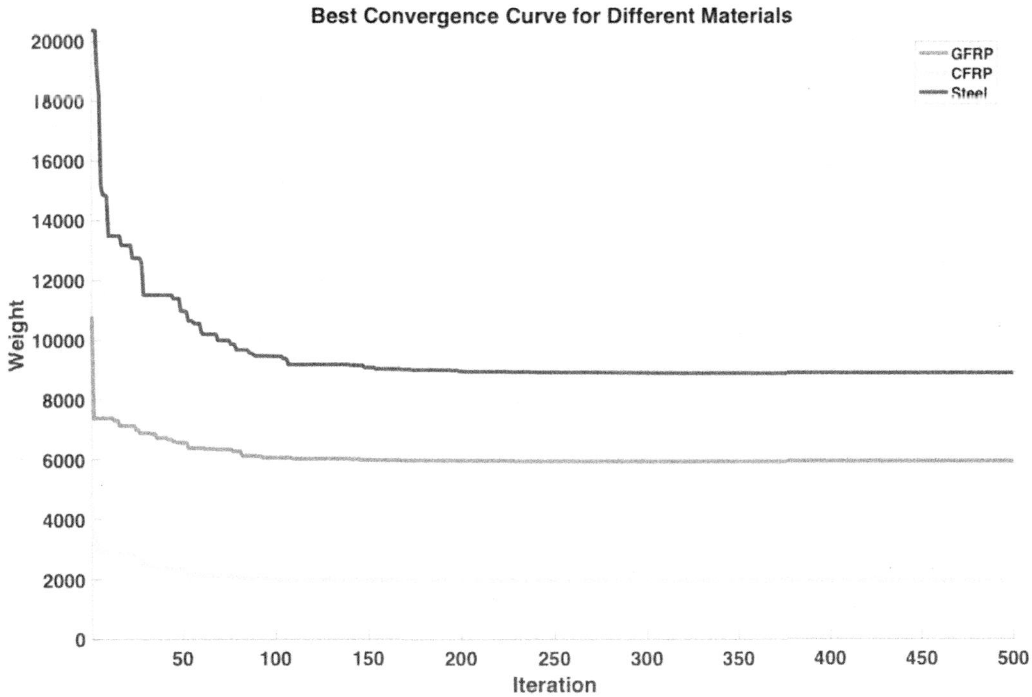

FIGURE 5.12 The best convergence curve of 20 runs for a 120-member truss.

Additionally, the anisotropic nature of CFRP allows for tailored mechanical performance, further improving dynamic behavior and vibrational control.

6. Conclusion

The chapter shows how to get the final optimized weight with the best set of natural frequencies for truss structures made of composites and optimized using QIO, which is still missing in the literature. The presented methodology gives high-quality optimal solutions with much reduced computational effort compared to traditional methods. The performances of the composite and steel materials are evaluated using the QIO algorithm, which can be a valuable contribution to knowing which material is more efficient to use and the best solution for specific structural designs. The results of carbon fiber reinforced polymer (CFRP), glass fiber reinforced polymer (GFRP), and steel materials show that the CFRP material is the best material to be used in the mentioned application of truss designs as it gave the minimum best and average weights, followed by the GFRP, and the steel material is the worst material due to it gave higher weights. The material showed the best responses concerning natural frequency constraints, and all those provided stable structural systems. CFRP and GFRP can be suggested as superior materials in lightweight, high-performance designs of truss forms.

References

[1] N. Khodadadi, S. Mirjalili, Truss optimization with natural frequency constraints using generalized normal distribution optimization, Appl. Intell. (2022) 1–14.
[2] A. Kaveh, S. Talatahari, N. Khodadadi, Stochastic paint optimizer: Theory and application in civil engineering, Eng. Comput. 38 (2022) 1921 1952, https://doi.org/10.1007/s00366-020-01179-5.
[3] G.-C. Luh, C.-Y. Lin, Optimal design of truss-structures using particle swarm optimization, Comput. Struct. 89 (2011) 2221–2232.
[4] C. V Camp, B.J. Bichon, Design of space trusses using ant colony optimization, J. Struct. Eng. 130 (2004) 741–751.
[5] C. V Camp, Design of space trusses using big bang–big crunch optimization, J. Struct. Eng. 133 (2007) 999–1008.
[6] S.D. Rajan, Sizing, shape, and topology design optimization of trusses using genetic algorithm, J. Struct. Eng. 121 (1995) 1480–1487.
[7] S.O. Degertekin, M.S. Hayalioglu, Sizing truss structures using teaching-learning-based optimization, Comput. Struct. 119 (2013) 177–188.
[8] G. Bekdaş, S.M. Nigdeli, X.-S. Yang, Sizing optimization of truss structures using flower pollination algorithm, Appl. Soft Comput. 37 (2015) 322–331.
[9] Y. Li, S. Wang, M. Han, Truss structure optimization based on improved chicken swarm optimization algorithm, Adv. Civ. Eng. 2019 (2019).

[10] R. Awad, Sizing optimization of truss structures using the political optimizer (PO) algorithm, in: Structures, Elsevier, 2021, pp. 4871–4894.

[11] A. Kaveh, M. Khayatazad, Ray optimization for size and shape optimization of truss structures, Comput. Struct. 117 (2013) 82–94.

[12] N. Khodadadi, H. Roghani, F. De Caso, E.-S.M. El-kenawy, Y. Yesha, A. Nanni, Data-driven PSO-CatBoost machine learning model to predict the compressive strength of CFRP-confined circular concrete specimens, Thin-Walled Struct. (2024) 111763.

[13] N. Khodadadi, H. Roghani, E. Harati, M. Mirdarsoltany, F. De Caso, A. Nanni, Fiber-reinforced polymer (FRP) in concrete: A comprehensive survey, Constr. Build. Mater. 432 (2024) 136634.

[14] L. Bank, Composites for Construction: Structural Design with FRP Materials, 2006.

[15] L.C. Bank, Reflections on 50 years of pultruded fiber-reinforced polymer materials in structural engineering, J. Compos. Construct. 27 (2023) 02523001.

[16] M. Zoghi, The International Handbook of FRP Composites in Civil Engineering, Crc Press, 2013.

[17] J. Qureshi, A review of fibre reinforced polymer structures, Fibers 10 (2022), https://doi.org/10.3390/fib10030027.

[18] H.V.S. GangaRao, W. Prachasaree, FRP Composite Structures: Theory, Fundamentals, and Design, CRC Press, 2021.

[19] W. Zhao, L. Wang, Z. Zhang, S. Mirjalili, N. Khodadadi, Q. Ge, Quadratic interpolation optimization (QIO): A new optimization algorithm based on generalized quadratic interpolation and its applications to real-world engineering problems, Comput. Methods Appl. Mech. Eng. 417 (2023) 116446.

[20] S. Liu, H. Zhu, Z. Chen, H. Cao, Frequency-constrained truss optimization using the fruit fly optimization algorithm with an adaptive vision search strategy, Eng. Optim. 52 (2020) 777–797.

[21] S.O. Degertekin, G.Y. Bayar, L. Lamberti, Parameter free Jaya algorithm for truss sizing-layout optimization under natural frequency constraints, Comput. Struct. 245 (2021) 106461.

[22] D. Wang, W.H. Zhang, J.S. Jiang, Truss optimization on shape and sizing with frequency constraints, AIAA J. 42 (2004) 622–630.

[23] A. Kaveh, A. Zolghadr, Truss shape and size optimization with frequency constraints using tug of war optimization, Asian J. Civil Eng. 7 (2017) 311–333.

[24] M. Farshchin, C. V Camp, M. Maniat, Multi-class teaching–learning-based optimization for truss design with frequency constraints, Eng. Struct. 106 (2016) 355–369.

[25] L. Wei, T. Tang, X. Xie, W. Shen, Truss optimization on shape and sizing with frequency constraints based on parallel genetic algorithm, Struct. Multidiscip. Optim. 43 (2011) 665–682.

Chapter 6

Binary Stochastic Paint Optimizer for feature selection problems with S-shaped transfer function

Nima Khodadadi[1], Ehsan Khodadadi[2], Ehsaneh Khodadadi[4], Khalid M. Mosalam[1] and Antonio Nanni[3]

[1]Department of Civil and Environmental Engineering, Pacific Earthquake Engineering Research (PEER) Center, University of California, Berkeley, CA, United States; [2]Department of Chemistry and Biochemistry, University of Arkansas, Fayetteville, AR, United States; [3]Department of Civil and Architectural Engineering, University of Miami, Coral Gables, FL, United States; [4]Department of Pathology, Stanford University School of Medicine, Stanford, CA, United States

1. Introduction

In recent years,volume of the data from various repositories has been tremendously growing. Data mining is a form of analysis and knowledge-based mode applied to different fields, including machine learning, statistics, and databases, which are used to analyze data and concepts in multiple computer files. All of the applications involve huge volumes of data and lengthy processes. The objective of data mining is to extract knowledge from data and exhibit it in a comprehensible form [1].

As a result of enormous technological progress, such as the Internet, a considerable number of novel databases with high dimensions of data have been created. These new dimensions increase the complexity and diversity of the database. On the other hand, there are some challenges in analyzing the high-dimensional datasets that are affected by longer times to build the models, fewer informative features, and generally reduced efficiency [2,3]. In an attempt to resolve these challenges, feature selection (FS) is a well-known data preprocessing step that can significantly reduce the number of features by reducing the dimensions of the dataset. This helps to enhance the performance of the classifiers by improving either the accuracy rate of the algorithm or by reducing the size of the framework, which facilitates learning and prediction. Consequently, the FS process can significantly improve the classifier's performance by selecting only a subset of features. FS identifies the most relevant attributes to be used in a classification problem [4]. The goal of FS is to select a subset of attributes that best represent the dataset, either by improving the accuracy rate or reducing the framework's size. Either way, this leads to a fast and accurate learning of the classifier by the machine and also speeds up the prediction process. The framework of FS techniques includes two main actions: search procedure and subset evaluation. First, the search procedure applies new methods to select subsets of FSs. Then, the FS process aims to evaluate these feature subsets and determine which best fits the problem. As presented in Fig. 6.1, the operational mechanism of the FS process consists of five essential components: original dataset, FS selection, subset evaluation, selection criterion, and validation [5].

FS approaches can be categorized into filter or wrapper methods based on the availability of an assessment tool. Filter-based methods first select the dataset's attributes and then train the learner. In contrast, wrapper-based methods explicitly use the classification model (e.g., classification) as a performance measure for the feature subset. The main idea is to treat subset selection as an optimization problem, generating various subsets, evaluating them, and comparing them to other configurations. While wrapper methods achieve higher classification accuracy than filter methods, they come with increased computational complexity [6,7].

Classical optimization techniques lead to poor solutions when faced with complex problems. This has caused researchers to seek alternatives to classical methods, and a more effective method called metaheuristic algorithms is now

Advanced Intelligence Methods for Data Science and Optimization. https://doi.org/10.1016/B978-0-443-28940-8.00004-X

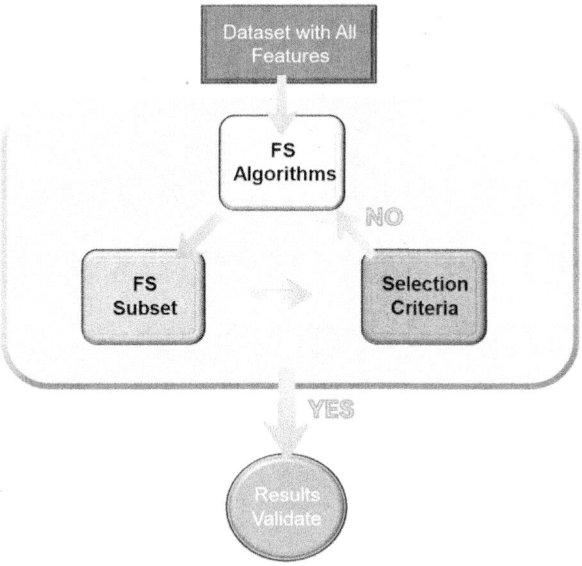

FIGURE 6.1 FS mechanism.

commonly used. Metaheuristic algorithms can be favored over classical methods because they require less effort, can be applied to nonspecified problem structures, do not require gradient information, and are less error-prone [8–10].

Many researchers have shown interest in metaheuristic algorithms in recent years due to their potential to address various problems across different fields [11]. As issues grow more complex and the number of variables rises, the prominence of high-dimensional challenges is increasing. Recently, several metaheuristics, such as been proposed to binary optimization problems such as Binary Battle Royale Optimizer [12] Binary Butterfly Optimization [13] Artificial Protozoa Optimizer [14] and Binary Particle Swarm Algorithm [15]. So far, all the aforementioned algorithms and their binary counterparts have been used for FS problems. One significant advantage of using these metaheuristics for FS problems is that they yieldoptimal result quickly, even for large problem sets.

This chapter examines the application of a novel optimizer, the Stochastic Paint Optimizer (SPO), within the realm of FS. Recently introduced by Kaveh et al. [16], the SPO draws inspiration from the concept of color harmony and has shown promising outcomes in various optimization challenges. This success forms the basis for exploring its potential in FS. The SPO has several variants, all of which have demonstrated strong performance across different challenges. However, a notable absence of a binary version of this algorithm presents an opportunity for development in this area.

As previously mentioned, heuristic methods are among the most effective for addressing FS problems. The current state of research necessitates a thorough investigation to identify new approaches that can not only determine the optimal subset of features but also enhance the performance of the underlying processes, minimize the number of selected features, and reduce execution time. Consequently, a binary adaptation of the SPO is proposed to tackle a range of high-dimensional FS problems. The primary contributions and innovations of this study can be summarized as follows:

- A binary adaptation of the SPO algorithm is introduced to address a range of feature selection tasks across diverse domains, including medical, artificial, gaming, and biological datasets.
- The KNN classifier is employed to assess the effectiveness of the selected feature subsets.
- To validate the reliability of the feature selection approach, experiments are conducted on 18 publicly available datasets.
- The performance of the proposed method is assessed using three widely recognized evaluation metrics.
- Comparative analysis with three established methods demonstrates the superior performance of the proposed BSPO algorithm.

2. Stochastic Paint Optimizer (SPO)

SPO [16] is a metaheuristic algorithm proposed in 2020 based on color theory. According to this algorithm, solutions are combined to generate a new population, similar to mixing colors to create new hues. As shown in Fig. 6.2, four basic

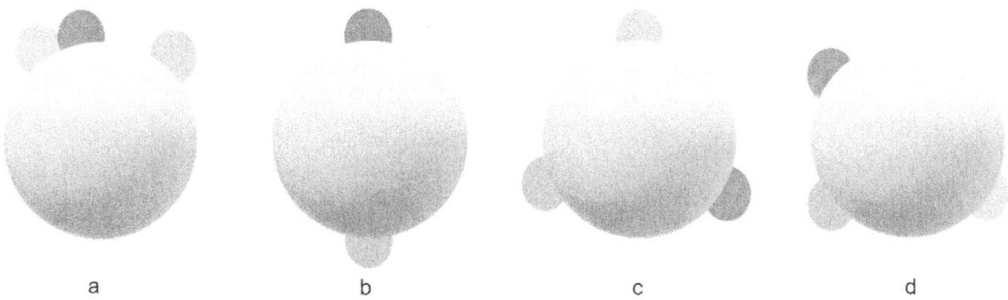

FIGURE 6.2 Four fundamental methods for combining colors.

methods are used to combine colors according to the color wheel, which are all used to generate new colors (Co_{new}). The following subsections explain the mathematical models that SPO applies to this color mixing rule.

2.1 Analogous combination technique (ACT)

This color mixing can involve two or four adjacent colors on the color wheel (Fig. 6.1(a)). This is translated to the SPO algorithm in the following equation:

$$Co^1_{new} = Co_i + rand \times (Co_{i+1} - Co_{i-1}) \tag{6.1}$$

Where Co_i, Co_{i+1} and Co_{i-1} are three individuals of the current population, *rand* is a random vector with values between [0, 1].

2.2 Complementary combination technique (CCT)

When combining colors in this manner, complementary colors are utilized, as shown in Fig. 6.1(b). In the SPO algorithm, this is simulated by randomly selecting a primary color (Co_p), a tertiary color (Co_T), and an existing color (Co_i). The following equation is employed for this process:

$$Co^2_{new} = Co_i + rand \times \left(Co_p - Co_T\right) \tag{6.2}$$

Where Co_p signifies a primary color, Co_T indicates a tertiary color, Co_i is an existing color, and rand is a random vector in the range [0, 1].

2.3 Triadic combination technique (TrCT)

This approach combines equidistant colors from around the color wheel (see Fig. 6.2(c)), while in SPO, this works as follows:

$$Co^3_{new} = Co_i + rand \times \left(\frac{Co_p + Co_s + Co_T}{3}\right) \tag{6.3}$$

Where Co_s is a secondary color, Co_T denotes a tertiary color and *rand* is a random vector within the range [0, 1].

2.4 Tetradic combination technique (TeCT)

This way of color mixing includes four mutually complementary colors, corresponding to the rectangular patterns on the color wheel (see Fig. 6.2(d)), which in the SPO runs with the following algorithm:

$$Co^4_{new} = Co_i + rand \times \left(\frac{rand_1 \times Co_p + rand_2 \times Co_s + rand_3 \times Co_T + rand_4 \times (lb + rand \times (ub - lb))}{4}\right) \tag{6.4}$$

Where *lb* and *ub* represent the lower and upper bounds of the design variable, and $rand_1$, $rand_2$, $rand_3$, and $rand_4$ are four random vectors within the range [0, 1].

Finally, you might wonder how colors are represented and mixed in the SPO algorithm. Since each solution is mapped to a color with *d* dimensions (where *d* corresponds to the number of problem variables), the "colors" of each solution depend only on their objective values. Essentially, the objective function acts as the color wheel. The primary color is the best solution, the secondary colors correspond to solutions with acceptable objective values, and the tertiary colors are solutions with poor objective values.

3. Binary Stochastic Paint Optimizer (BSPO)

FS is inherently a binary problem, which implies that the original SPO presented in the previous section cannot be used directly to tackle such tasks. This work proposes a binary variant of the SPO to better match FS's nature. In the original SPO, agents can move continuously in the search space because their position vectors are defined over the continuous real domain. The way of updating the position in the ACT and CCT phase introduced in Eq. (6.5) is modified as follows to facilitate the binary agents moving within a binary space:

$$B_1\left(x_{i,j}(t+1)\right) = \begin{cases} 1 \ \mathit{if} \ \mathit{sigmoid}\left(x_{i,j}(t+1)\right) \geq \mathit{rand} \\ 0 \ \mathit{otherwise} \end{cases} \tag{6.5}$$

where $x_{i,j}(t+1)$ represents the original ACT and CCT stage described in Eq. (6.7), $B_1\left(x_{i,j}(t+1)\right)$ is the binary updated position for the ACT and CCT phase at iteration t, *rand* is a random number drawn from a uniform distribution within the range [0, 1], and *sigmoid* (x) is the binary transfer function that converts the search space into binary form. The sigmoid function earns its place in neural networks and machine learning because of its S-shaped curve. The function produces almost 0 values when presented with large negative inputs and approaches 1 when handling large positive inputs. Its properties make the sigmoid function ideal for binary classification tasks because it helps estimate the probability of two possible outcomes. The sigmoid function is mathematically defined as follows:

$$\mathit{sigmoid}\ (x) = \frac{1}{1 + e^{-10(x-0.5)}} \tag{6.6}$$

Similarly, the position updating mechanism for the TrCT and TeCT phases described in Eq. (6.4) can be modified using the following equation:

$$B_2\left(x_{i,j}(t+1)\right) = \begin{cases} 1 \ \mathit{if} \ \mathit{sigmoid}\left(x_{i,j}(t+1)\right) \geq \mathit{rand} \\ 0 \ \mathit{otherwise} \end{cases} \tag{6.7}$$

where $x_{i,j}(t+1)$ denotes the original TrCT and TeCT stages as presented in Eq. (6.4), $B_2\left(x_{i,j}(t+1)\right)$ represents the binary updated position during the TrCT and TeCT phase at iteration t, *rand* is a randomly generated number from a uniform distribution within the range [0, 1], and *sigmoid(x)* is calculated as defined in Eq. (6.6).

The number of variables in the solution representation is defined by the length of the one-dimensional vector, where each dimension represents the status of the feature. If a feature is not selected, we assign the value zero to the corresponding dimension inside the vector. In the opposite case, if a feature is selected, we use a value of one. FS is a biobjective optimization problem that minimizes the number of selected features and maximizes classification accuracy. Therefore, we use the following fitness function to tackle both objectives based on the K-nearest neighbor (KNN) classifier.

$$\mathit{fitness} = \alpha \rho_R(Y) + \beta \frac{|K|}{|N|} \quad \alpha = [0, 1], \beta = (1 - \alpha) \tag{6.8}$$

Where $\rho_R(Y)$ represents the error rate of the KNN classifier. Furthermore, $|K|$ denotes the count of selected features, while $|M|$ indicates the total number of features present in the dataset.

4. Datasets

The BSPO method is tested and confirmed using 18 benchmark datasets sourced from the UC Irvine Machine Learning Repository (UCI) [17]. These datasets, frequently used by researchers for evaluating various FS methods, range in size from 73 to 5000 instances. Detailed information about these datasets is provided in Table 6.1.

The resulting feature subset is examined by using the KNN classifier, which is widely recommended. In this evaluation, a cross-validation scheme with $K = 5$ is employed, in which the data is split into three equal parts for training, testing, and validation.

TABLE 6.1 Dataset information.

No.	Dataset	Size	Name	Instances	No. Features	No. Classes
1	Breast cancer	Small	D1	699	9	2
2	BreastEW	Large	D2	569	30	2
3	CongressEW	Medium	D3	435	16	2
4	Exactly	Small	D4	1000	13	2
5	Exactly2	Small	D5	1000	13	2
6	HeartEW	Small	D6	270	13	2
7	IonosphereEW	Large	D7	351	34	2
8	KrvskpEW	Large	D8	3196	36	2
9	Lymphography	Medium	D9	148	18	2
10	M-of-n	Small	D10	1000	13	2
11	PenglungEW	Large	D11	73	325	2
12	SonarEW	Large	D12	208	60	2
13	SpectEW	Medium	D13	267	22	2
14	Tic-tac-toe	Small	D14	958	9	2
15	Vote	Medium	D15	300	16	2
16	WaveformEW	Large	D16	5000	40	3
17	WineEW	Small	D17	178	13	3
18	Zoo	Medium	D18	101	16	6

5. Performance metrics

This section will define the performance metrics that will be used to evaluate and compare the performance of different algorithms in the following section [1]:

5.1 The mean of classification accuracy (MCA)

This metric measures the classifier's accuracy based on a specific set of features when the algorithm is executed N times. It is calculated as follows:

$$MCA = \frac{1}{N}\sum_{k=1}^{N} AvgAcc^k \quad (6.9)$$

Where $AvgAcc^k$ is the average gain in accuracy at run k.

5.2 The average of selected feature (ASF)

It indicates the average proportion of selected features relative to the total features when the algorithm is executed N times. It is computed like this:

$$ASF = \frac{1}{N}\sum_{k=1}^{N} \frac{AvgSelection^k}{M} \quad (6.10)$$

Here, $AvgSelection^k$ represents the average number of features selected during run k, and M denotes the total number of features in the dataset.

5.3 The mean of fitness function (MFF)

This metric indicates the mean value of the fitness function obtained from N executions of algorithm executions. It is determined as follows:

$$MFF = \frac{1}{N}\sum_{k=1}^{N} g_k^* \tag{6.11}$$

In this context, g_k^* represents the average fitness achieved during the k -th run.

In this chapter, we employed three key performance metrics. MCA was used because it directly evaluates a classifier's predictive performance on various datasets. ASF measures how well the algorithm can lower data dimensionality by selecting a minimal set of informative features that supports model interpretability and reduces computational demands. The MFF delivers a complete evaluation by integrating classification accuracy alongside the number of selected features to achieve high performance and model simplicity. These metrics together create an evaluation framework that balances accuracy and efficiency while ensuring feature interpretability, which makes them vital for practical applications.

6. Results and discussion

This section details the results obtained from comparative methods based on the metrics employed. Table 6.2 summarizes the Mean Classification Accuracy (MCA) for four methods—BSPO, BDF, BPSO, and BGA—tested on 18 datasets. The BSPO method demonstrated superior performance, securing the highest accuracy in 13 of the 18 datasets. In contrast, BDF led in five instances, while BPSO and BGA did not lead in any instance. These results underscore the efficacy of BSPO in FS tasks, showcasing a clear performance advantage over the other methods. The overall average accuracy in

TABLE 6.2 The result of MCA for all methods.

Datasets	BSPO	BDF	BPSO	BGA
D1	**0.977**	0.945	0.935	0.948
D2	**0.973**	0.949	0.934	0.932
D3	**0.971**	0.954	0.931	0.934
D4	**0.974**	0.968	0.671	0.636
D5	0.782	**0.795**	0.755	0.764
D6	**0.853**	0.827	0.765	0.810
D7	**0.926**	0.924	0.825	0.814
D8	**0.966**	0.964	0.924	0.914
D9	0.854	**0.869**	0.641	0.634
D10	0.958	**0.989**	0.857	0.923
D11	**0.962**	0.885	0.710	0.704
D12	0.871	**0.908**	0.739	0.725
D13	**0.879**	0.877	0.746	0.777
D14	**0.819**	0.787	0.723	0.709
D15	**0.984**	0.942	0.886	0.881
D16	**0.859**	0.749	0.758	0.766
D17	**0.985**	0.912	0.944	0.925
D18	0.963	**0.976**	0.828	0.879
Average	0.920	0.901	0.810	0.815
Rank	**1**	2	4	3

Table 6.3 reveals BSPO at the forefront with an accuracy of 0.920, followed by BDF at 0.901, BGA at 0.815, and BPSO at 0.810.

Table 6.3 shows the Average Solution Fitness (ASF) results for four optimization methods—BSPO, BDF, BPSO, and BGA—across 18 datasets (D1 to D18). BSPO consistently shows the lowest ASF values in multiple datasets, such as D1 (3.623), D5 (1.161), and D15 (2.629), indicating its superior performance. On average, BSPO achieves the best performance with an average ASF of 103.551, significantly outperforming BDF, which has an average ASF of 249.083. In contrast, BGA and BPSO have higher average ASF values of 381.202 and 385.157, respectively, demonstrating lower efficiency. BSPO's robustness is particularly evident in datasets with high ASF variability.

BSPO is the most effective in securing the top rank when ranking these methods based on their average ASF values. BDF follows in second place, while BGA and BPSO are ranked third and fourth, respectively. BSPO's consistently low ASF values across most datasets underscore its reliability and efficiency in optimizing solutions.

Table 6.4 presents the Mean of Fitness Function (MFF) results for four optimization methods—BSPO, BDF, BPSO, and BGA—across 16 datasets (D1 to D16). The BSPO method generally achieves the lowest MFF values in several datasets, such as D1 (0.019), D3 (0.029), D4 (0.019), and D8 (0.018), indicating its efficiency in optimizing the fitness function. BDF also performs well in specific datasets, notably achieving the lowest MFF in D4 (0.009), D7 (0.068), D10 (0.010), and D12 (0.067). Comparatively, BPSO and BGA exhibit higher MFF values in most datasets, indicating lower optimization efficiency. For instance, BPSO has the highest MFF values in D4 (0.275) and D11 (0.216), while BGA has the highest in D4 (0.278) and D5 (0.245).

When examining the overall performance across datasets, BSPO consistently demonstrates lower MFF values, indicating superior optimization capabilities. In contrast, BDF shows competitive performance in specific datasets, outperforming other methods in a few cases. BPSO and BGA, while occasionally performing well, generally have higher MFF values, suggesting less effective optimization. BSPO's consistently low MFF values underscore its reliability and effectiveness in optimizing fitness functions, making it a preferable choice compared to BDF, BPSO, and BGA.

TABLE 6.3 The result of ASF for all methods.

Datasets	BSPO	BDF	BPSO	BGA
D1	**3.623**	4.846	5.697	5.088
D2	**9.712**	13.785	16.589	15.347
D3	**1.291**	3.596	6.789	6.619
D4	**3.945**	6.094	9.814	10.814
D5	**1.161**	2.714	6.115	6.175
D6	**5.042**	6.845	7.841	8.481
D7	**5.313**	10.987	18.952	16.299
D8	**7.519**	17.734	19.785	22.435
D9	**4.791**	7.147	9.015	10.002
D10	**5.935**	6.036	9.114	7.785
D11	**14.216**	95.994	178.784	176.125
D12	**8.945**	27.474	30.114	31.265
D13	**3.594**	7.896	12.457	11.698
D14	**5.089**	5.884	6.584	6.774
D15	**2.629**	3.154	8.744	6.589
D16	**12.412**	16.998	22.698	23.254
D17	**4.353**	5.911	8.366	7.351
D18	**5.051**	5.988	7.699	9.101
Average	**103.551**	249.083	385.157	381.202
Rank	**1**	2	4	3

TABLE 6.4 The result of MFF for all methods.

Datasets	BSPO	BDF	BPSO	BGA
D1	**0.019**	0.039	0.029	0.031
D2	0.033	0.035	**0.032**	0.041
D3	**0.029**	0.034	0.039	0.035
D4	0.019	**0.009**	0.275	0.278
D5	**0.218**	0.248	0.236	0.245
D6	0.176	0.167	0.148	**0.149**
D7	0.098	**0.068**	0.136	0.125
D8	**0.018**	0.026	0.041	0.069
D9	0.159	**0.129**	0.188	0.164
D10	0.027	**0.010**	0.107	0.075
D11	**0.079**	0.088	0.216	0.212
D12	0.119	**0.067**	0.125	0.126
D13	0.168	0.137	**0.126**	0.136
D14	**0.188**	0.209	0.232	0.244
D15	**0.018**	0.036	0.046	0.051
D16	**0.176**	0.231	0.219	0.206
D17	**0.009**	0.014	0.016	0.011
D18	**0.018**	0.032	0.101	0.085
Average	**1.571**	1.579	2.312	2.283
Rank	**1**	2	4	3

Fig. 6.3 for small datasets shows the FS numbers for BSPO, BDF, BPSO, and BGA, along with the total feature count for each dataset. BSPO generally selects fewer features, particularly evident in datasets like CONGRESSEW (D3), LYMPHOGRAPHY (D9), and SPECTEW (D13). For instance, in the SPECTEW dataset (D13), BSPO selects only 7.896 features, while BDF, BPSO, and BGA select 12.487, 9.836, and 12.487 features, respectively. This trend emphasizes BSPO's robustness and efficiency in FS across different dataset sizes, consistently minimizing the number of selected features while ensuring the retention of crucial information.

In Fig. 6.4 for medium datasets, FS numbers of BSPO, BDF, BPSO, and BGA are compared to the total feature count for each dataset. BSPO frequently selects fewer features than the other methods, particularly in datasets like CONGRESSEW (D3), LYMPHOGRAPHY (D9), and SPECTEW (D13). For example, in the CONGRESSEW dataset (D3), BSPO selects only 3.981 features, whereas BDF, BPSO, and BGA select 7.739, 6.619, and 6.619 features, respectively. This consistent performance underscores BSPO's efficiency in reducing the number of selected features without sacrificing the selection quality, making it a highly effective method for medium-sized datasets.

Fig. 6.5 for large datasets compares the FS numbers across four optimization methods—BSPO, BDF, BPSO, and BGA—and the total feature count for each dataset. BSPO consistently selects fewer features in datasets like BREASTEW (D2), IONOSPHEREEW (D7), KRVSPEW (D8), PENGUINEW (D11), and SONAREW (D12), indicating its efficiency in reducing feature dimensions. Notably, in the PENGUINEW dataset (D11), BSPO selects significantly fewer features (94.158) compared to BDF, BPSO, and BGA, which select 359.914, 579.794, and 737.151, respectively. This trend highlights BSPO's superior performance in effectively minimizing the feature set while maintaining essential information, which is crucial for handling large datasets.

7. Conclusion

In this chapter, we presented SPO in binary adaptation for feature selection problems called binary Stochastic Paint Optimizater (BSPO). The effectiveness of BSPO was verified on 18 selected benchmark classification datasets from the

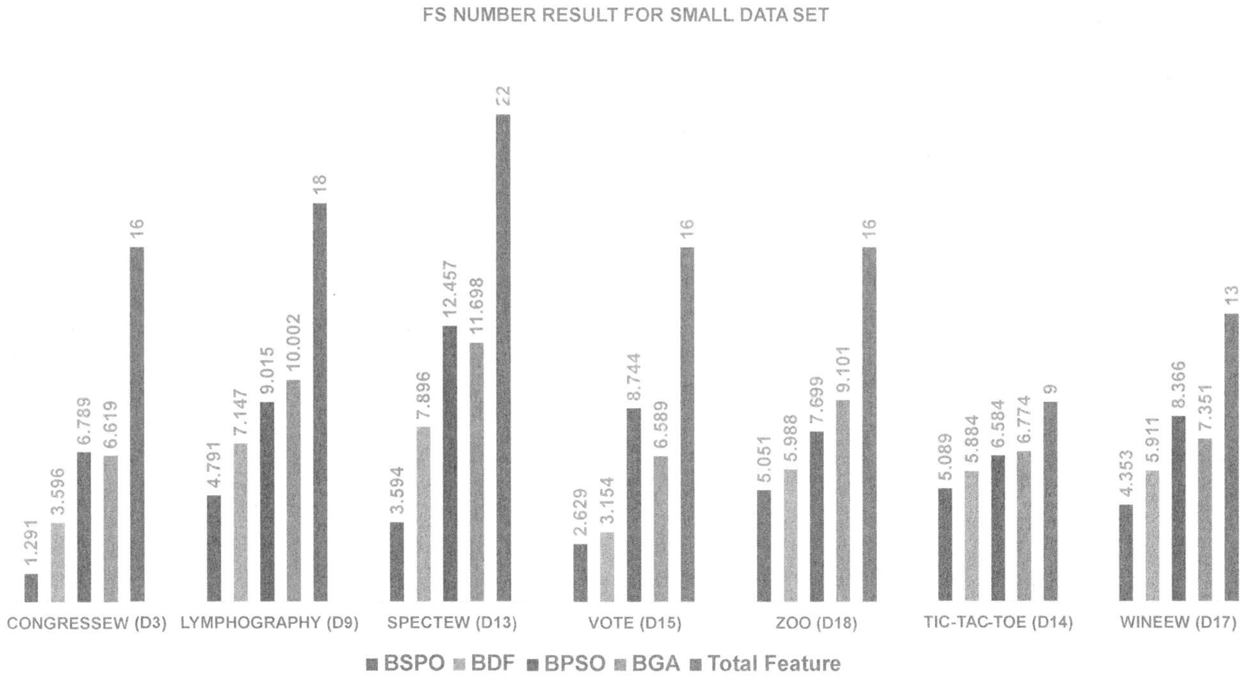

FIGURE 6.3 Comparison of small data sets based on the quantity of selected features.

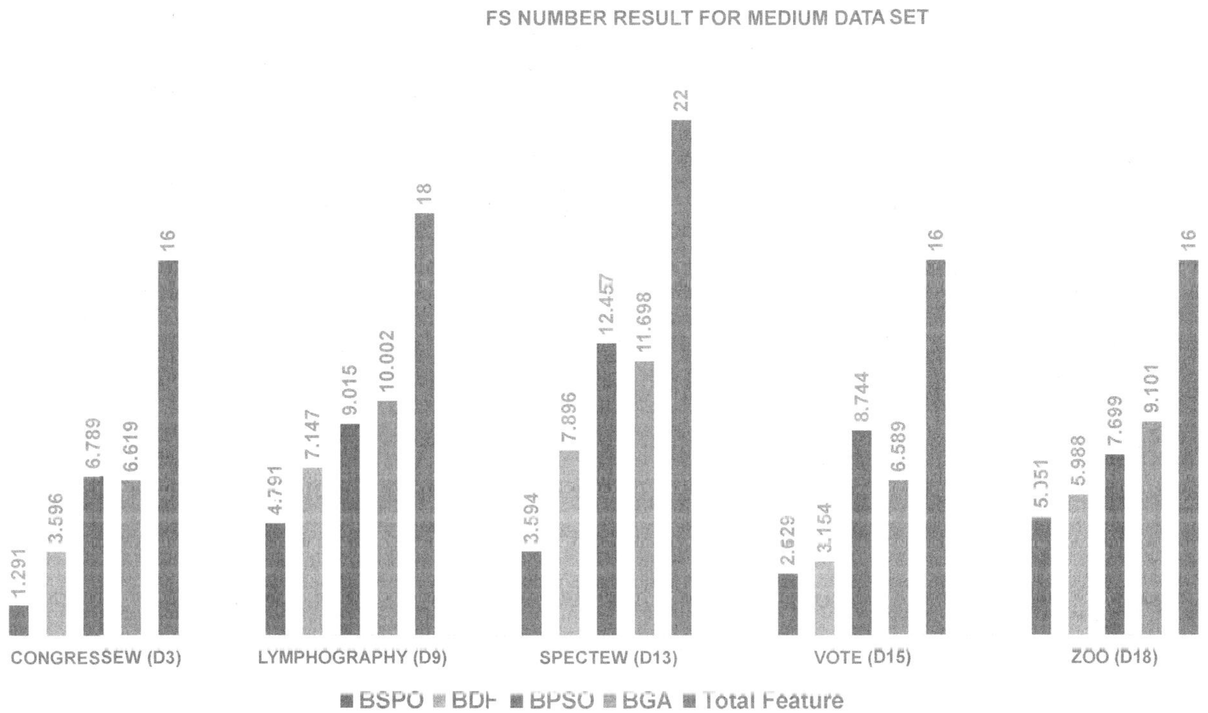

FIGURE 6.4 Comparison of medium data sets based on the quantity of selected features.

UCI machine learning repository. The performance of the proposed algorithm was evaluated using different performance metrics. To reveal the performance of the proposed technique, we compared the proposed method with three existing FS algorithms: BDF, BPSO, and BGA. Among the most benchmark UCI datasets, our proposed BSPO outperformed competing techniques regarding accuracy and the number of selected features. The comparison reveals the significant performance advantages of the proposed BSPO method over the existing state-of-the-art techniques. The better results

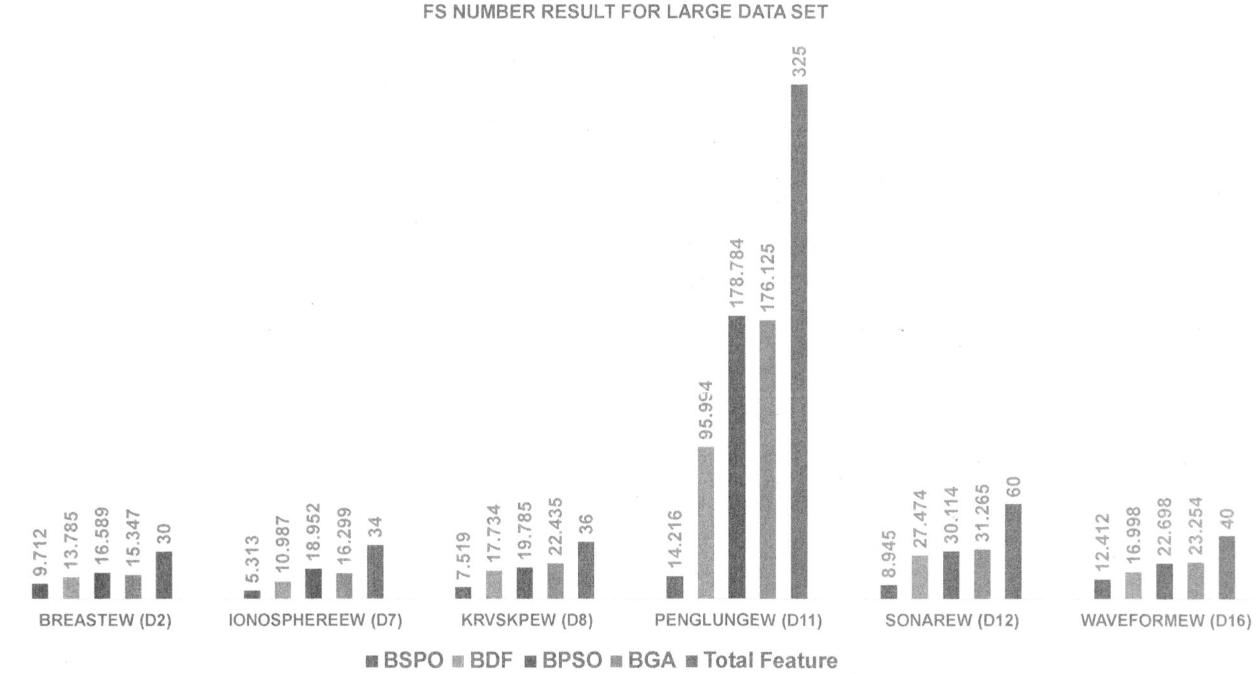

FIGURE 6.5 Comparison of large data sets based on the quantity of selected features.

achieved by the BSPO approach can be attributed to the fact that the proposed method can better balance the difference between exploration and exploitation dynamics during the optimization iterations for engineering problems. Future research will test the proposed algorithm with real-world datasets, such as high-dimensional medical data and complex engineering problems, to bridge theory with practical application. The investigation will reveal how well the solution performs and adapts to different application areas.

References

[1] N. Khodadadi, E. Khodadadi, Q. Al-Tashi, E.-S.M. El-Kenawy, L. Abualigah, S.J. Abdulkadir, A. Alqushaibi, S. Mirjalili, BAOA: Binary arithmetic optimization algorithm with K-nearest neighbor classifier for feature selection, IEEE Access 10 (2023) 106673–106698.

[2] Y. Xue, N. Wang, Y. Niu, P. Zhong, S. Niu, Y. Song, Robust re-weighted multi-view feature selection, Comput. Mater. Continua. 60 (2019) 741–756.

[3] H.H. Al-Baity, N. Al-Mutlaq, A new optimized wrapper gene selection method for breast cancer prediction, Comput. Mater. Continua 67 (2021).

[4] Y. Gültepe, Performance of lung cancer prediction methods using different classification algorithms, Comput. Mater. Continua 67 (2021).

[5] M. Dash, H. Liu, Consistency-based search in feature selection, Artif. Intell. 151 (2003) 155–176.

[6] N. El Aboudi, L. Benhlima, Review on wrapper feature selection approaches, in: 2016 International Conference on Engineering & MIS (ICEMIS), IEEE, 2016, pp. 1–5.

[7] S. Yu, J.C. Príncipe, Simple stopping criteria for information theoretic feature selection, Entropy 21 (2019) 99.

[8] E.-G. Talbi, Metaheuristics: From Design to Implementation, John Wiley & Sons, 2009.

[9] I. Boussaïd, J. Lepagnot, P. Siarry, A survey on optimization metaheuristics, Inf. Sci. 237 (2013) 82–117.

[10] X.-S. Yang, Nature-inspired Metaheuristic Algorithms, Luniver press, 2010.

[11] N. Khodadadi, H. Roghani, F. De Caso, E.-S.M. El-kenawy, Y. Yesha, A. Nanni, Data-driven PSO-CatBoost machine learning model to predict the compressive strength of CFRP-confined circular concrete specimens, Thin-Walled Struct. (2024) 111763.

[12] T. Akan, S. Agahian, R. Dehkharghani, Binbro: Binary battle royale optimizer algorithm, Expert Syst. Appl. 195 (2022) 116599.

[13] S. Arora, P. Anand, Binary butterfly optimization approaches for feature selection, Expert Syst. Appl. 116 (2019) 147–160.

[14] A. Seyyedabbasi, G. Hu, H.A. Shehadeh, X. Wang, P.J. Canatalay, V-shaped and S-shaped binary artificial protozoa optimizer (APO) algorithm for wrapper feature selection on biological data, Clust. Comput. 28 (2025) 163.

[15] J. Kennedy, R.C. Eberhart, A discrete binary version of the particle swarm algorithm, in: 1997 IEEE International Conference on Systems, Man, and Cybernetics. Computational Cybernetics and Simulation, IEEE, 1997, pp. 4104–4108.

[16] A. Kaveh, S. Talatahari, N. Khodadadi, Stochastic paint optimizer: Theory and application in civil engineering, Eng. Comput. 38 (2022) 1921–1952, https://doi.org/10.1007/s00366-020-01179-5.

[17] C.L. Blake, C.J. Merz, UCI repository of machine learning databases, Inf. Comput. Sci. 55 (1998). http://www.ics.uci.edu/~mlearn/MLRepository.html.

Chapter 7

Prediction of compressive strength of ultra-high-performance concrete with efficient training of ANN using four metaheuristic algorithms

Nima Khodadadi[1], Hossein Roghani[2], El-Sayed El-Kenawy[3], Francisco De Caso[2], Khalid M. Mosalam[1] and Antonio Nanni[2]

[1]*Department of Civil and Environmental Engineering, Pacific Earthquake Engineering Research (PEER) Center, University of California, Berkeley, CA, United States;* [2]*Department of Civil and Architectural Engineering, University of Miami, Coral Gables, FL, United States;* [3]*Jadara Research Center, Jadara University, Irbid, Jordan*

1. Introduction

Ultra-high-performance concrete (UHPC) is a group of advanced cement-based composites. They are known for their self-consolidating nature, outstanding mechanical strengths, and long-term durability [1]. It has a minimum specified compressive strength when cured for 28 days under standard curing conditions of more than 120 MPa [2]. Its high strength originates from its densified microstructure and ultra low porosity. It also has superior tensile and flexural strengths, owing to chopped fibers embedded in the cementitious matrix, which contribute to crack-bridging behavior [2]. Due to its compact microstructure and low porous connectivity, UHPC also exhibits excellent durability characteristics and thus can be employed to reinforce new structures and rehabilitate existing structures [3]. UHPC has been used in many civil engineering projects over the past decade, ranging from new infrastructure to existing infrastructure rehabilitation. Undoubtedly, UHPC is a promising material in modern construction.

UHPC is a promising addition to infrastructure and environmental sustainability. It is quite uncommon to find something extraordinary after it has cracked—in the case of UHPC, even when broken, if cured for 28 days, its CS can still exceed 120 MPa. This product is carefully designed with high- density material, contributing to most of its features. As a new category of innovative cement-based composite, it shows better mechanical strength and reliability than ordinary concrete. Fine aggregate, cement, silica fume, microsteel fibers, and high-range water-reducing additive (HRWR) all help to make UHPC. The material's outstanding features include inherent workability, remarkable toughness and strength, low water permeability, and superior durability. UHPC materials have a CS that is 3–16 times that of conventionally produced materials, and they offer the ductility and energy absorption of HPC [4].

UHPC's outstanding mechanical properties make it an excellent material for constructing structural elements where strength is a major design factor. UHPC offers a design advantage over standard concrete by reducing the dimensions of a component or structure that needs creep-proofing. This leads to smaller, thinner structural designs. UHPC is increasingly used in engineering design for building superstructures and long-span structures, for instance, to reduce the weight and improve the fire resistance of floor slabs. It is also used for sustainable ultra high-rise buildings. Thanks to its high mechanical strength, UHPC is suitable for use as the most critical structural element in the building area, thanks to its lower dead load and better resistance to corrosion and severe climatic conditions. It is also suitable for any type of structural application enhancing long-term sustainability and resilience of built facilities.

UHPC combines three major concrete technologies—fiber reinforcement, self-compaction, and high strength—into fresh and hardened concrete with exceptional properties. UHPC demonstrates minimum flexural, compressive, and tensile

Advanced Intelligence Methods for Data Science and Optimization. https://doi.org/10.1016/B978-0-443-28940-8.00006-3

strengths of about 30, 150, and 5 MPa, respectively, which makes UHPC a very durable, robust, and long-lasting civil engineering infrastructure to resist bad weather and prevent concrete from corroding steel reinforcement bars [5]. The unique microstructure of UHPC is supposed to break through the material limitations associated with conventional reinforced concrete (RC) [6]. Designing UHPC is not a trivial task, as the amount and proportions of its various chemicals and components differ by region. In most cases, how much of a specific element can be accommodated comes down to reading the particle size distribution (PSD) curve, a few density models, the systematic packing of particles, and the tried-and-tested method of trial and error [7].

Concrete is used for infrastructure projects all over the globe, and it has enormous environmental consequences: it contributes approximately 7% of global greenhouse gas emissions, while cement production accounts for close to 5% of annual anthropogenic CO_2 emissions worldwide. Therefore, integrating sustainability into structural design remains one of engineering's grand challenges. The cement industry needs to address these CO_2 emissions. So, each tone of cement-based construction helps emit as much CO_2 as possible. However, the benefits of UHPC will be seen only in years and decades. By not requiring frequent maintenance and rehabilitation (relative to conventional construction), UHPC would eliminate about 48% of greenhouse gas emissions. For this reason, UHPC is seen increasingly as a solution to the problem of CO_2 and the mitigation of global warming [8].

One of the major constraints slowing the wide use of UHPC for engineering purposes is its high material cost and high carbon footprint. High material cost and carbon footprint result from using expensive high-carbon materials such as steel fibers, cement, and organic admixtures. Different studies have investigated the development of more cost-effective and low-carbon UHPC mixtures by replacing cement and/or steel fibers with other alternative materials. For instance, Meng et al. [1] created four UHPC mixtures using local river sand, masonry sand, and supplementary cementitious materials (SCMs) such as fly ash and slag. Naturally, this takes time. Mechanical properties such as compressive and flexural strength usually require 28 days of curing following standard testing protocols. In contrast, more impactful tests on durability, such as resistance to external sulfate attacks, can take over 6 months. For example, the numerous possibilities in mixed design variables, such as the water-to-binder ratio, sand-to-binder ratio, and others, have a major influence on the properties of UHPC and entail a very demanding parameter screening process through experimental testing.

In addition, the complexity of the required experimentations increases in tandem with the coupling effects among these variables. Different engineering projects with varying performance requirements will have different requirements in balancing different properties with cost in materials. This also restricts the efficiency of the intensive experimental developments of new UHPC to time-consuming and costly operations. All these factors have hindered the wide application of new UHPC formulations in engineering applications. The rest of this chapter is structured as follows: Section 2 reviews related literature. Section 3 describes the data construction process. Section 4 introduces the metaheuristic optimization technique. Section 5 presents the results and discussion. Section 6 concludes the study.

2. Literature review

Machine learning (ML) methods effectively solve complex problems across various engineering disciplines. In civil engineering, ML is particularly beneficial for building materials, assisting with mix design, and optimizing cement performance. These models excel in analyzing large datasets and adapting to different data types.

The learning capabilities of ML systems have significantly expanded the application possibilities of practical problem-solving. This is facilitated by their capability to discover intricate and unpredictable patterns between the inputs and outputs in datasets. Many efficient and robust ML models, such as tree-based ensembles, support vector machines (SVMs), artificial neural networks (ANNs), and multivariate adaptive regression splines (MARSs), have good capability of simulating nonlinear engineering properties of the composition of material composites. For example, predicting the mechanical properties of MPC materials is widely achieved through the popular ML models, namely, extreme gradient boosting (XGBoost), random forest, and hybrid models. These are renowned for tree-based ensemble techniques. The mechanical properties of several types of advanced concrete, such as self-healing concrete [9], recycled aggregate concrete (RCA) [10], fiber-reinforced rubberized recycled aggregate concrete [11], high-strength concrete (HSC) and UHPC [12], have been predicted by many studies.

UHPC can also be produced by data-driven machine learning models, which are trained to predict UHPC properties by finding a calibrated relationship between the design variables and the concrete properties [12]. Some of the recent articles mention machine learning tools for UHPC development. For example, Fan et al. [12] trained a second-order polynomial regression model with 19 experimental data sets to predict the packing density of UHPC. Ghafari et al. [13] trained artificial neural networks with 53 datasets to predict UHPC's CS and flowability. Abellán-García and Guzmán-Guzmán [14] developed two random forest models with 600 datasets to predict the energy absorption and the ultimate strain capacities of UHPC.

Similarly, Sadrossadat et al. [15] used an artificial neural network in 53 datasets for predicting CS and flowability, while Fan et al. [16] used an artificial neural network in 80 and 26 datasets in different studies to predict particle packing density, CS, and flexural strength of UHPC. Several works have demonstrated that ML models can predict the material properties of concrete [17]. However, there is a research gap in predicting the CS of UHPC. Since the prediction of CS in the UHPC would be more accurate with the help of metaheuristic algorithms, the model is formed in this chapter.

The civil engineering field recognizes UHPC as a promising material because it possesses outstanding physical and mechanical properties. UHPC structural performance relies heavily on its compressive strength (CS). New research focuses on applying machine learning techniques, such as artificial neural networks, to estimate the compressive strength of UHPC. Finding the best parameters for ANN models presents a complex problem, which demands specialized knowledge and iterative testing methods. The use of metaheuristic optimization algorithms has grown to improve both accuracy and efficiency in ANN-based predictive models. The field has seen significant development, yet still shows a distinct gap when it comes to conducting systematic evaluations of numerous metaheuristic techniques under uniform experimental conditions.

The majority of past research concentrates on single algorithms while failing to provide comparisons or benchmarks with other techniques. This research addresses the identified research gap applying four metaheuristic algorithms to optimize ANN parameters for predicting UHPC compressive strength. In summary, this study contributes to the field by: The research tackles a lack of metaheuristic optimization techniques for UHPC strength prediction and compares four top algorithms while proving that the SPO-ANN model yields the highest accuracy for practical UHPC design.

3. Data construction

The effectiveness of ML in predicting the CS of UHPC hinges on having ample high-quality data. This prerequisite is essential for all artificial intelligence applications. Due to the novelty of UHPC and its recent implementation, gathering and organizing UHPC mix proportions along with corresponding CS values is a lot of work. Li et al. [18] compiled a 727 UHPC mix proportion group dataset. This dataset includes 12 input parameters: cement (C), silica fume (SF), slag (S), fly ash (FA), limestone powder (LP), nano silica (NS), water-to-binder ratio (w/b), quartz powder (QP), sand (Sa), steel fiber (Fi), superplasticizer (SP), and age (Ag). Fig. 7.1 provides details on these data characteristics. The dataset was divided randomly into training and testing sets, with 80% allocated for training and 20% for testing.

Machine learning models require input variables to be as independent as possible for accurate predictions. Therefore, Pearson correlation analysis identifies and removes highly correlated variables, reducing data redundancy and enhancing the model's prediction accuracy. The correlation between input parameters was examined using a correlation heatmap to assess the suitability of the selected variables. The Pearson correlation coefficient (R) was calculated to create the correlation matrix of the input parameters. An R-value exceeding 0.7 indicates multicollinearity among the input variables, suggesting a risk of redundant selection. The correlation analysis results, visually presented in Fig. 7.2, show no R-value surpassing 0.7, indicating no significant issues with redundant input variable selection.

4. Metaheuristic optimization technique

Metaheuristic algorithms are sophisticated optimization methods crafted to tackle challenging problems that conventional approaches struggle to solve. These algorithms navigate the search space to discover nearly optimal solutions by balancing exploration and exploitation. They often draw inspiration from natural phenomena or social behaviors, with well-known examples including genetic algorithms, simulated annealing, particle swarm optimization, and ant colony optimization. Renowned for their versatility, metaheuristic algorithms are employed across various disciplines, such as engineering, artificial intelligence, economics, and logistics, providing practical solutions for intricate, large-scale, and multidimensional problems. This study integrates artificial neural networks (utilizing feed-forward backpropagation) with the following meta-heuristic algorithms: Arithmetic Optimization Algorithm (AOA), African Vulture Optimization Algorithm (AVOA), Generalized Normal Distribution Optimization (GNDO), and Stochastic Paint Optimization (SPO). These meta-heuristic algorithms are employed within the neural network's training function to enhance performance.

4.1 AOA

Abualigah et al. [19] introduced the Arithmetic Optimization Algorithm (AOA). This algorithm is primarily inspired by applying arithmetic operators (division, multiplication, subtraction, and addition) to solve arithmetic problems. The AOA optimization process begins by generating a random set of candidate solutions called the population. As iterations

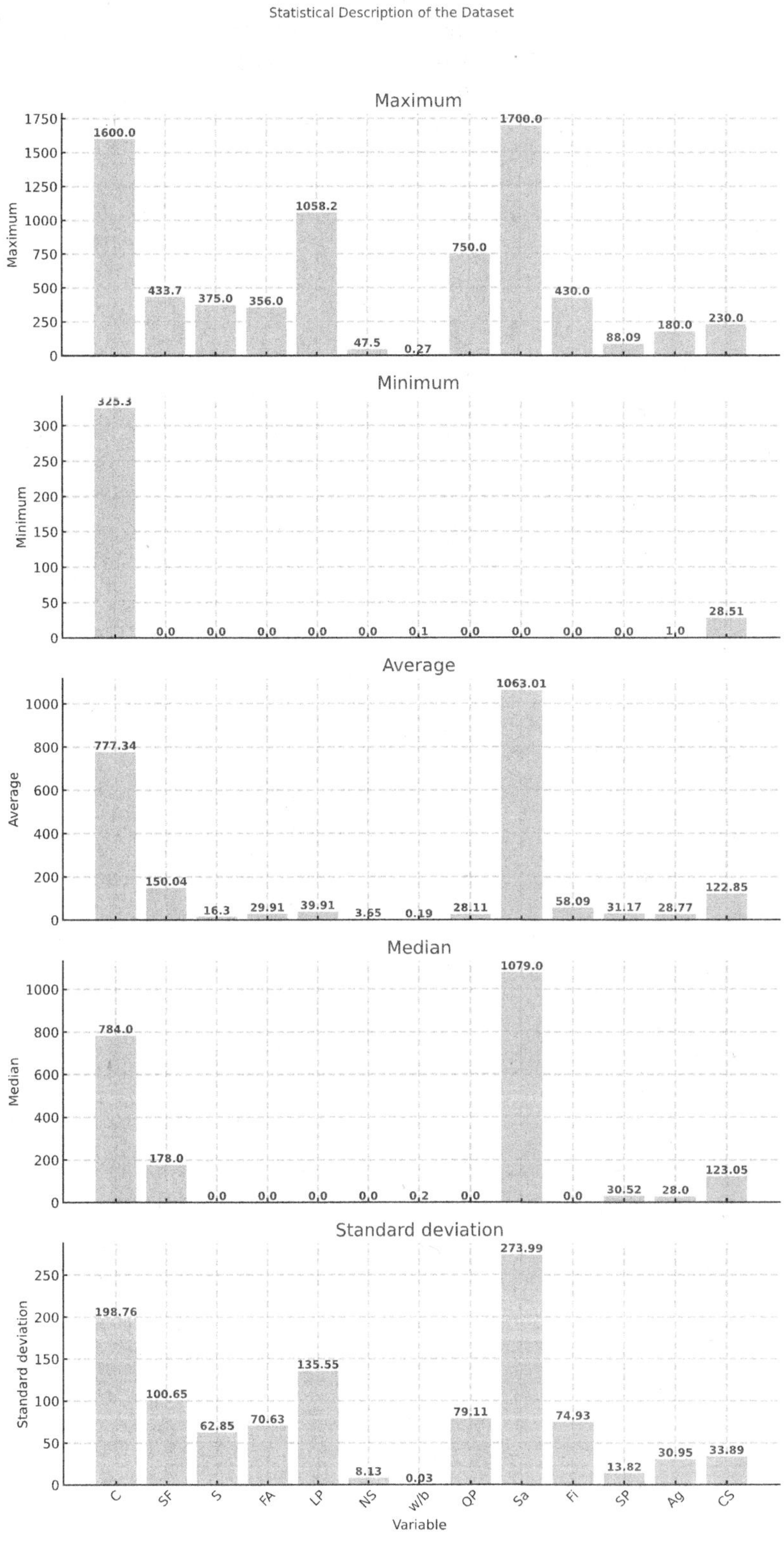

FIGURE 7.1 Statistical description of the dataset.

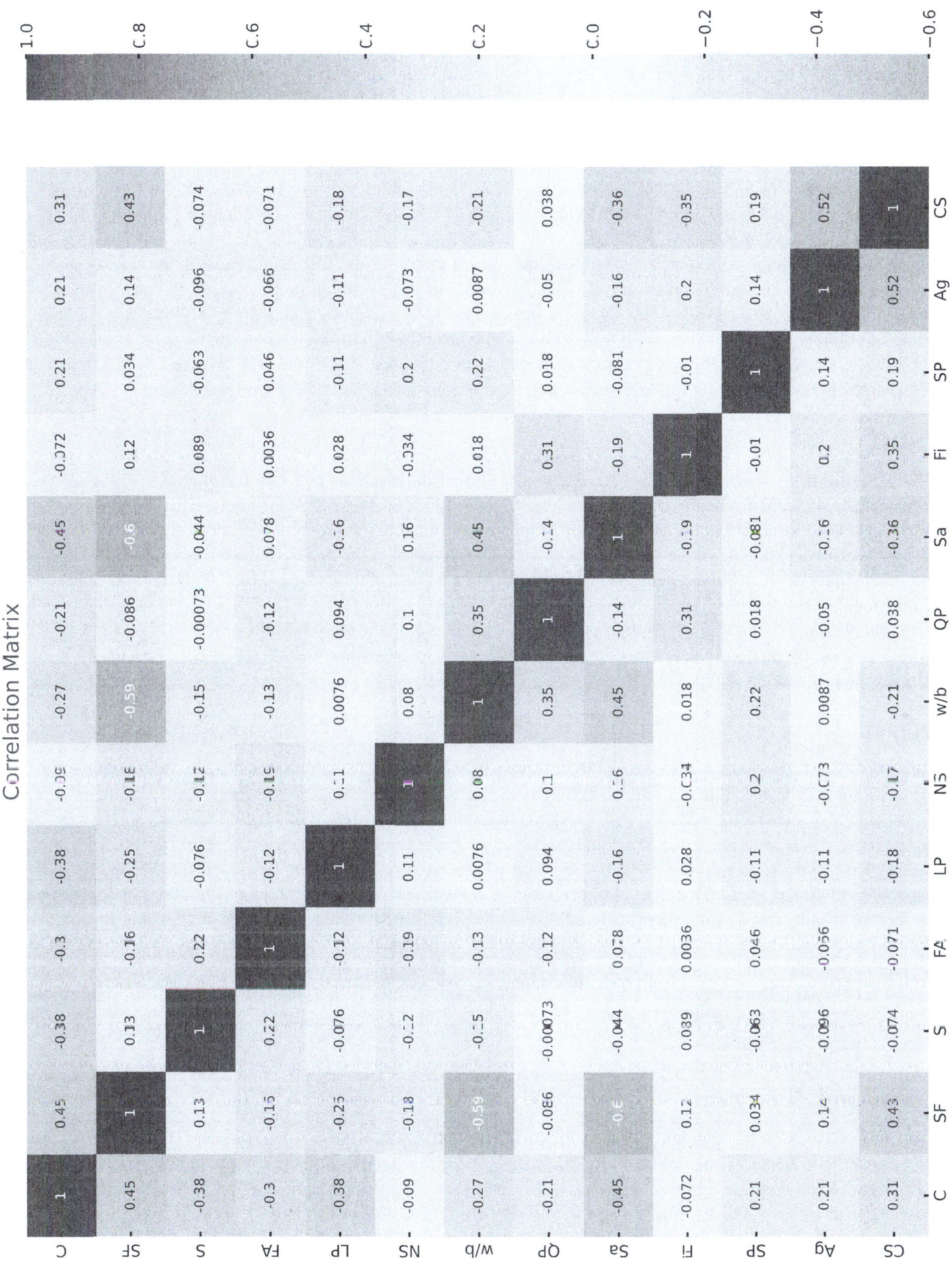

FIGURE 7.2 Pearson correlation of features.

proceed, the operators (division, multiplication, subtraction, and addition) guide the solutions toward the optimal position. Each solution updates its position based on the best solution identified. The Math Optimizer Accelerated (MOA) parameter gradually increases from 0.2 to 0.9 to balance exploration and exploitation. Candidate solutions move away from the near-optimal solution when a random number of r sub one exceeds the MOA and converge toward it when r sub 1 exceeds the MOA. The algorithm terminates once a predefined stopping criterion is met [20].

4.2 AVOA

The African Vulture Optimization Algorithm (AVOA), developed by Abdollahzadeh et al. [21], is inspired by African vultures' foraging behavior and living habits. These predatory birds are crucial to ecosystems, and their removal poses significant health risks to human communities. The simulation of AVOA relies on four key assumptions: the African vulture population consists of N_{POPF} vultures, each with an n-dimensional position, and the optimization process runs for a maximum number of iterations (*MaxIter*). The position of each vulture X_i^t at different iterations t represents its location in the solution space. The vulture population is divided into three groups based on their behavior: the first group identifies the best feasible solution, the second group finds the second-best solution, and the remaining vultures are the survivors. Each group of vultures has a distinct capability in finding and consuming food. The weakest and most starved vultures are considered the worst, while the strongest and most numerous are the best. In AVOA, the two best solutions are represented by the strongest vultures, and the other vultures aim to converge toward these optimal solutions.

4.3 GNDO

The GNDO algorithm is based on the characteristics of a normal distribution with two parameters: the mean (location parameter) and the standard deviation (scale parameter), which respectively represent the average and variation of random variables [22]. It has a straightforward structure and employs information-sharing heuristics conducive to balancing local exploitation and global exploration. Meanwhile, local exploitation searches for better solutions by considering the current positions of all individuals with the help of a generalized regular distribution model guided by current solutions and optimal positions. This is achieved by analyzing the relationship between the distribution of individuals in the population and the normal distribution. Global exploration performs a wide search in the whole solution space to find some promising areas, which is done by randomly selecting three individuals to help conduct the general search. The GNDO is used to solve various engineering problems [23,24].

4.4 SPO

The Stochastic Paint Optimization (SPO) algorithm, devised by Kaveh et al. [25], is inspired by the principles of color theory in painting. The algorithm progresses through initialization, clustering, combination, and termination control stages. The search space is imagined as a canvas, depicting solutions as paints with specific colors representing design parameters. These paints are assessed and ranked based on their beauty indices (objective function values), with each new color added to the canvas altering the overall perception of the artwork. Colors are classified into primary (best), secondary (good), and tertiary (least desirable) categories on the color wheel. The process begins with the random assignment of initial colors to all paints. Combining different colors generates new paints that serve as designs or solutions to optimization problems. These paints are evaluated and ranked based on their objective functions, classifying them into primary, secondary, and tertiary groups. New colors are created through analogous, complementary, triadic, or tetradic combination techniques. These new paints are then evaluated, and if their beauty index exceeds that of the previous iterations, they replace the older paints. The optimization continues until a specified termination condition is met, ensuring the optimal solution is identified.

5. Results and discussion

In this research, various metrics, including mean squared error (MSE), root mean squared error (RMSE), mean absolute error (MAE), and coefficient of determination (R^2), are employed to assess and contrast the models' performance. To ensure a fair analysis across all algorithms, each was run 20 times with a population size of 40 and 1000 iterations on a computer equipped with macOS Ventura, an Apple M2 Max chip, 96 GB of RAM, and MATLAB 2023b. The number of training data points is 582, while the number of test data points is 145. The workflow of the model is shown in Fig. 7.3.

Fig. 7.4 compares the convergence performance of four optimization algorithms: SPO, AOA, AVOA, and GNDO. Fig. 7.4(a) displays the best convergence curves, with the x-axis representing the number of iterations and the y-axis

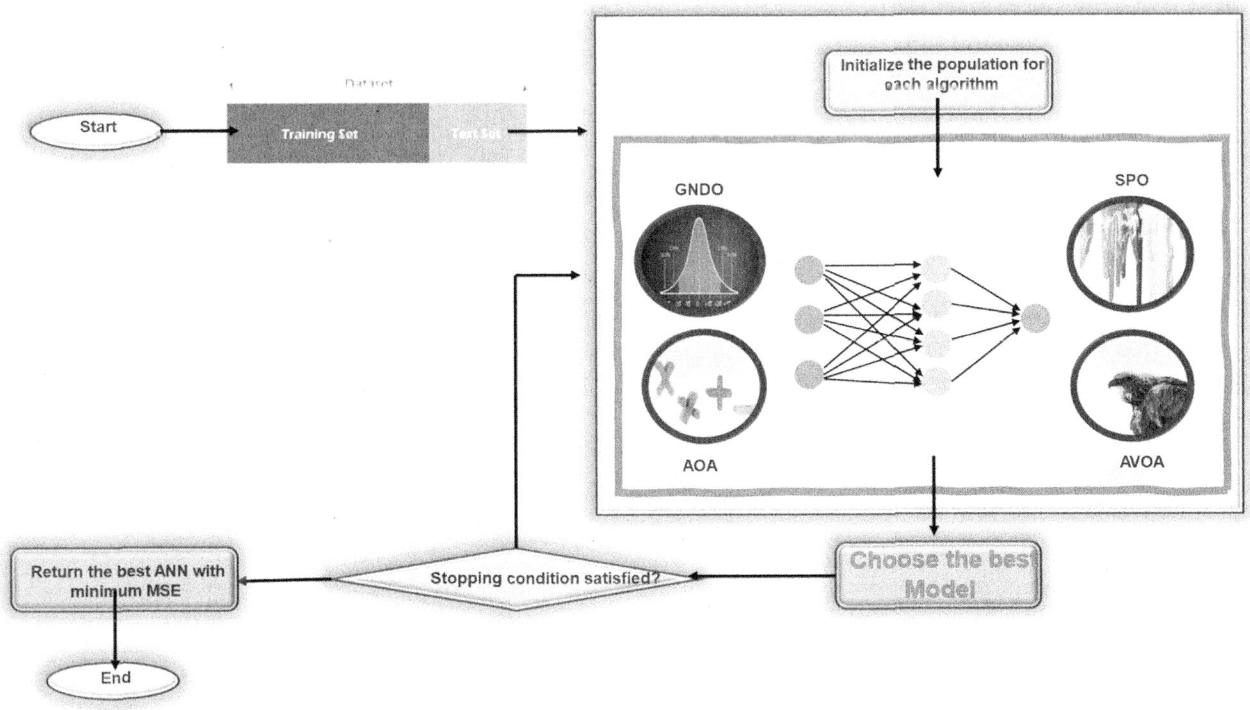

FIGURE 7.3 ML model based on four metaheuristic algorithms.

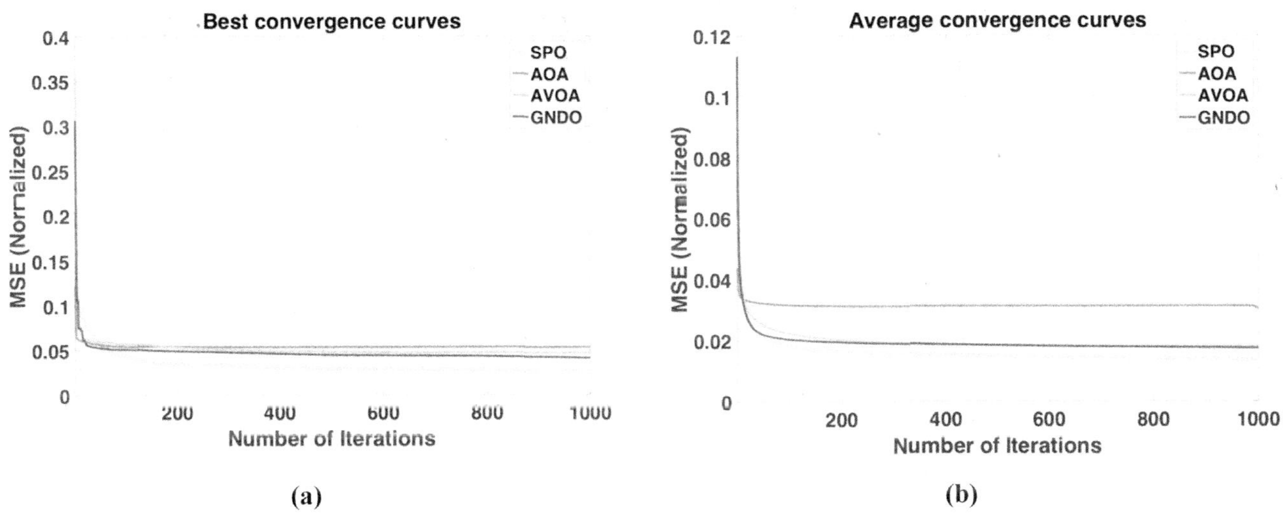

FIGURE 7.4 Best and convergence curves for all algorithms.

indicating the normalized MSE. Initially, all algorithms show a rapid decline in MSE, indicating fast convergence. However, as the number of iterations increases, the rate of improvement slows and eventually stabilizes. Among the algorithms, SPO consistently achieves the lowest MSE, demonstrating superior performance in minimizing the error compared with AOA, AVOA, and GNDO.

Fig. 7.4(b) illustrates the average convergence curves, providing a broader perspective on the algorithms' convergence behavior over 20 multiple runs. Similar to the best convergence curves, the x-axis shows the number of iterations, and the y-axis shows the normalized MSE. SPO again outperforms the other algorithms, maintaining a lower average MSE throughout the iterations. The AOA, AVOA, and GNDO algorithms exhibit higher average MSE values, with GNDO having the highest error. These plots highlight the effectiveness of the SPO algorithm in achieving lower MSE values in individual best-case scenarios and, on average, across multiple runs, suggesting its robustness and efficiency in optimization tasks.

Fig. 7.5 consists of four heatmaps, each representing the MSE results for a training dataset using different optimization algorithms: SPO, AOA, AVOA, and GNDO. Each heatmap visualizes how the MSE varies with various numbers of neurons and runs, with the color gradient indicating the MSE values. Notably, the SPO algorithm achieves the lowest MSE value of 0.0266, outperforming AOA (0.0533), AVOA (0.0381), and GNDO (0.0359) in error minimization. The minimum MSE values and their locations in the heatmaps depict the differences in the algorithms' efficiencies. Using various algorithms and configurations requires a thorough comparison to achieve the optimal training processes of neural networks and obtain greater accuracy and model performance. The main body of the heat maps gradually has different color gradients, from darker to lighter. The SPO heatmap generally has the darkest color gradients, which show lower MSE values than other algorithms' color gradients. Furthermore, the lowest MSE is recorded at 15 neurons for SPO, seven neurons for AOA, 14 neurons for AVOA, and 11 neurons for GNDO. The SPO algorithm has the smallest mean square error (MSE = 0.0266), meaning that this model (SPO) has the best ability to minimize errors and is chosen to build the predictive model.

Fig. 7.6 and 7.7 comparatively represent the capabilities of the SPO algorithm in predicting test and training datasets accordingly. In Fig. 7.6, we can see that the algorithm could predict the test data with minimal difference between the experimental and predicted values. Similarly, in Fig. 7.7, we can see that it can also train accurately with the experimental

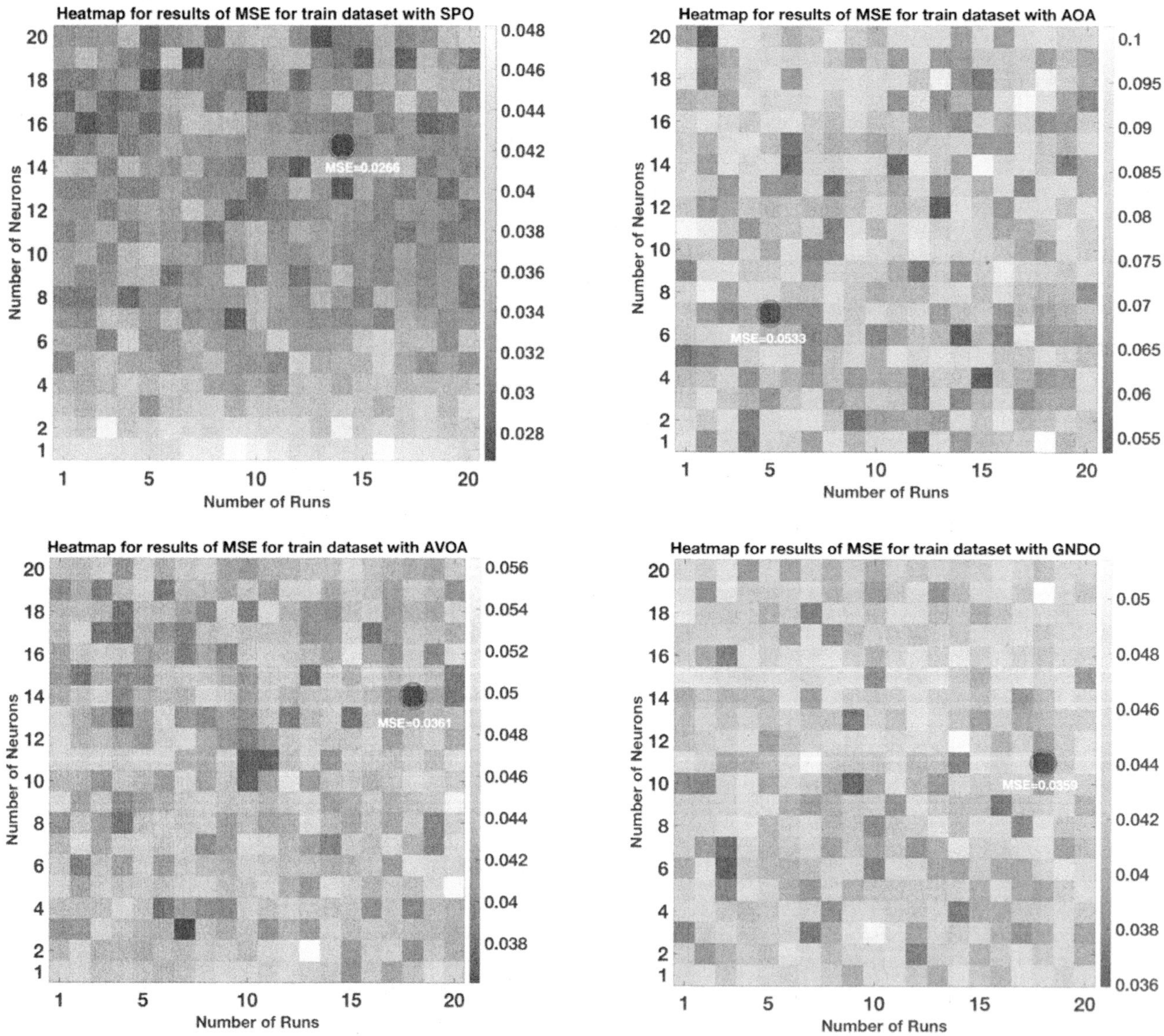

FIGURE 7.5 The MSE results of all algorithms for 20 runs.

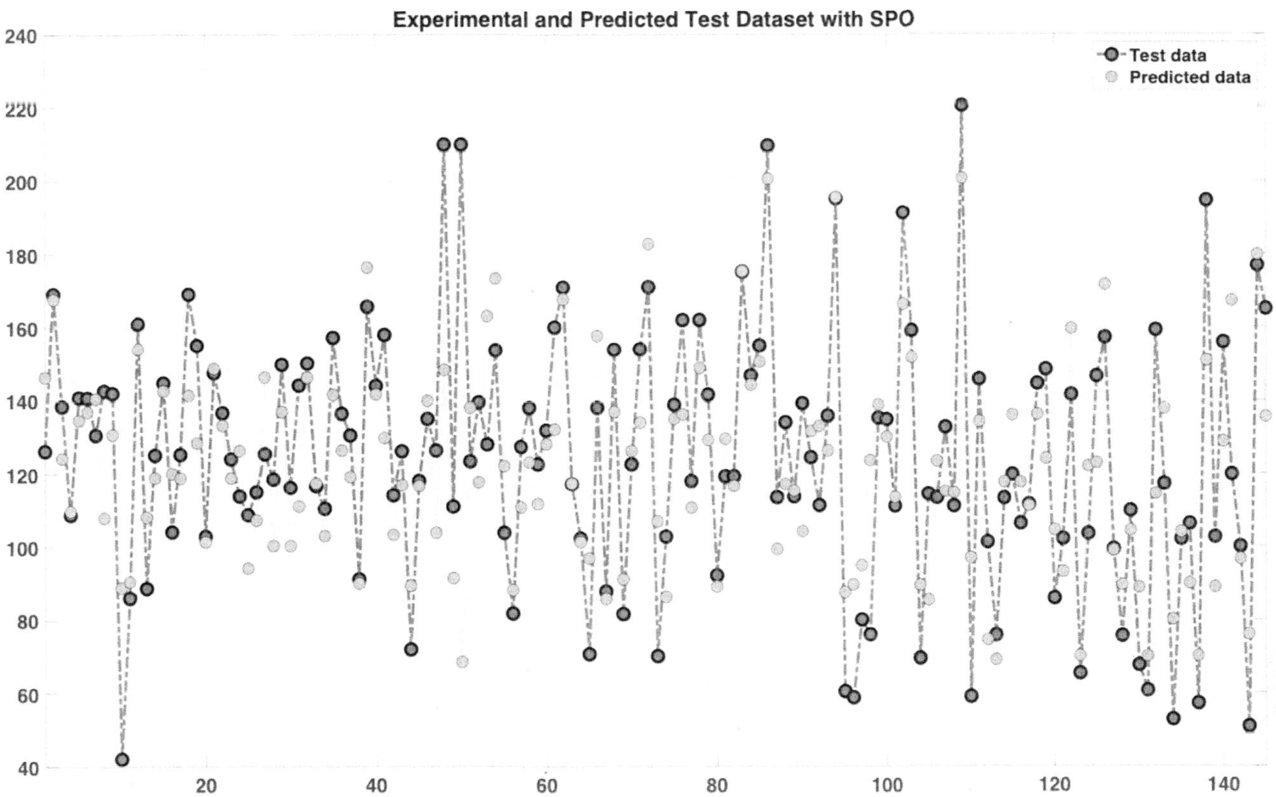

FIGURE 7.6 Comparing the experimental and predicted test dataset.

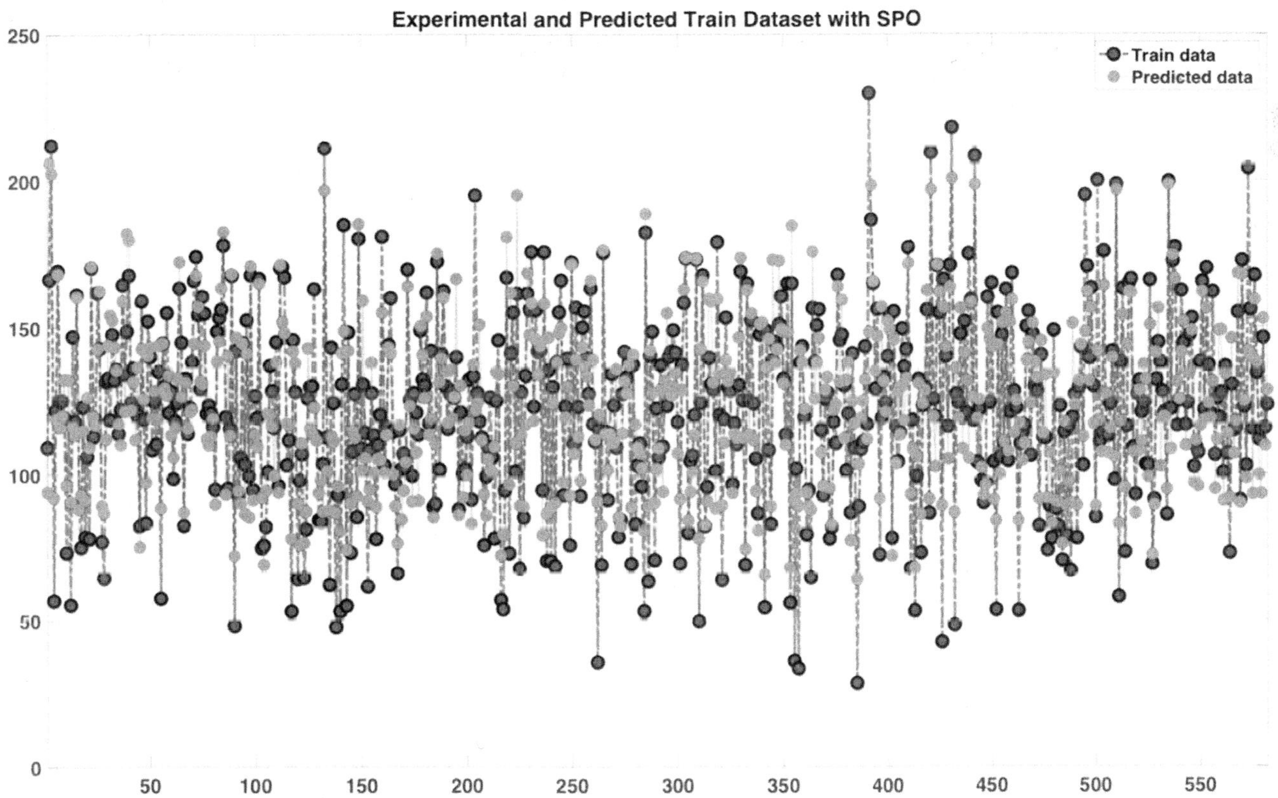

FIGURE 7.7 Comparing the experimental and predicted train dataset.

data by fitting it precisely with the predicted values. We can see that the model could predict the values of both the training and test datasets with utmost accuracy. This shows that the model can be applicable in many practical uses where predictive accuracy is crucial.

Table 7.1 compares the four different ANN architectures, such as the AOA-ANN, AVOA-ANN, GNDO-ANN, and SPO-ANN models. The MSE, MAE, RMSE, and R2 values are the performance metrics for both models. The table shows the highest, lowest, average, and STD values of the abovementioned parameters. Overall, the SPO-ANN model has given the minimum value across the board in all metrics. Its minimum value for MSE is 0.0286, with a mean of 0.0355 and a standard deviation of 0.0005. This makes SPO-ANN the most accurate and consistent. For the MAE metric, SPO-ANN has the lowest best value with 0.1258, the mean is 0.1400, and the standard deviation is again the smallest in the solution with 0.0008. For the RMSE metric, the SPO-ANN had the lowest best value of 0.1692, the lowest mean of 0.1882, and the smallest standard deviation of 0.0007. This result suggests that SPO-ANN is the most reliable in minimizing prediction errors. Furthermore, the SPO-ANN model has the highest coefficient of determination (R^2) with the best value of 0.8655, a mean of 0.8288, and a minor standard deviation of 0.0021, which reveals the best possible fit to the data.

The best MSE of AVOA-ANN was 0.0371, with a mean of 0.0454 and a standard deviation of 0.0004, while the best MAE was 0.1445, with a mean of 0.1618, and a standard deviation of 0.0009; its best RMSE was 0.1927, a mean of 0.2129, and a standard deviation of 0.0009; its best R^2 was 0.8197, a mean of 0.7741 and a standard deviation of 0.0022.

The third best model was GNDO-ANN, which got an outstanding result with the MSE best value of 0.0385, a mean of 0.0441, and a standard deviation of 0.0004. In MAE, GNDO-ANN got a best value of 0.1471, a mean of 0.1592, and a standard deviation of 0.0010. For RMSE, GNDO-ANN got a best of 0.1962, a mean of 0.2100, and a standard deviation of 0.0010. The R^2 values were also good, with a best of 0.8137, a mean of 0.7816, and a standard deviation of 0.0024.

The AOA-ANN model occupied the fourth position. Its best MSE was 0.0534, the mean was 0.0766, and the standard deviation was 0.0012. The best MAE value was 0.1740, the mean was 0.2144, and the standard deviation was 0.0020. The best value of RMSE was 0.2312, the mean was 0.2763, and the standard deviation was 0.0020. The best R^2 was 0.7531, the mean was 0.5895, and the standard deviation was 0.0134.

Fig. 7.8 displays a scatter plot contrasting the experimental dataset values (x-axis) with the predicted dataset values y-axis. The blue circles represent individual data points, showcasing the model's predicted values against the actual experimental values. The plot features a pink diagonal line (y = x), indicating the ideal scenario where predicted values

TABLE 7.1 Statistical results of performance metrics for all runs on the dataset.

Metrics		AOA-ANN	AVOA-ANN	GNDO-ANN	SPO-ANN
MSE	Best	0.0534	0.0371	0.0385	**0.0286**
	Worst	0.0999	0.0549	0.0497	**0.0465**
	Mean	0.0766	0.0454	0.0441	**0.0355**
	STD	0.0012	0.0004	0.0004	**0.0005**
MAE	Best	0.1740	0.1445	0.1471	**0.1258**
	Worst	0.2496	0.1792	0.1711	**0.1614**
	Mean	0.2144	0.1618	0.1592	**0.1400**
	STD	0.0020	0.0009	0.0010	**0.0008**
RMSE	Best	0.2312	0.1927	0.1962	**0.1692**
	Worst	0.3160	0.2343	0.2229	**0.2156**
	Mean	0.2763	0.2129	0.2100	**0.1882**
	STD	0.0020	0.0009	0.0010	**0.0007**
R^2	Best	0.7531	0.8197	0.8137	**0.8655**
	Worst	0.3670	0.7176	0.7492	**0.7672**
	Mean	0.5895	0.7741	0.7816	**0.8288**
	STD	0.0134	0.0022	0.0024	**0.0021**

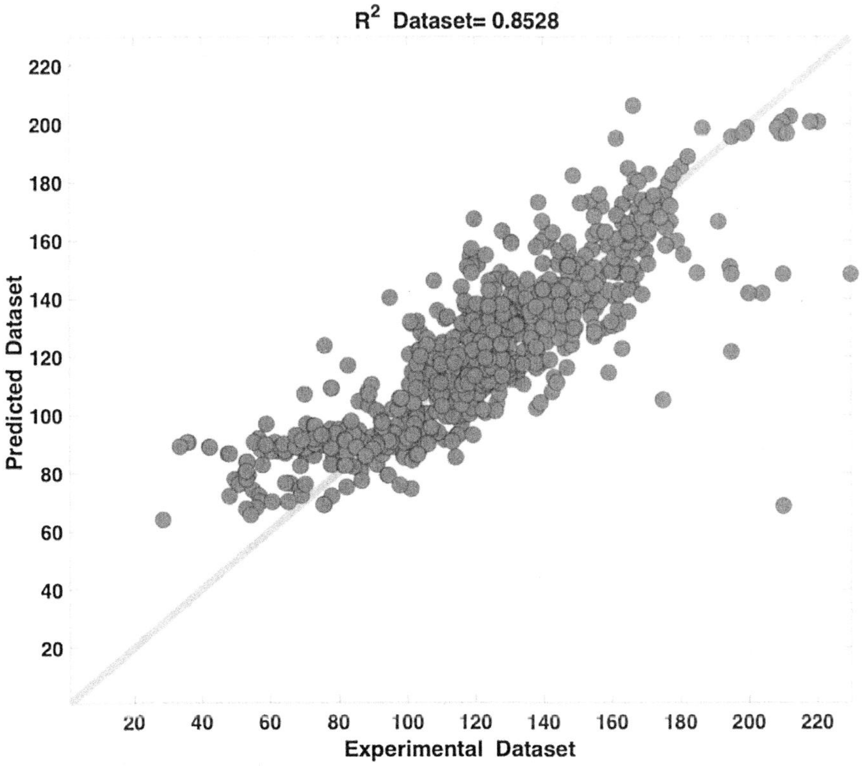

FIGURE 7.8 R-squared for dataset.

perfectly match experimental values. The closeness of the data points to this line demonstrates the model's accuracy. Moreover, the plot prominently shows an R^2 value of 0.8528 at the top, indicating that the predicted data account for 85.28% of the variability in the experimental data. This high R^2 value, coupled with the tight clustering of data points around the regression line, highlights the model's robust predictive capability and reliability in estimating the dataset values.

In summary, it seems that for all the datasets used, SPO-ANN performed with higher accuracy and was the most reliable model we applied to our test set. GNDO-ANN and AVOA-ANN illustrated a strong performance on the dataset, while the AOA-ANN did not.

6. Conclusion

This work demonstrated the potential of artificial intelligence (AI) and machine learning (ML) to predict the compressive strength of ultra-high-performance concrete (UHPC), which now attracts intensive attention in civil engineering. Since AI-based predictions are data-driven, the predictive accuracy of ML depends on the quality of data used to tune the hyperparameter, which is a critical issue for building ML models. To overcome this issue, it has now been proved that metaheuristic algorithms can successfully optimize modeling prediction for UHPC. Four metaheuristic algorithms (AOA, AVOA, GNDO, and SPO) were evaluated in training ANN models. It presented the performance metrics of all models in detail, and SPO-ANN was the best in MSE, MAE, and RMSE. It presented higher R^2 with the predictive model's highest predictive accuracy and reliability. This work may contribute to the development of UHPC and provide a research direction to develop further AI techniques to solve engineering problems.

References

[1] W. Meng, K.H. Khayat, Effect of hybrid fibers on fresh properties, mechanical properties, and autogenous shrinkage of cost-effective UHPC, J. Mater. Civ. Eng. 30 (2018) 4018030.

[2] J. Du, W. Meng, K.H. Khayat, Y. Bao, P. Guo, Z. Lyu, A. Abu-Obeidah, H. Nassif, H. Wang, New development of ultra-high-performance concrete (UHPC), Compos. B Eng. 224 (2021) 109220.

[3] Z. Lu, Z. Feng, D. Yao, X. Li, H. Ji, Freeze-thaw resistance of ultra-high performance concrete: Dependence on concrete composition, Constr. Build. Mater. 293 (2021) 123523.
[4] J. Li, Z. Wu, C. Shi, Q. Yuan, Z. Zhang, Durability of ultra-high performance concrete–A review, Constr. Build. Mater. 255 (2020) 119296.
[5] X. Ke, Y. Duan, A Bayesian machine learning approach for inverse prediction of high-performance concrete ingredients with targeted performance, Constr. Build. Mater. 270 (2021) 121424.
[6] M.G. Sohail, R. Kahraman, N. Al Nuaimi, B. Gencturk, W. Alnahhal, Durability characteristics of high and ultra-high performance concretes, J. Build. Eng. 33 (2021) 101669.
[7] K. Wille, A.E. Naaman, S. El-Tawil, G.J. Parra-Montesinos, Ultra-high performance concrete and fiber reinforced concrete: Achieving strength and ductility without heat curing, Mater. Struct. 45 (2012) 309–324.
[8] A.M. Ebid, A.F. Deifalla, H.A. Mahdi, Evaluating shear strength of light-weight and normal-weight concretes through artificial intelligence, Sustainability 14 (2022) 14010.
[9] J.A. Carneiro, P.R.L. Lima, M.B. Leite, R.D. Toledo Filho, Compressive stress–strain behavior of steel fiber reinforced-recycled aggregate concrete, Cem. Concr. Compos. 46 (2014) 65–72.
[10] Z.H. Duan, C.S. Poon, Properties of recycled aggregate concrete made with recycled aggregates with different amounts of old adhered mortars, Mater. Des. 58 (2014) 19–29.
[11] C. Cakiroglu, M. Shahjalal, K. Islam, S.M.F. Mahmood, A.H.M.M. Billah, M.L. Nehdi, Explainable ensemble learning data-driven modeling of mechanical properties of fiber-reinforced rubberized recycled aggregate concrete, J. Build. Eng. 76 (2023) 107279.
[12] Z. Shen, A.F. Deifalla, P. Kamiński, A. Dyczko, Compressive strength evaluation of ultra-high-strength concrete by machine learning, Materials 15 (2022) 3523.
[13] E. Ghafari, H. Costa, E. Júlio, Statistical mixture design approach for eco-efficient UHPC, Cem. Concr. Compos. 55 (2015) 17–25.
[14] J. Abellan-Garcia, J.S. Guzmán-Guzmán, Random forest-based optimization of UHPFRC under ductility requirements for seismic retrofitting applications, Constr. Build. Mater. 285 (2021) 122869.
[15] E. Sadrossadat, H. Basarir, A. Karrech, M. Elchalakani, Multi-objective mixture design and optimisation of steel fiber reinforced UHPC using machine learning algorithms and metaheuristics, Eng. Comput. 38 (2022) 2569–2582.
[16] F. Dingqiang, Y. Rui, S. Zhonghe, W. Chunfeng, W. Jinnan, S. Qiqi, A novel approach for developing a green ultra-high performance concrete (UHPC) with advanced particles packing meso-structure, Constr. Build. Mater. 265 (2020) 120339.
[17] N. Khodadadi, H. Roghani, F. De Caso, E.-S.M. El-kenawy, Y. Yesha, A. Nanni, Data-driven PSO-CatBoost machine learning model to predict the compressive strength of CFRP-Confined circular concrete specimens, Thin-Walled Struct. 198 (2024) 111763.
[18] Y. Li, X. Yang, C. Ren, L. Wang, X. Ning, Predicting the compressive strength of ultra-high-performance concrete based on machine learning optimized by meta-heuristic algorithm, Buildings 14 (2024) 1209.
[19] L. Abualigah, A. Diabat, S. Mirjalili, M. Abd Elaziz, A.H. Gandomi, The arithmetic optimization algorithm, Comput. Methods Appl. Mech. Eng. 376 (2021) 113609.
[20] N. Khodadadi, S. Vaclav, S. Mirjalili, Dynamic arithmetic optimization algorithm for truss optimization under natural frequency constraints, IEEE Access 10 (2022) 16188–16208.
[21] B. Abdollahzadeh, F.S. Gharehchopogh, S. Mirjalili, African vultures optimization algorithm: A new nature-inspired metaheuristic algorithm for global optimization problems, Comput. Ind. Eng. 158 (2021) 107408.
[22] Y. Zhang, Z. Jin, S. Mirjalili, Generalized normal distribution optimization and its applications in parameter extraction of photovoltaic models, Energy Convers. Manag. 224 (2020) 113301.
[23] N. Khodadadi, S. Mirjalili, Truss optimization with natural frequency constraints using generalized normal distribution optimization, Appl. Intell. 52 (2022) 1–14.
[24] N. Khodadadi, E. Khodadadi, B. Abdollahzadeh, E.-S.M. EI-Kenawy, P. Mardanpour, W. Zhao, F.S. Gharehchopogh, S. Mirjalili, Multi-objective generalized normal distribution optimization: A novel algorithm for multi-objective problems, Clust. Comput. 27 (2024) 1–43.
[25] A. Kaveh, S. Talatahari, N. Khodadadi, Stochastic paint optimizer: Theory and application in civil engineering, Eng. Comput. 38 (2022) 1921–1952, https://doi.org/10.1007/s00366-020-01179-5.

Chapter 8

Fuzzy logic applications in enhancing system safety and reliability: A brief analysis

Mohammad Yazdi[1] and Harish Garg[2]

[1]*Faculty of Science and Engineering, Macquarie University, Sydney, NSW, Australia;* [2]*Department of Mathematics, Thapar Institute of Engineering & Technology (Deemed University), Patiala, Punjab, India*

1. Introduction

The hydrogen energy sector has experienced rapid growth in recent years, driven by the increasing global demand for clean and sustainable energy solutions. However, handling hydrogen presents significant safety challenges due to its highly flammable and explosive nature. Failures in hydrogen systems can lead to catastrophic consequences, affecting both human life and the environment [1–4]. Therefore, it is crucial to identify potential risks associated with these systems and implement effective measures to mitigate them [5,6].

Traditional risk assessment techniques, such as Fault Tree Analysis (FTA), have been widely employed in hazardous industries to perform hazard analyses and prevent incidents [7,8]. FTA is particularly popular due to its systematic approach to identifying the root causes of system failures [9–11]. Despite its widespread use, FTA faces challenges when applied to complex hydrogen systems. One significant issue is the difficulty in obtaining precise failure data, often due to uncertainties arising from limited knowledge, scarcity of statistical data, ambiguous component behaviors, and varying operational environments [12–14].

These uncertainties hinder accurate quantitative analysis using conventional FTA, which typically assumes statistical independence among events—a condition not always met in real-world scenarios where events can be interdependent [15,16]. This assumption can lead to inaccurate system reliability and safety estimations, highlighting the need for improved methods that effectively handle uncertainties and dependencies.

Incorporating fuzzy logic into risk assessment is a promising solution to these challenges. The fuzzy set theory allows for handling imprecise and uncertain information by utilizing expert judgments and linguistic variables rather than relying solely on precise numerical data [17–20]. By integrating fuzzy logic with FTA, we can enhance the modeling of uncertainties and perform more reliable risk assessments even when complete failure data is lacking [21–24].

Furthermore, transforming the fuzzy fault tree into a Bayesian Network (BN) provides a robust framework for capturing dependencies among events and modeling scenarios with redundant components [25–27]. BNs illustrate causal relationships within a system, facilitating forward and backward analyses [15,28]. This integration allows for a more nuanced and accurate assessment of potential faults and their impacts, ultimately leading to better-informed decision-making regarding system safety and reliability [29,30].

This study aims to develop a novel approach for conducting risk analysis in the hydrogen energy sector under conditions of uncertainty. The proposed methodology involves using FTA for qualitative analysis to identify root causes of potential failures. Fuzzy set theory and expert judgment are employed to quantify the uncertainties associated with primary event data. The fault tree is then transformed into a Bayesian Network to perform quantitative analysis, capturing event dependencies and improving overall assessment accuracy.

By applying this methodology to a case study within the hydrogen energy sector, we demonstrate how integrating fuzzy logic and Bayesian Networks can significantly enhance the reliability of risk assessments. This approach addresses

Advanced Intelligence Methods for Data Science and Optimization. https://doi.org/10.1016/B978-0-443-28940-8.00001-4

traditional methods' limitations by effectively handling uncertainties and dependencies and supports diagnostic analysis crucial for developing effective maintenance and safety strategies. Our findings underscore the importance of uncertainty management and highlight fuzzy logic as a reliable alternative when conventional failure information is unavailable.

2. Methodological framework

The proposed methodology integrates fuzzy logic, fault tree analysis, and Bayesian Networks into a unified framework for risk assessment under uncertainty. The process begins with the construction of a fault tree, which serves as the foundation for modeling the system's failure structure. The top event, representing the system failure, is identified, and the fault tree is systematically developed by decomposing the system into intermediate and basic events. Logical gates such as AND and OR are used to represent the relationships between events. Once the fault tree structure is established, the next step involves the quantification of basic events using fuzzy logic. Instead of relying on exact probabilities, linguistic variables are assigned to represent the likelihood of each event. These linguistic terms are then converted into fuzzy numbers, typically using triangular or trapezoidal membership functions. Expert judgment plays a crucial role in this stage, as domain experts provide insights into the likelihood of failures based on their knowledge and experience. Fuzzy arithmetic is then applied to propagate uncertainty through the fault tree and compute the fuzzy probability of the top event. The final stage involves transforming the fuzzy fault tree into a Bayesian Network. This transformation allows for the modeling of dependencies among events, which is not possible in traditional FTA. Conditional probability tables are defined for each node in the network, capturing the probabilistic relationships between parent and child nodes. The Bayesian Network enables both forward and backward reasoning, providing a powerful tool for analyzing system behavior under different scenarios.

3. Comprehensive assessment and discussion

The integration of fuzzy logic with fault tree analysis and Bayesian Networks offers a significant advancement in the field of system safety and reliability. One of the most notable benefits of this approach is its ability to handle uncertainty in a structured and systematic manner. By incorporating fuzzy logic, the model can accommodate imprecise and ambiguous information, which is often unavoidable in real-world scenarios. This leads to more realistic and reliable risk assessments, particularly in data-scarce environments. Another important advantage is the ability to incorporate expert knowledge into the analysis. In many cases, experienced engineers and practitioners possess valuable insights that cannot be easily quantified using traditional methods. Fuzzy logic provides a means to capture this knowledge and integrate it into the modeling process, thereby enhancing the overall quality of the analysis. The use of Bayesian Networks further enhances the framework by enabling the modeling of dependencies among events. This is particularly important in complex systems where interactions between components can significantly influence system behavior. By capturing these dependencies, the model provides a more accurate representation of reality and reduces the likelihood of misleading conclusions. Additionally, the framework supports both predictive and diagnostic analyses. Predictive analysis allows for the estimation of system failure probabilities under different conditions, while diagnostic analysis helps identify the most likely causes of observed failures. This dual capability is highly valuable for decision-making, as it enables both proactive and reactive strategies for risk management. Despite its advantages, the proposed approach also presents certain challenges. The process of eliciting expert judgments and defining fuzzy membership functions can be subjective and time-consuming. Furthermore, the construction of Bayesian Networks and the definition of conditional probability tables require careful consideration to ensure accuracy and consistency. Nevertheless, these challenges can be addressed through structured methodologies and the use of specialized software tools.

4. Conclusion

This study has demonstrated the effectiveness of integrating fuzzy logic with Fault Tree Analysis and Bayesian Networks for enhancing system safety and reliability under conditions of uncertainty. Traditional risk assessment methods, while useful, are limited in their ability to handle incomplete data, ambiguity, and dependencies among events. The proposed hybrid framework addresses these limitations by combining the strengths of fuzzy logic, which handles uncertainty, and Bayesian Networks, which model probabilistic dependencies. The results indicate that this integrated approach provides more accurate and realistic risk assessments, particularly in complex and high-risk systems such as hydrogen energy applications. By enabling the incorporation of expert knowledge and facilitating both predictive and diagnostic analyses, the framework supports more informed decision-making and contributes to improved safety performance. In conclusion, the adoption of advanced computational techniques such as fuzzy logic and Bayesian reasoning represents a significant step forward in the field of reliability engineering. As systems continue to grow in complexity, the need for robust and flexible risk assessment methods will become increasingly important. Future research may focus on integrating machine learning techniques, real-time data analytics, and dynamic modeling approaches to further enhance the capabilities of the proposed framework.

References

[1] Z. Han, W. Weng, An integrated quantitative risk analysis method for natural gas pipeline network, J. Loss Prev. Process. Ind. 24 (2) (2011) 197–203.

[2] J. Taveau, Lessons learned from large LNG spills over water, J. Loss Prev. Process. Ind. 23 (6) (2010) 753–760.

[3] N. Khakzad, Application of dynamic bayesian network to risk analysis of domino effects in chemical infrastructures, Reliab. Eng. Syst. Saf. 138 (2015) 263–272.

[4] A. Escande, et al., Lessons learned from hydrogen safety public demonstrations and large-scale hydrogen refuelling stations, Int. J. Hydrogen Energy 41 (2) (2016) 2080–2086.

[5] N. Khakzad, et al., Safety analysis in process facilities: Comparison of fault tree and Bayesian network approaches, Reliab. Eng. Syst. Saf. 96 (8) (2011) 925–932.

[6] X. Yan, et al., An evidential reasoning-based CREAM to human reliability analysis in maritime accident process, Risk Anal. 36 (12) (2016) 2350–2366.

[7] W.E. Vesely, et al., Fault Tree Handbook with Aerospace Applications, NASA Office of Safety and Mission Assurance, 2002.

[8] V. De Dianous, C. Fiévez, ARAMIS project: A comprehensive methodology for the identification of reference accident scenarios in process industries, J. Hazard Mater. 130 (3) (2006) 200–219.

[9] S. Kabir, An overview of fault tree analysis and its application in model-based dependability analysis, Expert Syst. Appl. 77 (2017) 114–135.

[10] F.I. Khan, et al., Risk-based process plant design considering inherent safety measures, AIChE J. 54 (8) (2008) 2022–2035.

[11] Y. Wang, et al., Application of fault tree analysis to the probability assessment of subsea blowout preventer, Reliab. Eng. Syst. Saf. 75 (2) (2002) 179–189.

[12] H.-Z. Huang, et al., Fuzzy fault tree analysis of fault-tolerant systems, Reliab. Eng. Syst. Saf. 83 (1) (2004) 69–79.

[13] S. Kabir, et al., A review of applications of fuzzy fault tree analysis, J. Intell. Fuzzy Syst. 31 (1) (2016) 529–542.

[14] M. Omidvari, et al., Assessment of uncertainty in human error probability using fuzzy fault tree analysis, J. Loss Prev. Process. Ind. 32 (2014) 59–68.

[15] N. Khakzad, et al., Dynamic risk analysis using bayesian network, Reliab. Eng. Syst. Saf. 112 (2013a) 2–16.

[16] N. Khakzad, et al., Quantitative risk analysis of offshore drilling operations: A Bayesian approach, Saf. Sci. 57 (2013b) 108–117.

[17] X. Huang, et al., Bayesian network and simulation approach for railway risk analysis, Risk Anal. 26 (4) (2006) 1035–1049.

[18] M. Celik, et al., Risk assessment of the LNG terminal construction process using fuzzy fault tree analysis, Int. J. Shipp. Transp. Logist. (IJSTL) 2 (4) (2010) 409–423.

[19] S.M. Lavasani, et al., Application of fuzzy fault tree analysis for risk assessment of oil and gas offshore Wells, Ocean. Eng. 108 (2015a) 729–737.

[20] S.M. Lavasani, et al., Risk assessment of offshore drilling operations using fuzzy fault tree analysis, Saf. Sci. 78 (2015b) 248–255.

[21] R. Ferdous, et al., Handling data uncertainties in event tree analysis, Process Saf. Environ. Prot. 87 (5) (2009) 283–292.

[22] Y. Wang, et al., Fuzzy fault tree analysis for fire and explosion of crude oil tanks, J. Loss Prev. Process. Ind. 26 (6) (2013) 1390–1398.

[23] M. Yazdi, et al., A novel risk evaluation approach for petroleum tank farms using fuzzy fault tree analysis, J. Loss Prev. Process. Ind. 48 (2017a) 151–164.

[24] M. Yazdi, et al., Risk assessment based on novel intuitionistic fuzzy hybrid-modified TOPSIS approach, Saf. Sci. 91 (2017b) 174–186.

[25] M. Rausand, Risk Assessment: Theory, Methods, and Applications, John Wiley & Sons, 2011.

[26] S. Kabir, et al., A Bayesian network approach for reliability analysis of floating production storage and offloading vessel transfer system, Ocean. Eng. 92 (2014) 133–141.

[27] M. Hänninen, et al., Bayesian network modeling of port state control inspection findings and ship accident involvement, Expert Syst. Appl. 41 (4) (2014) 1632–1646.

[28] S. Barua, et al., Fault tree analysis of complex systems using bayesian networks, Reliab. Eng. Syst. Saf. 150 (2016) 200–209.

[29] M. Abimbola, F. Khan, N. Khakzad, Dynamic safety risk analysis of offshore drilling, J. Loss Prev. Process. Ind. 35 (2015) 139–150.

[30] A. Bouejla, et al., A dynamic Bayesian network-based approach to fault diagnosis application to a satellite power supply subsystem, Eng. Appl. Artif. Intell. 27 (2014) 58–70.

Chapter 9

A review on computational intelligence–based recommender systems: Recent progress, applications, challenges, and new future research avenues

Parijata Majumdar[1], Sanjoy Mitra[2] and Diptendu Bhattacharya[3]

[1]Dept. of IT, Tripura University, Agartala, Tripura, India; [2]Tripura Institute of Technology, Agartala, Tripura, India; [3]National Institute of Technology, Agartala, Tripura, India

Highlights

- It focuses on AI-based RS models, challenges, solutions, and awareness over RS domains.
- It reviews popular applications, performance metrics, datasets, and simulation platforms.
- Publications were gathered using inclusion/exclusion criteria for review.
- New trends are exposed that focus on various applications in implementation of RS.

1. Introduction

An ordinary user can now quickly access descriptions, reviews, and comments about nearly every type of goods or service. While having access to information is a desirable skill, people often face an overwhelming quantity of data sources, making it difficult for them to identify relevant and acceptable content and contributing to the issue of information overload. Information filtering solutions called recommender systems (RS) address this issue by giving consumers tailored access to potentially interesting content [1]. Nowadays, a lot of online retailers have recommendation engines installed on their platforms, and mostly the Internet users use these services for routine tasks like shopping, music streaming, and book reading. In most RSs, the product or service that the RSs recommends to its consumers is called the "item." An RS must either use the descriptive information about the products or evaluate the prior preferences of like-minded users in order to generate a list of recommended items for the user or estimate the extent to which the user will enjoy a specific item. The primary methods in RS are collaborative filtering (CF), demographic and content-based (CB) recommendation [2,3]. CF filtering can be memory and model-based. Memory-based approaches can be divided into item and user-based approaches. The advantages of these strategies can potentially be combined in hybrid techniques [4]. When using a CB approach, the recommendation method first verifies that the item descriptions match the user's profile before recommending related things whose contents are comparable to those of the previously liked items [5]. The most widely used technique for recommendation work is CF, which is predicated on identifying users who share similar interests. The main tenet is that individuals with similar ratings and opinions, as well as similar interests in the same products, will have similar preferences. Items are suggested in the demographic filtering (DF) approach based on the user's profile. It presumes that people with similar environments have similar preferences [5]. A hybrid RS combines recommendation approaches using the following hybridization strategies: Feature combination, weighted, switching,

Advanced Intelligence Methods for Data Science and Optimization. https://doi.org/10.1016/B978-0-443-28940-8.00013-0

mixed, cascading, feature augmentation, and meta-level hybridization [6]. In weighted RS, ratings from various recommendation systems are combined to provide a single recommendation output. In switching recommendation, either method produces output selectively based on the situation at hand. The simultaneous display of the results from both the methods is known as hybrid recommendation. When two approaches collaborate, the outputs from one method are improved upon by the other. Combining and utilizing features from both methods into a single algorithm is known as feature combination. The recommendation output of one strategy is used as the other approach's input in feature augmentation. A comparison of the benefits and drawbacks of various types of RS is presented in Table 9.1.

Nowadays, the majority of people's everyday demands must be met by machine learning-based intelligent systems. Among them, there are numerous applications for intelligent RS. These days, it is impossible to overstate the importance of RS in both academia and business. Many businesses use RS across a range of platforms to promote sales such as movies on YouTube [9]. Deep learning-based applications have achieved great success across domains of natural language processing (NLP) and computer vision. Deep learning has drawn interest from application fields due to its tremendous processing capacity, ability to manipulate large amounts of data, and ability to solve complicated problems with cutting edge results. Furthermore, latent data representations in higher layers and nonlinear user-item interactions are better captured by deep learning approaches. Furthermore, contextual information from diverse data sources can be learned by deep learning [10]. Researchers are also motivated to use deep architectures in preference prediction problems by deep learning techniques [11].

Despite technological advancements, research to date has demonstrated that internet and print media do not substantially differ in their definition of newsworthiness [12]. This could be due, in part, to the system's inability to more accurately anticipate user behavior and the absence of established protocols for providing a wide range of news timely. Thus, it is necessary to proceed in the direction of RS to deliver news updates based on readers' information requirements [5]. News readers can access a plethora of news sources and agencies from any location at any time, enabling them to peruse the most recent news via internet portals. These online portals are progressively using RS to enhance user experience on their sites in an effort to increase traffic to their websites. In the context of recommendations, "user experience" can mean various things, including usability, utility, efficacy, or a positive or satisfying encounter with the system [13]. It's difficult to suggest relevant and appropriate news articles to news readers. The rationale is that the news domain has distinct obstacles compared to other RS application domains.

Big data, artificial intelligence (AI), and Cloud computing have developed so quickly that the education sector has experienced a massive upheaval. Among the most famous outcomes of this revolution are Massive Open Online Courses or MOOCs. Over 100 million people have registered for MOOCs, which offer a wealth of curricular resources (roughly 11.4 million courses) [14]. With so many easy and high-quality online courses available, e-learning provides a geographically independent online education platform that might potentially improve educational outcomes for students worldwide. However, users find it challenging to make wise decisions due to the rapid expansion of network information. Information overload can now be effectively addressed with course RS. Compared to other RSs, course RS are frequently very distinct. First of all, there is a clear sequential relationship between the knowledge points across the courses, showing a close relationship. For instance, proficiency with the C programming language is required for a course on data structure. Understanding the material in a data structure course without first knowing the C programming language will be extremely challenging. Secondly, because most learners participate in learning activities with the intention of learning about a specific subject, it is crucial to take into account their long-term preferences and learning goals. Last but not least, the time spent watching online courses and other educational materials has a significant impact on the recommendations, as it indicates learner's preferences for particular courses as well as their level of proficiency in those courses. To locate objects of interest to users and provide individualized recommendations, RSs often create their lists according to user preferences, features of item, and user-item interactions including time or space.

These days, a wide range of applications are using RSs more and more which makes it essential to create high-end, distinctive RSs that can provide users with customized recommendations. Basically, in RSs, each user assigns a preference value (or rating) to a particular item (or product). Generally, approaches that are explicit or implicit are used to get user ratings. Implicit evaluations are gathered indirectly from the user interactions with the goods. On the contrary, the user directly provides explicit ratings by choosing a value from a predetermined point scale. For instance, implicit ratings for various goods may be obtained by a website from clickstream data, user duration on a webpage, and other sources. The majority of RSs use both these techniques to collect user evaluations. The user ratings are organized in a utility matrix, which is a user item matrix.

There are frequently a lot of missing values in the utility matrix. The primary challenge which RS is witnessing is identifying the values that the utility matrix is missing. Because consumers typically assess a limited number of things, the

TABLE 9.1 Comparison of the benefits and drawbacks of various RS.

Features	Content-based filtering	Collaborative filtering	Demographic filtering	Hybrid filtering
Benefits	The active user's user ratings are typically used only to develop his own profile. When making recommendations for things that no one has rated before, CB techniques are quite effective. First-rater problems do not exist. Because CB filtering leverage content description, it offers clear recommendations [7].	It can function in an environment where the objects related to the content are not readily available and in situations where the material like opinions is challenging to interpret [8].	Users interested in similar services might be identified by their demographics. DF groups individuals based on shared demographic traits, and then it tracks the aggregate purchasing preferences of these consumers group.	Applying a single methodology will not yield the same level of improvement and enhanced recommendation as integrating many RS methods. The shortcomings of a single technique can be mitigated by combining many techniques.
Drawbacks	Work well for recommending newly accessible things but not effective for recommending new users [5]. It does not make advantage of collective experience of similar users. This is not optimal because it tends to reduce the diversity of things to be recommended.	Cold-start problem arises when there is insufficient data on a user or an item to enable the system to make pertinent predictions. One issue that arises from inadequate information is data sparsity. Scalability is another problem.	Users' individuality may be lost due to an overly general classification, user-provided data is used. The data classification depends on customer's interests, which changes over time, and may be incomplete. The acceptance of changing the user profile is not supported. This approach suffers from how to identify the category that user belongs to when the user is new to the system. The accuracy is comparatively less.	—
User ratings history Usage history	A history of user ratings is necessary. The usage history is not necessary.	A history of user ratings is not necessary. The usage history is necessary.	A history of user ratings is not necessary. The usage history is not necessary.	A history of user ratings may be necessary. The usage history may be necessary.

initial matrix is typically relatively sparse, making this process challenging. The kind of algorithm and the type of data source have a major impact on RSs effectiveness.

The RSs utilized in tailored e-services were initially created, and for user profiling and preference discovery, methods and ideas from different AI domains were applied. The number of successful AI-driven applications has increased significantly in the last few years such as self-driving automobile, the AI-driven programs in the areas of computer vision. The remarkable progress in AI, data analytics, and big data offers RSs a fantastic chance to capitalize on AI's accomplishments.

In recent times, RSs have gained advantages from the utilization of diverse AI algorithms, leading to an enhanced user experience. In RSs, the development of sophisticated insights into the relationships between people and things, the presentation of even-more complex data representations, and the finding of vast amounts of information in contextual, virtual, textural, and demographic data is the new development. This study reviews the different contributions in RS, points out its shortcomings, and suggests new directions for future research and application of AI in RS. It will make an effort to examine the problems associated with AI powered RSs, as well as the ability of AI to facilitate the comprehension of massive datasets and transform data into knowledge.

This review paper's primary contributions are its responses to the following research queries (RQs):

- RQ 1: What are the domains of AI techniques and how are they applied in RS?
- RQ 2: What knowledge may be gained by pointing out interesting but unexplored research avenues?
- RQ 3: What problems and open research questions surround RS that point to potential future avenues for development?
- RQ 4: What datasets, simulation platforms, and performance evaluation metrics are employed to assess the effectiveness of AI-based RS?

From Fig. 9.1, it is evident that the number of papers using AI-based techniques for RS has been rising since the first notable work on RS was published. It was also evident that the majority of the AI-based RS articles that have been published are in the year of 2017 and 2022.

The objectives of this review are outlined.

1.1 Objectives

There is seldom any review work that thoroughly analyzed and synthesized the research across all RS categorization fields and application domains. The few published reviews of the literature on this domain only cover a small percentage of the articles such as system evaluation. Consequently, they do not provide an algorithmic categorization, as well as ranking of the most promising solutions. Review publications also frequently neglect examination of the description of the dataset and the platforms that were utilized for simulation. This chapter aims to review and contrast previous research on RS depending on a specified classification framework, algorithmic categorization, simulation platforms, applications, RSs features, challenges, solutions, and dataset description. In conclusion, we offer researchers and professionals an understanding of the most important avenues for more research in RSs.

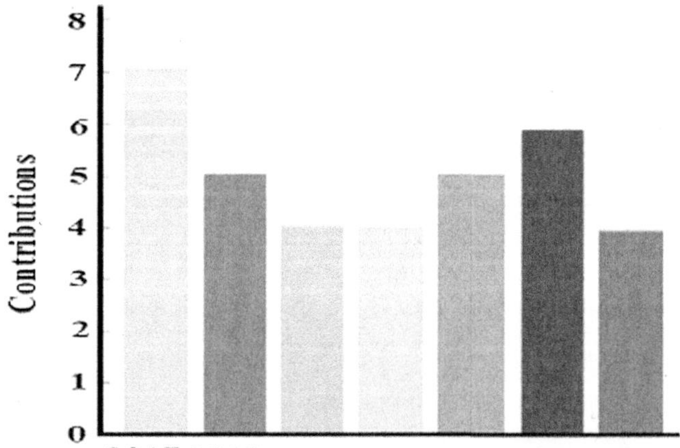

FIGURE 9.1 Number of RS articles using AI-based techniques published during last 7 years.

The rest of the section is organized as follows: Section 2 underlines the methodology used for inclusion and exclusion of research articles in the review. Section 3 discusses the related works related to the use of RS in various application domains such as AI, Evolutionary algorithms (EA), NLP, and Computer Vision and recent advances in RS research. Simulation platforms, commonly used datasets and performance metrics, are also identified. Section 4 addresses various challenges associated with the use of RS and possible solutions. In Section 5, classification of published works based on the experimental study target recommendation domains viz., movie, book, e-commerce, music, social networking, news and article recommendation, image and video is done. Section 6 presents the reader with insights and findings derived from the comprehensive analysis of deep learning-based RSs conducted throughout the study. Section 7 outlines future research directions on AI-driven RS and finally draws conclusion.

2. Methodology

Understanding the current research trends in RS is the aim of this review article. Because of the nature of RS research, it is challenging to assign any specific task to a particular RS. The fact that research publications on RS are distributed over a number of journals, including computer science, management, marketing, and information technology helps to further explain this. As a result, a large variety of journals and other research articles are examined in this literature study [15].

In order to locate the relevant literature, we identify and choose the bibliographic collections namely, Elsevier, SpringerLink, IEEE Xplore, and ACM Digital Library. In addition to those bibliographies, we look for relevant works using the academic search engines GoogleScholar, DBLP, CiteSeerX, MS Academic Search, Web of Science, Science Direct, and ResearchGate. Additionally, we search through journal transactions and conference proceedings for titles and abstracts in an effort to locate other publications that may have been overlooked during the original search.

Descriptors like "RS," "Recommendation systems," "Movie Recommend*," "Music Recommend*," "Personalized Recommend*," "Hybrid Recommend*," "CF," "Deep learning," and "Neural Network" were used to guide the search for online research publications, and studies unrelated to the review questions were among the research papers that were not included in our analysis. This evaluation does not include papers that do not adequately describe an experiment. A total of 350 publications have been screened by us based on the content and abstracts. Nevertheless, only studies that explained the applications of RS were selected. Only conference and journal publications are selected. Ultimately, 60 articles from prestigious international journals with Scopus or E-SCI indexes were chosen. The inclusion and exclusion procedure flowchart is now shown in Fig. 9.2. After a thorough evaluation process, each article was divided into three categories for system development methodologies and six categories for application domains. Expert Systems with Applications contributes the most relevant articles (23%), followed by IEEE (17%), Knowledge-Based System (17%), and Others (43%). The article distribution by journal title is shown in Fig. 9.3, while the article distribution by sector is shown in Fig. 9.4.

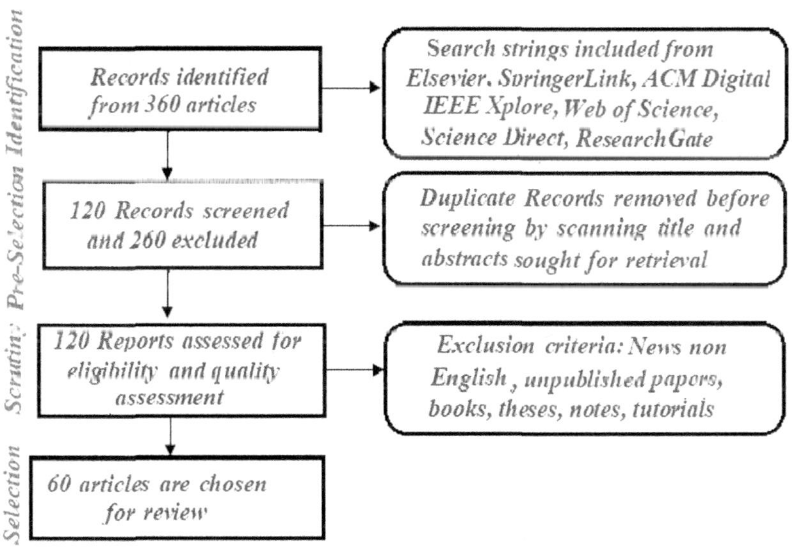

FIGURE 9.2 Inclusion and exclusion criteria of the articles in the methodology.

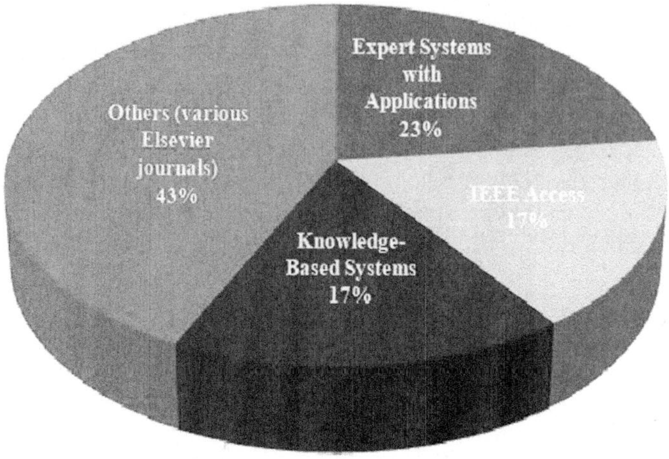

FIGURE 9.3 Distribution of articles by journal title.

Utilizing both forward and backward searching strategies, it was determined that the examination of 60 selected articles could adequately reflect the domain literature.

3. Related works

The big data information explosion has led to an increase in the demand for recommendation, hence several AI algorithms have been developed and deployed to RS.

3.1 Deep neural networks in recommender systems

The goal of recommendation involves the rating of items rather than the classification of items, neural networks are rarely used in RSs. To investigate the ordinal property of ratings, Salakhutdinov et al. first presented a restricted Boltzmann machine (RBM). Truyen et al. examines the parameterization options of RBM in recommendation [11]; this method gained popularity in 2009 Netflix Prize competition [16]. Deep learning has been very successful in computer vision and NLP. Factorization machines use multi-layer perceptrons to aid with feature engineering. It integrates into a single recommendation framework the benefits of both linear and nonlinear modeling [11]. Since the suggested factorization machines may be trained without the need for feature engineering, Guo et al. upgraded the deep model in Ref. [17]. To learn nonlinear latent representations of users or items, AutoRec combines matrix factorization with an autoencoder [18]. To create item feature representations from item content, AutoSVD++ combines matrix factorization and a contractive autoencoder [19]. For user profiling in RSs, autoencoder functions as a fundamental building component of representation learning.

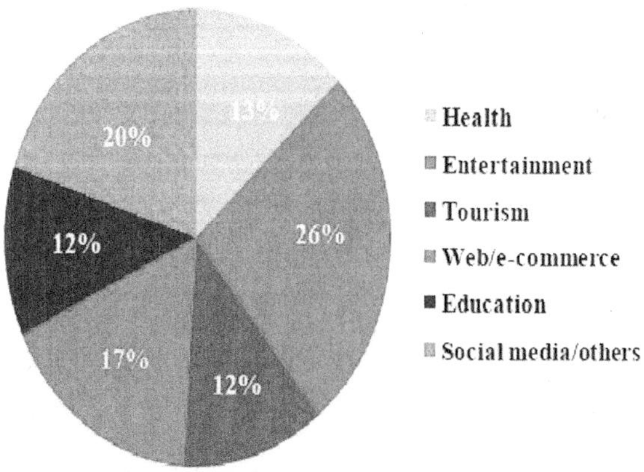

FIGURE 9.4 Distribution of articles by sector.

Deep Convolutional Neural Networks (DeepCoNN) uses reviews to jointly represent users and objects by merging two parallel neural networks [20]. Factorization machines enable a shared layer that connects the two Convolutional Neural Networks (CNN). ConvMF incorporates CNN into matrix factorization to increase accuracy [21].

Recurrent Neural Networks (RNNs) are mainly utilized to simulate and assess user interests or item attributes since they function well with sequential input. Applying RNN, a co-evolutionary latent feature process was introduced by Dai et al. to mimic the temporal dynamics of user-item interactions [22]. In order to determine whether to inherit current user behavior, Wu et al. employed a Long Short-Term Memory model to adopt the user behavior dynamics [23].

Generative adversarial network was included by Wang et al. into a single information retrieval framework. It consists of a generative retrieval model that learns the distribution over documents and tries to generate relevant documents that look like the ground truth [24]. This methodology demonstrates the promise of this system and emphasizes the need for more work, particularly in the RS domain. In the context of Bayesian personalized ranking.

3.2 Transfer learning in recommender systems

In reality, single domain RS focuses only on a single domain and ignores the user's interest in other domains, which exacerbates sparsity and cold start issues [25]. Cross-domain recommendation, which often makes use of the information gleaned from the domains to produce the target recommendation, can offer solutions to such issues. In machine learning, transfer learning has shown to be quite successful and has a bright future. It expands recommendation requests from one domain to several RS domains. The need for comprehensive and varied recommendations, along with the capability to mitigate the issue of data sparsity, has propelled the advancement of cross-domain RS (CDRS). In addition to solving the data sparsity issue, CDRS offers multi-domain recommendations to e-commerce merchants who sell a range of products. While CDRS can be deliberately structured as per overlap of users and objects, some techniques connect two domains through auxiliary information [26,27]. In Refs. [28–30], deep learning methods are used which demonstrate the efficacy of these methods in addressing generalization across multiple domains and offering improved recommendation on CDRS.

3.3 Active learning in recommender systems

Every user-item connection in an RS is important for user preference profiling and has a significant impact on system performance. In order to assist RS in choosing the most representative items and presenting them for user rating, active learning has been introduced. The active learning technique now includes complex aspects including user-acquired ratings [31]; the likelihood that a user can evaluate the system inquiry [32]; the influence of items [33]; and item properties [34]. Based on their evaluation criteria on unlabeled instances, active learning systems can be broadly categorized into numerous classes. These include density-weighted approaches, expected model change, expected error reduction, uncertainty sampling, query-by-committee, and variance reduction.

3.4 Reinforcement learning in recommender systems

Utilizing an RS involves a user-system interactive procedure with a sequence of states and actions that align with reinforcement learning. The difficulty with reinforcement learning is the sheer quantity of objects that users can choose from, which gives learning agents a lot of options and makes the system more complex. The main focus of the early research was bandit problems or the balance between exploration and exploitation [35]. In order to recommend the following item using the previous k consumed items, a direct implementation of MDP to RS is suggested in Ref. [36]. Reinforcement learning techniques are also widely used in industrial RS such Alibaba and YouTube.

3.5 Fuzzy techniques in recommender systems

In real-world RSs, item attributes and user actions are typically ambiguous, subjective, and incomplete. RS can benefit from the use of fuzzy set and fuzzy relation theories, which provide a useful solution to information uncertainty issues. Fuzzy approaches are used in two stages of the process of CB RS: matching relevant items and profiling. Fuzzy set theories are used in the development of recommendation techniques to ascertain user preferences and generate item representations [37]. Memory-based CF RS make use of fuzzy set theories to describe the level of uncertainty in user preferences. By using fuzzy relationships to describe user preferences and similarities, in Ref. [38] the CF framework expands to recommend a single item for personalized e-government. Zhang et al. [39] developed a fuzzy user-interest drift detection approach for dynamic user preferences. In model-based CF RS, a variety of approaches have been used, such as fuzzy Bayesian, fuzzy network, and fuzzy clustering. Nilashi et al. [40] used an adaptive neuro-fuzzy inference system for RS with a hybrid self-organizing map. Fuzzy C-means is a soft clustering technique that permits users or items to belong to several groups, in contrast to CF approaches with singular value decomposition (SVD) [41]. Kant et al. introduced a fuzzy Naive Bayesian classifier, which includes hybrid recommendation techniques [42].

3.6 Evolutionary algorithms in recommender systems

When treating the recommendation as a multi-objective optimization problem, evolutionary algorithms (EAs) are utilized to merge the outputs of numerous recommendation algorithms. These RS are optimized by EAs taking into account a variety of performance metrics [19]. Mu et al. [43] developed an innovative EA with elite population to discover the information core in order to accomplish accurate personalized recommendation. To speed up the evolution, the suggested algorithm adopts an elite population with an improved crossover technique. In Ref. [44]; a genetic algorithm (GA) is used to optimize the weights of the domains to weight their contributions inside the generalized cross domain triadic factorization model framework to solve data sparsity. EAs can be used to generate secure RS, where the model is less vulnerable to adversarial attacks by producing models that are less sensitive to detrimental data manipulation [45]. The Firefly algorithm (FA) [46] boosts recommendation efficiency and delivers quick results. It can cut down on the number of iterations needed to finish particular RS challenges. Additionally, it offers global and local sets of solutions.

Better search accuracy and reduced time complexity are provided by Beetle Antennae Search (BAS) [47], which enhances recommendation performance.

3.7 Natural language processing in recommender systems

NLP has already established a number of fine-grained opinion mining and topic modeling techniques, and there is a growing attempt to integrate these two fields in order to extract textual data and use it in recommendation processes. To augment the rating matrix and address the issue of data sparsity, NLP extracts review information that is advantageous to the majority of RS. Extreme circumstances in which ratings are unavailable lead to the generation of virtual ratings based on the emotion polarity discovered by review classification [48]. Topic models evaluate item metadata and combine matrix factorization techniques with them to handle cold start scenarios. In order to infer item similarity correlations, the neural embedding algorithm in the field of NLP has also been coupled with a CF framework [49]. Prior research has primarily concentrated on textual content, item descriptions, and static data from reviews. NLP techniques will be crucial in the development of an interactive RS with voice feedback, as digital voice systems like Siri and Google Home continue to advance in sophistication [50].

3.8 Computer vision in recommender systems

The advancement of computer vision technologies has been beneficial to RS, particularly in the domains of fashion analysis and things that are closely associated with looks, apparel, jewelry, and images. In order to map user preferences, a duel-net deep network was presented in Ref. [51]. Using deep neural network (DNN) to extract information from images, early works in various e-commerce recommendation domains combine this technology with preexisting techniques for clothing recommendation. Since images and user-posted images contain a lot of landmarks, visual content is used to recommend points of interest [52]. He et al. modeled nonvisual and visual variables using temporal dynamics and deep learning to uncover changing fashion trends among users [53].

3.9 Other recent contributions

An Internet of Things-based cancer rehabilitation RS utilizing the BAS algorithm was proposed by Han et al. [54] in 2020. It gave the patients a solution to the issue of an ideal diet program by taking the recurrence time into account as the objective function. An RS based on a tree model for tailored adverts in online broadcasting has been described in Ref. [55]. Dhelim et al. [56] used user interest mining and meta path finding approaches to create a personality-based product recommendation model in 2021. In comparison to deep learning and session-based models, this model performed better. In order to overcome the sparsity issue with RS, a web-based CF system was presented in Ref. [57] based on SVD, CF, and cosine similarity (CS). In real-time applications, it can learn from the decreased entropy loss mistake. In Ref. [58], a DNN-based DF is suggested that improves the CF process and solves the cold start issue for new users. This approach gives cold users individualized recommended things by making the recommendation task much more relevant.

The author tested the suggested method on two genuine multi-label datasets, 1 M and 100 K Movie Lens, in order to assess its efficacy.

A new meta-learning-based RS that can account for user period specific preferences that can mitigate the cold start issue was presented by Li et al. in Ref. [59]. Furthermore, utilizing period and user-specific gradients, a hierarchical meta-learning technique is presented to direct the recommendation model's learning process. HyperRS is a hyper-network-based RS that was presented by Lu et al. in Ref. [60]. It consists of a knowledge aware and a collaborative aware meta-learner to handle cold start problem by leveraging entity's knowledge and capturing meta users' preferences.

Liu et al. presented a novel cold start recommendation model in Ref. [61] that integrates meta-learning and the attention mechanism, to improve the capacity to model individualized user interest and thus optimizing the cold start recommendation performance. A novel meta-learning architecture, including a knowledge-aware and collaboration-aware meta learner, was proposed by Du et al. in Ref. [62] to gather meta user preferences for cold start recommendations.

A deep learning-based food RS is presented in Ref. [63] using a wide range of user and food characteristics and features, such as the users' preferences, demographics, food category, text description, and even the food images. This work creates a large-scale annotated dataset with numerous food-related records, user scores, and 54,554 food images to assess the RS. The quality of the recommendations can still be raised by modifying this work with a lot more user and food features. It is also possible to include text analysis of user comments, which provide useful features and data that might enhance the RS.

3.9.1 Simulation platforms, commonly used datasets, and performance metrics

Fig. 9.5 lists the several simulation platforms that were utilized to create distinct RS for diverse applications. Here, the Java platform accounts for 20%, MATLAB is used in 7%, cross-validation is used in 8%, the Python platform accounts for 7%, R-programming is used in 3%, Tensorflow, Weka and Android environments account for 1% of the research articles, respectively. Fifty percent of the contributions make use of other simulation platforms such as Facebook and web UI (User Interface), etc. The following are a few simulation platforms that are frequently used to create RS.

Java is utilized in social media, music, e-learning, health, and the web. Developing real-time RS can benefit from it. MATLAB is utilized in the fields of web, music, movies, and health. It includes a particular set of classes for research on RS. Python is utilized in the social media, web, music, film, and health fields. It works well for putting complex machine learning recommender algorithms with heavy processing demands into practice. News and education are two fields that use R programming. It requires a lot of RAM. TensorFlow is utilized in the e-learning and film industries. It works great for putting unsupervised algorithms into practice. Both the film making and e-learning industries use Weka. It works effectively with datasets for RS that need a lot of data preprocessing. Android has applications in the online, music, and tourism domains. Its processing power is restricted, but it works well for RS operating in real-time.

Fig. 9.6 shows the performance evaluation measures that were applied to the analysis of several RS articles. Out of the collection of research papers, 31% use recall measures, 16% use Mean Absolute Error (MAE), 11% use Root Mean Square Error (RMSE), 41% take precision into consideration, 30% analyze F1-measure, 31% use accuracy, and 6% use coverage measures to verify the effectiveness of RS.

A common metric to calculate RS performance does not exist. Out of 60 publications, the system performance was calculated using recall in 21, MAE in 10, precision in 25, F1-measure in 18, accuracy in 19, and RMSE in just 7 studies. It

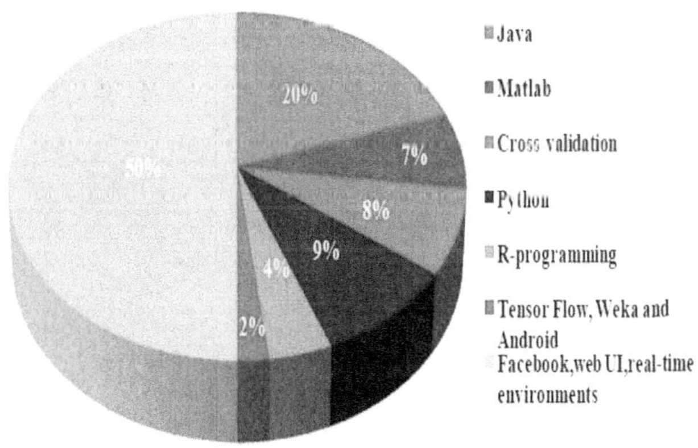

FIGURE 9.5 Distribution of simulation platforms utilized to create distinct RS for diverse applications.

FIGURE 9.6 Performance evaluation measures applied to the analysis of several RS articles.

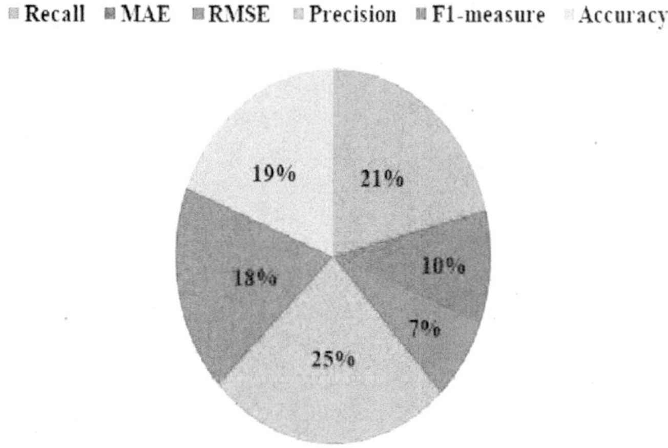

was found that very few systems performed well in two or more matrices. The majority of the studies are conducted using common and available datasets, however some researchers utilize customized and private datasets. Of all the datasets, 44% fall under the category "Others," which includes datasets that are only utilized in one study. Keeping this important information in mind, it is possible to see that the datasets from MovieLens, Netflix, and Yelp are popularly used in the trials, with MovieLens being used in 21% of the research, Netflix in 8%, and Yelp in 7% as shown in Fig. 9.7. There are 943 users, 1682 items, 100,000 total ratings, and a density of 6.30% on MovieLens 100 K.

MovieLens 1 M has a density of 4.19%, 6040 users, 3952 items, and 1,000,209 total ratings. MovieLens 10 M has a density of 1.31%, 10,681 items, 10,054 total ratings, and 71,567 users. There are 408,189 users on Netflix, 17,770 products, 100,480,507 total ratings, and a density of 1.39%.

4. Challenges

Numerous issues plague a large number of RS. It is acknowledged that the most significant obstacle to recommendation techniques is the cold start problem. This issue occurs when there are either too few rating records in the system or none at all for newly added individuals or objects. The system's efficiency is decreased and the recommendations' relevancy is adversely affected by a lack of information about both goods and users. Consequently, learning how to provide tailored recommendations during cold start is valuable. The following are a few ways to address this issue:

FIGURE 9.7 Distribution of commonly used datasets in several RS articles.

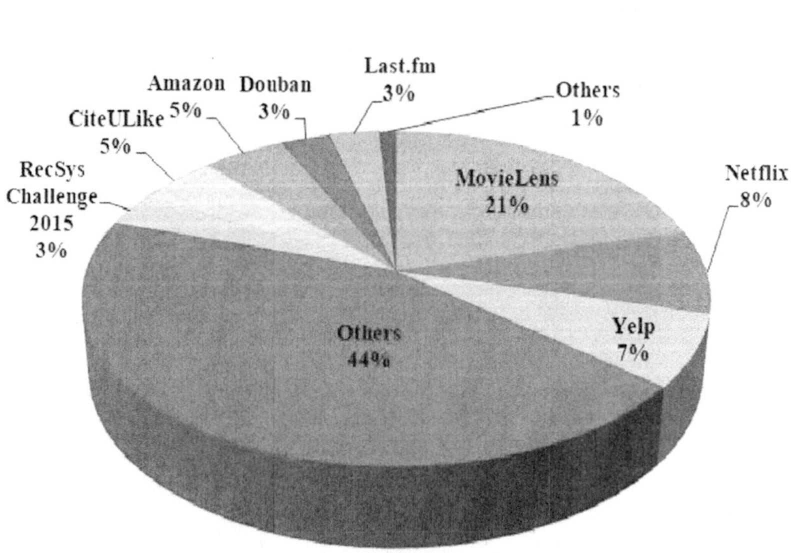

- Clearly state the item that they prefer when interacting with new users.
- Request that a new user rate a few items at the start.
- Gather user demographic data, often known as meta-data, and make item recommendations based on that information.

A novel hybrid RS called Collaborative and Deep Learning-based DF is proposed to avoid cold start issue [58]. This study makes a contribution by fusing improved CF with a DF based on DNNs. It employs user demographic data to offset the user information lacking that results in the cold start issue. In a classification task, the DNN model groups users into item categories according to their demographic information. This enables the algorithm to determine, independent of the item's rating history, the category of items for the new user. The model's increased CF component uses a neighborhood-based approach to carry out a personalized relevant recommendation task.

4.1 Shilling attack problem

When a malicious attacker joins the system under false pretenses and rates items falsely, this issue occurs [64]. This type of situation occurs when an adversarial user seeks to manipulate certain target products to increase or decrease their popularity. Shilling attacks drastically reduce the reliability of the system. Finding the attackers immediately and removing the fake user profiles are the different solutions to this problem.

4.2 Synonymy problem

This issue occurs when identical objects are represented when related or comparable items have various entries or names [8]. For instance, take baby clothes and baby clothing. The recommendation accuracy of many RS is decreased because they are unable to discern these changes. SVD, automatic term extension, and DF are employed to mitigate this issue [65].

4.3 Latency problem

The latency problem arises when new items are added to the database and is unique to CF techniques. The system's inability to suggest new products is what defines this issue. This occurs because, in a CF environment, new items are subject to evaluation prior to recommendation. This problem might be solved by using CB filtering, but it leads to overspecialization, reduce processing speed, and impair system performance. Clustering-based approaches and offline calculation environments are two ways to improve performance [65].

4.4 Sparsity problem

When some predicted values are missing from the dataset, a typical issue in large-scale data analysis is called data sparsity. This is the state that RS experience when there are very few active people rating products. This lowers the accuracy of the recommendations. DF, SVD, and the application of model-based collaborative methodologies are used to mitigate this problem [3].

4.5 Gray sheep problem

When a single user's feedback does not correspond with any user neighborhood, it presents a unique challenge of "gray sheep problem" in pure CF systems. The technology is unable to correctly predict pertinent things for that user in this scenario. Pure CB techniques, which base predictions on the user's profile and item qualities, can be used to tackle this issue [3].

4.6 Scalability problem

Scalability occurs because RS using CF approaches need a lot of training data. When the volume of data it receives as input grows rapidly increases then it leads to Scalability problem. Two popular methods for resolving the scalability issue are dimensionality reduction and the use of clustering algorithms to locate users in small clusters. While RS offer effective solutions to address the issue of information overload, they can present a variety of other difficulties [2]. The main problems of accuracy, sparsity, cold-start, and scalability are briefly discussed in this section. Providing users with engaging and pertinent content is one of a RSs most important needs. The quality of recommendations directly affects how much people trust the system. Users will clearly search for other systems if the recommendation engine does not offer them acceptable products and services, as this could be interpreted as insufficient in terms of customer satisfaction. Therefore, in order to increase preferability and efficacy, an RS needs to meet a certain level of prediction accuracy. The most frequently addressed issue with RS is accuracy, which is typically examined using three methods: rating prediction accuracy, usage predictions, and item ranking.

The object's rating history provided by system users is the foundation of CF systems. Since users only score a small portion of the accessible products, sparsity looks to be a significant issue, particularly for CF, making it difficult to provide predictions [2]. Benefitful associations between users and objects may go unnoticed by a CF algorithm when it is operating on a sparse dataset. Because there is not enough information to create a profile for a new user with few ratings, projections cannot be made for them. Similarly, it is also not possible to recommend recently added things to users because such items have not received any ratings. Nevertheless, CB RS can handle newly added users and things by using their content information, unlike CF approaches. The majority of RS are used in environments that are responsive. A user accessing a web page is typically presented with a list of recommended things based on their taste. A highly scalable system is needed to execute such a scenario effectively and offer the recommendations in a fair length of time.

Many algorithms have a tendency to require more processing resources as the number of users or things increases [66]. Scalability thus becomes a major issue that needs to be effectively handled.

5. Remedies for challenges of recommender systems

Developing practical answers to RS problems is one of the directions of using deep learning techniques in RS. In this section, we examine works that use deep learning to address the challenges that RS encounter.

5.1 Solutions for improving accuracy

Increasing the accuracy of predictions made by RS is one of the key goals of using deep learning techniques. Researchers use deep learning approaches to extract latent components because they are effective at extracting hidden features. Salakhutdinov et al. [16] show that the Netflix recommendation system is not as accurate at predicting future events as RBM models combined with SVD. According to Sedhain et al. [18], AutoRec is a predictor for missing ratings that makes use of autoencoders. In order to increase the accuracy of context-aware RS, Unger et al. [67] represent latent context features from sensor data using autoencoders and Principal Component Analysis (PCA). Additionally, they combine particular contextual with latent context features of autoencoders, comparing their performance to that of matrix factorization models. Their test findings validate that employing autoencoders to extract solely latent contextual features performs better, particularly when both positive and negative feedbacks are given. Deng et al. [68] employ a deep autoencoder to properly establish user and item-latent properties during the matrix factorization initialization phase, thereby enhancing accuracy in trust-aware RSs. According to their findings, the suggested approach is older than the most recent trust-aware recommendation algorithms. Studies show that deep learning's ability to uncover hidden features and combine data from multiple sources is what mostly drives its potential to increase recommendation accuracy. CF-Neural autoregressive distribution estimation (NADE), AutoRec, and CF-User Item-CoAutoregressive are very successful models compared to other methods, according to experiments conducted on the MovieLens 1M dataset [69]. Item-based algorithms outperform user-based ones in terms of accuracy. The average number of ratings per item is significantly higher than the average number of ratings per user, which accounts for the improvement. Predictions made in this manner increase in accuracy. U-CF-NADE with a single layer offers recommendations that are less accurate than U-CF-NADE with two layers. Consequently, I-CFNADE with one layer and two layers are subject to the same relation.

5.2 Solutions for sparsity and cold-start problems

Using deep learning techniques to convert the high-dimensional and sparse user-item matrix into a lower dimensional and denser set is one way to help CF-based RS to overcome the sparsity problem [70]. To address sparsity in context aware RS resulting from the integration of high context features, Unger et al. [67] use autoencoders to build low-dimensional latent representations of context features derived from sensors. Using additional side information enables RSs to mitigate the effects of the data sparsity problem. Deep learning techniques are utilized to handle sparsity and cold-start issues to extract high-level representations of users and goods based on preference matrices and side information [71].

In certain research [72], content information is directly incorporated to the recommendation process to address the sparsity issues. Side information is integrated into every denoising autoencoder (DAE) layer by Ref. [73]. Boltzmann machines are linked to content information of things to address the cold-start issue by Ref. [74]. Kim et al. [21] use CNN to extract characteristics from images with the goal of improving tag-aware RSs inability to detect missing tags. According to Tan et al. [75], RNNs can be used to provide predictions based on what users are currently doing. Ruocco et al. [76] employ RNN to combine the user's most recent sessions to solve cold-start concerns. As can be seen, deep learning techniques for feature engineering are primarily used to integrate extracted features from diverse data sources into recommendation processes, hence mitigating the sparsity and cold-start issues. Autoencoders, CNNs, and Deep Belief Networks (DBNs) are popularly used deep learning approaches for this kind of application.

5.3 Solutions for scalability problem

Scholars apply deep learning approaches to extract low-dimensional latent components of high-dimensional user preferences and item evaluations in an attempt to address the issue of scalability [29]. Boltzmann machines are used in Truyen et al. [11] to extract latent information from people and items and provide predictions across large-scale datasets. In order to address scalability, Elkahky et al. [29] set up multi-view DNNs to map high dimensional into lower dimensional features. They also use techniques like selecting the top k most relevant features, clustering similar features into a single cluster using the k-means algorithm, and applying local sensitive hashing on user features before network training in order to scale up their system. Optimizing scalability by partial modifications of deep learning models is the recommended method in RS. In order to scale up the learning process of their autoregressive model, Du et al. [77] present a neural co-autoregressive model for users and things using stochastic optimization.

6. Recommender system prevalence over application domains

For academicians who are interested in working on the topic, it is imperative that they are aware of and have access to deep learning-based models on recommendation domains. In this part, we classify published works based on the experimental study target recommendation domains. After placing closely related areas in context, we get eight major categories.

6.1 Movie recommendation

Salakhutdinov et al. [16] seminal work in this area demonstrates the potential of RBMs in making suggestions for the Netflix dataset. Many academics are now using Boltzmann machines for movie recommendation as a result of the study's success [11,74]. Autoencoders are introduced to CF tasks in Refs. [18,78], who assess their models using MovieLens datasets. Within the movie domain, the autoregressive models put forth in Refs. [77,79] are also assessed.

6.2 Book recommendation

As both of these final products have similar traits like consumption period and content, the book recommendation domain and the movie recommendation domain are closely related. Shen et al. [80] offer a technique that can give students with an online learning environment customized book recommendations. Shu et al. [81] look into enhancing an e-learning system's recommendations for a similar reason. In addition to these research, their models are evaluated on the movie and book domains in Suglia et al. [82] and Hsieh et al. [83].

6.3 E-commerce

One well-known area for deep learning applications in RS is e-commerce. A neural network model is put out by Tang et al. [84] to predict restaurant review ratings. Both Wu et al. [85] and Hidasi et al. [86] regularly examine user sessions on e-commerce websites. In order to increase the accuracy of clothing recommendations, Wakita et al. [87] employ deep learning to identify user's favorite brands. Using a sizable dataset of product shoppers that includes item descriptions as text and category, Nedelec et al. [88] suggest a novel architecture for item representation.

6.4 Music recommendation

Nowadays, majority of the people choose to listen to music digitally on websites like SoundCloud and Spotify1. Music recommendation has been a prominent research area due to the expansion of digital music consumption [89]. The articles in the music recommendation domain analysis depend on how different data sources are used such as audio signals, CB information, ratings, and usage data. Researchers employ deep models to propose music based on user ratings and usage statistics, others use these models to extract latent features from audio signals.

6.5 Social networking recommendation

Recommendation plays a significant part in social networking services, as defined by the concept of social networking. The terms "likes," "followers," "friends," "tags," "comments," and "followed" refer to user accounts. Ko et al. [90] use the check-in logs to apply a deep recurrent model to a location-based social network. In tag aware RS, Zuo et al. [91] and Xu et al. [92] test social bookmarking data. Point-of-interest recommendation is examined in relation to contextual elements in Ref. [67].

6.6 News and article recommendation

Large collections of news and articles make them particularly well-suited for CB recommendation. Ruocco et al. [76] monitor user sessions to enhance the quality of news recommendation. Dynamic deep models for article recommendation tasks are studied in Ref. [93]. Nguyen et al. [94] use images to find acceptable tags relating to each image using a tag RS.

6.7 Image and video recommendation

Given their significance in social networking, education, entertainment, and knowledge acquisition, images and videos are highly recommended goods. Lei et al. [51] extract visual information from images to provide individualized image recommendations. Ref. [95] have developed a model that can forecast which artworks people would likely buy in the future. Ref. [9] divided the YouTube video recommendation process into candidate generation and ranking and suggested different deep models for each phase.

The cross-domain recommendation unites several domains, according to the domain analysis's final finding. Ref. [29] integrated the company's many data sources on search queries, application downloads and movies in a Microsoft study.

7. Insights and discussions

This section presents the reader with insights derived from the comprehensive analysis of deep learning-based RS conducted in the review. Fig. 9.8 shows the yearwise article distribution of Conferences, Journals, Workshops, and Thesis related to the use of RS in various application domains.

DL is used in many recommendation strategies for various goals; they are not limited to any particular recommendation method. These methods are typically applied in CB filtering to extract features from heterogeneous data sources and create CB user profiles. Nonetheless, they are frequently applied in CF as a model-based method to extract latent features from user-item matrices. DL is used in hybrid RS to extract characteristics from auxiliary data and incorporate

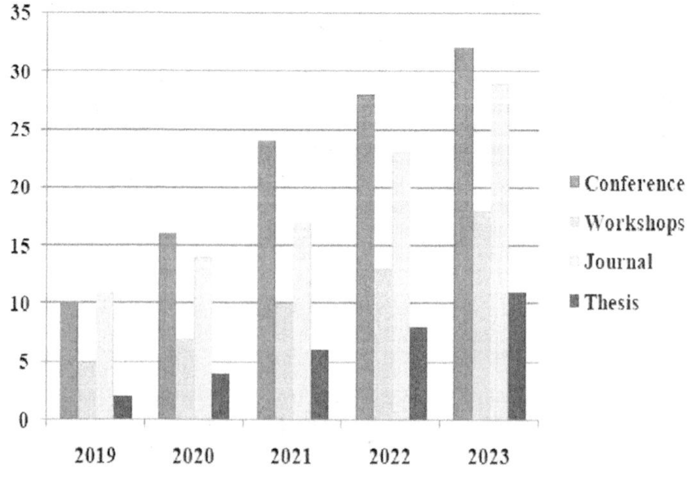

FIGURE 9.8 Yearwise article distribution related to the use of RS in various application domains.

them into the recommendation process. RBMs, autoencoders, and NADE are the most often utilized deep learning approaches in latent factor analysis. Because of their simple structure, ability to reduce dimensionality, suitability for feature engineering, and capacity for missing value estimation, autoencoders have gained greater traction in the field of RS research. RNNs are utilized for session-based recommendations, which combine the user's past choices with their current history to increase accuracy. Fig. 9.9 shows different widely used deep learning models used to develop an RS. The main use of CNNs and DBNs is feature engineering using inputs such as text, audio, and images. Nonlinear representations of user preferences provided by deep learning algorithms make it possible to identify unusual behavior. Deep learning-based techniques yield recommendations that are primarily more accurate than those produced by conventional RS. RS also employ deep learning-based techniques to handle large-scale datasets by decreasing dimensionality. Using deep learning techniques in conjunction with item- and user-based methodologies yields recommendations that are more accurate as well. Standard metrics used to assess deep learning-based recommendation systems include precision, recall, F1-measure, and receiver operating characteristic curve for classification accuracy; Mean-Square Error, MAE, and RMSE for prediction accuracy; and normalized discounted cumulative gain for ranking lists of recommended items. The assessment techniques that are most frequently used for the experimental examination of DL methods are comparable to those used in the ML area. These methods include the random split of input data into train and test sets, with k-fold cross validation to avoid overfitting.

8. Future research directions

We want to point the reader toward open research queries that demand more deep learning research in the area of RS. In RS, modifying deep learning models to increase their scalability remains a difficulty. Furthermore, as data volumes increase, solutions are required for optimizing the exponential rise of parameters. More data must be incorporated into user-item preferences in order to increase accuracy and reduce sparsity problems. Pattern recognition uses deep learning techniques to extract characteristics from texts, images, videos, and audio data. Unfortunately, there aren't many research that make use of deep learning approaches' ability to extract low-level information, particularly in the recommendations for images, videos, and music. Dynamic RS can be enhanced with the usage of deep sequential networks. Serendipity, uniqueness, variety, and coverage of generated recommendations are among the success characteristics of RS that can be enhanced by applying deep learning techniques. Studies on specialized RS are few, particularly for cross-domain, trust-aware, spatially aware, and group-based RS. It is difficult to strike a compromise between the competing objectives of accuracy and privacy levels in RS by using deep learning algorithms on privately obtained data. Another challenge is applying such strategies to dispersed or centrally stored private collections. In memory-based CF techniques, deep learning has not been applied to identify nearest neighbors of active users, which could lead to even greater accuracy improvements. Research on RS which combine data from various interactive websites such as Facebook, Twitter, and E-commerce sites, etc., is quite extensive. Other areas of interest for future research could include knowledge-based RS, techniques for handling real-time user feedbacks and techniques for processing implicit user data seamlessly. RS that rely on deep learning have been increasingly popular lately. Subsequent studies in this domain may incorporate new hybrid meta-heuristic variations with the highly effective deep learning models. Throughout this research, it became clear that

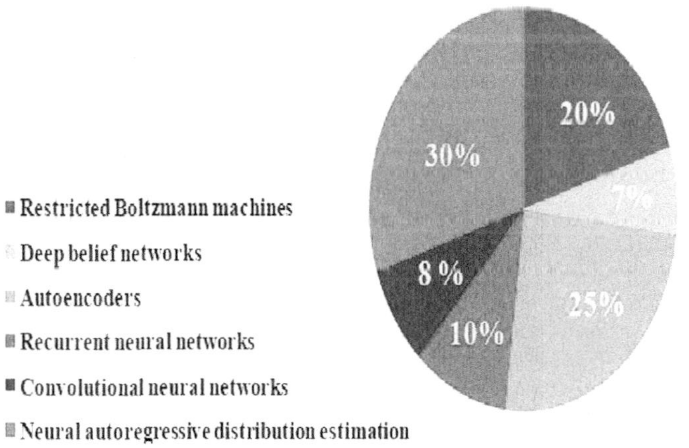

FIGURE 9.9 Widely used deep learning models used to develop an RS.

while contemporary RS have proven to function well, there isn't a single, accepted set of standards or methodology that can be applied to assess the effectiveness of all RS. Comparing system performance is challenging since many assessment matrices are typically used to measure it. RS are increasingly being used in real-time applications. The effectiveness of these RS is greatly dependent on user satisfaction and customization. New assessment standards that are able to gauge user satisfaction in real-time are required. Future studies should concentrate on gathering user feedback in real-time and use that data to modify the recommendation process.

9. Conclusion

Academicians and researchers have become interested in RS. Different methods for AI-based RS are compiled and examined in a comprehensive assessment of the literature. The purpose is to provide and guide practitioners and researchers in related domains in gaining a thorough grasp of AI-based RS. We have gathered and carefully examined research papers on RS with a variety of application areas. Numerous facts have been gathered for this evaluation, including the various application fields, strategies, simulation tools, and applications that have been focused on, as well as the performance metrics, datasets, system characteristics, challenges, and solutions associated with various RS. In addition, the challenges and research gaps were presented in order to examine the RS research outlook for the future. In summary, this chapter offers a thorough grasp of the current state of research on RS to offer guidance and future directions to scholars studying RS. This study intends to offer guidance to scholars and practitioners in the field of RS, while also highlighting the ways in which AI approaches might improve the RS. Even though the field of RS stands to benefit greatly from the application of AI, issues like accuracy and scalability still demand more research. One further potential area of investigation that was noted in the relevant studies was the use of larger datasets.

References

[1] J. Schafer, J. Konstan, J. Riedl, E-commerce recommendation applications, Data Min. Knowl. Discov. 5 (2001) 115–153.
[2] J. Bobadilla, F. Ortega, A. Hernando, A. Gutierrez, Recommender systems survey, Knowl. Base Syst. 46 (2013) 109–132.
[3] D. Roy, M. Dutta, A systematic review and research perspective on recommender systems, J. Big Data 9 (2022) 59.
[4] R. Burke, Hybrid recommender systems: Survey and experiments, User Model. User-Adapted Interact. 4 (2002) 331–370.
[5] G. Adomavicius, A. Tuzhilin, Toward the next generation of recommender systems: A survey of the state-of-the-art and possible extensions, IEEE Trans. Knowl. Data Eng. 17 (2005) 734–749.
[6] R. Burke, Personalized recommender system based on friendship strength in social network services, Expert Syst. Appl. 69 (2017) 135–148.
[7] J. Lu, D. Wu, M. Mao, W. Wang, G. Zhang, Recommender system application developments: A survey, Decis. Support Syst. 74 (2015) 12–32.
[8] F. Isinkaye, Y. Folajimi, B. Ojokoh, Recommendation systems: Principles, methods and evaluation, Egyptian Inform. J. 16 (2015) 261–273.
[9] P. Covington, J. Adams, E. Sargin, Deep neural networks for YouTube recommendations, in: Proceedings of the 10th ACM Conference on Recommender Systems, Boston, MA, USA, 2016, pp. 191–198.
[10] S. Zhang, L. Yao, A. Sun, Y. Tay, Deep learning based recommender system: A survey and new perspectives, ACM Comput. Surv. 52 (2019) 1–38.
[11] T. Truyen, D. Phung, S. Venkatesh, Ordinal Boltzmann machines for collaborative filtering, in: Proceedings of the 25th Conference on Uncertainty in Artificial Intelligence, 2009, pp. 548–556.
[12] P. Shoemaker, News and newsworthiness: A commentary, Communications 31 (2006) 105–111.
[13] J. Konstan, J. Riedl, Recommender systems: From algorithms to user experience, User Model. User-Adapted Interact. 22 (2012) 101–123.
[14] M. Premalatha, V. Viswanathan, G. Suganya, M. Kaviya, A. Vijaya, Educational data mining and recommender systems survey, Int. J. Web Portals (IJWP) 10 (2018) 39–53.
[15] D. Park, H. Kim, I. Choi, J. Kim, A literature review and classification of recommender systems research, Expert Syst. Appl. 39 (2012) 10059–10072.
[16] R. Salakhutdinov, H. MnihA, Restricted Boltzmann machines for collaborative filtering, in: Proceedings of the 24th International Conference on MachineLearning, 2007.
[17] H. Guo, R. Tang, Y. Ye, Z. Li, X. He, Deepfm: A factorization machine based neural network for CTR prediction, in: International Joint Conference on Artificial Intelligence, 2017, pp. 1725–1731.
[18] S. Sedhain, A.K. Menon, S. Sanner, L. Xie, Autorec: Autoencoders meet collaborative filtering, in: Proceedings of the 24th International Conference onWorldWideWeb, 2015, pp. 111–112.
[19] S. Zhang, L. Yao, X. Xu, Autosvd++: An efficient hybrid collaborative filtering model via contractive auto-encoders, in: Proceedings of the 40th International ACM SIGIR Conference on Research and Development in Information Retrieval, 2017, pp. 2–5.
[20] Q. Diao, M. Qiu, C. Wu, A. Smola, J. Jiang, C. Wang, Jointly modeling aspects, ratings and sentiments for movie recommendation, in: Proceedings of the 20th ACM SIGKDD International Conference on Knowledge Discovery and DataMining, 2014, pp. 193–202.

[21] D. Kim, C. Park, J. Oh, S. Lee, H. Yu, Convolutional matrix factorization for document context-aware recommendation, in: RecSys 2016-Proceedings of the 10thACMConference on Recommender Systems, 2016, pp. 233–240.
[22] H. Dai, Y. Wang, R. Trivedi, L. Song, Recurrent coevolutionary feature embedding processes for recommendation, in: Proceedings of the 1st Workshop on Deep Learning for Recommender Systems, 2016, pp. 1–11.
[23] C. Wu, A. Ahmed, A. Beutel, A. Smola, H. Jing, Recurrent recommender networks, in: Proceedings of the 10th ACM International Conference on Web Search and Data Mining, 2017, pp. 495–503.
[24] J. Wang, Y. Lantao, Z. Weinan, G. Yu, X. Yinghui, W. Benyou, Z. Peng, Z. Dell, Irgan: A minimax game for unifying generative and discriminative information retrieval models, in: Proceedings of the 40th International ACM SIGIR Conference on Research and Development in Information Retrieval, 2017, pp. 515–524.
[25] S. Seo, J. Huang, H. Yang, Y. Liu, Interpretable convolutional neural networks with dual local and global attention for review rating prediction, in: Proceedings of the Eleventh ACM Conference on Recommender Systems-RecSys, 2017, pp. 297–305.
[26] I. Cantador, I. Fernandez-Tobias, S. Berkovsky, P. Cremonesi, Cross-domain recommender systems, in: Recommender Systems Handbook, Springer, Berlin, 2015, pp. 919–959.
[27] Y. Shi, M. Larson, A. Hanjalic, Collaborative filtering beyond the user-item matrix: A survey of the state of the art and future challenges, ACM Comput. Surv. 47 (2014) 3.
[28] T. Ebesu, Y. Fang, Neural semantic personalized ranking for item cold-start recommendation, Inf. Retr. 22 (2017) 233–239.
[29] A. Elkahky, Y. Song, X. He, A multi-view deep learning approach for cross domain user modeling in recommendation systems, in: Proceedings of the 24th International Conference on World Wide Web, 2015, pp. 278–288.
[30] X. Wang, X. He, L. Nie, T. Chua, Item silk road: Recommending items from information domains to social users, in: Proceedings of the 40th International ACM SIGIR Conference on Research and Development in Information Retrieval, 2017, pp. 233–239.
[31] M. Wiesner, D. Pfeifer, Adapting recommender systems to the requirements of personal health record systems, in: Proceedings of the 1st ACM International Health Informatics Symposium, 2010, pp. 410–414.
[32] M. Elahi, F. Ricci, N. Rubens, Adapting to natural rating acquisition with combined active learning strategies, in: International Symposium on Methodologies for Intelligent Systems, 2012, pp. 254–263.
[33] N. Rubens, M. Sugiyama, Influence-based collaborative active learning, in: Proceedings of the 1st ACM Conference on Recommender Systems, 2007, pp. 145–148.
[34] L. He, N. Liu, Q. Yang, Active dual collaborative filtering with both item and attribute feedback, in: Proceedings of the National Conference on Artificial Intelligence 2, 2011, pp. 1186–1191.
[35] D. Berry, B. Fristedt, Bandit Problems: Sequential Allocation of Experiments (Monographs on Statistics and Applied Probability) 5, Chapman Hall, London, 1985, pp. 71–87.
[36] G. Shani, D. Heckerman, R. Brafman, An MDP-based recommender system, J. Mach. Learn. Res. 6 (2005) 1265–1295.
[37] A. Zenebe, L. Zhou, A. Norcio, User preferences discovery using fuzzy models, Fuzzy Set Syst. 161 (2010) 3044–3063.
[38] C. Cornelis, J. Lu, X. Guo, G. Zhang, One-and-only item recommendation with fuzzy logic techniques, Inf. Sci. 177 (2007) 4906–4921.
[39] Q. Zhang, D. Wu, G. Zhang, J. Lu, Fuzzy user-interest drift detection based recommender systems, in: International Conference on Fuzzy Systems, 2016, pp. 1274–1281.
[40] M. Nilashi, O. Bin-Ibrahim, N. Ithnin, Hybrid recommendation approaches for multi-criteria collaborative filtering, Expert Syst. Appl. 41 (2014) 3879–3900.
[41] K. Treerattanapitak, C. Jaruskulchai, Exponential fuzzy c-means for collaborative filtering, J. Comput. Sci. Technol. 27 (2012) 567–576.
[42] V. Kant, K. Bharadwaj, Integrating collaborative and reclusive methods for effective recommendations: A fuzzy Bayesian approach, Int. J. Intell. Syst. 28 (2013) 1099–1123.
[43] C. Mu, L. Jiao, Y. Liu, Y. Li, Multiobjective nondominated neighbor coevolutionary algorithm with elite population, Soft Comput. 19 (2015) 1329–1349.
[44] J. Koza, Genetic Programming: On the Programming of Computers by Means of Natural Selection, The MIT Press, Cambridge, 1992.
[45] L. Huang, A. Joseph, B. Nelson, B. Rubinstein, J. Tygar, Adversarial machine learning, in: Proceedings of the 4th ACM Workshop on Security and Artificial Intelligence, 2011, pp. 43–58.
[46] B. Settles, Active Learning Literature Survey, University of California, Santa Cruz, 2010.
[47] R. Sutton, A. Barto, Reinforcement Learning: An Introduction, MIT Press, Cambridge, 2011.
[48] W. Zhang, G. Ding, L. Chen, C. Li, C. Zhang, Generating virtual ratings from Chinese reviews to augment online recommendations, ACM Trans. Intell. Syst. Technol. 9 (2013) 1–17.
[49] O. Barkan, K. Noam, Item2vec: Neural item embedding for CF, in: IEEE 26th International Workshop on Machine Learning for Signal Processing, 2016, pp. 1–6.
[50] A. Iovinc, F. Narducci, G. Semeraro, Conversational recommender systems and natural language: A study through the converse framework, Decis. Support Syst. 131 (2020) 113250.
[51] C. Lei, D. Liu, W. Li, Z. Zha, H. Li, Comparative deep learning of hybrid representations for image recommendations, Decis. Support Syst. (2016), https://doi.org/10.48550/arXiv.1604.01252.
[52] S. Wang, Y. Wang, J. Tang, K. Shu, S. Ranganath, H. Liu, What your images reveal: Exploiting visual contents for point-of-interest recommendation, in: Proceedings of the 26th International Conference on World Wide Web, 2017, pp. 391–400.

[53] R. He, J. McAuley, Ups and downs: Modeling the visual evolution of fashion trends with one-class collaborative filtering, in: Proceedings of the 25th International Conference on World Wide Web, 2016, pp. 507–517.
[54] Y. Han, Z. Han, J. Wu, Y. Yu, S. Gao, D. Hua, A. Yang, Artificial intelligence recommendation system of cancer rehabilitation scheme based on iot technology, IEEE Access 8 (2020) 44924–44935.
[55] S. Kang, C. Jeong, K. Chung, Tree-based real-time advertisement recommendation system in online broadcasting, IEEE Access 8 (2020) 192693702.
[56] S. Dhelim, H. Ning, N. Aung, R. Huang, J. Ma, Personality-aware product recommendation system based on user interests mining and metapath discovery, IEEE Trans. Comput. Social Syst. 8 (2021) 86–98, https://doi.org/10.1109/TCSS.2020.3037040.
[57] N. Bhalse, R. Thakur, Algorithm for movie recommendation system using collaborative filtering, Mater. Today Proc. (2021), https://doi.org/10.1016/j.matpr.2021.01.235.
[58] J. Latrech, Z. Kodia, A. Ben, Codfi-dl: A hybrid recommender system combining enhanced collaborative and demographic filtering based on deep learning, J. Supercomput. 80 (2023) 1160–1182.
[59] Z. Li, D. Amagata, Y. Zhang, T. Maekawa, T. Hara, K. Yonekawa, M. Kurokawa, Hml4rec: Hierarchical meta-learning for cold-start recommendation in flash sale e-commerce, Knowl. Base Syst. 255 (2022) 109674.
[60] Y. Lu, K. Nakamura, R. Ichise, Hyperrs: Hypernetwork-based recommender system for the user cold-start problem, IEEE Access 11 (2023) 5453–5463.
[61] S. Liu, Y. Liu, X. Zhang, C. Xu, J. He, Y. Qi, Improving the performance of cold-start recommendation by fusion of attention network and meta-learning, Electronics 12 (2023) 376.
[62] Y. Du, X. Zhu, L. Chen, Z. Fang, Y. Gao, Metakg: Meta-learning on knowledge graph for coldstart recommendation, IEEE Trans. Knowl. Data Eng. 35 (2022) 9850–9863.
[63] O. Hamdollahi, M. Hashemzadeh, Foodrecnet: A comprehensively personalized food recommender system using deep neural networks, Knowl. Inf. Syst. 65 (2023) 3753–3775.
[64] I. Gunes, C. Kaleli, A. Bilge, H. Polat, Shilling attacks against recommender systems: A comprehensive survey, Artif. Intell. Rev. 42 (2012) 767–799.
[65] S. Khusro, Z. Ali, I. Ullah, Recommender systems: Issues, challenges, and research opportunities, Inf. Sci. Appl. (2016), https://doi.org/10.1007/978-981-10-0557-2_112.
[66] G. Shani, A. Gunawardana, Evaluating recommendation systems, in: F. Ricci, L. Rokach, B. Shapira, P.B. Kantor (Eds.), Recommender Systems Handbook, Springer, Boston, 2011, pp. 257–297.
[67] M. Unger, A. Bar, B. Shapira, L. Rokach, Towards latent context-aware recommendation systems, Knowl. Base Syst. 104 (2016) 165–178.
[68] S. Deng, L. Huang, G. Xu, X. Wu, Z. Wu, On deep learning for trust-aware recommendations in social networks, IEEE Transact. Neural Networks Learn. Syst. 28 (2017) 1164–1177.
[69] Z. Batmaz, A. Yurekli, A. Bilge, C. Kaleli, A review on deep learning for recommender systems: Challenges and remedies, Artif. Intell. Rev. 52 (2019) 1–37.
[70] J. Shu, X. Shen, H. Liu, B. Yi, Z. Zhang, A content-based recommendation algorithm for learning resources, Multimed. Syst. 24 (2018a) 163–173.
[71] Z. Xu, C. Chen, T. Lukasiewicz, Y. Miao, in: Hybrid Deep-Semantic Matrix Factorization for Tag-Aware Personalized Recommendation, 2017.
[72] D. Kim, C. Park, J. Oh, H. Yu, Deep hybrid recommender systems via exploiting document context and statistics of items, Inf. Sci. 417 (2017) 72–87.
[73] F. Strub, R. Gaudel, J. Mary, Hybrid recommender system based on autoencoders, in: Proceedings of the 1st Workshop on Deep Learning for Recommender Systems, Boston, MA, USA, 2016, pp. 11–16.
[74] A. Gunawardana, C. Meek, Tied Boltzmann machines for cold start recommendations, in: Proceedings of the 2nd ACM Conference on Recommender Systems, Lausanne, Switzerland, 2008, pp. 19–26.
[75] Y. Tan, X. Xu, Y. Liu, Improved recurrent neural networks for session-based recommendations, in: Proceedings of the 1st Workshop on Deep Learning for Recommender Systems, 2016, pp. 17–22.
[76] M. Ruocco, O. Skrede, H. Langseth, Inter-session modeling for session-based recommendation, in: Proceedings of the 2nd Workshop on Deep Learning for Recommender Systems, 2017, pp. 24–31.
[77] C. Du, C. Li, Y. Zheng, J. Zhu, C. Liu, H. Zhou, B. Zhang, in: Collaborative Filtering with User-Item Coautoregressive Models, 2016.
[78] Y. Ouyang, W. Liu, W. Rong, Z. Xiong, Autoencoder-based collaborative filtering, in: Proceedings of the 21st International Conference on Neural Information Processing, Kuching, Malaysia, 2014.
[79] Y. Zheng, C. Liu, B. Tang, H. Zhou, Neural autoregressive collaborative filtering for implicit feedback, in: Proceedings of the 1st Workshop on Deep Learning for Recommender Systems, Boston, MA, USA, 2016, pp. 2–6.
[80] X. Shen, B. Yi, Z. Zhang, J. Shu, H. Liu, Automatic recommendation technology for learning resources with convolutional neural network, in: Proceedings of the International Symposium on Educational Technology, Beijing, China, 2016, pp. 30–34.
[81] J. Shu, X. Shen, H. Liu, B. Yi, Z. Zhang, A content-based recommendation algorithm for learning resources, Multimed. Syst. 24 (2018b) 163–173.
[82] A. Suglia, C. Greco, C. Musto, M. de Gemmis, P. Lops, G. Semeraro, A deep architecture for content-based recommendations exploiting recurrent neural networks, in: Proceedings of the 25th Conference on User Modeling, Adaptation and Personalization, 2017, pp. 202–211.
[83] C. Hsieh, L. Yang, Y. Cui, T. Lin, S. Belongie, D. Estrin, Collaborative metric learning, in: Proceedings of the 26th International Conference on World Wide Web, 2017, pp. 193–201.

[84] J. Tang, X. Du, X. He, F. Yuan, Q. Tian, T. Chua, Adversarial training towards robust multimedia recommender system, IEEE Trans. Knowl. Data Eng. 32 (2019) 855–867.

[85] H. Wu, Z. Zhang, K. Yue, B. Zhang, R. Zhu, Content embedding regularized matrix factorization for recommender systems, in: Proceedings of the 2017 IEEE International Congress on Big Data, Boston, MA, USA, 2017, pp. 209–215.

[86] B. Hidasi, A. Karatzoglou, L. Baltrunas, D. Tikk, Session-based recommendations with recurrent neural networks, in: Proceedings of the 4th International Conference on Learning Representations, San Juan, Puerto Rico, 2016.

[87] Y. Wakita, K. Oku, K. Kawagoe, Toward fashion-brand recommendation systems using deep-learning: Preliminary analysis, Int. J. Knowl. Eng. 2 (2016) 128–131.

[88] T. Nedelec, E. Smirnova, F. Vasile, Toward fashion-brand recommendation systems using deep-learning: Preliminary analysis, in: Proceedings of the 2nd Workshop on Deep Learning for Recommender Systems, Como, Italy, 2017, pp. 10–18.

[89] A. Oord, S. Dieleman, B. Schrauwen, Deep content-based music recommendation, in: Proceedings of the 26th International Conference on Neural Information Processing Systems, Lake Tahoe, NV, USA, 2013, pp. 2643–2651.

[90] Y. Ko, L. Maystre, M. Grossglauser, Collaborative recurrent neural networks for dynamic recommender systems, in: Proceedings of the 8th Asian Conference on Machine Learning, Hamilton, New Zeland 63, 2016, pp. 366–381.

[91] Y. Zuo, J. Zeng, M. Gong, L. Jiao, Tag-aware recommender systems based on deep neural networks, Neurocomputing 204 (2016) 51–60.

[92] Z. Xu, T. Lukasiewicz, C. Chen, Y. Miao, X. Meng, Tag-aware personalized recommendation using a hybrid deep model, in: Proceedings of the 26th International Joint Conference on Artificial Intelligence, Melbourne, Australia, 2017, pp. 3196–3202.

[93] X. Wang, L. Yu, K. Ren, G. Tao, W. Zhang, Y. Yu, J. Wang, Dynamic attention deep model for article recommendation by learning human editors' demonstration, in: Proceedings of the 23rd ACM SIGKDD International Conference on Knowledge Discovery and Data Mining, Halifax, NS, Canada, 2017, pp. 2051–2059.

[94] H. Nguyen, M. Wistuba, J. Grabocka, L. Drumond, L. Schmidt-Thieme, Personalized deep learning for tag recommendation, in: Proceedings of the Pacific-Asia Conference on Knowledge Discovery and Data Mining, Jeju, South Korea, 2017, pp. 186–197.

[95] V. Dominguez, P. Messina, D. Parra, D. Mery, C. Trattner, A. Soto, Comparing neural and attractiveness based visual features for artwork recommendations, in: Proceedings of the 2nd Workshop on Deep Learning for Recommender Systems, Como, Italy, 2017, pp. 55–59.

Chapter 10

Multi-objective design optimization of point absorber wave energy converters

Mohammad Reza Nikoo[1], Mohammad Mehdi Hoseini Karani[2], Alireza Shadmani[3], Amir H. Gandomi[3, 4, 5] and Moharram Dolatshahi Pirooz[2]

[1]*College of Engineering, Department of Civil and Architectural Engineering, Sultan Qaboos University, Muscat, Oman;* [2]*College of Engineering, School of Civil Engineering, University of Tehran, Tehran, Iran;* [3]*Data Science Institute, Faculty of Engineering & Information Technology, University of Technology Sydney, Ultimo, NSW, Australia;* [4]*University Research and Innovation Center (EKIK), Óbuda University, Budapest, Hungary;* [5]*Department of Computer Science, Khazar University, Baku, Azerbaijan*

1. Introduction

Renewable energy is essential for addressing global challenges such as climate change, energy security, and resource depletion. As the world moves away from fossil fuels, the exploration and development of renewable energy sources become increasingly critical. Among these alternatives, wave energy converters (WECs) represent a promising and innovative technology. By tapping into the vast and largely untapped power of ocean waves, WECs play a key role in expanding the renewable energy mix, supporting sustainability, and reducing greenhouse gas emissions [1]. Although WEC technology is still in its early stages, it is gradually advancing toward commercial viability, especially with ongoing enhancements in areas such as geometry optimization. Integrating WECs with other renewable sources, such as solar and wind, offers a significant pathway toward a sustainable and carbon-neutral energy future, highlighting the essential role of renewable technologies [2]. Among various WEC types—including attenuators, overtopping devices, oscillating water columns, terminators, submerged pressure differential devices, oscillating wave surge converters, bulge wave technology, and rotating mass devices—point absorber WECs (PA-WECs) stand out for their efficiency in wave energy capture.

PA-WECs, designed as buoy-type converters, are built to capture wave energy from multiple motion directions, including heave, surge, sway, pitch, roll, and yaw [3]. This multidirectional capability makes them highly efficient and adaptable to various marine settings. Typically situated offshore, PA-WECs float on or just below the ocean surface, using a submerged buoy to absorb wave energy, which is then converted into electricity through mechanisms such as pistons or linear generators [4]. The FO3 PA-WEC, for instance, utilizes several heaving buoys attached to a rig, converting their vertical motion into rotational energy to produce electricity. Similarly, the Wave Star PA-WEC employs multiple floaters on articulated arms to capture and transform wave energy [5]. A major advantage of PA-WECs is their resilience in extremely storm conditions. The Wave Star system, for example, can elevate along support pillars to avoid damage during rough seas. PA-WECs showcase cutting-edge engineering with a highly effective approach to wave energy capture. Their limited water contact reduces the risk of physical damage, enhancing durability and effectiveness across diverse marine environments.

Designing and optimizing the geometry of PA-WECs is essential for ensuring their efficiency and commercial feasibility as renewable energy solutions. An optimal geometry maximizes energy extraction under various wave conditions, significantly boosting WEC performance, as supported in studies [6–8]. Additionally, thoughtful geometry design is critical for reducing construction and operational costs, a key factor for economic feasibility. An optimization approach that balances energy capture with cost minimization underscores the importance of geometry refinement during initial development stages, as seen in Ref. [9]. The adaptability of PA-WECs to diverse sea states is also largely influenced by their geometry, enabling consistent performance and energy production across varying wave conditions, as discussed in Refs. [10–12]. Geometry also plays a vital role in optimizing the interaction with control systems; for instance, refining

Advanced Intelligence Methods for Data Science and Optimization. https://doi.org/10.1016/B978-0-443-28940-8.00008-7

the geometry of a two-body PA-WEC in heave mode can significantly impact the efficiency of the power take-off (PTO) system, its control, and positioning, as noted in Ref. [13]. Ultimately, the commercial success of PA-WECs is closely tied to precise geometry optimization, which is vital for attracting investments and advancing toward large-scale deployment, as indicated in Ref. [14]. In essence, geometry design and optimization extend beyond technical factors—they are foundational to the goal of effectively and sustainably harnessing wave energy, marking a meaningful advance in global renewable energy efforts.

Numerous studies have been conducted on the optimization of the shape of PA buoys. For example, Gilloteaux and Ringwood [15] focused on optimizing the diameter and draft of a cylinder buoy in a single-body heaving PA system. De Backer [9] studied the hydrodynamic performance of a vertical cylinder buoy with conical and spherical bottoms in a PA system. Beirao and Mlca [16] evaluated stress concentration and induced displacement in spherical, cylindrical, and tulip-shaped buoys used in PAs, finding that the spherical buoy had the most advantageous structural properties. Blanco et al. [17] specifically optimized a two-body PA (2B-PA) to maximize power extraction while minimizing the system's volume. They considered key design parameters such as the diameters of the floating buoy, the secondary body, and the cylinder shaft.

Throughout the historical progression of shape optimization for PAs, the focus has largely been on buoys with cone-shaped, spherical, or cylindrical designs. The primary design specifications in these studies have typically encompassed the buoy's diameter, draft, and specific type. However, this narrow scope of parameters has occasionally fallen short of fulfilling all the design necessities. A notable issue is the significant drag encountered by floating cylindrical buoys. This high drag force often necessitates the use of either more or more robust mooring lines to maintain the system's stability against vertical (heave) movements. Xu et al. [18] conducted a study on the performance of a cylindrical shape PA that is outfitted with a three-hybrid-mooring system., utilizing various materials. The experimental outcomes revealed that the tension force exerted on the mooring line in the surge direction was approximately 50% higher compared with the tension on the remaining two mooring lines. This significant difference indicated that the cylindrical buoy experienced considerable drag force. Furthermore, an innovative hybrid wave-current energy converter was established by Jiang et al. [19] and Chen et al. [20]. This system integrated a 2B-PA with a turbine, integrating them into a single system sharing one PTO system. The experimental results demonstrated that the hybrid system was considerably more efficient in power harvesting, achieving a 24%–89% improvement over a traditional two-body point absorber (2B-PA). However, the system's design did face some challenges. In addition to the three mooring lines attached to the heave plate of the second body, an extra mooring line was added to the floating buoy to address instability in heave caused by surge and pitch motions from drag forces. These findings emphasize the need for diverse and flexible buoy shapes, enabling the optimization of a wider array of parameters, particularly under various constraints—an essential step for improving the efficiency and stability of wave-current energy converters. In related work, Abdelkhalik et al. [21] focused on designing an axisymmetric buoy for a single-body heaving PA, utilizing a combination of polynomial and Bezier curves with five control points. By adjusting polynomial coefficients and control point positions, the study explored a variety of buoy shapes to assess their energy extraction efficiency. However, limitations arose; the approach did not yield an optimal shape primarily due to computational time demands and the complex meshing needed for hydrodynamic simulations. The study underscored that an increase in simulation parameters leads to greater computational complexity, highlighting the need for a robust computational tool to improve simulation efficiency. Such a tool would be essential for managing computational demands effectively, ultimately aiding in the development of an optimal buoy design.

Lin et al. [22] aimed to identify an optimal buoy shape that would maximize wave energy capture while minimizing drag force from currents. They developed an advanced model using nonuniform rational B-splines (NURBS) for parametrization, which provided enhanced flexibility in buoy design. Additionally, they introduced a neural network to replace traditional hydrodynamic simulation tools, thereby reducing computational complexity. A genetic algorithm was also applied to solve the multiobjective optimization (MOO) problem, which was crucial in identifying the most efficient buoy shape. The case study results were impressive: the optimal buoy shape achieved a 68.7% reduction in drag force from currents compared with a standard cylindrical buoy, without any loss in wave energy capture efficiency. This innovation in buoy design represents a major step forward, highlighting the effectiveness of integrating advanced computational techniques with innovative design strategies in wave energy technology.

2. Point absorber WEC mechanism

The PA-WECs concept is widely regarded as a simple, versatile, and highly promising technology among the various WEC devices that have been extensively studied worldwide [23,24]. PA-WECs are devices with much smaller dimensions than one wavelength of the incident waves. These devices have the capability to function in both single and multiple degrees of freedom (DOFs) and can be located either nearshore or offshore. From a geometric standpoint, PAs can be classified into two subdivisions: 1B-PAs and 2B-PAs, as presented in Tables 10.1 and 10.2. Single-body PAs are typically anchored to the seabed or offshore structures and have a fixed point of reference, as shown in Fig. 10.1. On the other hand, 2B-PAs, illustrated in Fig. 10.2, are primarily self-referenced between the buoy and a submerged oscillating body [4]. As previously stated, single-body PAs are devices anchored to a fixed location. The main variations of single-body PAs are floating, semisubmerged, and fully submerged PAs. A single-body floating PA comprises a buoyant structure that interacts with oceanic waves while a PTO component remains secure on the seabed. The buoyant structure's oscillatory movement caused by the waves is harnessed by the PTO mechanism to produce electrical energy [25]. The shape of the floating body greatly influences the natural frequency and RAO. Therefore, by optimizing the shape of the hull, the hydrodynamic efficiency of floating single-body PAs can be significantly enhanced [25]. The operational mechanism of a submerged single-body PA is the same as its floating equivalent, with the only distinction being the position of the body, which can either rest on or anchor to the seabed using positive buoyancy. When comparing submerged single-body PA-WEC with floating counterparts, it is anticipated that submerged one will be less efficient in energy conversion but more resistant to extreme conditions. Furthermore, the depth at which the submerged PA-WEC is positioned plays a crucial role in geometric optimization. This is because the submergence depth substantially impacts on the hydrodynamic performance and the ability to capture power from the waves [26].

TABLE 10.1 Typical geometric shapes for one-body point absorbers from Ref. [25].

Schematic	Shape	Parameters
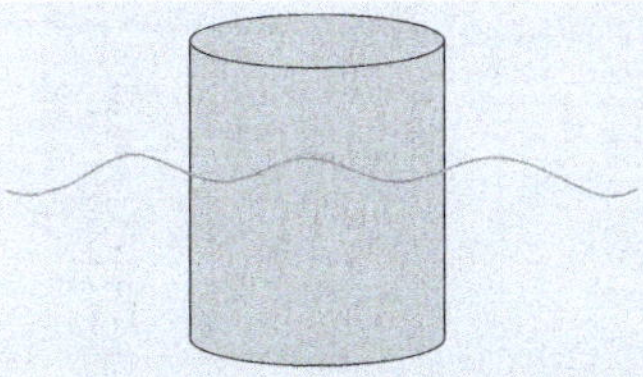	Cylinder	Radius Height Draught
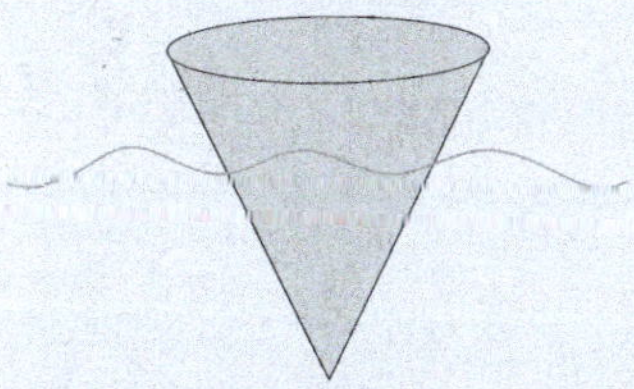	Cone	Radius Cone Angle Draught
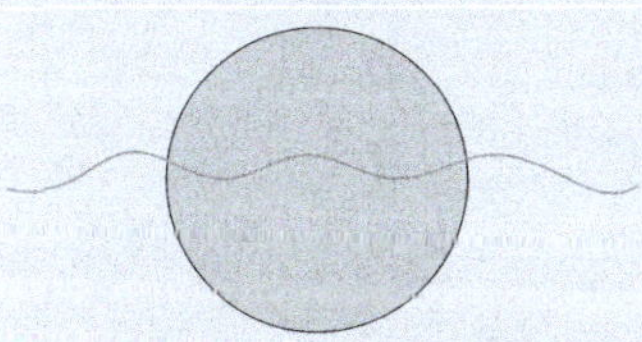	Sphere	Radius Draught
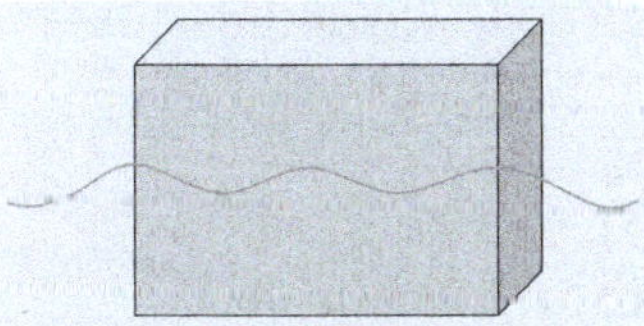	Cuboid	Length Width Height Draught
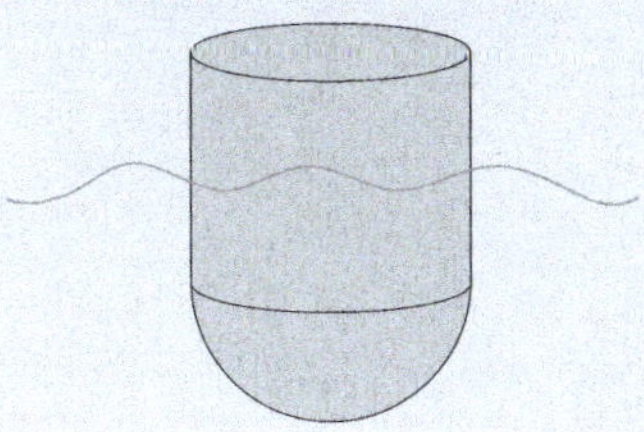	Cylinder–sphere	Radius Height Draught

TABLE 10.2 Typical geometric shapes for 2B-PAs from Ref. [25].

Schematic	Shape	Parameters
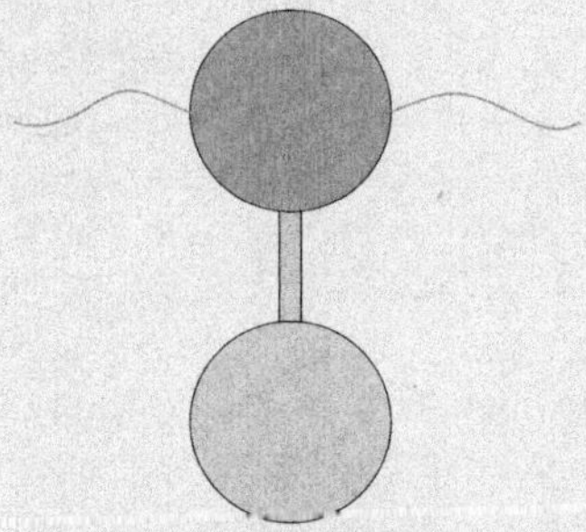	Sphere–sphere	Radii Draught Submergence
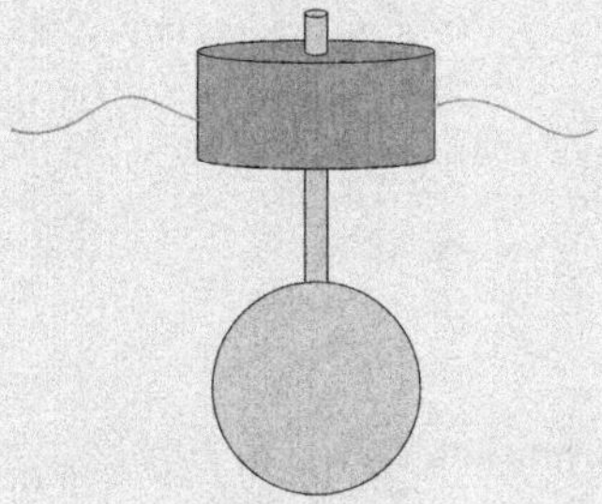	Cylinder–sphere	Radii Height Draught Submergence
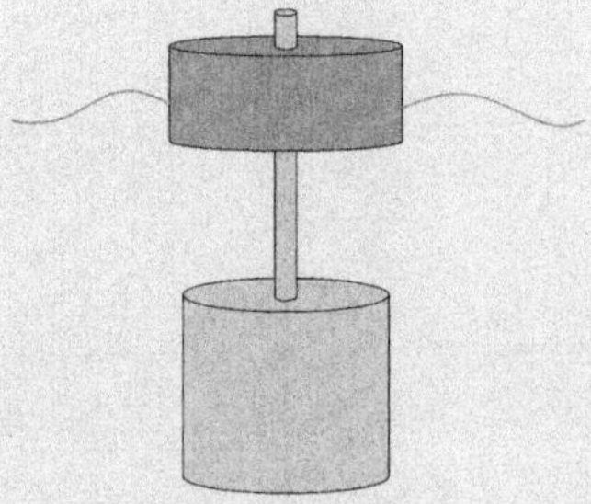	Cylinder–cylinder	Radii Height Draught
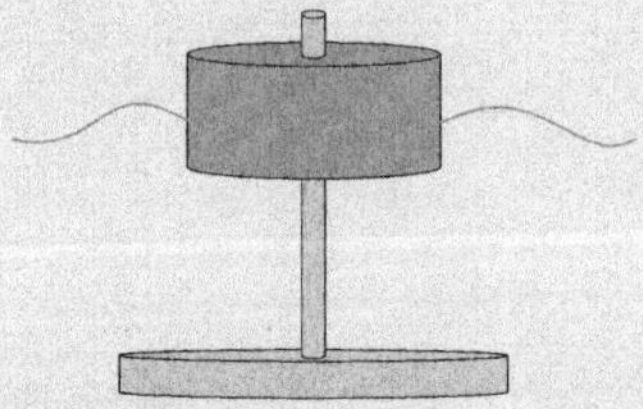	Cylinder–plate	Radii Draught
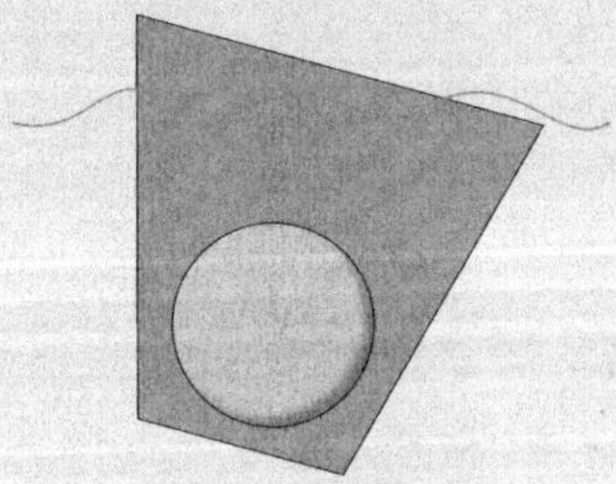	Hull-pendulum	Profile Draught
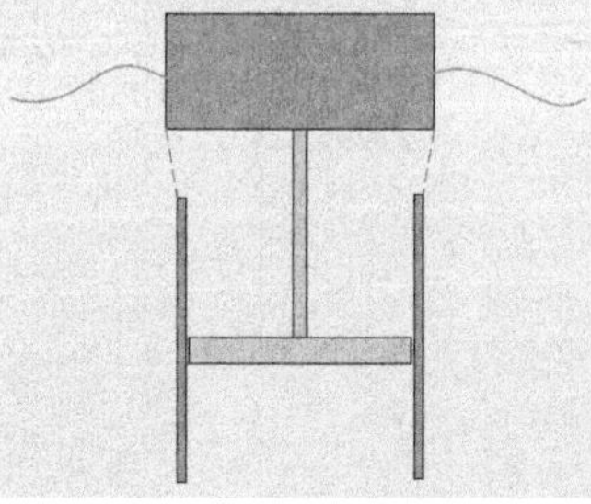	Cylinder–piston	Radii Height Draught Submergence

FIGURE 10.1 Representation of single-body (a) floating PA and (b) submerged PA.

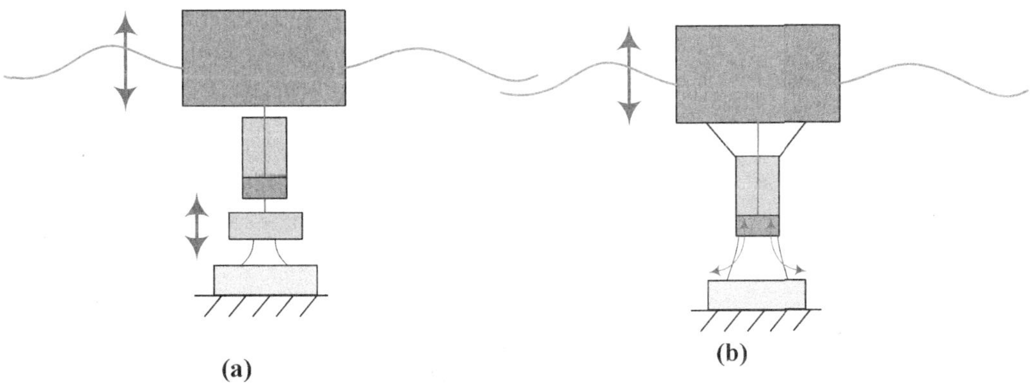

FIGURE 10.2 Two-body floating PAs with different mechanisms.

Conceptually, there are two types of 2B-PAs: self-referenced 2B-PA-WECs and self-contained 2B-PA-WECs [27]. The first type has been less frequently mentioned in literature. The self-referenced 2B-PA-WEC device has a floating body to interact with the surface wave to absorb the wave energy and a submerged body to create a reference point. This configuration enables energy extraction through the relative movement between these two bodies by the PTO mechanism. In regular and irregular waves, it has been discovered that the combined absorption capacity of a two-body system can be superior to that of a single-body system when both systems have an identical floating buoy [28]. Also, in comparison with single-body PAs, self-reacting 2B-PAs are not anchored to a fixed point. Hence, with a proper mooring design, 2B-PAs are appropriate for deep-water applications. On the other hand, a self-contained PA-WEC interacts solely with surface waves through its hull and employs a pendulum structure to produce electricity [29].

3. Multi-objective optimization procedure

Optimization can be described as identifying the most effective approach to utilizing available resources without violating any existing constraints. This procedure involves several sequential stages: mathematically formulating a model that accurately represents the system's behavior, identifying the variables and constraints involved, establishing the objective function, and ultimately, searching for the states that yield the most favorable outcomes by either maximizing or minimizing the objective functions [30,31]. In optimization problems, the presence of multiple local solutions necessitates the selection of an appropriate optimization method that does not solely focus on the vicinity of the best solution. It is crucial for the optimization algorithm to strike a balance between local and global searches. Conventional mathematical approaches may prove inadequate when faced with challenging optimization problems or expansive search spaces. Consequently, various meta-heuristic optimization methods have been established to tackle such complex optimization problems [31,32]. These algorithms intelligently discover near-optimal solutions, resulting in reasonable computation time. However, they do not guarantee the exact solution.

In addition, there is a growing need to solve multiple conflicting objectives due to the incapability of traditional single-objective algorithms. Therefore, MOO approaches are used to consider multiple alternative solutions instead of just one optimal solution, as is the case with single-objective problems. These algorithms aim to find a Pareto front of solutions that meet a set of constraints that may be present in the objective domain. Some well-known MOO algorithms that could be mentioned are NSGA-II [30], NSGA-III [33], R-NSGA-III [34], MOEA/D [35], RVEA [36], and AGE-MOEA [37]. A detailed overview of the steps involved in the MOO process is described in the following and illustrated in Fig. 10.3.

The first step in the MOO process is to clearly outline the objective functions, which represent the goals the optimization aims to achieve in mathematical terms. Quantifying each objective function is crucial, as it allows for measurable evaluations of optimization outcomes. With these objectives in place, the next step is to identify the decision variables—key factors adjusted during optimization. Selecting appropriate decision variables is vital for capturing the core performance aspects of the device, and they are chosen based on both their influence on the objective functions and their practicality [38]. In addition, constraints must be established within the optimization process to outline the limitations and requirements the optimized design must meet. These constraints ensure that the final solution is not only effective but also practical and feasible. By incorporating these elements, the optimization process can produce solutions that achieve performance goals while adhering to real-world limitations, thereby enhancing the design's reliability, safety, and usability. This balance is especially critical in complex engineering projects, where multiple factors must align to develop an optimal and viable solution [39,40].

The following step involves choosing an appropriate optimization algorithm. In MOO, algorithms such as MOEAs are frequently employed because they efficiently manage multiple conflicting objectives and navigate complex solution spaces. Once the algorithm is chosen, it is executed to explore the design space, aiming to identify a set of Pareto-optimal solutions. Each solution on the Pareto front represents a balance between the various objectives. These solutions are assessed based on their effectiveness in meeting the defined objectives, with attention also given to the diversity of the Pareto front, as a broader range provides more options for balancing different goals. The final step in the MOO process is the decision-making phase, where stakeholders select the most appropriate design from the Pareto front, guided by the specific priorities of the project [33,41].

4. Geometry optimization

Geometry optimization is one of the crucial design levels of WEC since it will directly affect efficiency in energy capture, stability in structure, and cost-effectiveness. This review is based on MOO concerning maximum energy extraction and minimum capital and environmental costs. It is usually an optimization process that requires great caution in defining objective functions and selecting comprehensive decision variables to ensure that the design space is explored for optimal performance. The process of geometry optimization in WEC technology encompasses several crucial elements, which can be summarized as follows:

- Choice of WEC technology: The selected WEC technology significantly impacts all subsequent elements of the optimization process. Different technologies have varying characteristics and constraints, influencing the overall approach to optimization.
- Initial geometry and decision variables: Defining the initial configuration and decision variables is critical, as it determines the scope of potential solutions. For instance, if the starting shape is a cylinder and the diameter and draft are considered decision variables, the optimization will inherently be limited to cylindrical shapes of various sizes.

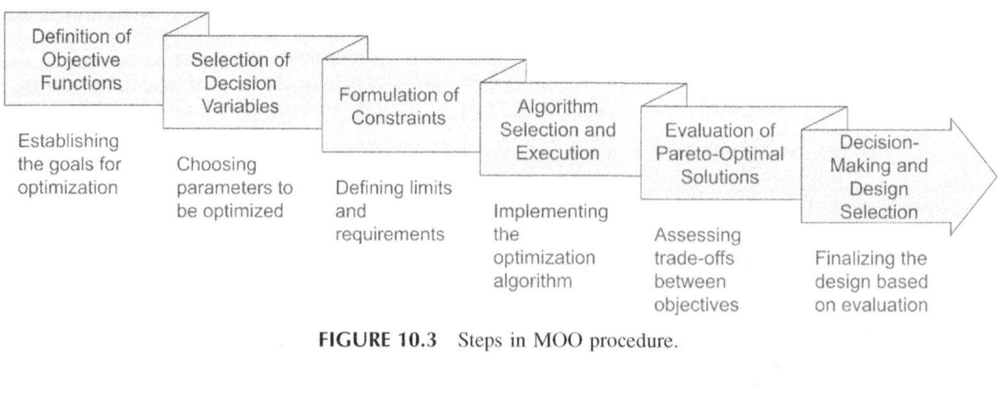

FIGURE 10.3 Steps in MOO procedure.

- Objective functions, models, and assumptions: The chosen metrics for objective functions, along with the models and assumptions used in their calculation, will inherently favor certain solutions over others. These factors shape the direction and focus of the optimization process.
- Optimization algorithm: The selection of an optimization algorithm affects two key areas:
  - Computational time: The efficiency of the algorithm influences the required computational resources and time, which in turn impacts the feasibility and depth of evaluations.
  - Convergence quality: The algorithm's effectiveness determines how well the optimization process converges, potentially leading to more or less optimal solutions.

It is important to note that this review encompasses studies focused on geometry optimization termed "geometry comparison studies." Unlike optimization studies, which involve the actual process of optimization, geometry comparison studies evaluate a predetermined set of geometries or their variations. Additionally, research that utilizes variation of parametric exploration also falls within this classification. These two types of studies will be distinctly reported and analyzed throughout this review [42–44].

Definition of the objective functions is one of the most important parts in the whole optimization process because it states what aspect should be prioritized in the WEC performance. Considering PA-WECs, objective functions were defined in order to catch those important features of the performance with prime relevance for energy capture efficiency maximization, construction cost minimization, and structural integrity while providing a reduced environmental impact. The usual primary objective functions sought to maximize the absorbed power of the WEC itself. It is quantified in terms of metrics such as capture width ratio and average power output. Secondary objectives included the minimization of the construction and installation costs by taking into account material costs, manufacturing complexity, and deployment logistics. Another important objective function was related to structural integrity, to deal with mechanical stability for different wave loading conditions to guarantee long-term reliability. Environmental targets centered around firing objectives, which were designed to reduce the effects of noise pollution, disturbance of seabed, and visual effects on marine ecosystems [45]. In addition to the aforementioned objectives, several other objective functions can be considered in WEC geometry optimization:

Fig. 10.4 illustrates that WEC design focuses on multiple essential aspects to maximize performance and sustainability. Survivability in extreme conditions is addressed by reinforcing structural integrity and enhancing energy dissipation to withstand harsh waves, while control system effectiveness is achieved by refining the geometry to support PTO systems, improving energy extraction across diverse wave conditions. Maintenance and reliability are optimized through design choices that minimize wear, simplify repairs, and extend operational life. Energy conversion efficiency is further improved by refining hydrodynamic characteristics to reduce PTO system losses and optimize wave coupling [46]. To streamline deployment and decommissioning, the structures are designed for ease of transport, installation, and removal, reducing lifecycle costs and environmental impact. Finally, scalability and modularity enable WEC adaptability to various sea conditions and power needs, supporting efficient deployment of arrays with uniform or flexible configurations. These

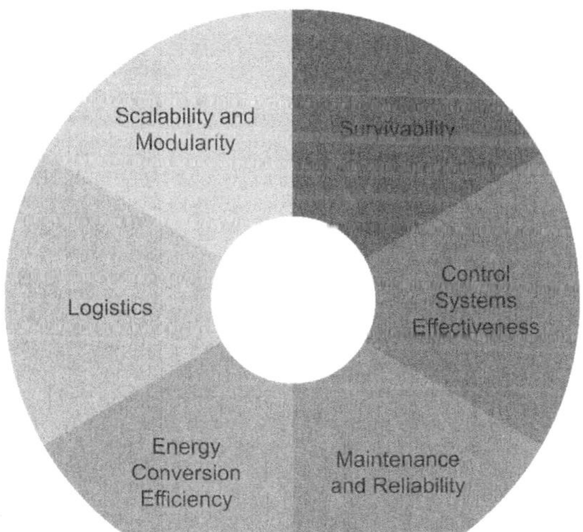

FIGURE 10.4 Several other objective functions applicable for WEC geometry optimization.

factors collectively ensure that WECs are durable, efficient, and adaptable for a range of marine environments and energy demands [26,27].

While any optimization process is concerned with the choice of decision variables, equally important are the decision variables that constitute those parameters that are adjusted to arrive at good performances. Decision variables have been selected based on their influence on defined objectives, including key geometric parameters of the PA: buoy dimensions are diameter, height, and draft, while shape includes cylindrical, hemispherical, and conical [45]. Selected geometric features include those that have a direct impact on the hydrodynamic performance of the WEC in wave energy absorption, buoyancy, and stability characteristics. The shape of the buoy influences the interaction of the WEC with incoming waves, consequently affecting the efficiency of capturing energy, while the draft does the same to the dynamic response of the WEC under different wave conditions [27,47,48].

The choice of the optimization algorithm for WEC geometry optimization is heavily problem-dependent, including but not limited to the nature of objective functions, characteristics of decision variables, and requirements for solution diversity. This is because MOEAs are especially more efficient in handling multiobjective issues featuring in WEC optimization problems, while capable of yielding a rich set of trade-off solutions that can meet potential variability in either operational conditions or design needs. These are, however, afflicted with computational costs that have to be judiciously handled. Gradient-based methods and direct search techniques are less effective for difficult, nonconvex problems but may be appropriate for simpler, well-defined optimization tasks. Probabilistic and swarm intelligence methods, such as simulated annealing and PSO, provide alternative approaches that, under specific conditions, can work well but could require extra measures to avoid premature convergence and loss of solution diversity [37,47].

The optimization algorithms involved in the comparison analysis include gradient descent, simulated annealing, and MOEAs, all of which are listed in Table 10.3. In the case of a class of methods such as the use of gradient descent, while there is effectiveness of convergence in the case of convex and well-behaved problems, in the case of nonlinear and multimodal WEC geometry optimizations, convergence to local optima will occur. Although the simulated annealing methods can escape local optima, compared with gradient descent, the availability of efficient methods for generating a diverse set of optimal solutions simultaneously is not as good as for MOO problems [49,50]. Accordingly, direct search methods also face similar difficulties in handling high-dimensional design spaces. In contrast, MOEAs handle multiple

TABLE 10.3 Comparison of different optimization algorithms applicable to WEC geometry optimization.

Algorithm	Type	Advantages	Limitations
MOEA	Evolutionary	• handles multiple conflicting objectives effectively • Maintains solution diversity • Finds global optima • Adaptable to varying conditions • Provides a Pareto front of optimal trade-offs	• Computationally expensive • Requires parameter tuning • Convergence can be slow in some cases
Gradient descent	Gradient-based	• Fast convergence for convex problems • Simple to implement	• Prone to getting trapped in local optima • Struggles with nonconvex or discontinuous search spaces • Lacks solution diversity
Simulated annealing	Probabilistic	• Capable of escaping local optima • Simple implementation	• Slow convergence • Does not effectively handle multiple conflicting objectives • Requires careful tuning of annealing schedule
Particle swarm optimization	Swarm intelligence	• Efficient search mechanism • Suitable for multiobjective problems • Less parameter sensitive than MOEAs	• May converge prematurely • Lacks diversity in solutions • Can struggle with complex discontinuous landscapes
Nelder-Mead	Direct search	• No need for gradient information • Simple to implement	• Inefficient for high-dimensional problems • Prone to local optima • Lacks scalability and robustness

conflicting objectives effectively and explore discontinuous design spaces, providing a diverse set of trade-off solutions. These algorithms are usually very time-consuming and sensitive to the proper choice of their parameters to yield good performance [51–53].

The well-known representatives MOEAs include NSGA, SPEA2, and MOEA/D. In fact, these MOEAs have already manifested considerable superiority for traditional optimization algorithms in convergence, solution diversity, and computational efficiency. MOEAs indeed outperform the others in achieving convergence to a diverse set of Pareto optimal solutions by means of population-based search mechanisms. Unlike the traditional gradient-based methods that may reach premature convergence to local optima, MOEAs use crossover, mutation, and selection operators for an extensive exploration in the solution space [40]. This allows this mechanism to enable MOEAs to successfully break through complex nonlinear, nonconvex solution landscapes typical of the WEC geometry optimization problem. Intrinsic parallel search in MOEAs increases the likelihood of convergence toward the true global optimum and makes the obtained solutions more robust [35,38].

The second most important strength of MOEAs consists of the fact that they offer an opportunity of preserving diversity of solutions during the optimization process. Classic methods, such as gradient descent or simulated annealing, are designed in a way that they usually provide an optimum solution, while giving little scope for diverse trade-off solutions when the problem of optimization involves more than one conflicting objective [36]. On the other hand, MOEAs employ diversity preservation techniques, such as crowding distance or clustering in order to keep the solution spread along the Pareto front wide. This becomes very important to a decision-maker, as the variability in solutions then presents them with a range of feasible solutions balancing different objectives [33].

While MOEAs are computationally intensive compared with traditional algorithms, these algorithms can generate a complete Pareto front in a single run rather than the multiple separate optimizations for different weightings of objectives. This computational burden may be mitigated through parallel processing and use of modern computational resources, which makes MOEAs particularly well-suited to large-scale and complex optimization problems such as WEC geometry optimization. Traditional algorithms, such as direct search or gradient-based methods, may demand substantial computational effort to explore the entire design space, particularly in cases with nonconvex or discontinuous objectives.

Previous studies have often used PAs with basic shapes to optimize both geometry and the control strategy for the PTO system. For instance, the role of control strategy was examined alongside geometry optimization in Ref. [15]. Babarit et al. [54] focused on optimizing the SEAREV WEC, a device with a pendulum within a floating hull that oscillates in heave, surge, and pitch. Their optimization process included three different shape families, with decision variables such as length, beam, draft, and the center of gravity's vertical position. Using a frequency-domain approach and genetic algorithms within a MOO process, the study aimed to maximize annual energy production AEP while minimizing submerged volume as a cost proxy. For each configuration, the optimal pendulum was identified using a gradient-based method in the inner loop optimization. The results highlighted the potential to reduce hull dimensions by optimizing both control strategy and geometry concurrently. The nested optimization method presented in Ref. [55] was effective for this purpose, ensuring an optimal PTO design and control strategy for each setup.

For single-body floating PA devices, research has prioritized geometry optimization through more flexible definitions to broaden solution possibilities. Generally, adaptable geometry definitions are key in optimization as they enable a wider array of shapes with enhanced performance characteristics [56–59]. When used in conjunction with shape definitions that are more flexible, cost proxies based on surface area in the objective function have been demonstrated to produce shapes that are more realistic and appropriate compared with cost proxies based on volume [60–62]. The analysis revealed that the submerged surface area resulted in simpler shapes with a greater cross-sectional area, facilitating improved load distribution and simplified manufacturing and reinforcement processes.

Blanco et al. [63] have conducted multiple investigations on the optimization of 2B-PA, primarily focusing on this shape but also comparing it with simpler geometries such as vertical cylinders. Several noteworthy points discussed in these studies involve the incorporation of various resonance strategies for WECs. In Ref. [49], three different approaches are mentioned: 1) aligning the resonance frequency of the WEC with the most frequently occurring sea state - for the 2B configuration, multiple resonance frequencies may exist; 2) considering only the highest resonance frequency; and 3) not considering resonance frequency as a constraint. Furthermore, in Ref. [17], several restrictions were imposed on the operation of the WEC. These constraints included requirements for minimum power generation and considerations for preventing slamming effects. However, it is important to note that these constraints were defined using relaxation coefficients, which assigned different weights to the constraints but were not explicitly detailed in the publication. A comprehensive approach to WEC optimization that considers diverse operational conditions and constraints can significantly improve device design by ensuring optimization for specific operating environments while mitigating potential hull damage.

The use of advanced computational models, such as nonuniform rational B-splines, has increased buoy shape flexibility, resulting in more effective energy capture and reduced hydrodynamic forces. Machine learning models have also reduced the computational demands typically linked to hydrodynamic simulations, marking a substantial improvement. Additionally, MOEAs have enabled efficient exploration across extensive design spaces, identifying configurations that balance energy efficiency with considerations such as structural integrity and cost. Nevertheless, challenges remain, particularly the complexity and computational demands of advanced hydrodynamic simulations, which intensify as optimization parameters grow. The balance between model accuracy and computational feasibility continues to be a central issue. While recent research has achieved notable advancements in optimizing individual WEC components, a holistic optimization of WEC systems, including their interactions with oceanic and environmental factors, remains underexplored. Moving forward, integrating advanced computational methods and enhancing the understanding of oceanic environments will be essential to address these limitations. Research in PA-WEC geometry optimization not only boosts the efficiency of renewable energy technologies but also supports the broader aim of creating sustainable and eco-friendly energy solutions.

Hydrodynamic simulations can be carried out using a boundary element method (BEM) solver, which introduces several important assumptions concerning linear wave theory and idealized boundary conditions. Setting the assumption for wave theory linearity, where wave height is small compared with the wavelength, the interactions between the wave and WEC are seriously simplified. This assumption is valid for moderate sea states but misses the nonlinear effects described by larger, steeper waves. As a result, linearizing the wave forces means that important phenomena, such as wave breaking, viscous damping, and strong nonlinear coupling, are not well represented [46].

Idealized boundary conditions are another assumption, where viscosity is neglected and perfect fluid flow is considered, both of which further reduce computational challenges. These conditions imply that in any real fluid interactions, viscous losses can be great, though totally ignored here. The idealization thus strips the model of accuracy with respect to the mechanisms of energy dissipation throughout, particularly in the case of turbulent flow or significant boundary layer effects. It also assumes potential flow for the BEM approach, relying on the assumption of irrotational flow; therefore, viscous effects are not considered [64]. Meanwhile, the potential flow theory works well in predicting the wave radiation and diffraction forces, but it fails to predict the drag forces together with viscous damping, which is essential for determining the overall power absorption and dynamic stability of the WEC [53].

These simplifications may have an important impact on the global results of optimization because it could overestimate energy capture efficiency and underestimate the structural loads on the WEC. For example, neglecting the rotational effects will provide a less dependable estimate of the forces acting on the device, which, in turn, would affect the reliability in the structural design and performance of the optimized geometry. In this regard, optimized designs using BEM may perform differently under real conditions and may require further validation through higher-fidelity models or experimental testing to ensure robustness and reliability [65,66].

Furthermore, most BEM solvers are based on frequency-domain analysis or linear time-domain simulations, hence further limiting the capability for modeling transient nonlinear phenomena adequately. Frequency-domain analysis is indeed informative with respect to the steady-state responses under regular wave conditions; however, it lacks the capability for representing transient dynamics characteristic of irregular, multidirectional, and extreme sea states. For example, sudden changes in wave height or wave-breaking events are challenging to model accurately, which may result in discrepancies when comparing actual performance with simulation results [67].

Additionally, such interactions, e.g., those in an array configuration of multiple WECs, are influenced by the assumptions inherent in the BEM approach. In fact, the common use of the linear superposition principle assumes that the effect of each device is independent of the others [27]. Afterward, the summation is used to derive the overall response. Thus, complex interactions—such as wave shadowing, constructive and destructive interference, and hydrodynamic coupling effects—present limitations for this model. These interactions, which can significantly enhance the overall power capture of a WEC array, require further improvements to be accurately represented [68].

In view of these limitations, it is usually advisable to validate the results obtained using BEM by experimental tests or higher-fidelity numerical methods such as computational fluid dynamics [69]. CFD is more detailed in representing fluid dynamics by solving the full Navier–Stokes equations, which include viscous, turbulent, and nonlinear effects, hence complexities of real fluid behavior. Greater confidence can be achieved through wave tank or field trials for nonlinear interactions, vortex-induced vibrations, and other phenomena that are challenging to model numerically. Finally, the three approaches using BEM, CFD, and experimental data together will allow a more complete and accurate understanding of WEC performance to obtain reliability in real ocean conditions.

5. Environmental impact of WECs

The environmental impact of the deployed PA-WECs should be taken into account for large-scale deployment. Other possible optimization goals include minimising disturbance to marine habitats and reducing the visual impact of surface buoys. These factors have been considered within the multiobjective framework in order to ensure that optimized WEC designs also provide environmental sustainability. Noise generated during WEC installation, operation, and maintenance may affect marine life [70,71].

In the optimization process, ecological preservation can be achieved by incorporating specific constraints and objectives. For instance, decision variables may be selected to minimize the WEC structure's footprint on the seabed, thereby reducing the risk of habitat disruption [72]. Simulations on various configurations can be conducted to assess local hydrodynamics and pinpoint designs that minimize adverse effects on marine currents and benthic habitats. These simulations are essential for understanding how different WEC geometries and placements impact water flow patterns, crucial for maintaining ecological balance.

Evaluating deployment configurations for their impact on marine habitats ensures that WEC solutions balance energy extraction with ecological sustainability. This includes considerations such as maintaining sediment stability, avoiding sensitive ecosystems, and exploring the potential of WEC arrays as artificial reefs, which could provide habitats for marine life [73]. By integrating these environmental considerations, the optimization process aims to develop solutions that meet energy goals while fostering marine biodiversity and ecosystem health. Minimizing disturbances to critical habitats, such as coral reefs, seagrass beds, and spawning grounds, helps mitigate potential negative impacts [74,75].

Additionally, positioning WEC arrays as artificial reefs presents an opportunity to create new habitats, supporting biodiversity by offering shelter and feeding areas for various species, thereby enhancing fish populations and aiding in marine habitat restoration. This approach not only avoids compromising marine ecological integrity but actively contributes to it. Integrating ecological benefits into WEC design and deployment demonstrates a commitment to sustainable development, aligning renewable energy initiatives with the conservation of natural ecosystems.

6. Conclusion and future works

The exploration of geometry optimization in PA-WECs, particularly through MOEAs, has uncovered a wealth of opportunities and challenges. Progress in this area reflects the innovative drive in renewable energy research, with advanced computational tools and algorithms enabling the optimization of intricate geometric designs, resulting in more efficient and effective WECs. Such advancements are essential for tapping into wave energy, a vast yet underutilized renewable resource. However, significant challenges persist, including the complexities of hydrodynamic simulations, the balancing of computational resources with model accuracy, and the integration of WECs within broader marine ecosystems. Furthermore, while geometry optimization has improved individual WEC components, there remains a need for system-level optimization that considers the dynamics among multiple WECs, their effects on marine life, and their resilience to extreme weather. Economic factors, particularly in reducing manufacturing and maintenance costs, are also critical for the commercial viability of these technologies, highlighting the ongoing need for research and innovation in this field.

Numerous paths for further exploration and advancement are emerging in PA-WEC technology. One major area is the integration of advanced machine learning and artificial intelligence algorithms into the optimization process, which could dramatically reduce computational demands and streamline design efficiency. Developing real-world testing and simulation environments to better replicate ocean conditions offers another promising direction, providing deeper insights into WEC performance in operational settings. Environmental impact assessment will also be crucial, given the growing global emphasis on sustainable and eco-friendly energy solutions. Understanding the long-term effects of WEC installations on marine ecosystems is vital for the sustainable expansion of wave energy projects. Additionally, researching new materials and manufacturing methods that could reduce costs while enhancing WEC durability and performance is essential.

In conclusion, PA-WEC technology has considerable potential, provided that hydrodynamic modelling, cost reduction, reliability, environmental effects, and system level optimization are addressed. By addressing current challenges and exploring these future directions, the development of efficient and sustainable wave energy conversion systems can accelerate, supporting the global transition toward cleaner energy solutions.

References

[1] R. Costello, K. Nielsen, J. Weber, N. Tom, J.D. Roberts, WaveSPARC: Evaluation of innovation techniques for wave energy, in: Conference: Proposed for presentation at the European Wave and Tidal Energy Conference held September 1-6, 2019 in Napoli, Italy, 2019. https://www.osti.gov/servlets/purl/1641798.

[2] A. Akpınar, P.J. Rosa-Santos, D. Carvalho, Editorial: Offshore wind and wave energy and climate change impacts, Front. Energy Res. 10 (2022). https://www.frontiersin.org/articles/10.3389/fenrg.2022.1002690.
[3] B. Drew, A.R. Plummer, M.N. Sahinkaya, A Review of Wave Energy Converter Technology, 2009.
[4] L.B. Hernandez, Modeling Link for Ocean Wave Energy of Point Absorbers: A Mathematical Framework, 2017.
[5] R.H. Hansen, M.M. Kramer, E. Vidal, Discrete displacement hydraulic power take-off system for the wavestar wave energy converter, Energies 6 (8) (2013) 4001–4044.
[6] T. Aderinto, H. Li, Conceptual design and simulation of a self-adjustable heaving point absorber based wave energy converter, Energies 13 (8) (2020) 1997, https://doi.org/10.3390/en13081997.
[7] B.C. Boren, P. Lomonaco, B.A. Batten, R.K. Paasch, Design, development, and testing of a scaled vertical axis pendulum wave energy converter, IEEE Trans. Sustain. Energy 8 (1) (2016) 155–163.
[8] E.B. Agyekum, S. PraveenKumar, A. Eliseev, V.I. Velkin, Design and construction of a novel simple and low-cost test bench point-absorber wave energy converter emulator system, Inventions 6 (1) (2021) 20.
[9] G. De Backer, Hydrodynamic design optimization of wave energy converters consisting of heaving point absorbers. Dep. Civ. Eng. Ghent Univ. Ghent Belg., 2009, 310 p, http://hdl.handle.net/1854/LU-1006160, ISBN: 9789085783169
[10] A. Garcia-Teruel, D.I. Forehand, H. Jeffrey, Wave energy converter hull design for manufacturability and reduced LCOE, Proc. 7th Int. Conf. Ocean Energy ICOE (2018) 1–9.
[11] A. Shadmani, M.R. Nikoo, R.I. Al-Raoush, N. Alamdari, A.H. Gandomi, The optimal configuration of wave energy conversions respective to the nearshore wave energy potential, Energies 15 (20) (2022), https://doi.org/10.3390/en15207734.
[12] A. Shadmani, M.R. Nikoo, A.H. Gandomi, R.-Q. Wang, B. Golparvar, A review of machine learning and deep learning applications in wave energy forecasting and WEC optimization, Energy Strategy Rev. 49 (2023) 101180, https://doi.org/10.1016/j.esr.2023.101180.
[13] A. Shadmani, M.R. Nikoo, A.H. Gandomi, Robust optimization of PTO settings for point absorber wave energy converter, in: Handbook of Formal Optimization, Springer, 2023, pp. 1–19.
[14] C.E. Clark, A. Garcia-Teruel, B. Dupont, D. Forehand, Towards Reliability-Based Geometry Optimization of a Point-Absorber with PTO Reliability Objectives, 2019.
[15] J.C. Gilloteaux, J. Ringwood, Control-informed geometric optimisation of wave energy converters, in: IFAC Proceedings Volumes (IFAC-PapersOnline), IFAC Secretariat, 2010, pp. 366–371, https://doi.org/10.3182/20100915-3-DE-3008.00072.
[16] P. Beirão, C. Malça, P. Beirão, C. Malça, Hydraulic power take-off and buoy geometries characterization for a wave energy converter, Energy Power Eng. 5 (2013) 72–77.
[17] M. Blanco, M. Lafoz, D. Ramirez, G. Navarro, J. Torres, L. Garcia-Tabares, Dimensioning of point absorbers for wave energy conversion by means of differential evolutionary algorithms, IEEE Trans. Sustain. Energy 10 (3) (2018) 1076–1085.
[18] G. Xue, Z. Zhang, J. Qin, S. Huang, Y. Liu, Control parameters optimization of accumulator in hydraulic power take-off system for eccentric rotating wave energy converter, J. Mar. Sci. Eng. 11 (4) (2023) 792.
[19] B. Jiang, et al., Performance analysis and tank test validation of a hybrid ocean wave-current energy converter with a single power takeoff, Energy Convers. Manag. 224 (2020) 113268.
[20] S. Chen, et al., Design, dynamic modeling and wave basin verification of a hybrid wave–current energy converter, Appl. Energy 321 (2022) 119320.
[21] O. Abdelkhalik, et al., Multiresonant feedback control of a three-degree-of-freedom wave energy converter, IEEE Trans. Sustain. Energy 8 (4) (2017) 1518–1527, https://doi.org/10.1109/TSTE.2017.2692647.
[22] W. Lin, B.H. Shanab, C. Lenderink, L. Zuo, Multi-objective optimization of the buoy shape of an ocean wave energy converter using neural network and genetic algorithm, 2nd Model. Estim. Control Conf. MECC 2022 55 (37) (2022) 145–150, https://doi.org/10.1016/j.ifacol.2022.11.175.
[23] A. Amiri, R. Panahi, S. Radfar, Parametric study of two-body floating-point wave absorber, J. Mar. Sci. Appl. 15 (1) (2016) 41–49, https://doi.org/10.1007/s11804-016-1342-1.
[24] R. Alamian, R. Shafaghat, M.R. Safaei, Multi-objective optimization of a pitch point absorber wave energy converter, Water Switz. 11 (5) (2019), https://doi.org/10.3390/w11050969.
[25] A. Garcia-Teruel, B. DuPont, D.I.M. Forehand, Hull geometry optimisation of wave energy converters: On the choice of the objective functions and the optimisation formulation, Appl. Energy 298 (2021) 117153, https://doi.org/10.1016/j.apenergy.2021.117153.
[26] H. Ding, et al., Optimization of the hydrodynamic performance of a wave energy converter in an integrated cylindrical wave energy converter-type breakwater system, J. Offshore Mech. Arctic Eng. 145 (5) (2023) 054501.
[27] A. Shadmani, M.R. Nikoo, A.H. Gandomi, Adaptive systematic optimization of a multi-axis ocean wave energy converter, Renew. Sustain. Energy Rev. 189 (2024) 113920.
[28] B. Guo, T. Wang, S. Jin, S. Duan, K. Yang, Y. Zhao, A review of point absorber wave energy converters, J. Mar. Sci. Eng. 10 (10) (2022) 1534.
[29] E.A. Shami, R. Zhang, X. Wang, Point absorber wave energy harvesters: A review of recent developments, Energies 12 (1) (2019), https://doi.org/10.3390/en12010047.
[30] K. Deb, S. Agrawal, A. Pratap, T. Meyarivan, A fast elitist non-dominated sorting genetic algorithm for multi-objective optimization: NSGA-II, in: Parallel Problem Solving from Nature PPSN VI: 6th International Conference Paris, France, September 18–20, 2000 Proceedings 6, Springer, 2000, pp. 849–858.

[31] J. Kennedy, R. Eberhart, Particle swarm optimization, in: Proceedings of ICNN'95-international Conference on Neural Networks, IEEE, 1995, pp. 1942–1948.
[32] S. Mirjalili, S.M. Mirjalili, A. Hatamlou, Multi-verse optimizer: A nature-inspired algorithm for global optimization, Neural Comput. Appl. 27 (2) (2016) 495–513, https://doi.org/10.1007/s00521-015-1870-7.
[33] K. Deb, H. Jain, An evolutionary many-objective optimization algorithm using reference-point-based nondominated sorting approach, part I: Solving problems with box constraints, IEEE Trans. Evol. Comput. 18 (4) (2014) 577–601, https://doi.org/10.1109/TEVC.2013.2281535.
[34] Y. Vesikar, K. Deb, J. Blank, Reference point based NSGA-III for preferred solutions, in: 2018 IEEE Symposium Series on Computational Intelligence (SSCI), 2018, pp. 1587–1594, https://doi.org/10.1109/SSCI.2018.8628819.
[35] Q. Zhang, H. Li, MOEA/D: A multiobjective evolutionary algorithm based on decomposition, IEEE Trans. Evol. Comput. 11 (6) (2007) 712–731, https://doi.org/10.1109/TEVC.2007.892759.
[36] R. Cheng, Y. Jin, M. Olhofer, B. Sendhoff, A reference vector guided evolutionary algorithm for many-objective optimization, IEEE Trans. Evol. Comput. 20 (5) (Oct. 2016) 773–791, https://doi.org/10.1109/TEVC.2016.2519378.
[37] A. Panichella, An adaptive evolutionary algorithm based on non-euclidean geometry for many-objective optimization, in: Proceedings of the Genetic And Evolutionary Computation Conference, in GECCO '19, Association for Computing Machinery, New York, NY, USA, 2019, pp. 595–603, https://doi.org/10.1145/3321707.3321839.
[38] K. Deb, Multi-objective Optimisation Using Evolutionary Algorithms: An Introduction, Springer, 2011.
[39] K. Deb, Multi-objective genetic algorithms: Problem difficulties and construction of test problems, Evol. Comput. 7 (3) (1999) 205–230, https://doi.org/10.1162/evco.1999.7.3.205.
[40] K. Deb, A. Sinha, S. Kukkonen, Multi-objective test problems, linkages, and evolutionary methodologies, in: Proceedings of the 8th Annual Conference on Genetic and Evolutionary Computation, in GECCO '06, Association for Computing Machinery, New York, NY, USA, 2006, pp. 1141–1148, https://doi.org/10.1145/1143997.1144179.
[41] F. Xue, A.C. Sanderson, R.J. Graves, Pareto-Based Multi-Objective Differential Evolution 2, The 2003 Congress on Evolutionary Computation, 2003. CEC '03, 2003, pp. 862–869, https://doi.org/10.1109/CEC.2003.1299757.
[42] A.F. de O. Falcão, Wave energy utilization: A review of the technologies, Renew. Sustain. Energy Rev. 14 (3) (2010) 899–918, https://doi.org/10.1016/j.rser.2009.11.003.
[43] B. Bouali, S. Larbi, Contribution to the geometry optimization of an oscillating water column wave energy converter, Energy Proc. 36 (2013) 565–573, https://doi.org/10.1016/J.EGYPRO.2013.07.065.
[44] A. Garcia-Teruel, D.I.M. Forehand, H. Jeffrey, Metrics for wave energy converter hull geometry optimisation, in: Proceedings of the 13th European Wave and Tidal Energy Conference, EWTEC, Napoli, Italy, 2019, pp. 1–6.
[45] A. Shadmani, M.R. Nikoo, A.H. Gandomi, M. Chen, An optimization approach for geometry design of multi-axis wave energy converter, Energy 301 (2024) 131714, https://doi.org/10.1016/j.energy.2024.131714.
[46] D.R. David, Wave Energy Converters in Arrays: Predicting Coastal Impacts, Multi-Objective Optimisation and Nonlinear Interactions, 2022.
[47] A. Shadmani, M.R. Nikoo, A.H. Gandomi, M. Chen, R. Nazari, Advancements in optimizing wave energy converter geometry utilizing meta-heuristic algorithms, Renew. Sustain. Energy Rev. 197 (2024) 114398, https://doi.org/10.1016/j.rser.2024.114398.
[48] A. Azam, et al., Wave energy evolution: Knowledge structure, advancements, challenges and future opportunities, Renew. Sustain. Energy Rev. 205 (2024) 114880, https://doi.org/10.1016/j.rser.2024.114880.
[49] J.C. Lagarias, J.A. Reeds, M.H. Wright, P.E. Wright, Convergence properties of the nelder-Mead simplex method in low dimensions, SIAM J. Optim. 9 (1) (1998) 112–147, https://doi.org/10.1137/S1052623496303470.
[50] S. Anosri, N. Panagant, S. Bureerat, N. Pholdee, Success history based adaptive multi-objective differential evolution variants with an interval scheme for solving simultaneous topology, shape and sizing truss reliability optimisation, Knowl.-Based Syst. 253 (2022) 109533.
[51] M. Peymani, A.H. Nikseresht, H.B. Bingham, A 3D numerical investigation of the influence of the geometrical parameters of an I-beam attenuator OWC on its performance at the resonance period, Energy 286 (2024) 129542, https://doi.org/10.1016/j.energy.2023.129542.
[52] M. Shadman, S.F. Estefen, C.A. Rodriguez, I.C.M. Nogueira, A geometrical optimization method applied to a heaving point absorber wave energy converter, Renew. Energy 115 (2018) 533–546, https://doi.org/10.1016/j.renene.2017.08.055.
[53] A. Mérigaud, B. Thiria, R. Godoy-Diana, Geometrical framework for hydrodynamics and control of wave energy converters, PRX Energy 2 (2) (2023) 023003, https://doi.org/10.1103/PRXEnergy.2.023003.
[54] A. Babarit, A.H. Clement, Shape optimization of the SEAREV wave energy converter, in: World Renewable Energy Conference, 2006.
[55] J. Capper, J. Mi, Q. Li, L. Zuo, Numerical analysis and parameter optimization of a portable two-body attenuator wave energy converter, in: Presented at the International Design Engineering Technical Conferences and Computers and Information in Engineering Conference, American Society of Mechanical Engineers, 2021. V010T10A005.
[56] Y. H. Yu, Y. Li, K. Hallett, C. Hotimsky, Design and analysis for a floating oscillating surge wave energy converter, in: Presented at the International Conference on Offshore Mechanics and Arctic Engineering, American Society of Mechanical Engineers, 2014. V09BT09A048.
[57] E. Renzi, F. Dias, Resonant behaviour of an oscillating wave energy converter in a channel, J. Fluid Mech. 701 (2012) 482–510, https://doi.org/10.1017/jfm.2012.194.
[58] E. Renzi, J. Leech, I. Phillips, WEC-GA Optimisation Tool for an Oscillating Wave Surge Converter, 2017. https://www.researchgate.net/publication/321300247.

[59] S.A. Mavrakos, G.M. Katsaounis, M.S. Apostolidis, Effect of floaters' geometry on the performance characteristics of tightly moored wave energy converters, in: Presented at the ASME 2009 28th International Conference on Ocean, Offshore and Arctic Engineering, American Society of Mechanical Engineers Digital Collection, 2010, pp. 1145–1152, https://doi.org/10.1115/OMAE2009-80133.

[60] M. Alves, A. Sarmento, Hydrodynamic Optimization of the Active Surface of a Heaving Point Absorber WEC, 2009.

[61] M. Alves, H. Traylor, A. Sarmento, Hydrodynamic Optimization of a Wave Energy Converter Using a Heave Motion Buoy, 2007.

[62] C. Sharp, B. DuPont, Wave energy converter array optimization: A genetic algorithm approach and minimum separation distance study, Ocean Eng 163 (2018) 148–156, https://doi.org/10.1016/j.oceaneng.2018.05.071.

[63] M. Blanco, P. Moreno-Torres, M. Lafoz, D. Ramírez, Design parameters analysis of point absorber WEC via an evolutionary-algorithm-based dimensioning tool, Energies 8 (10) (Oct. 2015) 11203–11233, https://doi.org/10.3390/en81011203.

[64] A. Elhanafi, A. Fleming, G. Macfarlane, Z. Leong, Underwater geometrical impact on the hydrodynamic performance of an offshore oscillating water column–wave energy converter, Renew. Energy 105 (2017) 209–231, https://doi.org/10.1016/j.renene.2016.12.039.

[65] H. Mirzaei, M.N. Moghim, B. Movahedian, Numerical solution of hydrodynamic efficiency equations for an oscillating water column wave energy converter using the method of fundamental solutions, Eng. Anal. Bound. Elem. 158 (2024) 270–288.

[66] L. Papillon, R. Costello, J.V. Ringwood, Boundary element and integral methods in potential flow theory: A review with a focus on wave energy applications, J. Ocean Eng. Mar. Energy 6 (3) (2020) 303–337, https://doi.org/10.1007/s40722-020-00175-7.

[67] R. Muduli, S.B. Patil, D. Karmakar, Hydrodynamic performance of pile restrained U-shaped OWC device using boundary element method, Eng. Anal. Bound. Elem. 158 (2024) 139–159.

[68] H. Abdulkadir, O. Abdelkhalik, Optimization of heterogeneous arrays of wave energy converters, Ocean Eng 272 (2023) 113818.

[69] P. Dafnakis, A.P.S. Bhalla, S.A. Sirigu, M. Bonfanti, G. Bracco, G. Mattiazzo, Comparison of wave–structure interaction dynamics of a submerged cylindrical point absorber with three degrees of freedom using potential flow and computational fluid dynamics models, Phys. Fluids 32 (9) (Sep. 2020) 093307, https://doi.org/10.1063/5.0022401.

[70] A. Rahman, O. Farrok, M.M. Haque, Environmental impact of renewable energy source based electrical power plants: Solar, wind, hydroelectric, biomass, geothermal, tidal, ocean, and osmotic, Renew. Sustain. Energy Rev. 161 (2022) 112279, https://doi.org/10.1016/j.rser.2022.112279.

[71] O. Farrok, K. Ahmed, A.D. Tahlil, M.M. Farah, M.R. Kiran, M.R. Islam, Electrical power generation from the Oceanic wave for sustainable advancement in renewable energy technologies, Sustainability 12 (6) (2020), https://doi.org/10.3390/su12062178.

[72] A.E. Copping, et al., Potential environmental effects of marine renewable energy development—The State of the Science, J. Mar. Sci. Eng. 8 (11) (2020), https://doi.org/10.3390/jmse8110879.

[73] B. Yang, et al., Wave energy converter array layout optimization: A critical and comprehensive overview, Renew. Sustain. Energy Rev. 167 (2022) 112668, https://doi.org/10.1016/j.rser.2022.112668.

[74] I. Galparsoro, et al., A new framework and tool for ecological risk assessment of wave energy converters projects, Renew. Sustain. Energy Rev. 151 (2021) 111539, https://doi.org/10.1016/j.rser.2021.111539.

[75] Q. Zhai, T. Li, Y. Liu, Life cycle assessment of a wave energy converter: Uncertainties and sensitivities, J. Clean. Prod. 298 (2021) 126719, https://doi.org/10.1016/j.jclepro.2021.126719.

Chapter 11

Hybrid intelligence for breast cancer biomarker discovery

Morteza Rakhshaninejad[1, 5, 6], Mohammad Fathian[1], Navid Yazdanjue[2] and Amir H. Gandomi[2, 3, 4]

[1]School of Industrial Engineering, Iran University of Science and Technology, Tehran, Iran; [2]Data Science Institute, Faculty of Engineering & Information Technology, University of Technology Sydney, Ultimo, NSW, Australia; [3]University Research and Innovation Center (EKIK), Obuda University, Budapest, Hungary; [4]Department of Computer Science, Khazar University, Baku, Azerbaijan; [5]Department of Data Analysis and Mathematical Modeling, Ghent University, Ghent, Belgium; [6]Institute for Computational Systems Biology, University of Hamburg, Hamburg, Germany

1. Introduction

Breast cancer (BC) stands as the most prevalent cancer among women and remains a significant public health challenge globally, particularly in both industrialized and developing nations. Characterized by the uncontrolled division and proliferation of breast cells, BC contributes to a high incidence and mortality rate. According to the World Health Organization (WHO) breast cancer fact sheet, in 2022, an estimated 2.3 million women were diagnosed with breast cancer worldwide, with approximately 670,000 deaths globally [1]. The early detection and accurate diagnosis of BC are crucial for improving treatment outcomes and personalizing therapeutic approaches [1,2]. Pathologists traditionally rely on the morphological examination of tissue samples, obtained through biopsies, to identify cancerous cells and assess the type, stage, and aggressiveness of the cancer. Although morphological assessment provides valuable diagnostic insights, it has inherent limitations that can lead to bias and diagnostic challenges [3]. Advancements in molecular biology, such as microarray technology and Next Generation Sequencing (NGS), have revolutionized gene expression profiling, making it widely accessible for clinical applications. As a result, gene expression profiling has become increasingly important in clinical oncology and translational cancer research, aiding in the early detection and treatment of various cancers, including BC [4]. The proliferation of computational techniques has further enhanced the ability to mine and analyze gene expression data, despite challenges such as small dataset sizes, high dimensionality, and data imbalance [5]. Consequently, a variety of machine learning (ML), deep learning (DL), and metaheuristic techniques have been developed and applied to improve the detection and classification of BC.

The discovery of significant biomarkers is pivotal for the early diagnosis and effective treatment of cancer, including BC. Biomarkers facilitate the identification and classification of tumors, thereby guiding the selection and recommendation of suitable therapeutic strategies [6]. By elucidating the critical genes and pathways involved in BC, researchers and clinicians can gain deeper insights into the disease's underlying mechanisms, which can lead to the identification of potential drug targets and the development of more effective treatments [7]. In the context of cancer-related datasets, artificial intelligence (AI), ML, and metaheuristic algorithms have proven effective in recognizing patterns and categorizing samples as either normal or cancerous [6,8]. To achieve accurate classification of BC samples using ML algorithms, data preprocessing and normalization are essential [9]. Properly processed data can then be fed into ML models, enabling precise classification and offering valuable diagnostic and therapeutic information. The integration of advanced computational methods in biomarker discovery can improve the identification and prioritization of cancer-related biomarkers, with the potential to support more targeted therapeutic research and, after clinical validation, improved patient outcomes [10]. This comprehensive approach underscores the critical role of biomarker discovery in advancing BC research and clinical practice.

Advanced Intelligence Methods for Data Science and Optimization. https://doi.org/10.1016/B978-0-443-28940-8.00021-X

Gene expression datasets are often characterized by high dimensionality and class imbalance, presenting significant challenges in biomarker discovery and classification tasks. Feature selection (FS) in high-dimensional datasets presents a combinatorial challenge that has been effectively addressed by metaheuristic algorithms [11]. These algorithms can provide useful approximate solutions for NP-hard search problems through population-based or stochastic search strategies. Notable metaheuristic algorithms include genetic algorithms (GA) [12], simulated annealing (SA) [13], whale optimization algorithm (WOA) [14], grey wolf optimizer (GWO) [15], and particle swarm optimization (PSO) [16], all of which have demonstrated efficacy in identifying relevant features within complex datasets. The recent trend toward hybrid methods, which combine the strengths of different metaheuristic algorithms, seeks to mitigate the limitations inherent in individual algorithms [17]. For example, the fusion of GA with the artificial bee colony (ABC) algorithm has shown enhanced capability in navigating complex search spaces [18]. Hybrid methods, such as the combination of the spotted hyena optimizer (MOSHO) with the salp swarm algorithm (SSA), have proven effective in enhancing FS in high-dimensional datasets [19]. A novel framework that integrates the cuckoo search (CS) algorithm with ABC and GA, termed CS-GA and ABC-CS, aims to balance exploration and exploitation in the search process, thereby improving computational efficiency and accuracy [20]. These hybrid approaches not only handle the high dimensionality of datasets but also deliver superior performance in FS tasks, making them invaluable in the context of BC research.

Hybrid metaheuristic algorithms play a crucial role in two significant ways within the realm of computational biology. Firstly, these algorithms are instrumental in fine-tuning the hyperparameters of ML [21] and DL [22] models. By leveraging the intelligent search strategies of hybrid metaheuristic algorithms, researchers can optimize the performance of ML and DL models [23], enhancing their accuracy and efficiency in processing complex biological data, such as gene expression profiles in BC research. Secondly, ML and DL models can reciprocally contribute to the effectiveness of metaheuristic algorithms by evaluating and calculating the fitness of solutions generated during the optimization process [6]. This relationship between metaheuristic algorithms and ML/DL models not only streamlines the parameter tuning process but also ensures that the solutions derived are robust and aligned with the specific objectives of biomarker discovery and feature selection in BC datasets.

This chapter presents a narrative review and conceptual framework for identifying potential breast cancer biomarkers by integrating ML, DL, and metaheuristic optimization techniques. It is intended as a conceptual and interpretive synthesis rather than a systematic review, and therefore does not apply a formal search strategy, inclusion criteria, or quality appraisal. We emphasize the deliberate use of hybrid metaheuristic optimization methods for feature selection in gene expression datasets. By leveraging the strengths of both ML and DL models, these approaches can support the identification and prioritization of relevant biomarkers for breast cancer research. In this chapter, we will review how ML and DL models are utilized for calculating the fitness of solutions generated by metaheuristic algorithms and how these algorithms can, in turn, tune the hyperparameters of ML and DL models. We will explore various approaches and case studies that demonstrate the application of these advanced computational techniques, providing insights into their practical implementation. By highlighting the synergy between metaheuristic optimization and ML/DL models, we aim to describe their potential to support breast cancer research and future clinical translation, leading to more effective and personalized therapeutic strategies.

2. Data science and optimization in cancer research

2.1 Data science

Data science has become an indispensable tool in cancer research, offering transformative potential in understanding, diagnosing, and treating the disease. The integration of ML and DL techniques has significantly enhanced the ability to analyze complex datasets, such as genomic sequences, medical images, and electronic health records, to identify patterns and correlations that are not discernible through traditional methods. For instance, ML algorithms like Decision Trees (DT), Random Forests (RF), and XGBoost have been employed to predict cancer stages and types with high accuracy, thereby aiding clinicians in making more informed decisions about patient care [24]. Deep learning, especially convolutional neural networks (CNNs), has achieved notable success in medical image processing. For example, CNNs have been used for automated tumor detection in medical imaging, including brain tumor identification from MRI data [25]. Accordingly, this chapter prioritizes breast cancer-specific and gene-expression-based studies. The application of big data in healthcare, encompassing genomic sequencing and medical imaging, has greatly advanced our understanding of cancer progression and treatment. Nevertheless, challenges such as data interoperability and quality continue to pose significant hurdles [26]. Moreover, the concept of digital twins in cancer research, which involves creating virtual representations of patients to simulate personalized diagnosis and therapy, exemplifies the cutting-edge applications of data science in oncology. This approach leverages physiologically based pharmacokinetic models and AI to optimize treatment plans, potentially improving patient outcomes by tailoring therapies to individual needs [27].

Optimization through data science in cancer research also extends to the discovery and application of biomarkers for early disease detection and personalized treatment. High-throughput profiling technologies, such as RNA sequencing and mass spectrometry, produce large omics datasets that can be analyzed using ML and DL methods to identify differentially expressed genes, transcripts, proteins, or other molecular features as candidate biomarkers. These biomarkers are crucial for developing personalized treatment strategies, as they account for the heterogeneity and polymorphism observed in oncogenes [28]. The application of AI and ML in oncology is not limited to diagnosis and treatment but also includes risk assessment and patient prognosis estimation, often achieving greater accuracy than traditional clinical methods [28]. Despite the promising advancements, several challenges persist, such as the need for large, high-quality datasets and the complexity of integrating multisource domain data. Traditional ML models may face limitations when applied to very large, high-dimensional, or complex datasets. In such settings, DL methods can offer advantages, particularly when sufficient training data and rigorous validation are available [29]. Furthermore, the financial burden of cancer treatment and the impact on patients' quality of life underscore the importance of optimizing healthcare delivery through data science. The rapid development of biomedical imaging and health management technologies, combined with the analytical power of ML and DL, holds the promise of more accurate prediction models and better health records, ultimately leading to improved cancer diagnosis and treatment [29]. The ongoing digitization of healthcare, although lagging in some areas, is crucial for realizing the full potential of data science in cancer research, as highlighted by the need for standardized infrastructure and incentives to support digital innovations in oncology [30].

2.2 Optimization techniques

Data science and optimization have become pivotal in cancer research, providing innovative solutions for early detection, diagnosis, and treatment. The integration of data mining, predictive analytics, ML, and AI has enabled researchers to analyze complex cancer-related data, identify significant patterns, and develop predictive models that enhance the understanding of cancer progression and treatment responses [31]. For instance, deep neural networks (DNNs) have been extensively used to extract valuable information from large datasets, although their training can be time-consuming and computationally intensive [32]. To address these challenges, meta-heuristic optimization techniques have been employed to optimize the hyperparameters and structures of DNNs, thereby improving their performance and efficiency [32]. Additionally, feature selection methods, such as Genetic Algorithm (GA), PSO, and ABC, have been utilized to reduce data dimensionality and enhance the classification accuracy of predictive models in BC detection [12]. These techniques not only improve the computational efficiency but also increase the accuracy of cancer detection models, as demonstrated by the Modified QPSO-LDA and Weighted Gradient Boosting methods, which achieved high accuracy rates in predicting breast, cervical, and lung cancers [33].

Furthermore, the use of hybrid meta-heuristic algorithms, such as the Gray Wolf-Whale Optimization Algorithm (GWWOA) combined with Support Vector Machine (SVM), has shown promising results in early stage BC detection, achieving high classification accuracy and robust performance metrics [14]. The application of these advanced optimization techniques in cancer research underscores their importance in developing reliable and efficient diagnostic tools, ultimately contributing to better patient outcomes and personalized treatment strategies. The importance of meta-heuristic optimization techniques in cancer research cannot be overstated, as they offer robust solutions to the inherent challenges of data complexity, computational resource constraints, and the need for high accuracy in predictive models. Meta-heuristic algorithms, inspired by natural processes, have been effectively used to optimize artificial neural networks (ANNs) and other ML models, enhancing their classification and prediction capabilities [34]. For example, the use of meta-heuristic-based hyperparameter optimization in DL models for BC detection on mammogram images has significantly improved the accuracy and efficiency of these models, as seen in the MHODL-BCDMI technique [35].

Moreover, the application of swarm intelligence (SI) and evolutionary computing (EC) methods has demonstrated their effectiveness in optimizing DNNs, making them more suitable for handling massive-scale data and complex cancer-related tasks [32]. The ability of these techniques to select optimal feature sets and reduce data size has also been crucial in speeding up the data mining process and improving the overall performance of cancer detection models [12]. Additionally, the advancements in deep meta-learning have further optimized the learning process of DNNs, addressing issues related to data scarcity and computational constraints [36]. The integration of these optimization techniques into cancer research not only enhances the accuracy and reliability of diagnostic models but also facilitates the development of personalized treatment plans, ultimately improving patient care and outcomes.

2.3 Integration of multi-disciplinary approaches

The integration of multidisciplinary approaches is crucial in advancing cancer research, particularly through the combination of gene expression analysis and AI. The high dimensionality and class imbalance in cancer datasets pose significant challenges, which are being addressed by innovative computational methods. For instance, a five-step integrative architecture incorporating proteomics data, protein-protein interaction (PPI) networks, and signaling pathways has been developed to identify protein biomarkers directly associated with cancer patients' overall survival and progression-free intervals. This approach utilizes a cluster-based gray wolf optimizer algorithm for feature selection and a deep stacked canonical correlation autoencoder for clinical endpoint prediction [37].

Additionally, DL techniques, such as Capsule Neural Networks combined with smart data augmentation strategies like Uniform Distributive Augmentation and Wasserstein-Generative Adversarial Networks, have been shown to enhance the classification accuracy, precision, and recall values in cancer diagnosis, reporting high accuracy in the evaluated datasets [38], although such results require careful interpretation because performance depends on validation design, sample size, and external testing. Integrative analysis of multiomic datasets, such as the INTEND algorithm, which merges gene expression and DNA methylation data, further exemplifies the power of combining different data types to uncover regulatory mechanisms in cancer, outperforming other state-of-the-art integration algorithms [39]. The use of DNA microarray technology to analyze gene expression levels has also been pivotal, with DL architectures like recurrent neural networks (RNN) optimized through meta-heuristic algorithms such as the quantum-inspired immune clone optimization algorithm (QICO) demonstrating superior performance in cancer classification [40]. These advancements underscore the importance of integrating gene expression analysis with AI and other computational techniques to enhance the precision and effectiveness of cancer diagnosis and treatment, ultimately contributing to better patient outcomes.

3. Machine learning techniques for biomarker discovery

3.1 Overview of machine learning algorithms

ML algorithms have become essential tools in the discovery of BC biomarkers, significantly improving early detection and treatment strategies. Among the most effective models are SVM, RF, XGBoost, and AdaBoost, each offering unique advantages in the classification and prediction of BC. SVM is widely used because it can perform well on high-dimensional datasets when properly regularized and validated, and because it can model complex decision boundaries. Studies have shown that SVM achieves an accuracy of 97.13%, with a specificity of 97.5% and sensitivity around 96%, supporting its use as a strong classifier in the evaluated diagnostic setting [41]. RF, another robust algorithm, excels in handling large datasets and capturing intricate patterns, which is crucial for identifying subtle biomarkers in BC data. It has been reported to achieve high test accuracies, such as 96.55%, and is particularly effective when combined with other models in ensemble learning approaches [42]. XGBoost, known for its efficiency and performance, has demonstrated remarkable accuracy in BC prediction, with studies indicating an accuracy of 98.6% [43]. This gradient boosting framework is adept at handling missing data and preventing overfitting, making it a valuable tool in biomarker discovery. AdaBoost, which combines multiple weak classifiers to form a strong classifier, has also shown significant promise. For instance, an AdaBoost-Logistic algorithm achieved an accuracy of 99.12%, outperforming several other models and highlighting its potential in precise classification of BC cases [44].

Additionally, ensemble methods that integrate these algorithms, such as combining SVM, RF, and Logistic Regression, have been proposed to leverage their collective strengths, thereby improving predictive performance and mitigating individual weaknesses [42]. Many diagnostic classification studies use datasets such as WDBC; however, these data are not gene-expression data and should be discussed separately from biomarker-discovery studies [45]. The integration of these ML algorithms not only enhances the accuracy of BC diagnosis but also aids in the discovery of novel biomarkers, ultimately contributing to better patient outcomes and more personalized treatment strategies [6]. The continuous advancements in ML and AI are thus playing a crucial role in the fight against BC, offering new avenues for research and clinical application.

3.2 Support Vector Machine

SVMs have shown significant promise in the field of BC biomarker discovery, leveraging their classification capabilities to enhance early detection and diagnosis. SVMs are particularly effective due to their ability to handle high-dimensional data and their strong generalization properties, making them suitable for analyzing complex biological datasets. For instance, SVMs have been employed to identify differentially expressed genes (DEGs) in BC, leading to the discovery of novel diagnostic and prognostic gene signatures. A study applied SVMs along with other ML methods to a large cohort of transcriptomics data, identifying a nine-gene diagnostic signature and an eight-gene prognostic signature, which were validated through experimental methods and cross-validation techniques [46]. Additionally, SVMs have been utilized in federated learning architectures to enhance data privacy while maintaining high accuracy in BC detection. This approach allows the integration of knowledge from multiple sources without sharing sensitive data, achieving an accuracy of 95.68% in early detection models [47]. The Wisconsin Diagnostic Breast Cancer (WDBC) dataset has commonly been used to benchmark SVM classifiers for breast cancer diagnosis, with some studies reporting high accuracy when optimized using techniques such as Grid Search [48]. However, it should be distinguished from transcriptomic datasets used for biomarker discovery.

Moreover, SVMs have been compared with other classification techniques such as logistic regression, DT, and RF, consistently demonstrating superior performance in predictive analytics for BC detection [49]. In another innovative approach, SVMs have been used in conjunction with thermography, a noninvasive technique that measures heat patterns on the skin surface, to detect abnormalities indicative of cancerous cells, achieving high sensitivity and accuracy [50]. The combination of SVM with ANN has also been explored, resulting in a hybrid model that significantly outperforms individual algorithms, achieving an accuracy rate of 97% [51]. Furthermore, SVMs have been applied in the spectral subspace of biomarkers, retaining diagnostically useful information while reducing data dimensionality, which enhances the efficacy of cancer detection [52]. Various types of SVMs, including proximal SVM, Lagrangian SVM, and linear programming SVM, have been analyzed for their performance in BC diagnosis, with linear programming SVM achieving the highest validation accuracy [53]. Lastly, feature selection algorithms based on SVM, such as the Constrained Search Sequential Floating Forward Search (CSSFFS), have been developed to minimize balanced error rates and optimize feature subsets, further improving the accuracy of BC detection models [54]. These studies underscore the versatility and effectiveness of SVM algorithms in advancing BC biomarker discovery and improving clinical outcomes.

3.3 Random Forest

The Random Forest algorithm has emerged as a powerful tool for BC biomarker discovery, leveraging its flexibility, robustness, and ability to handle high-dimensional data. This ML method excels in identifying relevant features from complex datasets, which is crucial for diseases like BC that exhibit significant heterogeneity. For instance, Park and Yi developed an 86 gene random forest model based on gene expression profiles to predict neoadjuvant chemotherapy response in patients with triple-negative breast cancer, highlighting the value of RF-based approaches for identifying clinically relevant predictive biomarkers [55]. Similarly, the Ensemble Feature Selection method (EFSmarker) employed RF to calculate feature importance, leading to the identification of 12 diagnostic biomarkers for BC, with COL10A1 reported as the most prominent candidate in that study [56]. Machine-learning models have also been applied to predict breast cancer treatment response using multi-omic and clinical data. For example, Sammut et al. developed a multi-omic machine-learning predictor of breast cancer therapy response and achieved an AUC of 0.87 for predicting pathological complete response in an external validation cohort [57]. Moreover, improved versions of the Nondominated Sorting Genetic Algorithm II (NSGA2) have been benchmarked against RF, showing that the latter can achieve high prediction accuracy with a small number of features, making it a valid alternative to established biomarker models like Pam50 and MammaPrint [58]. The integration of gene expression with network features, such as PPI networks, further enhances the predictive power of RF, as demonstrated by studies showing that edge-based features outperform gene-based features in various models [59].

Additionally, RF has been applied to breast cancer survival prediction using clinical and treatment related data, with studies showing that RF can identify important prognostic factors such as cancer stage, tumor size, lymph node status, and primary treatment type [60]. The algorithm's ability to handle sample heterogeneity is also noteworthy; by clustering data samples and applying modified PageRank to functional interaction networks, RF can identify cluster-specific prognostic genes, thereby improving prediction accuracy [61]. Furthermore, the GARBO algorithm, which optimizes accuracy and set size in biomarker discovery, has shown that RF can effectively model accurate classification systems using minimal subsets of relevant features [62]. Finally, the binomialRF technique extends the capabilities of RF by incorporating a correlated binomial distribution to analyze multiway interactions, demonstrating computational gains and high classification precision in identifying biomarkers' main effects and interactions [63].

3.4 XGBoost

XGBoost, a gradient boosting decision tree (GBDT) method, has outperformed other ML models in some breast cancer prediction studies, although its performance remains dataset- and validation-dependent. For instance, a study analyzing gene expression levels of 97 breast cancer patients identified key biomarker genes such as AL080059, Ubiquilin 1, CA9, PEX12, and CCN4, with the XGBoost model achieving an accuracy of 0.990, significantly higher than other algorithms like Naive Bayes and multilayer perceptron [64]. Another study optimized XGBoost using a grid search algorithm to identify a novel 6-gene signature (SQSTM1, GDF9, LINC01125, PTGS2, GVINP1, and TMEM64) for predicting metastatic breast tumors, achieving a mean AUC of 0.82and outperformed the evaluated DT, SVM, and RF classifiers in that specific experimental setting [65].

Additionally, XGBoost has been integrated into frameworks for identifying prognostic biomarkers, combining genomic and phenotypic data to address issues of data incompleteness and feature subjectivity, thereby enhancing the interpretability and predictive power of the biomarkers identified [66]. The algorithm's robustness is further demonstrated in studies where it was used in conjunction with other techniques, such as the Synthetic Minority Oversampling Technique to handle imbalanced data, resulting in an ensemble classifier that achieved 98.20% accuracy in early BC detection [67]. Moreover, XGBoost has been applied in radiogenomic studies, where it was used to construct models incorporating imaging features and clinical data, significantly improving the diagnostic accuracy of MRI BI-RADS 4 breast lesions [68]. The versatility of XGBoost is also evident in its application to histopathology images, where a combination of DL and XGBoost achieved 97% accuracy in classifying BC images into benign and malignant categories [69]. Furthermore, the development of the "Xsurv" R package, which integrates XGBoost for modeling right-censored survival outcomes, underscores its utility in screening a large number of prognostic candidate biomarkers, facilitating translational and clinical research [70]. The algorithm's ability to handle large datasets efficiently and its superior performance in various studies make it a valuable tool in the ongoing quest to identify reliable biomarkers for BC diagnosis, prognosis, and treatment [71].

Despite effectiveness of ML models in structured data analysis and small-to-medium datasets, ML techniques have limitations when handling high-dimensional structured datasets such as gene expression matrices. DL techniques may provide an alternative, but their performance depends strongly on sample size, architecture, regularization, and external validation.

4. Deep learning techniques for feature analysis

4.1 Deep learning in genomics

Deep Learning techniques have emerged as a solution to the limitations of traditional ML methods, particularly when sufficient data and suitable architectures are available, especially in analyzing high-dimensional, structured datasets such as gene expression profiles. Unlike ML, which relies on manual feature engineering, DL models automatically learn hierarchical representations, making them more effective for complex tasks such as cancer diagnosis using histopathology images. Deep learning techniques have expanded the available toolkit for genomic data analysis, particularly in the analysis of gene expression profiles, by providing powerful tools to uncover complex patterns and relationships within vast datasets. These techniques, which include various architectures such as DNN, CNN, RNN, and autoencoders, have shown significant promise in enhancing our understanding of genomic data and its implications for disease diagnosis and treatment [72]. One of the primary applications of DL in genomics is feature selection, where algorithms identify the most informative genes for specific medical conditions. For instance, a novel algorithm leveraging autoencoders and Explainable AI (XAI) scores has been developed to select key genes for diagnosing and prognosing Chronic Lymphocytic Leukemia, demonstrating the effectiveness of DL in pinpointing critical genetic markers [73]. Moreover, DL models excel in capturing the intricate structures within genomic data, which traditional methods might overlook. This capability is particularly beneficial in cancer detection, where models like multilayer perceptrons and CNNs have been used to classify patients based on their gene expression profiles, achieving high accuracy and precision [74]. The integration of DL with other analytical methods, such as Empirical Bayes Harmonization (EBS) and Jensen–Shannon Divergence (JSD), further enhances the detection precision by focusing on pertinent features and visualizing decision boundaries in high-dimensional spaces [75]. Despite these advancements, challenges remain, particularly concerning the small sample sizes typical of genomic datasets, which can hinder the performance of complex DL models. Studies have shown that nondeep ML methods sometimes outperform DL models in genomic data analysis, especially when sample sizes are limited [76]. However, as sample sizes increase, the performance gap narrows, suggesting that DL methods could become more advantageous with larger datasets [76].

Additionally, dimensionality reduction techniques, such as those based on convolutional autoencoders, have been employed to manage the high dimensionality of genomic data, preserving global and local structures more effectively than traditional methods like principal component analysis [77]. The application of DL in genomics is not without its hurdles, but the potential benefits, such as improved disease diagnostics and personalized treatment strategies, make it a compelling area of research. As the field progresses, the development of more sophisticated models and the integration of diverse data types will likely enhance the utility of DL in genomics, paving the way for more precise and comprehensive genetic analyses [25].

4.2 Autoencoders for feature analysis

DL techniques, particularly autoencoders, have emerged as powerful tools for feature analysis in gene expression profiles, offering significant advancements in the field of functional genomics and disease diagnosis. Autoencoders, a type of ANN, are designed to learn efficient coding of input data, making them highly suitable for high-dimensional data such as gene expression profiles. These networks consist of an encoder that compresses the input into a latent space representation and a decoder that reconstructs the input from this representation. The ability of autoencoders to perform dimensionality reduction and feature extraction is particularly beneficial in genomics, where datasets often contain thousands of genes but only a limited number of samples. For instance, a novel algorithm leveraging autoencoders was proposed to perform feature selection on genomic-scale data, effectively identifying meaningful genes for chronic lymphocytic leukemia diagnosis and prognosis [73]. Similarly, in the context of oral cancer, an autoencoder-based DL model was used to extract features from gene expression profiles, leading to the identification of prognostic biomarkers that predict the time-to-development of oral cancer and survival stratification of patients [78]. The versatility of autoencoders extends beyond feature extraction to include applications in various types of biomedical data processing. For example, the Tissue-AdaPtive autoEncoder was developed to connect bulk RNA-seq and single-cell RNA-seq data, achieving precise deconvolution and predicting cell-type-specific gene expression profiles with high biological significance [79]. This method demonstrates the potential of autoencoders in integrating different types of omics data, thereby enhancing the accuracy and robustness of gene expression analysis.

The integration of autoencoders with other DL architectures, such as CNNs and graph neural networks (GNNs), further enhances their capability in feature analysis. For instance, a study proposed a Graph Feature Auto-Encoder framework that utilizes the structure of gene networks to predict node features, outperforming state-of-the-art imputation methods that do not use protein interaction information [80]. This approach highlights the benefit of combining autoencoders with graph-based models to exploit the close relationship between molecular interaction networks and functional genomics data. Moreover, the use of autoencoders in conjunction with feature selection techniques, such as the ABC algorithm, has been shown to improve classification accuracy by removing redundant information and selecting the most relevant genes for cancer prediction and diagnosis [81]. In summary, autoencoders play a crucial role in the analysis of gene expression profiles by enabling efficient feature extraction, dimensionality reduction, and integration with other DL models. Their application spans various domains, from disease diagnosis and prognosis to the deconvolution of complex biological data, making them indispensable tools in the advancement of precision medicine and genomics research [79].

4.3 Neural network architectures

DL techniques have revolutionized feature analysis in gene expression profiles, leveraging various neural network architectures to enhance the accuracy and interpretability of predictive models. One of the primary challenges in gene expression data analysis is the "n $\ll$ p" problem, where the number of samples is significantly smaller than the number of features, making traditional DL methods prone to overfitting. To address this, innovative architectures like the Forest Deep Neural Network integrate deep neural networks with supervised forest feature detectors, enabling the learning of sparse feature representations and mitigating overfitting issues [82]. Similarly, the Graph-Embedded Deep Feedforward Networks incorporate external relational information of features into the neural network architecture, achieving sparse connections between network layers and enhancing classification accuracy [83]. Spectral graph convolutional neural networks have also been adapted to handle multiple gene networks, extracting features from gene-specific expression profiles and prioritizing the most important genes for disease classification [84]. Moreover, DL models like Scaden utilize gene expression data to infer cellular composition, demonstrating robustness to bias and noise without the need for complex preprocessing or feature selection [85]. The use of biologically-constrained neural network models combined with unsupervised pathway attribution methods, such as PAUSE, further enhances the interpretability of DL models by identifying major sources of transcriptomic variation [86]. Data augmentation techniques are also employed to overcome the dimensionality problem in gene expression datasets, generating synthetic samples to increase data diversity and improve model performance [72]. DL architectures like CNNs, autoencoders (AEs), and RNNs have been extensively reviewed for their efficacy in classifying and predicting cancer types through gene expression data analysis [72]. The development of contrastive feature analysis (CFA) provides a computational framework to explore the feature space of deep neural networks, improving the performance of AI in various applications, including gene expression data analysis [87].

Additionally, the integration of DL with optimized feature selection methods has shown promise in diagnosing chronic diseases and assisting medical decision making, as evidenced by the classification of multiple cancer types using different optimizers like AdaGrad and Adam [88]. Despite the challenges, DL has produced strong results in several healthcare applications, where models such as CNNs, GANs, and RNNs are frequently used. However, its performance depends on data quality, sample size, model design, and validation [89]. The development of hybrid conventional DL architectures and the potential dominance of capsule architectures in the future further highlight the evolving landscape of DL in feature analysis. Overall, the integration of DL techniques with innovative neural network architectures and feature analysis methods holds significant promise for advancing gene expression data analysis and improving disease diagnosis and treatment outcomes.

However, the performance of DL models is highly dependent on optimized architectures and hyperparameters. Selecting the right features and fine-tuning these models are critical steps that are computationally challenging, especially with high-dimensional data. Metaheuristic optimization techniques address these challenges, enhancing DL's ability to process complex biological datasets effectively.

5. Metaheuristic optimization techniques

5.1 Metaheuristic algorithms

Metaheuristic optimization techniques complement ML and DL by addressing critical challenges such as feature selection and hyperparameter tuning. These algorithms are particularly effective in high-dimensional datasets, where traditional methods struggle to balance exploration and exploitation. Metaheuristic optimization techniques are useful tools in solving complex optimization problems across various domains, including cancer research. These algorithms are designed to efficiently search large solution spaces to find optimal or near-optimal solutions, making them particularly useful in medical applications where precision and efficiency are paramount. GAs and Simulated Annealing (SA) are among the classical metaheuristic techniques widely used in cancer research for optimizing treatment plans and resource allocation, thereby improving patient outcomes [12,13]. PSO and Differential Evolution (DE) are also prominent classical algorithms that have shown effectiveness in solving complex objective functions and constraints, often outperforming other classical methods in benchmark problems [16]. The Quantum-Based Avian Navigation Optimizer and the Al-Biruni Earth Radius (BER) algorithms are newer additions to the metaheuristic family, offering innovative approaches to optimization problems by mimicking natural phenomena and historical scientific methods, respectively [90]. The spider monkey algorithm and the shuffled frog leaping algorithm are inspired by social behaviors in nature and have been applied to various healthcare data, including cancer diagnosis, to enhance the accuracy and efficiency of predictive models [91].

Grey Wolf Optimizer (GWO), Symbiotic Organism Search (SOS), and Krill Herd (KH) algorithms are part of the new generation of metaheuristics that have demonstrated superior performance in solving highly complex problems with multiple local optima, making them suitable for intricate cancer research applications [92]. These algorithms have been particularly effective in optimizing high-dimensional spaces and maintaining population diversity, which is crucial for avoiding local optima and finding global solutions [93]. The versatility and robustness of these metaheuristic algorithms are further highlighted by their successful application in various engineering and medical problems, including cancer research, where they have been used to optimize diagnostic and treatment processes [94]. The continuous development and hybridization of these algorithms, such as the integration of PSO and DE into a novel hybrid algorithm (ihPSODE), have further enhanced their capability to solve unconstrained optimization problems more efficiently and accurately [95]. Despite the challenges associated with data quality, privacy, and the complexity of high-dimensional spaces, metaheuristic algorithms continue to evolve, offering promising solutions to some of the most pressing issues in cancer research and healthcare [96]. The ongoing advancements in metaheuristic optimization techniques underscore their critical role in improving clinical decision-making and patient care, making them useful tools for computational cancer research [97].

5.2 Genetic algorithms

Genetic algorithms have shown significant promise in the field of BC research, especially when applied to gene expression data. GAs, inspired by the principles of natural selection and genetics, are powerful tools for solving high-dimensional optimization problems, such as identifying relevant genes associated with BC prognosis and metastasis. For instance, the Pyramid Gravitational Search Algorithm (PGSA), a population-based metaheuristic method, effectively reduces the dimensionality of gene expression data, achieving high classification accuracy (84.5%) with a reduced gene set, highlighting genes such as HSP90AA1, PTK2, and SRC that are crucial in BC pathways [98]. Moreover, the application of Recursive Feature Elimination (RFE) combined with ML algorithms, including GA, has been instrumental in identifying gene signatures that differentiate TNBC from other subtypes, with XGBoost performing best for subsets of 25 and 20 genes, respectively [99]. The integration of metaheuristic techniques in healthcare, as reviewed in a study analyzing 173 papers, underscores the efficacy of algorithms like GA in diagnosing diseases, including BC, by optimizing feature selection and improving prediction accuracy [91].

Additionally, a recently proposed metaheuristic algorithm, Coronavirus Metamorphosis Optimization Algorithm (CMOA), further exemplifies the potential of these techniques in providing robust and optimized solutions for complex problems, including those in BC research [93]. In the context of radiation therapy benefit prediction in breast cancer, Shen et al. developed an 11-gene signature based on treatment responsiveness to predict radiotherapy survival benefit, showing that gene-expression-based models may support more personalized radiation therapy decision-making [100]. Overall, the integration of GAs in BC research, particularly through the analysis of gene expression data, offers a powerful approach to uncovering critical genetic markers, optimizing diagnostic models, and ultimately improving patient outcomes through personalized treatment strategies.

5.3 Particle swarm optimization

Metaheuristic optimization techniques, particularly PSO, have shown significant promise in addressing complex problems, including those in the medical field such as BC diagnosis and treatment through gene expression analysis. PSO, inspired by the social behavior of birds and fish, is a stochastic optimization approach that simulates a simplified social network where each particle adjusts its position based on its own experience and that of its neighbors to find the optimal solution [16]. In the context of BC, gene expression profiling is crucial for developing personalized medicine strategies. Traditional methods often focus on identifying a single gene signature, but recent studies have demonstrated that multiple highly predictive signatures can be derived from the same dataset, enhancing the robustness and applicability of the findings [16]. Enhanced Binary PSO (EBPSO) has been particularly effective in this domain, offering improved runtime and optimization performance over traditional BPSO by producing more succinct feature sets. This method has reported very high accuracy in some datasets, underscoring its potential for identifying prognostic gene signatures. However, such results should be interpreted cautiously and further verified using external validation before drawing conclusions about clinical applicability [16]. Comparative studies of various metaheuristic algorithms, including PSO, have shown that while classical algorithms like PSO and Differential Evolution (DE) perform well, newer algorithms such as Symbiotic Organism Search (SOS) and Krill Herd (KH) often yield better results for complex optimization problems [92]. However, PSO remains a robust choice, particularly when enhanced versions like EBPSO are employed. The versatility of metaheuristic algorithms, including PSO, is further highlighted by their application across diverse fields, from engineering to medicine, where they optimize different objective functions to achieve desired outcomes [93]. The development of new algorithms, such as the CMOA, which has outperformed many existing methods, indicates the ongoing evolution and improvement of metaheuristic techniques [93].

In the realm of power systems, metaheuristic optimization algorithms have been effectively used to solve various challenges, demonstrating their broad applicability and effectiveness in optimizing complex systems [101]. This versatility is mirrored in their application to BC gene expression analysis, where the ability to handle sparse or inaccurate information and limited computational resources is particularly valuable. The success of PSO and its enhanced versions in identifying accurate and prognostic gene signatures for BC highlights the potential of metaheuristic optimization techniques in advancing personalized medicine. By leveraging the strengths of these algorithms, researchers can develop more effective diagnostic and treatment strategies, ultimately improving patient outcomes. The integration of PSO in gene expression analysis for BC exemplifies the powerful synergy between advanced computational methods and medical research, paving the way for more precise and individualized healthcare solutions.

5.4 Simulated annealing

Metaheuristic optimization techniques, such as Simulated Annealing (SA), have shown significant promise in various fields, including the medical domain, particularly in BC research using gene expression data. BC remains a leading cause of mortality among women, and its metastasis to other organs exacerbates the mortality rate. The study of gene expression in predicting BC metastasis is crucial, as gene expression profiles can provide insights into the disease's progression and potential treatment pathways [102]. Simulated Annealing, inspired by the annealing process in metallurgy, is a probabilistic technique used to approximate the global optimum of a given function. It is particularly useful in handling the high-dimensional and complex nature of gene expression data, which often involves a large number of genes but a relatively small sample size. This characteristic makes traditional optimization methods prone to overfitting, a challenge that SA can effectively mitigate through its iterative improvement process and ability to escape local optima by accepting worse solutions with a certain probability [93]. The application of SA in optimizing gene expression data for BC can be seen as part of a broader trend of employing metaheuristic algorithms to solve complex optimization problems in various domains [101]. Moreover, the effectiveness of metaheuristic algorithms like the CMOA in providing optimized solutions for real-world problems underscores the potential of SA in similar applications. CMOA's success in preserving population diversity and preventing local optima entrapment further validates the applicability of SA in gene expression optimization for BC research [93]. By leveraging SA, researchers can develop more accurate and cost-effective predictive models for BC metastasis, ultimately contributing to better clinical outcomes and personalized treatment strategies. The integration of SA with advanced computational models and regularization techniques can lead to significant advancements in the early detection and prognosis of BC, demonstrating the profound impact of metaheuristic optimization in the medical field.

5.5 Binary Grey Wolf Optimizer

Metaheuristic optimization techniques, particularly the Binary Grey Wolf Optimizer (BGWO), have shown significant promise in the field of BC research, especially when applied to gene expression data. The BGWO algorithm, a variant of the Gray Wolf Optimizer (GWO), is inspired by the social hierarchy and hunting behavior of gray wolves. This algorithm has been effectively utilized to enhance the performance of SVM for BC diagnosis, achieving high accuracy rates by optimizing the selection of gene expression features [15]. The integration of BGWO with gene expression profiling, which measures the expression levels of thousands of genes simultaneously, allows for the identification of gene signatures that can predict clinical outcomes more accurately than single-gene analyses [103]. This approach is particularly beneficial in BC, where patient outcomes such as survival, recurrence, and response to treatment can vary significantly based on the molecular characteristics of the tumor [104]. By employing BGWO, researchers can optimize the selection of gene subsets that are most predictive of these outcomes, thereby improving the precision of prognostic models and therapeutic strategies. Additionally, the adaptive control parameter scheme and RNA crossover-operation in advanced versions of GWO, such as RNA-GWO, further enhance the algorithm's ability to balance exploration and exploitation during the optimization process, leading to more accurate and reliable solutions [105]. The application of these metaheuristic algorithms in BC research is part of a broader trend of using nature-inspired optimization techniques to tackle complex problems, such as the combinatorial explosion in test case generation for combinatorial t-way testing [106]. The continuous improvement and application of metaheuristic algorithms like BGWO in BC research hold great potential for advancing personalized medicine, enabling more accurate predictions of patient outcomes and more targeted therapeutic interventions. The integration of these advanced optimization techniques with gene expression profiling represents a significant step forward in the fight against BC, offering new avenues for research and clinical application.

5.6 Comparative analysis of metaheuristic optimization algorithms

Metaheuristic algorithms such as GA, PSO, and SA have demonstrated significant utility in optimizing high-dimensional gene expression data for biomarker detection [92]. Each of these algorithms possesses unique strengths and limitations, making them suitable for specific aspects of this complex task. This section provides a comparative analysis of these algorithms, focusing on computational efficiency, convergence speed, and accuracy in biomarker detection.

GAs are particularly effective in exploring large, high-dimensional solution spaces due to their stochastic nature [107]. The use of crossover and mutation operations ensures diversity within the population, allowing GA to robustly handle noisy and incomplete datasets, which are common in gene expression analysis. This capability enables GA to focus on the evolutionary fitness of solutions, reducing the risk of premature convergence and making it well-suited for complex optimization problems like biomarker discovery. However, GA is computationally intensive, especially when the population size or number of generations is large, and its convergence speed is slower compared to other algorithms like PSO. The performance of GA is also highly dependent on the fine tuning of its parameters, such as mutation rate, crossover probability, and population size. Despite these limitations, GA-based feature-selection methods have been used in breast cancer research to reduce gene-expression datasets containing more than 20,000 genes to smaller subsets of candidate biomarkers. In specific datasets, these reduced gene sets have been reported to achieve high classification accuracy when paired with classifiers such as Random Forest, although such performance remains dependent on the dataset, validation design, and external testing.

PSO offers a more computationally efficient alternative, with fewer parameters to tune compared to GA [92]. Its ability to leverage the swarm's collective intelligence allows for rapid convergence, making it particularly effective in selecting minimal subsets of relevant features for classification tasks. PSO's computational simplicity and speed are advantageous in scenarios requiring real-time or near-real-time decision-making. However, PSO is prone to premature convergence, particularly in optimization landscapes with multiple local optima, and may lose diversity in the population during later iterations, leading to suboptimal solutions. Enhanced versions of PSO, such as EBPSO, have demonstrated superior performance in gene expression datasets, reporting very high accuracy in certain benchmark datasets while selecting fewer features than traditional methods.

Simulated Annealing excels in its ability to escape local optima by probabilistically accepting worse solutions during the optimization process [108,109]. This characteristic makes it highly effective in rugged optimization landscapes, where conventional algorithms often struggle. SA's simplicity and minimal parameter requirements add to its accessibility. However, SA's convergence speed is generally slower compared to GA and PSO, as it explores solutions sequentially rather than in parallel. The algorithm's performance is also sensitive to the cooling schedule, which must be carefully designed to achieve effective optimization. Despite these limitations, SA has proven valuable in optimizing hyperparameters for machine learning models. For instance, SA has been reported to improve classifier performance in some studies. For instance, in breast cancer diagnostic tasks using SVMs, SA has shown better performance than grid search-based methods, although the size of the improvement depends on the dataset, model, and tuning protocol.

Each algorithm's strengths and weaknesses make it suitable for specific biomarker detection tasks. GA is ideal for exploring high-dimensional spaces and managing noisy data, making it a robust choice for global optimization tasks. PSO is preferred for applications requiring rapid convergence and efficient computation, such as real-time clinical decision-making. SA, with its ability to navigate complex optimization landscapes, is best suited for problems where escaping local optima is critical. Hybrid approaches combining these algorithms could further enhance their individual capabilities, leveraging the exploration strengths of GA, the convergence efficiency of PSO, and the adaptability of SA. Together, these algorithms provide a powerful toolkit for advancing biomarker discovery and improving breast cancer diagnosis and treatment.

5.7 Role in feature selection

Metaheuristic optimization techniques have emerged as powerful tools in the realm of feature selection for BC diagnosis using gene expression data. These techniques are particularly effective in handling the high dimensional nature of gene expression datasets, which often contain thousands of genes but only a limited number of observations. The primary goal of these methods is to identify the most informative genes that contribute to accurate cancer classification while minimizing redundancy and noise. For instance, the PGSA has been employed to cyclically reduce the number of genes, achieving high classification accuracy with a reduced gene set, as demonstrated in BC datasets [98]. Similarly, the Relief filter method combined with a novel version of the spider wasp optimizer (RSWO-MPA) has shown remarkable success in selecting relevant genes, achieving high accuracy across multiple datasets, including BC [110]. The integration of metaheuristic algorithms like the QICO with DL models such as RNN has further enhanced the classification performance, outperforming traditional ML methods [40]. Additionally, the use of RFE in conjunction with ML algorithms like XGBoost has been effective in identifying gene signatures that differentiate TNBC from other subtypes, providing insights into potential prognostic biomarkers [99]. The ensemble of filter methods, such as Symmetrical Uncertainty, chi-square, and Relief, followed by optimization using GAs, has also proven to be a robust approach for feature selection, leading to improved classification accuracy in cancer gene expression data [111]. Despite their effectiveness, these techniques face challenges related to data quality, privacy, and high dimensionality, which require further research for clinical use. In cancer diagnosis, metaheuristic algorithms show potential for improving model optimization and supporting better clinical decision-making [112]. The advancements in DL and optimized feature selection methods have further solidified the role of metaheuristic techniques in the analysis of gene expression data, enabling the early and accurate detection of various cancer types, including BC [88]. Overall, the integration of metaheuristic optimization techniques in feature selection processes represents a significant advancement in bioinformatics, offering practical solutions to the challenges posed by high-dimensional gene expression data and paving the way for more precise and personalized cancer diagnostics and treatment strategies.

High-dimensional datasets pose a significant challenge in biomarker discovery, often requiring robust feature selection methods to isolate relevant genes. Metaheuristic algorithms like GA and PSO excel in this regard, as their iterative optimization strategies ensure the selection of features that contribute to accurate classifications. Enhanced algorithms such as Binary PSO (BPSO) and hybrid variants like PSO-GWO demonstrate superior performance by balancing exploration and exploitation, thereby avoiding premature convergence while effectively reducing dimensionality.

5.8 Role in hyperparameter tuning

Metaheuristic algorithms play a crucial role in hyperparameter tuning [113,114], especially in complex datasets such as those involving breast cancer gene expression. In breast cancer research, effective model performance often depends on the careful optimization of parameters that control the learning process, such as learning rates, regularization parameters, network structure, and the number of selected features. Metaheuristic algorithms can support this process by exploring large and nonconvex search spaces without requiring gradient information, making them useful for optimizing ML and DL models in complex biomedical datasets. By systematically searching the hyperparameter space, these algorithms may help identify model configurations that improve predictive performance and stability when appropriate validation is applied. For example, Punitha et al. introduced HABC for breast cancer diagnosis by hybridizing ABC with modified AIS [108]. An employee bee phase based on Tabu was suggested to enhance ABC's local search. HABC was employed for selecting input features and parameter tuning of the ANN. HABC attained a high accuracy of 99.14% using the Wisconsin Diagnostic Breast Cancer Dataset. Therefore, metaheuristic algorithms can be useful for hyperparameter tuning, particularly when conventional search methods are inefficient.

6. Hybrid intelligence framework

6.1 Combining machine learning and deep learning

The hybrid intelligence framework leverages the complementary strengths of ML, DL, and metaheuristic optimization to address the complexities of BC biomarker detection. ML provides interpretable models for structured datasets, DL extracts patterns from high-dimensional data, and metaheuristics optimize feature selection and hyperparameters, enhancing the performance of both ML and DL models. Fig. 11.1 illustrates this synergistic workflow, which integrates the techniques seamlessly to improve accuracy and efficiency in biomarker discovery.

The integration of ML and DL techniques into a hybrid intelligence framework offers a promising approach to enhance BC diagnosis and prognosis using gene expression data. This hybrid framework leverages the strengths of both ML and DL to address the complexities and heterogeneity inherent in BC. For instance, the study by Mirza et al. demonstrated the application of ML methods to identify valuable gene signatures for BC diagnosis and prognosis, resulting in a nine-gene diagnostic model and an eight-gene prognostic model, which were validated through qRT-PCR and additional ML methods, showcasing the potential for precise and cost-effective healthcare management [46]. Similarly, the work by Li et al. utilized a deep neural network model trained on single-cell RNA-Seq data to screen small molecules for their ability to induce differentiation in cancer stem cells, highlighting the potential for targeted therapies against BC stem cells [115]. Moreover, the BrST-Net framework developed by Rahaman et al. exemplifies the use of DL architectures to predict gene expression from histopathology images, achieving significant improvements over previous studies by identifying 237 genes with positive correlation, thus providing a more affordable alternative to spatial transcriptomics technologies [116]. The DeepCME model proposed by Kim et al. further illustrates the application of DL in predicting BC metastasis, addressing the issue of overfitting through regularization methods and identifying key genes related to metastasis, which could lead to cost-effective and time-efficient diagnostic tests [102].

Additionally, the study by Takeshita et al. developed a recurrence prediction model (RPM) using a logistic progression model to extract nine prognosis-related genes, effectively stratifying high- and low-risk hormone receptor-positive BC patients and reflecting major therapeutic target pathways and tumor immune microenvironment [117]. Howard et al. also showcased a DL model that predicts recurrence assay results using digital histology and clinical risk factors,

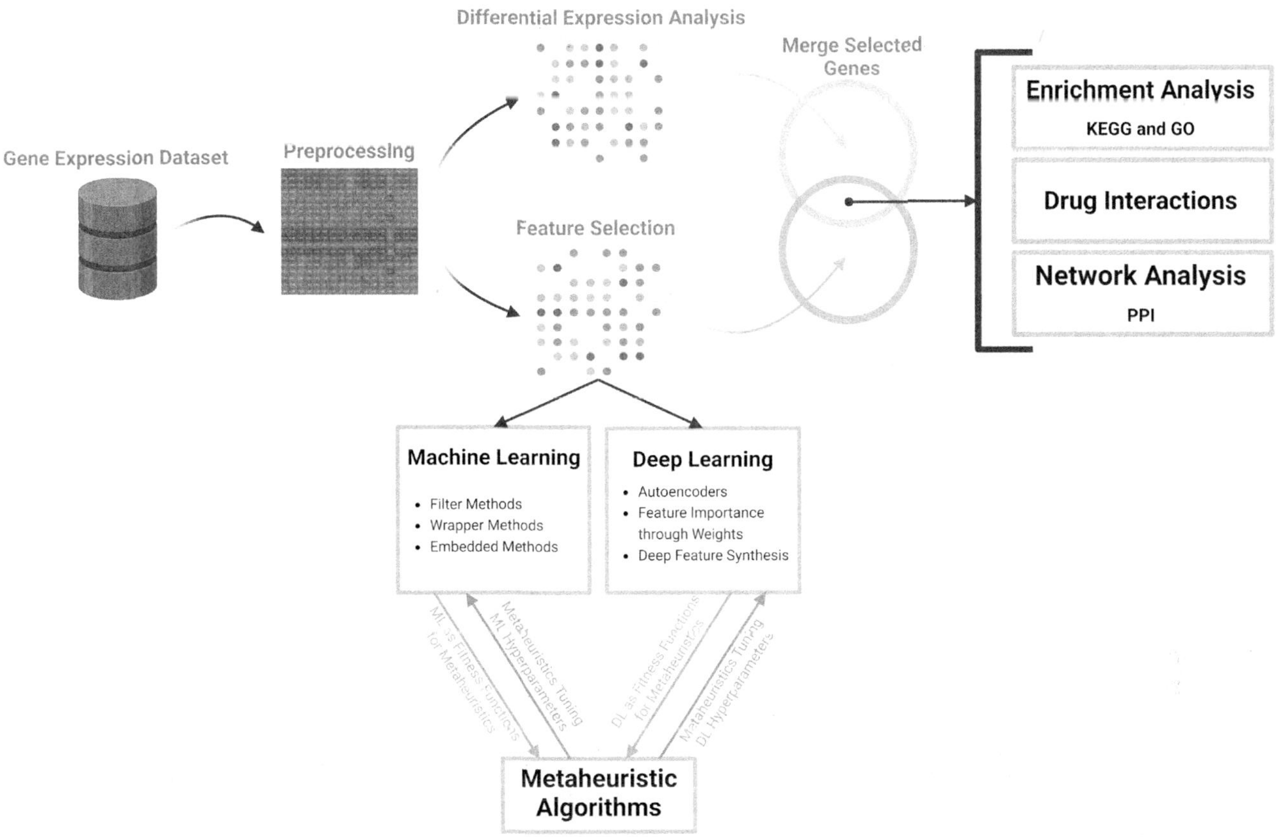

FIGURE 11.1 Conceptual workflow for hybrid breast cancer biomarker discovery, including preprocessing, differential expression analysis, feature selection, ML/DL modelling, metaheuristic optimization, enrichment analysis, drug–gene interaction analysis, and network analysis.

outperforming established clinical nomograms and identifying patients with excellent prognoses who may not need further genomic testing [118]. The hist2RNA approach by Mondol et al. predicted gene expression from digital images of stained tissue samples, enabling personalized treatments and improving patient survival without the need for expensive molecular tests [119]. Furthermore, Zarif et al. proposed a hybrid DL model (CNN + EfficientNetV2B3) for classifying BC in histopathology images, achieving outstanding performance metrics and supporting pathologists in making accurate diagnoses [120]. Lastly, Wang et al. developed Deep-ITH, a method to predict and measure intratumor heterogeneity from whole slide images, providing independent prognostic value and enabling prediction of patient survival from routine histopathology images [121].

Collectively, these studies underscore the transformative potential of a hybrid intelligence framework that combines ML and DL in advancing BC diagnosis, prognosis, and treatment.

6.2 Integration of metaheuristic optimization

Hybrid metaheuristic optimization algorithms have shown significant promise in the detection of BC biomarkers using gene expression datasets. These algorithms combine the strengths of various optimization techniques to enhance the accuracy and efficiency of biomarker identification. For instance, the hybrid artificial bee colony with whale optimization algorithm (HAW) integrates the exploitative employee bee phase of the ABC with the bubble net attacking method of whale optimization, improving the accuracy of BC diagnosis by optimizing the parameters of an ANN model. This approach has demonstrated high accuracy across multiple BC datasets, achieving up to 99.2% accuracy with the HAW-RP variant [122]. Another notable hybrid method is the combination of the Eagle Strategy Optimization (ESO) and Gravitational Search Optimization algorithms, which has been applied to the WDBC dataset. This hybrid approach has achieved remarkable results, with an accuracy of up to 98.9578% and an AUC of 0.9980, by selecting the most relevant features and reducing the complexity of the dataset [123]. Additionally, the two-stage hybrid biomarker selection method based on ensemble filter and binary differential evolution incorporating binary African vultures optimization (EF-BDBA) has been effective in reducing the dimensionality of microarray data and identifying optimal biomarkers. This method combines an improved fast correlation-based filter algorithm with Fisher score in the first stage and uses an improved binary differential evolution algorithm in the second stage, achieving classification accuracy above 0.93 on eight microarray datasets [124].

Furthermore, the hybrid feature selection method (NHFSM) that combines the bat algorithm and PSO has been proposed to enhance the efficiency of patient classification. This method uses a quick selection module based on information gain and a feature selection module that combines the strengths of both algorithms, resulting in improved accuracy, precision, sensitivity, and F1-score [17]. The Harris Hawks Optimization (HHO) algorithm has also been utilized in conjunction with SVM and k-nearest neighbors (k-NN) to determine a small gene subset for high-accuracy classification. This approach has shown excellent performance in terms of classification accuracy and the number of selected genes across six microarray datasets [125]. Moreover, the integration of GAs with SVM (GA-SVM) has been employed to classify triple-negative and nontriple-negative breast cancer patients, outperforming other feature selection SVM hybrid models and demonstrating superior predictive accuracy [126]. These hybrid metaheuristic optimization algorithms leverage the strengths of multiple techniques to effectively handle the high-dimensionality and complexity of gene expression data, thereby improving the detection and classification of BC biomarkers.

7. Gene expression datasets

Gene expression datasets are critical resources for identifying candidate biomarkers for breast cancer, providing invaluable information that enhances diagnosis, prognosis, and treatment strategies. These datasets offer a detailed view of the molecular alterations in BC, enabling the identification of differentially expressed genes (DEGs) crucial for distinguishing cancerous tissues from normal ones. For example, studies have identified novel diagnostic and prognostic gene signatures, validated through experimental or independent computational analyses, depending on the study, that significantly aid in clinical decision-making [5,6]. Gene expression data also reveal the heterogeneity and complexity of BC, providing insights for personalized medicine by identifying drugs and biomarkers sensitive to treatments and radiation. Additionally, integrating spatial context with gene expression data enhances molecular phenotype predictions and addresses intratumor heterogeneity. The ability to monitor obesity-related biomarkers linked to cancer risk and progression further underscores the importance of these datasets in BC research [46].

The primary sources of gene expression databases for BC detection include repositories such as the Gene Expression Omnibus (GEO) [127], The Cancer Genome Atlas (TCGA) [128], and the Breast Cancer Gene Database (BCGD) [129]. Because BCGD is an older resource, it should be complemented by current resources such as TCGA, GEO, METABRIC, cBioPortal, and Ensembl-based resources. These databases offer a wealth of data, from microarray and RNA-Seq profiles to integrated multi-omics datasets, facilitating predictions of recurrence, molecular classification, and treatment planning. The integration of these diverse data sources enhances the robustness of gene expression analysis, allowing for the identification of technology-independent biomarkers and improved classification accuracy. Although spatial transcriptomics technologies are expensive, frameworks like BrST-Net provide cost-effective alternatives for large-scale studies [116]. Overall, these gene expression databases are essential for advancing BC research, enabling significant strides in identifying prognostic biomarkers, optimizing treatment strategies, and ultimately improving patient outcomes.

8. Workflow and methodology

The workflow and methodology of a hybrid intelligence framework for BC biomarker detection using gene expression datasets involve several critical steps, integrating ML, DL, and metaheuristic algorithms. The process begins with downloading the gene expression datasets from repositories such as The Cancer Genome Atlas (TCGA) and Gene Expression Omnibus (GEO) databases [130]. Preprocessing these datasets involves normalization, handling missing values, and filtering out low-expression genes to ensure data quality and consistency [46]. These preprocessing steps are crucial to prepare the data for robust and accurate analysis, which forms the basis for subsequent steps in the workflow.

Gene selection is a crucial step where metaheuristic algorithms like GA or PSO can be employed to identify the most relevant genes, reducing dimensionality and enhancing model performance [46,102]. Metaheuristic algorithms are particularly useful in exploring large solution spaces efficiently and finding optimal or near-optimal gene subsets that contribute significantly to BC detection and prognosis. This step not only improves the interpretability of the model but also ensures that only the most informative genes are used for further analysis.

Following gene selection, a PPI network is constructed to understand the interactions between the selected genes, which can be visualized using tools like Cytoscape [46]. The PPI network provides insights into the functional interactions and biological pathways in which these genes are involved. By identifying hub proteins and key interaction partners, researchers can gain a deeper understanding of the molecular mechanisms underlying BC, which can aid in the discovery of new therapeutic targets.

Enrichment analysis, including Gene Ontology and Kyoto Encyclopedia of Genes and Genomes pathways, is then performed to identify the biological processes, cellular components, and molecular functions associated with the selected genes, providing insights into the underlying mechanisms of BC [46]. This step involves mapping the selected genes to known biological functions and pathways to determine their roles in cancer biology. Enrichment analysis helps in elucidating the biological significance of the gene sets and identifying potential biomarkers and therapeutic targets.

Drug-gene interaction analysis is conducted to explore potential therapeutic targets, leveraging databases such as DrugBank to identify drugs that interact with the identified biomarkers [46]. This analysis is critical for translating the identified biomarkers into clinical applications. By understanding how drugs interact with the selected genes, researchers can identify existing drugs that could be repurposed for BC treatment or discover new drug candidates that specifically target the biomarkers. This step is essential for developing personalized treatment strategies and improving patient outcomes.

Metaheuristic algorithms are also valuable for hyperparameter tuning of ML and DL models, optimizing their performance in predicting BC outcomes [102]. For instance, DL models like CNNs and hybrid models (e.g., CNN + EfficientNetV2B3) have shown high accuracy in classifying BC subtypes and predicting metastasis, with metaheuristics enhancing their predictive capabilities [102,120]. Hyperparameter tuning using metaheuristics ensures that the models are fine-tuned for the best possible performance, leading to more accurate and reliable predictions.

Additionally, RF- and SVM-based models have been widely used to develop diagnostic and prognostic gene signatures from breast cancer gene-expression profiles. To improve these models, metaheuristic-based feature selection can reduce the number of genes, remove redundant features, and focus on the most informative biomarkers. For example, Yaqoob et al. combined Seagull Optimization Algorithm-based gene selection with RF classification, showing that feature reduction in high-dimensional expression data can improve classification performance while making the model more interpretable [131]. Such approaches can support patient classification and outcome prediction, although further validation is needed before clinical application.

This approach can support the identification of candidate biomarkers and may improve diagnostic modelling, subject to independent and clinical validation. By combining ML, DL, and metaheuristic algorithms, researchers can leverage the strengths of each method to develop a robust and efficient framework for biomarker detection. This hybrid intelligence framework is summarized in Fig. 11.1, and may support future personalized medicine studies if validated on independent datasets.

9. Future prospects and current limitations

Future research in the domain of BC biomarker discovery could greatly benefit from integrating advanced metaheuristic algorithms. These integrations promise to improve computational efficiency and accuracy in feature selection tasks. Additionally, there is significant potential in enhancing deep learning models with sophisticated data augmentation strategies, aiming to achieve higher classification accuracy, precision, and recall in cancer diagnosis. Furthermore, future work could focus on the integrative analysis of multiomic datasets, such as combining gene expression and DNA methylation data, to uncover comprehensive regulatory mechanisms in cancer and improve biomarker discovery. Optimization of hyperparameters in deep learning models using metaheuristic techniques also presents a promising area for research, which could significantly enhance the performance and efficiency of these models in BC detection. Using metaheuristic algorithms to optimize ensemble classifier weights is another promising direction. Lastly, the development of novel hybrid frameworks that balance exploration and exploitation in the search process, and use federated learning or privacy-preserving learning models to reduce data-sharing risks in real-world applications, could more effectively handle high-dimensional datasets.

Despite these promising directions, several current limitations must be addressed. Data quality and privacy issues are critical in clinical settings, and ensuring high-quality, privacy-compliant data remains a significant challenge. The complexity of high-dimensional gene expression data also poses difficulties, necessitating ongoing research and development to manage and analyze such data effectively. Overfitting in deep learning models, particularly when dealing with the "$n \ll p$" problem (where the number of samples is significantly smaller than the number of features), is another concern. Additionally, the application of advanced optimization techniques and deep learning models can be computationally intensive, requiring significant resources for training and implementation. There is a persistent need for large, high-quality datasets to improve the robustness and accuracy of predictive models, and the integration of multisource domain data adds to this complexity. Finally, while these techniques show promise in research settings, their generalization and applicability in real-world clinical settings require further validation and adaptation. Addressing these limitations will be crucial for translating research advancements into practical clinical applications that can significantly impact patient care and outcomes in BC treatment.

While challenges such as data quality, privacy, and computational intensity persist, hybrid intelligence frameworks present a promising solution. By combining ML, DL, and metaheuristic optimization, these frameworks can address many of these limitations, providing robust, interpretable, and efficient solutions for BC biomarker discovery.

10. Conclusion

The integration of Machine Learning (ML), Deep Learning (DL), and Metaheuristic Optimization techniques holds significant promise for advancing the discovery of biomarkers in breast cancer (BC) research. This chapter has reviewed selected recent methodologies that leverage the strengths of these computational techniques to analyze gene expression datasets, thereby enhancing the accuracy and efficiency of BC diagnosis and treatment. By employing hybrid intelligence approaches, researchers can more effectively identify critical biomarkers, optimize hyperparameters, and calculate the fitness of solutions generated by metaheuristic algorithms. These methods not only improve the precision of cancer detection but also support the development of personalized medicine, leading to better patient outcomes and more targeted therapies.

The comprehensive review presented in this chapter underscores the potential of combining ML and DL models with metaheuristic optimization to tackle the complexities inherent in BC research. Through the application of advanced algorithms such as GA, PSO, and Simulated Annealing (SA), alongside sophisticated ML and DL models like SVM, RF, and CNNs, significant strides can be made in biomarker discovery. The synergy between these techniques facilitates robust feature selection, efficient hyperparameter tuning, and accurate classification, ultimately supporting future improvements in breast cancer research and clinical translation. The findings and insights from this chapter highlight the transformative potential of hybrid intelligence in improving BC diagnosis, prognosis, and treatment, paving the way for future advancements in the field.

References

[1] World Health Organization, Breast Cancer (2026). https://www.who.int/news-room/fact-sheets/detail/breast-cancer. (Accessed 17 May 2026).

[2] A.A. Tabl, A. Alkhateeb, W. ElMaraghy, L. Rueda, A. Ngom, A machine learning approach for identifying gene biomarkers guiding the treatment of breast cancer, Front. Genet. 10 (2019), https://doi.org/10.3389/fgene.2019.00256.

[3] T.I.A. Mohamed, A.E. Ezugwu, J.V. Fonou-Dombeu, A.M. Ikotun, M. Mohammed, A bio-inspired convolution neural network architecture for automatic breast cancer detection and classification using RNA-seq gene expression data, Sci. Rep. 13 (2023) 14644, https://doi.org/10.1038/s41598-023-41731-z.

[4] A. Triantafyllou, N. Dovrolis, E. Zografos, C. Theodoropoulos, G.C. Zografos, N.V. Michalopoulos, et al., Circulating miRNA expression profiling in breast cancer molecular subtypes: Applying machine learning analysis in bioinformatics, Cancer Diagnosis Progn. 2 (2022) 739–749, https://doi.org/10.21873/cdp.10169.

[5] A. Sahu, S. Qazi, K. Raza, A. Singh, S. Verma, Machine learning-based approach for early diagnosis of breast cancer using biomarkers and gene expression profiles 1016, 2022, https://doi.org/10.1007/978-981-16-9221-5_17.

[6] M. Rakhshaninejad, M. Fathian, R. Shirkoohi, F. Barzinpour, A.H. Gandomi, Refining breast cancer biomarker discovery and drug targeting through an advanced data-driven approach, BMC Bioinf. 25 (2024), https://doi.org/10.1186/s12859-024-05657-1.

[7] H. MotieGhader, P. Tabrizi-Nezhadi, M. Deldar Abad Paskeh, B. Baradaran, A. Mokhtarzadeh, M. Hashemi, et al., Drug repositioning in non-small cell lung cancer (NSCLC) using gene co-expression and drug–gene interaction networks analysis, Sci. Rep. 12 (2022), https://doi.org/10.1038/s41598-022-13719-8.

[8] A.U. Mazlan, N.A. Sahabudin, M.A. Remli, N.S.N. Ismail, M.S. Mohamad, H.W. Nies, et al., A review on recent progress in machine learning and deep learning methods for cancer classification on gene expression data, Processes 9 (2021), https://doi.org/10.3390/pr9081466.

[9] M. Kenn, D. Cacsire Castillo-Tong, C.F. Singer, M. Cibena, H. Kölbl, W. Schreiner, Microarray normalization revisited for reproducible breast cancer biomarkers, BioMed Res. Int. 2020 (2020), https://doi.org/10.1155/2020/1363827.

[10] H. Chai, X. Zhou, Z. Zhang, J. Rao, H. Zhao, Y. Yang, Integrating multi-omics data through deep learning for accurate cancer prognosis prediction, Comput. Biol. Med. 134 (2021), https://doi.org/10.1016/j.compbiomed.2021.104481.

[11] N. Alromema, A.H. Syed, T. Khan, A hybrid machine learning approach to screen optimal predictors for the classification of primary breast tumors from gene expression microarray data, Diagnostics 13 (2023), https://doi.org/10.3390/diagnostics13040708.

[12] N.A. Abujabal, A.B. Nassif, Meta-heuristic algorithms-based feature selection for breast cancer diagnosis: A systematic review, Int. Conf. Electr. Comput. Commun. Mechatronics Eng. ICECCME (2022, 2022) 1–6, https://doi.org/10.1109/ICECCME55909.2022.9988285.

[13] B. Haznedar, M.T. Arslan, A. Kalinli, Optimizing ANFIS using simulated annealing algorithm for classification of microarray gene expression cancer data, Med. Biol. Eng. Comput. 59 (2021) 497–509, https://doi.org/10.1007/s11517-021-02331-z.

[14] I. Singh, R. Bansal, A. Gupta, A. Singh, A hybrid grey wolf-whale optimization algorithm for optimizing SVM in breast cancer diagnosis, PDGC 2020 - 2020 6th Int. Conf. Parallel, Distrib. Grid Comput. (2020) 286–290, https://doi.org/10.1109/PDGC50313.2020.9315816.

[15] E. Badr, S. Almotairi, M.A. Salam, H. Ahmed, New sequential and parallel support vector machine with grey wolf optimizer for breast cancer diagnosis, Alex. Eng. J. 61 (2022) 2520–2534, https://doi.org/10.1016/j.aej.2021.07.024.

[16] R.G. Murphy, A. Gilmore, S. Senevirathne, P.G. O'Reilly, M.L. Wilson, S. Jain, et al., Particle swarm optimization artificial intelligence technique for gene signature discovery in transcriptomic cohorts, Comput. Struct. Biotechnol. J. 20 (2022) 5547–5563, https://doi.org/10.1016/j.csbj.2022.09.033.

[17] W.M. Shaban, Insight into breast cancer detection: New hybrid feature selection method, Neural Comput. Appl. 35 (2022) 6831–6853, https://doi.org/10.1007/s00521-022-08062-y.

[18] H.M. Alshamlan, G.H. Badr, Y.A. Alohali, Genetic Bee Colony (GBC) algorithm: A new gene selection method for microarray cancer classification, Comput. Biol. Chem. 56 (2015) 49–60, https://doi.org/10.1016/j.compbiolchem.2015.03.001.

[19] A. Sharma, R. Rani, C-Hmoshssa, Gene selection for cancer classification using multi-objective meta-heuristic and machine learning methods, Comput. Methods Progr. Biomed. 178 (2019) 219–235, https://doi.org/10.1016/J.CMPB.2019.06.029.

[20] R.M. Aziz, Nature-inspired metaheuristics model for gene selection and classification of biomedical microarray data, Med. Biol. Eng. Comput. 60 (2022) 1627–1646, https://doi.org/10.1007/s11517-022-02555-7.

[21] N. Tavasoli, K. Rezaee, M. Momenzadeh, M. Sehhati, An ensemble soft weighted gene selection-based approach and cancer classification using modified metaheuristic learning, J. Comput. Des. Eng. 8 (2021) 1172–1189, https://doi.org/10.1093/jcde/qwab039.

[22] S. Thirumalaisamy, K. Thangavilou, H. Rajadurai, O. Saidani, N. Alturki, S kumar Mathivanan, et al., Breast cancer classification using synthesized deep learning model with metaheuristic optimization algorithm, Diagnostics 13 (2023), https://doi.org/10.3390/diagnostics13182925.

[23] B. Akay, D. Karaboga, R. Akay, A comprehensive survey on optimizing deep learning models by metaheuristics, Artif. Intell. Rev. 55 (2022) 829–894, https://doi.org/10.1007/s10462-021-09992-0.

[24] N.K. Mudaliar, S. Redekar, N.M. Kadam, I. Ramachandran, Machine learning-based prediction model for cancer detection, Proc. 2nd Int. Conf. Appl. Artif. Intell. Comput. ICAAIC (2023, 2023) 383–388, https://doi.org/10.1109/ICAAIC56838.2023.10140323.

[25] D. Hari Krishna, M. Anand, D. Saravanan, K. Pushpalatha, Optimization of machine learning and deep learning algorithms for diagnosis of cancer, ECS Trans. 107 (2022) 9389–9401, https://doi.org/10.1149/10701.9389ecst.

[26] S.M. Sweeney, H.K. Hamadeh, N. Abrams, S.J. Adam, S. Brenner, D.E. Connors, et al., Challenges to using big data in cancer, Cancer Res. 83 (2023) 1175–1182, https://doi.org/10.1158/0008-5472.CAN-22-1274.

[27] J. Brosch-Lenz, C. Uribe, A. Rahmim, B. Saboury, Theranostic digital twins: An indispensable prerequisite for personalized cancer care, J. Nucl. Med. 64 (2022) 501, https://doi.org/10.2967/jnumed.122.264929.

[28] V.B. Mathema, P. Sen, S. Lamichhane, M. Orešič, S. Khoomrung, Deep learning facilitates multi-data type analysis and predictive biomarker discovery in cancer precision medicine, Comput. Struct. Biotechnol. J. 21 (2023) 1372–1382, https://doi.org/10.1016/j.csbj.2023.01.043.

[29] Y. Zhang, J. Hong, Challenges of deep learning in cancers, Technol. Cancer Res. Treat. 22 (2023) 153303382311734, https://doi.org/10.1177/15330338231173495.

[30] S. Patel, J.C. Goldsack, G. Cordovano, A.S. Downing, K.K. Fields, C. Geoghegan, et al., Advancing digital health innovation in oncology: Priorities for high-value digital transformation in cancer care, J. Med. Internet Res. 25 (2023) e43404, https://doi.org/10.2196/43404.

[31] T.F.G.G. Cova, D.J. Bento, S.C.C. Nunes, Computational approaches in theranostics: Mining and predicting cancer data, Pharmaceutics 11 (2019), https://doi.org/10.3390/PHARMACEUTICS11030119.

[32] M.A. Elaziz, M.A. Elaziz, A. Dahou, L. Abualigah, L. Yu, M. Alshinwan, et al., Advanced metaheuristic optimization techniques in applications of deep neural networks: A review, Neural Comput. Appl. 33 (2021) 14079–14099, https://doi.org/10.1007/S00521-021-05960-5.

[33] P. Saranya, P. Asha, Cancer prognosis with machine learning-based modified meta-heuristics and weighted gradient boosting algorithm, Comput. Methods Biomech. Biomed. Eng. Imaging Vis. (2023) 1–17, https://doi.org/10.1080/21681163.2023.2219772.

[34] D. Devikanniga, K. Vetrivel, N. Badrinath, Review of meta-heuristic optimization based artificial neural networks and its applications, J. Phys., Conf. Ser. 1362 (2019), https://doi.org/10.1088/1742-6596/1362/1/012074.

[35] P. Ashwini, N. Suguna, N. Vadivelan, Modelling of hybrid Meta heuristic based parameter optimizers with deep convolutional neural network for mammogram cancer detection, Int. J. Recent Innov. Trends Comput. Commun. 11 (2023) 146–156, https://doi.org/10.17762/ijritcc.v11i9s.7406.

[36] P.H. Sulibhavi, R.A. Hallyal, R.K. Katti, A.E. Kabade, S.S. Thadal, S.M. Meena, et al., A study on Meta learning optimization techniques, IEEE 7th Int. Conf. Converg. Technol. I2CT (2022) 1–7, https://doi.org/10.1109/I2CT54291.2022.9824942.

[37] I. Zenbout, A. Bouramoul, S. Meshoul, M. Amrane, Efficient bioinspired feature selection and machine learning based framework using omics data and biological knowledge data bases in cancer clinical endpoint prediction, IEEE Access 11 (2023) 2674–2699, https://doi.org/10.1109/ACCESS.2023.3234294.

[38] U. Ravindran, C. Gunavathi, Cancer disease prediction using integrated smart data augmentation and capsule neural network, IEEE Access 12 (2024) 81813–81826, https://doi.org/10.1109/access.2024.3411633.

[39] Y. Itai, N. Rappoport, R. Shamir, Integration of gene expression and DNA methylation data across different experiments, Nucleic Acids Res. 51 (2023) 7762–7776, https://doi.org/10.1093/nar/gkad566.

[40] N.R. Eluri, G.R. Kancharla, S. Dara, V. Dondeti, Cancer data classification by quantum-inspired immune clone optimization-based optimal feature selection using gene expression data: Deep learning approach, Data Technol. Appl. 56 (2) (2021) 247–282, https://doi.org/10.1108/DTA-05-2020-0109.

[41] A.J. Zaylaa, S. Kourtian, Advancing breast cancer diagnosis through breast mass images, machine learning, and regression models, Sensors 24 (2024), https://doi.org/10.3390/s24072312.

[42] S. Abirami, R.B. Sri Vignesh, V. Srihariprasath, U. Mathialahan, T.S. Yaswanth, Early breast cancer prediction using machine-learning algorithms, Int. Conf. Adv. Data Eng. Intell. Comput. Syst. ADICS (2024) 1–7, https://doi.org/10.1109/ADICS58448.2024.10533612.

[43] S.K. Saini, U. Parmar, G. Chandel, Breast cancer prediction using machine learning algorithms, Int. Conf. Adv. Comput. Commun. Inf. Technol. ICAICCIT 2023 (2023) 94–99, https://doi.org/10.1109/ICAICCIT60255.2023.10465997.

[44] S. Zhou, C. Hu, S. Wei, X. Yan, Breast cancer prediction based on multiple machine learning algorithms, Technol. Cancer Res. Treat. 23 (2024), https://doi.org/10.1177/15330338241234791.

[45] D.S. Mohammed, F. Saaduldeen, M.H. Ahmed, Z.S. Hussain, Enhancing breast cancer detection with ensemble machine learning models, J. Electr. Syst. 20 (2024) 2255–2265, https://doi.org/10.52783/jes.2585.

[46] Z. Mirza, M.S. Ansari, N. Ahmad, N. Alganmi, H. Banjar, M.H. Al-Qahtani, et al., Identification of novel diagnostic and prognostic gene signature biomarkers for breast cancer using artificial intelligence and machine learning assisted transcriptomics analysis, Cancers (Basel) 15 (2023) 3237, https://doi.org/10.3390/cancers15123237.

[47] Y. Supriya, G. Chemmalar Selvi, G. Yenduri, G. Srivastava, T.R. Gadekallu, Firefly optimized federated SVM model for breast cancer prediction, Can. Conf. Electr. Comput. Eng. 2023 (2023) 130–135, https://doi.org/10.1109/CCECE58730.2023.10288828.

[48] S. Kalyanapu, A.R. Kandula, P. Madhuri, P. Ganta, H.N. Sai Sri Vattikuti, U. Darapu, Enhancing breast cancer prediction through SVM-based analysis, Annu. Int. Conf. Emerg. Res. Areas Int. Conf. Intell. Syst. AICERA/ICIS 2023 (2023) 1–6, https://doi.org/10.1109/AICERA/ICIS59538.2023.10420106.

[49] B.J. Brearley, Investigating the prediction of breast cancer diagnosis by use of support vector machines, Int. J. Healthc. Inf. Syst. Inf. 18 (2023) 1–16, https://doi.org/10.4018/ijhisi.325219.

[50] T. Zavvar, I Al Ridhawi, A. Abbas, Thermography-based early-stage breast cancer detection using SVM, Int. Conf. Intell. Data Sci. Technol. Appl. IDSTA 2023 (2023) 27–34, https://doi.org/10.1109/IDSTA58916.2023.10317862.

[51] S. Nathiya, J. Sumith, M. Varun, S. Sugany, G. Sathana, SVM-ANN optimized algorithm for the classification of breast cancer data as benign and malignant. Smart Technol. Commun. Robot, IEEE, 2022, pp. 1–7, https://doi.org/10.1109/STCR55312.2022.10009301.

[52] Y. Sun, Y. Pu, Y. Yang, R.R. Alfano, Biomarkers spectral subspace for cancer detection, J. Biomed. Opt. 17 (2012) 107005, https://doi.org/10.1117/1.JBO.17.10.107005.

[53] A.T. Azar, S.A. El-Said, Performance analysis of support vector machines classifiers in breast cancer mammography recognition, Neural Comput. Appl. 24 (2014) 1163–1177, https://doi.org/10.1007/S00521-012-1324-4.

[54] S. Aruna, S.P.R. Dr, A novel SVM based CSSFFS feature selection algorithm for detecting breast cancer, Int. J. Comput. Appl. 31 (2011) 14–20.

[55] S. Park, G. Yi, Development of gene expression-based random forest model for predicting neoadjuvant chemotherapy response in triple-negative breast cancer, Cancers 14 (2022) 881, https://doi.org/10.3390/cancers14040881.

[56] Z.-P. Liu, L. Li, Y.A. Algabri, Identifying diagnostic biomarkers of breast cancer based on gene expression data and ensemble feature selection, Curr. Bioinf. 18 (2023) 232–246, https://doi.org/10.2174/1574893618666230111153243.

[57] S.J. Sammut, M. Crispin-Ortuzar, S.F. Chin, E. Provenzano, H.A. Bardwell, W. Ma, et al., Multi-omic machine learning predictor of breast cancer therapy response, Nature 601 (2022) 623–629, https://doi.org/10.1038/s41586-021-04278-5.

[58] L. Cattelani, V. Fortino, Improved NSGA-II algorithms for multi-objective biomarker discovery, Bioinformatics 38 (Suppl) (2022) ii20–ii26, https://doi.org/10.1093/bioinformatics/btac463.

[59] N. Adnan, C. Lei, J. Ruan, Robust edge-based biomarker discovery improves prediction of breast cancer metastasis, BMC Bioinf. 21 (2020) 359, https://doi.org/10.1186/S12859-020-03692-2.

[60] M.D. Ganggayah, N.A. Taib, Y.C. Har, P. Lio, S.K. Dhillon, Predicting factors for survival of breast cancer patients using machine learning techniques, BMC Med. Inform. Decis. Mak. 19 (2019) 48, https://doi.org/10.1186/s12911-019-0801-4.

[61] J. Choi, S. Park, Y. Yoon, J. Ahn, Improved prediction of breast cancer outcome by identifying heterogeneous biomarkers, Bioinformatics 33 (2017) 3619–3626, https://doi.org/10.1093/BIOINFORMATICS/BTX487.

[62] V. Fortino, G. Scala, G. Scala, D. Greco, D. Greco, Feature set optimization in biomarker discovery from genome scale data, Bioinformatics 36 (2020) 3393–3400, https://doi.org/10.1093/BIOINFORMATICS/BTAA144.

[63] S.R. Zaim, C. Kenost, J. Berghout, W. Chiu, L. Wilson, H.H. Zhang, et al., binomialRF: Interpretable combinatoric efficiency of random forests to identify biomarker interactions, BMC Bioinf. 21 (2020) 374, https://doi.org/10.1186/S12859-020-03718-9.

[64] F. Inceoglu, F.H. Yagin, Genomic Biomarkers of Metastasis in Breast Cancer Patients: A Machine Learning Approach, J Cogn Syst, 2022, https://doi.org/10.52876/jcs.1211185.

[65] Q. Li, H. Yang, P. Wang, X. Liu, K. Lv, M. Ye, XGBoost-based and tumor-immune characterized gene signature for the prediction of metastatic status in breast cancer, J. Transl. Med. 20 (2022), https://doi.org/10.1186/s12967-022-03369-9.

[66] Q. Liu, P. Hu, A novel integrative computational framework for breast cancer radiogenomic biomarker discovery, Comput. Struct. Biotechnol. J. 20 (2022) 2484–2494, https://doi.org/10.1016/j.csbj.2022.05.031.

[67] T.R. Mahesh, V.V. Kumar, V. Muthukumaran, H.K. Shashikala, B. Swapna, S. Guluwadi, Performance analysis of XGBoost ensemble methods for survivability with the classification of breast cancer, J. Sens. 2022 (2022) 1–8, https://doi.org/10.1155/2022/4649510.

[68] W. Tang, T. Quan, X. Chen, H. Zhang, Y. Lin, R. Wu, XGboost prediction model based on 3.0T diffusion kurtosis imaging improves the diagnostic accuracy of MRI BiRADS 4 masses, Front. Oncol. 12 (2022), https://doi.org/10.3389/fonc.2022.833680.
[69] X.Y. Liew, N. Hameed, J. Clos, An investigation of XGBoost-based algorithm for breast cancer classification, Mach. Learn with Appl. 6 (2021) 100154, https://doi.org/10.1016/j.mlwa.2021.100154.
[70] K. Li, S. Yao, Z. Zhang, B. Cao, C.M. Wilson, D. Kalos, et al., Efficient gradient boosting for prognostic biomarker discovery, Bioinformatics 38 (2022) 1631–1638, https://doi.org/10.1093/bioinformatics/btab869.
[71] M. Razmjouei, H.-R. Hamidi, A parallel feature selection algorithm for detection of cancer biomarkers, Intell. Decis. Technol. 16 (2022) 441–447, https://doi.org/10.3233/idt-210227.
[72] U. Ravindran, C. Gunavathi, A survey on gene expression data analysis using deep learning methods for cancer diagnosis, Prog. Biophys. Mol. Biol. 177 (2022) 1–13, https://doi.org/10.1016/j.pbiomolbio.2022.08.004.
[73] C. Adornetto, G. Greco, A new deep learning and XAI-based algorithm for features selection in genomics, ArXivOrg 2023;abs/2303 1 (2023), https://doi.org/10.48550/arXiv.2303.16914.
[74] S. Majumder, P.V. Yogita, A. Yadav, A. Chakrabarty, Performance analysis of deep learning models for binary classification of cancer gene expression data, J. Healthc. Eng. 2022 (2022) 1–11, https://doi.org/10.1155/2022/1122536.
[75] V.K. Venkatesan, K.R.K. Murugesan, K.A. Chandrasekaran, M.T. Ramakrishna, S.B. Khan, A. Almusharraf, et al., Cancer diagnosis through contour visualization of gene expression leveraging deep learning techniques, Diagnostics 13 (22) (2023), https://doi.org/10.3390/diagnostics13223452.
[76] Y. Dong, S. Zhou, L. Xing, Y. Chen, Z. Ren, Y.-L. Dong, et al., Deep learning methods May not outperform other machine learning methods on analyzing genomic studies, Front. Genet. 13 (2022), https://doi.org/10.3389/fgene.2022.992070.
[77] C. Nettelblad, A deep learning framework for characterization of genotype data, G3 Genes, Genomes, Genet 12 (2022), https://doi.org/10.1093/g3journal/jkac020.
[78] L. Tapak, M.K. Ghasemi, S. Afshar, H. Mahjub, A.R. Soltanian, H. Khotanlou, Identification of gene profiles related to the development of oral cancer using a deep learning technique, BMC Med. Genom. 16 (2023), https://doi.org/10.1186/s12920-023-01462-6.
[79] M. Li, F. Spotswood, Deep autoencoder for interpretable tissue-adaptive deconvolution and cell-type-specific gene analysis, Nat. Commun. 13 (2022), https://doi.org/10.1038/s41467-022-34550-9.
[80] R. Hasibi, T. Michoel, A graph feature auto-encoder for the prediction of unobserved node features on biological networks, BMC Bioinf. 22 (2021), https://doi.org/10.1186/S12859-021-04447-3.
[81] H. Almarzouki, Deep-learning-based cancer profiles classification using gene expression data profile, J. Healthc. Eng. 2022 (2022) 1–13, https://doi.org/10.1155/2022/4715998.
[82] Y. Kong, T. Yu, A deep neural network model using random forest to extract feature representation for gene expression data classification, Sci. Rep. 8 (2018) 16477, https://doi.org/10.1038/S41598-018-34833-6.
[83] Y. Kong, T. Yu, A graph-embedded deep feedforward network for disease outcome classification and feature selection using gene expression data, Bioinformatics 34 (2018) 3727–3737, https://doi.org/10.1093/BIOINFORMATICS/BTY429.
[84] H. Yang, Z. Zhuang, W. Pan, A graph convolutional neural network for gene expression data analysis with multiple gene networks, Stat. Med. 40 (2021) 5547–5564, https://doi.org/10.1002/SIM.9140.
[85] K. Menden, M. Marouf, S. Oller, A. Dalmia, D.S. Magruder, K. Kloiber, et al., Deep learning–based cell composition analysis from tissue expression profiles, Sci. Adv. 6 (2020), https://doi.org/10.1126/SCIADV.ABA2619.
[86] J.D. Janizek, A.L. Spiro, S. Celik, B.W. Blue, T.-I. Lee, M. Kaeberlin, et al., PAUSE: Principled feature attribution for unsupervised gene expression analysis, Genome Biol. 24 (2023), https://doi.org/10.1186/s13059-023-02901-4.
[87] M.T. Islam, L. Xing, Deciphering the feature representation of deep neural networks for high-performance AI, IEEE Trans. Pattern Anal. Mach. Intell. 46 (8) (2024) 5273–5287, https://doi.org/10.1109/tpami.2024.3363642.
[88] S. Gupta, M.K. Gupta, M. Shabaz, A. Sharma, Deep learning techniques for cancer classification using microarray gene expression data, Front. Physiol. 13 (2022), https://doi.org/10.3389/fphys.2022.952709.
[89] S.F. Ahmed, M.S.B. Alam, M.A.A. Hassan, M.R. Rozbu, T. Ishtiak, N. Rafa, et al., Deep learning modelling techniques: Current progress, applications, advantages, and challenges, Artif. Intell. Rev. (2023) 1–97, https://doi.org/10.1007/s10462-023-10466-8.
[90] K. Deep, S. Das, An exhaustive review of the metaheuristic algorithms for search and optimization: Taxonomy, applications, and open challenges, Artif. Intell. Rev. (2023) 1–71, https://doi.org/10.1007/s10462-023-10470-y.
[91] S. Kaur, Y. Kumar, A. Koul, S.K. Kamboj, A systematic review on metaheuristic optimization techniques for feature selections in disease diagnosis: Open issues and challenges, Arch. Comput. Methods Eng. 30 (2022) 1863–1895, https://doi.org/10.1007/s11831-022-09853-1.
[92] T. Sadhu, S. Chowdhury, S. Mondal, J. Roy, J. Chakrabarty, S.K. Lahiri, A comparative study of metaheuristics algorithms based on their performance of complex benchmark problems, Decis Mak. Appl. Manag. Eng. 6 (2023) 341–364, https://doi.org/10.31181/dmame0306102022r.
[93] D. Nazarpour, A novel metaheuristic algorithm inspired by COVID 19 for real-parameter optimization, Neural Comput. Appl. 35 (14) (2023) 10147–10196, https://doi.org/10.1007/s00521-023-08229-1.
[94] A. Momenikorbekandi, M.F. Abbod, A novel metaheuristic hybrid parthenogenetic algorithm for job shop scheduling problems: Applying an optimization model, IEEE Access 11 (2023) 56027–56045, https://doi.org/10.1109/ACCESS.2023.3278372.
[95] R.P. Parouha, P. Verma, State-of-the-Art reviews of meta-heuristic algorithms with their novel proposal for unconstrained optimization and applications, Arch. Comput. Methods Eng. 28 (2021) 4049–4115, https://doi.org/10.1007/S11831-021-09532-7.

[96] M. Rakhshaninejad, M. Fathian, R. Shirkoohi, F. Barzinpour, A.H. Gandomi, P3DE: A novel integration of deep ensemble learning and parameter-less optimization for superior breast cancer biomarker discovery, Neural Comput. Appl. 38 (5) (2026) 101, https://doi.org/10.1007/s00521-026-11896-5.

[97] M. Rakhshaninejad, M. Fathian, N. Yazdanjue, A.H. Gandomi, F. Barzinpour, Breast cancer biomarker discovery using an enhanced quantum-based avian navigation optimizer and ensemble learning model, IEEE Trans. Comput. Biol. Bioinform. (2026) 1–13, https://doi.org/10.1109/TCBBIO.2026.3692410.

[98] A.A. Tahmouresi, E. Rashedi, M. Yaghoobi, M. Rezaei, Gene selection using pyramid gravitational search algorithm, PLoS One 17 (2022) e0265351, https://doi.org/10.1371/journal.pone.0265351.

[99] A. Thalor, H. Kumar Joon, G. Singh, S. Roy, D. Gupta, Machine learning assisted analysis of breast cancer gene expression profiles reveals novel potential prognostic biomarkers for triple-negative breast cancer, Comput. Struct. Biotechnol. J. 20 (2022) 1618–1631, https://doi.org/10.1016/j.csbj.2022.03.019.

[100] J. Shen, D. Yan, L. Bai, R. Geng, X. Zhao, H. Li, Y. Dong, J. Cao, Z. Tang, S.B. Liu, An 11-gene signature based on treatment responsiveness predicts radiation therapy survival benefit among breast cancer patients, Front. Oncol. 11 (2022) 816053, https://doi.org/10.3389/fonc.2021.816053.

[101] A.M. Nassef, M.A. Abdelkareem, H.M. Maghrabie, A. Baroutaji, Review of metaheuristic optimization algorithms for power systems problems, Sustainability 15 (2023) 9434, https://doi.org/10.3390/su15129434.

[102] J. Kim, M. Lee, J. Seok, Deep learning model with L1 penalty for predicting breast cancer metastasis using gene expression data, Mach. Learn. Sci. Technol. 4 (2023) 25026, https://doi.org/10.1088/2632-2153/acd987.

[103] R. Rouzier, P. Wagner, P. Morandi, L. Pusztai, Gene expression profiling of primary breast cancer, Curr. Oncol. Rep. 7 (2005) 38–44, https://doi.org/10.1007/S11912-005-0024-Y.

[104] R.M. Hallett, A. Dvorkin, C.M. Gabardo, J.A. Hassell, An algorithm to discover gene signatures with predictive potential, J. Exp. Clin. Cancer Res. 29 (2010) 120, https://doi.org/10.1186/1756-9966-29-120.

[105] X. Liu, N. Wang, A novel gray wolf optimizer with RNA crossover operation for tackling the non-parametric modeling problem of FCC process, Knowl. Base Syst. 216 (2021), https://doi.org/10.1016/J.KNOSYS.2021.106751.

[106] A.A. Muazu, A.S. Hashim, A. Sarlan, Review of nature inspired metaheuristic algorithm selection for combinatorial t-Way testing, IEEE Access 10 (2022) 27404–27431, https://doi.org/10.1109/ACCESS.2022.3157400.

[107] L. Meenachi, S. Ramakrishnan, Metaheuristic search based feature selection methods for classification of cancer, Pattern Recogn. 119 (2021), https://doi.org/10.1016/J.PATCOG.2021.108079.

[108] S. Punitha, T. Stephan, A.H. Gandomi, A novel breast cancer diagnosis scheme with intelligent feature and parameter selections, Comput. Methods Progr. Biomed. 214 (2022) 106432, https://doi.org/10.1016/j.cmpb.2021.106432.

[109] I. Boussaïd, J. Lepagnot, P. Siarry, A survey on optimization metaheuristics, Inf. Sci. 237 (2013) 82–117, https://doi.org/10.1016/J.INS.2013.02.041.

[110] S. Osama, A.A. Ali, A.A. Ali, Gene selection based on recursive spider wasp optimizer guided by marine predators algorithm, Neural Comput. Appl. 36 (28) (2024) 17327–17344, https://doi.org/10.1007/s00521-024-09965-8.

[111] U. Uzma, Z. Halim, An ensemble filter-based heuristic approach for cancerous gene expression classification, Knowl. Base Syst. 234 (2021), https://doi.org/10.1016/J.KNOSYS.2021.107560.

[112] A. Lameesa, M. Hoque, M.S.B. Alam, S.F. Ahmed, A.H. Gandomi, Role of metaheuristic algorithms in healthcare: A comprehensive investigation across clinical diagnosis, medical imaging, operations management, and public health, J. Comput. Des. Eng. 11 (2024) 223–247, https://doi.org/10.1093/jcde/qwae046.

[113] A. Bahrami, M. Rakhshaninejad, R. Ghousi, A. Atashi, Enhancing machine learning performance in cardiac surgery ICU: Hyperparameter optimization with metaheuristic algorithm, PLoS One 20 (2) (2025) e0311250, https://doi.org/10.1371/journal.pone.0311250.

[114] A. Gheysarbeigi, M. Rakhshaninejad, M. Fathian, F. Barzinpour, An ensemble-based auto insurance fraud detection using bqana hyperparameter tuning, IEEE Access 13 (2025) 42997–43012, https://doi.org/10.1109/ACCESS.2025.3548529.

[115] Z. Li, A. Napolitano, M. Fedele, X. Gao, F. Napolitano, AI identifies potent inducers of breast cancer stem cell differentiation based on adversarial learning from gene expression data, Briefings Bioinf. 25 (2024), https://doi.org/10.1093/bib/bbae207.

[116] M.M. Rahaman, E.K.A. Millar, E. Meijering, Breast cancer histopathology image-based gene expression prediction using spatial transcriptomics data and deep learning, Sci. Rep. 13 (2023), https://doi.org/10.1038/s41598-023-40219-0.

[117] T. Takeshita, H. Iwase, R. Wu, D.N. Ziazadeh, L. Yan, K. Takabe, Development of a machine learning-based prognostic model for hormone receptor-positive breast cancer using nine-gene expression signature, World J. Oncol. 14 (5) (2023) 406–422, https://doi.org/10.14740/wjon1700.

[118] F.M. Howard, J.M. Dolezal, S. Kochanny, G. Khramtsova, J. Vickery, A. Srisuwananukorn, et al., Integration of clinical features and deep learning on pathology for the prediction of breast cancer recurrence assays and risk of recurrence, npj Breast Cancer 9 (2023), https://doi.org/10.1038/s41523-023-00530-5.

[119] R.K. Mondol, E.K.A. Millar, P. Graham, L. Browne, A. Sowmya, E. Meijering, hist2RNA: An efficient deep learning architecture to predict gene expression from breast cancer histopathology images, Cancers (Basel) 15 (2023) 2569, https://doi.org/10.3390/cancers15092569.

[120] S. Zarif, H. Abdulkader, I. Elaraby, A. Alharbi, W.S. Elkilani, P. Pławiak, Using hybrid pre-trained models for breast cancer detection, PLoS One 19 (2024), https://doi.org/10.1371/journal.pone.0296912.

[121] Y. Wang, M.A. Ali, J. Vallon-Christersson, K. Humphreys, J. Hartman, M. Rantalainen, Transcriptional intra-tumour heterogeneity predicted by deep learning in routine breast histopathology slides provides independent prognostic information, Eur. J. Cancer (2023) 112953, https://doi.org/10.1016/j.ejca.2023.112953.

[122] P. Stephan, T. Stephan, R. Kannan, A. Abraham, A hybrid artificial bee colony with whale optimization algorithm for improved breast cancer diagnosis, Neural Comput. Appl. 33 (2021) 13667–13691, https://doi.org/10.1007/S00521-021-05997-6.

[123] L.K. Singh, M. Khanna, R. Singh, Artificial intelligence based medical decision support system for early and accurate breast cancer prediction, Adv. Eng. Software 175 (2023) 103338, https://doi.org/10.1016/j.advengsoft.2022.103338.

[124] W. Liu, Y. Chi, K. Yu, W. Xie, A two-stage hybrid biomarker selection method based on ensemble filter and binary differential evolution incorporating binary African vultures optimization, BMC Bioinf. 24 (2023), https://doi.org/10.1186/s12859-023-05247-7.

[125] H. AlMazrua, H. AlShamlan, A new algorithm for cancer biomarker gene detection using harris Hawks optimization, Sensors 22 (2022), https://doi.org/10.3390/s22197273.

[126] S. Sarkar, K. Mali, Breast cancer subtypes classification with hybrid machine learning model, Methods Inf. Med. 61 (2021) 68–83, https://doi.org/10.1055/s-0042-1751043.

[127] S. Dashti, M. Taheri, S. Ghafouri-Fard, An in-silico method leads to recognition of hub genes and crucial pathways in survival of patients with breast cancer, Sci. Rep. 10 (2020), https://doi.org/10.1038/S41598-020-76024-2.

[128] B. Haibe-Kains, D.W. Cescon, Gene expression analyses in breast cancer: Sample matters, JNCI Cancer Spectr. 2 (2018), https://doi.org/10.1093/JNCICS/PKY019.

[129] R.A. Baasiri, S.R. Glasser, D. Steffen, D.A. Wheeler, The breast cancer gene database: A collaborative information resource, Oncogene 18 (1999) 7958–7965, https://doi.org/10.1038/SJ.ONC.1203335.

[130] C. Zhang, W. Zhai, Y. Ma, M. Wu, Q. Cai, J. Huang, et al., Integrating machine learning algorithms and multiple immunohistochemistry validation to unveil novel diagnostic markers based on costimulatory molecules for predicting immune microenvironment status in triple-negative breast cancer, Front. Immunol. 15 (2024), https://doi.org/10.3389/fimmu.2024.1424259.

[131] A. Yaqoob, N.K. Verma, M.A. Mir, G.G. Tejani, N.H.B. Eisa, H. Mamoun Hussien Osman, M.A. Shah, SGA-Driven feature selection and random forest classification for enhanced breast cancer diagnosis: A comparative study, Sci. Rep. 15 (2025) 10944, https://doi.org/10.1038/s41598-025-95786-1.

Chapter 12

A bibliometric analysis of adversarial attacks and countermeasures in AI/ML cybersecurity

Navid Yazdanjue[1], Juuso Itkonen[2,3], Mikko S. Niemelä[3] and Amir H. Gandomi[1,4]

[1]*Data Science Institute, Faculty of Engineering & Information Technology, University of Technology Sydney, Ultimo, NSW, Australia;* [2]*Macquarie University, Sydney, NSW, Australia;* [3]*Cyber Intelligence House (CIH), Singapore, Singapore;* [4]*University Research and Innovation Center (EKIK), Obuda University, Budapest, Hungary*

1. Introduction

In the fast-evolving landscape of artificial intelligence (AI) and machine learning (ML), the increasing sophistication of these technologies has accelerated their use across many fields. ML refers to the capability of systems to learn from data, recognize patterns, and make decisions with minimal human intervention, which has led to its deployment in various critical applications. For example, ML models are utilized to support decision-making in healthcare [1], improve fraud detection [2], enhance intrusion detection systems [3], and ensure the safety and efficiency of autonomous vehicles [4]. These developments have not only enhanced the capabilities of these systems but have also improved their accuracy, sometimes surpassing human performance in tasks such as image classification and natural language processing.

However, the ubiquity and critical reliance on ML technologies have made them prime targets for adversarial attacks, where malicious actors seek to manipulate or deceive these systems for harmful intents. These adversarial attacks include but are not limited to training data poisoning, which can decrease the accuracy of the model or lead to error-specific attacks; the insertion of well-designed backdoors in training data, which can trigger catastrophic consequences; evasion through carefully crafted adversarial samples that mislead models during testing; and more sophisticated threats such as model inversion, model extraction, and membership inference attacks, which can expose sensitive information, infer training-set membership, or reveal aspects of model behaviour. Recent high-profile attacks further illustrate the practical impact of these vulnerabilities. For example, Sadasivan et al. introduced the beam search-based adversarial attack (BEAST), which targeted large language models like LLaMA-2 [5]. They found that BEAST successfully breached the security of Vicuna-7B-v1.5, a chat assistant developed by fine-tuning LLaMA-2 with user-generated dialogs, achieving a success rate of 89% in less than a minute. Also, Zou et al. demonstrated the feasibility of adversarial attacks by successfully breaching popular AI platforms, such as ChatGPT, Claude, and Bard, achieving an inference accuracy of 50% on GPT-4 and 86.6% on GPT-3.5 [6]. Moreover, Gong X. et al. achieved a 97% success rate in breaching the security of the commercial Alibaba API [7].

These adversarial attacks underscore the critical need for comprehensive security-by-design solutions that enhance the ML systems' resilience throughout the development process rather than solely fortifying individual models. Hence, Adversarial Machine Learning (AML) is an emerging and rapidly growing field at the intersection of cybersecurity and AI, concerned primarily with the ML systems' security against such adversarial threats.

Despite the growing research efforts directed toward understanding and mitigating these adversarial threats in ML, there remains a need for a bibliometric analysis focused specifically on adversarial attacks and countermeasures in AI/ML cybersecurity. Such an analysis is crucial to understanding this domain's historical development, key contributions, and prevailing challenges. This paper seeks to address this gap by conducting a bibliometric study of the literature on adversarial attacks and countermeasures within AI/ML deployments in the cybersecurity realm. This research is of

Advanced Intelligence Methods for Data Science and Optimization. https://doi.org/10.1016/B978-0-443-28940-8.00007-5

significant importance, as it assists both academics and industry experts in grasping the latest research trends and developments, thereby facilitating the creation of robust and secure ML models.

In this regard, we initially retrieved publications spanning from 2015 to 2024 via the open-source Elsevier Developer Portal, utilizing the Scopus API (Elsevier 2024). After applying the inclusion and exclusion criteria, 141 records were retained for analysis. Subsequently, we preprocessed and visualized the authors' keywords with network visualization tools. We then performed an initial analysis using statistical methods to identify the most prominent keywords or themes and tracked their growth within the AI/ML security domain. Finally, our results enabled us to provide a discussion of the most common attacks and defensive measures since the early days of this research area.

The structure of this paper is organized as follows. Section 2 provides an in-depth review of the existing literature on adversarial attacks and their countermeasures in the context of AI/ML. Section 3 outlines the methods used in this study, detailing the collection and preprocessing of relevant literature corpora. In Section 4, the statistical measures are used to determine the most significant keywords or themes in this field and also indicate their growth and trends. Section 5 provides a detailed discussion of the most common attacks and their defensive mechanisms in the field of AI/ML security. Also, in Section 6, some future research directions based on the conducted analysis will be provided. Section 7 concludes the study by summarizing the findings.

2. Literature review

Over the past decade, ML-based methods have become increasingly important in cybersecurity. These algorithms extend traditional cybersecurity procedures to detect and respond to threats. Nevertheless, despite the continued success, there are considerable obstacles to maintaining the trustworthiness of ML systems. Some malicious actors in cyberspace seek to exploit ML vulnerabilities by devising various adversarial attacks targeting ML-based models employed in cybersecurity. In contrast, a growing amount of research has examined defense mechanisms and responses against the mentioned adversarial attacks in recent years. In the following paragraphs, several research studies and state-of-the-art surveys on ML adversarial attacks and associated defense mechanisms will be reviewed and elaborated upon.

In 2014, Mozaffari-Kermani et al. investigated the vulnerability of healthcare ML systems to poisoning attacks [8]. The authors developed a systematic, algorithm-independent approach to generate malicious input data that could be added to training datasets. These attacks aimed to cause either a targeted error (e.g., increasing classification into a specific category) or an arbitrary error in the algorithm's output. The attacks were effective across 6 ML models on five healthcare datasets. Furthermore, the authors proposed countermeasures based on monitoring accuracy metrics to detect deviations caused by poisoning attacks. Afterward, in 2018, Liu et al. conducted a review of existing ML security threats and presented a structured survey, analyzing them from two perspectives: the training phase and the testing or inference phase [9]. The authors then categorized current defensive techniques into four groups, comprising security assessment mechanisms, countermeasures in the training phase, countermeasures in the testing/inferring phase, and data privacy. In the same year, Guan et al. explored the use of machine learning in cybersecurity, examined security threats and defenses in ML-based systems, and addressed the security challenges associated with emerging mobile devices [10]. Specifically, the authors introduced malware detection, intrusion detection, phishing detection, advanced persistent threat (APT) concerns, and biometrical recognition for the application of machine learning in cybersecurity. After that, the potential security threats against an ML system and defensive techniques from the testing phase, training phase, and data privacy were examined. Moreover, Goodfellow et al. stated that machine learning has traditionally been developed based on the assumption that the environment is benign during training and testing the model [11]. While this assumption is useful for designing efficient algorithms, it implicitly precludes the possibility that an adversary could alter the distribution during training or testing. For the numerous attacks that have been proven, few robust responses exist in the context of adversarial test inputs. In order to answer the question of what can be done to defend models from adversarial samples, they also examined several existing defenses, including model training, input validation, and architecture modifications.

In another attempt, Biggio et al. presented a comprehensive review of research on the security of machine learning, pattern recognition, and deep neural networks, aiming to provide a detailed historical perspective along with practical guidelines for evaluating and improving their defenses against adversarial attacks [12]. Additionally, they categorized the defense techniques as reactive and proactive, with reactive defenses including timely detection of attacks, frequent retraining, and decision verification, and proactive defenses including secure/robust learning, attack detection, information hiding and randomization, and detection of probing attacks. Afterward, in 2019, Yuan et al. reviewed recent discoveries regarding adversarial samples in deep neural networks and examined existing strategies for producing adversarial samples [13]. They also provided a taxonomy of defenses with the reactive defense tactics consisting of adversarial detecting, input reconstruction, and network verification, whereas proactive defense strategies consisted of network distillation, adversarial (re)training, and classifier robustifying. Moreover, Pitropakis et al. developed a taxonomy and conducted a survey of attacks targeting machine learning systems. They categorized these attacks into poisoning and evasion types, recognizing the potential for malicious modification of both training and test data [14]. The authors aimed to organize existing knowledge in AML to identify areas where researchers from different disciplines could make contributions.

The following year, in 2020, Shaukat et al. presented an overview of the challenges that ML techniques face in the cybersecurity field by providing literature on ML models in intrusion detection, spam detection, and malware detection on computer networks and mobile networks over the past decade [15]. Therefore, the authors provided a brief overview of each ML method, the commonly used security datasets, essential ML tools, and the evaluation metrics required for assessing classification models. Finally, they discussed adversarial attacks and their respective defense mechanisms for employing the ML approaches mentioned in the cybersecurity field. In addition, Xi reviewed research on AML with an emphasis on cybersecurity and computer vision [16]. The author first described three primary categories of machine learning technology attacks (i.e., poisoning attacks, evasion attacks, and privacy attacks). Then, she attempted to present the related defense strategies with the weaknesses and restrictions of the existing ones. Simultaneously, Xue et al. studied the security challenges of machine learning, concentrating on existing attacks on ML systems, related defenses, and evaluation methodologies for security [17]. This research examined all areas of ML security, from the training phase to the testing phase, instead of focusing on a single type of attack. Initially, the ML model's behavior in adversarial settings was introduced, followed by an analysis of the vulnerabilities that make machine learning susceptible to attacks. The difficulties associated with ML security were then categorized into five groups, including training set poisoning, backdoors in the training set, adversarial example attacks, model theft, and recovery of sensitive training data.

In 2021, Hu et al. reviewed the challenges and recent advancements in AI security to create a comprehensive framework for addressing AI security issues [18]. The lifecycle of an AI-based system is used as a framework for identifying security threats at each stage, followed by a thorough review of corresponding solutions. The presented framework proposed a variety of protective methods to combat security concerns in the data collecting (detection and filtering, data provenance and authentication, standardized management), data preprocessing (image reconstruction, quality monitoring, randomization), training (Reject On Negative Impact (RONI)), robust training, inference (modified networks or training process or input data, model enhancement, additional network, validation network), and integration (homomorphic encryption, differential privacy, model watermarking, fuzzy test, learning fair representations, and bias diagnostic) phases of the AI lifecycle. In addition, Anthi et al. studied how adversarial learning might target supervised learning systems by producing adversarial samples with the Jacobian-based Saliency Map attack and analyzing the Random Forest (RF) and J48 classification behaviors [19]. In addition, they examined how such samples can enhance the robustness of classification algorithms employing an adversarial training defense mechanism. Furthermore, Alazab et al. demonstrated how Federated Learning (FL) might improve cybersecurity and prevent real-time cyber-attacks [20]. The authors presented an overview of various FL models currently under development for authentication, privacy, trust management, and threat detection. Additionally, they discussed several recently deployed real-time use cases and demonstrated how FL is applied to safeguard data privacy and improve system performance. Finally, they outlined a number of adversarial attacks on FL as well as current defense mechanisms designed to counteract the problems. Zhou et al. also conducted a literature review on adversarial attacks in deep learning [21]. The authors also proposed a framework for understanding adversarial attacks and their defense mechanisms in a systematic manner. In a different study, Kuppa et al. carried out a detailed security analysis of explainable artificial intelligence (XAI) methods that reveal counterfactual explanations [22]. They designed four black-box attacks using XAI methods to compromise underlying classifiers' confidentiality and privacy properties. Also, the defense methods (i.e., modified training/input, modifying the network, and network add-ons) were discussed and compared in terms of their advantages and disadvantages.

A year later, Khamaiseh et al. reviewed the most current adversarial attacks on deep learning methods by analyzing and explaining the functioning of these attacks [23]. They emphasized the mathematical concepts and terminology of adversarial attacks. In addition, they evaluated the efficiency of the most recent defense mechanisms and countermeasures (i.e., modifications to the artificial neural networks (ANN), modifications to the training set, additions to the ANN model, and defense against poisoning attacks) in protecting deep neural networks from adversarial attacks. Moreover, Pawlicki et al. examined the main issues posed by the deployment of AI/ML in the form of an ANN in the cybersecurity field, particularly in intrusion detection systems [24]. In this regard, the authors disclosed the details of using ANNs in intrusion detection systems to examine the challenges, such as security, explainability, and societal issues, that must be resolved. In addition, they categorized and addressed the new defensive techniques against adversarial attacks on ANN (i.e., gradient masking, defensive distillation, input reconstruction, and detectors) separately.

In contrast to several researchers who studied the adversarial attack vulnerability of deep learning-based intrusion detection systems, Jmila et al. investigated the adversarial attack vulnerability of shallow classifiers, which are still extensively employed in ML-based intrusion detection systems because of their maturity and ease of implementation [25]. The authors evaluated the robustness of seven shallow ML-based intrusion detection systems, including Adaboost, Bagging, Gradient Boosting (GB), Logical Regression (LR), Decision Tree (DT), RF, Support Vector Classifier (SVC), and a deep learning network, against several widely used adversarial attacks. Additionally, they utilized a Gaussian data augmentation defense method and assessed its effectiveness in improving the robustness of the classifier. The acquired results revealed that different attacks impact classifiers to varying degrees, with a classifier's robustness depending on the type of attack. Furthermore, the findings highlighted the need to balance performance and robustness based on the specific network intrusion detection scenario. Similarly, Wazid et al. reviewed papers related to the two distinct concepts of combining cybersecurity and ML (i.e., "ML in cybersecurity," in which ML methods are used to provide cybersecurity, and "cybersecurity in ML," in which cybersecurity mechanisms are used to provide secure ML algorithms) [26]. They highlighted the benefits, concerns, and challenges of combining cybersecurity and ML, as well as the cybersecurity mechanisms (encryption techniques, signature generation and verification techniques, and hashing mechanisms) used to secure ML against cyber attacks. In another attempt, Mehta et al. analyzed the influence of cybersecurity on machine learning, the adversarial attacks that can be encountered in an ML-based system, and their respective defense mechanisms [27]. The authors present a comprehensive review of the use of machine learning in cybersecurity, as well as defensive approaches (i.e., Defensive Distillation, Adversarial Training, Data Randomization, and Detector Network) in machine learning-based models. Furthermore, in a different study, Goldblum et al. discussed and systematically categorized a vast diversity of dataset vulnerabilities and exploits, machine learning-based ways for protecting against these threats, and a variety of outstanding issues in this domain [28]. The following categories and methods were included in a taxonomy of defenses against training-only and backdoor attacks. Their taxonomy includes identifying poisoned data (outlier in input space, latent space signature, and predictions signatures), identifying poisoned models (trigger reconstruction and trigger-agnostic detection), repairing poisoned models after training (randomized smoothing, majority vote mechanisms, differential privacy, and input preprocessing), defenses for FL (robust federated aggregation, robust federated training, and posttraining defenses).

A year later, and in a recent study, Rodrguez-Barroso et al. reviewed the threats posed by FL and their respective countermeasures [29]. They provided a taxonomy of adversarial attacks and defense methods that provide a broad picture of the vulnerability of FL in terms of its server, client, and communication channel components, as well as the means to overcome it. Moreover, Lahe and Singh conducted a survey analyzing various security attacks on ML systems [30]. They categorized these attacks based on their position within the ML pipeline, examining threats at every stage, from training to testing. A year later, in 2024, Paracha et al. investigated the security and privacy threats facing ML systems [31]. They analyzed how adversaries exploit publicly available ML models through feature engineering, model architecture understanding, and targeted system knowledge to develop adversarial attacks. The authors found that successful attacks can trigger a cascade effect, with one attack leading to others, such as poisoning attacks resulting in membership inference and backdoor attacks. They also reviewed the existing mitigation techniques, such as data sanitization, adversarial training, and differential privacy. In the same year, Bajaj and Vishwakarma conducted a comprehensive survey of adversarial attacks against ML models used in computer vision applications [32]. They categorized these attacks into several types, including data poisoning during training, test-time evasion attacks using adversarial images, and oracle attacks. The authors focused on the potent threat of test-time evasion, explaining how adversarial images are generated and discussing various attack algorithms. They also explored the transferability of adversarial examples and provided insights into building more robust models against these attacks. The survey highlights areas requiring further research and identifies limitations in existing methods. In a different study in 2024, Paya et al. introduced Apollon, a novel defense system designed to defend intrusion detection systems against AML attacks [33]. Apollon utilizes multiple classifiers and a multi-armed bandit algorithm with Thompson sampling to dynamically select the most effective classifier for each input, blocking attackers' ability to learn and exploit the intrusion detection system behavior. In another recent study, Merkle et al. investigated the application of game theory in AML [34]. They developed a framework that allows for any number of actions for both the attacker and defender, and analytically determined equilibrium strategies and conditions for mixed strategies when considering two arbitrary actions. The authors modeled adversaries as White Box, Gray Box, and Black Box entities and conducted extensive experiments across various architectures, training procedures, and attacks. These experiments produced data on accuracy, robustness, and computational costs. Using algorithmic game theory, they analyzed the obtained data and revealed insights, such as the effectiveness of previously disregarded "cheap" attacks like universal adversarial perturbations and transfer attacks with minimal optimization steps.

3. Research methodology

This study employs a bibliometric analysis to investigate research on adversarial attacks and countermeasures in AI/ML, following the process outlined in Fig. 12.1. We collected relevant literature from the Scopus database using selected keywords to ensure broad coverage. Scopus was chosen for this study due to its extensive coverage of peer-reviewed journal articles and conference proceedings, particularly in fields relevant to this research, such as computer science and engineering. While other databases, such as Web of Science (WoS), also provide valuable resources, Scopus offers a larger collection of journals and broader interdisciplinary coverage [35], making it well-suited for capturing the diverse research landscape on adversarial attacks. The collected data were preprocessed by removing duplicates, standardizing author names and keywords, and filtering out incomplete or non-English entries. We utilized VOSviewer to analyze author keywords, uncovering key themes and patterns within the research landscape. Statistical analyses were conducted to examine research growth over time and validate the significance of emerging trends. The insights gained from these steps were synthesized to identify current research gaps and suggest future research directions. The following subsections describe each step.

3.1 Data collection and pre-processing

As previously mentioned, the dataset for this study consists of author keywords from papers focused on AI/ML adversarial attacks and countermeasures. These papers were collected through the Scopus API, accessed via the Elsevier Developer Portal (Elsevier, 2024). The Scopus API enabled advanced filtering and retrieval of bibliometric data by providing access to essential metadata, such as article titles, journal names, publication years, author affiliations, authors' keywords, citation counts, and references.

To gather relevant studies, a structured search was conducted in the Elsevier Scopus database using the following Boolean query: TITLE-ABS-KEY ("Machine Learning Security and Privacy" OR "Adversarial Machine Learning" OR "Machine Learning Attacks" OR "Machine Learning Adversarial Attacks" OR "Machine Learning Attacks and Defenses" OR "Machine Learning Security Threats and Countermeasures"). The search was performed on June 2024 and was limited to publications indexed between 2015 and 2024. The search was applied to the title, abstract, and keyword fields of documents. Only English-language publications were considered. In addition, the document types were restricted to journal articles, conference papers, and review papers to ensure the inclusion of peer-reviewed and high-quality studies

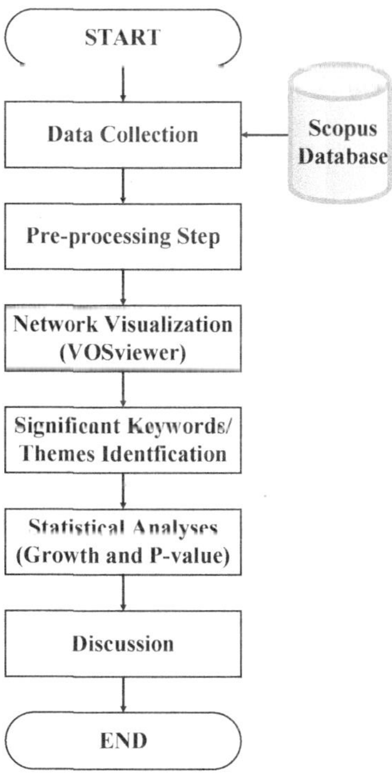

FIGURE 12.1 Research methodology.

relevant to AI/ML security and privacy. The API allowed us to refine the search by limiting results to peer-reviewed journal articles and conference papers published in English, improving the consistency of the retrieved dataset.

After retrieving the initial dataset, several preprocessing steps were applied to enhance the dataset's quality and consistency. Duplicate keywords were removed to reduce noise, and stemming and lemmatization were performed to group variations of the same word and capture their core meaning. Special characters were eliminated to improve the dataset's readability. For papers missing author-supplied keywords, we substituted indexed keywords provided by the Scopus API to ensure completeness. Additionally, Python scripts were developed to correct misspelled keywords. These steps improved the consistency of the dataset before analysis.

The final dataset consisted of 141 articles published between 2015 and 2024. To observe how research interest evolved, the data were divided into five 2-year intervals: 2015–16, 2017–18, 2019–20, 2021–22, and 2023–24. Fig. 12.2 illustrates the distribution of publications across these intervals, showing a steady growth in research activity. The trend line added to the chart, with an R-squared value of 0.8879, suggests that approximately 89% of the variability in publication numbers can be explained by the trend across these periods. The fitted trend line indicates a general increase in publications across the five subperiods. However, despite the relatively high R-squared value, the observed trend should be interpreted with caution due to the limited number of aggregated observations. However, the remaining 11% of variability, not explained by the trend line, could be due to other factors such as shifts in the research environment, variations in funding availability, or other external factors.

These articles were published in various journals and conference proceedings. The top-20 ranked publication venues that featured a considerable number of these articles are shown visually in Fig. 12.3.

Additionally, Fig. 12.4 displays a visual breakdown of article contributions by country, including countries with at least four published articles. Full counting was adopted, whereby each collaborating country received one full publication count per article. The leading contributors include the United States of America (USA), China, Italy, the United Kingdom (UK), India, and Germany. The USA is at the forefront, accounting for 25% of the articles reviewed in this study. Following closely are China with 18%, Italy and the UK each with 7%, India with 6%, and Germany with 5% of the total articles published.

Regarding the data preprocessing phase, it should be noted that several steps were undertaken to enhance the quality and clarity of the keywords within the dataset, making them appropriate for subsequent analysis. These preprocessing steps include:

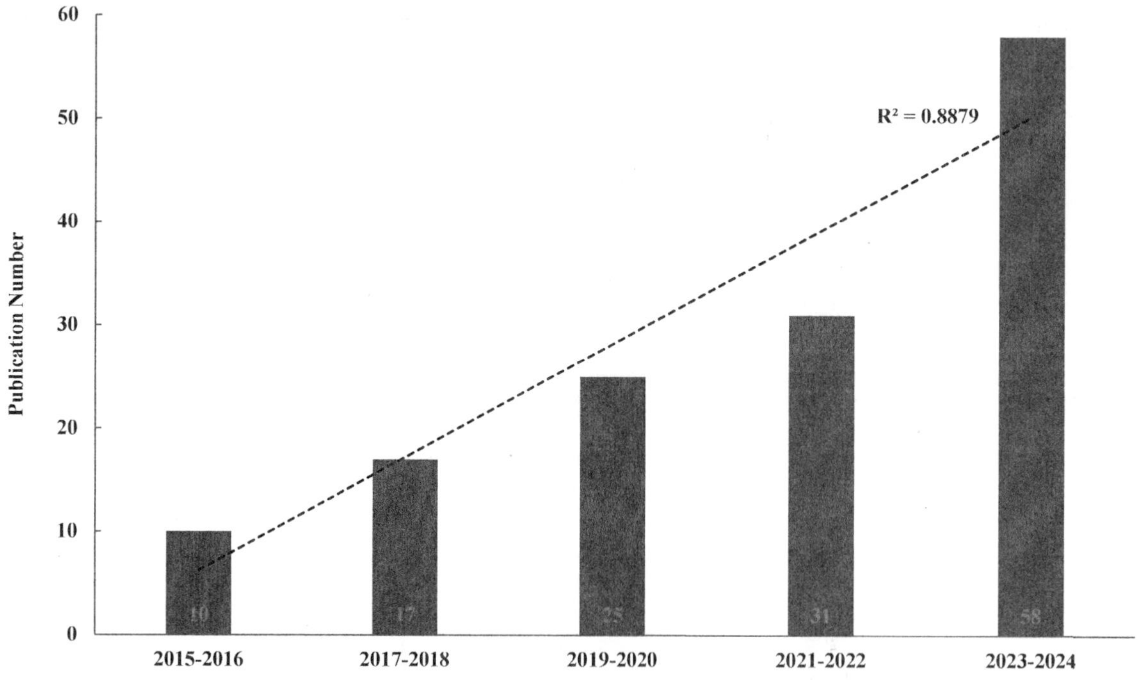

FIGURE 12.2 Number of published articles in each subperiod and its trendline.

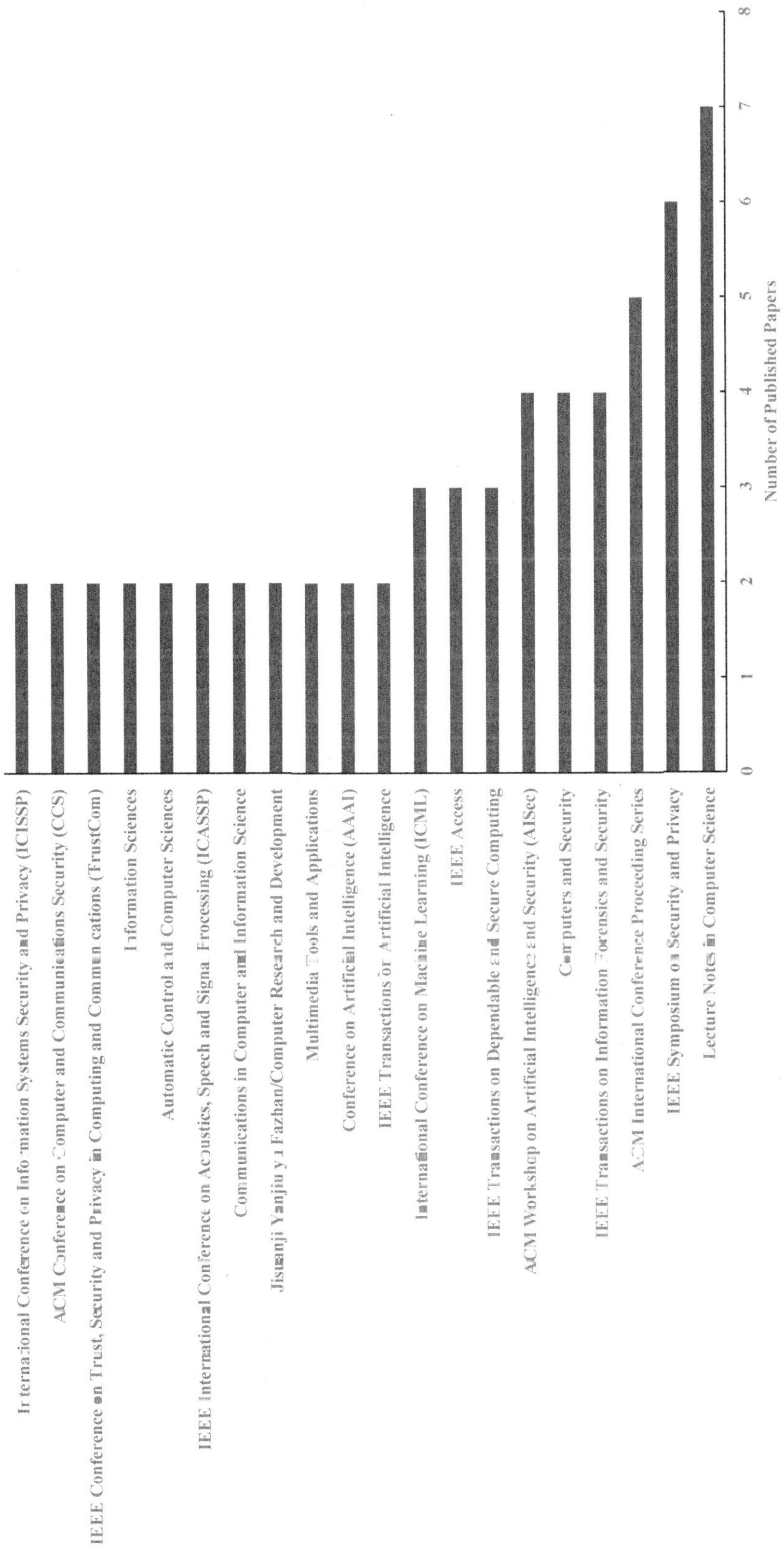

FIGURE 12.5 Top-20 ranked publication venues for the studied field.

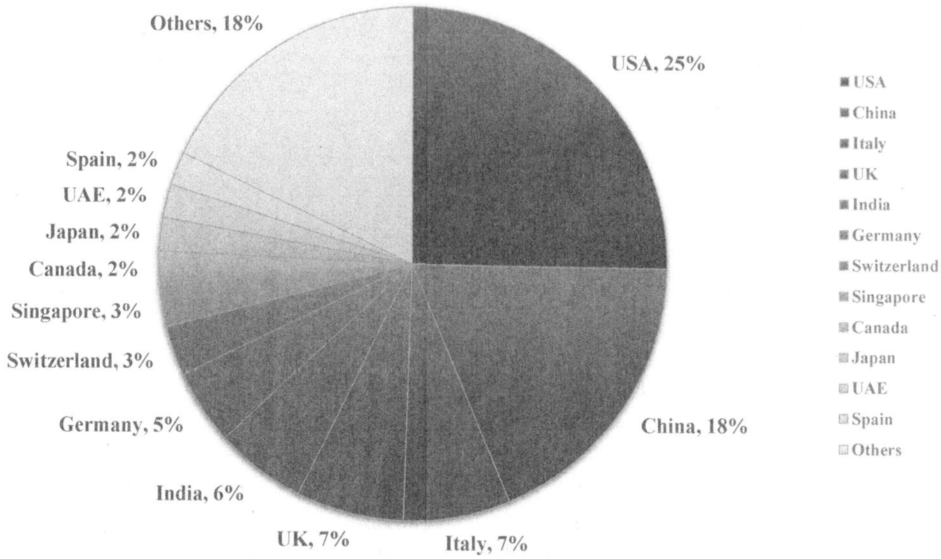

FIGURE 12.4 The countries with the most published articles in the studied field.

- Removing duplicate keywords: Duplicate keywords were eliminated to decrease dataset noise.
- Stemming: Words were modified to their base forms to integrate various versions of the same word.
- Lemmatization: Words were transformed into their root form.
- Eliminating special characters: Special characters were removed to enhance the dataset's readability.
- Missing values: Indexed keywords from the Elsevier Scopus API (Elsevier 2024) were used as replacements for papers that did not include authors' keywords.
- Correcting Misspelled Keywords: Some of the extracted articles had incorrectly spelled keywords. To solve this issue, we utilized Python scripts that detect and substitute misspelled keywords with their correctly spelled counterparts, ensuring accuracy in keyword identification.

After implementing the described preprocessing steps, the characteristics of the dataset are summarized as follows: the total number of keywords identified in the dataset is 684, with 281 of these being unique. It is also worth mentioning that, on average, each paper in the dataset includes approximately 4.85 keywords. Furthermore, the dataset shows that the keyword with the highest frequency occurs 94 times, which is related to the "Machine Learning Security" keyword, whereas the least frequent keywords appear just once. These figures give a basic overview of keyword distribution within the dataset, aiding in the comprehension of research traits in the area of machine learning security.

3.2 Authors' keywords network visualization

This section uses the preprocessed author-keyword data to develop a keyword association network via VOSviewer software. This network visualizes keywords as nodes and connects them through edges that reflect the cooccurrence frequency of keyword pairs. Analysis of this network helps identify relationships among keywords. Additionally, the generated networks include clusters of keywords based on the strength of these relationships [36,37]. With the keyword frequency data, the generated network illustrates the relationships among keywords, where node size indicates keyword frequency, while edge thickness indicates the co-occurrence strength between keywords. Hence, we could obtain critical insights into the most pertinent keywords/themes in the field of machine learning security.

After building the keyword-keyword network using the VOSviewer software, an analysis is carried out to reveal the hidden patterns and connections between the keywords and the most significant keywords. The following figures illustrate the keywords cooccurrence networks for the five defined subperiods.

In the network shown in Fig. 12.5 for the 2015–16 subperiod, keywords such as "Machine Learning Security", "Machine Learning Privacy", "Machine Learning", "Artificial Neural Network", and "Poisoning Attacks" are notably larger compared to other keywords within their respective clusters. This highlights their continued relevance and the focus of researchers on them within the machine learning security field in the mentioned subperiod. These keywords not only dominate their clusters but also suggest a robust engagement with core issues in machine learning. Additionally, terms like

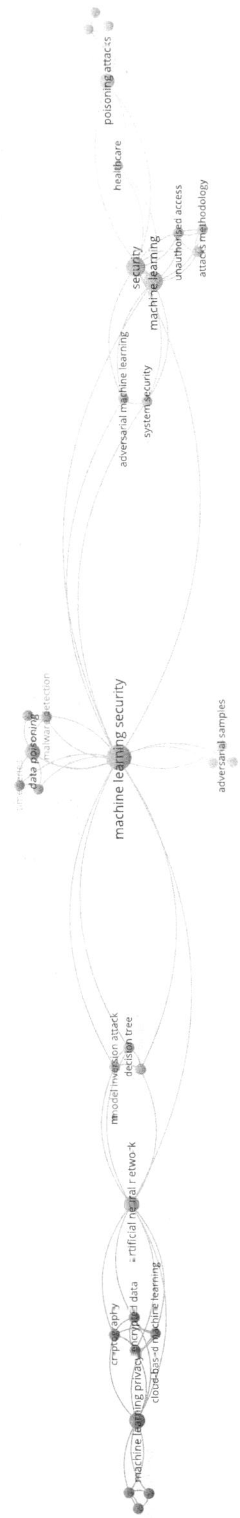

FIGURE 12.5 The 2015–16 cooccurrence network of the authors' keywords. Node size indicates keyword frequency; edge thickness indicates co-occurrence strength; colours indicate VOSviewer clusters. Minimum occurrence threshold: 2. Counting method: full counting.

"Adversarial Machine Learning", "Decision Tree", "Cryptography", and "Deep Neural Networks" are closely linked to these central keywords across various clusters, illustrating their frequent cooccurrence within the studied field.

Moreover, the 2017–18 network depicted in Fig. 12.6 highlights significant keywords such as "Machine Learning Security", "Adversarial Machine Learning", "Deep Learning", "Artificial Neural Network", "Convolutional Neural Networks", "Machine Learning", and "Machine Learning Privacy". These terms, centrally positioned within their clusters and represented by larger nodes, indicate their substantial influence and centrality in the machine learning security research landscape. Importantly, "Adversarial Samples", "Deep Neural Networks", "Membership Inference Attacks", and "Poisoning Attacks" show a strong connection with these influential keywords. These connections highlight the intricate relationships between machine learning techniques and security challenges, emphasizing the critical need for integrated approaches that address both innovation in machine learning and its vulnerabilities to attacks. The cooccurrence of these terms not only points to a robust academic focus on these issues but also underscores the practical urgency of developing sophisticated defense mechanisms and countermeasures against the evolving adversarial threats in machine learning security.

In the 2019–20 network illustrated in Fig. 12.7, prominent keywords such as "Machine Learning Security", "Machine Learning Privacy", "Adversarial Attacks", "Deep Learning", "Adversarial Machine Learning", and "Adversarial Samples" are again highlighted as key terms within the clusters of this timeframe. Additionally, several keywords, including "Deep Neural Networks", "Convolutional Neural Networks", "Poisoning Attacks", "Generative Adversarial Network", "Artificial Neural Network", "Membership Inference Attacks", and "Robustness", are strongly linked to these central nodes. This pattern indicates a significant interest among researchers in these interconnected keywords during the 2019–20 subperiod. It should be noted that the strong connections between these keywords reflect a concentrated effort in the community to address complex challenges in machine learning security, such as enhancing the robustness of ML systems against adversarial threats and improving privacy measures. Integrating deep learning techniques with adversarial defense strategies highlights the dynamic evolution of research that aims to fortify ML models against increasingly sophisticated attacks, ensuring their reliability and safety in critical applications.

In the 2021–22 subperiod's network, shown in Fig. 12.8, keywords such as "Machine Learning Security", "Adversarial Machine Learning", "Machine Learning", "Adversarial Samples", "Adversarial Attacks", "Deep Learning", "Artificial Neural Network", and "Backdoor Attacks" are prominent within various clusters, highlighting their importance in shaping the machine learning security related studies in the mentioned subperiod. Alongside these, terms like "Evasion Attacks", "Byzantine Attack", "Machine Unlearning", "Robustness", "Federated Learning", "Generative Models", "Cybersecurity", "Intrusion Detection", and "Poisoning Attacks" exhibit strong connections with the central nodes, illustrating a dense network of interrelated themes. These connections highlight a robust academic and practical focus on developing strategies to fortify machine learning systems against sophisticated adversarial threats and systemic vulnerabilities, such as "Poisoning Attacks" and "Evasion Attacks". Particularly, the emphasis on "Federated Learning" and "Machine Unlearning" reflects cutting-edge approaches to enhancing data privacy and model integrity in distributed environments. Such interconnectedness in the network not only illustrates the complexity of challenges in machine learning security but also points to the collaborative efforts and countermeasures to address them, aiming to create more resilient, secure, and trustworthy AI systems.

In the network of the latest subperiod, 2023–24, shown in Fig. 12.9, keywords such as "Machine Learning Security", "Adversarial Machine Learning", "Machine Learning", "Adversarial Samples", "Adversarial Attacks", "Artificial Intelligence", "Deep Learning", "Deep Neural Networks", "Backdoor Attacks", "Federated Learning", and "Poisoning Attacks" stand out as central nodes. These terms represent the core themes in the studied domain in this subperiod. Additionally, terms such as "Artificial Neural Network", "Machine Learning Privacy", "Membership Inference Attacks", "Machine Unlearning", "Cryptography", "Adversarial Robust Toolbox", "Ensemble Models", "Robustness", "Artificial Intelligence Security", "Federated Learning Security", "Distributed Machine Learning", "Byzantine Attack", "Backdoor Defenses", "AI Code Assistant", "Audio Adversarial Attacks", "Convolutional Neural Networks", and "Generative Adversarial Network" are tightly connected with these central nodes. This connection of keywords underscores the complexity of machine learning security and highlights the interdisciplinary approach needed to tackle these issues effectively. The continuing emphasis on "Federated Learning" as a distributed machine learning approach and its strong linkage with "Federated Learning Security" shows the growing importance of protecting collaborative and distributed machine learning systems from breaches and data leaks, reflecting a shift toward more privacy-preserving methodologies in AI/ML. The connection between "Deep Learning" and "Adversarial Machine Learning" illustrates the dual-edged nature of deep learning advancements. They enhance capabilities but also increase vulnerability to sophisticated attacks, necessitating ongoing innovations in defensive strategies. Also, the linkage of "Cryptography" with "Machine Learning" through the "Security" node underscores the critical role of encryption and secure protocols in protecting data

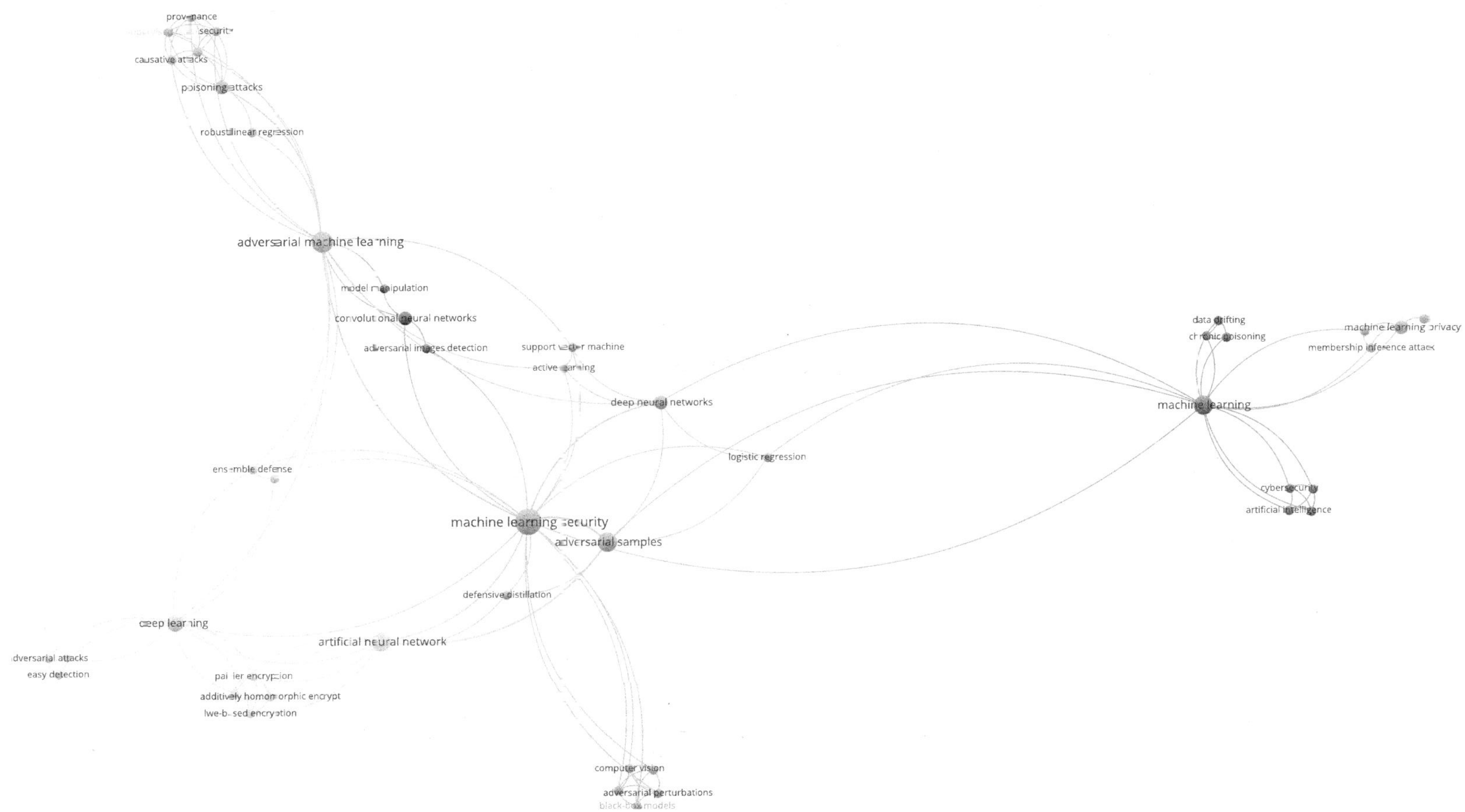

FIGURE 12.6 The 2017–18 co-occurrence network of the authors' keywords. Node size indicates keyword frequency; edge thickness indicates co-occurrence strength; colours indicate VOSviewer clusters. Minimum occurrence threshold: 2. Counting method: full counting.

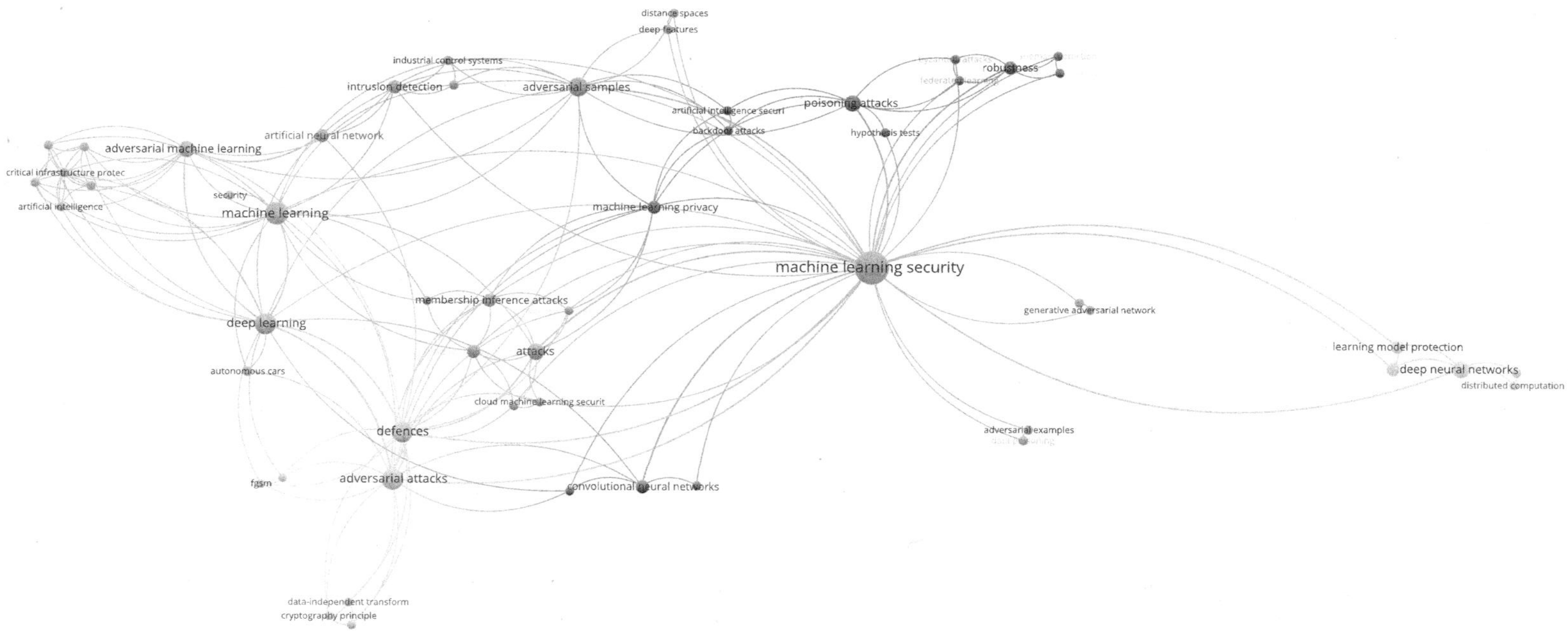

FIGURE 12.7 The 2019–20 cooccurrence network of the authors' keywords. Node size indicates keyword frequency; edge thickness indicates co-occurrence strength; colours indicate VOSviewer clusters. Minimum occurrence threshold: 2. Counting method: full counting.

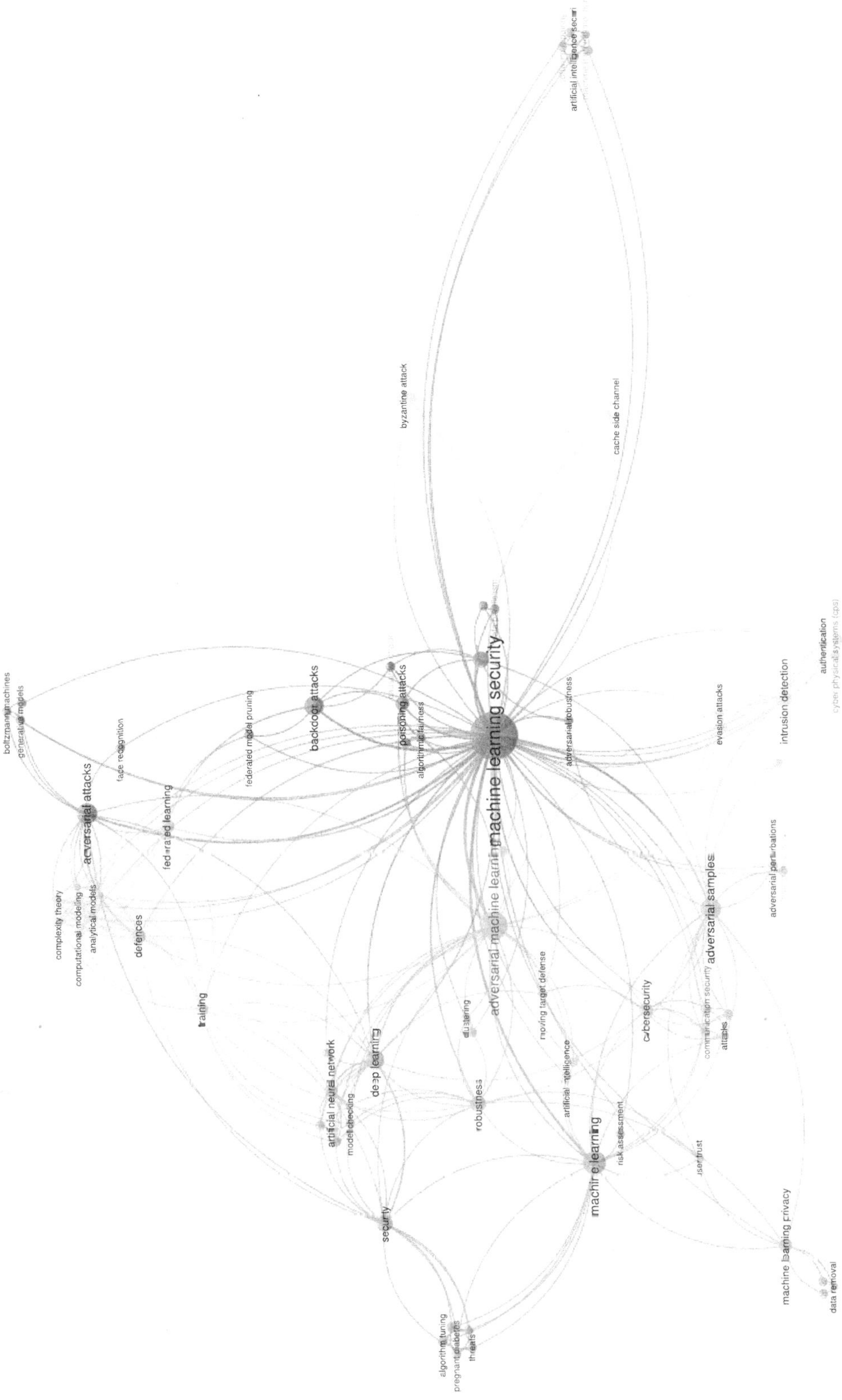

FIGURE 12.8 The 2021–22 cooccurrence network of the authors' keywords. Node size indicates keyword frequency; edge thickness indicates co-occurrence strength; colours indicate VOSviewer clusters. Minimum occurrence threshold: 2. Counting method: full counting

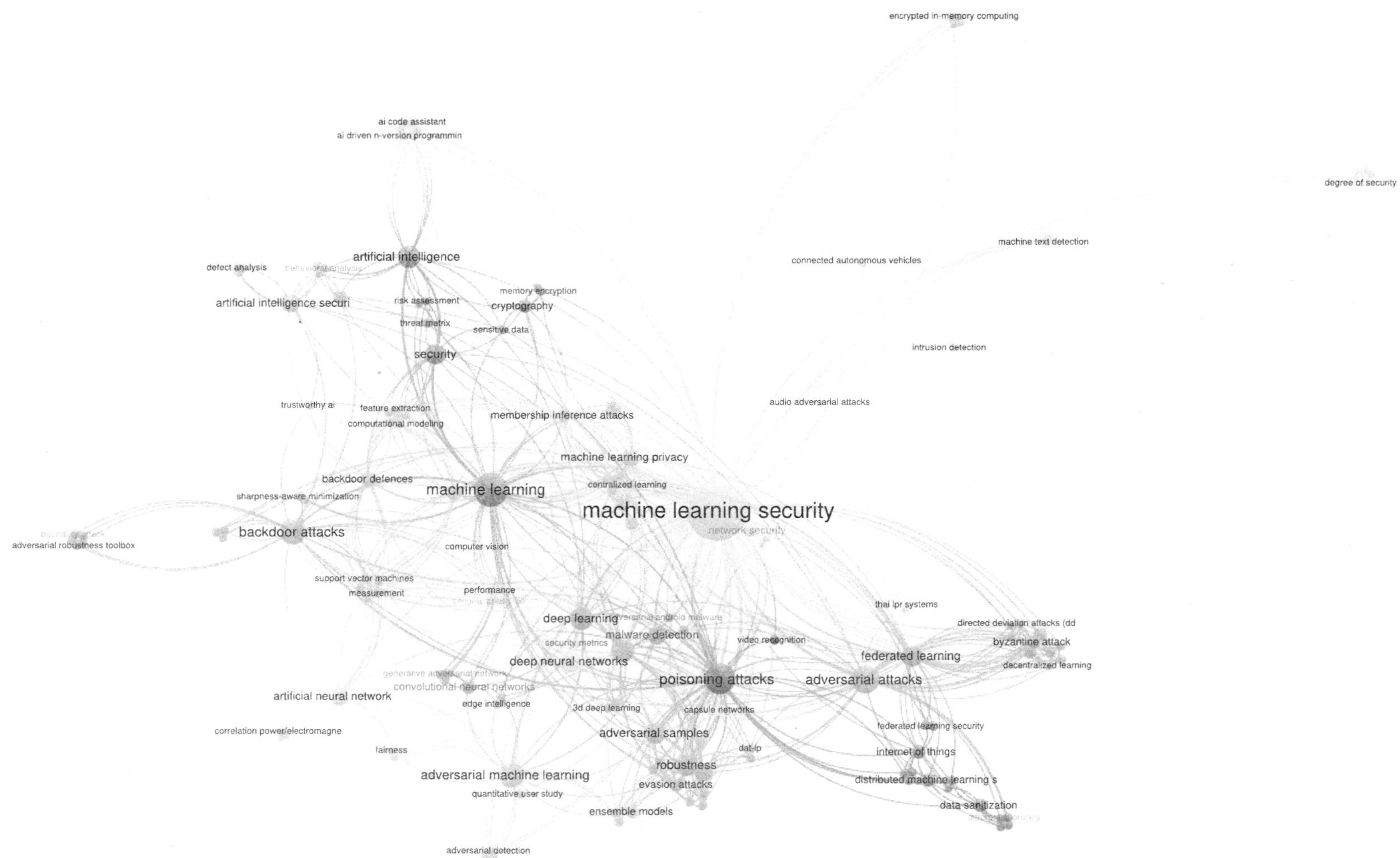

FIGURE 12.9 The 2023–24 cooccurrence network of the authors' keywords. Node size indicates keyword frequency; edge thickness indicates co-occurrence strength; colours indicate VOSviewer clusters. Minimum occurrence threshold: 2. Counting method: full counting.

integrity and user privacy in AI/ML applications. Moreover, the appearance of newer terms like "AI Code Assistant" and "Audio Adversarial Attacks" indicates emerging areas in AI applications and their corresponding security challenges, pointing to the need for specialized defensive mechanisms and countermeasures that can adapt to these novel contexts. Each keyword's link in the network shows how AI development must constantly adapt to keep pace with growing security threats.

Furthermore, Fig. 12.10 presents a map showing how frequently the authors' keywords appeared together in the published articles throughout the period of 2015–2024. This decade-spanning network in Fig. 12.10 shows keyword co-occurrence patterns in the analysed records to the dual challenges of enhancing AI's capabilities while ensuring its safety and integrity against evolving cyber threats. Moreover, this network indicates the persistence of foundational keywords and the adaptive strategies the field has employed, demonstrating a complex and proactive engagement with the ever-evolving challenges in machine learning security.

The keyword cooccurrence network presented in Fig. 12.10 for the period 2015–24 includes the core themes and dynamic shifts within the field of machine learning security. Central to this network are key terms such as "Machine Learning Security", "Machine Learning", "Machine Learning Privacy", "Adversarial Machine Learning", "Poisoning Attacks", "Adversarial Attacks", "Adversarial Samples", "Backdoor Attacks", "Artificial Intelligence", "Artificial Intelligence Security", "Artificial Neural Network", "Deep Learning", "Deep Neural Networks", "Convolutional Neural Networks", "Robustness", "Defenses", "Security", and "Federated Learning". These keywords represent the most significant and central terms across the decade and illustrate the expanding interconnectivity of concepts as the field has matured. In the 2015–16 subperiod, the research community's focus on "Machine Learning Security" and "'Machine Learning Privacy" and its related aspects, such as "Poisoning Attacks", underscored a foundational concern for securing emerging AI technologies. As depicted in the subsequent subperiod networks, there has been a consistent emphasis on advancing security measures alongside the rapid development of machine learning capabilities. In the 2017–18 subperiod, the "Adversarial Machine Learning" and "Deep Learning" keywords showed a deeper understanding and response to sophisticated cyber threats, integrating more complex security strategies with more complex ML models, including "Deep Neural Networks" and "Convolutional Neural Networks". The 2019–20 subperiod highlighted a significant interest in robustness and defensive strategies against "Adversarial Attacks", reflecting a shift toward not only understanding but actively countering adversarial threats. This period also noted the integration of "Federated Learning", indicating some efforts toward securing decentralized machine learning frameworks, which continued into the 2021–22 subperiod. Here, the focus expanded to the security implications of "Machine Unlearning" and securing AI-enhanced systems, such as "Generative Models". The 2023–24 network reaffirms the importance of these themes, with "Deep Neural Networks", "Backdoor Attacks", and emerging areas such as "AI Code Assistant" and "Audio Adversarial Attacks" pointing to new frontiers in machine learning security.

4. Most significant keywords/themes

This section provides statistical analyses of the authors' keywords of the dataset across successive subperiods. This includes a frequency analysis of keywords, an examination of their growth rates, and the evaluation of P-values. In the subsequent paragraphs, we describe the mentioned statistical analysis methods used to examine the authors' keywords.

The technique for analyzing growth is utilized to assess the development of different topics within the research domain [38]. This is achieved by tracking the rise or fall in the frequency of certain keywords, which helps identify trends in topic growth over successive subperiods. The growth metric is calculated using Eq. (12.1), where the variable X_i indicates the frequency of a particular keyword in the i'th subperiod. To avoid division-by-zero issues when a keyword is absent in a previous subperiod, the denominator is adjusted using $\max(1, X_{i-1})$. The resulting average growth values are subsequently normalized using the maximum observed average growth value among all keywords.

$$\text{Growth} = \frac{X_i - X_{i-1}}{max(1, X_{i-1})} \times 100 \tag{12.1}$$

Additionally, the P-value analysis provides an exploratory measure for evaluating the significance of keyword frequencies, offering insights into which keywords are truly impactful in the field of machine learning security. The P-value helps determine whether the observed frequency of a keyword is significantly different from the expected average frequency. This assessment helps to identify keywords that are unusually common or rare in the dataset. The P-value is derived from the T-score using the t-distribution. In this regard, we will calculate the T-score using the following

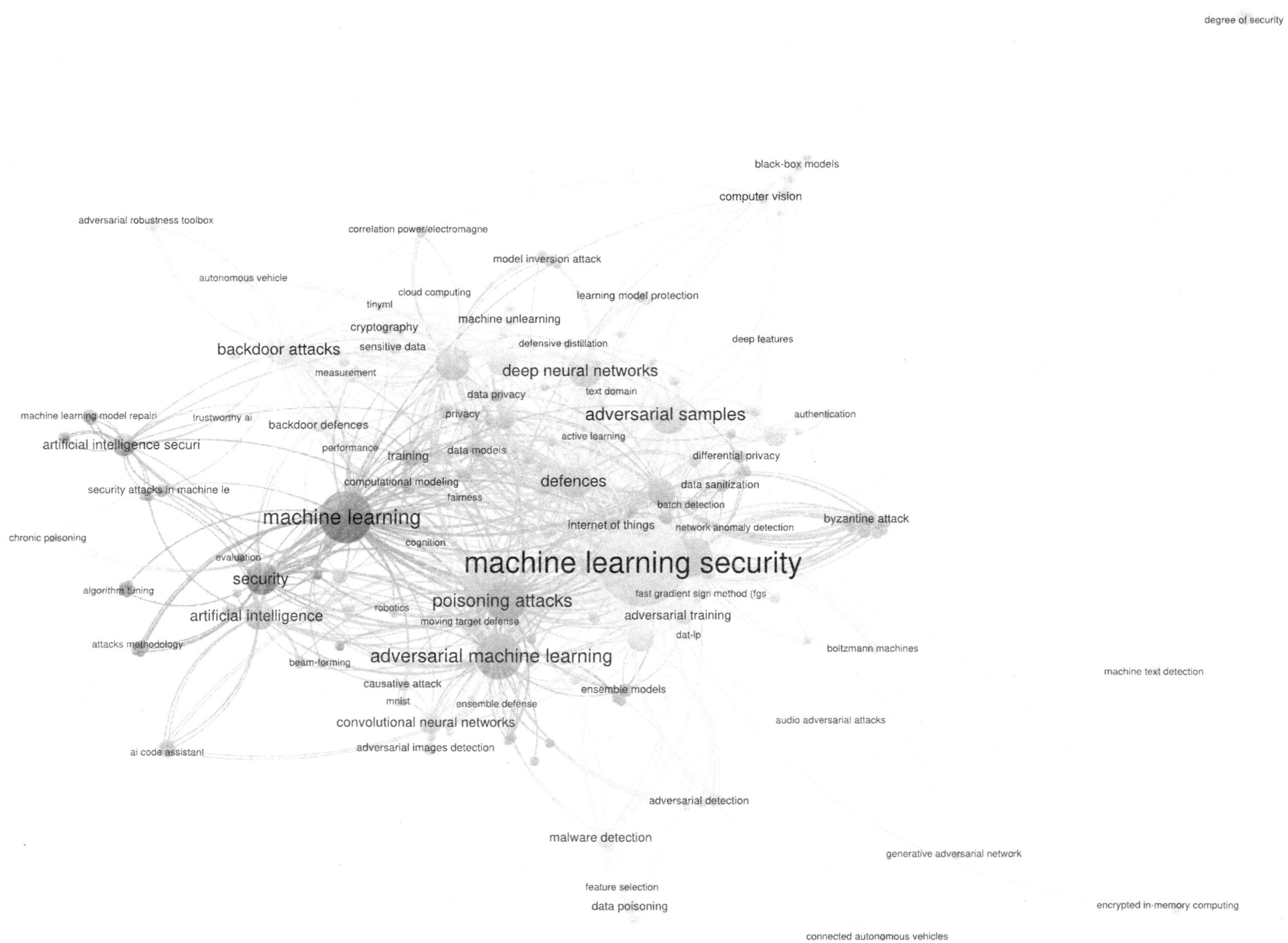

FIGURE 12.10 The 2015–24 cooccurrence network of the authors' keywords. Node size indicates keyword frequency; edge thickness indicates co-occurrence strength; colours indicate VOSviewer clusters. Minimum occurrence threshold: 2. Counting method: full counting.

Eq. (12.2), where X is the keyword frequency, μ indicates the mean, σ denotes the standard deviation, and n is the number of samples (keywords).

$$T - \text{Score} = \frac{X - \mu}{\left(\frac{\sigma}{\sqrt{n}}\right)} \tag{12.2}$$

The *P*-value indicates the probability of obtaining a result as extreme as the T-score under the assumption of the null hypothesis. It is calculated using the t-distribution with n-1 degree of freedom through the following formula:

$$p - \text{value} = 2 \times P(T > |T|) \tag{12.3}$$

Where $P(T>|T|)$ is the probability of the absolute T-score being greater than the observed T-score, which can be looked up in t-distribution tables. It is worth mentioning that keywords with low *P*-values (typically less than 0.05) indicate that their observed frequencies differ more noticeably from the average frequency within the analysed dataset. Therefore, these keywords may reflect relatively prominent or emerging research topics in the field. Conversely, higher *P*-values suggest that the observed keyword frequencies are closer to the overall average distribution within the dataset.

Using the previously mentioned statistical measures, we have calculated the frequency and *P*-values for the top 20 frequently used keywords in publications on machine learning security over five different time periods, which is shown in the following Table 12.1.

The analysis of the reported keyword frequency, growth rate, and *P*-values in Table 12.1 provides a comprehensive understanding of the key themes and emerging trends in the field of machine learning security.

As shown in the table, the term "Machine Learning Security" emerges as the most frequently used keyword, with 94 occurrences. Its growth rate of 0.61 and a *P*-value of 2.04E-03 highlight both its rapid increase in usage and its statistical significance. This reflects the growing recognition of security as a critical component of machine learning systems, driven by the increasing integration of AI into sensitive domains such as healthcare, finance, and autonomous vehicles. The rise of adversarial attacks and vulnerabilities in ML models has intensified research efforts to develop secure frameworks that ensure the reliability, confidentiality, and integrity of these systems. Additionally, the prominence of this keyword signals a shift from traditional cybersecurity to AI-specific security challenges, underscoring the need for novel defense mechanisms tailored to the unique threats faced by machine learning applications.

Similarly, "Machine Learning", with 32 occurrences and a growth rate of 0.47, has a *P*-value of 2.92E-04, highlighting its foundational role in the machine learning security domain. Despite a lower frequency compared to "Machine Learning Security", its consistent presence and low *P*-value emphasize its essential nature in the literature, serving as a base for discussions on security within machine learning. The prominence of this keyword reflects the dual focus in the literature, on both advancing machine learning algorithms and addressing the vulnerabilities they introduce.

"Adversarial Machine Learning," appearing 25 times with a growth rate of 1.00 and a *P*-value of 3.69E-04, represents a rapidly emerging and increasingly critical area of research. The high reported growth rate and frequency increase underscore the rising focus on identifying, understanding, and mitigating adversarial threats that exploit vulnerabilities in machine learning models. This surge in interest aligns with the growing deployment of AI systems in security-sensitive environments, such as autonomous vehicles, healthcare diagnostics, and financial services, where adversarial attacks can have severe consequences. As adversarial techniques evolve, ranging from evasion and poisoning attacks to model inversion, research in this area is crucial for developing resilient models capable of maintaining performance and reliability in the face of malicious inputs. The prominence of this keyword highlights the urgency of advancing both theoretical and practical defenses to safeguard machine learning applications in real-world scenarios.

Keywords such as "Poisoning Attacks" and "Adversarial Attacks," each with 20 occurrences, exhibit substantial growth rates of 0.89 and 0.91, respectively, along with statistically significant *P*-values of 5.30E-03 and 3.32E-03. The mentioned values underscore the growing concern within the research community about these specific types of adversarial threats and their impact on the integrity of machine learning models. Poisoning attacks, which compromise models by injecting malicious data during the training phase, have gained attention due to the rise of decentralized data sources and collaborative frameworks like FL. Meanwhile, the broader term "Adversarial Attacks" reflects the increasing diversity of attack methods, ranging from evasion and backdoor attacks to membership inference and model inversion.

"Adversarial Samples", with 19 occurrences, has a growth rate of 0.67 and a very low *P*-value of 2.25E-05, suggesting it is a significant term in AML and adversarial attacks-related research studies. Its significance is further emphasized by the consistent increase in its usage over the analyzed periods. These samples are inputs that are designed to deceive and compromise the integrity of the models, providing insights into vulnerabilities and potential defenses.

TABLE 12.1 Top 20 frequent keywords, growth rates, and *P*-values.

Frequent Keywords	2015–16 Frequency	2017–18 Frequency	2019–20 Frequency	2021–22 Frequency	2023–24 Frequency	Total Frequency	Growth Rate	*P*-value
Machine Learning Security	5	7	13	27	42	94	0.61	2.04E-03
Machine Learning	3	4	6	6	13	32	0.47	2.92E-04
Adversarial Machine Learning	1	5	3	9	7	25	1.00	3.69E-04
Poisoning Attacks	2	2	3	2	11	20	0.89	5.30E-03
Adversarial Attacks	0	1	5	5	9	20	0.91	3.32E-03
Adversarial Samples	1	4	4	5	5	19	0.67	2.25E-05
Deep Learning	0	3	5	4	6	18	0.62	3.98E-04
Deep Neural Networks	1	2	3	3	6	15	0.55	3.36E-04
Artificial Neural Network	2	4	2	2	4	14	0.39	1.02E-05
Defenses	0	0	5	3	6	14	0.88	5.50E-03
Security	3	1	1	3	5	13	0.47	4.16E-04
Backdoor Attacks	0	0	1	4	8	13	0.78	2.02E-02
Machine Learning Privacy	2	2	2	2	4	12	0.31	6.89E-06
Artificial Intelligence	1	1	1	1	6	10	0.94	9.89E-03
Robustness	0	0	2	3	5	10	0.50	7.71E-03
Federated Learning	0	0	1	3	5	9	0.57	1.38E-02
Intrusion Detection	1	1	2	3	1	8	0.29	1.55E-04
Artificial Intelligence Security	0	0	1	1	4	6	0.63	2.31E-02
Convolutional Neural Networks	0	2	2	0	2	6	0.47	3.56E-03
Membership Inference Attacks	0	0	2	1	2	5	0.39	5.75E-03

The term "Deep Learning", appearing 18 times, has a growth rate of 0.62 and a *P*-value of 3.98E-04. The observed frequency and growth pattern suggest continued attention of deep learning techniques in the context of machine learning security, making it a vital area of study. Closely related is "Deep Neural Networks", which appears 15 times with a growth rate of 0.55 and a *P*-value of 3.36E-04, indicating focused research on the specific architectures of neural networks in security contexts. The widespread adoption of these models in critical domains such as healthcare, autonomous vehicles, and finance has raised concerns about their susceptibility to adversarial attacks. As these complex architectures become more prevalent, ensuring their robustness against threats, such as evasion and poisoning attacks, is paramount.

Although the "Artificial Neural Network" keyword appears 14 times, it has a very low *P*-value of 1.02E-05 and a growth rate of 0.39. This highlights the significance of security concerns on neural network-based ML models. Similarly, "Defenses", with 14 occurrences, shows a high growth rate of 0.88 and a significant *P*-value of 5.50E-03, pointing to increasing research on defensive measures and countermeasures in machine learning security.

The keyword "Security", with 13 occurrences, has a growth rate of 0.47 and a *P*-value of 4.16E-04. This broad term remains significant, indicating a sustained focus on security aspects within the machine learning community. "Backdoor Attacks", with the same frequency, have a growth rate of 0.78 and a *P*-value of 2.02E-02, pointing to a specialized area of concern and reflecting attention on hidden threats embedded within models.

"Machine Learning Privacy", appearing 12 times, has a growth rate of 0.31 and a very low *P*-value of 6.89E-06. This indicates the growing importance of privacy discussions within the context of machine learning, emphasizing the need for protecting personal data in these systems.

"Artificial Intelligence", with 10 occurrences, has a high growth rate of 0.94 and a *P*-value of 9.89E-03. While broader and less frequent, its significant *P*-value suggests it is a fundamental term that occasionally overlaps with more specific security concerns in machine learning. "Robustness", also with 10 occurrences, has a growth rate of 0.50 and a *P*-value of 7.71E-03, highlighting its critical role in research studies to ensure that machine learning models can withstand various attacks.

"Federated Learning", with nine occurrences, has a growth rate of 0.57 and a *P*-value of 1.38E-02. As a relatively new area, the *P*-value suggests it is an emerging trend with significant interest due to its privacy-preserving characteristics. This trend highlights the increasing demand for decentralized AI frameworks that allow multiple parties to collaboratively train models without directly sharing sensitive data, making FL particularly relevant in healthcare, finance, and IoT environments. Similarly, "Intrusion Detection," with eight occurrences, shows a growth rate of 0.29 and a highly significant *P*-value of 1.55E-04, underscoring its continuing relevance in addressing machine learning security threats. Intrusion detection systems (IDS) remain a critical focus for researchers, as they are essential for identifying and mitigating attacks in real time. The steady research interest in this area reflects the ongoing need for advanced IDS solutions that use machine learning techniques to detect increasingly sophisticated cyberattacks.

Finally, "Artificial Intelligence Security", with six occurrences, has a growth rate of 0.63 and a *P*-value of 2.31E-02, indicating that while it is still a developing topic, it is gradually becoming more prominent. "Convolutional Neural Networks", also with six occurrences, has a growth rate of 0.47 and a *P*-value of 3.56E-03, indicating that CNNs are a significant topic in the field. This is particularly relevant as many researchers focus on addressing machine learning security threats in computer vision problems, where CNNs are extensively used. "Membership Inference Attacks", which appeared five times, have a growth rate of 0.39 and a *P*-value of 5.75E-03. These attacks enable adversaries to identify whether a specific data point was included in the training set of a machine learning model. The relatively low *P*-value indicates that this is a statistically significant area of research. The growth rate suggests increasing interest and awareness within the community, reflecting the rising concern over privacy and the need for effective defenses to protect machine learning models from such attacks.

From the provided analyses, it could be understood that keywords with low *P*-values and high growth rates, such as "Machine Learning Security", "Adversarial Machine Learning", and "Poisoning Attacks", highlight critical areas of ongoing research and interest. In addition to these well-established topics, the presence of significant but less frequent keywords, such as "Federated Learning" and "Membership Inference Attacks", indicates areas that might attract increasing attention within the research community.

5. Discussion

The current section presents two taxonomies of AI/ML attacks and their corresponding countermeasures. These taxonomies synthesize the reviewed literature and are informed by the bibliometric results. Examining the authors' keywords has provided valuable insights into the trends and central themes within the field of ML security. This examination has enabled the identification of patterns, connections, and groupings of keywords, indicating their roles within the broader body of research and literature on ML security.

In this regard, our focus was on the keywords/themes directly related to specific methods used in the field of ML security. From the results of our research, we pinpointed key attacks and their countermeasures within this domain. Hence, regarding the ML attacks taxonomy, shown in Fig. 12.11, we capture the two primary dimensions that define the landscape of ML adversarial attacks, including the timing of the attack relative to the ML model's lifecycle and the knowledge level of the attacker.

Machine learning system attacks can be categorized according to the timing of the attack relative to the model's lifecycle. This categorization helps in understanding whether the adversarial actions occur during the training phase, where the model's learning process is targeted, or during the testing phase, where the attack seeks to exploit the already trained model.

The training phase adversarial attacks could be categorized into poisoning (causative) attacks and Backdoor attacks. Poisoning attacks involve the malicious modification of the training dataset. By injecting or altering training data, attackers aim to corrupt the learning algorithm, resulting in a compromised model that behaves as the attacker desires under specific circumstances. There are two primary methods to achieve this disruption, comprising label poisoning, where the labels of the data samples are altered, and clean-label poisoning, where the features of the data samples are perturbed, but the labels remain unchanged. Therefore, these attacks fundamentally corrupt the model's integrity, affecting its behavior across all uses. In backdoor attacks, attackers can embed a backdoor within the training data or a pretrained model. This hidden-natured backdoor remains inactive, not influencing the model's typical operations; however, upon the activation of a specific trigger, the backdoor could be deceptive, causing the model to misclassify the input to an attacker-designated label.

Furthermore, the testing phase adversarial attacks could be classified into three main attacks, including evasion attacks, model inversion (model extraction) attacks, and membership inference (MI) attacks. Evasion attacks take place during the testing phase of a machine learning model, involving carefully designed adversarial inputs intended to deceive the model and diminish its accuracy. This type of attack targets the integrity of machine learning by altering testing data to provoke incorrect predictions. These attacks not only compromise the operational reliability and accuracy of machine learning models but also emphasize the importance of implementing robust defenses to protect against this attack's vulnerabilities. Model inversion attacks are designed to compromise the privacy of machine learning systems by enabling adversaries to reconstruct or infer sensitive input data. These attacks pose considerable privacy risks, as they allow attackers not only to infer sensitive information contained within the training data but also to expose the structural integrity of the model itself. In this attack, the attackers employ systematic queries with diverse datasets to extract and replicate the underlying behavior of the model, thereby gaining insights into its information. To make it clear, the attackers seek to see how the

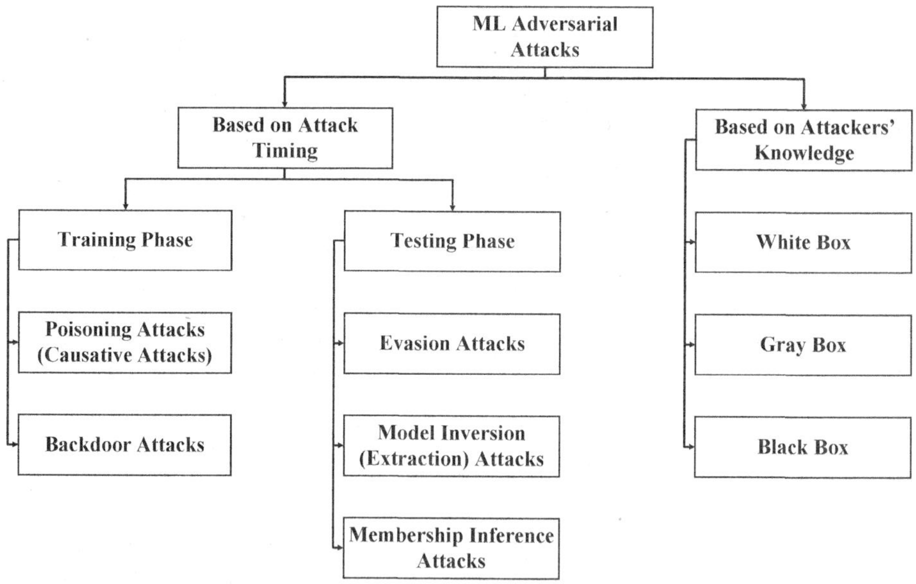

FIGURE 12.11 The taxonomy of ML adversarial attacks.

predictive outputs of a model can be exploited to infer sensitive features, reconstruct representative inputs, or approximate aspects of model behaviour. The MI attacks directly threaten the confidentiality and privacy of the training data. In these attacks, an adversary exploits the ability to query a machine learning model and analyze its outputs to determine whether specific data points were used in the model's training set. By observing how the model responds differently to seen (trained on) versus unseen data, the attacker can infer sensitive details about the dataset. These attackers analyze the responses from their queries to regenerate parts of the targeted model's training dataset, revealing insights into the model's privacy settings and operational parameters.

Adversarial attacks on machine learning models can also vary significantly based on the extent of attackers' knowledge about the target system. This categorization represents attacks into three distinct types, including White Box, Gray Box, and Black Box.

The White Box attacks occur under the assumption that the adversary has complete access to the model's architecture, parameters, and training data. Such transparency allows the attacker to exploit the model's vulnerabilities with precision, utilizing detailed insights into its functioning. Such conditions make these attacks particularly effective for poisoning and evasion attacks, where full transparency and precise manipulations are crucial for success. In Gray Box scenarios, the attacker has partial knowledge, such as the model's architecture, but lacks access to the exact parameters or the training dataset. This partial insight is often sufficient to trigger substantial attacks. Such attacks are particularly relevant to ML systems where some components are open source. The Black Box attacks, which are the most common in real-world applications, are characterized by the attacker having no internal knowledge of the model, interacting with it solely through input-output pairs. Despite these constraints, effective strategies have been developed to manipulate model behavior. Typically, the attack aims to degrade the overall performance or reduce the model's accuracy rather than to manipulate it with a specific, targeted approach.

As mentioned earlier, we also provide a taxonomy of the defense mechanisms for adversarial ML attacks, as shown in Fig. 12.12. These countermeasures are classified into two categories regarding the attack time, which are the training phase and the testing phase.

During the training phase, countermeasures focus on ensuring that the model is trained securely without being compromised by malicious data or tampered training processes.

If an attacker tries to launch a poisoning attack, four defense mechanisms could be applied to serve as countermeasures to this attack, including data sanitization, adding adversarial noise to data samples, adversarial training, and model hardening.

Data sanitization involves preprocessing the training data to detect and remove any instances that appear anomalous or poisonous to maintain the integrity and reliability of the training data. Techniques such as statistical anomaly detection, clustering, and outlier analysis can be employed to clean the dataset [31,39–42]. Adding adversarial noise to training samples introduces controlled noise to the training data to make it harder for an attacker to inject precise malicious data without detection [43,44]. Introducing controlled perturbations to the data enables the model to develop resilience against minor alterations, hindering attackers from embedding malicious data. This technique increases the difficulty for adversaries in introducing effective poisoning attacks, thereby enhancing the model's robustness and resilience. Adversarial training involves training the model using both clean and adversarial examples [45]. The model is exposed to malicious inputs during training, allowing it to learn how to recognize and mitigate these inputs during testing. Model hardening is another technique aimed at making the model resilient against poisoning attacks [46,47]. This is achieved by training the model to achieve large class distances, which means that the decision boundaries between different classes are maximized. As a result, the model becomes less likely to accept outliers or data points that do not fit well into any established class. This approach makes it significantly more challenging for adversaries to introduce poisoned data that can influence the model's decisions. By creating large class distances and making the model more resistant to outliers, model hardening effectively mitigates the risk of poisoning attacks, ensuring the integrity and reliability of the trained model.

Moreover, five well-known countermeasures, including activation clustering, pruning and fine-tuning, input filtering, neural cleanse (neuron pruning), and unlearning, input anomaly detection, autoencoders, and retraining, and real-time trojan detection, could be applicable regarding the backdoor attack scenario. The activation clustering method is designed to detect poisoned training samples that insert backdoors into deep neural networks [48]. This method analyzes the neural network activations of the training data to determine whether the dataset has been poisoned and, if so, identifies which data points are poisonous. This technique effectively identifies and mitigates backdoors by examining the internal behavior of the model, ensuring the removal of hidden malicious functionalities and maintaining the integrity of the training process. The pruning and fine-tuning approach minimizes the size of the backdoored network by removing neurons inactive on clean inputs, effectively neutralizing the backdoor behavior [49]. Fine-tuning involves a small amount of local retraining on a clean training dataset. By reducing the model's complexity through pruning and improving its

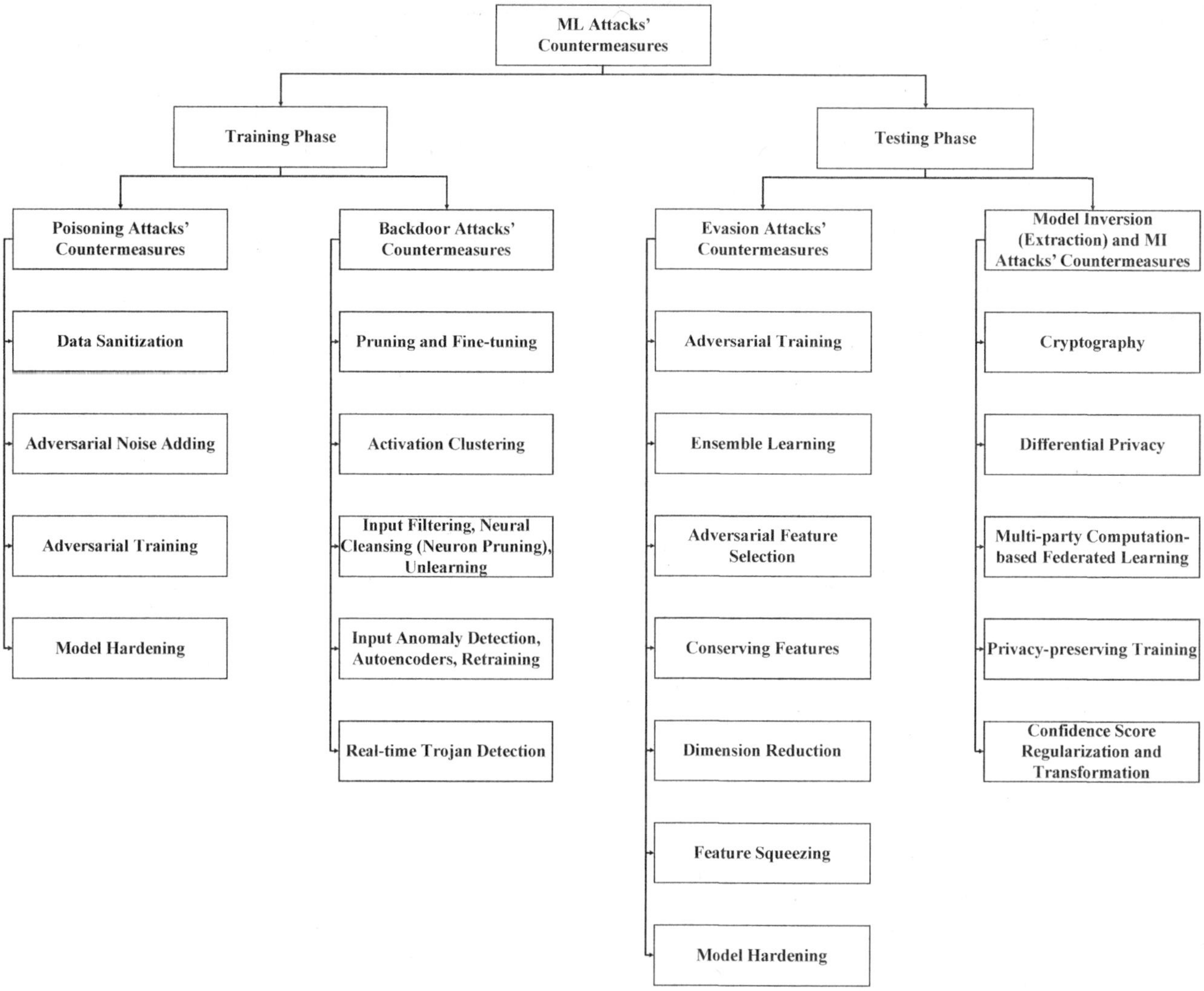

FIGURE 12.12 The taxonomy of ML attacks' countermeasures.

accuracy with fine-tuning, pruning and fine-tuning can reduce or neutralise some backdoor behaviours while maintaining the model's performance. The input filtering, neural cleanse (neuron pruning), and unlearning approach involve multiple steps [50]. First, a filter is created to identify and reject any backdoor trigger input. This filter relies on neuron activation profiles for reversed triggers, calculated by measuring the average activation of the top 1% of neurons in the second-to-last layer. The filter identifies inputs with activation profiles surpassing a specified threshold, which is adjustable based on clean input data. Then, once backdoor-related neurons are identified through their abnormal activation patterns, two techniques could be applied, including neuron cleansing and unlearning. By utilizing neuron cleansing, the backdoor-related neurons are pruned, meaning their output values are set to zero during inference. The pruning targets neurons with the largest activation gaps between clean and adversarial inputs, focusing on the second-to-last layer. Pruning continues until the model no longer reacts to the backdoor trigger, while ensuring minimal impact on the clean inputs' classification accuracy. Additionally, the unlearning technique involves retraining the model to unlearn the backdoor behavior by using the reversed trigger. The model is trained to recognize correct labels even when the trigger is present, allowing it to adjust problematic weights rather than removing entire neurons. This layered defense effectively cleans both the inputs and the model, removing backdoor influences and enhancing the model's security. By using neuron pruning and unlearning, the model is robust against detected backdoor triggers without significantly degrading performance on clean data. The input anomaly detection, autoencoders, and retraining methods strengthen neural network models against backdoors by employing three techniques [51]. This method first uses Support Vector Machines (SVM) or DT to detect unusual input patterns that might indicate backdoor triggers. Then, it adds an input preprocessor in the form of an autoencoder trained on legitimate training data. This autoencoder preprocesses input data based on the expected data distribution, effectively filtering out anomalous inputs. Finally, it continuously retrains the model on clean data, helping it to unlearn the malicious behaviors introduced by the backdoor. It should be noted that it enhances model robustness by detecting and filtering out anomalous inputs and continuously adapting the model to clean data, reducing the likelihood of backdoor activation. Also, the real-time Trojan detection method works by perturbing the input data and observing the randomness of the model's predictions regarding entropy [52]. If the input contains a Trojan trigger, the model's prediction remains stable despite the perturbations, indicating the presence of a backdoor. Conversely, for clean inputs, the predictions vary significantly with perturbations.

Furthermore, during the testing phase, defenses focus on ensuring that the deployed model behaves securely and accurately in response to various input queries and does not leak sensitive information.

If an attacker decides to launch an evasion attack, seven defense mechanisms are applicable. Adversarial training is one of the defense mechanisms that could also countermeasure the evasion attack by enhancing the model's ability to resist adversarial examples during operation, maintaining accuracy and reliability. Another defense mechanism in this scenario is the utilization of ensemble learning. This mechanism involves combining multiple classifiers to improve the robustness and overall performance of the model. This approach utilizes the diversity of classifiers, making it significantly more challenging for an adversary to successfully attack all models within the ensemble simultaneously [53]. The underlying motivation is that the adversary must evade multiple classifiers, which enhances the security and reliability of the model. Besides, adversarial feature selection is another defense mechanism for this scenario. This method selects features not just based on the classifier's ability to generalize in the absence of attacks, as traditional methods do, but also considering the model's robustness against adversarial data manipulations [54]. It integrates assumptions about how an adversary might alter data into the feature selection process. By embedding security considerations into the feature selection process, this method improves the model's defense against adversarial attacks, resulting in a robust classifier that sustains high accuracy even when under attack. Another defense mechanism is conserving features. This method involves training the model to extract features that are crucial for performance and cannot be modified without compromising the malicious functionality of adversarial inputs [55]. For example, in the context of malware detection, it focuses on extracting features that are essential for malware operation and thus cannot be easily altered without nullifying the malware's functionality. Dimension reduction is also a defense mechanism in evasion attack scenarios. This method uses techniques like Principal Component Analysis (PCA) to reduce the number of features, simplifying the feature space and minimizing the attack surface [56]. However, these methods might reduce the performance of the ML system. Moreover, the feature squeezing could also defend against the evasion attack. Feature squeezing, such as reducing the color depth of each pixel and performing spatial smoothing, involves reducing the complexity of input data to limit the adversary's ability to make subtle but harmful changes [57]. Model hardening at the testing phase could also develop a security barrier against adversarial evasion attacks by training the model until it reaches a state where it can effectively reject adversarial samples [58,59]. By reaching the state of hardening, the model becomes resilient and robust, capable of identifying and discarding poisoned input data during testing.

Furthermore, in the scenario of model inversion (extraction attacks) and membership inference attacks, four well-known countermeasures exist. Differential privacy is one of the defense mechanisms in these attack scenarios. To safeguard the privacy of machine learning models, differential privacy adds controlled noise to the model's outputs or training process, hindering adversaries from extracting sensitive information. Techniques such as applying differential privacy with stochastic gradient descent (SGD) can significantly enhance data privacy [60]. Another countermeasure for this attack scenario is cryptography-based approaches. This countermeasure technique utilizes cryptographic techniques such as secure multi-party computation and encryption to provide strong guarantees against unauthorized access and manipulation, ensuring the security of the model and its data while maintaining high accuracy. For instance, using asynchronous stochastic gradient descent and homomorphic encryption could improve the distributed learning framework for privacy protection [61]. This ensures the security and privacy of the training data without affecting the model's accuracy, although it inevitably introduces high computational overhead during the training process. Moreover, multi-party computation-based FL also preserves the privacy of each participant's data during the collaborative training process, ensuring that sensitive information is not exposed while still benefiting from the collective learning effort [62]. This method is able to protect gradient information in distributed learning. In FL, multiple parties collaborate to train a model without sharing their raw data. Secure aggregation ensures that the gradients contributed by each party are encrypted and aggregated in a way that individual contributions remain confidential. The privacy-preserving training method, as another countermeasure in this scenario, involves training multiple teacher models on disjoint subsets of sensitive data [63]. A student model is then trained based on the aggregated outputs of these teacher models, with added noise to preserve privacy. The student model does not have direct access to the sensitive data or the individual teacher model parameters.

This method effectively balances privacy and utility by ensuring that the model's training process does not leak sensitive information, providing robust defenses against membership inference attacks and maintaining high accuracy in the presence of noisy data. The confidence score regularization and transformation are also a countermeasure for membership inference attacks to reduce the risk of this attack by making it challenging for adversaries to infer training data membership based on prediction confidences [64,65]. This method involves modifying the confidence scores output by the model to obscure differences between training and nontraining data. It transforms the confidence score vectors predicted by the target classifier to make them indistinguishable in individual shape, statistical distribution, and prediction label between members and nonmembers. Another technique to achieve this countermeasure is to enforce less confident predictions by the model using high-entropy soft labels and an entropy-based regularizer. This technique ensures that the model behaves similarly on both training and testing samples, obscuring differences in confidence scores between members and nonmembers.

6. Future research directions

This study has identified key trends, attack types, and defense mechanisms within AI/ML security. As the landscape of AI continues to evolve, several new technologies and challenges demand further exploration. Below are critical future research directions that might shape the next generation of secure AI systems.

6.1 Development of proactive defense mechanisms

With the increasing sophistication of adversarial attacks, future research could focus on developing proactive and adaptive defenses. Current solutions, including adversarial training and model hardening, could be enhanced with continuous monitoring techniques that detect attacks in real time and dynamically adjust models to mitigate threats without compromising performance. Additionally, research into self-healing models capable of automatically recovering from attacks could present a promising avenue.

6.2 Security of large language models

As large language models (LLMs), such as GPT, Llama, and their successors continue to grow in size and capability, new security challenges arise. Future research should explore how adversarial attacks, such as prompt injection, model extraction, and backdoor triggers, impact these models and develop specialized defenses for LLMs in real-world deployments. Investigating the risks posed by unintended biases or hallucinations in LLM-generated outputs will be critical, especially in sensitive areas including healthcare, law, and finance. Furthermore, research is needed to secure the fine-tuning and reinforcement learning processes used for adapting LLMs to specific applications, ensuring they remain robust against manipulation.

6.3 Addressing the security-performance trade-off

Many existing countermeasures, such as feature squeezing and dimension reduction, improve security but can degrade model performance. Future research could explore new methods that strike a better balance between robustness and performance, ensuring that secure AI systems remain effective in real-world applications, particularly in safety-critical domains, including healthcare and autonomous vehicles.

6.4 Research on secure decentralized learning systems

As FL and multi-party computation gain traction, new challenges arise in ensuring the security and privacy of distributed systems. Future work could explore novel attack vectors, such as collusion attacks or gradient poisoning, and investigate defenses that are computationally efficient for large-scale deployments. Emerging paradigms, such as federated reinforcement learning, offer additional complexity, requiring innovative strategies to safeguard against adversarial behaviors.

6.5 Sector-specific security solutions

Given the varied deployment contexts of AI systems, ranging from finance and healthcare to transportation and defense, future research could investigate sector-specific security challenges. For example, research in financial fraud detection might focus on backdoor attacks on transaction models, while healthcare research could prioritize robust defenses against membership inference to safeguard patient privacy. In addition, autonomous systems in transportation will require new methods to defend against attacks targeting sensor data and navigation models.

7. Conclusion

This work presents a comprehensive bibliometric analysis of adversarial attacks and countermeasures in AI/ML security, offering several insights into the field's evolution and emerging trends. Using the Scopus database, we collected and preprocessed 141 relevant publications from 2015 to 2024 by removing duplicates, standardizing author names and keywords, and filtering incomplete or non-English entries. VOSviewer software was employed to analyze author keywords, uncovering key themes, patterns, and interconnections within the research landscape. Our statistical analysis highlighted keywords' growth over time and pinpointed emerging topics, providing a robust foundation for identifying influential contributions and evolving trends.

The analysis revealed that adversarial attacks vary based on the timing relative to the model's lifecycle, with poisoning and backdoor attacks occurring during training, and evasion, model inversion, and membership inference attacks targeting the testing phase. Additionally, attacks differ in sophistication depending on the attacker's knowledge, ranging from White Box scenarios with full access to black-box scenarios with limited knowledge. Alongside these attacks, we identified defensive strategies for each attack type, such as data sanitization for poisoning attacks, pruning and fine-tuning for backdoor attacks, adversarial training for evasion attacks, and privacy-preserving techniques, including differential privacy and homomorphic encryption, for model inversion attacks.

Our findings emphasize that as adversarial threats grow more sophisticated, defensive strategies must evolve to meet these challenges. The results also highlight emerging trends toward interdisciplinary solutions, combining AI security with privacy-preserving frameworks. However, the analysis uncovered gaps, such as the need for scalable defenses against backdoor attacks and the challenge of maintaining performance while applying complex security techniques.

By offering both a historical perspective and actionable insights, this study not only outlines the current state of research but also identifies directions for future work. As the field continues to evolve, we hope these findings will guide researchers toward addressing underexplored areas and inspire innovative solutions to secure AI/ML systems in increasingly adversarial environments.

Acknowledgments

We gratefully acknowledge funding from the Digital Finance CRC, supported by the Cooperative Research Centers program, an initiative of the Australian Government. We also express our gratitude to Cyber Intelligence House (CIH) for their invaluable contributions, which have greatly enhanced our research.

References

[1] S.G. Finlayson, H.W. Chung, I.S. Kohane, A.L. Beam, Adversarial Attacks against Medical Deep Learning Systems, 2018 arXiv preprint arXiv:1804.05296.

[2] J. Park, M.-H. Kim, S. Choi, I.S. Kweon, D.-G. Choi, Fraud detection with multi-modal attention and correspondence learning, in: 2019 International Conference on Electronics, Information, and Communication (ICEIC), IEEE, 2019, pp. 1–7.

[3] N. Pitropakis, A. Pikrakis, C. Lambrinoudakis, Behaviour reflects personality: Detecting co-residence attacks on Xen-based cloud environments, Int. J. Inf. Secur. 14 (2015) 299–305.

[4] G. Loukas, E. Karapistoli, E. Panaousis, P. Sarigiannidis, A. Bezemskij, T. Vuong, A taxonomy and survey of cyber-physical intrusion detection approaches for vehicles, Ad Hoc Netw. 84 (2019) 124–147.

[5] V.S. Sadasivan, S. Saha, G. Sriramanan, P. Kattakinda, A. Chegini, S. Feizi, Fast Adversarial Attacks on Language Models in One GPU Minute, 2024 arXiv preprint arXiv:2402.15570.

[6] A. Zou, Z. Wang, J.Z. Kolter, M. Fredrikson, Universal and Transferable Adversarial Attacks on Aligned Language Models, 2023 arXiv preprint arXiv:2307.15043.

[7] X. Gong, Y. Chen, W. Yang, H. Huang, Q. Wang, b3: Backdoor attacks against black-box machine learning models, ACM Transactions on Privacy and Security 26 (4) (2023) 1–24.

[8] M. Mozaffari-Kermani, S. Sur-Kolay, A. Raghunathan, N.K. Jha, Systematic poisoning attacks on and defenses for machine learning in healthcare, IEEE J. Biomed. Health Inform. 19 (6) (2014) 1893–1905.

[9] Q. Liu, P. Li, W. Zhao, W. Cai, S. Yu, V.C. Leung, A survey on security threats and defensive techniques of machine learning: A data driven view, IEEE Access 6 (2018) 12103–12117.

[10] Z. Guan, L. Bian, T. Shang, J. Liu, When machine learning meets security issues: A survey, in: 2018 IEEE International Conference on Intelligence and Safety for Robotics (ISR), IEEE, 2018, pp. 158–165.

[11] I. Goodfellow, P. McDaniel, N. Papernot, Making machine learning robust against adversarial inputs, Commun. ACM 61 (7) (2018) 56–66.

[12] B. Biggio, F. Roli, Wild patterns: Ten years after the rise of adversarial machine learning, in: Proceedings of the 2018 ACM SIGSAC Conference on Computer and Communications Security, 2018, pp. 2154–2156.

[13] X. Yuan, P. He, Q. Zhu, X. Li, Adversarial examples: Attacks and defenses for deep learning, IEEE Transact. Neural Networks Learn. Syst. 30 (9) (2019) 2805–2824.

[14] N. Pitropakis, E. Panaousis, T. Giannetsos, E. Anastasiadis, G. Loukas, A taxonomy and survey of attacks against machine learning, Computer Science Review 34 (2019) 100199.

[15] K. Shaukat, S. Luo, V. Varadharajan, I.A. Hameed, M. Xu, A survey on machine learning techniques for cyber security in the last decade, IEEE Access 8 (2020) 222310–222354.

[16] B. Xi, Adversarial machine learning for cybersecurity and computer vision: Current developments and challenges, Wiley Interdiscip. Rev.: Comput. Stat. 12 (5) (2020) e1511.

[17] M. Xue, C. Yuan, H. Wu, Y. Zhang, W. Liu, Machine learning security: Threats, countermeasures, and evaluations, IEEE Access 8 (2020) 74720–74742.

[18] Y. Hu, et al., Artificial intelligence security: Threats and countermeasures, ACM Comput. Surv. 55 (1) (2021) 1–36.

[19] E. Anthi, L. Williams, M. Rhode, P. Burnap, A. Wedgbury, Adversarial attacks on machine learning cybersecurity defences in industrial control systems, J. Inf. Secur. Appl. 58 (2021) 102717.

[20] M. Alazab, S.P. Rm, M. Parimala, P.K.R. Maddikunta, T.R. Gadekallu, Q.-V. Pham, Federated learning for cybersecurity: Concepts, challenges, and future directions, IEEE Trans. Ind. Inf. 18 (5) (2021) 3501–3509.

[21] S. Zhou, C. Liu, D. Ye, T. Zhu, W. Zhou, P.S. Yu, Adversarial attacks and defenses in deep learning: From a perspective of cybersecurity, ACM Comput. Surv. 55 (8) (2022) 1–39.

[22] A. Kuppa, N.-A. Le-Khac, Adversarial XAI methods in cybersecurity, IEEE Trans. Inf. Forensics Secur. 16 (2021) 4924–4938.

[23] S.Y. Khamaiseh, D. Bagagem, A. Al-Alaj, M. Mancino, H.W. Alomari, Adversarial deep learning: A survey on adversarial attacks and defense mechanisms on image classification, IEEE Access 10 (2022) 102266–102291.

[24] M. Pawlicki, R. Kozik, M. Choraś, A survey on neural networks for (cyber-) security and (cyber-) security of neural networks, Neurocomputing 500 (2022) 1075–1087.

[25] H. Jmila, M.I. Khedher, Adversarial machine learning for network intrusion detection: A comparative study, Comput. Netw. 214 (2022) 109073.

[26] M. Wazid, A.K. Das, V. Chamola, Y. Park, Uniting cyber security and machine learning: Advantages, challenges and future research, ICT Express 8 (3) (2022) 313–321.

[27] C. Mehta, P. Harniya, S. Kamat, Comprehending and detecting vulnerabilities using adversarial machine learning attacks, in: 2022 2nd International Conference on Artificial Intelligence and Signal Processing (AISP), IEEE, 2022, pp. 1–5.

[28] M. Goldblum, et al., Dataset security for machine learning: Data poisoning, backdoor attacks, and defenses, IEEE Trans. Pattern Anal. Mach. Intell. 45 (2) (2022) 1563–1580.

[29] N. Rodríguez-Barroso, D. Jiménez-López, M.V. Luzón, F. Herrera, E. Martínez-Cámara, Survey on federated learning threats: Concepts, taxonomy on attacks and defences, experimental study and challenges, Inf. Fusion 90 (2023) 148–173.

[30] A.D. Lahe, G. Singh, A Survey on security threats to machine learning systems at different stages of its pipeline, Int. J. Inf. Technol. Comput. Sci. 15 (2) (2023) 23–34.

[31] A. Paracha, J. Arshad, M.B. Farah, K. Ismail, Machine learning security and privacy: A review of threats and countermeasures, EURASIP J. Inf. Secur. 2024 (1) (2024) 1–23.

[32] A. Bajaj, D.K. Vishwakarma, A state-of-the-art review on adversarial machine learning in image classification, Multimed. Tool. Appl. 83 (3) (2024) 9351–9416.

[33] A. Paya, S. Arroni, V. García-Díaz, A. Gómez, Apollon: A robust defense system against adversarial machine learning attacks in intrusion detection systems, Comput. Secur. 136 (2024) 103546.

[34] F. Merkle, M. Samsinger, P. Schöttle, T. Pevny, On the economics of adversarial machine learning, IEEE Trans. Inf. Forensics Secur. 19 (2024) 4670–4685, https://doi.org/10.1109/TIFS.2024.3379829.

[35] P. Mongeon, A. Paul-Hus, The journal coverage of web of science and scopus: A comparative analysis, Scientometrics 106 (2016) 213–228.

[36] N. Van Eck, L. Waltman, Software survey: VOSviewer, a computer program for bibliometric mapping, Scientometrics 84 (2) (2010) 523–538.

[37] N. Yazdanjue, H. Yazdanjouei, H. Gharoun, M.S. Khorshidi, M. Rakhshaninejad, A.H. Gandomi, A Comprehensive Bibliometric Analysis on Social Network Anonymization: Current Approaches and Future Directions, 2023 *arXiv preprint arXiv:2307.13179*.

[38] B. Amiri, R. Karimianghadim, N. Yazdanjue, L. Hossain, Research topics and trends of the hashtag recommendation domain, Scientometrics 126 (2021) 2689–2735.

[39] P.P. Chan, Z.-M. He, H. Li, C.-C. Hsu, Data sanitization against adversarial label contamination based on data complexity, Int. J. Mach. Learn. Cybern. 9 (2018) 1039–1052.

[40] S. Ho, A. Reddy, S. Venkatesan, R. Izmailov, R. Chadha, A. Oprea, Data sanitization approach to mitigate clean-label attacks against malware detection systems, in: MILCOM 2022-2022 IEEE Military Communications Conference (MILCOM), IEEE, 2022, pp. 993–998.

[41] P.W. Koh, J. Steinhardt, P. Liang, Stronger data poisoning attacks break data sanitization defenses, Mach. Learn. (2022) 1–47.

[42] S. Venkatesan, H. Sikka, R. Izmailov, R. Chadha, A. Oprea, M.J. De Lucia, Poisoning attacks and data sanitization mitigations for machine learning models in network intrusion detection systems, in: MILCOM 2021-2021 IEEE Military Communications Conference (MILCOM), IEEE, 2021, pp. 874–879.

[43] T.Y. Liu, Y. Yang, B. Mirzasoleiman, Friendly noise against adversarial noise: A powerful defense against data poisoning attack, Adv. Neural Inf. Process. Syst. 35 (2022) 11947–11959.

[44] Z. You, J. Ye, K. Li, Z. Xu, P. Wang, Adversarial noise layer: Regularize neural network by adding noise, in: 2019 IEEE International Conference on Image Processing (ICIP), IEEE, 2019, pp. 909–913.

[45] M. Jagielski, A. Oprea, B. Biggio, C. Liu, C. Nita-Rotaru, B. Li, Manipulating machine learning: Poisoning attacks and countermeasures for regression learning, in: 2018 IEEE Symposium on Security and Privacy (SP), IEEE, 2018, pp. 19–35.

[46] G. Apruzzese, M. Andreolini, M. Colajanni, M. Marchetti, Hardening random forest cyber detectors against adversarial attacks, IEEE Trans. Emerg. Top. Comput. Intell. 4 (4) (2020) 427–439.

[47] G. Tao, et al., Model orthogonalization: Class distance hardening in neural networks for better security, in: 2022 IEEE Symposium on Security and Privacy (SP), IEEE, 2022, pp. 1372–1389.

[48] B. Chen, et al., Detecting Backdoor Attacks on Deep Neural Networks by Activation Clustering, 2018 arXiv preprint arXiv:1811.03728.

[49] K. Liu, B. Dolan-Gavitt, S. Garg, Fine-pruning: Defending against backdooring attacks on deep neural networks, in: International Symposium on Research in Attacks, Intrusions, and Defenses, Springer, 2018, pp. 273–294.

[50] B. Wang, et al., Neural cleanse: Identifying and mitigating backdoor attacks in neural networks, in: 2019 IEEE Symposium on Security and Privacy (SP), IEEE, 2019, pp. 707–723.

[51] Y. Liu, Y. Xie, A. Srivastava, Neural trojans, in: 2017 IEEE International Conference on Computer Design (ICCD), IEEE, 2017, pp. 45–48.

[52] Y. Gao, C. Xu, D. Wang, S. Chen, D.C. Ranasinghe, S. Nepal, Strip: A defence against trojan attacks on deep neural networks, in: Proceedings of the 35th Annual Computer Security Applications Conference, 2019, pp. 113–125.

[53] B. Biggio, G. Fumera, F. Roli, Multiple classifier systems for robust classifier design in adversarial environments, Int. J. Mach. Learn. Cybern. 1 (2010) 27–41.

[54] F. Zhang, P.P. Chan, B. Biggio, D.S. Yeung, F. Roli, Adversarial feature selection against evasion attacks, IEEE Trans. Cybern. 46 (3) (2015) 766–777.

[55] L. Tong, B. Li, C. Hajaj, C. Xiao, N. Zhang, Y. Vorobeychik, Improving robustness of {ML} classifiers against realizable evasion attacks using conserved features, in: 28th USENIX Security Symposium (USENIX Security 19), 2019, pp. 285–302.

[56] A.N. Bhagoji, D. Cullina, C. Sitawarin, P. Mittal, Enhancing robustness of machine learning systems via data transformations, in: 2018 52nd Annual Conference on Information Sciences and Systems (CISS), IEEE, 2018, pp. 1–5.

[57] W. Xu, D. Evans, Y. Qi, Feature Squeezing: Detecting Adversarial Examples in Deep Neural Networks, 2017 arXiv preprint arXiv:1704.01155.

[58] E. Anthi, L. Williams, A. Javed, P. Burnap, Hardening machine learning denial of service (DoS) defences against adversarial attacks in IoT smart home networks, Comput. Secur. 108 (2021) 102352.

[59] G. Apruzzese, M. Andreolini, M. Marchetti, A. Venturi, M. Colajanni, Deep reinforcement adversarial learning against botnet evasion attacks, IEEE Trans. Netw. Serv. Manag. 17 (4) (2020) 1975–1987.

[60] M. Abadi, A. Chu, I. Goodfellow, H.B. McMahan, I. Mironov, K. Talwar, L. Zhang, Deep learning with differential privacy, in: Proceedings of the 2016 ACM SIGSAC Conference on Computer and Communications Security, Association for Computing Machinery (ACM), New York, NY, USA, 2016, pp. 308–318.

[61] Y. Aono, T. Hayashi, L. Wang, S. Moriai, Privacy-preserving deep learning via additively homomorphic encryption, IEEE Trans. Inf. Forensics Secur. 13 (5) (2017) 1333–1345.

[62] K. Bonawitz, et al., Practical Secure Aggregation for Federated Learning on User-Held Data, 2016 *arXiv preprint arXiv:1611.04482*.

[63] E. Raff, M. Benaroch, A.L. Farris, You Don't Need Robust Machine Learning to Manage Adversarial Attack Risks, 2023 arXiv preprint arXiv:2306.09951.

[64] Z. Chen, K. Pattabiraman, Overconfidence Is a Dangerous Thing: Mitigating Membership Inference Attacks by Enforcing Less Confident Prediction, 2023 arXiv preprint arXiv:2307.01610.

[65] Z. Yang, et al., Purifier: Defending data inference attacks via transforming confidence scores, Proc. AAAI Conf. Artif. Intell. 37 (9) (2023) 10871–10879.

Chapter 13

Gene structures in genetic programming: A taxonomic and functional survey

Mohammad Sadegh Khorshidi[1], Mohammad Reza Nikoo[2], Fang Chen[1], and Amir H. Gandomi[1, 3]

[1]Data Science Institute, Faculty of Engineering & Information Technology, University of Technology Sydney, Ultimo, NSW, Australia; [2]College of Engineering, Department of Civil and Architectural Engineering, Sultan Qaboos University, Muscat, Oman; [3]University Research and Innovation Center (EKIK), Obuda University, Budapest, Hungary

1. Introduction

Symbolic regression aims to uncover the underlying analytical expressions that best describe empirical data, offering an interpretable alternative to black-box models commonly used in machine learning. Unlike parametric regression or neural networks, symbolic regression searches for parameters and the form of the predictive function itself. Among the methods designed for this purpose, GP is a versatile, stochastic optimization framework that evolves symbolic expressions represented as executable programs. Since its inception by Ref. [1], GP has been extensively applied to symbolic regression tasks across various scientific and engineering domains, primarily due to its flexibility in evolving nonlinear, interpretable, and compact solutions from data.

At the heart of GP's functionality lies the genetic representation of solutions—commonly referred to as gene structure. The gene structure defines the format in which candidate solutions are encoded, which in turn determines the operability of evolutionary operators, the expressiveness of the solution space, and the algorithm's ability to generalize. While early GP systems employed tree-structured genes inspired by LISP-based expressions, subsequent developments introduced a range of alternative representations including linear, stack-based, graph-based, grammar-guided, and probabilistic structures. These diverse representations were motivated by limitations observed in the standard tree-based approach—such as code bloat, weak locality, and inefficient recombination—prompting researchers to reconsider how structure affects evolutionary dynamics.

Among these innovations, multigene GP (MGGP) and related modular structures have gained considerable traction. In contrast to traditional GP, which evolves single, monolithic expressions, MGGP represents individuals as a weighted ensemble of multiple gene components, often with each gene contributing a subexpression or partial solution. This architectural modification facilitates a more interpretable decomposition of the regression task and enhances the evolutionary process by enabling modularity, reuse, and ensemble-based generalization. Prominent frameworks such as GPTIPS [2,3] have demonstrated the potential of MGGP in producing parsimonious models with competitive accuracy, especially in symbolic regression benchmarks where complex functional relationships are involved.

The diversity of gene structures in GP is not merely a matter of representation; it induces profound implications for the exploration-exploitation balance, semantic diversity, bloat control, and fitness landscape smoothness. For instance, linear GP [4] operates on imperative sequences rather than expression trees, which alters how crossover and mutation affect program semantics. Similarly, grammar-based GP [5,6] leverages formal grammars to constrain the syntactic space of solutions, thereby encoding domain knowledge and ensuring structural validity. Cartesian GP [7] and its extensions represent individuals as directed acyclic graphs (DAGs), introducing redundancy and neutrality that impact evolvability and robustness.

Despite these conceptual advances, the literature on GP still lacks a unified analytical synthesis of how different gene structures influence the efficiency, scalability, and interpretability of symbolic regression models. Most studies either focus on operator design (e.g., crossover variants), empirical comparisons over a limited number of datasets, or propose

Advanced Intelligence Methods for Data Science and Optimization. https://doi.org/10.1016/B978-0-443-28940-8.00002-6

new representations without contextualizing them within a broader structural taxonomy. Moreover, the field has seen a surge in hybrid and differentiable approaches, including neuro-symbolic regression [8] and differentiable GP [9], yet their relationship to classical gene structures remains poorly understood. As symbolic regression applications expand to high-dimensional and noisy domains—such as physics-informed modeling and automated scientific discovery—the need for a principled understanding of gene structure design becomes increasingly critical.

This survey aims to fill that gap by providing a systematic, representation-centered review of GP in the context of symbolic regression, with a particular emphasis on multigene and modular gene structures. Our goal is not merely to catalog existing methods but to analyze the design principles, strengths, and limitations of various gene structures with respect to symbolic regression goals such as model parsimony, interpretability, semantic alignment, and search efficiency. We focus on how representation choices constrain or empower genetic operators, affect the dynamics of evolutionary search, and influence performance on standard symbolic regression benchmarks.

To this end, we organize the paper into the following parts. Section 2 revisits foundational concepts of GP, emphasizing its components and the mechanics of symbolic regression. Section 3 presents a comprehensive taxonomy of gene structures, covering tree-based, linear, stack-based, grammar-guided, graph-based, probabilistic, and strongly-typed GP variants. Special attention is given to modular and multigene representations, including their architectural rationale and empirical benefits. Section 4 discusses how gene structure interacts with variation operators—particularly crossover and mutation—highlighting structure-specific design challenges and their impact on population diversity and convergence. Section 5 reviews symbolic regression benchmarks and evaluates gene structures in terms of their expressiveness, generalization performance, and computational complexity. Section 6 synthesizes insights into comparative tables and decision guidelines, while Section 7 identifies open challenges and future directions, including differentiable representations, semantic-aware evolution, and hybrid neuro-symbolic models.

The intended audience of this survey includes researchers and practitioners in evolutionary computation, machine learning, and symbolic AI who seek to understand the representational underpinnings of GP in symbolic regression. We adopt a technically deep, citation-grounded approach, balancing historical perspective with critical analysis of current and emerging trends. By providing a structure-oriented lens on GP, we aim to advance the theoretical understanding and practical development of more robust, expressive, and interpretable symbolic regression models.

The survey methodology followed a structured, representation-centric workflow that integrates source identification, inclusion filtering, structured data extraction, and multidimensional synthesis (Fig. 13.1). Literature retrieval targeted peer-reviewed venues and authoritative software/toolbox releases using queries aligned with the representation families reviewed in Section 3. Inclusion was contingent on the study providing substantive technical detail on GP representations or on representation–operator dependencies, irrespective of the downstream application domain. Eligible works were mapped to the taxonomy of gene structures, and representation-specific operator design, bloat-control strategies, evaluation protocols, and benchmark usage were extracted in a standardized format. These data were then synthesized into comparative analyses and classification tables to enable cross-family evaluation of expressiveness, interpretability, modularity, evolvability, and structural efficiency. The workflow thereby formalizes a consistent basis for the technical synthesis and critical evaluation that follow in subsequent sections.

2. Foundations of GP

GP is a population-based evolutionary algorithm that extends the principles of genetic algorithms to the evolution of computer programs, typically expressed in symbolic or functional form [1]. Unlike fixed-length chromosomes in genetic algorithms, GP individuals are structured as variable-length programs, usually represented through expression trees that encode functional compositions of variables, constants, and operators [10]. This flexible representation makes GP suitable for nonlinear, model-free learning tasks such as symbolic regression, where both the structure and parameters of the solution are subject to optimization [4,11].

2.1 Representation and initialization

The most canonical form of GP representation is the tree structure, where internal nodes correspond to function operators (e.g., addition, multiplication, trigonometric functions), and leaves correspond to terminal symbols (variables or constants) [1,12]. Alternative representations have emerged, including linear instruction sequences [13], postfix stacks [14], grammatically constrained derivations [5], and graph-based encodings such as Cartesian GP [7]. The choice of representation influences both the expressiveness of the hypothesis space and the semantics and locality of genetic operators [15].

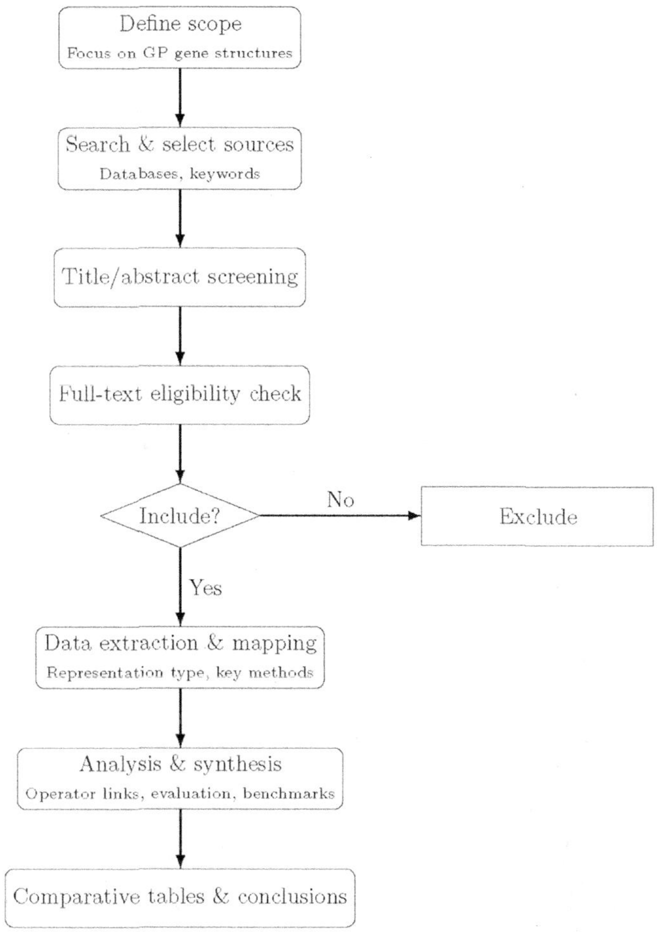

FIGURE 13.1 Streamlined workflow for the GP gene-structure survey. Detailed lists of representation families, datasets, and characteristics are given in the text and tables.

Initialization procedures define the structural characteristics of the first generation of individuals and thus shape the early exploration dynamics of the evolutionary process [16]. Common strategies include the GROW, FULL, and Ramped Half-and-Half methods introduced by Koza [1], which generate trees of varying depths and arities to promote structural diversity. More recent probabilistic initialization approaches, such as Probabilistic Tree Creation (PTC1 and PTC2), allow users to control the expected size of initial trees while satisfying syntactic constraints [16]. Given that premature structural homogeneity can impair exploration, initialization remains a critical component of GP's search behavior [17].

2.2 Population evolution and genetic operators

The core of GP lies in its population-based search, where candidate solutions evolve over generations through variation and selection operators [10]. At each generation, individuals are evaluated against a fitness function that quantifies their performance on a given task, commonly through root-mean-squared error (RMSE) is commonly used to measure predictive error, while expression complexity is usually treated as a secondary objective, penalty, or parsimony measure [18]. Selection mechanisms—such as tournament selection, fitness-proportionate selection, or rank-based selection—probabilistically favor individuals with better fitness for reproduction [19].

Variation is primarily introduced through crossover and mutation. Crossover typically exchanges subtrees between two parent programs, preserving syntactic validity while allowing partial reuse of structural components [1]. However, conventional subtree crossover has been shown to produce large offspring and introduce structural bloat, often without proportional gains in fitness [20]. As a result, numerous alternative crossover strategies have been proposed, including context-aware crossover [21], homologous crossover [15], and semantic-aware crossover [22]. Mutation may involve replacing subtrees with randomly generated expressions or perturbing constants within the terminals [23]. Although generally less disruptive than crossover, mutation plays a vital role in maintaining diversity and escaping local optima [24].

Beyond standard operators, advanced frameworks have introduced mechanisms such as automatically defined functions [11], epigenetic operators [25], and memetic crossovers [26], each altering the inheritance and adaptation of genetic material in ways informed by problem structure or semantic feedback.

2.3 Control parameters and bloat management

GP performance is sensitive to several control parameters, including population size, number of generations, selection pressure, and operator probabilities [27]. Larger populations tend to maintain higher diversity but incur higher computational costs, while smaller populations may converge prematurely or stagnate [28]. The depth and size of trees are particularly prone to unbounded growth—a phenomenon known as bloat—which can degrade generalization performance and hinder interpretability [29].

Various strategies have been proposed to counter bloat, including static depth/size limits [1], dynamic depth constraints [30], parsimony pressure [31], and resource-limited evolution [17]. Multiobjective approaches also model parsimony and fitness jointly, yielding trade-off solutions along the Pareto front [18,32].

2.4 Fitness evaluation and termination

Fitness evaluation in symbolic regression is typically based on minimizing the error between predicted outputs and ground truth values, but this may be augmented with structural complexity penalties or domain-specific constraints [33]. In multigene systems, the fitness of an individual may result from an ensemble prediction that linearly combines the outputs of subexpressions, requiring additional regression steps [2].

Termination criteria include fixed generation counts, fitness thresholds, or convergence-based halting conditions [34]. More adaptive strategies incorporate stagnation detection or dynamic restarts to balance computational efficiency and solution quality [35].

3. Taxonomy of gene structures in GP

The representation of individuals in GP directly determines the search-space structure, operator behavior, and the semantic expressiveness of evolved programs. Gene structure—the format and organization of symbols within individuals—not only conditions the efficiency of variation/selection but also constrains the classes of functions discoverable in symbolic regression. We therefore adopt a representation-centric taxonomy (Fig. 13.2) comprising nine families: Tree, Linear, Stack/Postfix (PushGP), Grammar/GE, Graph/CGP, Probabilistic/Model-based, Strongly-Typed/Constrained, Multigene/Ensemble, and Hybrid & Differentiable. Each class is evaluated for expressiveness, semantic locality, interpretability, and suitability to symbolic regression; for legibility, studies are assigned to a primary family in Fig. 13.2, with cross-family links (e.g., typed trees, neural/LLM-guided search) discussed in their respective subsections.

3.1 Tree-based GP

Tree-based representations remain the canonical structure in GP, introduced by Ref. [1], where individuals are expression trees with function nodes as internal operators and terminals as leaves. Trees allow for recursive functional composition and align naturally with parseable symbolic expressions, making them suitable for symbolic regression [10]. Subtree crossover and mutation are structurally intuitive and maintain syntactic closure [36].

However, tree-based GP suffers from weak locality—small structural changes often yield disproportionate semantic shifts—and from bloat, where nonfunctional code accumulates without improving fitness [20]. Several extensions have attempted to mitigate these limitations. Strongly Typed GP (STGP) introduces data-type constraints to maintain type safety during crossover [37], while Context-Aware and Size-Fair crossover aim to preserve structural semantics [12]. More recently, semantic-aware crossover operators have been developed to guide recombination based on output similarity rather than syntax alone [22].

3.2 Linear GP

Linear GP (LGP) encodes individuals as imperative instruction sequences acting on registers, drawing from classical machine code representations [13]. Unlike tree-based GP, LGP executes sequentially and allows for explicit reuse of intermediate computations, improving computational efficiency and expressiveness.

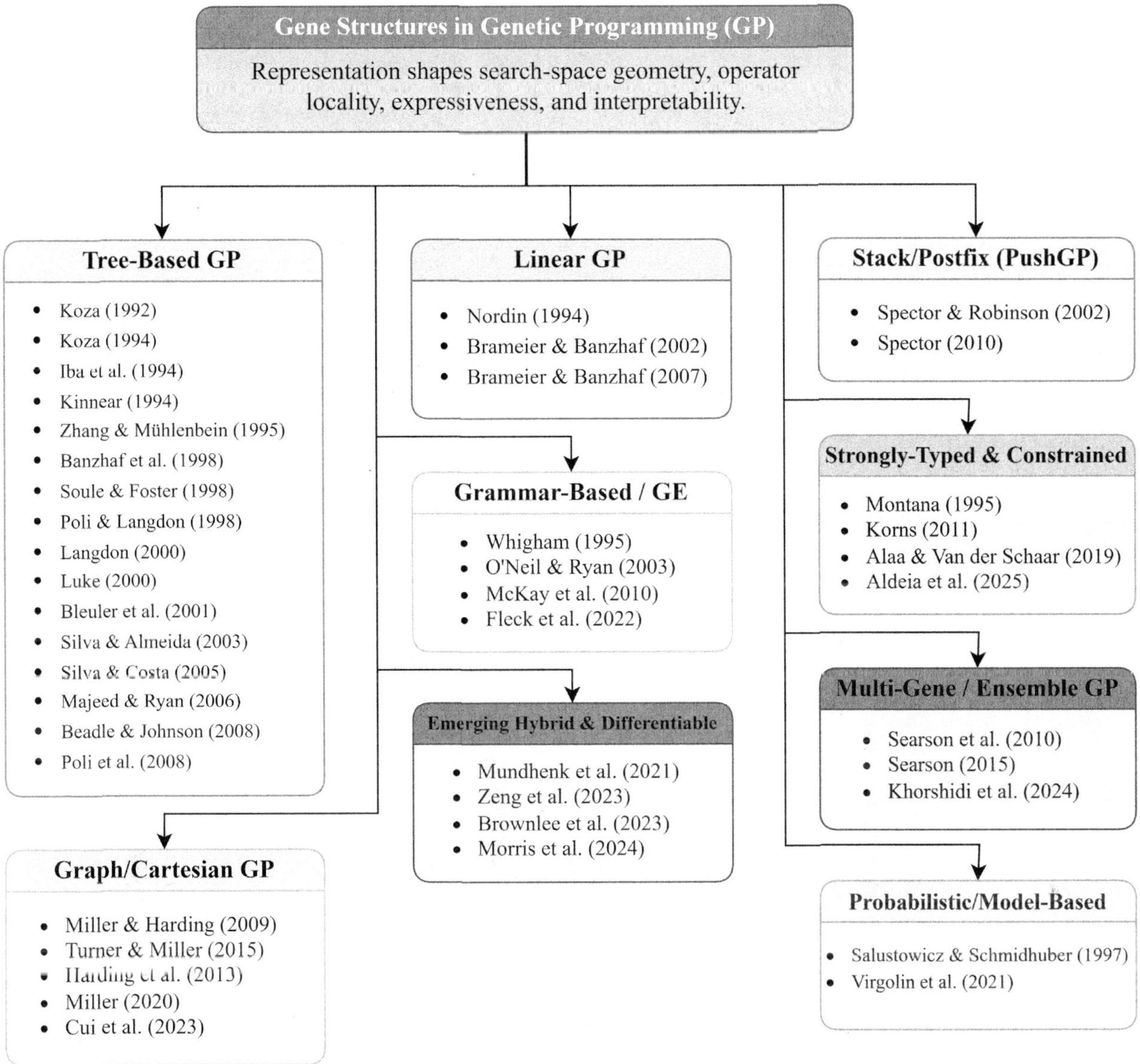

FIGURE 13.2 Taxonomy of GP gene structures. Literature is organized into nine representation families: Tree, linear, stack/postfix (PushGP), Grammar/GE, Graph/CGP, probabilistic/model-based, strongly-typed/constrained, multigene/ensemble, and hybrid & differentiable. Panels list representative studies (not exhaustive), colored by family; items are placed by primary representation.

The primary advantage of LGP lies in its compactness and hardware alignment. LGP typically produces shorter programs with lower redundancy and exhibits better resistance to bloat due to its flat structure [38]. However, LGP often sacrifices interpretability, as evolved sequences are less intuitive than symbolic expressions. Recent LGP variants for symbolic regression combine structural search with local optimisation or constant tuning; this claim should be supported by LGP-specific sources.

3.3 Stack-based and postfix GP

Stack-based GP, exemplified by PushGP [14], represents programs in postfix notation and uses multiple data stacks to handle different types (e.g., integer, float, boolean). This approach enables implicit control flow and allows operations to be composed dynamically during execution.

PushGP has demonstrated utility in evolving compositional structures with emergent modularity, particularly when combined with autoconstructive evolution [39]. However, stack-based execution is harder to analyze formally, and symbolic output extraction for regression remains a challenge.

3.4 Grammar-based GP

Grammar-Based GP (GBGP) leverages context-free grammars to generate syntactically valid expressions, embedding domain knowledge directly into the search process [5]. Grammatical Evolution (GE) further generalizes this by evolving codon-based genomes that map to grammar productions [40]. By constraining the syntactic space, GBGP can avoid invalid solutions and enforce priors such as dimensional consistency, function restrictions, or semantic templates [6]. More recent work on grammar-guided symbolic regression has shown improved convergence in problems with known structure [41].

3.5 Graph-based and Cartesian GP

Cartesian GP (CGP) encodes individuals as directed acyclic graphs (DAGs) where nodes represent operations and edges represent data flow [7]. CGP introduces neutrality and redundancy through inactive nodes, which enhances evolvability by allowing neutral mutations [42].

CGP is useful for symbolic regression because it enables subgraph reuse and compact expression encoding; its hardware-synthesis uses should be discussed separately. Extensions such as Embedded CGP (ECGP) [43] and Weighted CGP (W-CGP) enhance expressiveness by introducing continuous weights and local structures [44].

3.6 Probabilistic and model-based GP

Model-based GP approaches, including Probabilistic Incremental Program Evolution (PIPE) and Estimation of Distribution Programming (EDP), construct probabilistic models over program components to guide the generation of offspring [45,46].

These techniques reduce reliance on blind stochastic variation and are often less susceptible to bloat. However, their scalability is limited by the complexity of accurately estimating distributions over large symbolic spaces. Recent advancements have explored hybridization with neural density estimators and symbolic priors [47].

3.7 Strongly-typed and constrained GP

Strong typing introduces syntactic and semantic restrictions on allowable subtrees, improving program validity and evolutionary efficiency [37]. Type-safe GP prevents invalid compositions, encourages modularization, and enables polymorphic function evolution.

Constraints have been extended to include units-of-measure [48], dimensional consistency [49], and symbolic logic templates [50], all of which increase the relevance of evolved expressions in scientific contexts.

3.8 Multigene and ensemble GP structures

Multigene GP (MGGP) represents individuals as a linear combination of subprograms (genes), with scalar weights optimized by a separate regression step [2]. Each gene encodes a simple symbolic expression, and their combination enables modular approximation of complex functions.

MGGP has demonstrated superior generalization, parsimony, and stability in symbolic regression tasks, especially when the target function exhibits additive or weakly interacting structure [51]. Recent approaches have extended MGGP with semantic distance regularization [52]. Hybrid ensemble variants, including multiview GP approaches, may improve robustness in high-dimensional settings, although classification-focused evidence should not be treated as direct symbolic regression evidence [53].

3.9 Emerging hybrid and differentiable structures

Recent work has blurred the line between GP and deep learning through differentiable GP (DGP), where expression trees are relaxed into continuous parameter spaces and optimized with gradient-based methods [9]. These approaches improve scalability and enable end-to-end integration with other machine learning systems.

Neural-Guided Symbolic Regression [8] uses neural predictors to bias the search toward promising subexpressions. LLM-augmented GP is an emerging direction in which pretrained language models may guide expression synthesis, repair, or variation, but its role in symbolic regression remains under active evaluation [54].

Recent work has begun exploring the integration of large language models (LLMs) into the mutation pipeline of evolutionary systems, effectively hybridizing symbolic GP with pretrained transformer models. In the domain of genetic improvement (GI), Brownlee et al. [55] demonstrated that LLMs can serve as mutation operators to diversify edits and improve the rate of valid patches. While this work centers on software repair, it provides an adjacent example of LLM-guided mutation in genetic improvement, but direct evidence in symbolic regression should be cited separately.

4. Variation operators and their dependency on structure

The behavior and efficacy of GP critically depend on the design of variation operators—primarily crossover and mutation—which guide the traversal of the search space. These operators are intimately tied to the underlying gene structure, as they manipulate syntactic elements that encode semantic information. Therefore, understanding the interaction between structure and variation is fundamental to achieving desirable trade-offs between exploration and exploitation, controlling bloat, and preserving functional diversity in symbolic regression.

4.1 Structure-specific crossover mechanisms

4.1.1 Tree-based representations

In canonical tree-based GP, crossover is typically implemented as subtree crossover, which replaces a randomly selected subtree in one parent with a subtree from another [1]. While syntactically valid and structurally expressive, this operator lacks semantic awareness and often produces disruptive changes, particularly when subtrees encode semantically critical or fragile components [20]. As a result, it tends to exacerbate bloat by favoring larger offspring without consistent fitness gain [29].

To address these issues, several crossover strategies have been proposed. Size-Fair Crossover constrains the exchanged subtrees to be similar in size, reducing the likelihood of exponential growth [12]. Context-Aware Crossover biases the choice of crossover points based on node context or parent structure, thus maintaining functional locality [21]. Homologous Crossover aligns nodes with similar positions or roles across both parents to preserve structural correspondences [15]. More recently, Semantic-Aware Crossover selects crossover points based on the similarity of program behavior—evaluated over input-output traces—to reduce destructive recombination [22].

4.1.2 Linear representations

In Linear LGP, crossover operates on instruction sequences. Variants include two-point crossover, homologous instruction exchange, or insertion-based recombination, all of which preserve execution order and register dependencies [13]. The low structural overhead and high modularity of LGP reduce the probability of syntactic disruption, but semantic consistency across recombined code segments remains an open challenge [38].

4.1.3 Stack-based representations

PushGP employs stack-aware crossover strategies where program fragments are exchanged while ensuring that the stack behavior is preserved or restored postrecombination [14]. This is crucial because control flow and data routing in PushGP rely on multiple concurrent stacks (e.g., integer, boolean, float). Autoconstructive variants of PushGP evolve crossover operators themselves, introducing a meta-evolutionary layer to optimize variation behavior [39].

4.1.4 Grammar-based representations

In Grammar-Based GP, crossover operates on derivation trees or codon arrays. Grammar-Guided Crossover swaps subtrees that correspond to identical grammar production rules, maintaining syntactic constraints [5,6]. In Grammatical Evolution (GE), codon level crossover may disrupt mappings if not aligned with derivation boundaries, motivating the use of sensible crossover and syntax-aware slicing to preserve grammatical validity [40].

4.1.5 Graph-based representations

Crossover in CGP is complicated by the DAG structure and the presence of inactive nodes. Standard strategies include node-level uniform crossover and slice-based crossover, both of which can alter connectivity without breaking acyclic constraints [7]. CGP's redundancy—through noncoding genes—enables neutral crossover, which introduces genetic drift while preserving output behavior [42].

4.2 Structure-specific mutation mechanisms

Mutation operators vary substantially across representations, reflecting their syntactic structure and execution semantics.

4.2.1 Tree-based mutation

Mutation in tree-based GP is typically implemented as subtree mutation, where a random subtree is replaced with a newly generated one. This operation can be highly disruptive if large or semantically important subtrees are replaced [1]. To mitigate such effects, point mutation (changing a node's operator or terminal), depth-limited mutation, and semantic-aware mutation have been proposed [20,52].

4.2.2 Linear and stack-based mutation

In LGP, mutation may involve instruction replacement, operand mutation, or constant tuning, allowing finer-grained edits [4]. The sequential nature of execution enables local mutations to yield coherent effects, though register reuse can introduce epistasis. Stack-based systems such as PushGP permit instruction set mutation and stack manipulation edits, often coevolved with domain-specific macros [14].

4.2.3 Grammar and graph-based mutation

Grammar-based mutation modifies codons or subtrees while respecting grammar constraints. For example, rule-constrained subtree mutation ensures that the replacement subtree derives from the same nonterminal symbol as the original [6]. In CGP, mutation typically acts at the node level, modifying functions, connections, or output nodes, often with fixed mutation rates [43]. CGP's neutral networks allow mutations to accumulate silently, facilitating nondestructive exploration.

4.2.4 Probabilistic and differentiable variants

In model-based GP frameworks such as PIPE, mutation is implicitly realized by sampling from learned probabilistic models [45]. In differentiable GP, gradient-driven mutation replaces stochastic edits, adjusting both structure and parameters through continuous relaxation [9]. This form of mutation introduces inductive biases and allows for backpropagation-compatible optimization, albeit at the cost of full symbolic transparency.

4.3 Effect of gene structure on operator design

The structural encoding of individuals directly determines the feasibility and performance of variation operators. For example, tree-based and stack-based representations favor compositionality but are vulnerable to bloat and semantic destructiveness. Linear and CGP structures allow modular recombination but require careful management of dependencies and neutrality. Grammar-guided representations enable constrained exploration but impose syntactic rigidity. Multigene representations introduce a new axis of variation: intergene recombination and weighting, which has been exploited in softmax ensembling and elastic combination models [2,53].

Recent hybrid systems augment traditional GP operators with neural guidance, semantic distance metrics, or LLM-generated edits to enhance variation diversity and alignment with task objectives [8,54,55]. These advances highlight the shift from purely stochastic to more informed, adaptive variation mechanisms, emphasizing the importance of structure-aware operator design.

5. Evaluation in symbolic regression context

The evaluation of GP in symbolic regression involves assessing not only the accuracy of the evolved models but also their structural complexity, interpretability, and generalization performance. These criteria are tightly coupled to the underlying gene structure, which influences the representation's inductive bias, expressiveness, and convergence behavior. This section outlines standard evaluation metrics, benchmark datasets, and structural considerations relevant to symbolic regression, with an emphasis on how different gene structures impact performance outcomes.

5.1 Metrics for performance assessment

The most commonly used metric in symbolic regression is RMSE, which quantifies the average deviation between predicted and actual values [1]. While effective for capturing overall accuracy, RMSE can obscure overfitting tendencies, especially when models achieve low training error at the expense of generalization [17]. Consequently, test error and validation error are routinely reported to evaluate generalization under distributional shifts [56].

To assess model simplicity, measures such as tree depth, node count, or expression length are used. These indicators are essential in detecting and mitigating code bloat, which can degrade interpretability and inflate computational costs [20]. Some studies employ model parsimony scores, combining error and complexity into a single composite objective [18].

When comparing symbolic regression models with black-box alternatives (e.g., XGBoost, neural networks), additional interpretability metrics are considered. For instance, structural transparency—the degree to which model components map to understandable functional elements—is emphasized in grammar-based GP [41], while semantic alignment is evaluated in semantic-aware GP [25]. In multigene GP, the contribution of each gene can be inspected through ensemble weights or feature attributions, which are particularly relevant when evaluating model modularity [3].

Beyond accuracy and complexity, runtime performance and convergence dynamics are increasingly used to assess scalability. These metrics are critical when evaluating differentiable GP methods or hybrid neuro-symbolic approaches that incorporate computational overhead from external models [9,57].

5.2 Benchmark datasets

Symbolic regression benchmarks fall into three main categories: synthetic function approximations, real-world datasets, and physics-informed expressions.

5.2.1 Synthetic benchmarks

Classic functions such as Nguyen, Keijzer, Korns, and Pagie-1 serve as de facto standards in GP research due to their analytical tractability and varying degrees of difficulty [58]. These functions allow for systematic assessment of overfitting, generalization, and bloat behavior. Benchmarks such as Friedman 1–3 are also used to evaluate feature interactions and epistasis sensitivity [59].

5.2.2 Scientific datasets

Recent efforts emphasize the use of symbolic regression for scientific discovery, where models are expected to reveal interpretable laws from empirical data. The Feynman dataset contains equations derived from physics, with varying levels of noise and variable count, serving as a testbed for models requiring dimensional consistency and symbolic complexity [60].

5.2.3 Real-world datasets

General-purpose datasets, such as those from the UCI repository, are less interpretable but are included for comparative performance testing against black-box regressors. Their use is prominent in studies validating hybrid approaches that combine GP with neural guidance or probabilistic modeling [47,61].

Recent works have also proposed benchmarking suites such as SRBench, which unify evaluation protocols across multiple datasets, error metrics, and model types [49]. These frameworks facilitate fair comparisons and support reproducibility.

5.3 Impact of gene structure on evaluation criteria

The choice of gene structure affects how models trade off between accuracy, complexity, and robustness. Tree-based GP, while expressive, often produces bloated solutions with redundant subtrees unless regularization is explicitly enforced [29]. LGP and CGP tend to produce more compact and reusable components, but at the cost of interpretability due to register dependencies or DAG semantics [4,7].

Grammar-based GP constrains expressiveness using prior knowledge, which can improve generalization and enforce domain-relevant properties, as seen in symbolic physics discovery and chemical equation modeling [6,41]. However, excessive constraint tightens the search space and may exclude viable solutions.

Multigene GP explicitly facilitates modular composition, enabling sparse additive models that better reflect the structure of many real-world target functions [51,53]. The ensemble nature of MGGP allows for decomposition of complex tasks into interpretable subcomponents and can improve convergence by decoupling optimization across genes.

Differentiable and hybrid GP models introduce new challenges for evaluation. While these models often outperform traditional GP in test error and convergence speed, they may introduce opacity through black-box guidance, undermining the interpretability that symbolic regression seeks to preserve [8,55]. Evaluating such models requires multiobjective analysis that includes fidelity, complexity, semantic novelty, and transparency.

5.4 Considerations for fair comparison

Comparing GP variants requires standardized experimental protocols, including:

- Multiple random seeds ($\geq$30) to account for stochastic variation,
- Consistent hyperparameter settings or tuned baselines,
- Statistical testing (e.g., Wilcoxon signed-rank, Friedman tests),
- Effect size reporting (e.g., Cliff's delta, Cohen's d).

Without these safeguards, performance differences may result from experimental artifacts rather than structural superiority. Modern studies increasingly employ open-source benchmarks, reproducibility checklists, and runtime audits to establish reliability [49,59].

6. Comparative summary and synthesis

The heterogeneity of gene structures in GP reflects a spectrum of trade-offs among expressiveness, interpretability, generalization, computational overhead, and evolvability. While previous sections introduced each structure in isolation, a cross-comparative synthesis is essential to delineate how representational choices impact symbolic regression performance. This section summarizes these relationships and outlines design guidelines for selecting gene structures based on problem requirements.

6.1 Expressiveness versus parsimony

Tree-based GP offers a maximally expressive representation space, allowing arbitrary functional compositions. However, this expressiveness often results in structural bloat unless regularization is applied [20]. In contrast, linear GP restricts expressiveness through instruction sequencing but achieves better parsimony and code compactness, especially for procedural tasks [4]. Grammar-based GP limits search space to grammatically valid expressions, which may reduce overfitting but risks excluding valid solutions when the grammar is overly constrained [5,41]. Cartesian GP balances expressiveness and reuse by enabling DAG-based encoding, but the presence of inactive genes introduces redundancy requiring management [7].

Multigene GP architectures distribute complexity across subexpressions, achieving higher parsimony than monolithic trees for additive or weakly coupled problems [3,51]. Differentiable GP and hybrid neuro-symbolic approaches introduce latent expressiveness through parameter tuning and model bias, but often at the cost of symbolic clarity [8,9].

6.2 Interpretability and modularity

Interpretability is fundamental in symbolic regression, where human comprehension of the output model is often as important as predictive accuracy. Tree-based and grammar-based GP structures are directly interpretable in symbolic form and are thus preferred in domains requiring analytical transparency [1,41]. Linear GP and CGP tend to obscure symbolic structure due to low-level operations and implicit computation flow, making post-hoc interpretation more difficult [7].

Multigene GP provides a modular structure, where each gene's contribution can be isolated and analyzed, supporting both interpretability and feature relevance estimation [53]. This decomposition aligns with ensemble principles in machine learning, facilitating robustness and clarity simultaneously [2].

Stack-based and autoconstructive systems (e.g., PushGP) offer unique advantages in self-adaptive behavior and code evolution but suffer from steep interpretability trade-offs due to dynamic stack state and nonobvious control flow [14].

6.3 Evolutionary efficiency and operator compatibility

The efficiency of evolutionary search depends on how gene structure interacts with genetic operators. Tree-based GP allows structurally diverse recombination through subtree crossover, but this often introduces semantic disruption unless semantic-aware or homologous methods are used [22]. LGP and CGP show better locality and evolvability due to modular, flat encodings and nondisruptive variation [42].

Grammar-based systems constrain the operator space to valid derivations, improving the success rate of crossover but limiting exploration diversity [6]. Probabilistic and model-based GP approaches reduce reliance on variation by guiding generation through learned distributions, though scalability and expressiveness remain concerns [46,47].

Hybrid models incorporating language models or neural guidance improve search efficiency and convergence but introduce opaque decision pathways, requiring careful evaluation of transparency and fairness [54,55].

6.4 Problem suitability and domain alignment

The suitability of a gene structure depends on the domain's structural and interpretive needs:

- Tree-based and grammar-based GP are favored in scientific modeling, where symbolic interpretability is crucial [60].
- LGP and CGP are effective in signal processing, control, or image domains where modular reuse and compactness are prioritized [62].
- Multigene GP and ensemble extensions may be useful for high-dimensional or multioutput regression, but this should be supported by symbolic-regression evidence rather than classification-only evidence.
- Differentiable and hybrid GP excel in data-intensive or black-box environments, but care must be taken to retain interpretability if symbolic output is required [8,9].

6.5 Summary

The gene structures explored in this survey exhibit distinct strengths and limitations across multiple symbolic regression evaluation axes. Table 13.1 presents a comparative synthesis of these structures with respect to key design considerations, including representational expressiveness, interpretability, evolvability, modularity, risk of structural bloat, and typical application suitability. High expressiveness is characteristic of tree-based and differentiable GP, though this flexibility often leads to increased bloat unless constrained by regularization or semantic awareness. Interpretability is most naturally supported by tree-based, grammar-based, and multigene GP, whereas stack-based and linear variants often obscure symbolic semantics due to low-level procedural encoding. Evolvability—defined as the structure's compatibility with variation operators while preserving semantic stability—is enhanced in Cartesian and linear GP due to their locality and redundancy properties, and further improved in multigene and probabilistic models by modular recombination or learned variation distributions. Modularity, crucial for decomposing complex symbolic relationships, is most explicit in multigene

TABLE 13.1 Comparative analysis of major gene structures in GP across key evaluation dimensions relevant to symbolic regression.

Gene structure	Expressiveness	Interpretability	Evolvability	Modularity	Bloat risk	Suitable tasks
Tree-based	High	High	Moderate	Low	High	General SR, interpretable tasks
Linear GP	Moderate	Low	High	Moderate	Low	Procedural modeling, signals
Stack-based	Moderate	Low	Variable	Low	Moderate	Autoconstructive evolution
Grammar-based	Constrained	High	Moderate	High	Low	Physics, engineering, chemistry
Cartesian GP	High	Low–Moderate	High	High	Low	Reuse-intensive regression
Multigene GP	High	High	High	High	Low	Modular or additive systems
Probabilistic GP	Moderate	Moderate	High	Low	Low	Structured priors, optimization
Differentiable GP	High	Low	Very high	Low	Controlled	Deep regression, hybrid models
LLM-hybrid GP	High	Variable	High	High	Controlled	Symbol synthesis, repair

GP and CGP, where component reuse or ensemble combination is intrinsic. Finally, bloat risk is highest in unconstrained tree-based GP and lowest in structured or regularized variants such as grammar-based GP, CGP, and differentiable GP. This synthesis highlights that no single structure dominates across all criteria, and effective deployment requires alignment between the representational characteristics and task-specific priorities.

7. Open challenges and research opportunities

Despite considerable advancements in gene structures for GP, several fundamental challenges remain unresolved, particularly in the context of symbolic regression. These challenges span expressiveness-control trade-offs, semantic generalization, operator design, modularization, and reproducibility. Addressing them is essential for evolving interpretable and generalizable models in increasingly complex domains.

7.1 Balancing expressiveness and generalization

A persistent issue across GP variants is the tension between representational expressiveness and model generalization. Structures that allow unrestricted composition, such as tree-based and differentiable GP, tend to explore vast hypothesis spaces, increasing the likelihood of fitting spurious patterns or redundant substructures [9,20]. Conversely, grammar-based or strongly typed systems restrict solution space but risk excluding viable formulations, especially when the underlying grammar lacks domain completeness [6]. Future work must explore adaptive representation constraints, where the expressive scope of the gene structure evolves in tandem with population semantics or predictive uncertainty.

7.2 Semantic preservation in variation

While semantic-aware operators have improved the locality of crossover and mutation in recent years [22,25], they remain limited in generality and scalability. Existing methods often rely on expensive behavioral evaluations or static semantics captured from training data, which may not generalize across input domains. There is a need for learning-based variation operators that adapt mutation and recombination strategies based on contextual embeddings or behavioral equivalence classes. This direction aligns with recent trends in LLM-guided mutation and reinforcement-learning-enhanced GP, which offer dynamic operator tuning [8,55].

7.3 Structural modularity and decomposition

While modularity is recognized as beneficial for both interpretability and evolvability, the automated discovery of functional substructures remains underexplored. Multigene GP provides an explicit compositional framework, but the determination of gene granularity, intergene interactions, and ensemble weighting is typically heuristic [3,53]. Novel mechanisms for data-driven modularity detection, potentially leveraging information-theoretic segmentation, semantic clustering, or network-based community detection, could enhance model decomposition. Additionally, hybrid models should formalize the semantic roles of symbolic and neural components to preserve transparency while enabling scale.

7.4 Evolutionary efficiency and scalability

Many gene structures suffer from poor scalability when applied to high-dimensional or large-scale symbolic regression tasks. Tree-based GP becomes inefficient as tree sizes grow, while LGP and CGP often require large populations and deep pipelines to evolve reusable components [7,63]. Differentiable GP and probabilistic models address scalability to some extent, but often require gradient information or probabilistic approximations that are incompatible with hard syntactic constraints [9,47]. There remains an unmet need for representation-agnostic search frameworks that combine symbolic flexibility with neural optimization and probabilistic sampling in a modular and interpretable pipeline.

7.5 Integration with domain knowledge

Encoding domain knowledge into GP remains a double-edged sword. While grammars and type systems can enforce validity and dimensional consistency, they often require expert-defined templates that are brittle or task-specific [5,41]. Emerging approaches, such as grammar induction, unit-checking neural priors, or meta-GP frameworks that evolve both the program and the structural bias, offer potential directions for balancing flexibility with correctness. However, these techniques require principled evaluation to avoid over-constraining the hypothesis space.

7.6 Reproducibility and benchmarking

The lack of standardized evaluation protocols has historically limited the reproducibility of GP studies. Differences in dataset splits, variation operator implementations, and termination criteria obscure cross paper comparisons [25,59]. Recent efforts such as SRBench and OpenSR provide baseline models and reproducibility checklists, but more comprehensive benchmarking ecosystems are required. These should include multiple problem classes, evaluation across model complexity metrics, and standardized logging of search trajectories and operator behavior.

8. Conclusion

The architecture of gene structures in GP fundamentally shapes the search dynamics, representational scope, and interpretability of symbolic regression models. This survey has reviewed the landscape of gene representations, from classical tree-based encodings to contemporary modular, probabilistic, and hybrid neuro-symbolic variants. We classified these structures into nine families and evaluated them against core criteria, including expressiveness, modularity, evolvability, and compatibility with variation operators. The analysis revealed that structural decisions are rarely neutral: each form imposes inductive biases that influence both convergence behavior and model generalization.

Tree-based GP offers syntactic transparency and expressive power but requires explicit mechanisms to manage bloat and semantic disruption. Linear and Cartesian GP prioritize evolutionary locality and computational efficiency but often trade off interpretability. Grammar-based and strongly typed systems encode domain priors, facilitating constraint-aware exploration, while probabilistic and differentiable GP introduce parametric smoothness into symbolic spaces at the cost of symbolic purity. Multigene structures, particularly those employing ensemble-based composition, demonstrate favorable convergence and generalization behavior for high-dimensional, decomposable tasks, especially when guided by information-theoretic or semantic criteria.

The survey also identified emerging frontiers, including adaptive constraint learning, operator coevolution, differentiable symbolic models, and LLM-guided mutation. These developments underscore the field's shift toward hybrid frameworks that integrate symbolic transparency with neural scalability. However, realizing this integration without compromising model auditability, modularity, or reproducibility remains a significant research challenge.

Future work should pursue structured evaluations of gene representation under standardized benchmarking protocols, develop semantics-preserving operator libraries, and formalize theoretical frameworks that relate gene structure to convergence rates and functional diversity. Such efforts are necessary not only to improve symbolic regression performance but also to fulfill its broader promise as an interpretable and generalizable modeling paradigm across scientific and engineering domains.

Acknowledgment

The Australian Government supported this work through the Australian Research Council, Australia, under Project DE210101808.

References

[1] J.R. Koza, Genetic Programming: On the Programming of Computers by Means of Natural Selection, MIT Press, 1992.

[2] D.P. Searson, D.E. Leahy, M.J. Willis, GPTIPS: An open source genetic programming toolbox for multigene symbolic regression, in: Proceedings of the International Multiconference of Engineers and Computer Scientists, 2010.

[3] D.P. Searson, GPTIPS 2: An open-source software platform for symbolic data mining, in: Handbook of Genetic Programming Applications, Springer, 2015, pp. 551–573.

[4] M. Brameier, W. Banzhaf, A comparison of linear genetic programming and neural networks in medical data mining, IEEE Trans. Evol. Comput. 5 (1) (2002) 17–26.

[5] P.A. Whigham, Grammatically-based genetic programming, in: Proceedings of the Workshop on Genetic Programming: From Theory to Real-World Applications, Vol 16, July 1995, pp. 33–41.

[6] R.I. McKay, N.X. Hoai, P.A. Whigham, Y. Shan, M. O'neill, Grammar-based genetic programming: A survey, Genet. Program. Evolvable Mach. 11 (3) (2010) 365–396.

[7] J.F. Miller, S.L. Harding, Cartesian genetic programming, in: Proceedings of the 11th Annual Conference Companion on Genetic and Evolutionary Computation Conference: Late Breaking Papers, July 2009, pp. 3489–3512.

[8] T. Mundhenk, M. Landajuela, R. Glatt, C.P. Santiago, B.K. Petersen, Symbolic regression via deep reinforcement learning enhanced genetic programming seeding, Adv. Neural Inf. Process. Syst. 34 (2021) 24912–24923.

[9] P. Zeng, X. Song, A. Lensen, Y. Ou, Y. Sun, M. Zhang, J. Lv, Differentiable Genetic Programming for High-Dimensional Symbolic Regression, 2023 arXiv preprint arXiv:2304.08915.
[10] W. Banzhaf, P. Nordin, R.E. Keller, F.D. Francone, Genetic Programming: An Introduction: on the Automatic Evolution of Computer Programs and its Applications, Morgan Kaufmann Publishers Inc, 1998.
[11] J.R. Koza, Genetic Programming II: Automatic Discovery of Reusable Programs, MIT press, 1994.
[12] W.B. Langdon, Size fair and homologous tree genetic programming crossovers, Genet. Program. Evolvable Mach. 1 (1/2) (2000) 95–119.
[13] M.F. Brameier, W. Banzhaf, Basic Concepts of Linear Genetic Programming, Springer US, 2007, pp. 13–34.
[14] L. Spector, A. Robinson, Genetic programming and autoconstructive evolution with the push programming language, Genet. Program. Evolvable Mach. 3 (2002) 7–40.
[15] R. Poli, W.B. Langdon, Schema theory for genetic programming with one-point crossover and point mutation, Evol. Comput. 6 (3) (1998) 231–252.
[16] S. Luke, Two fast tree-creation algorithms for genetic programming, IEEE Trans. Evol. Comput. 4 (3) (2000) 274–283.
[17] S. Silva, E. Costa, Comparing tree depth limits and resource-limited GP, in: 2005 IEEE Congress on Evolutionary Computation, vol 1, IEEE, September 2005, pp. 920–927.
[18] S. Bleuler, M. Brack, L. Thiele, E. Zitzler, Multiobjective genetic programming: Reducing bloat using SPEA2, in: Proceedings of the 2001 Congress on Evolutionary Computation (IEEE Cat. No. 01TH8546), vol 1, IEEE, May 2001, pp. 536–543.
[19] A.E. Eiben, J.E. Smith, Introduction to Evolutionary Computing, springer, 2015.
[20] W.B. Langdon, R. Poli, Why ants are hard, in: Proceedings of the Genetic Programming Conference, 1998.
[21] H. Majeed, C. Ryan, Using context-aware crossover to improve the performance of GP, in: Proceedings of the 8th Annual Conference on Genetic and Evolutionary Computation, July 2006, pp. 847–854.
[22] L. Beadle, C.G. Johnson, Semantically driven crossover in genetic programming, in: 2008 IEEE Congress on Evolutionary Computation (IEEE World Congress on Computational Intelligence), IEEE, June 2008, pp. 111–116.
[23] H. Iba, H. De Garis, T. Sato, 12 principle genetic programming using a minimum description length, in: Advances in Genetic Programming, 1, 1994, p. 265.
[24] C.Y. Lee, X. Yao, Evolutionary programming using mutations based on the Lévy probability distribution, IEEE Trans. Evol. Comput. 8 (1) (2004) 1–13.
[25] W. La Cava, T. Helmuth, L. Spector, K. Danai, Genetic programming with epigenetic local search, Proceedings of the 2015 Annual Conference on Genetic and Evolutionary Computation 27 (3) (2015) 1055–1062.
[26] B.E. Eskridge, D.F. Hougen, Imitating success: A memetic crossover operator for genetic programming, in: Proceedings of the 2004 Congress on Evolutionary Computation (IEEE Cat. No. 04TH8753), vol. 1, IEEE, June 2004, pp. 809–815.
[27] S. Luke, Modification point depth and genome growth in genetic programming, Evol. Comput. 11 (1) (2003) 67–106.
[28] S. Luke, G.C. Balan, L. Panait, Population implosion in genetic programming, in: Genetic and Evolutionary Computation—GECCO 2003: Genetic and Evolutionary Computation Conference Chicago, IL, USA, July 12–16, 2003 Proceedings, Part II, Springer Berlin Heidelberg, 2003, pp. 1729–1739.
[29] T. Soule, J.A. Foster, Effects of code growth and parsimony pressure on populations in genetic programming, Evol. Comput. 6 (4) (1998) 293–309.
[30] S. Silva, J. Almeida, Dynamic maximum tree depth: A simple technique for avoiding bloat in tree-based gp, in: Genetic and Evolutionary Computation—GECCO 2003: Genetic and Evolutionary Computation Conference Chicago, IL, USA, July 12–16, 2003 Proceedings, Part II, Springer Berlin Heidelberg, 2003, pp. 1776–1787.
[31] B.T. Zhang, H. Mühlenbein, Balancing accuracy and parsimony in genetic programming, Evol. Comput. 3 (1) (1995) 17–38.
[32] E. Zitzler, L. Thiele, Multiobjective evolutionary algorithms: A comparative case study and the strength Pareto approach, IEEE Trans. Evol. Comput. 3 (4) (2002) 257–271.
[33] K.E. Kinnear, Alternatives in Automatic Function Definition: A Comparison of Performance, 1994.
[34] M.D. Kramer, D. Zhang, Gaps: A genetic programming system, in: Proceedings 24th Annual International Computer Software and Applications Conference. COMPSAC2000, IEEE, October 2000, pp. 614–619.
[35] G. Folino, G. Spezzano, P-cage: An environment for evolutionary computation in peer-to-peer systems, in: European Conference on Genetic Programming, Springer Berlin Heidelberg, Berlin, Heidelberg, April 2006, pp. 341–350.
[36] R. Poli, W.B. Langdon, N.F. McPhee, J.R. Koza, A Field Guide to Genetic Programming, Lulu. com, 2008.
[37] D.J. Montana, Strongly typed genetic programming, Evol. Comput. 3 (2) (1995) 199–230.
[38] P. Nordin, 14 A compiling genetic programming system that directly manipulates the machine code, in: Advances in Genetic Programming, 1, 1994, p. 311.
[39] L. Spector, Towards practical autoconstructive evolution: Self-evolution of problem-solving genetic programming systems, in: Genetic Programming Theory and Practice VIII, Springer New York, New York, NY, 2010, pp. 17–33.
[40] M. O'Neill, C. Ryan, M. O'Neil, C. Ryan, Grammatical Evolution. Grammatical Evolution: Evolutionary Automatic Programming in an Arbitrary Language, Springer US, 2003, pp. 33–47.
[41] P. Fleck, S. Winkler, M. Kommenda, M. Affenzeller, Grammar-based vectorial genetic programming for symbolic regression, in: Genetic Programming Theory and Practice XVIII, Springer Nature Singapore, Singapore, 2022, pp. 21–43.
[42] A.J. Turner, J.F. Miller, Neutral genetic drift: An investigation using Cartesian genetic programming, Genet. Program. Evolvable Mach. 16 (2015) 531–558.

[43] J.F. Miller, Cartesian genetic programming: Its status and future, Genet. Program. Evolvable Mach. 21 (1) (2020) 129–168.
[44] H. Cui, D. Pätzel, A. Margraf, J. Hähner, Weighted mutation of connections to mitigate search space limitations in Cartesian genetic programming, in: Proceedings of the 17th ACM/SIGEVO Conference on Foundations of Genetic Algorithms, August 2023, pp. 50–60.
[45] R. Salustowicz, J. Schmidhuber, Probabilistic incremental program evolution, Evol. Comput. 5 (2) (1997) 123–141.
[46] M. Virgolin, T. Alderliesten, C. Witteveen, P.A. Bosman, Improving model-based genetic programming for symbolic regression of small expressions, Evol. Comput. 29 (2) (2021) 211–237.
[47] L. Rodriguez-Coayahuitl, A. Morales-Reyes, H.J. Escalante, Evolving autoencoding structures through genetic programming, Genet. Program. Evolvable Mach. 20 (2019) 413–440.
[48] M.F. Korns, Accuracy in symbolic regression, in: Genetic Programming Theory and Practice IX, Springer New York, New York, NY, 2011, pp. 129–151.
[49] M. Durasevic, D. Jakobovic, M. Scoczynski Ribeiro Martins, S. Picek, M. Wagner, Fitness landscape analysis of dimensionally-aware genetic programming featuring feynman equations. International Conference on Parallel Problem Solving from, Nature, Springer International Publishing, Cham, 2020, pp. 111–124.
[50] A.M. Alaa, M. Van der Schaar, Demystifying black-box models with symbolic metamodels, Adv. Neural Inf. Process. Syst. 32 (2019).
[51] A.H. Gandomi, D.A. Roke, Assessment of artificial neural network and genetic programming as predictive tools, Adv. Eng. Software 88 (2015) 63–72.
[52] W. La Cava, J.H. Moore, Semantic variation operators for multidimensional genetic programming, in: Proceedings of the Genetic and Evolutionary Computation Conference, July 2019, pp. 1056–1064.
[53] M.S. Khorshidi, N. Yazdanjue, H. Gharoun, D. Yazdani, M.R. Nikoo, F. Chen, A.H. Gandomi, Enhancing classification through multi-view synthesis in multi-population ensemble genetic programming, in: Proceedings of the Genetic and Evolutionary Computation Conference Companion, July 2024, pp. 2099–2102.
[54] C. Morris, M. Jurado, J. Zutty, Llm guided evolution-the automation of models advancing models, in: Proceedings of the Genetic and Evolutionary Computation Conference, July 2024, pp. 377–384.
[55] A.E.I. Brownlee, J. Callan, K. Even-Mendoza, A. Geiger, C. Hanna, J. Petke, F. Sarro, D. Sobania, Enhancing Genetic Improvement Mutations Using Large Language Models (arXiv:2310.19813v1), 2023 arXiv, https://arxiv.org/abs/2310.19813.
[56] J. McDermott, G. Kronberger, P. Orzechowski, L. Vanneschi, L. Manzoni, R. Kalkreuth, M. Castelli, Genetic programming benchmarks: Looking back and looking forward, ACM SIGEVOlution 15 (3) (2022) 1–19.
[57] L. Rovito, Genetic Programming Across Domains: Leveraging Evolutionary Computation to Address Practical Problems, 2025.
[58] J. Woodward, S. Martin, J. Swan, Benchmarks that matter for genetic programming, in: Proceedings of the Companion Publication of the 2014 Annual Conference on Genetic and Evolutionary Computation, July 2014, pp. 1397–1404.
[59] P. Orzechowski, W. La Cava, J.H. Moore, Where are we now? A large benchmark study of recent symbolic regression methods, in: Proceedings of the Genetic and Evolutionary Computation Conference, July 2018, pp. 1183–1190.
[60] S.M. Udrescu, M. Tegmark, AI Feynman: A physics-inspired method for symbolic regression, Sci. Adv. 6 (16) (2020) eaay2631.
[61] W. La Cava, B. Burlacu, M. Virgolin, M. Kommenda, P. Orzechowski, de França, Y. Jin, J.H. Moore, Contemporary symbolic regression methods and their relative performance, Advances in neural information processing systems, 2021 (DB1) (2021) 1.
[62] S. Harding, J. Leitner, J. Schmidhuber, Cartesian genetic programming for image processing, In: Genetic Programming Theory and Practice X, Springer New York, New York, NY, 2013, pp. 31–44.
[63] B. Burlacu, G. Kronberger, M. Kommenda, Operon C++ an efficient genetic programming framework for symbolic regression, in: Proceedings of the 2020 genetic and evolutionary computation conference companion, 2020, pp. 1562–1570.

Chapter 14

Convolutional neural network ensembles for improving plant leaf disease severity estimation

Mohamed Rayane Lakehal, Hassiba Nemmour, Naouel Arab, Mohamed Lamine Bouibed and Youcef Chibani

Faculty of Electrical Engineering, Laboratoire d'Ingénierie des Systèmes Intelligents et Communicants (LISIC), University of Sciences and Technology Houari Boumediene (USTHB), Algiers, Algeria

1. Introduction

Pests and phyto-pathological complications driven by various factors, such as population growth, climate change, and industrial and economic expansion, conduct to sever diseases in plant leaves which constitute a significant threat to food security. Reliable and precise estimation of disease severity is a key element for understanding evolutions of plant diseases and predicting yield loss through epidemic monitoring and forecasting [1,2]. Recently, artificial intelligence and deep learning have emerged as promising solutions for plant leaf severity estimation. These techniques outperform traditional estimation based on visual inspection of changes in leaf color, texture, and morphology, which is characterized by high human labor intensity, low speed, and a high misjudgment rate [3–5]. Similar to many computer vision models, plant leaf disease severity classification systems are typically composed of three main steps, preprocessing such as background removal, resizing, and image filtering to facilitate information extraction, the feature generation, and the classification. These steps aim to extract relevant information for estimating the severity level [6]. In this respect, several studies have explored color and texture features of plant leaves. For instance, in Ref. [7], the GLCM (Gray-Level Co-occurrence Matrix) was used as a textural feature descriptor with gray level images of wheat leaves. Also, in Ref. [8], authors employed different color spaces, including LAB and HSV, as features improving severity estimation in diseased tea leaves. Furthermore, recent advances in artificial intelligence have introduced more accurate and plant leaf representative features. CNN are at the forefront of this progress, as they have the ability to recognize patterns yielding promising results for image classification through multiple abstraction layers [3,7]. CNN are known by the deep feature learning that is performed by convolutional layers using convolutions between the image and a set of filters. They count also fully connected layers that handle the classification task through backpropagation, which updates internal parameters based on computations and representations from the previous layers [8]. Therefore, CNN can be used as end-to-end classification systems or as deep feature generators. For tasks with high complexity such as plant disease severity classification, common systems combining multiple CNN are used to improve the classification accuracy. The present work is focused on the use of CNN ensembles for severity estimation in diseased plant leaves. Precisely, two CNN ensembles are proposed by fusing deep features or by stacking output probabilities of multiple CNN models. In both cases, an SVM classifier is employed as a series of binary classifiers to achieve the multi-level severity classification. Experiments are conducted to classify six severity levels of the Stripe Rust in wheat leaf images.

2. Related works

CNN models are considered as a recent breakthrough due to their capability for both automatic feature extraction and classification from the input images [9,10]. In precision agriculture, CNN are the core of several successful systems of

Advanced Intelligence Methods for Data Science and Optimization. https://doi.org/10.1016/B978-0-443-28940-8.00014-2

plant disease detection and severity classification. Various studies have shown that CNN allow more accurate and reproducible results than classical machine learning techniques. For instance, in Ref. [10], a multitask system was designed to identify and estimate stress severity caused by biotic agents on coffee leaves. The proposed system is based on ResNet50 architecture, which yields an overall accuracy of 86.5%. Additionally, authors in Ref. [11] introduced the PD2SE-Net network that is based on the ResNet50 architecture, with additional shuffle units serving as auxiliary structures to reduce computational complexity. The severity estimation performance achieved an accuracy of 91%. To enhance the recognition of spots severity in cucumber leaves within complex backgrounds a two-stage model was employed in Ref. [5]. In the first stage, leaf segmentation was performed using the DeepLabV3+ network. The resulting segmented leaf images were then utilized as input for the U-Net architecture to identify the spots severity. Experimental results reveal that the proposed framework achieved an impressive overall accuracy of 92.85% in severity estimation. For the early diagnosis of the severity level in pear crops, a model was proposed in Ref. [12], featuring a multi-output system based on five pretrained CNN architectures such as VGG16, VGG19, ResNet50, InceptionV3, and MobileNetV2. The same dataset was employed in Ref. [13], where an ensemble of CNN models was elaborated using Fuzzy logic fusion rules. Based on the VGG16, InceptionV3, MobileNetV2, and ResNet152, the CNN ensemble improves the severity estimation with 4% in the overall accuracy. On the other hand, the Yellow Rust severity in wheat crops was investigated in Refs. [14,15] by using various CNN models as end-to-end classification systems. Results highlighted the superiority of CNN over classical systems associating SVM with handcrafted features. As the state-of-the-art reports variable estimation performance, it seems necessary to combine multiple CNN models to reach a robust severity estimation of plant leaf diseases. Presently, two CNN ensembles are proposed for Yellow Rust severity estimation in wheat leaves.

3. Proposed CNN ensembles

The proposed framework for severity estimation based on CNN ensembles is exhibited in Fig. 14.1. Initially, a size normalization is applied to scale all images at 120×120 pixels to expedite system development. Then, three CNN models are trained to predict six severity levels of the Yellow Rust disease. The first ensemble is elaborated by training fused deep

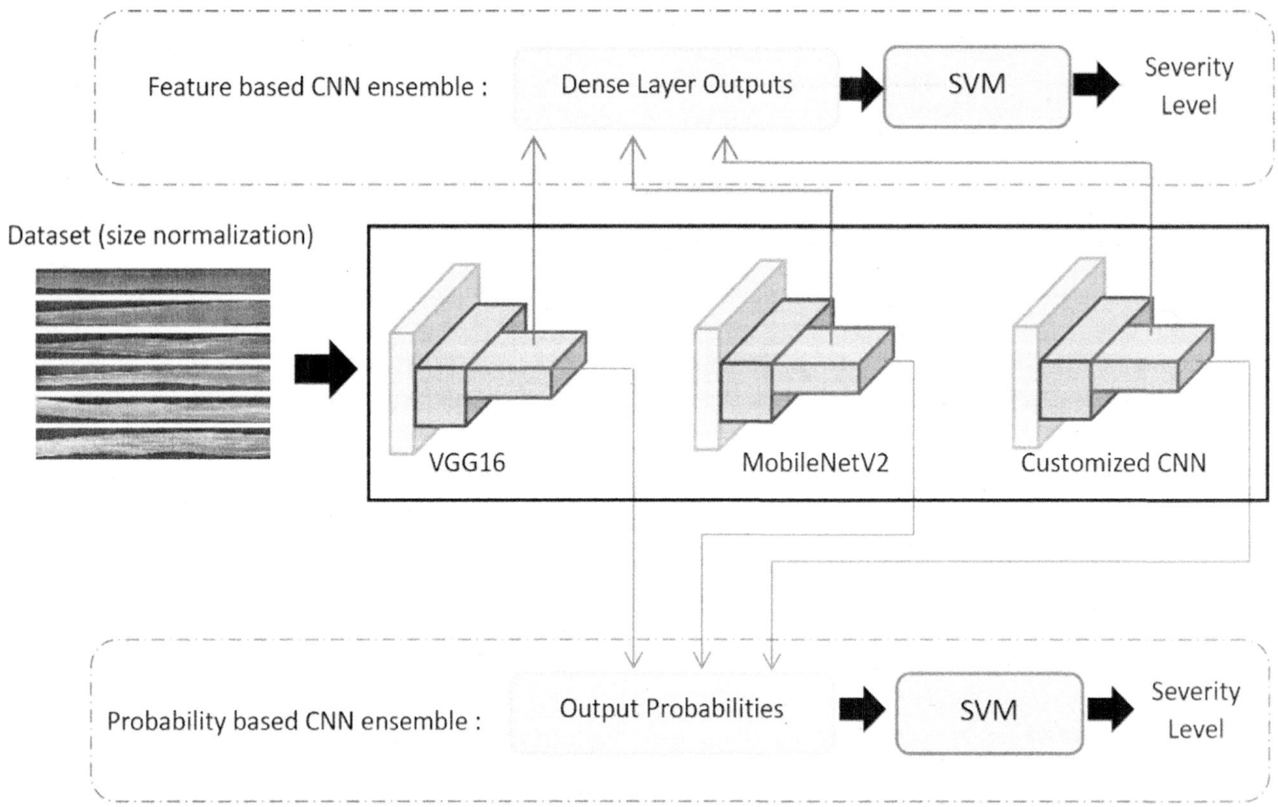

FIGURE 14.1 Pipeline of the proposed CNN ensembles for wheat disease severity estimation.

features generated from fully connected layers of the different CNN models, while the second ensemble is established by training stacked output probabilities of CNN.

3.1 CNN models

Convolutional neural networks are designed by stacking interconnected convolution and fully connected dense layers. The core component of the network is the convolutional phase, which can be envisioned as a small sliding filter passed over the image, generating a layer of features across the image. These features are discriminative characteristics extracted from the data [15]. The role of dense layers consists of mapping deep features to output classes. They are responsible for classifying patterns presented to input units based on the summation operation performed by the output unit of each input, multiplied by its corresponding weight [16]. Presently, VGG16 and MobileNetV2 are utilized based on the transfer learning technique, leveraging their ImageNet weights through a fine-tuning process. During this operation, weights of fully connected layers are optimized while freezing those of convolution layers. The prediction block is composed of a flatten layer followed by a fully connected layer of 1024 nodes and then, a SoftMax output layer. Additionally, a customized CNN is introduced to ensure diversity in deep features.

- **VGG16:** This CNN has been introduced by the Visual Geometry Group of Oxford university. It is composed of five sets of convolution layers based on 3×3 filters, and separated by a 2×2 Max-pooling layers. The convolution block is composed of 13 convolution layers and is concluded with a flatten layer. The prediction block contains two dense layers of 4096 nodes, culminating in an output layer with a SoftMax function [17].
- **MobileNetV2:** is a CNN model designed to reduce the computation cost of deep models by using the depth-wise separable convolution and bottleneck layers. The depth-wise separable convolution is a technique that divides the convolution process into two distinct stages to reduce the computational complexity, while Bottleneck layers are used for expansion and compressing the number of channels of input features before and after depth convolution. Roughly, the MobileNetV2 is composed of a convolution layer with 32 filters, followed by 19 residual bottleneck layers [18].
- **Customized CNN:** Our proposed architecture comprises four convolutional layers with a 3×3 kernel size. Max-pooling operations are applied after each convolution step. Additionally, a dropout of 20% of the network's parameters is applied at the input of the last convolution layer. The prediction block consists of three dense layers containing 256, 128, and 80 nodes, respectively. The last SoftMax layer provides output decisions where each node corresponds to a class of interest (see Fig. 14.2). Batch normalization is applied at the end of the convolution block and after the first and the second dense layers.

3.2 SVM classification

Presently, two CNN ensembles are developed by using an SVM classifier. The first ensemble is elaborated by fusing deep features extracted from fully connected layers of multiple CNN models, in order to ensure complementary characterization of the disease severity. These features are trained by an SVM classifier implemented according to the One-Against-All approach to yield a decision about the severity level of the input image. The second CNN ensemble is

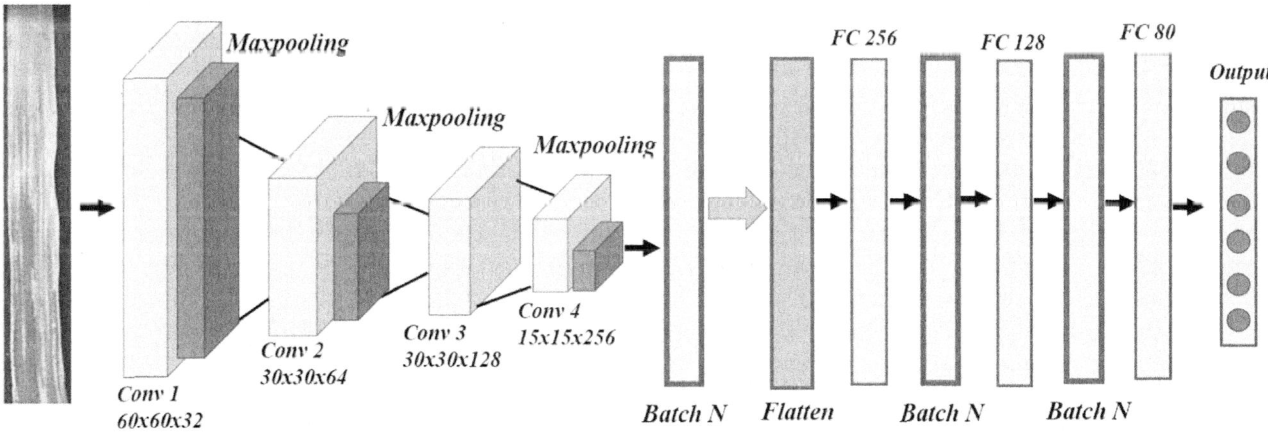

FIGURE 14.2 Proposed customized CNN architecture for yellow rust severity estimation. *Batch N*, Batch normalization; *FC*, Fully connected.

developed by handling CNN output probabilities. In this respect, a new training set is developed by substituting each training image by the concatenation of CNN outputs. Obtained vectors are trained by an SVM classifier which indicates the severity level of input images.

Recall that SVM was introduced in 1995 to automatically find a flat surface that maximally separates points from two categories, making it a powerful tool for binary classification with the primary goal of maximizing the margin criterion [19]. To address multi-class problems, commonly, the SVM divides the classification task into a set of binary classification problems resolved by the One-Against-All approach [20,21]. An input datum X which is presently fused deep features or a vector containing CNN output probabilities is classified by using the decision function reported in Eq. (14.1):

$$F(X) = sign\left(\sum_{i=1}^{s_V} \alpha_i K(X_i, X) + b\right) \tag{14.1}$$

α_i: Lagrange multipliers associated with a training sample X_i
s_V: Number of support vectors
b: Bias
K: Kernel function

There are several mathematical functions that can be used as SVM kernels but the RBF (Radial Basis Function) is the classical choice for pattern recognition tasks. It can be computed as follows:

$$RBF(X_i, X) = \exp\left(-\|X_i - X\|^2/\delta^2\right) \tag{14.2}$$

δ: a user defined parameter.

4. Experimental analysis

Experiments are carried out on images extracted from Yellow-Rust-19 dataset, which focuses on the severity of Yellow Rust disease in wheat under field conditions.[1] Yellow Rust (known as Stripe rust) is a fungal disease that affects the wheat leaves. It can devastate wheat crops and induce a significant loss in the yields when it reaches high severity levels. The experimental dataset was initially introduced in Ref. [14]; it emphasizes six degrees of infection severity, ranging from minimal to severe. The wheat leaf images were processed through several steps prior to analysis, including background separation through thresholding, morphological transformation, filtering, masking to suppress the background, and finally, the addition of a transparency channel to lessen the background suppression impact. The dataset was created from the ground up and collected in Haymana, Ankara, Turkey, in a cultivation area dedicated to cereal fungus disease experiments. Each leaf image was subsequently labeled by two experts: an agricultural engineer and a food engineer. For further details, refer to the dataset's introductory article [14]. The total number of samples is 15,000 leaf images, with 2500 samples per class, the corresponding labels to the six classes are as follows: **0** (Healthy: No signs of infection), **R** (Resistant: Minor signs of infection), **MR-MS** (Moderately Resistant-Moderately Susceptible), **MR** (Moderately Resistant: Small and medium signs of infection), **MS** (Moderately Susceptible: Medium signs of infection), and **S** (Susceptible: Major signs of infection). Fig. 14.3 showcases a sample from each class of the experimental set.

According to several research works, CNN are developed by using 90% of samples and tested on the remaining 10% samples due to the high complexity of the severity estimation [12]. The dataset was split via the train_test_split function in scikit-learn library, setting the random_state to 0 in each experiment to ensure reproducibility of CNN results. This generated 1500 test images, with slight class imbalances since the train_test_split function does not enforce equal class distribution. All experiments were carried out in Spyder environment, utilizing the following hardware configuration: an Intel Core i7-2600 CPU @ 3.4GHz $\times$ 4, 32 GB RAM, and an NVIDIA Corporation GP107GL.

In the first step, experiments were conducted for severity level estimation by training each CNN as an end-to-end classification system. The CNN training followed the hyper-parameters reported in Table 14.1.

Confusion matrices obtained depicted in Figs. 14.4–14.6 are obtained for the VGG16, MobileNetV2, and the customized CNN, respectively. The inspection of these matrices reveals that there is no CNN model that can give the best accuracy in all classes. Also, the estimation of severity is a challenging problem, since there are several misclassifications. The MR-MS (Moderately Resistant—Moderately Susceptible) is the most critical class since it overlaps with both MR and MS classes yielding substantial confusion scores. The VGG16 is the best individual CNN in distinguishing closely

1. YELLOW-RUST-19 (kaggle.com).

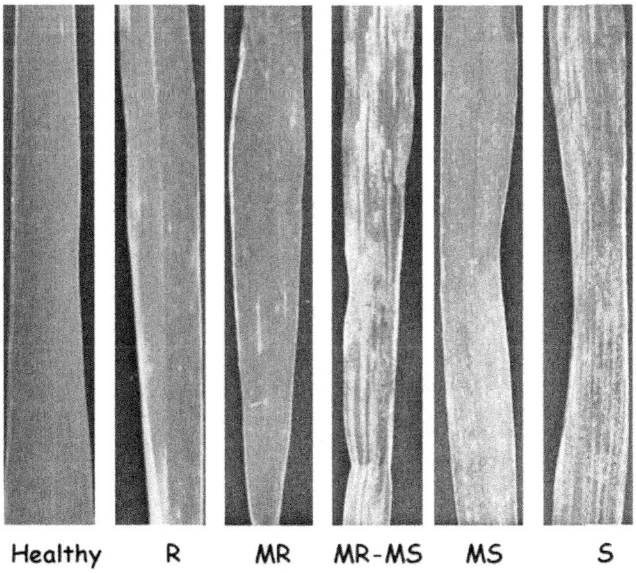

FIGURE 14.3 Images from the experimental dataset.

TABLE 14.1 Selected hyper-parameters utilized with CNN models.

Hyperparameter	Value
Input shape	120 × 120 pixels
Optimizer	RMS-prop
Learning rate	0.0002
Momentum	0.9
Batch-size	32

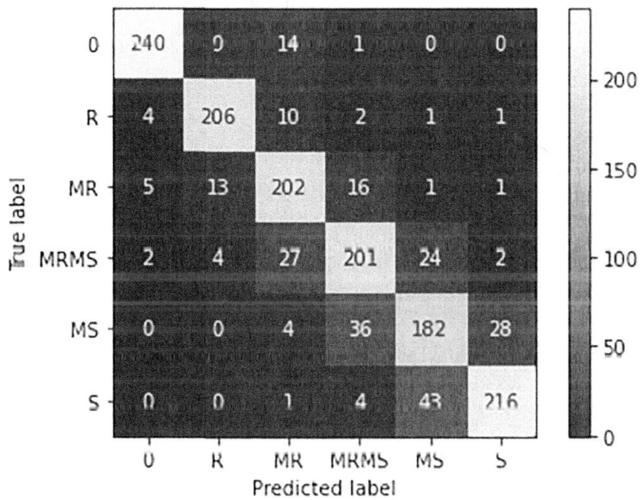

FIGURE 14.4 Confusion matrix obtained for VGG16.

related severity levels, labeled as R, MR, and MR-MS. VGG16 demonstrates higher precision in these classes compared to MobileNetV2 and the customized CNN. Besides, most of classification errors occurred within these similar severity levels. For instance, as shown in Fig. 14.4, the severity level R is misclassified as MR, while MR is commonly confused with R and MR-MS, with 29 classification errors.

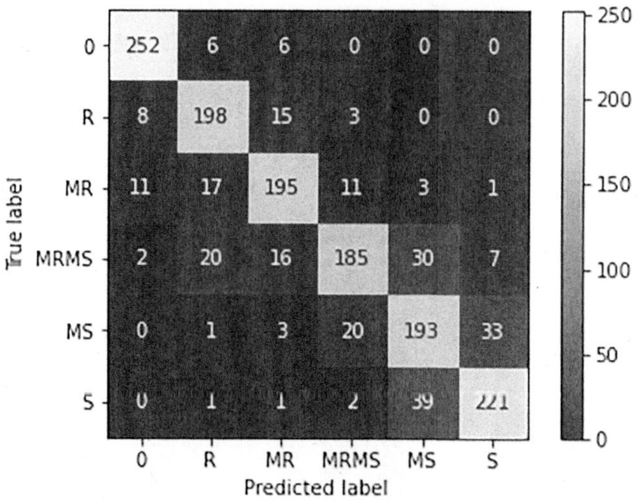

FIGURE 14.5 Confusion matrix obtained for MobileNetV2.

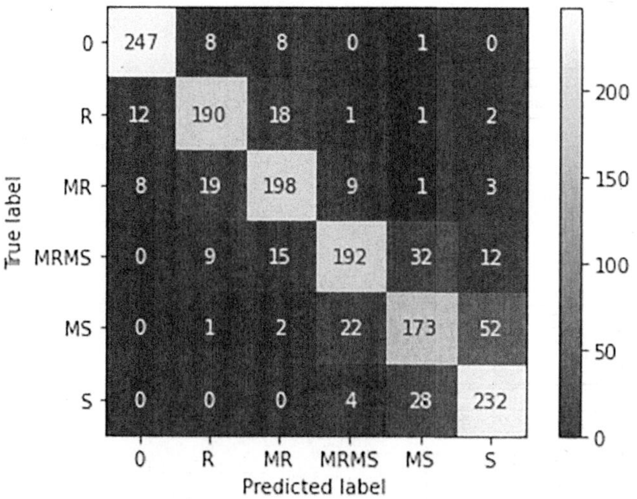

FIGURE 14.6 Confusion matrix obtained for the customized CNN.

After the VGG16, the MobileNetV2 performs better than the customized CNN in several classes including the Healthy and the MS (Moderately Susceptible) classes. Nevertheless, our customized CNN model performs exceptionally well on the S (Susceptible) level class, with fewer misclassifications compared to both VGG16 and MobileNetV2. These findings highlight the complementarity between CNN models and confirm the usefulness of using ensembles.

Furthermore, the overall classification accuracy obtained by using the proposed CNN ensembles are reported in Table 14.2 along with those derived from individual CNN. As expected, the deep feature fusion ensemble provides an improvement of 1.33% where the overall accuracy reaches 84.26%. Nevertheless, the second CNN ensemble that is based on learning stacked probabilities allows a better classification enhancing the overall accuracy to 85.53%. Furthermore, the inspection of the confusion matrices reported in Fig. 14.7, indicates that CNN ensembles improve the classification score in several classes while keeping similar performance as individual CNN in some others. Upon analyzing the confusion matrices, both ensembles reveal similar performance for the Healthy and MR-MS severity levels. As previously noted, the MR-MS class is the most prone to misclassifications, with 59 samples incorrectly predicted across both strategies. Nevertheless, the probability-based ensemble performs better on the R, MR, and MS classes, while the deep feature fusion ensemble excels with the S class, both in correctly and incorrectly classified samples.

TABLE 14.2 Overall classification accuracy obtained for severity estimation systems.

Severity estimation system	Overall accuracy (%)
Customized CNN	82.13
MobileNetV2	82.93
VGG16	83.13
Deep feature fusion ensemble	84.26
Probability stacking based ensemble	85.53

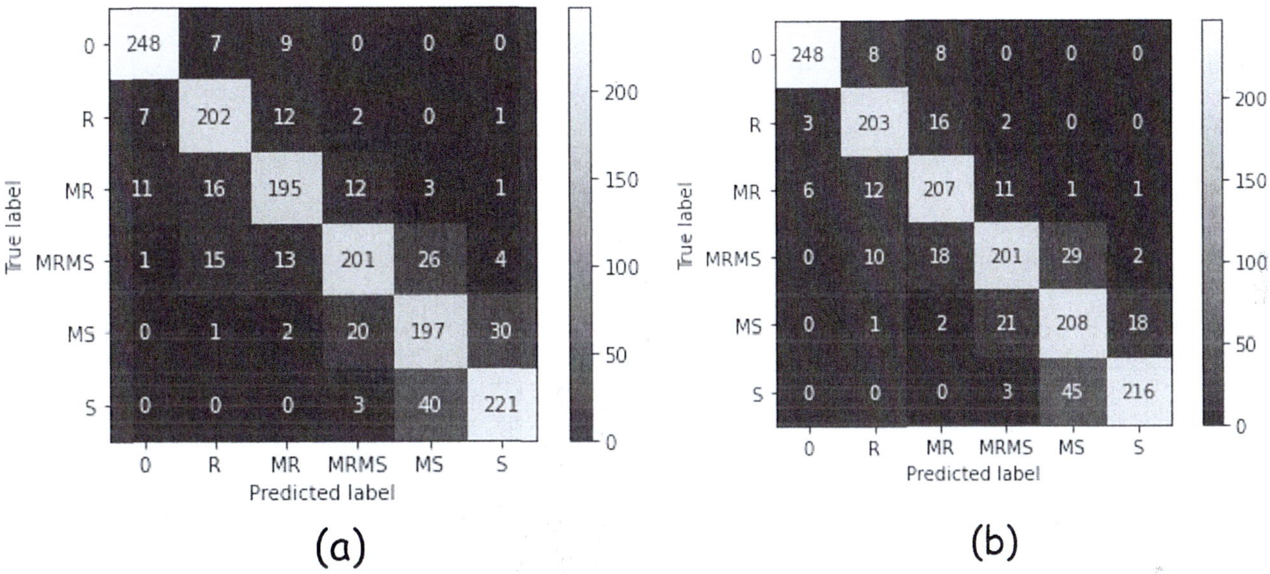

FIGURE 14.7 Confusion matrices. (a) CNN ensemble based on stacked probabilities, (b) CNN ensemble based on deep feature fusion.

5. Discussion

Experimental results reveal that CNN ensembles have improved the overall classification accuracy, but there are still notable confusions between some severity classes. Precisely, the MR (Moderately Resistant) is particularly prone to confusion with MR-MS, which contains samples with both Moderately Resistant and Moderately Susceptible severities at once. That is the reason for which classifying infection severity levels turns out to be particularly complex, as evidenced by the fact that none of the systems achieved an overall accuracy of 90%. This complexity is largely due to the similarities between certain infection classes, which lead to notable confusion. For example, the MR and MR-MS classes are often

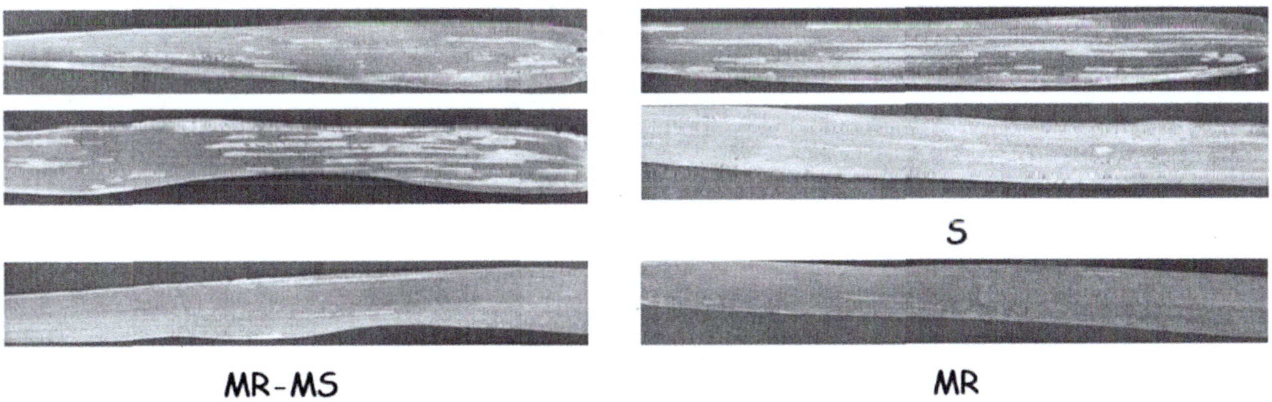

FIGURE 14.8 Similar test samples having different severity levels.

confused due to their similar visual characteristics. Likewise, there is a notable confusion between S and MR-MS classes, which reflects the difficulty of differentiating very similar severity levels. Fig. 14.8 presents examples that highlight the difficulty we encounter in visually distinguishing between severity levels for these classes.

Finally, CNN ensembles are well-suited for implementation in a wheat crop monitoring system, similar to the one in which the dataset was originally created. Additionally, an embedded system could facilitate monitoring across large-scale farms by integrating the framework with a real-time camera mounted on a drone. Given the moderate computational demands, the CNN ensembles require a simple preprogrammed Python concatenation function, and the CNN models have a small-scale architecture, totaling 30 M parameters across three models. Fine-tuning VGG16 and MobileNetV2 reduces their trainable parameters to 5 and 10 M, respectively, with the customized CNN at 15 M parameters. This results in a system that is efficient, fast, and easy to implement.

6. Conclusion

In the present work, two approaches for combining CNN models are introduced to improve the Yellow Rust severity estimation in wheat crops. First, three CNN models that are VGG16, MobileNetV2 and a customized CNN were employed as end-to-end severity estimation systems. Then, two CNN ensembles were elaborated by fusing deep features or by stacking CNN output probabilities. In both ensembles, an SVM classifier was used to perform the severity classification task. Across all experiments, the results showed that end-to-end CNN provides medium performance with variable accuracies among different classes. Also, the customized CNN which is a lightweight architecture provides similar performance as the VGG16 while having a small computation cost. Meanwhile, for the Yellow-Rust-19 dataset, the CNN based on training stacked probabilities provides the best classification improvement. With this ensemble, the SVM input vector has a reduced size that is composed of 18 output probabilities corresponding to 6 class probabilities for each CNN. On the contrary, the deep feature fusion ensemble collects 1024 deep features from both VGG16 and MobileNetV2, and 80 deep features of the customized CNN. Therefore, we infer that the CNN ensemble based on stacked probabilities allows the best tradeoff between accuracy improvement and the size of the SVM input. Another advantage of this ensemble is the time required to estimate the severity of a test image which is less than 1 s, making it suitable for mobile and real time severity estimation platforms. Further tests including more advanced deep learning architectures could help to improve the severity estimation. In this respect, we plan to investigate deep features extracted from vision transformers and compact convolutional transformers to reinforce the response of the proposed deep learning ensemble.

References

[1] C. Boke, T. Gottwald, G. Poole, Plant disease severity estimated visually, by digital photography and image analysis and by hyperspectral imaging, Plant Sci. 25 (2010) 59–107.

[2] S. Verma, A. Chug, A. Singh, Application of convolutional neural networks for evaluation of disease severity in tomato plant, J. Discrete Math. Sci. Cryptogr. 23 (2020) 273–282.

[3] R. Misra, N. Kesswani, M. Rajarajan, B. Veeravalli, A. Patel, Wheat disease severity estimation: A deep learning approach, in: Proceedings on 6th International Conference on Internet of Things and Connected Technologies (ICIoTCT), July 29-30, New Delhi 340, 2022, pp. 185–193.

[4] J. Lu, M. Zhou, Y. Gao, H. Jiang, Using hyperspectral imaging to discriminate yellow leaf curl disease in tomato leaves, Precis. Agric. 19 (2018) 379–394.

[5] C. Wang, P. Due, H. Wu, J. Li, C. Zhao, H. Zhu, A cucumber leaf disease severity classification method based on the fusion of DeepLabV3+ and U-Net, Comput. Electron. Agric. 189 (2021) 106373.

[6] A. Mezenner, H. Nemmour, Y. Chibani, A. Hafiane, Comparison of CNN-based features with gradient features for tomato plant leaf disease detection, in: Multimedia Data Processing and Computing, 2023, pp. 32–42.

[7] T. Hayıt, H. Erbay, F. Varcın, F. Hayıt, N. Akci, The classification of wheat yellow rust disease based on a combination of textural and deep features, Multimed. Tool. Appl. 82 (2023) 47405–47423.

[8] G. Hu, M. Wan, K. Wei, R. Ye, Computer vision based method for severity estimation of tea leaf blight in natural scene images, Eur. J. Agron. 144 (2023) 126756.

[9] Y. LeCun, Y. Bengio, G. Hinton, Deep learning, Review 521 (2015) 436–444.

[10] J. Esgario, R. Krohlin, J. Ventura, Deep learning for classification and severity estimation of coffee leaf biotic stress, Comput. Electron. Agric. 169 (2020) 105–162.

[11] Q. Liang, S. Xiang, Y. Hu, G. Coppola, D. Zhang, W. Sun, PD^2SE-Net : Computer assisted plant disease diagnosis and severity estimation network, Comput. Electron. Agric. 157 (2019) 518–529.

[12] G. Fenu, F. Malloci, Using multioutput learning to diagnose plant disease and stress severity, Complexity 2021 (2021) 1–11.

[13] M. Lakehal, H. Nemmour, M. Bouibed, Y. Fetmouche, M. Harchaoui, Y. Chibani, CNN ensembles for pear leaf disease severity estimation, in: 30th IEEE International Conference on Electronics, Circuits and Systems (ICECS), Istanbul, Turkiye, 2023, pp. 1–5.

[14] T. Hayit, H. Erbay, F. Varcin, F. Hayit, N. Akci, Determination of the severity level of yellow rust disease in wheat by using convolutional neural networks, J. Plant Pathol. 103 (2021) 923–934.
[15] H. Aghdam, E. Heravi, Guide to Convolutional Neural Networks, Springer International Publishing, 2017, p. 282.
[16] T.J. Sejnowski, The Deep Learning Revolution, MIT Press, 2018, p. 352.
[17] R. Venkatesan, B. Li, Convolutional Neural Networks in Visual Computing, CRC Press, 2018, p. 186.
[18] A. Howard, M. Zhu, B. Chen, D. Kalenichenko, W. Wang, T. Weyand, M. Andreetto, H. Adam, in: MobileNets: Efficient Convolutional Neural Networks for Mobile Vision Applications, 2017.
[19] C. Cortes, V. Vapnik, Support-vector networks, Mach. Learn. 20 (1995) 273–297.
[20] Y. Ma, G. Guo, Support Vector Machines Applications, Springer, Cham, 2014, p. 302.
[21] U. Fayyad, A tutorial on support vector machines for pattern recognition, Data Min. Knowl. Discov. 2 (1998) 121–167.

Chapter 15

Leveraging ontology engineering for enhanced big data science

Bryar A. Hassan[1, 2], Tarik A. Rashid[3], Aram M. Ahmed[1], Alla A. Hassan[4], Aabdulhady A. Abdullah[3] and Salar Farahmand-Tabar[5]

[1]Computer Science and Engineering Department, University of Kurdistan Hewler, Erbil, Iraq; [2]Department of Computer Science, College of Science, Charmo University Sulaimani, KRI, Iraq; [3]Artificial Intelligence and Innovations Centre, University of Kurdistan Hewler, Erbil, Iraq; [4]Department of Database Technology, Computer Science Institute, Sulaimani Polytechnic University, Sulaimani, KRI, Iraq; [5]Department of Civil Engineering, Faculty of Engineering, University of Zanjan, Zanjan, Iran

1. Introduction and background

The digital revolution has fundamentally transformed how enterprises operate, leading to the automation of many business processes, including procurement, sales, and customer relationship management. This shift has resulted in the comprehensive digitization of product information and business processes, which enterprises manage as electronic data within their information systems [1]. However, this digitization brings its own set of challenges, particularly as the complexity of handling large volumes of data increases. The concept of "big data" encapsulates these vast and intricate datasets, which traditional data processing applications find difficult to manage efficiently.

Enterprises face the daunting task of integrating and managing extensive datasets spread across various information systems such as enterprise resource planning (ERP) systems, product data management (PDM) systems, customer relationship management (CRM) systems, and content management systems (CMS). Often, these systems are not well-integrated, leading to data redundancy, inconsistencies, and inefficiencies in managing and utilizing product information. Additionally, capturing and representing relationships between products or product features is crucial for both internal management and customer interactions but remains a challenging task.

Additionally, addressing the complexity of modern product information datasets necessitates innovative approaches to big data management [2]. Big data management involves various processes, including analysis, capture, querying, sharing, storage, visualization, and updating. Essential to these processes are suitable algorithms for modeling, representing different data types, and linking dynamic datasets. In 2011, Gartner identified three dimensions of big data: volume, variety, and velocity. IBM later added a fourth dimension, veracity, emphasizing the reliability of data sourced from diverse origins [3].

1.1 Big data

Big data is characterized by its vast volume, encompassing enormous datasets; variety, incorporating diverse data types such as tabular data, documents, emails, multimedia, and transactional data; velocity, indicating the rapid generation and processing of data; and veracity, highlighting the importance of data accuracy and reliability [4]. Effective big data management must account for these dimensions, ensuring that data are processed efficiently and meets stakeholders' requirements.

I. ***Volume***: The sheer amount of data generated daily is staggering, ranging from terabytes to petabytes. Managing this data requires robust storage solutions and efficient processing techniques to handle the large volume without compromising performance.

Advanced Intelligence Methods for Data Science and Optimization. https://doi.org/10.1016/B978-0-443-28940-8.00016-6

II. ***Variety***: Data comes in various forms, including structured data (e.g., databases), semistructured data (e.g., XML files), and unstructured data (e.g., text documents, images). Managing this variety necessitates flexible systems capable of processing different data types and formats.

III. ***Velocity***: The speed at which data are generated and needs to be processed is critical. Real-time or near-real-time processing capabilities are essential for applications requiring immediate insights and actions based on incoming data.

IV. ***Veracity***: Ensuring the accuracy and reliability of data is crucial for making informed decisions. Data from various sources can have differing levels of quality, and it's important to validate and clean data to maintain its integrity.

1.2 Semantic technologies

Semantic technologies facilitate the creation and representation of complex information and relationships between concepts by identifying the corresponding context [5]. These technologies enable a better understanding of data's meaning and purpose, enhancing information retrieval and knowledge sharing. Metadata, providing additional information about data, plays a crucial role in semantic technologies, necessitating standardized rules for formal representation and exchange between systems.

1.3 Semantic ontologies

Ontologies, defined as "explicit specifications of conceptualizations," enable the formal definition of concepts and their relationships [6–8]. They provide a high degree of semantic richness, surpassing other models such as glossaries, taxonomies, thesauri, and topic maps. Ontologies use mathematical logic to infer new knowledge, forming the foundation of the semantic web, which integrates ontology-based technologies with web resources using core technologies such as XML and URI/IRI.

I. ***Glossaries***: Simple collections of terms and their definitions within a specific domain. They provide basic semantic understanding but lack detailed relationships between terms.

II. ***Taxonomies***: Hierarchical structures that classify terms into categories and subcategories. They offer a more organized way to understand relationships between concepts compared with glossaries.

III. ***Thesauri***: More complex than glossaries and taxonomies, thesauri include synonyms, antonyms, and hierarchical relationships between terms. They enhance information retrieval by providing alternative terms and more detailed relationships.

IV. ***Topic Maps***: Extend the capabilities of taxonomies and thesauri by allowing for more complex relationships and associations between topics. They enable richer representations of knowledge domains.

V. ***Ontologies***: The most advanced model, ontologies provide a formal specification of concepts and their interrelationships. They enable sophisticated data integration and analysis by offering a common framework for representing knowledge across different systems.

The structure of this book chapter unfolds as follows. Section 2 explores the applications of ontological engineering in big data science, supported by various experimental scenarios. Section 3 offers insights from two case studies showcasing the utilization of semantic ontologies in both big data management and healthcare systems. Specifically, Section 3.1 discusses the integration of semantic technologies in big data management, while Section 3.2 examines ontology-based approaches in healthcare data systems. Moving forward, Section 4 introduces a proposed framework designed to harness ontology engineering for advancing big data science. Following this, Section 5 critically assesses the challenges associated with these approaches and proposes potential solutions, providing a balanced view of their practical implications. The chapter concludes in Section 6 with a summary of key findings and implications drawn from the preceding sections. Finally, Section 7 outlines potential avenues for future research and development in this evolving field.

2. Applications of semantic web ontology in big data

Semantic Web Ontologies play a crucial role in resolving data heterogeneity and interoperability challenges in Big Data environments. Big Data typically involves diverse data sources, formats, and structures, making integration a significant challenge. Ontologies provide a shared and common understanding of a domain, which enables the seamless integration of these diverse data sources. They define the relationships and constraints within the data, ensuring that different systems can interpret and process the data consistently. For example, in healthcare, ontologies can integrate data from electronic health records, lab results, and medical imaging, providing a unified view for better patient care and research [9,10]. This semantic integration is essential for leveraging the full potential of Big Data, allowing for comprehensive data analysis and informed decision-making.

2.1 Knowledge representation

Ontologies are used to encode domain-specific knowledge, enhancing the understanding and interpretation of Big Data. By representing knowledge in a structured and formalized manner, ontologies make data more accessible and meaningful. This structured representation supports advanced analytics and automates knowledge extraction processes. For instance, in the financial sector, ontologies can represent complex financial instruments and regulatory requirements, enabling automated compliance checks and risk assessments [11,12]. In Big Data scenarios, this capability is particularly valuable for handling large volumes of data, where traditional methods of data understanding are inadequate. Ontologies facilitate the creation of a rich metadata layer that describes the data's semantics, aiding in tasks such as data discovery, integration, and analysis.

2.2 Data querying and reasoning

Leveraging ontological structures, Semantic Web technologies enable advanced querying and reasoning over Big Data. SPARQL, for example, is a powerful query language designed to query RDF (Resource Description Framework) data. It allows users to perform complex queries that consider the semantic relationships within the data, going beyond simple keyword-based searches to exploit the rich structure of the data [9]. Additionally, ontologies support reasoning, which involves inferring new knowledge from existing data based on the defined relationships and rules. This reasoning capability is crucial for uncovering hidden insights and patterns within Big Data, driving more informed and intelligent decision-making. For example, in smart cities, ontologies and reasoning can be used to infer traffic patterns and optimize urban planning and resource allocation [13].

3. Case studies

In this section, two use cases are presented on the use of Semantic Ontology Learning, which are big data management and healthcare sector.

3.1 Semantic technologies in big data management

This chapter presents three use cases to illustrate how ontologies can improve big data management. Each use case demonstrates the practical application of ontologies in addressing specific challenges related to data integration, data quality, and business process integration.

3.1.1 Data integration

Integrating disparate data sources into a cohesive system is a significant challenge for many enterprises. Data often exists in silos, spread across different departments and systems, making it difficult to achieve a unified view. Ontology-based solutions can streamline data integration processes by providing a common semantic framework that aligns different data sources [14]. For example, in a manufacturing company, data from the production floor, inventory management, and sales systems can be integrated using an ontology that defines common concepts such as "product," "order," and "inventory." This common framework allows data from different systems to be mapped and understood in a consistent way, reducing redundancy and inconsistencies.

By adopting an ontology-based approach, enterprises can achieve more efficient data integration, ensuring that all relevant information is accessible and interconnected. This approach also facilitates better decision-making by providing a comprehensive view of the data, enabling stakeholders to gain insights and make informed decisions. Fig. 15.1 gives a simplified example of ontology alignment.

3.1.2 Data quality

Maintaining high data quality is essential for effective big data management. Poor data quality can lead to incorrect analyses and misguided business decisions. Ontologies can enhance data quality by imposing syntactical and semantical

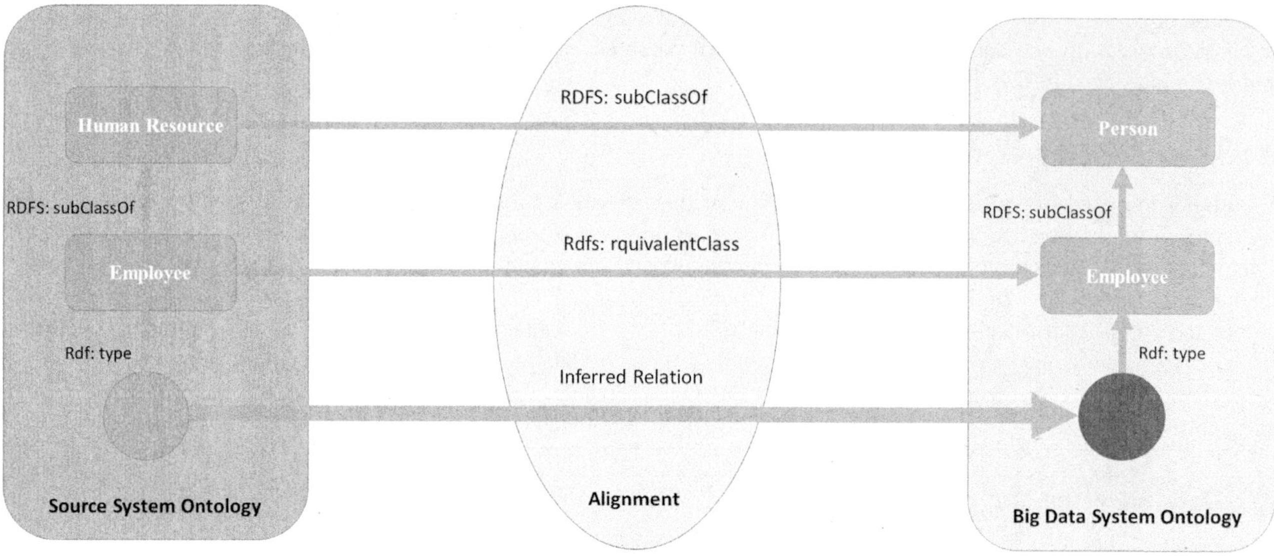

FIGURE 15.1 Ontology alignment.

restrictions on data [15]. These restrictions ensure that data adheres to predefined standards and is consistent across different systems.

For instance, in a healthcare organization, an ontology can define standards for patient records, ensuring that data such as patient ID, name, and medical history is entered in a consistent format. This reduces errors and improves the reliability of patient information, which is crucial for providing high-quality care.

By implementing ontology-based data quality measures, enterprises can ensure that their data are accurate, reliable, and fit for purpose. This leads to improved operational efficiency, reduced costs associated with data errors, and enhanced trust in the data used for decision-making.

3.1.3 Business process integration

Integrating business processes across various systems is often a complex and time-consuming task. Different systems may use different terminologies and data formats, making it difficult to achieve seamless integration. Ontologies can facilitate smoother business process integration by providing a common semantic framework that aligns different processes [16]. For example, in a retail company, an ontology can define the processes involved in order fulfillment, from receiving an order to delivering the product to the customer. By mapping these processes to a common framework, the company can ensure that all systems involved in order fulfillment work together seamlessly; improving efficiency and reducing errors.

Ontology-based business process integration enables enterprises to streamline their operations, reduce duplication of efforts, and enhance collaboration across departments. This leads to more efficient workflows, faster response times, and better overall performance.

3.2 Ontology-based data management in the healthcare sector

The healthcare sector offers a compelling case study for the application of ontology-based big data management. The complexity and critical nature of healthcare data make it an ideal candidate for the benefits of semantic technologies.

3.2.1 Data integration in healthcare

Healthcare organizations manage a vast array of data, including patient records, treatment histories, diagnostic images, and research data [17]. These data are often dispersed across various systems, such as electronic health records (EHRs), laboratory information systems (LIS), and radiology information systems (RIS). Integrating these data is crucial for providing comprehensive patient care and supporting research and analytics. An ontology-based approach can provide a unified framework for integrating these disparate data sources. For example, an ontology can define common concepts such as "patient," "diagnosis," and "treatment," enabling data from different systems to be mapped to a consistent semantic model. This integration facilitates a holistic view of patient information, supporting better clinical decision-making and more effective treatment plans.

3.2.2 Enhancing data quality

Ensuring the quality and consistency of healthcare data is paramount, as inaccuracies can have serious implications for patient care. Ontologies can impose strict standards and validation rules on healthcare data, ensuring that it is entered and maintained in a consistent and accurate manner [18]. For instance, an ontology can define the structure and format of patient records, including mandatory fields and acceptable values for each field. This ensures that all data adheres to predefined standards, reducing the risk of errors and improving the overall reliability of patient information.

3.2.3 Integrating business processes

Healthcare organizations must coordinate numerous processes, from patient admission and treatment to billing and insurance claims. These processes often span multiple systems and departments, making integration a complex task. Ontologies can streamline business process integration by providing a common framework that aligns different processes and terminologies [16]. For example, an ontology can define the workflow for patient discharge, including the steps involved and the data required at each stage. By mapping this process to a common semantic framework, healthcare organizations can ensure that all systems and departments work together seamlessly, improving efficiency and reducing the risk of errors.

4. Proposed framework for leveraging ontology engineering for enhanced big data science

The diagram illustrates a proposed framework that integrates ontology engineering with big data science to achieve enhanced insights. The framework is divided into two main areas (Fig. 15.2):

I. Ontology Engineering:
   a. ***Knowledge Representation***: Structures and organizes information in a way that enables effective understanding and usage [19].

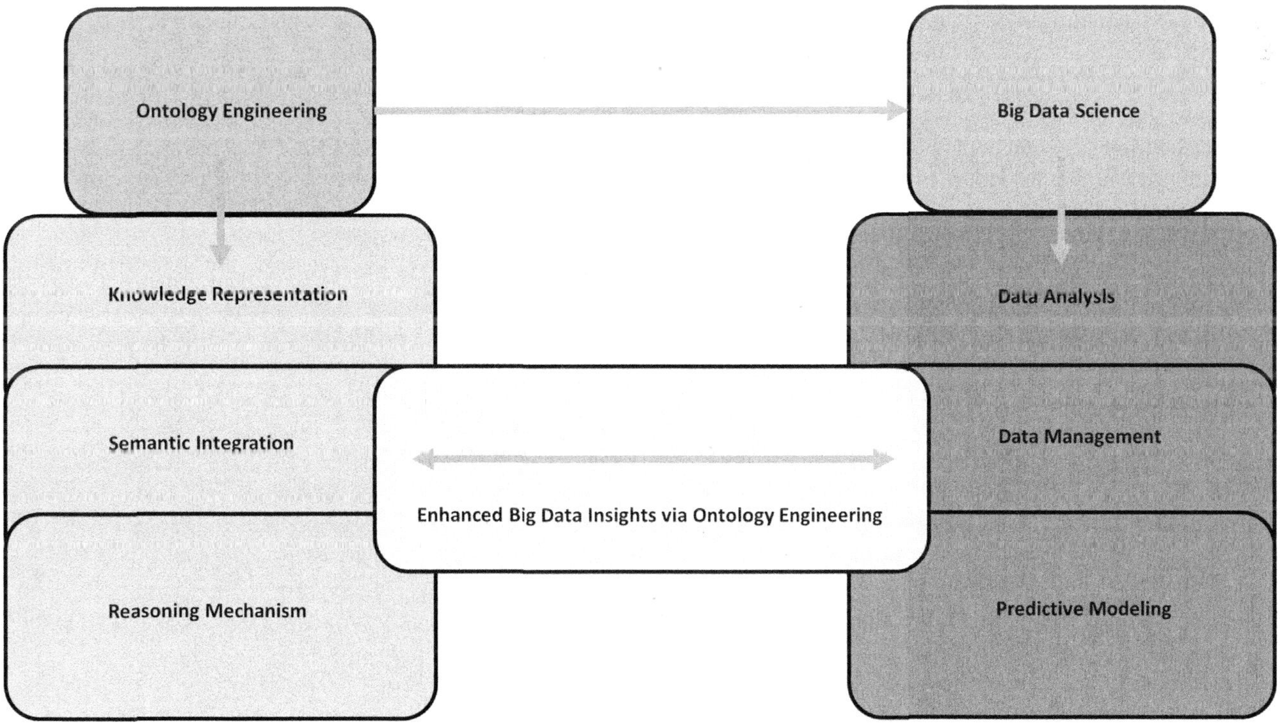

FIGURE 15.2 A proposed framework for leveraging ontology engineering for enhanced big data science.

   b. ***Semantic Integration***: Merges data from various sources, ensuring that different systems can work together seamlessly [20].
   c. ***Reasoning Mechanisms***: Applies logical rules to the data to infer new information and insights [21].

II. *Big Data Science*:
   a. ***Data Analysis***: Examines large datasets to uncover patterns, trends, and associations [22].
   b. ***Data Management***: Involves storing, organizing, and maintaining data for easy access and use [23].
   c. ***Predictive Modeling***: Uses statistical and machine learning techniques to predict future outcomes based on historical data [24].

The central interaction between these two areas is depicted as Enhanced Big Data Insights through Ontology Engineering, highlighting how the combination of ontology engineering techniques with big data processes leads to improved data analysis, management, and predictive modeling. This synergy enhances the ability to extract meaningful and actionable insights from large datasets, ultimately benefiting various applications such as healthcare and data management systems.

5. Challenges and solutions

While the proposed ontology-based approaches offer promising solutions, they are not without their limitations. This section critically evaluates the challenges and potential solutions associated with these approaches, providing a balanced view of their practical implications.

Ontologies provide a high degree of semantic richness, which can significantly improve data integration, quality, and process integration. They offer a common framework that aligns different data sources and processes, reducing redundancy and inconsistencies. By imposing syntactical and semantical restrictions, ontologies can enhance data quality and reliability. Also, ontology-based approaches facilitate better decision-making by providing a comprehensive and interconnected view of the data. This leads to more accurate analyses, improved operational efficiency, and enhanced collaboration across different departments and systems.

5.1 Challenges

I. ***Scalability***: One of the primary challenges in ontology learning for big data management is scalability. Big data involves vast volumes of data generated at high velocity from diverse sources. Traditional ontology learning techniques often struggle to process and analyze such large-scale data efficiently. The computational complexity and resource requirements of these techniques can hinder their application in big data environments [25]. Furthermore, the dynamic nature of big data requires continuous updates and learning, adding another layer of complexity.

II. ***Data Quality and Heterogeneity***: Big data is often characterized by its variability, which includes diverse data formats, structures, and sources. This heterogeneity poses significant challenges for ontology learning, as integrating and harmonizing disparate data sources is complex. Additionally, big data can contain noisy, incomplete, and inconsistent information, which can adversely affect the accuracy and reliability of the learned ontologies [26]. Ensuring high-quality data preprocessing and integration is essential for effective ontology learning.

III. ***Semantic Ambiguity***: Another challenge is dealing with semantic ambiguity in big data. Different data sources may use varying terminologies and conceptualizations for similar concepts, leading to ambiguities and inconsistencies. Resolving these ambiguities and achieving semantic interoperability is critical for accurate ontology learning and meaningful data integration [27]. This challenge is exacerbated in big data contexts where the volume and variety of data are immense.

5.2 Expected solutions

I. ***Scalable Algorithms and Frameworks***: To address scalability, researchers are developing scalable ontology learning algorithms and frameworks that leverage distributed computing and parallel processing. Approaches such as MapReduce and Apache Spark are being utilized to handle large-scale data processing efficiently [28]. These frameworks enable the distribution of computational tasks across multiple nodes, significantly improving the speed and efficiency of ontology learning processes.

II. ***Advanced Data Preprocessing Techniques***: Improving data quality and handling heterogeneity in big data requires advanced data preprocessing techniques. Techniques such as data cleaning, normalization, and transformation are essential to prepare data for ontology learning. Additionally, the use of machine learning and natural language processing (NLP) techniques can help in automatically identifying and resolving inconsistencies and ambiguities in the data [29]. Semantic enrichment techniques, such as entity recognition and linking, can further enhance the quality of data integration.

III. ***Hybrid and Ensemble Methods***: To mitigate semantic ambiguity, hybrid and ensemble methods that combine mul tiple ontology learning approaches are being explored. These methods leverage the strengths of different techniques, such as statistical methods, machine learning, and expert knowledge, to improve the robustness and accuracy of ontology learning [30]. By integrating various approaches, these methods can better handle the complexities and nuances of big data.

IV. ***Interactive and Incremental Learning***: Interactive and incremental learning approaches are gaining attention as they allow for continuous updates and refinement of ontologies based on new data. These approaches involve human-in-the-loop mechanisms where domain experts can provide feedback and corrections, ensuring that the learned ontologies remain accurate and relevant over time [31]. Incremental learning techniques enable the system to adapt to the evolving nature of big data without requiring complete retraining.

6. Conclusion

In conclusion, the increasing complexity of electronic data and business processes necessitates advanced approaches to big data management. Semantic technologies, particularly ontologies, offer promising solutions for improving data integration, quality, and business process integration. Despite the challenges, the adoption of semantic technologies can significantly enhance enterprises' ability to manage and utilize complex datasets effectively, driving operational efficiency and business success. By leveraging the power of ontologies, enterprises can achieve a more comprehensive and interconnected view of their data, leading to better decision-making, improved operational efficiency, and enhanced collaboration across different departments and systems. As the volume, variety, velocity, and veracity of data continue to grow, the importance of innovative approaches to big data management will only increase, making semantic technologies a crucial component of modern enterprise information systems. For future reading, the authors advise the reader could optionally read the following research works [32–44].

7. Future work and directions

While ontology-based big data management has shown great promise, there are several areas where further research and development are needed. Future work could explore the following directions:

7.1 Scalability and performance

As the volume of data continues to grow, scalability and performance become increasingly important. Research is needed to develop more efficient algorithms and techniques for handling large-scale ontology-based data integration and analysis.

7.2 Automation and machine learning

Integrating machine learning with ontology-based approaches could automate many aspects of data management, from data integration to quality assurance. Future research could explore how machine learning algorithms can be used to automatically generate and maintain ontologies, reducing the need for manual intervention.

7.3 Standardization and interoperability

Standardization of ontologies and semantic technologies is crucial for ensuring interoperability across different systems and platforms. Future work could focus on developing and promoting industry-wide standards for ontologies and semantic data management.

7.4 Privacy and security

Managing big data, particularly in sensitive domains such as healthcare, requires robust privacy and security measures. Future research could explore how ontology-based approaches can enhance data privacy and security, ensuring that sensitive information is protected while still being accessible for legitimate use.

Acknowledgments

The authors wish to express sincere thanks to their universities for providing facilities and continuous support in conducting this study.

Compliance with ethical standards

Conflict of interest: Not declared.
Funding: Still waiting to be received.
Competing Interests: Authors declare that there are not any competing interests.
Ethical and informed consent for data used: Not applicable.

References

[1] C. Collins, D. Dennehy, K. Conboy, P. Mikalef, Artificial intelligence in information systems research: A systematic literature review and research agenda, Int. J. Inf. Manag. 60 (2021) 102383, https://doi.org/10.1016/J.IJINFOMGT.2021.102383.

[2] K. Węcel, Big Data Organization Challenge, 2022, pp. 73–112, https://doi.org/10.1007/978-3-031-07147-8_4.

[3] R. Gaire, C. Sriharsha, D. Puthal, et al., Internet of Things (IoT) and Cloud Computing Enabled Disaster Management, 2020, pp. 273–298, https://doi.org/10.1007/978-3-030-43795-4_12.

[4] M. Naeem, T. Jamal, J. Diaz-Martinez, et al., Trends and future perspective challenges in big data. Smart innovation, Syst. Technol. 253 (2022) 309–325, https://doi.org/10.1007/978-981-16-5036-9_30.

[5] Hassan B, Dasmahapatra S *Towards Semantic Web: Challenges and Needs.*

[6] B.A. Hassan, T.A. Rashid, Artificial Intelligence Algorithms for Natural Language Processing and the Semantic Web Ontology Learning, 2021 arXiv preprint arXiv:210813772.

[7] A. Bryar, T.A.R. Hassan, Formal context reduction in deriving concept hierarchies from corpora using adaptive evolutionary clustering algorithm, Complex Intell. Syst. (2020).

[8] B.A. Hassan, T.A. Rashid, S. Mirjalili, Formal context reduction in deriving concept hierarchies from corpora using adaptive evolutionary clustering algorithm star, Complex Intell. Syst. (2021) 1–16.

[9] C. Bizer, T. Heath, T. Berners-Lee, Linked data - The story So far, in: Linking the World's Information, 2023, pp. 115–143, https://doi.org/10.1145/3591366.3591378.

[10] J. Euzenat, P. Shvaiko, Ontology matching, in: Ontology Matching, second ed., 2013, pp. 1–511, https://doi.org/10.1007/978-3-642-38721-0/COVER.

[11] N. Burkart, M.F. Huber, A survey on the explainability of supervised machine learning, J. Artif. Intell. Res. 70 (2021) 245–317, https://doi.org/10.1613/JAIR.1.12228.

[12] R. Angles, M. Arenas, P. Barceló, et al., Foundations of modern query languages for graph databases, ACM Comput. Surv. 50 (2017), https://doi.org/10.1145/3104031/SUPPL_FILE/ANGLES.ZIP.

[13] I. Horrocks, P.F. Patel-Schneider, F. Van Harmelen, From SHIQ and RDF to OWL: The making of a web ontology language, J. Web Semant. 1 (2003) 7–26, https://doi.org/10.1016/J.WEBSEM.2003.07.001.

[14] A. Rhayem, M.B.A. Mhiri, F. Gargouri, Semantic web technologies for the internet of things: Systematic literature review, Internet Things 11 (2020) 100206, https://doi.org/10.1016/J.IOT.2020.100206.

[15] L. Ehrlinger, W. Wöß, A survey of data quality measurement and monitoring tools, Front. Big Data 5 (2022) 850611, https://doi.org/10.3389/FDATA.2022.850611/BIBTEX.

[16] M. Yahya, J.G. Breslin, M.I. Ali, Semantic web and knowledge graphs for industry 4.0, Appl. Sci. 11 (2021), https://doi.org/10.3390/APP11115110, 5110 11:5110.

[17] S. Balakrishna, M. Thirumaran, V.K. Solanki, IoT sensor data integration in healthcare using semantics and machine learning approaches, Intell. Syst. Ref. Libr. 165 (2020) 275–300, https://doi.org/10.1007/978-3-030-23983-1_11.

[18] A.K.M.B. Haque, B.M. Arifuzzaman, S.A.N. Siddik, et al., Semantic web in healthcare: A systematic literature review of application, research gap, and future research avenues, Int. J. Clin. Pract. 2022 (2022) 6807484, https://doi.org/10.1155/2022/6807484.

[19] J. Dörpinghaus, S. Klante, M. Christian, et al., From social networks to knowledge graphs: A plea for interdisciplinary approaches, Soc. Sci. Humanit. Open 6 (2022) 100337, https://doi.org/10.1016/J.SSAHO.2022.100337.

[20] N. Noy, Y. Gao, A. Jain, et al., Industry-scale knowledge graphs: Lessons and challenges, ACM Queue 17 (2019), https://doi.org/10.1145/3329781.3332266.

[21] S. Ji, S. Pan, E. Cambria, et al., A survey on knowledge graphs: Representation, acquisition, and applications, IEEE Transact. Neural Networks Learn. Syst. 33 (2022) 494–514, https://doi.org/10.1109/TNNLS.2021.3070843.

[22] A. Gandomi, M. Haider, Beyond the hype: Big data concepts, methods, and analytics, Int. J. Inf. Manag. 35 (2015) 137–144, https://doi.org/10.1016/J.IJINFOMGT.2014.10.007.

[23] A. Cuzzocrea, I.Y. Song, K.C. Davis, Analytics over large-scale multidimensional data: The big data revolution, in: International Conference on Information and Knowledge Management, Proceedings, 2011, pp. 101–103, https://doi.org/10.1145/2064676.2064695.

[24] G. Shmueli, O.R. Koppius, Predictive analytics in information systems research, MIS Q. 35 (2011) 553–572, https://doi.org/10.2307/23042796.

[25] I. Mountasser, B. Ouhbi, F. Hdioud, B. Frikh, Semantic-based big data integration framework using scalable distributed ontology matching strategy, Distributed Parallel Databases 39 (2021) 891–937, https://doi.org/10.1007/S10619-021-07321-6/METRICS.
[26] I. Salvadori, A. Huf, F. Siqueira, Data linking as a service: An infrastructure for generating and publishing linked data on the web, in: Proceedings - 2020 IEEE 44th Annual Computers, Software, and Applications Conference, COMPSAC, 2020, pp. 262–271, https://doi.org/10.1109/COMPSAC48688.2020.00042.
[27] J. Kozák, M. Ne Č Aský, J. Pokorný, Drug encyclopedia – Linked data application for physicians, Lect. Notes Comput. Sci. 9367 (2015) 41–56, https://doi.org/10.1007/978-3-319-25010-6_3.
[28] Y.K. Gupta, S. Kumari, A study of big data analytics using Apache spark with python and scala, in: Proceedings of the 3rd International Conference on Intelligent Sustainable Systems, ICISS, 2020, pp. 471–478, https://doi.org/10.1109/ICISS49785.2020.9315863.
[29] J. Luengo, D. García-Gil, S. Ramírez-Gallego, et al., Big Data Preprocessing: Enabling Smart Data, 2020, pp. 1–186, https://doi.org/10.1007/978-3-030-39105-8/COVER.
[30] A. Alsayat, H. Ahmadi, A hybrid method using ensembles of neural network and text mining for learner satisfaction analysis from big datasets in online learning platform, Neural Process. Lett. 55 (2023) 3267–3303, https://doi.org/10.1007/S11063-022-11009-Y/TABLES/21.
[31] E.A. Kardinata, N.A. Rakhmawati, Online incremental learning based on crowdsourcing for Indonesian ontology relation extraction, Intel. Artif. 26 (2023) 124–136, https://doi.org/10.4114/INTARTIF.VOL26ISS72PP124-136.
[32] B.A. Hassan, N.B. Tayfor, A.A. Hassan, A.M. Ahmed, T.A. Rashid, N.N. Abdalla, From A-to-Z review of clustering validation indices, Neurocomputing (Jul. 2024) 128198, https://doi.org/10.1016/J.NEUCOM.2024.128198.
[33] S.U. Umar, T.A. Rashid, A.M. Ahmed, B.A. Hassan, M.R. Baker, Modified bat algorithm: A newly proposed approach for solving complex and real-world problems, Soft Comput. (Jul. 2024) 1–16, https://doi.org/10.1007/S00500-024-09761-5/METRICS.
[34] H.K. Hamarashid, B.A. Hassan, T.A. Rashid, Modified-improved fitness dependent optimizer for complex and engineering problems, Knowl. Base Syst. 300 (Sep. 2024) 112098, https://doi.org/10.1016/J.KNOSYS.2024.112098.
[35] R.K. Muhammed, et al., Comparative analysis of AES, blowfish, twofish, Salsa20, and ChaCha20 for image encryption, Kurd. J. Appl. Res. 9 (1) (May 2024) 52–65, https://doi.org/10.24017/SCIENCE.2024.1.5.
[36] T.A. Rashid, et al., NSGA-II-DL: Metaheuristic optimal feature selection with deep learning framework for HER2 classification in breast cancer, IEEE Access 12 (2024) 38885–38898, https://doi.org/10.1109/ACCESS.2024.3374890.
[37] A.M. Ahmed, et al., Balancing exploration and exploitation phases in whale optimization algorithm: An insightful and empirical analysis, in: Handbook of Whale Optimization Algorithm: Variants, Hybrids, Improvements, and Applications, Jan. 2024, pp. 149–156, https://doi.org/10.1016/B978-0-32-395365-8.00017-8.
[38] B.A. Hassan, et al., Equitable and fair performance evaluation of whale optimization algorithm. Handbook of Whale Optimization Algorithm: Variants, Hybrids, Improvements, and Applications, Jan. 2024, pp. 157–168, https://doi.org/10.1016/B978-0-32-395365-8.00018-X.
[39] M.H. Abdalla, et al., Sentiment analysis based on hybrid neural network techniques using binary coordinate ascent algorithm, IEEE Access 11 (2023) 134087–134099, https://doi.org/10.1109/ACCESS.2023.3334980.
[40] B.A. Hassan, Ontology Learning Using Formal Concept Analysis and WordNet, Nov. 2023. https://arxiv.org/abs/2311.14699v1. (Accessed 24 July 2024).
[41] T.A. Rashid, et al., Awareness requirement and performance management for adaptive systems: A survey, J. Supercomput. 79 (9) (Jun. 2023) 9692–9714, https://doi.org/10.1007/S11227-022-05021-1/METRICS.
[42] M.T. Abdulkhaleq, et al., Fitness dependent optimizer with neural networks for COVID-19 patients, Comput. Methods Programs Biomed. Update 3 (Jan. 2023) 100090, https://doi.org/10.1016/J.CMPBUP.2022.100090.
[43] S. Farahmand-Tabar, T.A. Rashid, Steel plate fault detection using the fitness dependent optimizer and neural networks, in: A.J. Kulkarni, A.H. Gandomi (Eds.), Handbook of Formal Optimization, Springer, Singapore, 2023, https://doi.org/10.1007/978-981-19-8851-6_41-1.
[44] B.A. Hassan, T.A. Rashid, Artificial Intelligence Algorithms for Natural Language Processing and the Semantic Web Ontology Learning, 2021.

Chapter 16

Strength prediction of concrete materials with fly ash additive using optimized TSK model

Salar Farahmand-Tabar[1] and Sina Shirgir[2]
[1]Department of Civil Engineering, Faculty of Engineering, University of Zanjan, Zanjan, Iran; [2]Department of Structural Engineering, Faculty of Civil Engineering, University of Tabriz, Tabriz, Iran

1. Introduction

Engineering challenges are frequently tackled with the aid of artificial intelligence (AI), specifically through training frameworks [1–5]. A variety of simulation techniques grounded in artificial neural networks (ANN) and fuzzy logic (FL) systems has recently emerged. These techniques have been applied across different engineering domains, including structural control [6], prediction of concrete mechanical properties [7–9], strength estimation of structural components [10,11], and seismic behavior forecasting in structures [12,13]. Developing models using ANNs and FL systems generally involves training the system with a comprehensive dataset. If this dataset sufficiently represents the system's behavior, the trained ANN or FL system can model the system effectively. These models not only replicate experimental outcomes but also predict results for new experiments.

Fuzzy logic is particularly useful for problems involving uncertainty in specific criteria. Fuzzy set theory's systematic linguistic computation addresses these issues by employing numerical calculations based on membership functions, which describe relative rather than absolute membership to a set. These functions can range from 0 to 1 [14]. The four main components of a Fuzzy Inference System (FIS) are fuzzification, a fuzzy rule base, fuzzy inference, and defuzzification. There are rules within fuzzy rule base in an "if-then" format that depict potential fuzzy relationships between outputs and inputs. The fuzzy inference engine processes these rules to convert inputs to the related outputs [15].

FIS with *if-then* rules can emulate the qualitative aspects of human reasoning, capturing and mimicking human-like inference without relying solely on quantitative data. This capability makes them valuable for nonlinear behavior simulation. These systems are categorized into Sugeno and Mamdani [16,17] types. In the Sugeno approach, the fuzzy rule results are determined by a specific output function. Developed by Takagi, Sugeno, and Kang [17], this system has been widely implemented in control, prediction, and inference applications [18–20]. The adaptive neuro-FIS (ANFIS) merges FIS and ANN to leverage the advantages of both, offering a unified solution for engineering problems. ANFIS has proven effective in various civil engineering fields [21–24], demonstrating strong predictive capabilities for system performance.

In construction, concrete plays a critical role in binding stone and brick elements, with fly ash often used as an additive alongside binder materials and aggregates. While cement is the primary binding material in modern construction, ongoing research is exploring alternative materials to decrease the cement's environmental impact and improve the life cycle assessment of concrete. Fly ash is one such material, known for enhancing the properties of concrete. However, despite extensive research, investigating an exact tool to quantitatively aid in optimizing the design of cement-based concrete is required [25]. The challenge lies in creating a predictive model [26–28] for concrete properties due to the significant nonlinearity introduced by various compositional parameters, making accurate predictions with deterministic methods difficult.

Advanced Intelligence Methods for Data Science and Optimization. https://doi.org/10.1016/B978-0-443-28940-8.00019-1

This chapter focuses on predicting the concrete's mechanical properties through AI methods, particularly the FIS. It aims to predict the compressive strength of the concrete by developing and optimizing Takagi-Sugeno-Kang (TSK) models utilizing the CryStAl. The model is developed using a dataset of 104 specimens from the literature, with input parameters including synthesis parameters such as the water-to-binder ratio, fine aggregate ratio, fly ash replacement ratio, and the content of air-entraining and superplasticizers. The output parameters are the concrete slump and compressive strength. The optimum model of TSK proves to be both efficient and reliable in its performance.

This chapter contributes to the field of engineering and materials science by addressing the challenge of predicting the compressive strength of concrete, a critical property in construction, using advanced artificial intelligence techniques. Specifically, it develops and optimizes Takagi-Sugeno-Kang (TSK) models utilizing the innovative Crystal Structure Algorithm (CryStAl) to accurately simulate concrete behavior. By leveraging a dataset of 104 specimens with key input parameters, including water-to-binder ratio, fine aggregate ratio, fly ash replacement ratio, and additive content, the research demonstrates the superior efficiency and reliability of the optimized TSK model. This work not only enhances predictive capabilities for concrete properties but also provides a robust tool for designing eco-friendly, high-performance concrete mixtures, contributing to sustainability and innovation in civil engineering.

2. Methods and materials

2.1 Crystal structure algorithm

Metaheuristic algorithms were introduced following the development of gradient-based methods [29], with early examples including classic Genetic Algorithms [30–33] and Ant Colony Optimization methods [34–36]. Given the complex nature of various problems, numerous advanced methods have since been proposed, addressing both single-objective [37–45] and multiobjective optimization [46–48]. One of the more recent contributions in this field is the Crystal Structure Algorithm [49]. Crystals are solid minerals characterized by a regular and repetitive arrangement of their constituent molecules, atoms, or ions in three-dimensional space, known as crystallographic order. These crystalline solids exhibit a variety of properties, which can be either isotropic or anisotropic. The term "crystal" derives from Greek, meaning "frozen by cold," reflecting the ancient belief that water, when sufficiently cooled, becomes a stable solid. Additionally, the word has Arabic roots from the Greek "berlis," meaning emerald [50]. Fig. 16.1a showcases a typical crystal example. Historical references to the orderly arrangement of particles in crystals date back to Johannes Kepler in 1619. In 1690, Christine Hogens furthered this understanding by studying the optical properties of calcite crystals, suggesting that they consist of tiny particles with distinct shapes. Over the centuries, numerous chemical and physical theories regarding crystals have been proposed and tested [50]. Moreover, the diverse symmetries of crystals have inspired the design and creation of various human-made artworks, mechanisms, and structures.

The fundamental components of a crystal include the "lattice," a periodic array of points in defined spaces that does not specify the precise atoms' location within the material. In contrast, the "basis" determines the positions of atoms in a crystal structure, related with each lattice point. Thus, crystals are defined by the combining these elements—the lattice and the basis—as presented in Fig. 16.1b. While the lattice dictates the shape of the crystal, various geometric forms can be constructed, reflecting the infinite variety of natural shapes. Here, we highlight some of the most recognized regular shapes, depicted in Fig. 16.1c. The basis considers various arrangements of atoms within the lattice, including atoms positioned at the corners and other irregular patterns, as exemplified in Fig. 16.1d within a simple cubic crystal system. For mathematical and numerical representation, the Bravais model [51] is commonly employed to define crystal configurations. This model describes a periodic crystal structure where each lattice point is identified by its coordinates using vector notation, such as:

$$r = \sum n_i a_i, \tag{16.1}$$

In this context, n_i represents an integer, a_i denotes the shortest vector along the principal crystallographic directions, and i signifies the quantity for crystal corners. The mathematical framework of CryStAl is explained here, integrating fundamental principles of crystal structures with specific adaptations (Algorithm 16.1). In the optimization process of this model, the space is visualized as containing individual crystals, each representing a candidate solution. The iterative process begins by randomly selecting a set number of crystals for initialization.

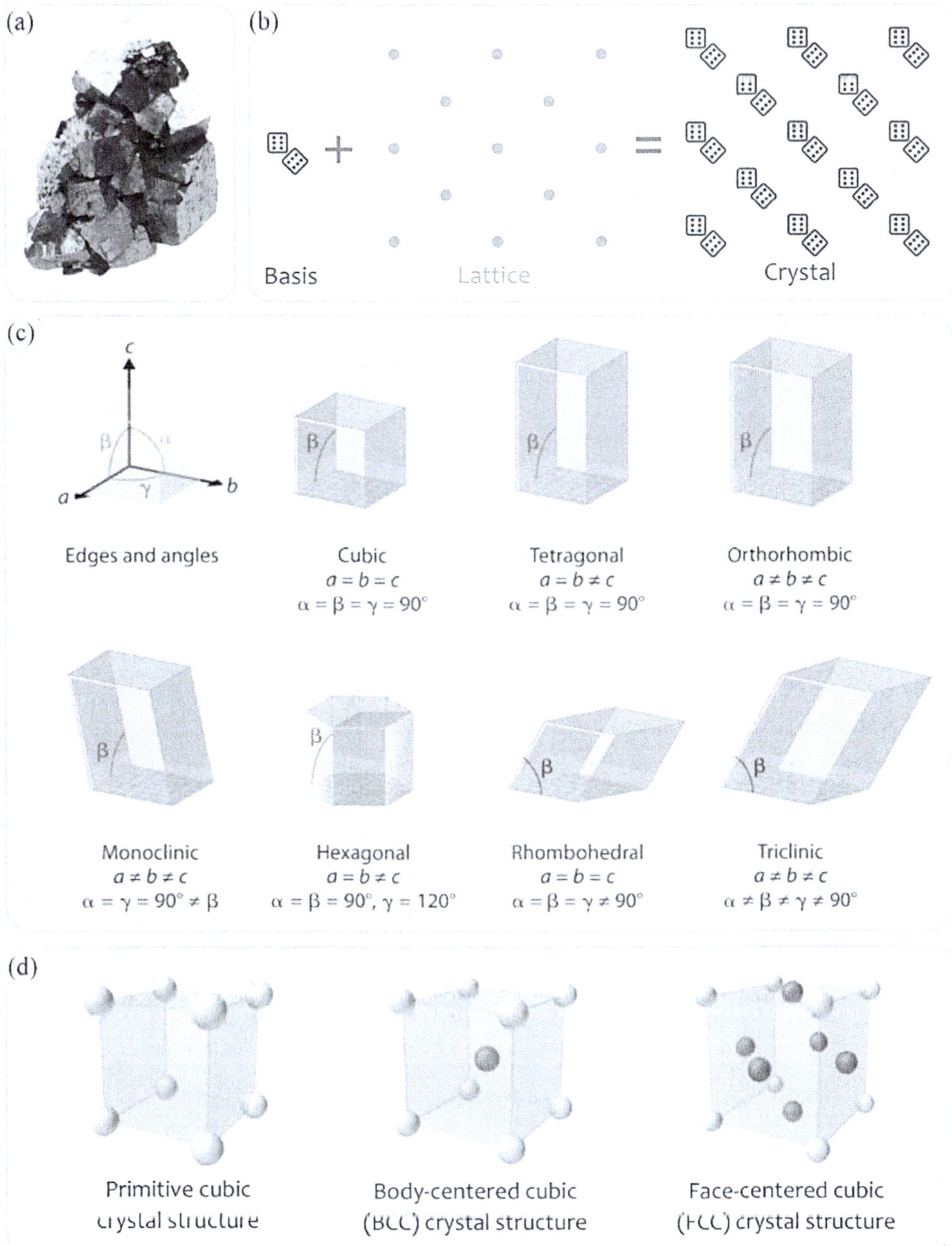

FIGURE 16.1 Different aspects related to crystals: (a) A typical natural crystal known as galena. (b) A crystal with an added basis on a lattice. (c) Different options for lattice configurations. (d) Common varieties within the cubic crystal system [50].

$$Cr = \begin{bmatrix} Cr_1 \\ Cr_2 \\ \vdots \\ Cr_i \\ \vdots \\ Cr_n \end{bmatrix} = \begin{bmatrix} x_1^1 & x_1^2 & \cdots & x_1^j & \cdots & x_1^d \\ x_2^1 & x_2^2 & \cdots & x_2^j & \cdots & x_2^d \\ \vdots & \vdots & \vdots & \vdots & \vdots & \vdots \\ x_i^1 & x_i^2 & \cdots & x_i^j & \cdots & x_i^d \\ \vdots & \vdots & \vdots & \vdots & \vdots & \vdots \\ x_n^1 & x_n^2 & \cdots & x_n^j & \cdots & x_n^d \end{bmatrix}, \begin{cases} i = 1, 2, \ldots, n \\ j = 1, 2, \ldots, d \end{cases} \tag{16.2}$$

Here, n denotes the crystal numbers (equal to candidate solutions), and d represents the dimensionality of the problem. The procedure for assigning the initial crystal positions within the search space involves random placement according to the following method:

$$x_i^j(0) = x_{i,min}^j + \xi\left(x_{i,max}^j - x_{i,min}^j\right), \begin{cases} i = 1, 2, \ldots, n \\ j = 1, 2, \ldots, d \end{cases} \tag{16.3}$$

To clarify, in the context of crystallography, $x_i^j(0)$ represents the initial crystal positions. $x_{i,min}^j$ and $x_{i,max}^j$ denote the lower and upper allowable values, respectively, for the j-th decision variable of the i-th candidate solution. The random number of ξ defined within the range [0, 1]. According to the crystallographic concept of the 'basis,' primary crystals, labeled Cr_{main}, are those located at the corners and are randomly selected from the initial set of candidate solutions, with the current crystal, Cr, excluded from selection. The optimal crystal configuration is referred to as Cr_b, and the mean values of randomly chosen crystals are represented by F_c. The candidate solutions' positions are updated within the search space utilizing fundamental lattice principles, which involve four distinct updating processes outlined as follows:

(I) Simple cubic:

$$Cr_{new} = Cr_{old} + r_1 Cr_{main} \tag{16.4}$$

(II) Cubic with the best crystals:

$$Cr_{new} = Cr_{old} + r_1 Cr_{main} + r_2 Cr_b \tag{16.5}$$

(III) Cubic with the mean crystals:

$$Cr_{new} = Cr_{old} + r_1 Cr_{main} + r_2 F_c \tag{16.6}$$

(IV) Cubic with the mean and best crystals:

$$Cr_{new} = Cr_{old} + r_1 Cr_{main} + r_2 Cr_b + r_3 F_c \tag{16.7}$$

In the four equations mentioned above, Cr_{new} represents the updated position of the crystal, Cr_{old} denotes the current position of the crystal, and r, r_1, r_2 and r_3 are random numbers used in the updating process.

Algorithm 16.1. The pseudo-code of the CryStAl [49].

procedure CryStAl
  Generate initial random positions (x_i^j) of crystals (Cr_i)
  Calculate fitness of each crystal
  while ($iter < max\_iter$)
   for $i = 1$: No. initial crystals
    Generate Cr_{main}
    Generate new crystals using Eq. (16.4)
    Generate Cr_b
    Generate new crystals using Eq. (16.5)
    Generate F_c
    Generate new crystals using Eq. (16.6)
    Generate new crystals using Eq. (16.7)
    if new crystals violate the boundary conditions
     Modify the new violated position
    end if

Calculate the new crystals' fitness
Update Global Best
end for
iter = *iter* + 1
end while
Return GB
end procedure

2.2 Fuzzy inference system

The TSK model as an FIS, proposed by Takagi, Sugeno, and Kang in 1985, is essential for modeling systems through the creation of fuzzy rules based on input–output data [17]. A crucial component of adaptive neuro-fuzzy inference systems (ANFIS), this method shares its initial steps with the Mamdani approach, including the use of fuzzy inputs and a rule base. "If-then" statements are employed in the Mamdani FIS, as illustrated by Eq. (16.8) [16].

$$if\ (x_1\ is\ A_1) and\ (x_j\ is\ A_j)\ and\ \dots\ and\ (x_n\ is\ A_n)\ then\ (y\ is\ B) \tag{16.8}$$

Creating an optimal fuzzy system is crucial for obtaining the best possible output, given that the rules within the FIS are according to human expertise. The challenge lies in the complexity, which escalates as the number of rules in the system's rule base increases to m^n, where n represents the number of inputs and m denotes the membership functions for each input. This makes the task of designing an optimal fuzzy system difficult. To overcome this complexity, the inference system of TSK is employed, in which the outcome of the rule base is a function of the input variables. The TSK model-based fuzzy system can be outlined as follows [17]:

$$if\ (x_1\ is\ A_1^r), (x_j\ is\ A_j^r), \dots, (x_n\ is\ A_n^r)\ then\ (y^r = a_0^r + a_1^r x_1 + \dots + a_n^r x_n) \tag{16.9}$$

In the TSK model, for each rule r (where $r = 1, 2, \dots, m$), the inputs x_j and the output y^r are utilized. The model uses m fuzzy rules, each linked to the degree of match between the inputs and the rules. Designing a TSK system involves determining the optimum fuzzy rule parameters by leveraging a training dataset. This dataset is divided into three distinct subsets: training-, checking-, and test-data. Accurate determination of the output parameters of the rules is crucial. Several techniques, such as NNs, and evolutionary algorithms have been suggested to achieve this. Adaptive networks adjust the parameter set according to the training data to ensure the system produces the desired results. ANFIS utilizes a sophisticated approach to train and fine-tune the parameters of an FIS. Fig. 16.2 depicts an adaptive network representing a first-order FIS with two rules.

$$\begin{aligned} &1)\ If\ x\ is\ A_1\ and\ y\ is\ B_1\ Then\ f_1 = p_1.x + q_1.y + r_1 \\ &2)\ If\ x\ is\ A_2\ and\ y\ is\ B_2\ Then\ f_2 = p_2.x + q_2.y + r_2 \end{aligned} \tag{16.10}$$

Following the development of the ANFIS approach, numerous methods have been introduced to train the rules and establish the optimum rule set. To identify the regulatory parameters of fuzzy membership functions, several training algorithms have been explored. In addition, metaheuristic (MH) optimization techniques have been utilized to define both the membership functions of input variables and the structure of the rule base. Key factors for developing an accurate ANFIS model include the type and number of fuzzy rules, as well as the type of membership functions. To address this, an optimization problem is formulated to identify the parameters of the TSK fuzzy rules and the distribution parameters of the membership functions associated with each input variable. MH algorithms are then used for training the ANFIS model by minimizing the relative deviation of the data while training.

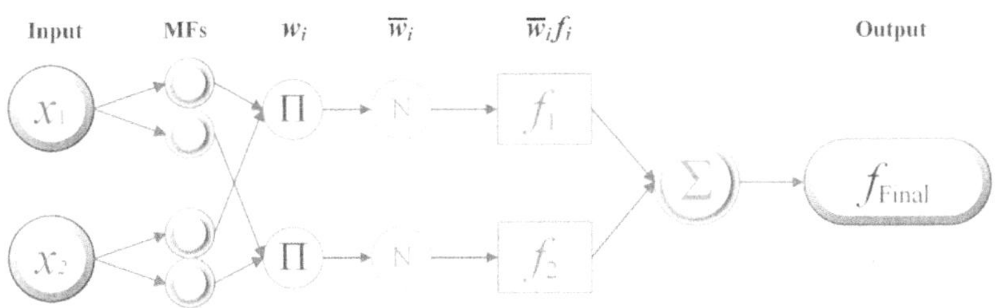

FIGURE 16.2 Structure of the FIS.

2.3 An efficient optimum FIS (CryStAl-FIS)

This section is developed an adaptive procedure to train the fuzzy inference system based on the optimization problem. By integrating an FIS with an optimization technique, the method aims to minimize prediction errors. The system is trained with a data set, refining the model through this process. The training utilizes a feedforward scheme, and afterward, the system's predictive accuracy is tested in a closed-loop setting. This technique has proven to be effective in predicting the behavior of complex systems. In this regard, the crystal metaheuristic optimization algorithm is combined with the TSK inference model to solve the training problem in optimum manner. Each crystal (candidate solution) represents a set of parameters for the FIS (e.g., mean, standard deviation of MFs, and rule coefficients). The FIS is trained by minimizing an objective function (e.g., RMSE) that measures how well the FIS predicts outputs for given inputs. The algorithm iteratively updates crystals and evaluates their performance until convergence criteria are met. The pseudo-code and flowchart of the proposed method are depicted in Algorithm 16.2 and Fig. 16.3.

Algorithm 16.2. The pseudo code of the Crystal FIS.

1. Initialize Fuzzy Inference System (FIS):
   a. Define input variables and their membership functions (MFs) with initial parameters (e.g., mean and standard deviation).
   b. Define the rule base with initial coefficients.
2. Define the Optimization Objective:
   a. Select a performance criterion to optimize (e.g., RMSE, accuracy).
   b. Create an objective function that evaluates FIS performance for given input–output data.
3. Initialize the Crystal Algorithm:
   a. Set parameters for the algorithm, such as: Number of crystals (particles). - Reflection factor, absorption factor, and other hyperparameters.
   b. Randomly initialize the positions of crystals (candidate solutions) in the search space.

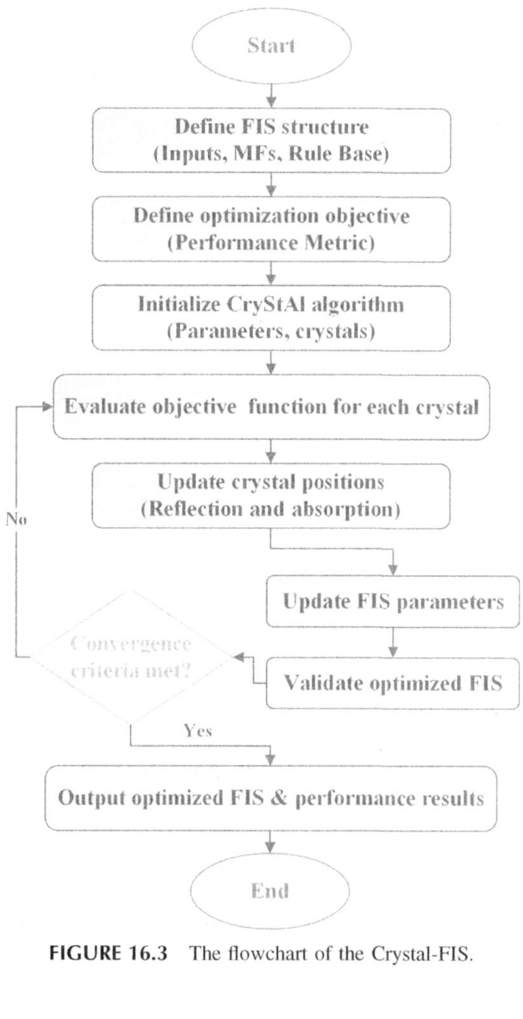

FIGURE 16.3 The flowchart of the Crystal-FIS.

4. Main Optimization Loop:
   a. Evaluate the objective function for each crystal.
   b. Identify the best-performing crystal (global best).
   c. Update the positions of crystals:
      - Reflect crystals toward the global best based on reflection factor.
      - Perform absorption based on absorption factor to avoid stagnation.
   d. Check convergence criteria (e.g., maximum iterations or minimum error threshold):
      - If met, exit the loop.
      - Otherwise, go to step 4a.
5. Update FIS Parameters:
   a. Set the FIS membership function parameters and rule coefficients to the values found by the best crystal.
6. Validate the Optimized FIS:
   a. Test the optimized FIS with validation data.
   b. Report performance metrics.
7. Output:
   a. Return the optimized FIS parameters.
   b. Plot/visualize the results (e.g., optimized membership functions, error plots).

3. Problem definition

This section details an adaptive method designed to predict concrete's compressive strength utilizing a material data set. By integrating an FIS with an optimization technique, the method aims to minimize prediction errors. The system is trained with data on concrete ingredients, refining the model through this process. The training utilizes a feedforward method, and afterward, the system's predictive accuracy is tested in a closed-loop setting. Here, the properties of the ingredients in each sample are used as inputs to forecast outcomes within a feedback loop. This technique has proven to be efficient in the behavioral prediction of complex systems. A schematic diagram for the structure of the inference system is presented in Fig. 16.4.

The system output focuses on estimating the compressive strength of each concrete sample. The inputs to the inference system include the ingredients and specifications of the samples. This design is flexible enough to predict various properties of concrete. The adaptive FIS for predicting responses is fully interconnected. The system's design dictates that the number of inputs and outputs is based on the specific response being predicted and the count of input variables. Here, the input variables reflect the concrete's characteristics and ingredients, while the output parameter indicates the predicted compressive strength. The framework of this method is shown in Fig. 16.5.

An optimization problem is formulated to identify the TSK model parameters in the FIS. The objective is to minimize the error between the predicted response and the experimental data. The mean squared error (MSE) is used to compare the predicted time–history response $\widetilde{f}(t_i|\mathbf{p})$ with the actual time-history response $f(t_i)$ at each time step. The parameters of the TSK model are optimized to reduce this prediction error. The formal definition of the objective function is provided in Eq. (16.11)

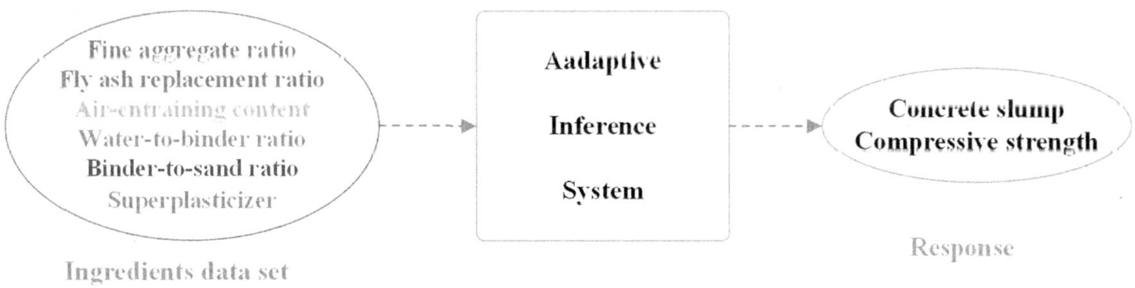

FIGURE 16.4 Schematic presentation of the inference system.

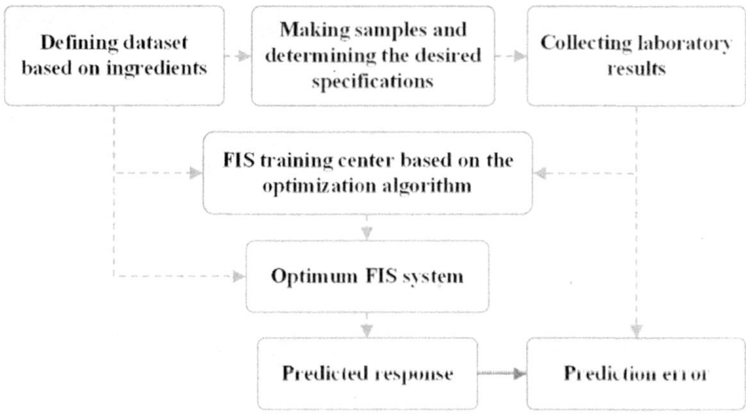

FIGURE 16.5 The design process of the inference system.

$$OF(p) = \frac{\sum_{i=1}^{N} \left(f(t_i) - \widetilde{f}(t_i|\mathbf{p})\right)^2}{N.\sigma_f^2} \tag{16.11}$$

The vector denoted as p represents the design variables, while the variance in the set of analytical responses is symbolized by σ_f^2. N signifies the number of data sets. In the FIS, Gaussian membership functions, determined by their statistical values, represent the input variables. The outputs of the rules are generated by integrating these input variables. To accurately predict the system's response, optimizing the TSK model involves identifying the mean and standard deviation of the membership functions for input variables, along with the rule coefficients governing the output variable. In the TSK inference system, these parameters serve as design variables and are refined using metaheuristic optimization methods. Specifically, the optimization process focuses on the characteristics of the membership functions (σ_i and μ_i) for each input and the rule coefficients (a_i^r) associated with the output variable. The formulation of the optimum training problem is presented in Eq. (16.12).

$$\begin{cases} Design\ Variables: \left[InputsMFs\left(\sigma_{i,A^r}, \mu_{i,A^r}\right) \quad Output\left(a_i^r\right)\right] \\ To\ Minimize: Objective\ Function = MSE \end{cases} \tag{16.12}$$

The input variables of the inference system are defined by membership functions (MF). In this case, four Gaussian membership functions labeled ZR, PS, PM and PL are used. These labels represent qualitative values: zero, small, medium, and large positive, respectively. The global domain for the input variables is determined by the range of variation within the data set. To precisely estimate concrete's compressive strength with a fuzzy inference system, a thorough dataset that covers all potential conditions is required. Data from laboratory-generated samples, as referenced in various sources, is employed for this purpose.

4. Database for concrete materials with fly ash additive

4.1 Procedure

A total of 104 sets of mixtures were utilized in this experimental program. According to the results of the mixing tests, an inference system was developed using these 104 sets of mixtures. Subsequently, the TSK model was implemented within the CryStal algorithm using MATLAB. The results obtained from TSK-CryStal were then compared against two sets of test mixtures, one for training and the other for testing the inference system. The composition of fly ash can vary considerably depending on factors such as its source, the combustion process, and storage conditions. Variations in its chemical composition (e.g., silica and alumina content) and physical characteristics (e.g., fineness and density) can influence concrete performance. Additionally, factors such as cement type, aggregate size, and admixture properties may introduce further variability. The model's ability to adapt depends on how well the dataset captures these variations. External influences, such as curing conditions (e.g., temperature and humidity), also play a significant role in hydration and strength development. Moreover, geographic and climatic factors during sample production could introduce biases if the dataset predominantly represents specific environmental conditions. If the dataset prioritizes certain properties, such as compressive strength, over others such as durability or thermal resistance, the model may become specialized and less effective for broader applications. With only 104 samples, the dataset may not fully represent the diverse range of real-world fly ash concrete properties. However, for studies focusing on specific concrete types, addressing these aspects enhances the analysis and provides a clearer perspective on the model's practical strengths and limitations. To better understand the relationships between input and output variables, sensitivity analysis is conducted. Furthermore, the dataset is divided into training and testing subsets to evaluate model performance, using validation techniques to assess how well the model generalizes.

4.2 Material properties

Materials for this experiment were all sourced from South Korea. ASTM Type I Portland cement was utilized [52]. The aggregate mixture consisted of crushed granite as the coarse aggregate, which had a fineness modulus of 7.2, a specific gravity of 2.7, and a maximum particle size of 19 mm, combined with quartz sand as the fine aggregate, featuring a fineness modulus of 2.94 and a specific gravity of 2.61. To achieve a very low water-to-binder ratio, a naphthalene superplasticizer and an air-entraining agent were incorporated. Additionally, Class *F* fly ash from Elkem, Norway, was included in the mixture. Table 16.1 provide detailed properties of these materials.

TABLE 16.1 Mixture properties of the concrete.

Cement			**Fly ash**				
Properties	**Value**		**Properties**		**Value**		
Specific gravity	3.15		Specific gravity		2.13		
Fineness (m^2/kg)	310		Fineness (m^2/kg)		360		
SiO_2 (%)	21.3		SiO_2 (%)		63.5		
Al_2O_3 (%)	4.7		Al_2O_3 (%)		28.5		
Fe_2O_3 (%)	3.1		Fe_2O_3 (%)		4.2		
CaO (%)	63.1		CaO (%)		1.2		
MgO (%)	3		MgO (%)		0.8		
Loss on ignition (%)	0.8		Moisture content (%)		0.2		
			Loss on ignition (%)		3.6		
Superplasticizer			**Air-entraining agent**				
Properties	**Value**		**Properties**		**Value**		
Color tone	Deep brown		Color tone		Colorless		
State	Liquid		State		Liquid		
Specific gravity	1.22		Specific gravity		1.05		
Solid content (%)	40.9		Solid content (%)		6		
pH	7.5						
Aggregates			**Mix proportion (40–80 MPa)**				
Properties	**Coarse**	**Fine**	G_{max}	**W/B (%)**	**W(kg/m^3)**	G_v	**FA (%)**
Fineness modulus	7.2	2.94	19 mm	30	160	32	0
Specific gravity	2.7	2.61		35	170	34	10
Water absorption (%)	0.6	0.8		40	180	36	20
Unit weight (kg/cm3)	1480	1590		45			
Abrasion (%)	18.6	-	G_v: Volume of coarse aggregate				

4.3 Mix proportions

Table 16.1 provides the mix proportions needed to achieve compressive strengths ranging from 40 to 80 MPa. The water-to-binder ratio varies from 0.30 to 0.45, and the fly ash content ranges up to 20% of the total binder. The volume of coarse aggregate (G_v) is between 32% and 36%. The water content varies between 160 and 180 kg/m^3, while the superplasticizer content fluctuates by up to 2%. The air-entraining agent content ranges from 0.010% to 0.013%, both expressed as a percentage of dry solids relative to the binder content.

According to Table 16.1, a total of 104 batches were mixed for this experiment. Of these, 91 mixtures were selected for training based on compressive strength and slump of concrete. Additionally, 13 mixtures were selected for verification and validation of the algorithm. The training and test datasets were compiled through random selection, and details of the verification dataset are presented in Table 16.2. For compressive strength testing, specimens were prepared using 100 × 200 mm cylinder molds and tested in compliance with ASTM C 684–95. After demolding, which occurred 24 h later, the specimens were cured in nonlime water at 20°C for a duration of 28 days before testing. Immediately after mixing, the slump of the fresh concrete was measured based on ASTM C 143-90a. The evaluation of the air content in the fresh concrete was conducted following the guidelines set by ASTM C 231-91b.

Training data points are represented as vectors containing ratio parameters such as water-to-binder, fine aggregate, fly ash replacement, along with the quantities of air-entraining agent and superplasticizer. These parameters are extracted from the provided dataset. The output vectors include the slump and compressive strength values of the concrete specimens. Table 16.3 presents a summary of the statistical values for these output vectors. To develop AI models that are robust, reliable, and optimized, achieving high correlation coefficients between input and output parameters is crucial. Whether negative or positive, high correlation coefficients can introduce inefficiencies into the approaches and complicate the understanding of how explanatory variables influence the response.

Table 16.4 presents the computed correlation coefficients used to analyze the relationships between different variables. The results reveal that the independent input variables do not exhibit significant correlations with one another. However, a strong relationship is evident between the compressive strength of the mortar and certain input parameters, such as water-to-binder ratio, and the content of air-entraining agent, and superplasticizer. Furthermore, Fig. 16.6 visualizes the distribution of mortar parameters and their association with compressive strength. These graphical representations highlight the intricate and nonlinear nature of mortar mixtures, demonstrating the difficulties deterministic approaches encounter when attempting to predict compressive strength through analytical equations.

TABLE 16.2 Selected data set for train and test.

		Group 1			Group 2	
		Case 1	Case 2		Case 3	Case 4
Number	Sample	Slump (mm)	Fc (MPa)	Sample	Slump (mm)	Fc (MPa)
1	8	225	65	5	205	69
2	16	260	63	13	200	63
3	24	210	61	26	145	63
4	32	185	63	31	245	59
5	40	225	58	37	200	56
6	48	170	48	47	190	51
7	56	205	49	53	95	49
8	64	190	47	61	205	49
9	72	205	43	67	170	47
10	80	140	46	74	200	44
11	88	175	46	81	130	45
12	96	180	42	94	200	43
13	104	170	38	101	185	41

TABLE 16.3 Employed parameters as input/output in the model.

			Statistics			
Variable	**Symbol**	**Units**	**Min**	**Max**	**Avg**	**STD**
Water-to-binder ratio	W/B	(%)	30	45	37.596	5.573
Water content	W	(kg/m^3)	160	180	170	8.244
Fine aggregate ratio	S/A	(%)	37	53	46	3.639
Fly ash replacement ratio	FA	(%)	0	20	10.096	8.302
Air-entraining agent	AE	(kg/m^3)	0.036	0.078	0.0541	0.0149
Superplasticizer	SP	(kg/m^3)	1.89	8.5	4.482	2.302
Slump of concrete	SL	(mm)	95	260	198.990	31.418
Compressive strength	Fc	(MPa)	38	74	52.683	9.431

Evaluating the effectiveness of created models is essential for tackling engineering and scientific problems. In this research, various performance metrics were utilized to assess the models. These metrics encompass the coefficient of determination (R^2), variance accounted for (VAF), mean absolute error (MAE), root mean square error ($RMSE$), and a10-index. These indices are frequently employed in previous studies to evaluate the efficacy of AI methodologies. Below are the formulas used to compute these metrics:

$$R^2 = 1 - \frac{\sum_i \left(x_{\text{imes}} - x_{\text{ipred}}\right)^2}{\sum_i \left(x_{\text{imes}} - \overline{x}\right)^2} \tag{16.13}$$

$$VAF = \left[1 - \frac{var\left(x_{\text{imes}} - x_{\text{ipred}}\right)}{var\left(x_{\text{imes}}\right)}\right] \times 100 \tag{16.14}$$

$$RMSE = \sqrt{\frac{1}{N}\sum_{i=1}^{N}\left(x_{\text{imes}} - x_{\text{ipred}}\right)^2} \tag{16.15}$$

TABLE 16.4 Correlation matrix of the input variables.

		Input						Output	
Variable		**W/B**	**W**	**S/A**	**FA**	**AE**	**SP**	**SL**	**F_c**
Input	W/B	1.00							
	W	−0.0317	1.00						
	S/A	0.5721	−0.3819	1.00					
	FA	0.0159	−0.0142	−0.1221	1.00				
	AE	−0.8983	−0.2095	−0.4819	0.0244	1.00			
	SP	−0.9577	0.2075	−0.6222	0.0117	0.8631	1.00		
Output	SL	−0.5574	0.0975	−0.4518	0.1251	0.4936	0.5096	1.00	
	Fc	−0.9087	−0.2860	−0.3330	−0.0678	0.9218	0.8407	0.4803	1.00

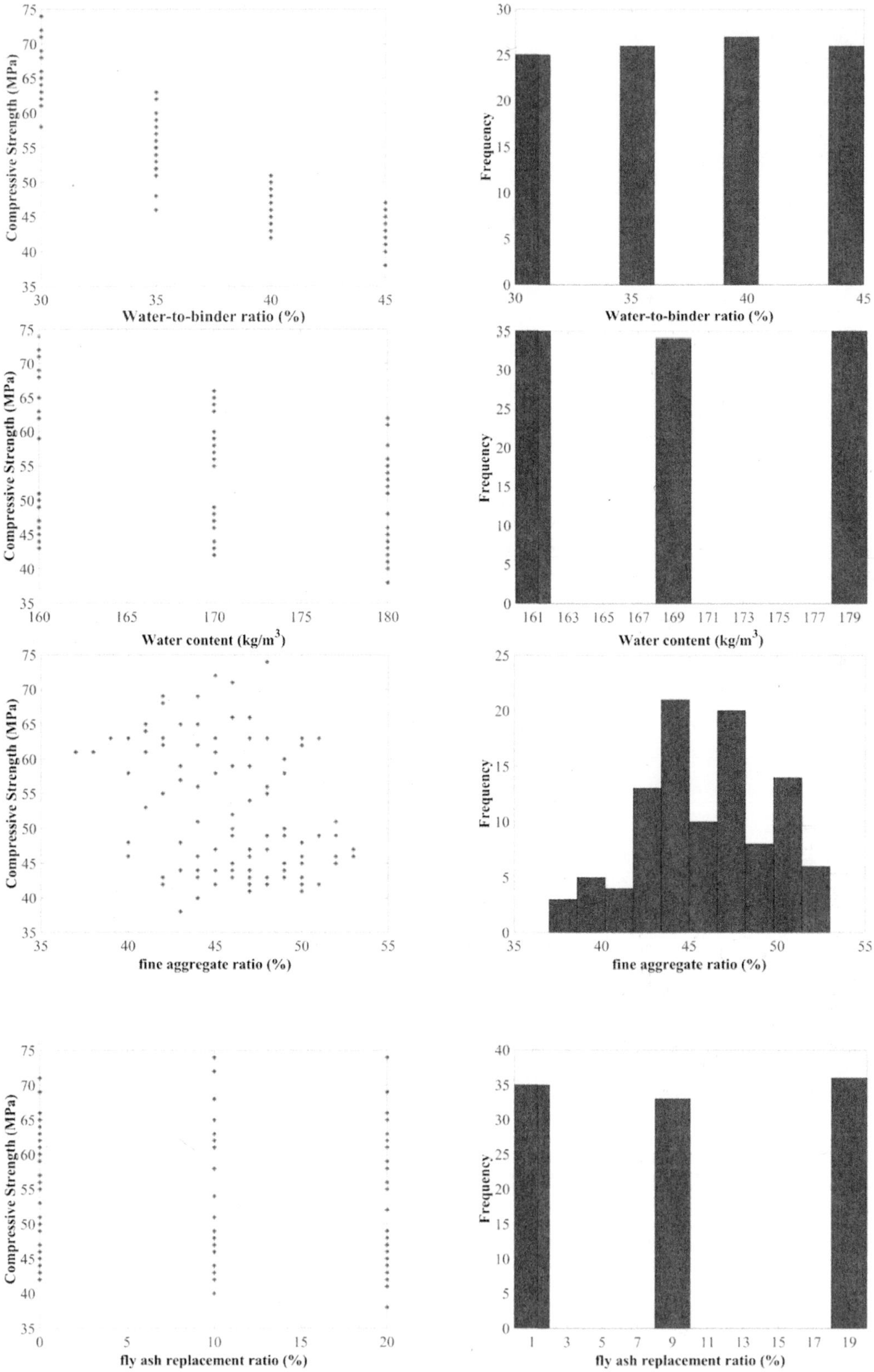

FIGURE 16.6 Histograms of the parameters.

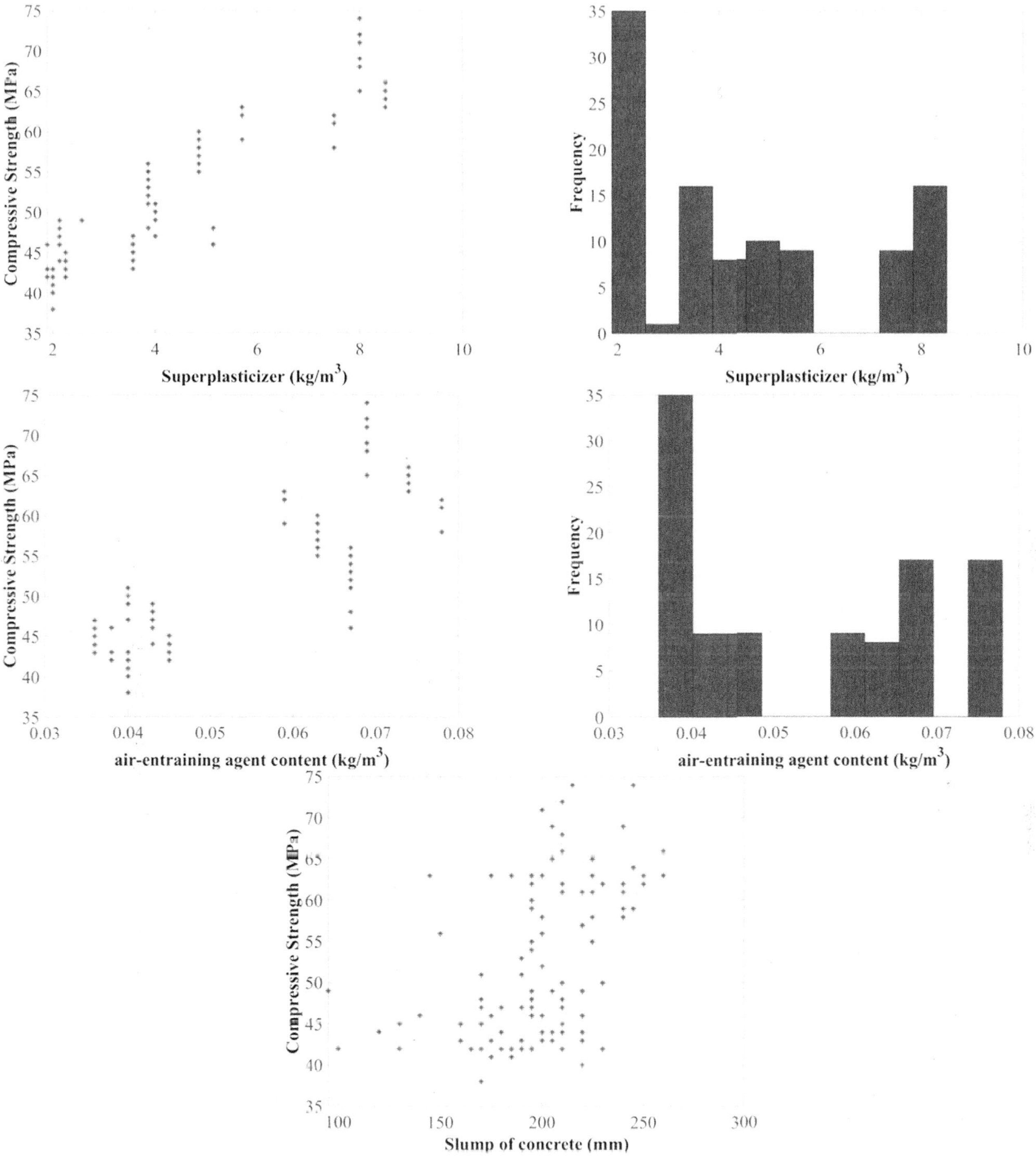

FIGURE 16.6 cont'd

$$MAE = \frac{1}{N}\sum_{i=1}^{N}\left|x_{\text{imes}} - x_{\text{ipred}}\right| \tag{16.16}$$

$$a10 - index = \frac{m10}{N} \tag{16.17}$$

The measured values are labeled as x_{imes}, and x_{ipred} indicates the values predicted by the model. The symbol $\overline{x}$ represents the mean of all measured data points across N total datasets. Several metrics assess model accuracy: MAE, RMSE, VAF, R^2, and a10, each calculated according to their respective Eq. A perfect prediction model would achieve an R^2 value of 1, VAF of 100%, zero for both RMSE and MAE measurements, and an a10 score of 1. The m10 metric counts how many data points show agreement between predicted and measured values within a 10% margin (specifically between 0.9 and 1.1).

5. Results and discussion

The TSK model's design to predict the concrete's compressive strength was optimized utilizing the proposed algorithms. A thorough evaluation included statistical tests analyzing the mean, best, and standard deviation of solutions to assess algorithm performance. These tests were specifically conducted during the training phase of the TSK model. Table 16.5 presents the algorithm's performance based on training RMSE across various scenarios.

Table 16.6 presents a comparative analysis of MSE performance between Crystal-FIS and ANFIS, evaluating both training and testing data. The data demonstrates superior accuracy of the Crystal-FIS across all model configurations, with consistently lower MSE values than ANFIS. Looking at Model one specifically, Crystal-FIS achieved a training MSE of 0.07,322 and testing MSE of 12.74,561, outperforming ANFIS with the corresponding values of 0.15,493 and 13.06,997. Crystal-FIS exhibits more stable performance, evidenced by the minimal difference between its training and testing errors. In contrast, ANFIS shows a wider gap between training and testing MSE, suggesting issues with overfitting and limited generalization abilities. The enhanced performance of Crystal-FIS can be traced to its optimized FIS, which processes complex data patterns more efficiently. These results establish Crystal-FIS as the more reliable option for accurate predictions in complex systems, given its proven ability to minimize errors and maintain consistency.

TABLE 16.5 Statistical results for RMSE of training.

	Experiment type			
Model	Best	Mean	STD	C_{best}
# 1	0.2706	0.5653	0.3112	324
# 2	0.2050	0.5012	0.3301	366
# 3	0.2373	0.4967	0.2984	307
# 4	0.2631	0.5459	0.3475	349

TABLE 16.6 Comparison of best results of MSE for ANFIS and Crystal-FIS.

	Train		Test	
Model	ANFIS	Crystal-FIS	ANFIS	Crystal-FIS
# 1	0.15493	0.07322	13.06997	12.74561
# 2	0.11485	0.04202	2.08421	1.25238
# 3	0.14098	0.05631	4.71594	2.37622
# 4	0.12827	0.06922	1.69025	0.80085

Researchers often use statistical or performance metrics to evaluate computational simulations. Table 16.7 presents the results of five evaluation indices computed for the TSK model in this study. The assessment included both training datasets and those utilized to validate the simulation's accuracy. According to all performance metrics, the optimized TSK model demonstrated effective performance across both training and testing datasets. These results highlight the TSK model as the preferred choice among alternative models, as it consistently outperformed them across all evaluated indices. The results presented in Table 16.7 demonstrate the robust prediction capability of the models across both training and testing datasets. During training, all models achieve perfect A10-index values of 1.00, indicating optimal prediction accuracy. The R^2 values are exceptionally high, ranging from 0.9992 to 0.9999, reflecting excellent model fit. Furthermore, the RMSE values during training are very low, with a minimum of 0.2050, and the MAPE values are also minimal, underscoring the models' high accuracy. The VAF during training exceeds 99.9% in all cases, further highlighting the models' effectiveness in explaining the variance in the data. On the test dataset, while the models maintain high performance, there is a slight drop in R^2, with values ranging from 0.9841 to 0.9983, indicating a small decrease in predictive accuracy. However, the RMSE and MAPE values are still relatively low, particularly in Model 4, which exhibits the best testing performance with the lowest RMSE (0.8949) and MAPE (0.8554), and a VAF of 99.03%. These results suggest that the models generalize well, with only minor performance loss in the testing phase, affirming their strong prediction capability and reliability.

In Fig. 16.7, the predicted compressive strength data from all TSK models optimized with CryStAl is compared with experimental data, covering both training and testing datasets. The models reliably demonstrated an accurate approximation of both the slump and compressive strength of the concrete. Based on the train data, the developed model demonstrates excellent predictive performance. The targets and outputs show that the model accurately captures the underlying pattern in the training dataset. The small values of MSE, confirm the minimal discrepancy between predicted and actual values. The error histogram shows that errors are distributed approximately normally, centered around zero with a small standard deviation (Std). This indicates that the model is unbiased and consistent in its predictions during the training phase. But in test data, the model's performance declines when applied to unseen data. Although the targets and outputs in the upper plot follow a similar trend, there is a more noticeable deviation between the two, especially in certain regions. The MSE increases significantly and the error histogram reveals a wider spread of errors with a slight bias and the standard deviation. This highlights greater variability and less reliable predictions on the test data.

The comparison between train and test data in all Cases highlights a common issue: while the model performs exceptionally well on the training data (low errors, high alignment), its performance deteriorates on the test data due to larger prediction errors and variability. This discrepancy suggests that the model may be overfitting to the training data, capturing noise or patterns specific to the training dataset instead of generalizing to new, unseen data. The significant increase in MSE and RMSE during testing underscores the need for further model tuning, such as regularization or additional data validation, to improve its generalization capability.

As previously mentioned, the dataset generation process for both training and testing is consistent across conditions one and 2, with a 7:1 ratio, where seven parts are used for training and one part for testing, applied to both the slump and

TABLE 16.7 The prediction capability.

		Performance indices				
Datasets	Model	A10-index	R^2	RMSE	MAPE	VAF
Training	# 1	1.00	0.9999	0.2706	0.1667	99.9927
	# 2	1.00	0.9995	0.2050	0.1417	99.9534
	# 3	1.00	0.9999	0.2373	0.1581	99.9935
	# 4	1.00	0.9992	0.2631	0.2117	99.9291
Test	# 1	1.00	0.9856	3.5701	3.1803	98.6086
	# 2	1.00	0.9841	1.1191	1.0699	98.4169
	# 3	1.00	0.9983	1.5415	1.4530	99.8346
	# 4	1.00	0.9891	0.8949	0.8554	99.0294

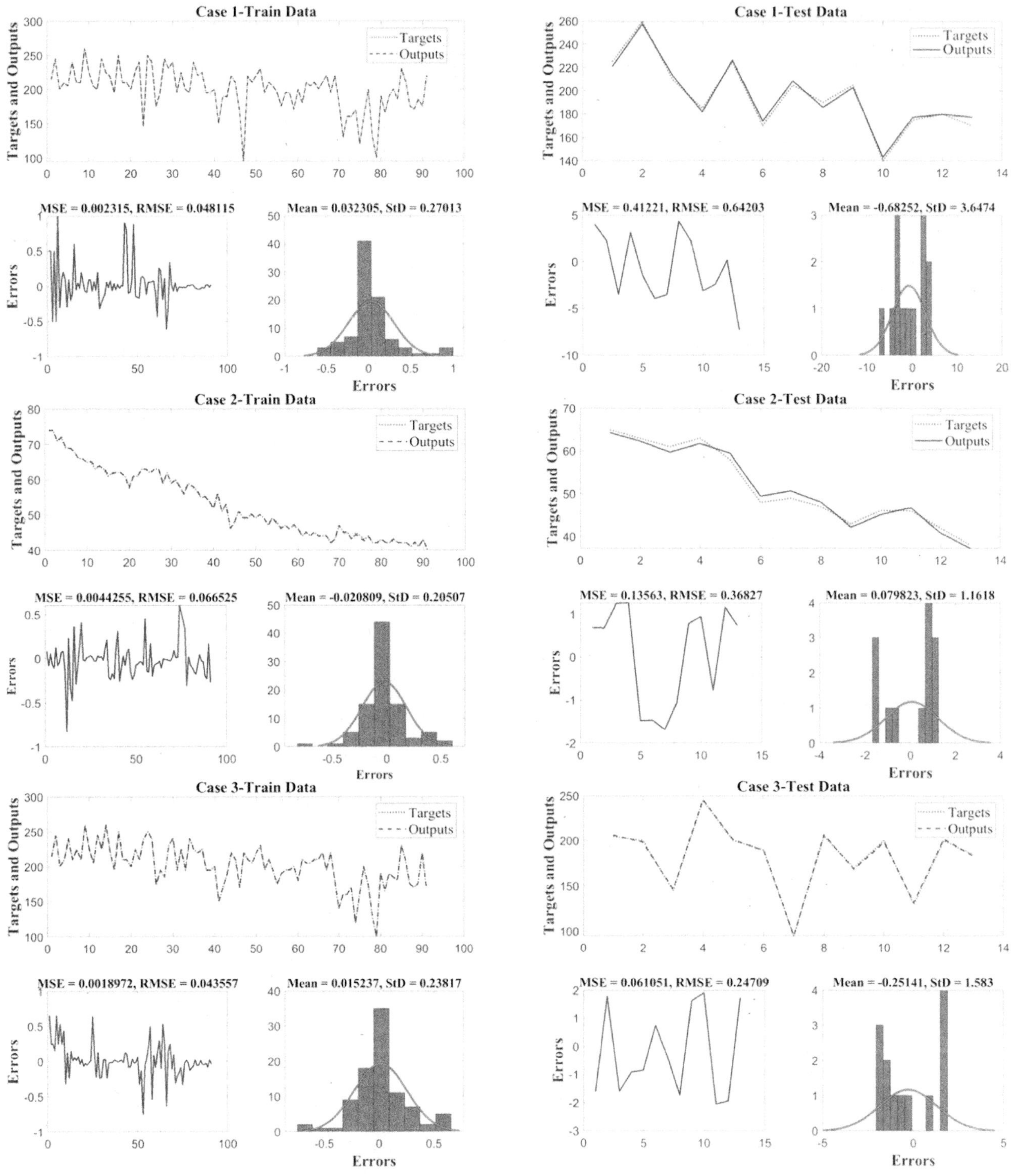

FIGURE 16.7 Performance of the optimized TSK model considering the datasets.

compressive strength results of the concrete. Fig. 16.8 presents the comparison between the predicted and actual results for concrete using the optimal inference system based on the concrete slump data (case 1).

According to this figure, the scale of implementation and distribution of the results of the prediction of concrete slump based on the training and testing data is evident in case 1.

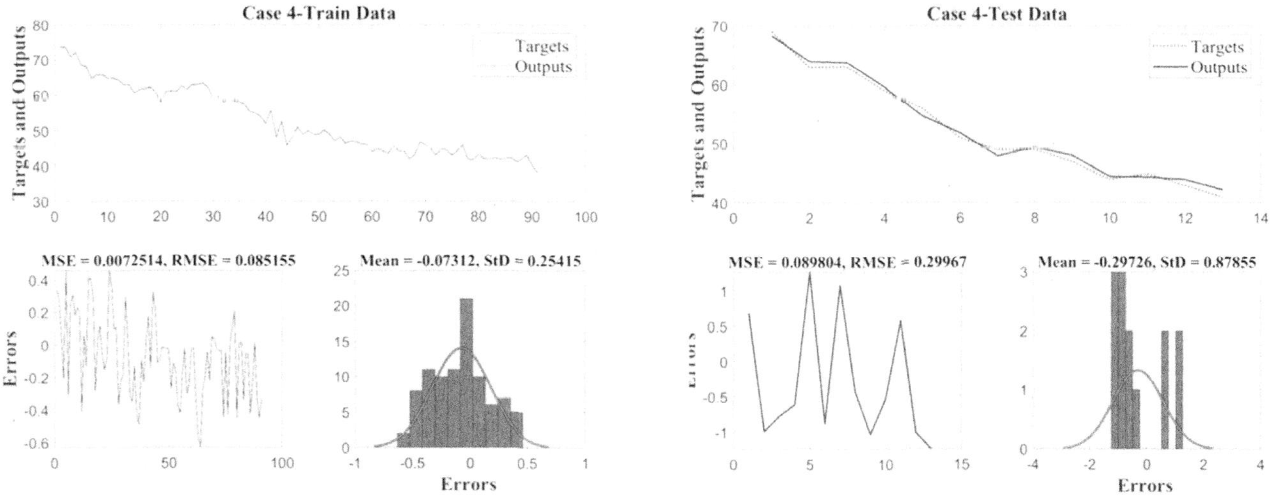

FIGURE 16.7 cont'd

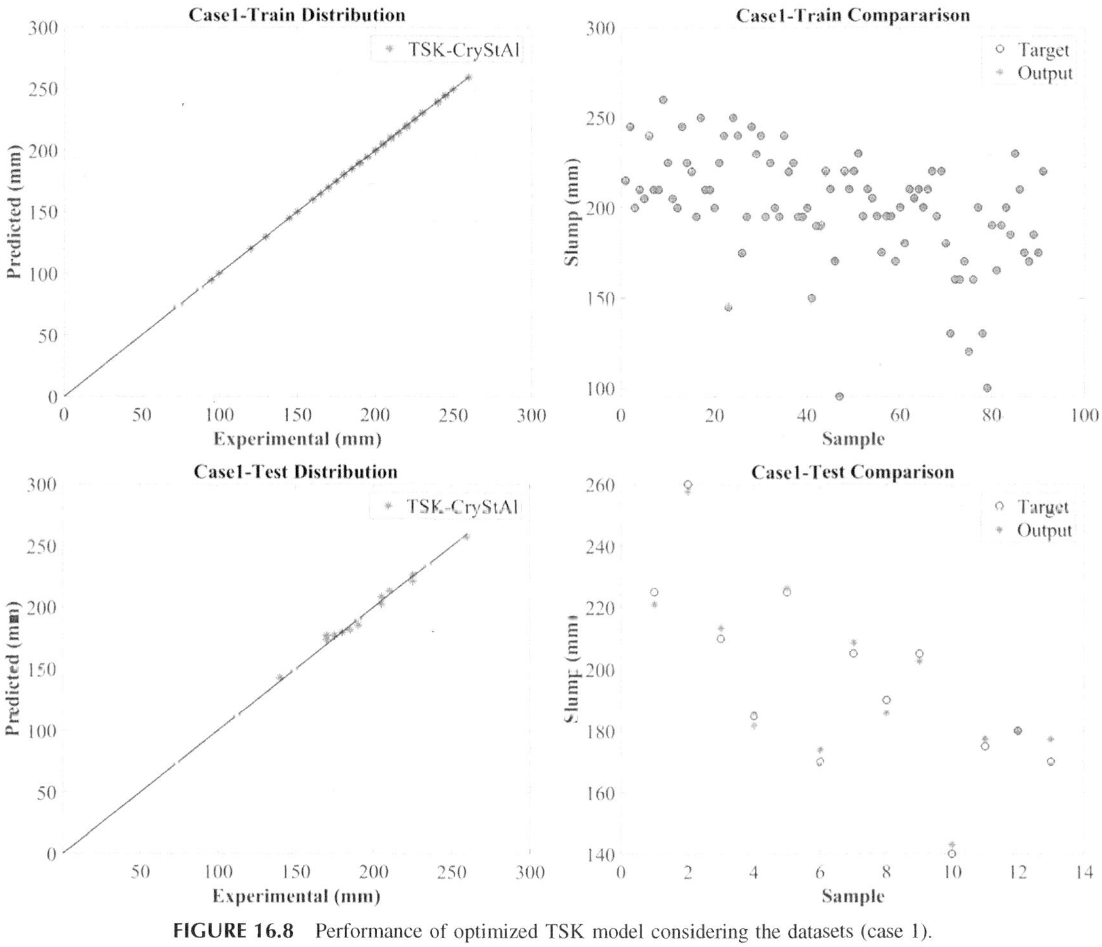

FIGURE 16.8 Performance of optimized TSK model considering the datasets (case 1).

Fig. 16.9 illustrates the comparison between the predicted and actual results for the compressive strength of concrete (case 2) using the optimal inference system. According to this figure, the accuracy and distribution of the prediction of the concrete's compressive strength according to the dataset is evident. It can be seen that the trained system also has a good performance in predicting the slump and concrete's compressive strength in the test stage.

A random selection pattern was used for data set in cases 3 and 4. Fig. 16.10 shows the comparison between the predicted and actual results for concrete using the optimal inference system. This figure clearly illustrates the scale of implementation and the distribution of results for predicting concrete slump in the dataset used for training and testing in case 3.

Fig. 16.11 illustrates the comparison between the actual results and the predicted results for the concrete's compressive strength using the optimal inference system and based on case 4 dataset. According to this figure, the distribution and distribution of the scale of the prediction of the concrete's compressive strength according to the data of training and testing case 4 is evident. It can be seen that the system trained in the test stage also has a good performance in predicting the creep and compressive strength of concrete.

The comparison between all cases for compressive strength and slump of concrete highlights the difference in the model's performance on training and test datasets. In the train data, the predicted outputs align closely with the target values across the entire range, indicating that the model effectively learns the underlying patterns with minimal error. However, in the test data, there are more noticeable deviations between the targets and outputs, particularly in specific samples where the model struggles to replicate the actual values accurately. The model successfully captures the general trend of the test data, but the presence of errors highlights a potential overfitting issue, where the model performs well on training data but fails to generalize effectively to new, unseen inputs. Improving generalization techniques, such as regularization or additional data validation, may help address this limitation.

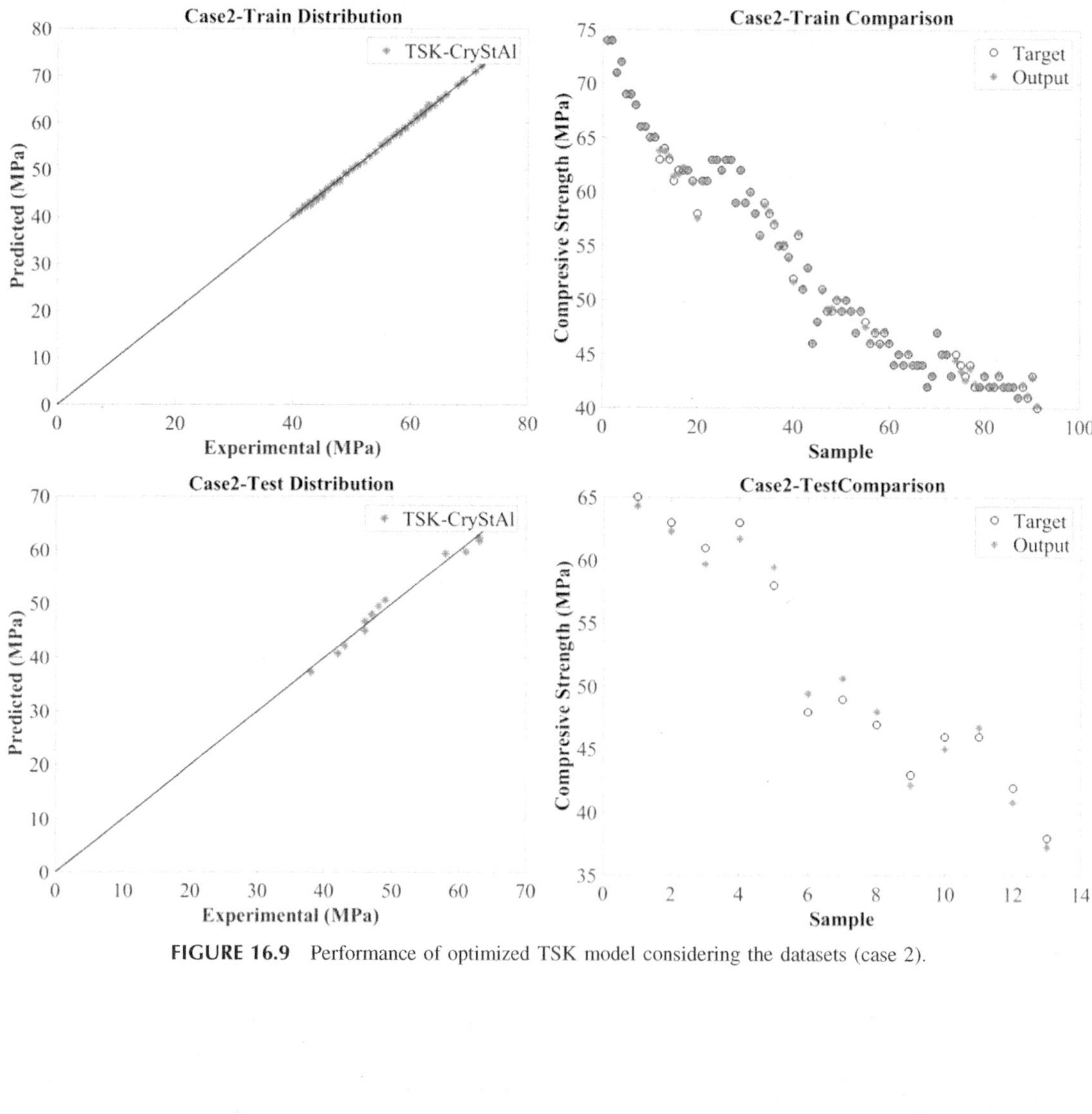

FIGURE 16.9 Performance of optimized TSK model considering the datasets (case 2).

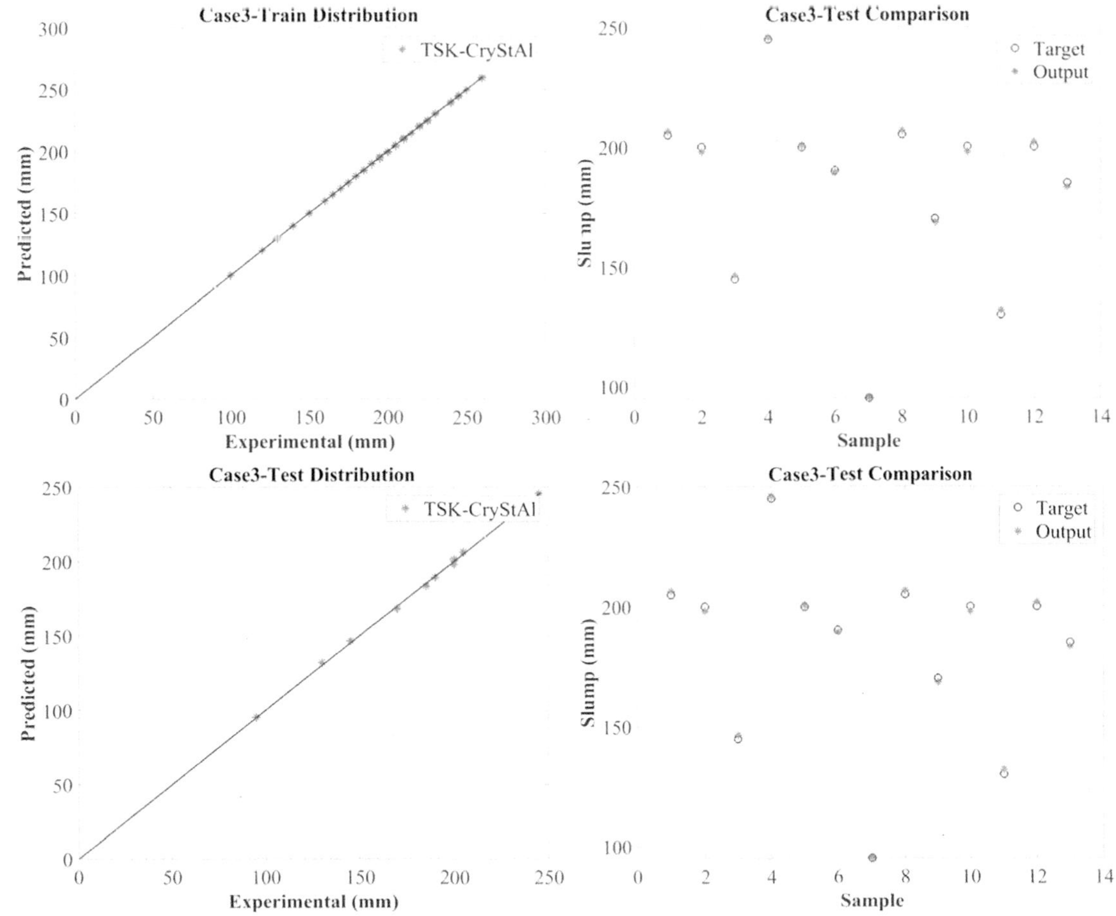

FIGURE 16.10 Performance of optimized TSK model considering the datasets (case 3).

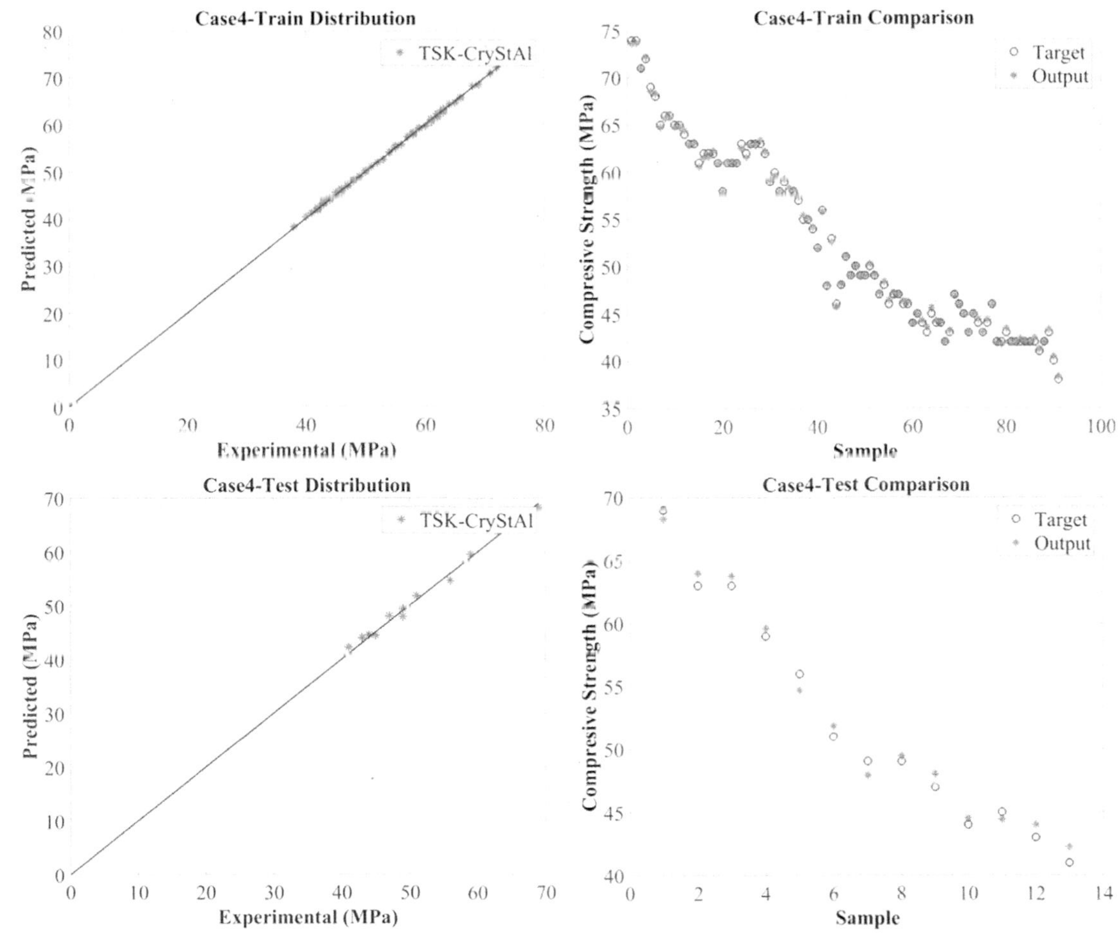

FIGURE 16.11 Performance of optimized TSK model considering the datasets (case 4).

6. Conclusions

This chapter highlights the importance of developing a reliable method to accurately predict the concrete's compressive strength, given its extensive use in construction. The nonlinear and complex relationship between concrete composition and its strength necessitates the use of AI techniques for effective predictive modeling.

By applying the TSK model to predict concrete's compressive strength using literature-based experimental data, the study achieved accurate and reliable results. The effectiveness of the model was evident, and to ensure it remained generalizable and avoided overfitting with new data, the optimization was conducted utilizing the MSE criterion.

The Efficient TSK model was developed using the CryStAl algorithm by expanding the dataset to include 104 samples with diverse input parameters. Through comprehensive investigation and comparison utilizing performance metrics such as MAE, RMSE, VAF, R^2, and the A10-index, the TSK model consistently demonstrated superior performance in predicting concrete's compressive strength.

In conclusion, the TSK model developed in this study serves as a robust predictive tool for predicting compressive strength in concrete. It provides reliable insights for the construction industry, promising enhanced accuracy and efficiency in future construction practices.

Appendix 1.

Dataset								
	Inputs						Outputs	
Number	W/B (%)	W (kg/m^3)	S/A (%)	FA (%)	AE (kg/m^3)	SP (kg/m^3)	Slump (mm)	Fc (MPa)
1	30	160	48	10	0.069	8	215	74
2	30	160	48	20	0.069	8	245	74
3	30	160	46	0	0.069	8	200	71
4	30	160	45	10	0.069	8	210	72
5	30	160	44	20	0.069	8	205	69
6	30	160	42	0	0.069	8	240	69
7	30	160	42	10	0.069	8	210	68
8	30	160	41	20	0.069	8	225	65
9	30	170	47	0	0.074	8.5	210	66
10	30	170	46	20	0.074	8.5	260	66
11	30	170	44	0	0.074	8.5	225	65
12	30	170	43	10	0.074	8.5	205	65
13	30	170	42	20	0.074	8.5	200	63
14	30	170	41	0	0.074	8.5	245	64
15	30	170	40	10	0.074	8.5	225	63
16	30	170	39	20	0.074	8.5	260	63
17	30	180	45	0	0.078	7.5	220	61
18	30	180	44	10	0.078	7.5	195	62
19	30	180	44	20	0.078	7.5	250	62
20	30	180	42	0	0.078	7.5	210	62
21	30	180	41	10	0.078	7.5	210	61
22	30	180	40	20	0.078	7.5	200	58

—cont'd

	Dataset								
	Inputs							Outputs	
Number	W/B (%)	W (kg/m³)	S/A (%)	FA (%)	AE (kg/m³)	SP (kg/m³)	Slump (mm)	Fc (MPa)
23	30	180	38	0	0.078	7.5	225	61
24	30	180	38	10	0.078	7.5	210	61
25	30	180	37	20	0.078	7.5	240	61
26	35	160	51	0	0.059	5.71	145	63
27	35	160	50	10	0.059	5.71	250	63
28	35	160	50	20	0.059	5.71	240	62
29	35	160	48	0	0.059	5.71	175	63
30	35	160	47	10	0.059	5.71	195	63
31	35	160	47	20	0.059	5.71	245	59
32	35	160	45	0	0.059	5.71	185	63
33	35	160	44	10	0.059	5.71	230	62
34	35	160	43	20	0.059	5.71	240	59
35	35	170	49	0	0.063	4.86	195	60
36	35	170	49	10	0.063	4.86	225	58
37	35	170	48	20	0.063	4.86	200	56
38	35	170	46	0	0.063	4.86	195	59
39	35	170	45	10	0.063	4.86	240	58
40	35	170	45	20	0.063	4.86	225	58
41	35	170	43	0	0.063	4.86	220	57
42	35	170	42	20	0.063	4.86	225	55
43	35	180	48	0	0.067	3.86	195	55
44	35	180	47	10	0.067	3.86	195	54
45	35	180	46	20	0.067	3.86	200	52
46	35	180	44	0	0.067	3.86	150	56
47	35	180	44	10	0.067	3.86	190	51
48	35	180	43	20	0.067	3.86	170	48
49	35	180	41	0	0.067	3.86	190	53
50	35	180	40	10	0.067	5.14	220	46
51	35	180	40	20	0.067	5.14	210	48
52	40	160	52	0	0.04	4	170	51
53	40	160	52	10	0.04	2.57	95	49
54	40	160	51	20	0.04	4	220	49
55	40	160	49	0	0.04	4	210	50
56	40	160	49	10	0.04	4	205	49
57	40	160	48	20	0.04	4	220	49
58	40	160	46	0	0.04	4	230	50

Continued

—cont'd

Dataset								
	Inputs						Outputs	
Number	W/B (%)	W (kg/m^3)	S/A (%)	FA (%)	AE (kg/m^3)	SP (kg/m^3)	Slump (mm)	Fc (MPa)
59	40	160	46	10	0.04	4	195	49
60	40	160	45	20	0.04	4	210	47
61	40	170	51	0	0.043	2.13	205	49
62	40	170	50	10	0.043	2.13	195	48
63	40	170	50	20	0.043	2.13	175	46
64	40	170	48	0	0.043	2.13	190	47
65	40	170	47	10	0.043	2.13	195	47
66	40	170	47	20	0.043	2.13	195	46
67	40	170	45	0	0.043	2.13	170	47
68	40	170	44	10	0.043	2.13	200	46
69	40	170	44	20	0.043	2.13	180	44
70	40	180	49	0	0.045	2.25	210	45
71	40	180	49	10	0.045	2.25	205	44
72	40	180	48	20	0.045	2.25	205	43
73	40	180	46	0	0.045	2.25	210	45
74	40	180	46	10	0.045	2.25	200	44
75	40	180	45	20	0.045	2.25	210	44
76	40	180	43	0	0.045	2.25	220	44
77	40	180	42	10	0.045	2.25	195	42
78	40	180	42	20	0.045	2.25	220	43
79	45	160	53	0	0.036	3.56	180	47
80	45	160	53	10	0.036	3.56	140	46
81	45	160	52	20	0.036	3.56	130	45
82	45	160	50	0	0.036	3.56	160	45
83	45	160	50	10	0.036	3.56	160	43
84	45	160	49	20	0.036	3.56	170	45
85	45	160	47	0	0.036	3.56	120	44
86	45	160	47	10	0.036	3.56	160	43
87	45	160	46	20	0.036	3.56	200	44
88	45	170	52	0	0.038	1.89	175	46
89	45	170	51	10	0.038	1.89	130	42
90	45	170	51	20	0.038	1.89	100	42
91	45	170	49	0	0.038	1.89	190	43
92	45	170	48	10	0.038	1.89	165	42
93	45	170	48	20	0.038	1.89	190	42
94	45	170	46	0	0.038	1.89	200	43

—cont'd

Dataset								
	Inputs						Outputs	
Number	W/B (%)	W (kg/m^3)	S/A (%)	FA (%)	AE (kg/m^3)	SP (kg/m^3)	Slump (mm)	Fc (MPa)
95	45	170	45	10	0.038	1.89	185	42
96	45	170	45	20	0.038	1.89	180	42
97	45	180	51	0	0.04	2	230	42
98	45	180	50	10	0.04	2	210	42
99	45	180	50	20	0.04	2	175	41
100	45	180	47	0	0.04	2	170	42
101	45	180	47	20	0.04	2	185	41
102	45	180	44	0	0.04	2	175	43
103	45	180	44	10	0.04	2	220	40
104	45	180	43	20	0.04	2	170	38

References

[1] M. Woźniak, D. Połap, Soft Trees with Neural Components as Image-Processing Technique for Archeological Excavations, Pers Ubiquit Comput, 2020, https://doi.org/10.1007/s00779-019- 01292-3.

[2] M. Woźniak, D. Połap, Intelligent home systems for ubiquitous user support by using neural networks and rule based approach, IEEE Trans. Ind. Inf. 16 (2019) 2651–2658, https://doi.org/10.1109/TII. 2019.2951089.

[3] M. Woźniak, D. Połap, Hybrid neuro-heuristic methodology for simulation and control of dynamic systems over time interval, Neural Netw. 93 (2017) 45–56.

[4] J. Zhou, E. Li, S. Yang, M. Wang, X. Shi, S. Yao, H.S. Mitri, Slope stability prediction for circular mode failure using gradient boosting machine approach based on an updated database of case histories, Saf. Sci. 118 (2019) 505–518.

[5] J. Zhou, X. Li, H.S. Mitri, Comparative performance of six supervised learning methods for the development of models of hard rock pillar stability prediction, Nat. Hazards 79 (1) (2015) 291–316.

[6] M. Azizi, R.G. Ejlali, S.A.M. Ghasemi, S. Talatahari, Upgraded whale optimization algorithm for fuzzy logic based vibration control of nonlinear steel structure, Eng. Struct. 192 (2019) 53–70, https://doi.org/10.1016/j.engstruct.2019.05.007.

[7] P.G. Asteris, A.D. Skentou, A. Bardhan, P. Samui, K. Pilakoutas, Predicting concrete compressive strength using hybrid ensembling of surrogate machine learning models, Cement Concr. Res. 145 (2021) 106449, https://doi.org/10.1016/j.cemconres.2021.106449.

[8] M. Charrier, C.M. Ouellet-Plamondon, Artificial neural network for the prediction of the fresh properties of cementitious materials, Cement Concr. Res. 156 (2022) 106761, https://doi.org/10.1016/j.cemconres.2022.106761.

[9] R.K. Tipu, V.R. Panchal, K.S. Pandya, An ensemble approach to improve BPNN model precision for predicting compressive strength of high-performance concrete, Structures 45 (2022) 500–508, https://doi.org/10.1016/j.istruc.2022.09.046.

[10] S. İpek, E. Güneyisi, E.M. Güneyisi, Data-driven models for prediction of peak strength of R-CFST circular columns subjected to axial loading, Structures 46 (2022) 1863–1880, https://doi.org/10.1016/j.istruc.2022.10.137.

[11] M.S. Sandeep, K. Tiprak, S. Kaewunruen, P. Pheinsusom, W. Pansuk, Shear strength prediction of reinforced concrete beams using machine learning, Structures 47 (2023) 1196–1211, https://doi.org/10.1016/j.istruc.2022.11.140.

[12] H. Peng, J. Yan, Y. Yu, Y. Luo, Time series estimation based on deep learning for structural dynamic nonlinear prediction, Structures 29 (2021) 1016–1031, https://doi.org/10.1016/j.istruc.2020.11.049.

[13] O. Yazdanpanah, M. Chang, M. Park, C.Y. Kim, Seismic response prediction of RC bridge piers through stacked long short term memory network, Structures 45 (2022) 1990–2006, https://doi.org/10.1016/j.istruc.2022.10.015.

[14] L.A. Zadeh, Fuzzy sets, Int. Control 8 (1965) 338–353, https://doi.org/10.1142/9789814261302_0021.

[15] G. Feng, Analysis and Synthesis of Fuzzy Control Systems: A Model-Based Approach, Taylor & Francis Group, Boca Raton, 2010.

[16] E.H. Mamdani, Applications of fuzzy algorithms for simple dynamic plants, Procedings of IEEE 121 (12) (1974) 1585–1588.

[17] T. Takagi, M. Sugeno, Fuzzy identification of systems and its applications to modeling and control, IEEE Trans. Syst. Man Cybern. 15 (1) (1985) 116–132, https://doi.org/10.1109/TSMC.1985.6313399.

[18] D. Kukolj, Design of adaptive takagi-sugeno-kang fuzzy models, Appl. Soft Comput. 2 (2002) 89–103, https://doi.org/10.1016/S1568-4946(02)00032-7.

[19] G. Acampora, A TSK neuro-fuzzy approach for modeling highly dynamic systems, IEEE International Conference on Fuzzy Systems (2011) 146–152, https://doi.org/10.1109/FUZZY.2011.6007638.

[20] F. Raeesi, B.F. Azar, H. Veladi, S. Talatahari, An inverse TSK model of MR damper for vibration control of nonlinear structures using an improved grasshopper optimization algorithm, Structures 26 (2020) 406–416, https://doi.org/10.1016/j.istruc.2020.04.026.

[21] M. Stojčić, Application of ANFIS model in road traffic and transportation: A literature review from 1993 to 2018, Oper Res Eng Sci Theory Appl 1 (2018) 40–61.

[22] T. Abunama, F. Othman, M.K. Younes, Predicting sanitary landfill leachate generation in humid regions using ANFIS modeling, Environ. Monit. Assess. 190 (2018) 597.

[23] D.Y. Kebria, M. Ghavami, S. Javadi, M. Goharimanesh, Combining an experimental study and ANFIS modeling to predict landfill leachate transport in underlying Soil—A case study in north of Iran, Environ. Monit. Assess. 190 (2018) 26.

[24] F. Jafari, B. Badarloo, Finite element analysis and ANFIS investigation of seismic behavior of sandwich panels with different concrete material in two story steel building, Frat ed Integrita` Strutt 13 (2019) 209–230.

[25] S. Farahmand-Tabar, S. Shirgir, Synergistic collaboration of motion-based metaheuristics for the strength prediction of cement-based mortar materials using TSK model, in: A.J. Kulkarni, A.H. Gandomi (Eds.), Handbook of Formal Optimization, Springer, Singapore, 2023, https://doi org/10.1007/978-981-19-8851-6_43-1.

[26] S. Farahmand-Tabar, T.A. Rashid, Steel plate fault detection using the fitness dependent optimizer and neural networks, in: A.J. Kulkarni, A. H. Gandomi (Eds.), Handbook of Formal Optimization, Springer, Singapore, 2023, https://doi.org/10.1007/978-981-19-8851-6_41-1.

[27] S. Farahmand-Tabar, P. Ashtari, M. Babaei, Gaussian cross-entropy and organizing intelligence for design optimization of the outrigger system with inclined belt truss in real-size tall buildings, Probab. Eng. Mech. 76 (2024) 103616, https://doi.org/10.1016/j.probengmech.2024.103616.

[28] S. Farahmand-Tabar, P. Ashtari, M. Babaei, Dynamic intelligence of self-organized map in the frequency-based optimum design of structures, in: A.J. Kulkarni, A.H. Gandomi (Eds.), Handbook of Formal Optimization, Springer, Singapore, 2023, https://doi.org/10.1007/978-981-19-8851-6_45-1.

[29] S. Farahmand-Tabar, F. Abdollahi, M. Fatemi, Robust conjugate gradient methods for non-smooth convex optimization and image processing problems, in: A.J. Kulkarni, A.H. Gandomi (Eds.), Handbook of Formal Optimization, Springer, Singapore, 2023, https://doi.org/10.1007/978-981-19-8851-6_42-1.

[30] S. Farahmand-Tabar, P. Ashtari, Simultaneous size and topology optimization of 3D outrigger-braced tall buildings with inclined belt truss using genetic algorithm, Struct. Des. Tall Special Build. 29 (13) (2020) e1776, https://doi.org/10.1002/tal.1776.

[31] S. Farahmand-Tabar, Genetic algorithm and accelerating fuzzification for optimum sizing and topology design of real-size tall building systems, in: N. Dey (Ed.), Applied Genetic Algorithm and its Variants. Springer Tracts in Nature-Inspired Computing, Springer, Singapore, 2023, https://doi.org/10.1007/978-981-99-3428-7_9.

[32] P. Ashtari, R. Karami, S. Farahmand-Tabar, Optimum geometrical pattern and design of real-size diagrid structures using accelerated fuzzy-genetic algorithm with bilinear membership function, Appl. Soft Comput. 110 (2021) 107646, https://doi.org/10.1016/j.asoc.2021.107646.

[33] S. Farahmand-Tabar, P. Ashtari, Bilinear fuzzy genetic algorithm and its application on the optimum design of steel structures with semi-rigid connections, in: A.J. Kulkarni, A.H. Gandomi (Eds.), Handbook of Formal Optimization, Springer, Singapore, 2023.

[34] S. Farahmand-Tabar, S. Shirgir, Antlion-facing ant colony optimization in parameter identification of the MR damper as a semi-active control device, in: N. Dey (Ed.), Applications of Ant Colony Optimization and its Variants, Springer, Singapore, 2023, https://doi.org/10.1007/978-981-99-7227-2_8.

[35] S. Farahmand-Tabar, S. Shirgir, Opposed pheromone ant colony optimization for property identification of nonlinear structures, in: N. Dey (Ed.), Applications of Ant Colony Optimization and its Variants, Springer, Singapore, 2023, https://doi.org/10.1007/978-981-99-7227-2_5.

[36] S. Farahmand-Tabar, Frequency-based optimization of truss dome structures using ant colony optimization (ACOR) with multi-trail pheromone memory, in: N. Dey (Ed.), Applications of Ant Colony Optimization and its Variants, Springer, Singapore, 2023, https://doi.org/10.1007/978-981-99-7227-2_11.

[37] S. Farahmand-Tabar, M. Babaei, Memory-assisted adaptive multiverse optimizer and its application in structural shape and size optimization, Soft Comput. 27 (2023) 11505–11527, https://doi.org/10.1007/s00 500-023-08349-9.

[38] S. Farahmand-Tabar, Memory-driven metaheuristics: Improving optimization perfor-mance, in: A.J. Kulkarni, A.H. Gandomi (Eds.), Handbook of Formal Optimization, Springer, Singapore, 2023, https://doi.org/10.1007/978-981-19-8851-6_38-1.

[39] S. Shirgir, S. Farahmand-Tabar, P. Aghabeigi, Optimum design of real-size reinforced concrete bridge via charged system search algorithm trained by nelder-mead simplex, Expert Syst. Appl. (2023) 121815, https://doi.org/10.1016/j.eswa.2023.121815.

[40] S. Farahmand-Tabar, S. Shirgir, Incorporating nelder mead simplex as an accelerating operator to improve the performance of metaheuristics in nonlinear system identification, in: A.J. Kulkarni, A.H. Gandomi (Eds.), Handbook of Formal Optimization, Springer, Singapore, 2023, https://doi.org/10.1007/978-981-19-8851-6_39-1.

[41] S. Farahmand-Tabar, N. Sadrekarimi, Overcoming constraints: The critical role of penalty functions as constraint handling methods in structural optimization, in: A.J. Kulkarni, A.H. Gandomi (Eds.), Handbook of Formal Optimization, Springer, Singapore, 2023, https://doi.org/10.1007/978-981-19-8851-6_40-1.

[42] S. Farahmand-Tabar, S. Shirgir, Positron-enabled atomic orbital search algorithm for improved reliability-based design optimization, in: A. J. Kulkarni, A.H. Gandomi (Eds.), Handbook of Formal Optimization, Springer, Singapore, 2023, https://doi.org/10.1007/978-981-19-8851-6_44-1.

[43] S. Farahmand-Tabar, S. Shirgir, Boosting the efficiency of metaheuristics through opposition-based learning in optimum locating of control systems in tall buildings, in: A.J. Kulkarni, A.H. Gandomi (Eds.), Handbook of Formal Optimization, Springer, Singapore, 2023, https://doi.org/10.1007/978-981-19-8851-6_37-1.

[44] V. Goodarzimehr, S. Talatahari, S. Shojaee, S. Hamzehei-Javaran, Special relativity search for applied mechanics and engineering, Comput. Methods Appl. Mech. Eng. 403 (A) (2023) 115734, https://doi.org/10.1016/j.cma.2022.115734.

[45] M. Azizi, S. Talatahari, A.H. Gandomi, Fire hawk optimizer: A novel metaheuristic algorithm, Artif. Intell. Rev. 56 (2023) 287–363, https://doi.org/10.1007/s10462-022-10173-w.

[46] S. Farahmand-Tabar, S. Shirgir, Multi-objective adaptive guided differential evolution for passively controlled structures equipped with a tunned mass damper, in: N. Dey (Ed.), Applied Multi-Objective Optimization. Springer Tracts in Nature-Inspired Computing, Springer, Singapore, 2024, https://doi.org/10.1007/978-981-97-0353-1_3.

[47] S. Farahmand-Tabar, Multi-objective lichtenberg algorithm for the optimum design of truss structures, in: N. Dey (Ed.), Applied Multi-Objective Optimization. Springer Tracts in Nature-Inspired Computing, Springer, Singapore, 2024, https://doi.org/10.1007/978-981-97-0353-1_5.

[48] S. Farahmand-Tabar, P. Afrasyabi, Multi-modal routing in urban transportation network using multi-objective quantum particle swarm optimization, in: N. Dey (Ed.), Applied Multi-Objective Optimization. Springer Tracts in Nature-Inspired Computing, Springer, Singapore, 2024, https://doi.org/10.1007/978-981-97-0353-1_7.

[49] S. Talatahari, M. Azizi, M. Tolouei, B. Talatahari, P. Sareh, Crystal structure algorithm (CryStAl): A metaheuristic optimization method, IEEE Access 9 (2021) 71244–71261, https://doi.org/10.1109/ACCESS.2021.3079161.

[50] B.A. Averill, P. Eldredge, Chemistry: Principles, patterns, and applications (2019, June 23). Retrieved April 6, from, https://chem.libretexts.org/@go/page/3999, 2021.

[51] B.A. Averill, P. Eldredge, Chemistry: Principles, patterns, and applications, Apr. 6, 2021. [Online]. Available: https://chem.libretexts.org/go/page/3, 2019.

[52] C.-H. Lim, Y.-S. Yoon, J.-H. Kim, Genetic algorithm in mix proportioning of high-performance concrete, Cement Concr. Res. 34 (3) (2004) 409–420, https://doi.org/10.1016/j.cemconres.2003.08.018.

Chapter 17

Artificial intelligence applications for earthquake and tsunami damage assessment: An overview

Atousa Nasertork[1], Mohammad Reza Nikoo[2], Ghazi Al-Rawas[2] and Amir H. Gandomi[3, 4]

[1]Department of Civil & Environmental Engineering, Amirkabir University of Technology (Tehran Polytechnic), Tehran, Iran; [2]College of Engineering, Department of Civil and Architectural Engineering, Sultan Qaboos University, Muscat, Oman; [3]University Research and Innovation Center (EKIK), Óbuda University, Budapest, Hungary; [4]Department of Computer Science, Khazar University, Baku, Azerbaijan

1. Introduction

Combining RS for data acquisition with AI for analysis provides a powerful approach for monitoring and responding to natural disasters such as earthquakes and tsunamis. Automated earthquake- and tsunami-damage assessment often involves two broad steps: first, locating exposed assets such as buildings, roads, and infrastructure; second, classifying the type or severity of observed damage. Firstly, a building- or asset-localization model is applied, treating it as a localization problem where a system estimates a binary map indicating structures and non-structures in an input image. Secondly, the localization map is used to assess damage at locations marked as structures. AI-powered systems can continuously monitor impacted regions, providing ongoing assessments of damage extent and supporting recovery tracking. AI can support early warning when combined with seismic, buoy, tide-gauge, Global Navigation Satellite System (GNSS), and RS data; however, post-event damage assessment usually relies on imagery collected after the event. The use of these technologies in decision-making and resource allocation can be broken down into several key steps, as summarized in Fig. 17.1.

AI methods, particularly machine learning (ML), deep learning (DL), and transfer learning (TL), have been crucial in processing RS data to assess disaster damage. These algorithms can analyze images captured before and after a disaster to identify changes in land cover, infrastructure, and water bodies. For instance, changes in coastal landforms or the presence of debris fields can signal tsunami impacts. They can also recognize specific objects such as buildings, roads, and vegetation; by comparing pre- and postevent imagery, damaged structures can be automatically detected. AI algorithms are able to focus on relevant image features, such as changes in pixel intensity, texture, or spectral signatures, and recognize specific patterns associated with various types of damage, including collapsed buildings, flooded areas, and landslides. Common methods are summarized in Fig. 17.2 and discussed below [1–3].

To provide a representative overview of recent AI-based post-disaster damage-assessment approaches, relevant studies published between 2019 and 2023 were collected from the Google Scholar database using combinations of keywords related to earthquake damage assessment, tsunami damage assessment, and artificial intelligence. The retrieved studies were screened based on relevance, methodological clarity, application of AI techniques, and availability of methodological or performance-related details. After removing duplicate and unrelated records, 45 papers were retained from an initial set of 456 results and categorized according to their primary AI approach. To ensure consistency and accessibility, only English-language journal papers and review articles were included in this chapter.

Given the diversity of recent AI algorithms and novel techniques, their extensive application across various fields, and the rapid evolution of these strategies, a structured overview can help researchers identify suitable methods, data sources,

Advanced Intelligence Methods for Data Science and Optimization. https://doi.org/10.1016/B978-0-443-28940-8.00020-8

FIGURE 17.1 Workflow for AI-supported post-disaster damage assessment and decision support, from data acquisition and preprocessing to labeling, training, mapping, and resource allocation. *Source: Author-created schematic synthesized from prior literature and publicly available imagery.*

and validation strategies for different damage-assessment tasks. It can assist them in identifying the most effective approaches for tackling problems and improving assessment results more efficiently.

Combining complementary AI methods may improve damage assessment, provided that the input data, labels, and validation methods are appropriate. RS is typically used to identify large-scale damage patterns, and with the advantages of high-resolution imagery and advanced techniques, it can also assess damage at the level of individual structures. While computer vision techniques excel at detecting damaged buildings in urban areas, ML models can be effective in rural damage assessment when appropriate features, labels, and validation data are available.

2. Machine learning (ML) methods

Recent studies have combined diverse ML techniques with RS data. ML includes supervised learning for prediction and classification, unsupervised learning for clustering and representation learning, and semi-supervised learning that combines labeled and unlabeled data. ML classifiers, favored for classifying images using training samples, can benefit from feature engineering. These methods can be used to analyze limited ground-truth data and identify damage patterns based on terrain characteristics and historical data. They can also be extended to non-imagery data, such as sensor records or reports, to identify patterns of damage and resource needs, although the present chapter focuses mainly on RS imagery. The following outlines common ML algorithms employed in postdisaster damage assessment [4,5].

2.1 Decision tree (DT)

DT is a widely used algorithm, valued for its simplicity and user-friendly nature. The core concept involves constructing a tree structure consisting of a root node, internal decision nodes, branches, and terminal leaf nodes. The highest node, referred to as the top root node, signifies the most crucial feature for labeling data. DT aims to maximize information while minimizing entropy or tree impurity. Branches split from the top node down to the bottom leaves, providing classification results based on the DT algorithm. DTs can handle continuous variables by selecting split thresholds [6,7]. Random Forests (RFs), Rotation Forests (RoFs), and Canonical Correlation Forests (CCFs) are among the popular decision forests [8].

2.2 Random forest (RF)

RF, a nonparametric ensemble learning technique akin to DTs, constructs multiple DTs and combines them for accurate and stable predictions in classifying objects. At each node, input features are randomly chosen to grow a DT, and each tree contributes a single vote for the most common class. RF uses bootstrap samples of the training data and random subsets of features at each split. Bootstrap aggregation and random feature selection reduce variance and help limit overfitting, while

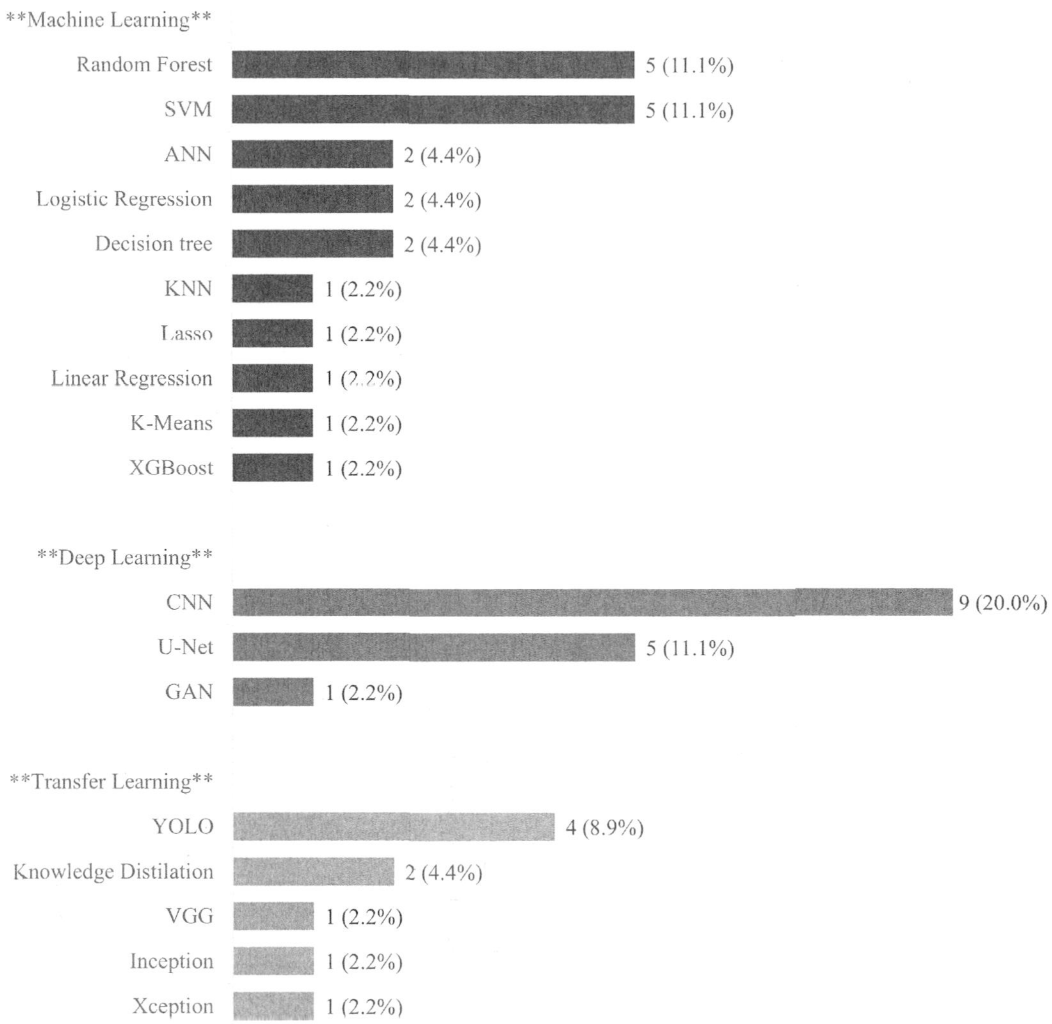

FIGURE 17.2 Distribution of AI methods reported in recent post-disaster damage-assessment studies, published between 2019 and 2023. The analysis includes 45 papers selected according to the search strategy and inclusion criteria described in the Introduction. Each study was categorized based on its primary AI methodology. Algorithms were broadly classified into Machine Learning (e.g., SVM, RF), Deep Learning (e.g., CNNs, U-Net), and Transfer Learning (e.g., VGG, YOLO) approaches.

parallel implementation mainly improves computational efficiency [6,9–12]. A seamless combination of cGAN-driven image simulation, features extracted from residual networks, and classification through tree-based ensemble learning has also proven to be successful in this field [13]. RF can also serve as a feature selector [14,15].

2.3 Gradient boosted tree (GBT)

Gradient boosting builds an additive sequence of weak learners, usually shallow DTs, where each new learner corrects errors from the current ensemble. While similar to DT and RF procedures, GBT utilizes a sequential approach to address errors at each step, often resulting in high predictive accuracy [6]. Although training speed depends on the dataset size, model depth, and the specific implementation, modern gradient boosting frameworks including XGBoost, LightGBM, and CatBoost provide significantly more efficient and optimized implementations through techniques such as histogram-based splitting, parallelization, and advanced regularization.

2.4 K-nearest neighbor (KNN)

KNN, inherently nonparametric and commonly used for pattern recognition, calculates the distance between an unlabeled sample and the labeled samples in the training set. The class of the unknown sample is usually determined by majority voting or distance-weighted voting among its K nearest neighbours, often computed using the Euclidean formula [11].

2.5 Support vector machine (SVM)

SVM algorithm is a commonly employed and effective classifier for various datasets, including linearly nonseparable and high-dimensional ones. It aims to find optimal hyperplanes to separate classes, with support vectors being the samples closest to these hyperplanes [11]. The SVM model's performance is influenced by kernel functions, with the Radial Basis Function (RBF) being highly effective for nonlinear classification [16]. Researchers have utilized soft-margin SVM with two regularization parameters to provide varying tolerance levels for subsets differing from the standard SVM that uses a single regularization parameter [17].

2.6 Logistic regression (LR)

LR is a dependable algorithm for solving binary classification tasks. The s-shaped logistic function forms the foundation of LR, and the curve of this function signifies the likelihood of the target class [9].

2.7 K-means

K-Means, a widely used clustering algorithm, establishes K clusters with their own centroid points as centers in order to segment the dataset by assigning each member to a cluster. This process is conducted based on their proximity, normally measured by the Euclidean distance, to the respective cluster center, minimizing the distance. The clustering process can operate on multivariate feature vectors. The number of clusters can be selected using criteria such as the Davies-Bouldin Index (DBI), silhouette score, elbow method, or task-specific validation. The Davies-Bouldin index is minimized, whereas the silhouette score is maximized; the elbow method is interpreted from the change in within-cluster variance [6].

2.8 Hybrid machine-learning technique (HMLT)

The cited HMLT combines SVM and ANN components. It is employed for classification based on superior features. This method finds a hyperplane to separate features into two sets, namely damaged and undamaged, and assesses building damage levels. A hybrid preprocessing method named HFSM is utilized to enhance efficiency and identify significant features [18].

2.9 Methods using feature engineering

Several studies use feature engineering to improve post-disaster image interpretation using methods such as Phase Correlation (PC) [19], fuzzy geometric features [20], proxy tsunami inundation metrics such as height and area [21], and the combination of the matrix elements and copolarization correlation coefficient [22]. The presence of similar scattering mechanisms in collapsed structures and undamaged structures with nonparallel orientation to the Synthetic-Aperture Radar (SAR) movement path can lead to potential confusion. Nevertheless, these two types of structures exhibit distinct textures. To address this, the Optimization of Polarimetric Contrast Enhancement (OPCE) method is utilized to boost the textural contrast ratio for both undamaged and collapsed structures [10]. Additionally, a Precision-Weighted Multi-Feature Fusion (PWMF) method merges multiple texture features. Notably, the proposed method is adaptable, requiring only adjustments to the classification threshold values during PWMF operation when implemented on different datasets. Utilizing Lagrange optimization on the disparity between two polarimetric covariance matrices amplifies the distinctions in scattering characteristics between data acquired pre- and postevent. This approach exhibits superior damage sensitivity compared with traditional coherence-based single and dual-polarization methods [23].

Integrating maps derived from optical and SAR images can improve damage mapping. Utilizing Interferometric Synthetic-Aperture Radar (InSAR) coherence mapping, complemented by the Normalized Difference Vegetation Index (NDVI) for vegetation masking and Modified Normalized Difference Water Index (MNDWI) for extraction of water bodies before the event, allows the creation of a comprehensive damage assessment map. Geographic Information System (GIS) tools facilitate mapping based on area characteristics. Additionally, an NDVI-based change detection process was incorporated to assess damage in vegetation areas [24]. The schematic is given in Fig. 17.3.

3. Deep learning (DL) methods

DL, a specific form of ML utilizing neural networks, employs an architecture with multiple layers to extract numerous features from raw data automatically. The output from a layer serves as the input for the next, involving various data conversion and processing steps. Hidden layers facilitate the learning of data structures across different training layers, allowing the adjustment of parameters. This versatile architecture can handle diverse data types, such as images or signals.

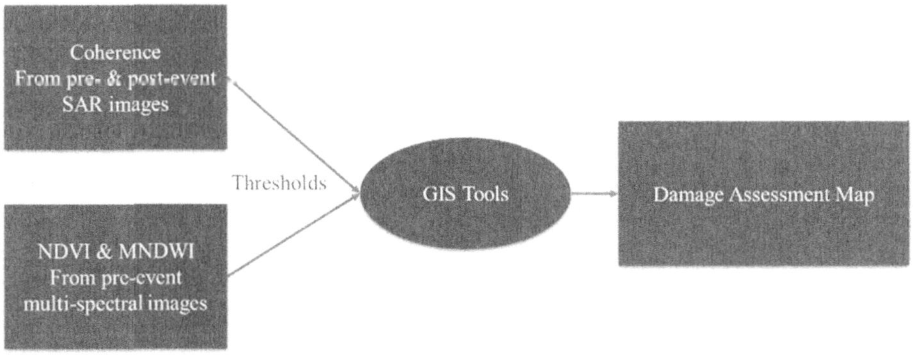

FIGURE 17.3 Workflow for generating a damage-assessment map from SAR coherence, NDVI/MNDWI masks, threshold selection, and GIS-based integration.

Today, various architectures exist, and deeper networks can learn more complex hierarchical representations, although performance depends on data volume, architecture, regularization, and training strategy [4]. These methods are well-suited for detailed damage assessment of individual buildings and infrastructure. High-resolution photographs can be used to train and deploy these models.

3.1 Artificial neural network (ANN)

ANN finds applications in pattern recognition and image classification across various fields. The Multilayer Perceptron (MLP) neural network, featuring fully connected layers, can be employed to tackle complex situations. Its layers are categorized as input, hidden, and output, enabling the network to address nonlinear classification tasks. In feed-forward neural networks trained by back-propagation, predictions are computed in a forward pass and weights are updated during the backward pass [18]. The DL architecture, illustrated in Fig. 17.4, involves the main steps of preprocessing data, model development, and evaluation [4,5,15,16].

3.2 Convolutional neural network (CNN)

CNNs are widely used in damage assessment due to their ability to learn hierarchical spatial features directly from image data and to model complex patterns using convolutional filters and hierarchical feature learning. Their performance on limited datasets often relies on techniques such as data augmentation, transfer learning, or the use of pretrained architectures to improve generalization and mitigate overfitting. A basic CNN includes pooling, convolution, and Fully Connected Layers (FCL), allowing the construction of various network models [25]. Composite, Twin, and Fusion, demonstrated in Fig. 17.5, are three variations of CNN that have proven effective in damage detection. They utilize three bands (RGB) of orthophoto imagery, demonstrating their suitability in handling pre- and postevent images. The Composite network tackles overfitting with dropout and includes convolution layers, filters, activation functions, and max-pooling. Twin and Fusion networks employ parallel CNNs for pre- and postevent images, with Fusion differing by using one 2D CNN for predisaster and two 2D CNNs for postdisaster images [26].

3.3 Faster R–CNN

Faster R CNN stands out as a CNN driven object detection framework that utilizes shared network weights for both region proposal and object classification. It integrates a convolutional backbone for feature extraction and a Region Proposal Network (RPN) that generates candidate object regions in a unified and end-to-end trainable architecture. This design leads to significantly faster and more precise predictions compared with its predecessor, R–CNN. It is essential to highlight that within the Faster R–CNN model, key components such as bounding-box regression and classification layers are retained alongside the two core networks, RPN and CNN. The CNN image feature extractors can be Zeiler and Fergus (ZF), a modified version of the AlexNet architecture, ResNet-50 or other suitable convolutional backbones [27].

3.4 Deep embedding clustering (DEC)

Given that disaster-induced alterations in pre- and postevent images constitute a small portion amid various clusters such as luminosity, weather effects, and crop changes, a dual-phase process is introduced. Initially, a combined autoencoder

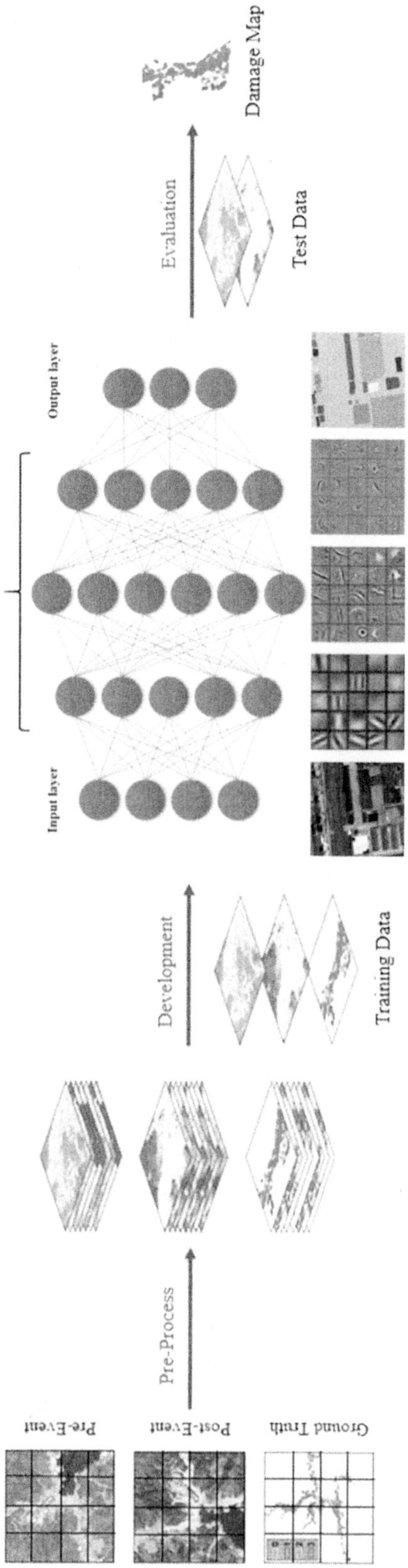

FIGURE 17.4 General deep-learning workflow for preprocessing, training, validation, testing, and damage-map generation.

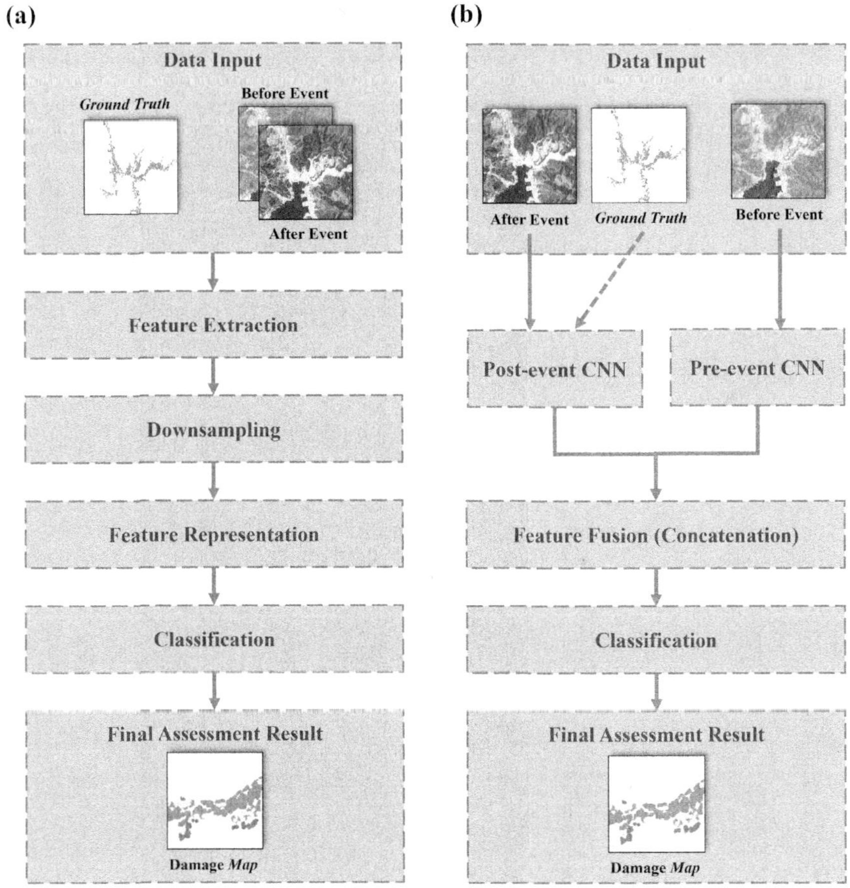

FIGURE 17.5 Schematic workflow of (a) the composite NN, and (b) the fusion or twin CNN models, for pre- and post-event image analysis.

identifies areas with significant changes. Subsequently, the detected regions with significant alterations are utilized as a mask, allowing a clustering algorithm to be applied exclusively to those areas. The DEC algorithm is contrasted with conventional methods such as the K-Means algorithm, showcasing enhanced effectiveness, particularly when applied to concatenated versions of pre- and postevent images [28].

3.5 Pyramid pooling module-based Semi-Siamese network (PPM-SSNet)

This network employs a Semi-Siamese approach, sharing parameters at early layers between images from before and after the event to collectively learn low-level features. Deeper layers use independent branches, merging them by taking the difference between them across channels to learn differences. A single branch produces the final network output. Squeeze-and-Excitation (SE) block and Residual Blocks (RBs) are employed along with dilated convolution, allowing feature extraction from both small and large receptive fields. SE blocks concentrate on significant features while diminishing less relevant ones. A PPM is used preceding an SE and a convolutional layer at the end of the network to aggregate features [1]. The outline is illustrated in Fig. 17.6.

3.6 U-net

U-Net, a CNN-based framework widely used for monitoring disaster-damaged structures, exhibits high precision, fast processing capabilities, and minimal reliance on extensive datasets or complex computational resources [4]. For the specific task of building localization, U-Net can effectively utilize pre-event imagery. However, for comprehensive damage assessment, a comparison between bi-temporal pre- and post-event imagery is typically necessary. When employing only preevent images for tasks like semantic segmentation, the architecture leverages an encoder-decoder structure. The encoder, composed of 2D-convolution layers, batch-normalization operations, and activation functions,

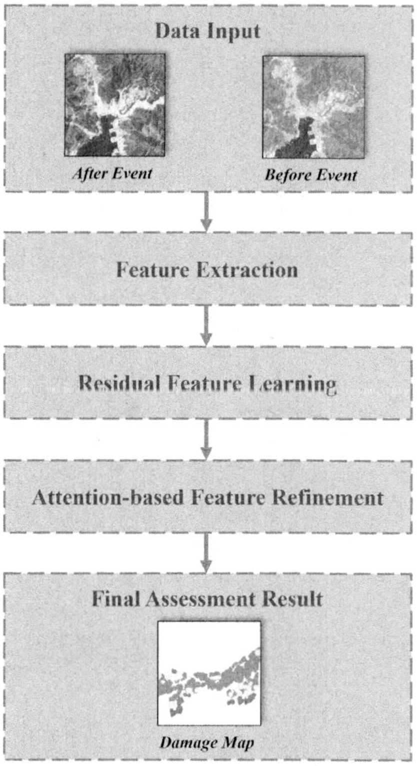

FIGURE 17.6 Architecture of PPM-SSNet. C: Convolutional layer, D: Dropout layer, R: ReLU layer, B: Batch normalization layer.

progressively reduces spatial resolution while increasing feature dimensionality, thereby extracting high-level feature representations. A modified encoder design, often incorporating two parallel streams, can process both pre- and post-disaster datasets distinctly. The decoder mirrors the encoder's structure, utilizing transpose convolutions for up-sampling and incorporating skip connections to facilitate the propagation of fine-grained spatial information from earlier layers. To address class imbalance in damage categories, specific weighting schemes can be applied [2,3]. Furthermore, attention gate mechanisms can enhance the model's ability to focus on relevant structures across diverse scenarios. Finally, SoftMax activation generates multi-channel probability maps, where the final categorical prediction for each pixel is determined by selecting the channel with the highest probability [29,30]. A schematic U-Net is given in Fig. 17.7.

3.7 Graph convolutional network (GCN)

Graph neural networks (GNNs) are deemed impactful considering the spatial characteristics of natural disaster damage. For instance, BLDNet employs a hybrid architecture that integrates CNN and GCN. This framework utilizes graph convolutions to aggregate information from neighboring samples, building an undirected spatial graph from building-footprint polygons. Nodes correspond to building subimages, and edges are formed based on spatial proximity. Meta-features are embedded at the node level to incorporate domain knowledge. The graph structure is used to classify damage levels in each building. Another hybrid model, GCN + CNN, effectively uses high-resolution remote-sensing (HRS) images, location, and temporal data for building damage assessment. Concatenating components into a dense layer enables nonlinear aggregation, followed by a SoftMax layer for a category probability distribution. Semisupervised GCN involves training on a single graph with labeled nodes, propagating labels along the graph edges to unlabeled nodes [31,32]. The GCN can be simplified, as illustrated in Fig. 17.8.

3.8 Generative adversarial network (GAN)

CycleGAN can be trained to convert SAR images into optical-like images, leveraging unlabeled pairs of optical and SAR images. The CycleGAN involves two generators: one transcodes SAR imagery into optical images, and the other projects optical imagery into SAR images. After unsupervised training, the SAR-to-optical generator serves as a deep feature

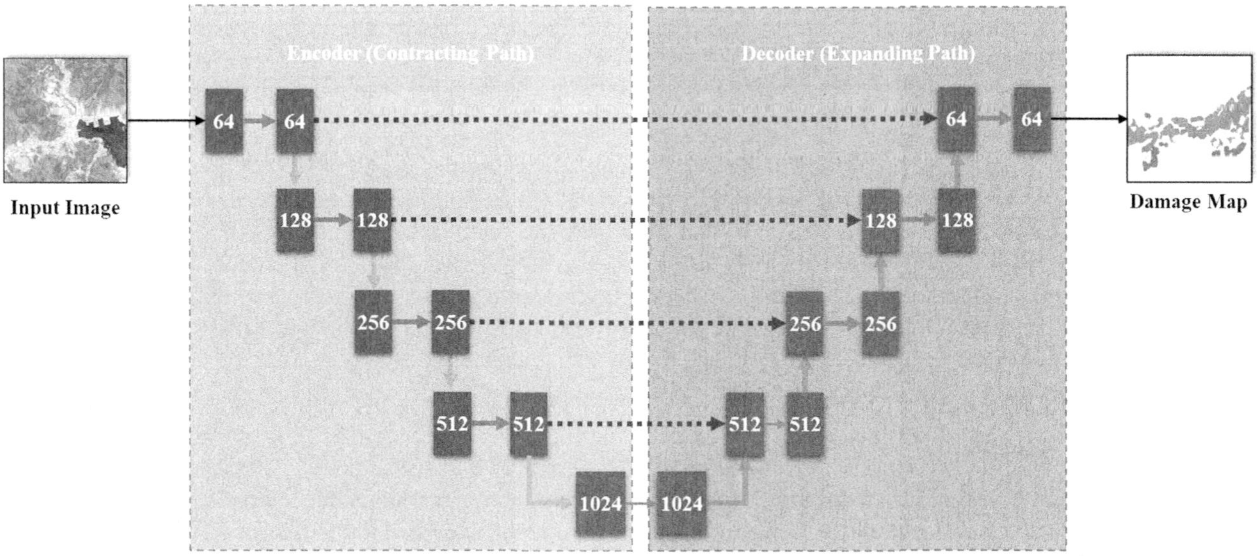

FIGURE 17.7 Standard U-Net architecture showing encoder blocks, decoder blocks, skip connections, and the output segmentation map. The network consists of an encoder (contracting path; green shaded area) and a decoder (expanding path; red shaded area) connected through skip connections at corresponding levels. Blue rectangles denote convolutional blocks composed of two consecutive 3×3 convolution + ReLU operations. Blue arrows indicate convolution operations, green arrows represent 2×2 max pooling for down-sampling, and red arrows indicate 2×2 transpose convolutions for up-sampling. Black dashed arrows denote skip connections with feature-map concatenation, while the black solid arrow represents the final 1×1 convolution used to generate the segmentation map.

FIGURE 17.8 Graph-based networks: Edges represent similarity-based or spatial-proximity relationships between nodes; node colors indicate classes.

extractor for bi-temporal data, enabling fuzzy rules and Deep Change Vector Analysis (DCVA) for identifying changed structures. The interaction of generators and discriminators in CycleGAN follows adversarial and cycle-consistency criteria, optimizing both the generator and discriminator together and ensuring that consecutively transformed patches result in the original patches [33].

4. Knowledge transfer techniques in DL

Leveraging the knowledge of pretrained models to improve both performance and training speed has become increasingly common. Such techniques also address challenges such as data scarcity by utilizing prior knowledge. TL is one such approach, where a pretrained model is adapted to solve similar tasks, utilizing the information gained from one problem to generalize more effectively to others. TL adapts pretrained architectures or weights to a related task, either by using the model as a feature extractor or by fine-tuning some or all layers. Although not universally applicable, it can be efficient for related tasks when the source and target domains are sufficiently similar. Popular methods used for TL, such as VGGNet, Inception, DenseNet, and Resnet, investigate the feature extraction capabilities of various CNN architectures. Fine-tuning is the process of adapting a pretrained model to a specific task. Additionally, Knowledge Distillation (KD) is a technique for model compression in which a smaller and simpler model, referred to as the student, learns to replicate the behavior of a larger and more complex model, known as the teacher, capturing its information and performance. While KD focuses on transferring knowledge within the same task to enhance model efficiency, TL generally involves repurposing a model's knowledge for a different task or domain [34,35].

4.1 VGGNet

As a deep CNN, VGG is a powerful algorithm with a profound structure comprising 16 and 19 layers in VGG-16 and VGG-19, respectively. The ImageNet dataset, containing about 1.2 million training images, was used to train the original model. VGG-16 is comparatively shallower in depth compared with Inception and ResNet. VGG-16 may be useful for TL on small datasets, but its large number of parameters can also increase overfitting risk. Modifications can be made to the original VGG-16 model in the SoftMax and fully connected layers to classify two object types [36]. VGG-19 model is trained to categorize into 1000 classes, processing 224×224 -pixels color images. Although it has an extensive architecture, VGG-19 stands out for its simplicity, employing 3×3 convolutional layers stacked in increasing depth. Notably, it utilizes small-sized kernels within the deep structure [37].

4.2 Inception (GoogLeNet)

Inception, a multilayer CNN algorithm developed by Google, utilizes a wider architecture, incorporating 1×1, 3×3, and 5×5 convolutions in the same module. When pretrained on ImageNet, it classifies images into 1000 object classes. Notably, it secured first place in the 2014 ImageNet competition, outperforming VGG-19, which was the runner-up. The Inception algorithm functions as a multilevel feature extractor, stacking filters across the channels and adding them to the subsequent network layer. Additionally, Inception-v3 replaces large filters with smaller ones, a distinctive feature of this model [38].

4.3 Xception model

Xception is an improved version of the Inception architecture, introducing depth-wise separable convolutions to replace standard Inception modules. This distinctive feature involves depth-wise convolution succeeded by point–wise convolution. The input data undergoes eight middle cycles concluding with the exit progression. All convolutional and separable convolutional layers are adjusted with batch normalization [25].

4.4 You only look once (YOLO)

YOLO is an end-to-end network model designed for efficient object detection. YOLOv5, a lightweight version, excels at detecting small objects with a balance of accuracy and speed. It automatically learns and uses anchor boxes during training, improving adaptability to different datasets. Anchor boxes are predefined bounding-box shapes used as priors for object localization. It consists of a backbone for essential feature extraction, a neck for combining features, and a head for predicting image features, bounding boxes, and object types. YOLOv5 offers various models, including YOLOv5n, YOLOv5s, YOLOv5m, YOLOv5l, and YOLOv5x, denoting nano, small, medium, large, and extra-large variants, respectively [39].

4.5 DenseNet

DenseNet has been used in image-based earthquake-damage monitoring studies. DenseNet-201 has been selected as the input pretrained network in a Color-Base Damage Feature Enhanced Support Vector Classifier [40]. The Spatial and Channel Attention Module U-Net (SCAMU-Net) model is an extended U-Net with hyperparameter tuning, incorporating a Spatial Channel Attention Module (SCAM). It employs a single U-Net with shared weights and various backbones, such as DenseNet, with 121, 169, and 201 layers. Unlike recent ResNet studies, this model explores a deeper backbone for optimal solutions. The U-Net utilizes an Atrous Spatial Pyramid Pooling (ASPP) module at the conclusion of the encoder block to capture global context information. The ASPP-enhanced U-Net incorporates a BottleNeck layer. The U-Net Decoder configuration includes concatenation, ensuring all context information extracted by DenseNet contributes to accurate classification. Modifications can be made to the Dense layers in the Channel Attention Module, changing a single Dense Layer into a double dense layer [41].

4.6 ResNet

As a sample of ResNet application in this field, Two-Stream ResNet50 has been used. It utilizes the ImageNet-pretrained ResNet50 backbone in a dual-path U-Net architecture, employing separate encoders whose encodings are subtracted before being provided as input to the decoder. The encoders are initialized with ImageNet-pretrained weights, while separate encoder weights allow pre- and post-event images to be represented differently. Ranked fifth in the xView2 challenge, the Dual-HRNet integrates heads for building detection and damage assessment, fusion blocks in the middle, and two HRNetV2 backbones pretrained on ImageNet [42].

Another semantic segmentation network is designed by putting U-Net as the baseline and benefiting from ResNet architecture. Images before the event are utilized as input, leveraging intact predisaster building features. The building damage grading stage focuses on damage classification, utilizing a Siamese Network to segment structures based on their damages. Pre- and postevent images are used as input, with shared weights in the encoder part initialized with the weight from the building segmentation network. Network improvements include Extra Skip Connection (ESC) addition in the decoder, replacing partial convolution with an Asymmetric Convolution Block (ACB), and incorporating a Shuffle Attention module in the Siamese Network decoder to enhance attention to building correlations before and after the disaster [30].

The PRESS-Net model comprises the Pyramid Scene Parsing Network (PSPNet), utilizing a Spatial Attention Module (SAM) and a ResNet50 to enhance performance in segmenting images. PSPNet is a CNN that uses a PPM to grasp contextual details across various scales (both global and local). Compared with channel attention, the SAM generates a spatial attention map by considering interspatial relationships between features. SAM enables the model to efficiently prioritize important characteristics while suppressing less informative ones by selectively focusing on relevant regions. This involves a concatenation of Average and Max Pooling along the channel axis to create an effective feature extractor [43].

The AR-CDNet utilizes a shared feature extractor with an encoder-decoder structure for bitemporal feature extraction, where ResNet18 is a potential backbone for the encoder. The decoder follows a U-shape structure, incorporating a Feature Aggregation Module (FAM) to progressively fuse multilevel context information from high to low levels. FAM calibrates low-level features using element-wise weights computed from high-level features, and the fused features pass through a convolution layer. The decoder captures multilevel bitemporal features for change detection. Temporal Symmetric Transformer achieves Temporal Difference Extraction (TDE), concatenating bitemporal features with two temporal orders and passing them through 3D convolution layers. However, the U-shape structure neglects long dependencies between high and low-level features, impacting distinctive knowledge. To address this, Knowledge Review Modules (KRM) are introduced to gather complementary details from multilevel temporal difference features, enhancing change detection accuracy. Additionally, an Online Uncertainty Estimation (OUE) branch evaluates pixel-wise uncertainty, combining uncertainty-aware features with multilevel temporal difference features to focus on less reliable regions for improved attention [44].

4.7 Knowledge distillation (KD)

KD is utilized to compress a large model for building damage assessment. Unlike traditional training methods with binary labels, KD teaches the student model the predictive and hidden outputs of the teacher model, resulting in more accurate and extensive knowledge. The teacher-student algorithm, a form of knowledge distillation, reduces the number of model parameters, enhancing operational speed. Curriculum learning initializes the classification model using a localization model as the teacher, and a Siamese network structure can be employed in KD for encoding similar feature maps from pre- and postdisaster images. Multi-teacher-supervised KD combines information from multiple sources to instruct student models, enhancing performance. The dual-teacher guidance approach simplifies curriculum learning using two similar-structured teacher models with distinct output layer structures. This method proves effective in computer vision tasks. Based on the number of teachers and students, this method can have either an indirect or a direct knowledge-flow approach [34,35]. A schematic diagram is given in Fig. 17.9.

This KD method is categorized into feature distillation and target distillation. Distillation through feature extraction aligns the middle-layer resulting features from the student and teacher models, while prediction-based distillation uses the teacher model's output as pseudo-labels. Combining these forms results in an ensemble T-S method.

5. Metrics of performance

The choice of metrics depends on the specific task and the desired outcome. By carefully selecting and interpreting these metrics, it is possible to evaluate the effectiveness of various AI models and identify the most suitable approach for disaster damage detection. The most common metrics are calculated based on the confusion matrix. To evaluate classifiers' efficiency against validation data, a confusion matrix is formed as the basis of many common metrics. It consists of

FIGURE 17.9 Schematic of multi-teacher ensemble KD.

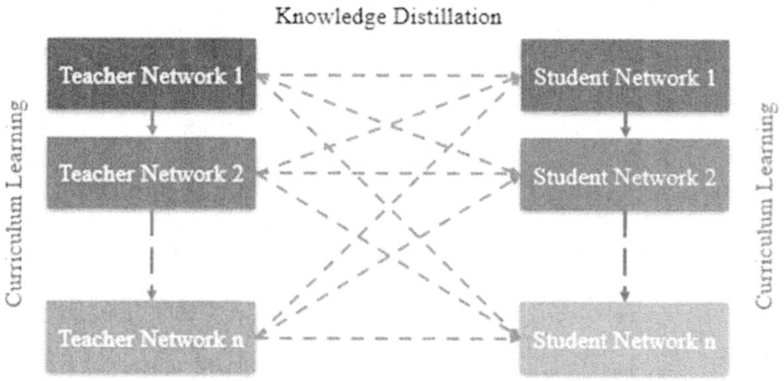

True Positive (TP) as an indicator for the correctly identified positive sample, True Negative (TN) representing the negative samples predicted correctly, False Positive (FP) counting the negative sample predicted incorrectly, and False Negative (FN) denoting the positive sample incorrectly classified as negative [45]. Some frequently used evaluation metrics in the field of tsunami damage assessment are summarized below.

5.1 Overall accuracy (OA)

OA measures the proportion of reference classes that are correctly mapped [45,46]. It is calculated as the number of correctly classified samples divided by the total number of samples [7].

$$\mathrm{OA} = (\mathrm{TP} + \mathrm{TN})/(\mathrm{TP} + \mathrm{TN} + \mathrm{FP} + \mathrm{FN})$$

While OA provides an average measure throughout the classification procedure, it conceals the technique's class-wise performance [26]. In some cases, accuracy alone may not fully capture model performance.

5.2 Average accuracy (AA)

Average accuracy is defined as the mean of individual per-class accuracies, offering a more representative metric in imbalanced scenarios than OA.

For C classes:

$$\mathrm{AA} = (1/\mathrm{C})\sum_{\mathrm{i}=1}^{\mathrm{C}} (\mathrm{TP}_\mathrm{i})/(\mathrm{TP}_\mathrm{i} + \mathrm{FN}_\mathrm{i})$$

While OA assesses aggregate performance, AA mitigates the bias introduced by varying instance counts across classes. Nonetheless, both metrics may fail to provide a complete picture of model efficacy when dealing with highly skewed training distributions [27].

5.3 Producer accuracy (PA)

It is a metric applied to a specific class that measures the likelihood of correct classification [26]. PA represents the likelihood that a value within a specific class is accurately classified [7]. It focuses on the map's ability to accurately represent real-world features by calculating the ratio of correctly classified pixels to the total number of pixels of that class in the reference data. This metric is mathematically equivalent to recall, for a specific class.

5.4 User accuracy (UA)

This metric is used for an individual class and corresponds to the commission error (incorrectly identifying a feature). UA indicates the probability of correct class assignment [7,26]. It focuses on how accurately a map user can interpret the map by dividing the number of correctly classified pixels for a class by the total number of pixels classified as that class on the map. This metric is mathematically equivalent to precision, for a specific class.

5.5 Precision

Precision is the percentage of correctly labeled positives out of all positively labeled points [18,44]. It measures the model's ability to avoid false positives [27,47].

$$\text{Precision} = (TP)/(TP + FP)$$

5.6 Recall

Recall, also known as sensitivity, represents the proportion of correctly identified positive samples to the total number of actual positive samples. It assesses the model's sensitivity to positive cases [27].

$$\text{Recall} = (TP)/(TP + FN)$$

Recall measures how well the model identifies all actual positive cases, while precision tells us how accurate it is when it does find them [18,47].

5.7 F1 score

Precision and recall individually may not provide a comprehensive evaluation of the model's overall performance, especially when dealing with imbalanced datasets, as high precision could be achieved with poor recall, or vice versa [47]. The F1 score, the harmonic mean of precision and recall, provides a balanced measure of a classification model's performance by considering both its ability to correctly identify positive instances and its ability to avoid false positives.

$$F1 = (2 \times \text{Precision} \times \text{Recall})/(\text{Precision} + \text{Recall}) = (2TP)/(2TP + FP + FN)$$

Macroaveraging for metrics provides a more comprehensive explanation of the uneven distribution of samples across different classes [26,45]. Macro-averaged F1 is commonly used when class frequencies are imbalanced, but it should not be treated as identical to the binary F1 score. F1 score metric is one of the most widely used metrics for evaluating classification tasks [18,30,35].

By varying the classification threshold, precision and recall can be assessed across operating points; a threshold of 0.5 should not be assumed optimal. A Precision-Recall Curve (PRC) can be generated by differing the threshold. The optimal F1-score and threshold can be identified from the PRC curve [27,44].

It can also be modified based on the topic. An F1 score based on individual pixels is calculated for the binary classification problem of damage localization, and the harmonic mean of pixel wise F1 score for each class is computed for multiclass damage classification. The overall standard xView2 metric is calculated as the weighted sum of the localization and damage classification scores [48].

5.8 Receiver operating characteristic (ROC)

A graphical evaluation approach, known as the ROC curve, is frequently referenced in the ML literature. The ROC curve plots the true-positive rate (sensitivity) against the false-positive rate, where the false-positive rate equals (1 – specificity), for various classification thresholds. When examining a PRC or ROC for a classification model, it is typically observed that as sensitivity increases, precision and specificity often decrease, depending on the classification threshold. With the ROC curve, the Area Under the ROC Curve (AUC) serves as a consolidated metric that reflects the overall performance of the model [27].

5.9 Intersection over union (IoU)

IoU, also known as the Jaccard index, measures the overlap between predicted and actual positive regions relative to their union, assessing the quality of the detection outcomes.

$$\text{IoU} = (TP)/\ (TP + FP + FN)$$

In the building identification procedure, the model classifies each pixel as either a building or a nonbuilding. The prediction improves when the predicted building area overlaps with the actual one, leading to higher recall. However, increasing recall may increase false positives, depending on the threshold and model calibration. Therefore, the goal is to maximize the intersection while minimizing the union of the predicted and actual areas [30,35,44].

5.10 Loss function

The loss curve is another metric utilized to assess the network performance, illustrating the optimization progress and relative learning advancements over multiple epochs [26]. Categorical Cross-Entropy (CE) is a commonly used loss function for multiclass classification problems, while loss functions such as Dice Coefficient (DC) are particularly effective for addressing class imbalance issues [26,44]. Dice loss, commonly employed for binary semantic segmentation tasks, can exhibit instability when dealing with smaller targets. To mitigate this issue, a weighted combination of losses may be used [30]. The primary objective of building detection is to accurately classify each pixel in an image as either belonging to a building or the background, thereby delineating the boundaries of building structures. In HRS images, the significant disparity in the number of background pixels compared with building pixels leads to a class imbalance problem, where the majority class (background) overwhelms the minority class (buildings). Here a combined loss function, such as a weighted combination of Dice loss and Focal loss, can help. Focal loss possesses an adjustable balance factor α, which can address class imbalance [30].

5.11 Kappa coefficient (κ)

When the sample distribution is imbalanced, Kappa can provide information beyond OA, although it should be interpreted alongside class-wise metrics. Kappa evaluates agreement between model predictions and reference labels and can range from -1 to 1, although values between 0 and 1 are common in practice. The results exhibit moderate consistency when the Kappa coefficient exceeds 0.4 [45].

$$\kappa = \left(\mathrm{OA} - \left(\left(\sum\nolimits_{m} f_i g_i\right)/n^2\right)\right) \Big/ \left(1 - \left(\left(\sum\nolimits_{m} f_i g_i\right)/n^2\right)\right)$$

where n is the total number of samples, m is the number of classification categories, f_i is the sum of elements in row i of the corresponding confusion matrix, and g_i is the sum of elements in column i.

This metric offers a comprehensive evaluation of classification performance in comparison to a reference random classifier. In particular, Kappa values below 0 indicate worse-than-random performance, 0 means no better than random, and values closer to one indicate significantly better performance [44].

5.12 Mean squared error (MSE) or mean squared deviation (MSD)

MSE is a statistical measure quantifying the average squared difference between predicted and actual values.

$$\mathrm{MSE} = (1/n)\sum_{i=1}^{n}(y_i - \gamma_i)^2$$

where y_i is the ground-truth value, γ_i is the predicted value, and n is the number of samples.

When a model's predictions are perfectly accurate, the MSE is zero. As the model's prediction errors increase, the MSE value also increases proportionally [11].

5.13 Root mean square error (RMSE)

RMSE is derived from the MSE by taking its square root. By employing this standard statistical metric, the discrepancy between the predicted and true values of a model parameter can be readily plotted, facilitating the analysis of the model's accuracy and potential biases [11].

$$\mathrm{RMSE} = \sqrt{\left((1/n)\sum_{i=1}^{n}(y_i - \gamma_i)^2\right)}$$

where y_i is the ground-truth value, γ_i is predicted value, and n is number of samples.

5.14 Mean absolute error (MAE)

MAE measures the average deviation between the predicted and true values. It is referred to as scale-dependent accuracy because it evaluates errors within observations captured on the same scale. It is commonly used to assess many ML regression models [11].

$$\mathrm{MAE} = (1/n)\sum_{i=1}^{n} |y_i - \gamma_i|$$

where y_i is the ground-truth value, γ_i is predicted value, and n is number of samples.

5.15 Frames per second prediction (FPS)

FPS measures the frame rate of a video stream. In image processing tasks it refers to the quantity of images a model can process and classify within a 1-s timeframe, as an evaluation for the model's prediction speed [35].

$$\mathrm{FPS} = N_f/T$$

where N_f is the number of processed frames, and T is the total processing time.

6. Challenges

In disaster damage detection, common challenges include class feature similarities and data scarcity, both of which can greatly affect AI model performance. Below are several strategies to help address these issues. These techniques can improve robustness and accuracy, but their benefit should be verified through independent validation.

6.1 Class feature similarities

Issues with class feature similarities can be addressed through feature engineering and advanced DL techniques. Feature engineering [13,21,22] allows models to focus on specific handcrafted features, such as texture, shape, and color, helping to distinguish between similar classes. Additionally, feature selection techniques [17] can aid in reducing dimensionality and preventing overfitting, thereby enhancing model performance.

Among DL strategies, attention mechanisms can be highly effective by directing focus toward the most informative parts of the input data. Furthermore, training with difficult or perturbed examples can improve generalization under domain shift, sensor noise, and other real-world variations.

6.2 Data scarcity

Data scarcity can be addressed with techniques such as TL, semisupervised learning, data augmentation, synthetic data generation, and active learning. TL, for example, leverages models pretrained on massive datasets, such as ImageNet, and adapts them to disaster damage detection, enabling accurate assessments even with limited data. Semisupervised learning, which leverages both unlabeled and labeled data, is particularly useful in data-scarce situations, employing methods such as self-training and consistency regularization to make effective use of unlabeled data [31]. In addition, unsupervised learning can further support these efforts by identifying patterns in unlabeled data, enhancing the robustness of the model under low-data conditions [20,33,34].

When time constraints limit data availability, active learning can be valuable for selecting the most informative unlabeled data, allowing human experts to prioritize labeling efforts strategically. Data augmentation enhances the training dataset by creating variations through geometric transformations (such as rotating, flipping, and scaling images) or by altering color channels and adding noise, thus increasing data diversity. Additionally, generative models such as GANs can produce synthetic data, which can expand and diversify the training set, although their realism and effect on model bias should be validated.

7. Conclusion

AI has demonstrated strong potential for improving earthquake–tsunami damage assessment across multiple spatial and temporal scales. However, no single approach is universally optimal, as methodological suitability depends on assessment scale, data availability, and operational constraints.

For rapid regional mapping, DL-based semantic segmentation approaches, particularly CNN architectures such as U-Net and ResNet-derived models, provide an effective balance between accuracy and computational efficiency. Supported by TL and cloud-based geospatial platforms, these models enable near–real-time extraction of inundation extents and heavily damaged areas from satellite and aerial imagery. In contrast, feature-engineering-based ML methods remain useful in computationally constrained environments, although they generally offer lower scalability and automation.

For building-level damage classification, object detection and hybrid architectures demonstrate superior performance due to their ability to capture both local structural features and spatial context. Models such as Faster R-CNN, YOLO, and hybrid CNN–GCN frameworks (e.g., BLDNet) enable accurate localization and characterization of structural damage from high-resolution imagery. In addition, multi-sensor fusion using UAV, LiDAR, optical, and SAR data significantly improves the identification of subtle damage patterns and complex urban damage distributions.

In limited-label or data-scarce settings, classical ML methods, including SVM, RF, and GBTs, remain competitive because of their robustness and lower data requirements. Within DL frameworks, TL, domain adaptation, and KD improve generalization by leveraging pretrained representations, while data augmentation, attention mechanisms, and feature-engineering strategies help mitigate limited labeled data and class imbalance.

For operational deployment, lightweight CNN-based frameworks and optimized object detection models, such as real-time YOLO variants, offer practical solutions for time-sensitive disaster response applications. Their integration with GIS platforms and human-in-the-loop workflows enhances reliability, interpretability, and usability in real-world decision-support systems.

Despite substantial progress, several challenges remain, including limited availability of labeled post-disaster datasets, domain transferability across geographic regions and hazard types, class imbalance, multimodal data integration complexity, and the need for standardized evaluation frameworks. Future research should therefore focus on improving model generalizability, robust multi-sensor fusion, and scalable operational implementation for real-world disaster management applications.

References

[1] Y. Bai, J. Hu, J. Su, X. Liu, H. Liu, and X. He, "Pyramid pooling module-based semi-siamese network : A benchmark model for assessing building damage from xBD satellite imagery datasets", doi: 10.3390/rs12244055.

[2] I. Learning *et al.*, "Intelligent learning using remote sensing dataset from previous earthquakes to assess building damage in," 2020.

[3] B. Adriano, J. Xia, N. Yokoya, H. Miura, Damage characterization in urban environments from multitemporal remote sensing datasets built from previous events geoinformatics unit, in: RIKEN Center for Advanced Intelligence Project , Japan Graduate School of Engineering, Hiroshima University, Japan, 2020, pp. 3751–3754.

[4] M. Moradi and R. Shah-Hosseini, "Earthquake damage assessment based on deep learning method using VHR images," no. December, p. 16, 2021, https://doi.org/10.3390/iecg2020-08545.

[5] S. Karimzadeh, M. Ghasemi, M. Matsuoka, K. Yagi, A.C. Zulfikar, A deep learning model for road damage detection after an earthquake based on synthetic aperture radar (SAR) and field datasets, IEEE J. Sel. Top. Appl. Earth Obs. Remote Sens. 15 (2022) 5753–5765, https://doi.org/10.1109/JSTARS.2022.3189875.

[6] K. Saengtabtim, et al., Predictive analysis of the building damage from the 2011 great east Japan tsunami using decision tree classification related algorithms, IEEE Access 9 (2021) 31065–31077, https://doi.org/10.1109/ACCESS.2021.3060114.

[7] E. Ferrentino, F. Nunziata, C. Bignami, L. Graziani, A. Maramai, M. Migliaccio, Multi-polarization C-band SAR imagery to quantify damage levels due to the central Italy earthquake, Int. J. Rem. Sens. 42 (15) (2021) 5971–5986, https://doi.org/10.1080/01431161.2021.1933247.

[8] B. Adriano, J. Xia, G. Baier, N. Yokoya, S. Koshimura, Multi-source data fusion based on ensemble learning for rapid building damage mapping during the 2018 Sulawesi earthquake and tsunami in palu, Indonesia, Remote Sens. 11 (7) (2019), https://doi.org/10.3390/RS11070886.

[9] W. Liu and Y. Maruyama, "Detection of collapsed bridges from multi-temporal sar intensity images by machine learning techniques," 2021.

[10] Y. Nie, Q. Zeng, H. Zhang, Q. Wang, Building damage detection based on opce matching algorithm using a single post-event polsar data, Remote Sens. 13 (6) (2021) 1–36, https://doi.org/10.3390/rs13061146.

[11] G. Cakra, A. Wibowo, S. Yulianto, J. Prasetyo, I. Sembiring, Tsunami vulnerability and risk assessment using machine learning and landsat 8, MATRIK: Jurnal Manajemen, Teknik Informatika dan Rekayasa Komputer 22 (2) (2023) 365–380, https://doi.org/10.30812/matrik.v22i2.2677.

[12] J. Hou *et al.*, "Tsunami risk change analysis for qidong county of China based on land use classification," 2023.

[13] B. Adriano, N. Yokoya, J. Xia, G. Baier, and S. Koshimura, "Cross-domain-classification of tsunami damage via data simulation and residual-network-derived features from multi-source images geoinformatics unit , RIKEN center for advanced intelligence project , Japan international research institute of disaster scie," igarss 2019, pp. 4947–4950, 2019.

[14] W. Jeon, Y. Kim, Investigation of hybrid polarimetric features for tsunami-induced damage assessment of urban areas, Remote Sens. Lett. 10 (10) (2019) 988–997, https://doi.org/10.1080/2150704X.2019.1637957.

[15] K. Chaurasia, S. Kanse, A. Yewale, V.K. Singh, B. Sharma, B.R. Dattu, Predicting damage to buildings caused by earthquakes using machine learning techniques, in: Proc. 2019 IEEE 9th Int. Conf. Adv. Comput, IACC, 2019, pp. 81–86, https://doi.org/10.1109/IACC48062.2019.8971453.

[16] M. Syifa, P.R. Kadavi, C.W. Lee, An artificial intelligence application for post-earthquake damage mapping in palu, Central Sulawesi, Indonesia, Sensors 19 (3) (2019), https://doi.org/10.3390/s19030542.
[17] L. Moya, C. Geis, M. Hashimoto, E. Mas, S. Koshimura, G. Strunz, Disaster intensity-based selection of training samples for remote sensing building damage classification, IEEE Trans. Geosci. Rem. Sens. 59 (10) (2021) 8288–8304, https://doi.org/10.1109/TGRS.2020.3046004.
[18] V.V.R. Maa, A. Chaparala, P.K. Jain, H. Karamti, W. Karamti, Monitor the strength status of buildings using hybrid machine learning technique, IEEE Access 11 (January) (2023) 26441–26458, https://doi.org/10.1109/ACCESS.2023.3247499.
[19] L. Moya, et al., Detecting urban changes using phase correlation and ℓ1-based sparse model for early disaster response: A case study of the 2018 Sulawesi Indonesia earthquake-tsunami, Remote Sens. Environ. 242 (July 2019) (2020) 111743, https://doi.org/10.1016/j.rse.2020.111743.
[20] D. Pirrone, F. Bovolo, L. Bruzzone, An approach to unsupervised detection of fully and partially destroyed buildings in multitemporal VHR SAR images, IEEE J. Sel. Top. Appl. Earth Obs. Remote Sens. 13 (2020) 5938–5953, https://doi.org/10.1109/JSTARS.2020.3026838.
[21] K. Goda, N. Mori, T. Yasuda, Rapid tsunami loss estimation using regional inundation hazard metrics derived from stochastic tsunami simulation, Int. J. Disaster Risk Reduct. 40 (2019) 101152, https://doi.org/10.1016/j.ijdrr.2019.101152.
[22] H. Fan, S. Quan, D. Dai, X. Wang, S. Xiao, Refined model-based and feature-driven extraction of buildings from PolSAR images, Remote Sens. 11 (11) (2019) 1–15, https://doi.org/10.3390/rs11111379.
[23] E. Ferrentino, A. Marino, F. Nunziata, M. Migliaccio, A dual–polarimetric approach to earthquake damage assessment, Int. J. Rem. Sens. 40 (1) (2019) 197–217, https://doi.org/10.1080/01431161.2018.1511935.
[24] S. Havivi, S.R. Rotman, D.G. Blumberg, S. Maman, Damage assessment in rural environments following natural disasters using multi-sensor remote sensing data, Sensors 22 (24) (2022), https://doi.org/10.3390/s22249998.
[25] F. Chollet, "Xception : Deep learning with depthwise separable convolutions," in 2017 IEEE Conference on Computer Vision and Pattern Recognition, pp. 1251–1258, 2017, arXiv:1610.02357.
[26] B. Kalantar, N. Ueda, H. A. H. Al-najjar, and A. A. Halin, "Assessment of convolutional neural network architectures for earthquake-induced building damage detection based on pre- and post-event orthophoto images," 2020.
[27] S. Tang, Z. Chen, Understanding natural disaster scenes from Mobile images using deep learning, Appl. Sci. 11 (9) (2021), https://doi.org/10.3390/app11093952.
[28] J. Sublime, E. Kalinicheva, Automatic post-disaster damage mapping using deep-learning techniques for change detection: Case study of the tohoku tsunami, Remote Sens. 11 (9) (2019), https://doi.org/10.3390/rs11091123.
[29] B. Adriano, et al., ISPRS journal of photogrammetry and remote sensing learning from multimodal and multitemporal Earth observation data for building damage mapping, ISPRS J. Photogrammetry Remote Sens. 175 (February) (2021) 132–143, https://doi.org/10.1016/j.isprsjprs.2021.02.016.
[30] L. Deng, Y. Wang, Post-disaster building damage assessment based on improved U-Net, Sci. Rep. 12 (1) (2022) 1–13, https://doi.org/10.1038/s41598-022-20114-w.
[31] A. Ismail and M. Awad, "BLDNet: A semi-supervised change detection building damage framework using graph convolutional networks and urban domain knowledge," 2022, [Online]. Available: http://arxiv.org/abs/2201.10389.
[32] R. Trevino, V. Sawal, and K. Yang, "GIN & TONIC : Graph infused networks with topological neurons for inference & classification," 2020, [Online]. Available: http://cs230.stanford.edu/projects_winter_2020/reports/32621646.pdf.
[33] S. Saha, G. S. Member, F. Bovolo, S. Member, and L. Bruzzone, "Building change detection in VHR SAR images via unsupervised deep transcoding," pp. 1–13, 2020.
[34] J. Xia, N. Yokoya, and B. Adriano, "Building damage mapping with self-positiveunlabeled learning," 2021, [Online]. Available: http://arxiv.org/abs/2111.02586.
[35] Y. Bai, J. Su, Y. Zou, B. Adriano, Knowledge distillation based lightweight building damage assessment using satellite imagery of natural disasters, GeoInformatica 27 (2) (2023) 237–261, https://doi.org/10.1007/s10707-022-00480-3.
[36] F. Wu, C. Wang, B. Zhang, H. Zhang, L. Gong, Discrimination of collapsed buildings from remote sensing imagery using deep neural networks, Int. Geosci. Remote Sens. Symp. 28 (2019) 2646–2649, https://doi.org/10.1109/IGARSS.2019.8898183.
[37] K. Simonyan, A. Zisserman, Very Deep Convolutional Networks for Large-Scale Image Recognition. arXiv:1409.1556, 2015.
[38] C. Szegedy, V. Vanhoucke, S. Ioffe, J. Shlens, Z. Wojna, Rethinking the inception architecture for computer vision, in: Proceedings of the IEEE Conference on Computer Vision and Pattern Recognition (CVPR), 2016, pp. 2818–2826, https://doi.org/10.1109/CVPR.2016.308.
[39] J. Sakamoto, "Proposal of a disrupted road detection method in a tsunami event using deep learning and spatial data," 2023.
[40] T. Yasuno, M. Amakata, J. Fujii, Y. Shimamoto, Color-Base Damage Feature Enhanced Support Vector Classifier for Monitoring Quake Image, LNCS. Springer International Publishing, 2019, https://doi.org/10.1007/978-3-030-13940-7_20.
[41] C.S. Widjaja, A.A.S. Gunawan, E. Irwansyah, Tsunami building damage assessment using multiclass segmentation model, Int. J. Intell. Syst. Appl. Eng. 10 (4) (2022) 498–506.
[42] V. Benson, A. Ecker, Assessing Out-Of-Domain Generalization for Robust Building Damage Detection, NeurIPS, 2020, pp. 1–8.
[43] D.A.D.A. Nathania, A.A.S. Gunawan, E. Irwansyah, PRESSNet: Assessment of building damage caused by the earthquake, Int. J. Adv. Comput. Sci. Appl. 14 (9) (2023) 888–894, https://doi.org/10.14569/IJACSA.2023.0140993.
[44] Z. Li, C. Tang, X. Liu, X. Hu, X. Li, N. Li, C. Li, Hard Region Aware Network for Remote Sensing Change Detection. arXiv:2305.19513, 2024.
[45] W. Yang, X. Zhang, P. Luo, Transferability of convolutional neural network models for identifying damaged buildings due to earthquake, Remote Sens. 13 (3) (2021) 1–20, https://doi.org/10.3390/rs13030504.

[46] J. Rodwell and J. H. Williams, "Empirical fragility assessment of three-waters and railway infrastructure damaged by the 2015 illapel tsunami, Chile," 2023.

[47] S.M.S. Ahmed, H. Güneyli, Automatic post-tsunami loss modeling using deep learning CNN case study: Miyagi and Fukushima Japan tsunami, Nat. Hazards 117 (3) (2023) 3371–3397, https://doi.org/10.1007/s11069-023-05991-2.

[48] Z. Zheng, Y. Zhong, J. Wang, A. Ma, L. Zhang, Remote sensing of environment building damage assessment for rapid disaster response with a deep object-based semantic change detection framework : From natural disasters to man-made disasters, Remote Sens. Environ. 265 (July) (2021) 112636, https://doi.org/10.1016/j.rse.2021.112636.

Chapter 18

Intersection of chaos theory and artificial intelligence: Concepts, enhancements, and future directions

Behnaz Nouhi[1], Siamak Talatahari[1, 2, 3], Amin Beheshti[2], Fang Chen[1] and Amir H. Gandomi[1, 4]

[1]*Data Science Institute, Faculty of Engineering & Information Technology, University of Technology Sydney, Ultimo, NSW, Australia;* [2]*School of Computing, Macquarie University, Sydney, NSW, Australia;* [3]*Department of Computer Science, Khazar University, Baku, Azerbaijan;* [4]*University Research and Innovation Center (EKIK), Óbuda University, Budapest, Hungary*

1. Introduction

In recent decades, artificial intelligence (AI) has revolutionized numerous fields, ranging from healthcare [1] and finance [2] to robotics [3] and scientific discovery [4]. At the same time, chaos theory has provided valuable insights into nonlinear and unpredictable behaviors in nature and engineered systems [5–7]. The intersection of these two domains presents a compelling frontier for exploration, as chaotic systems can enhance AI methodologies [8], while AI can, in turn, provide new perspectives on understanding and controlling chaotic phenomena [9,10]. This synergy has led to innovative applications in Optimization [11], Machine Learning (ML) [12], and Dynamical Systems [13], opening pathways for more efficient and resilient computational models [14,15].

This chapter explores how chaos theory enhances AI by examining existing methods and identifying future opportunities. It delves into fundamental concepts of chaos theory, including dynamical systems and key characteristics of chaotic behavior, and their role in improving AI techniques. Specifically, the review focuses on optimization algorithms and machine learning, demonstrating how chaos-driven methodologies enhance performance and adaptability.

This chapter is organized as follows. Section 2 presents the fundamental principles of chaos theory, highlighting its core properties and various types of dynamical and chaotic systems. Section 3 examines the integration of chaos into AI methods, showcasing its impact on optimization and machine learning. Section 4 discusses key challenges and open questions in this field while also exploring future directions and potential advancements in chaos-driven AI. Finally, the chapter concludes with a summary of key insights and reflections on the broader implications of this interdisciplinary approach.

2. Fundamentals of chaos theory

2.1 Definition of a dynamical system

A system refers to a set of interrelated components or variables that collectively influence its overall function or behavior [16]. These components may be physical entities, abstract concepts, or a combination of both. The system is defined by the relationships and interactions between these components, which collectively describe a process, phenomenon, or set of behaviors [17]. In mathematical terms, a system is often described by a set of state variables that capture specific characteristics of its condition at any given moment.

A dynamical system specifically refers to systems where the state evolves over time, driven by these rules or equations, [18,19]. This evolution is governed by mathematical formulations that describe the relationship between the state variables and related rates of change. For continuous systems, this evolution is often expressed through differential

Advanced Intelligence Methods for Data Science and Optimization. https://doi.org/10.1016/B978-0-443-28940-8.00022-1

equations, which describe the infinitesimal changes in state over time. In contrast, discrete systems are modeled using difference equations, where the state changes at discrete intervals.

Dynamical systems can vary widely in their complexity. On one end of the spectrum, they might represent simple mechanical systems, such as the motion of a pendulum [20] or the oscillation of a spring [21], where the interactions and equations are relatively straightforward. On the other end, they can describe highly complex systems, such as ecological networks [22], the spread of diseases [23], or economic markets [24], where multiple interdependent variables interact in intricate ways. These systems may demonstrate a range of behaviors, including periodic oscillations, chaotic behavior, or steady-state equilibrium.

2.2 Types of dynamical systems

Dynamical systems can be categorized in different ways according to their configuration, evolution patterns, and governing mathematical models [25]. These include the following categories.

2.2.1 Linear versus nonlinear systems

- **Linear Systems:** In linear dynamical systems, the relationships between variables are proportional and additive. The state variables evolve in a predictable, straightforward manner. A linear system can be represented by a simple equation [26]:

$$\dot{x}(t) = Ax(t) \tag{18.1}$$

where $x(t)$ is the state vector and A is a constant matrix. Solutions to such systems typically exhibit simple behaviors such as exponential growth or decay, making them easier to analyze and predict.

- **Nonlinear Systems:** In nonlinear dynamical systems, the relationships between variables are more complex, and the system's behavior can change drastically depending on parameters and initial conditions. Nonlinear systems are described by equations where state variables are raised to higher powers or multiplied by one another [27]. For example, the Lotka-Volterra model of predator-prey dynamics is a nonlinear system [28]:

$$\begin{aligned} \frac{dx}{dt} &= \alpha x - \beta xy \\ \frac{dy}{dt} &= \delta xy - \gamma y \end{aligned} \tag{18.2}$$

In these equations, x is the prey population, y is the predator population, and α, β, δ, and γ are constants.

2.2.2 Conservative versus dissipative systems

- **Conservative Systems:** These systems are those where certain quantities, such as energy, remain constant over time. In dynamical systems, this means that there is no net loss or gain in the system's total state—whatever is "conserved" (whether it's energy, momentum, or another property) does not change as the system evolves [29]. A classic example of a conservative system is the Hamiltonian system, where the total energy (kinetic plus potential) remains constant throughout the system's evolution. The general form of a Hamiltonian system is described by Hamilton's equations [30], as follows:

$$\frac{d}{dt}\begin{pmatrix} q \\ p \end{pmatrix} = \begin{pmatrix} \frac{\partial H}{\partial p} \\ -\frac{\partial H}{\partial q} \end{pmatrix} \tag{18.3}$$

where q and p are generalized coordinates and momenta, and $H(q,p)$ is the Hamiltonian function. The solutions to these systems typically exhibit periodic or quasi-periodic motion, where energy is preserved over time.

- **Dissipative Systems:** These systems are characterized by the loss of certain quantities over time, such as energy, which tends to degrade or dissipate through processes such as friction, resistance, or external forces [31]. This dissipation results in a gradual reduction of the system's energy or other conserved quantities, often leading to the system settling into a steady state or equilibrium. In more general terms, dissipative systems are often modeled in contexts such as optimization algorithms or signal processing, where the system loses efficiency or reduces noise over time. For example, in a damped harmonic oscillator (as a model in mechanical systems), energy is lost with each oscillation, and the amplitude of the oscillations gradually decreases over time. Mathematically, this can be expressed by the equation [32]:

$$\frac{d^2x}{dt^2} + \gamma\frac{dx}{dt} + \omega^2 x = 0 \tag{18.4}$$

where γ is the damping coefficient and ω is the angular frequency. In optimization, such systems can represent convergence dynamics, where the "energy" (or error) decreases as the system approaches an optimal solution.

2.2.3 Stable, periodic and unstable systems

- **Stable Systems:** A stable system is characterized by its ability to resist major behavioral changes in response to minor disturbances or shifts from equilibrium, [33]. In other words, when the system is disturbed, it returns to its equilibrium state or oscillates around it without diverging uncontrollably. Mathematically, a system is stable if, after a small perturbation, the state of the system either returns to a fixed point or remains bounded around it. The concept of stability is formalized using Lyapunov's stability criteria [34], which helps in determining whether the system remains close to equilibrium over time. For a system to be asymptotically stable, its state variables must tend toward a fixed point as time progresses, even in the presence of small disturbances. For example, consider a damped harmonic oscillator governed by the differential equation [32]:

$$\frac{d^2x}{dt^2} + 2\xi\omega\frac{dx}{dt} + \omega^2 x = 0 \tag{18.5}$$

where, $x(t)$ is the position of the mass, ω is the natural angular frequency, and ξ is the damping ratio. In this case, any perturbation results in oscillations that gradually decay to zero, meaning the system returns to equilibrium over time, making it a stable system.

- **Marginally Stable Systems:** A system is considered marginally stable or neutrally stable if disturbances do not cause the system to grow indefinitely, nor do they cause the system to decay back to equilibrium. Instead, the system remains in a new state indefinitely or oscillates around equilibrium without returning to a fixed point. The behavior of these systems can be oscillatory without decaying over time [35]. A classic example is a simple harmonic oscillator [36], which the following second-order differential equation can model:

$$\frac{d^2x}{dt^2} + \omega^2 x = 0 \tag{18.6}$$

where $x(t)$ represents the position of the mass, and ω is the angular frequency. The solution to this equation describes oscillations around the equilibrium point $x = 0$. If the system is disturbed, it will oscillate around the equilibrium without growing unbounded confirming system stability. In this case, the system will oscillate indefinitely without any damping, meaning the amplitude of oscillation remains constant and does not return to a fixed point, making it marginally stable.

- **Periodic Systems:** A periodic system exhibits repeating cycles or behaviors over time, meaning the system's state returns to its initial configuration after a fixed time interval, [37]. The defining characteristic of a periodic system is the existence of a period T such that:

$$x(t+T) = x(t) \ \ for\ all\ t \tag{18.7}$$

where T is the period of the system. These systems oscillate or evolve cyclically, with the same pattern repeating indefinitely. A classic example of a periodic system is the motion of planets around the sun, which follows elliptical orbits as described by Kepler's laws, [38]. The gravitational force between the planet and the sun leads to an oscillatory motion, where the planet repeatedly moves along the same orbit after a fixed period. The equation governing the motion of a planet in a two-body system (simplified version) [39] can be written as:

$$\frac{d^2\boldsymbol{r}}{dt^2} = -\frac{GM}{|\boldsymbol{r}|^3}\boldsymbol{r} \tag{18.8}$$

where $\boldsymbol{r}$ denotes the position vector of the planet, M is the mass of the sun, G is the gravitational constant, and t is time. This equation describes the orbital motion of a planet, and the system's behavior is periodic, with the planet returning to the same position after each orbit.

- **Unstable Systems:** Conversely, an unstable system responds to minor variations in initial conditions with significantly divergent outcomes as time progresses. In an unstable system, disturbances do not decay over time; instead, they cause the system's state to diverge further from equilibrium, often leading to unpredictable and complex behavior, [40]. Such behavior is frequently seen in systems governed by nonlinear dynamics, where the interaction between system variables is not proportional and can result in exponential growth or decay, [41]. For example, consider the Lorenz system [42], which is a set of nonlinear differential equations used to model atmospheric convection:

$$\begin{aligned} \frac{dx}{dt} &= \sigma(y - x) \\ \frac{dy}{dt} &= x(\rho - z) - y \\ \frac{dz}{dt} &= xy - \beta z \end{aligned} \tag{18.9}$$

where σ, ρ, and β are system parameters. For certain values of these parameters, small differences in initial conditions can result in exponentially diverging trajectories, characteristic of chaotic behavior. For chaotic parameter regimes, trajectories do not settle to a fixed equilibrium; instead, they remain bounded while showing sensitive dependence on initial conditions.

2.2.4 Continuous versus discrete systems

- **Continuous systems:** These systems evolve continuously over time, typically governed by ordinary or partial differential equations (ODEs or PDEs). They model processes where time progresses without interruption, and state variables change smoothly [43]. The general form is as follows:

$$\frac{dx}{dt} = f(x, t) \tag{18.10}$$

where, $x(t)$ is the state vector as a function of time, $f(x,t)$ represents the system's dynamics, which can depend on both the state and time.

A well-studied example of a continuous dynamical system is the motion of a pendulum [44], which the following second-order differential equation can model:

$$\frac{d^2\theta}{dt^2} + \frac{g}{L}\sin(\theta) = 0 \tag{18.11}$$

where $\theta(t)$ is the angular displacement, L is the length of the pendulum, and g is the acceleration due to gravity. The pendulum's motion is continuous, and the system follows the laws of motion governed by this differential equation. Another important example of continuous systems is fluid dynamics, which describes the motion of fluids. This can be represented by the Navier–Stokes equations [45], which are a set of PDEs describing the flow of incompressible fluids:

$$\frac{\partial \boldsymbol{u}}{\partial t} + (\boldsymbol{u}.\nabla)\boldsymbol{u} = -\nabla p + \nu\nabla^2\boldsymbol{u} \tag{18.12}$$

where, $\boldsymbol{u}$ is the velocity field, ν is the kinematic viscosity of the fluid, and p is the pressure. These equations describe how velocity and pressure fields evolve over time in a fluid, taking into account forces such as pressure gradients and viscosity.

- **Discrete Systems:** Discrete systems evolve in discrete steps, where the state changes at distinct time intervals, often governed by different equations or iterative maps. In these systems, the evolution of the state is described in terms of values at different time points, rather than continuously over time, [46]. The general form is as follows:

$$x_{n+1} = f(x_n) \tag{18.13}$$

where, x_n represents the state at the nth time step, $f(x_n)$ describes how the system evolves from one state to the next.

As an example, a basic model of population growth is represented by the logistic map. The population at the next time step is determined by the population at the current time step and a growth function:

$$x_{n+1} = rx_n(1 - x_n) \tag{18.14}$$

where x_n is the population at the nth time step (normalized to the range $0 \leq x_n \leq 1$), and r denotes the growth rate. This discrete model captures the idea of a population growing exponentially at first but then slowing down as resources become limited. The dynamics of this system can lead to stable populations, periodic oscillations, or chaotic behavior, depending on the value of r [47,48].

2.3 Chaotic systems

Chaos theory studies deterministic nonlinear dynamical systems that can show sensitive dependence on initial conditions, aperiodic behaviour, and bounded long-term dynamics. [49]. This concept suggests that even small variations in initial conditions can result in drastically different outcomes over time, making prediction highly challenging.

Initially popularized by Edward Lorenz in the 1960s through his research on weather prediction [50], chaos theory has since found applications in physics, biology, engineering, meteorology, economics, and computer science, [49]. At its core, it examines how deterministic systems—those governed by well-defined equations—can exhibit seemingly random or unpredictable behavior due to complex internal feedback mechanisms.

This unpredictability underscores the importance of precise measurements and calculations, as even minor inaccuracies can cause significant deviations in system behavior over time. While this sensitivity poses challenges for forecasting and control, it has also driven advances in computational modeling and AI, enabling better analysis of chaotic systems. Despite its inherent difficulties, chaos theory has provided profound insights into unpredictability, complex system dynamics, and real-world phenomena, influencing fields ranging from climate science to financial markets, [51].

2.4 Key features of chaotic systems

Chaotic systems exhibit several distinct characteristics that differentiate them from simple deterministic or purely random systems. These properties highlight the intricate balance between order and unpredictability in chaotic behavior [49].

- **Sensitivity to Initial Conditions:** A key characteristic of chaotic systems is their heightened sensitivity to initial conditions, often called the butterfly effect. This means that even the tiniest variations in initial conditions can result in significantly divergent outcomes as time progresses. In practical terms, this makes long-term prediction virtually impossible, as small measurement errors or external influences can rapidly amplify, causing the system to diverge unpredictably.
- **Deterministic Nature:** Despite their apparent randomness, chaotic systems are fundamentally deterministic, meaning they are governed by well-defined mathematical rules and equations. Unlike purely random systems, where outcomes are entirely unpredictable due to stochastic processes, chaotic systems evolve according to specific laws of motion. However, due to their nonlinearity and sensitivity to initial conditions, their behavior appears random and unpredictable in practice. This deterministic yet unpredictable nature makes chaotic systems distinct from both orderly mechanical systems and completely random processes.
- **Nonlinearity:** Chaotic systems are inherently nonlinear, meaning their behavior cannot be described by simple proportional relationships. Small changes in inputs do not lead to proportional changes in outputs; instead, they can cause disproportionate and complex effects. This nonlinearity arises from feedback loops and interactions within the system, making chaotic dynamics difficult to model using traditional linear equations.

- **Aperiodicity:** In contrast to periodic systems, which exhibit repeating cycles over time, chaotic systems display aperiodic behavior—their trajectories never settle into a repetitive pattern, even though they remain bounded within a finite range. This means that while a chaotic system does not exhibit regular cycles, its state variables do not diverge to infinity either. Instead, they fluctuate within a certain range, following complex but structured dynamics. This property is particularly relevant in natural systems such as heart rhythms and fluid turbulence, where signals appear irregular but are still constrained within physical limits.
- **Fractal Structures:** Many chaotic systems exhibit self-similar fractal patterns when analyzed in phase space. These fractal structures arise because chaotic dynamics often involve repeated patterns at different scales, a property known as self-similarity. For example, the Lorenz attractor, a well-known chaotic system, forms a fractal-like structure when visualized (Fig. 18.1a). These fractals are a direct consequence of the system's intricate internal feedback loops and recursive behavior, making fractal analysis an essential tool for studying chaos.
- **Strange Attractors:** In dynamical systems, an attractor refers to a set of states that a system naturally gravitates toward over time. While simple systems may have fixed-point attractors (where the system settles to a single state) or limit-cycle attractors (where the system follows a stable periodic orbit), chaotic systems display strange attractors—intricate, nonrepeating patterns that govern their behavior over time. These attractors demonstrate the underlying order within chaos, revealing how chaotic trajectories remain confined to a structured yet nonrepetitive region in phase space. The Lorenz attractor (Fig. 18.1a) and the Rössler attractor (Fig. 18.1b) are classic examples of strange attractors, illustrating the intricate and highly sensitive nature of chaotic motion.
- **Mixing and Ergodic Property:** Chaotic systems exhibit strong mixing behavior, meaning that trajectories that start close together in phase space will eventually become completely uncorrelated over time. In systems where ergodicity holds, long trajectories sample the accessible region of phase space in a statistically representative way. Ergodicity is often linked to statistical mechanics, where chaotic motion helps distribute energy efficiently in physical systems.
- **Topological Transitivity:** Chaotic systems demonstrate topological transitivity, meaning that for any two open regions of the attractor, some trajectory starting in one region eventually enters the other. This implies that the system does not remain confined to localized regions of phase space but rather explores a broad range of possible states, contributing to its apparent randomness.
- **Long-Term Unpredictability:** Unlike periodic or stable systems, where future states can be accurately predicted, chaotic systems display an exponential divergence of nearby trajectories (quantified by the Lyapunov exponent). Even though they are governed by deterministic rules, their long-term evolution becomes unpredictable due to the compounding effects of small perturbations.
- **Bifurcations and Route to Chaos:** Chaotic behavior often emerges through bifurcations, where small parameter changes cause a system to shift from stable periodic motion to progressively more complex dynamics. A common pathway to chaos is the period-doubling route, where a system undergoes a sequence of successive period doublings before entering a chaotic regime. This phenomenon is observed in fluid turbulence, electrical circuits, and population dynamics.

2.5 Chaotic systems versus unstable systems

Chaotic systems show local sensitivity to initial conditions, but they may remain bounded on attracting sets. They should therefore be distinguished from simple divergence from equilibrium. However, chaos is typically treated as a distinct class because its behavior is fundamentally different from other types of instability. Therefore, we may consider chaotic systems as a distinct class. Here's why chaos is treated as a separate class, despite its inherent instability [18].

2.5.1 Divergence, instability, and sensitivity to initial conditions

- Unstable Systems: Small perturbations lead to divergence from equilibrium in a straightforward manner with a relatively predictable and consistent pattern.
- Chaotic Systems: Even minor variations in initial conditions can result in vastly different outcomes as time progresses. The divergence is more complex, exhibiting nonlinear and intricate instability due to the butterfly effect.

2.5.2 Predictability and unpredictability

- Unstable Systems: While they diverge from equilibrium, they do not exhibit the highly unpredictable patterns seen in chaotic systems.
- Chaotic Systems: Despite being deterministic, chaotic systems appear random and unpredictable over time, even though they follow deterministic equations.

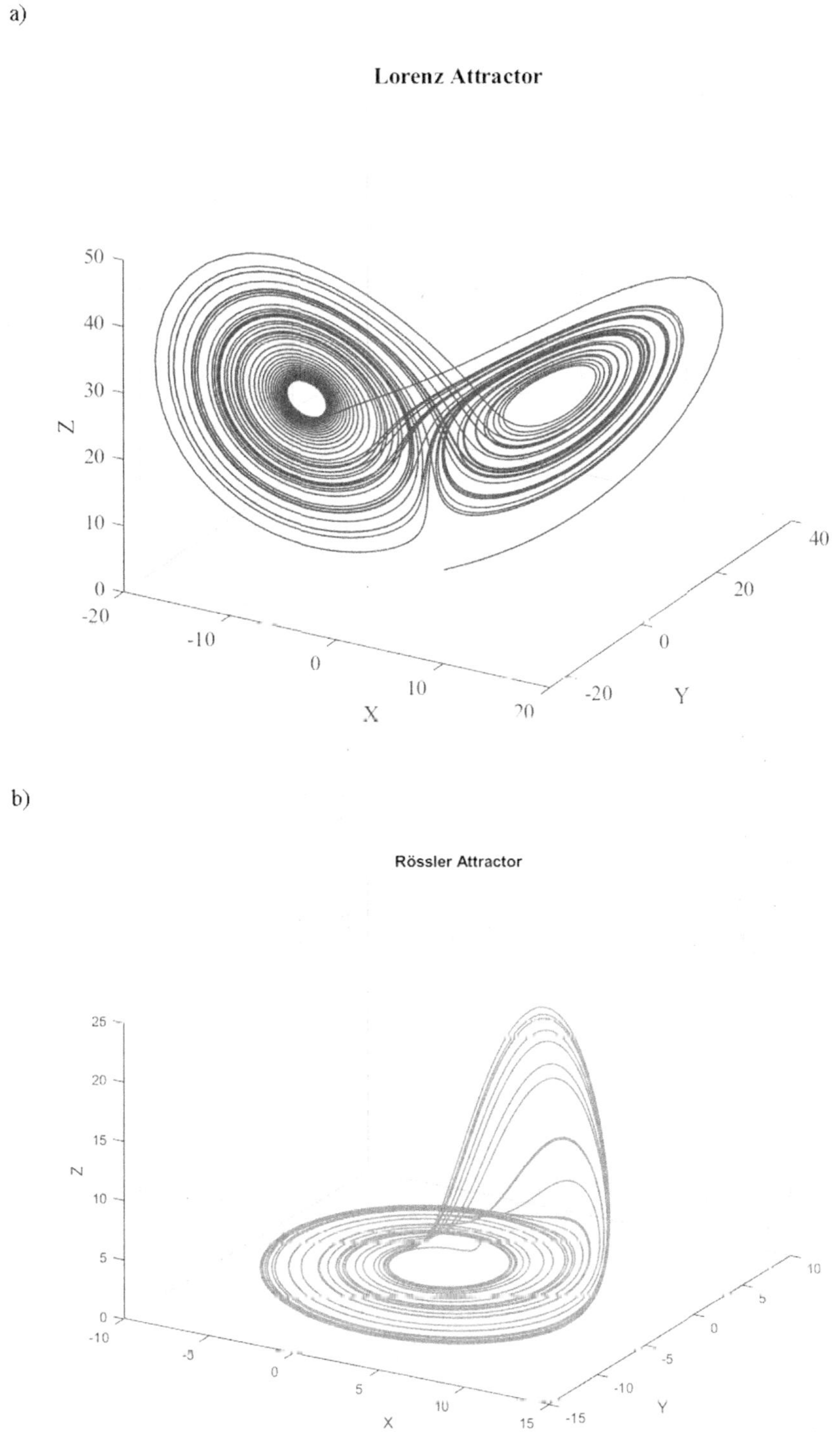

FIGURE 18.1 Visualization of chaotic attractors: (a) Lorenz attractors; (b) Rossler attractor.

2.5.3 Long-term behavior and predictability

- Unstable Systems: These systems diverge straightforwardly, often exponentially, leading to eventual divergence to infinity or a runaway state. While they are unpredictable in the long term, their divergence follows a simple, predictable pattern.

- Chaotic Systems: Chaotic systems also diverge but in a more complex, nonlinear manner. Despite being deterministic, their behavior is highly unpredictable. They do not follow simple, predictable trajectories, instead exhibiting irregular and bounded behavior over time, often with oscillations or complex dynamics.

2.5.4 Complexity and fractal behavior

- Unstable Systems: These systems exhibit simple instability, typically lacking the fractal behavior or complex patterns characteristic of chaotic systems.
- Chaotic Systems: Chaotic systems often display fractal structures in their state space, with strange attractors reflecting the complexity and deterministic unpredictability that distinguishes chaos from simple instability.

2.5.5 Nonlinear dynamics and mathematical framework

- Unstable Systems: These systems are usually represented by nonlinear differential equations, which can result in exponential growth or simple divergence in their behavior. The dynamics are governed by deterministic laws, but they tend to follow relatively predictable patterns over time.
- Chaotic Systems: Chaotic systems arise from nonlinear dynamics, where feedback loops and complex interactions lead to irregular yet deterministic behavior. While chaotic systems are also described by nonlinear differential equations, their sensitivity to initial conditions leads to unpredictable long-term behavior, resulting in a more intricate and detailed form of instability compared with other unstable systems.

2.5.6 Phase space behavior

- Unstable Systems: They show simple, often exponential divergence in phase space, with trajectories moving away from equilibrium in a predictable manner.
- Chaotic Systems: These systems exhibit strange attractors in phase space, where behavior is confined to a bounded region but appears irregular and unpredictable.

To sum up, although chaotic systems share some characteristics with unstable systems (such as sensitivity to initial conditions and divergence from equilibrium), their complex behavior, unpredictability, and fractal-like trajectories are what often justify treating them as a distinct class. Chaos represents a unique type of instability that is not just about divergence but about nonlinear, complex dynamics that don't fit neatly into the broader category of instability. Therefore, treating chaos as a separate class allows for a better understanding of its unique properties and behaviors.

3. Enhancing artificial intelligence using chaos theory

In traditional methods, systems are typically designed to follow a set of well-defined, deterministic rules, where the output is predictable given the input, [52]. However, real-world problems often exhibit complex, nonlinear, and unpredictable behaviors that are difficult to capture using conventional techniques. To address this challenge, AI has been developed as a powerful solution, enabling systems to learn patterns and adapt to uncertainties. At the same time, chaos theory has recently gained significant attention for its ability to model and analyze such complex behaviors. Moreover, incorporating AI techniques with principles from chaos theory can improve the ability of models to represent complex dynamics to tackle complex problems, enhancing both accuracy and adaptability across various fields of applications. This integration empowers AI systems to better simulate real-world complexities, driving progress in fields such as forecasting, optimization, pattern recognition, and machine learning.

The growing intersection of chaos theory and AI has sparked significant research interest, as evidenced by the recent trends in the number of publications in this area. Fig. 18.2(a) illustrates the number of related publications, as recorded by Scopus [53], using the keywords "chaos" or "chaotic" in combination with "machine learning" or "artificial intelligence". The data demonstrates a significant rise in interest in this area over recent years. This growing interest can be attributed to several factors: the increasing availability of complex, high-dimensional datasets that demand more advanced modeling techniques; the recognition that traditional methods often fail to capture the inherent unpredictability of real-world systems; and the increasing need for more robust and adaptive AI systems capable of handling dynamic, uncertain environments.

The distribution of research output across different fields reveals the significant contributions from various disciplines to the growing interest in chaos theory and AI. As shown in Fig. 18.2(b), the majority of research in this area originates

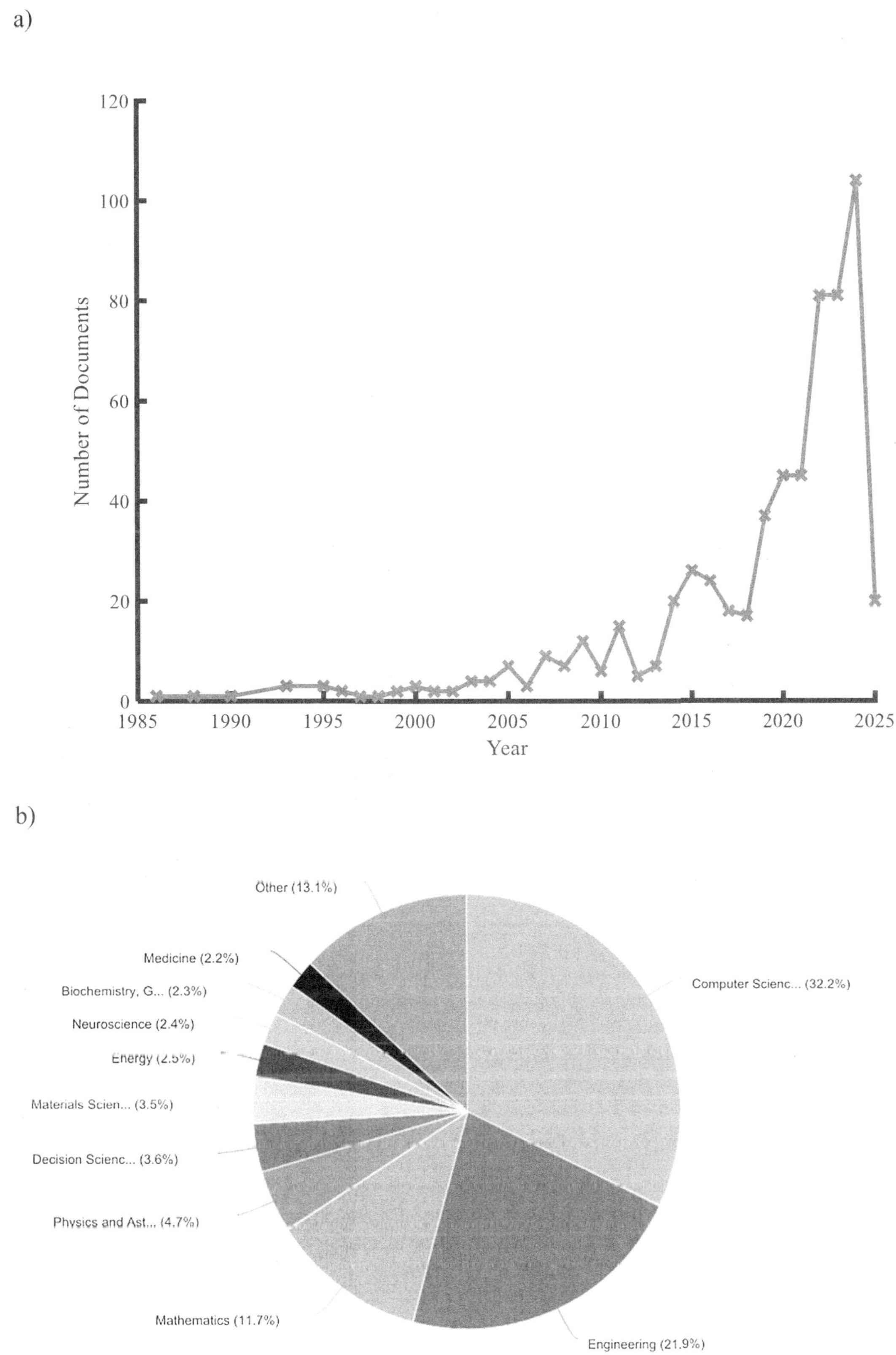

FIGURE 18.2 Growth and distribution of research on chaos theory in AI: (a) Number of publications over time and (b) Research distribution across fields, [53].

from the field of computer science, accounting for approximately 32% of the total publications, followed by engineering, which contributes 22%, [53]. Together, these two fields represent over 50% of the total research output. In the field of computer science, AI models are being enhanced or modified to incorporate chaos theory, improving their ability to handle complex, nonlinear data and to simulate dynamic processes. In engineering, the combination of chaos theory and AI is particularly valuable for addressing some of the most challenging problems where traditional methods often fall short in dealing with system unpredictability. Further exploration of other domains reveals that mathematics, physics, and decision science follow in research contributions. These fields often focus on the theoretical foundations and applications of chaos theory in AI, providing critical insights into its implementation and limitations.

One key feature of chaotic systems is their deterministic unpredictability. While the system follows deterministic rules, the outputs lead to complex and seemingly random behavior. This characteristic of chaos theory has opened new avenues for AI, particularly in enhancing predictive models, optimization techniques, and neural networks. By applying chaos theory, AI researchers have developed more robust, adaptive, and accurate models, which are capable of handling complex problems. The following subsections explore how chaos theory is integrated into AI.

3.1 Chaos-based optimization techniques

Optimization is a key challenge across many fields to identify the best solutions from large and complex solution spaces, [54]. Traditional optimization algorithms, such as gradient-based methods, are effective for many problems but often face difficulties when dealing with nonlinear, high-dimensional, or complex systems. AI-based optimization techniques incorporating metaheuristic concepts have been developed to address these challenges by offering more adaptive and versatile approaches, [55]. However, these methods are not without their limitations. They are suitable for many problems but require adaptation based on specific problem characteristics. Parameter tuning, which greatly influences the performance of these algorithms, is crucial and can be a time-consuming process. Furthermore, balancing exploration (searching for new solutions) and exploitation (refining known good solutions) remains a critical issue that must be carefully managed [56]. As a result, these algorithms often necessitate further steps and modifications to improve their efficiency and effectiveness, [57]. Introducing chaotic optimization methods offers a promising solution to overcome these challenges. By integrating chaotic dynamics, these techniques introduce an element of unpredictability and diversity into the search process, helping algorithms avoid local optima, allowing for a more comprehensive exploration of the solution space, and enhancing the chances of identifying the global optimum. This enhanced exploration ultimately leads to better results in fewer iterations, improving the overall performance of optimization algorithms.

Several chaos-based optimization techniques have emerged, each utilizing chaos theory in different ways to address challenges in optimization methods, [58,59]. Fig. 18.3 presents the publication trends in this field based on Scopus data [53], using the keywords "chaos" or "chaotic" and "optimization" or "optimum." The data highlights a growing interest in chaos-based optimization, driven by the limitations of traditional methods in capturing real-world problems and the demand for more adaptive optimum solutions. As depicted in Fig. 18.2(b), computer science and engineering together account for over half of the research output [53].

These techniques can be broadly categorized into two main classes: those that develop new optimization methods based on chaos theory and those that enhance existing optimization algorithms by incorporating chaotic maps. The first class of methods is centered around the development of entirely new optimization techniques inspired by chaos theory. Chaos Game Optimization (CGO) [60,61] is a prominent example in this category. This method is based on the concept of chaotic systems and is designed to mimic the behavior of chaotic dynamics to perform optimization. The CGO algorithm utilizes a process where solutions evolve through iterative updates, guided by chaotic behavior, allowing for an efficient exploration of complex solution spaces, [60,62]. Another example is the Stochastic Fractal Search (SFS), [63]. This method is inspired by the fractal structures often seen in chaotic systems. It employs stochastic processes that mimic the fractal nature of chaotic dynamics, enhancing the algorithm's ability to search efficiently across high-dimensional and complex spaces. The search process in SFS is designed to exploit self-similar patterns that can emerge in problem spaces, offering improvements in convergence speed and robustness compared with traditional search algorithms. The chaos optimization algorithm proposed by Feng et al. [64] leverages chaotic sequences generated through various chaotic maps. It employs different strategies, using these chaotic maps to transform chaotic variables into optimization variables, enhancing the exploration of the solution space.

The second class focuses on integrating chaos into existing optimization algorithms to improve their performance. The core idea of this approach is to replace random values used in traditional optimization algorithms with values generated by chaotic maps, which introduces greater unpredictability and diversity into the search process. Many studies have incorporated chaos theory into optimization methods to improve their performance. In this section, we highlight a few

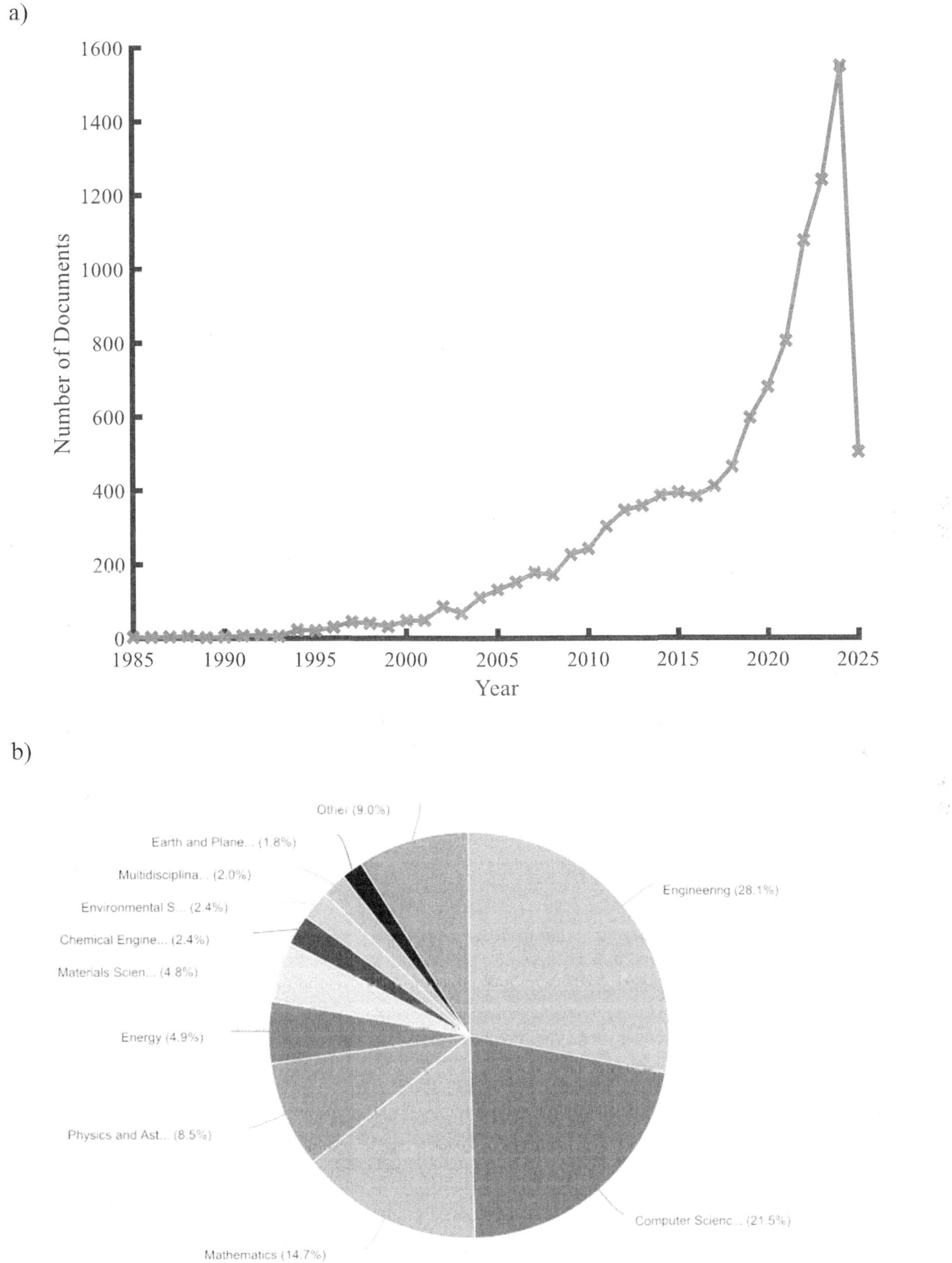

FIGURE 18.3 Growth and distribution of research on chaos theory in optimization: (a) Number of publications over time and (b) Research distribution across fields, [53].

notable examples. One well-known technique in this class is Chaotic Particle Swarm Optimization (CPSO), [65,66], which combines the standard Particle Swarm Optimization (PSO) algorithm with chaotic sequences. In CPSO, the traditional particle velocity update is influenced by chaotic values, enhancing the exploration capabilities of the algorithm and helping it avoid premature convergence. This results in a more thorough and effective search of the solution space, particularly in complex, high-dimensional optimization problems. Similarly, the Chaotic Firefly Algorithm (CFA), [67], is another example of an algorithm in this category. The Firefly Algorithm is enhanced by chaotic behavior to prevent the algorithm from becoming stuck in local optima. The chaotic components modify the movement of fireflies, improving their exploration abilities and improving the exploration of the search space. The Chaotic Imperialist Competitive Algorithm (CICA) [68] is another example that incorporates chaos into the Imperialist Competitive Algorithm (ICA). In this method, chaotic sequences are used to perturb the movement of imperialists and colonies, increasing the diversity of solutions and improving the global search capabilities of the algorithm. This incorporation of chaos helps overcome issues such as premature convergence and stagnation. Furthermore, Chaotic Charged System Search (CCSS) [69] is another chaotic optimization method that combines the principles of chaos theory with a charged system search mechanism. The CCSS algorithm simulates a system of charged particles in an electric field representing potential solutions to the optimization problem. The movement of these particles is influenced by both their charge (fitness) and chaotic dynamics, leading to a better balance exploration/exploitation. This combination of chaos and charged particle dynamics has proven effective in handling complex optimization problems as it facilitates a robust search that adapts to the problem's landscape, ensuring more accurate and efficient convergence to global optima.

3.2 Chaos-based neural networks

Neural networks have revolutionized various fields, including signal processing, pattern recognition, and decision-making, due to their learning ability [70]. However, traditional neural networks face several challenges, particularly in handling highly nonlinear and unpredictable data. Issues such as overfitting, slow convergence, and getting trapped in local minima hinder their effectiveness in complex problem-solving tasks. To address these challenges, researchers have explored integrating chaos theory into neural networks, leading to the development of "chaos-based neural networks". Chaos-based neural networks leverage chaotic dynamics to enhance learning capabilities and improve robustness in handling real-world problems. These methods introduce chaos at different levels of neural network design, such as weight initialization, activation functions, learning rules, and training algorithms. Fig. 18.4 presents the publication statistics from 1985 onwards, shedding light on the growth trajectory of research related to chaos neural networks. As illustrated in Fig. 18.4(a), the overall trend reveals a consistent upward growth in the number of publications, with a brief plateau observed between 2012 and 2015. However, following this period, there has been a notable resurgence in interest, with the number of publications surpassing 1000 in 2024. This indicates a renewed focus and heightened attention from researchers in the field. Fig. 18.4(b) further clarifies the main disciplines contributing to the study of chaos neural networks. Similar to the previous findings, the fields of computer science and engineering dominate, occupying the leading positions in the publication count. This trend underscores the integral role these disciplines play in advancing the application of chaos theory in neural network research.

Chaotic Neural Networks (CNNs), first introduced by Aihara et al. [71], utilize chaotic neurons, which exhibit nonlinear dynamical properties, to enhance network flexibility and stability. Unlike traditional neurons, chaotic neurons operate in a regime where minor disturbances can result in substantial variations in network behavior, allowing for more dynamic information processing [72]. Another example is the Chaotic Hopfield Network (CHN), which integrates chaos into the Hopfield network structure, [73]. In CHNs, the activation dynamics of neurons are governed by chaotic functions, improving the network's ability to escape local minima and converge to better solutions.

Another major approach to chaos-based neural networks focuses on improving learning efficiency by incorporating chaotic sequences into training algorithms. This method involves replacing conventional random weight initialization and training strategies with chaotic maps, which generate more diverse and structured search patterns. For example, Chaotic Backpropagation (CBP) uses chaotic sequences to initialize weights and adjust learning rates dynamically. Traditional backpropagation algorithms often suffer from slow convergence and susceptibility to local minima. By introducing chaotic weight updates, CBP enhances the network's capacity to navigate the solution space more effectively, leading to faster and more accurate training [74,75]. Similarly, Chaotic Learning Rate Adjustment modifies the learning rate of a neural network using chaotic maps instead of fixed or adaptive rate schedules. Conventional neural networks rely on fixed learning rates, which may be inefficient for handling different learning phases. In contrast, chaotic learning rate strategies dynamically adjust step sizes based on chaotic sequences, allowing for a better balance between exploration and exploitation during training [76,77].

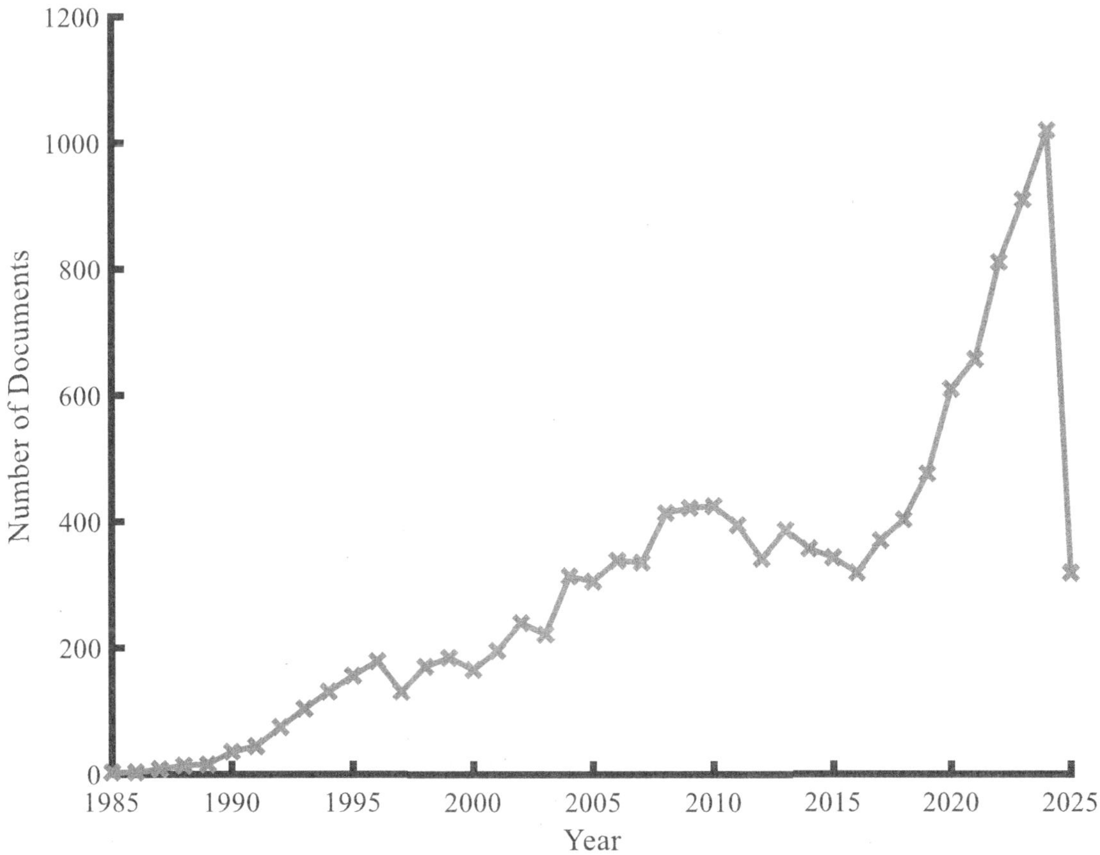

b)

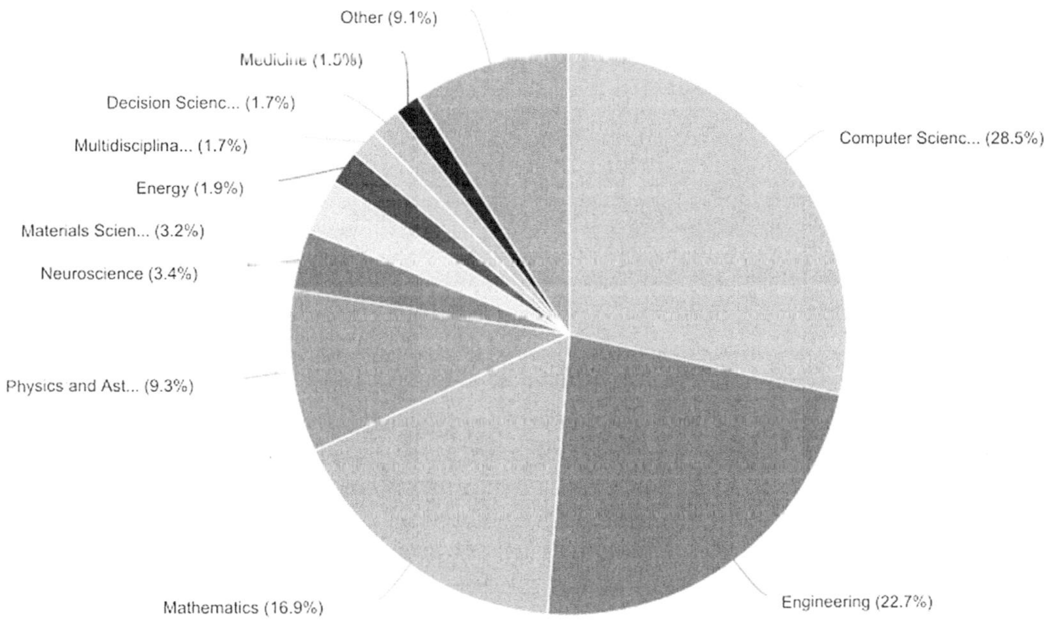

FIGURE 18.4 Growth and distribution of research on chaos neural networks: (a) Number of publications over time and (b) Research distribution across fields, [53].

Another important method is Chaos-Based Stochastic Gradient Descent (CSGD), which introduces chaotic perturbations into the gradient descent process to prevent premature convergence. Unlike traditional SGD, where updates follow a predefined trajectory, CSGD incorporates chaos-induced fluctuations that enable the network to escape poor local minima and explore more optimal solutions [78,79].

3.3 Applications of chaos-based AI

Chaos-based AI has demonstrated substantial potential across various domains, particularly in handling complex, noisy, and nonlinear data. Some key application areas include the following subsections.

3.3.1 Time series prediction

Chaos-based AI models are particularly adept at forecasting chaotic time series data, such as financial markets and weather patterns. By utilizing chaotic dynamics, these models can capture the intricate dependencies within time series data more accurately than traditional methods. For example, chaos-based models have been shown to outperform conventional approaches in financial forecasting and climate prediction [80–82].

3.3.2 Image recognition

In the realm of computer vision, chaotic dynamics have been integrated into convolutional neural networks (CNNs) to enhance feature extraction and classification. Chaotic CNNs employ chaotic activation functions to improve sensitivity to subtle image features, leading to more robust and accurate recognition models [83,84].

3.3.3 Healthcare and medical diagnosis

Chaos-enhanced AI models have found applications in medical imaging and diagnosis, where the ability to detect nonlinear patterns in biological signals is critical. For instance, chaotic deep learning models have shown improvements in the early detection of diseases such as Alzheimer's and cancer by analyzing MRI and CT scan data with greater precision than conventional models [85–87]. These methods offer better adaptability to the complex nature of medical data.

3.3.4 Control systems

Chaos-based AI methods are widely employed in control systems where dynamic adaptability is crucial. These systems are used to improve the stability and performance of control mechanisms in robotics, autonomous vehicles, and industrial automation. Chaos theory enables better handling of unpredictable system behaviors, optimizing performance across a range of real-time applications [88].

3.3.5 Engineering

In engineering, AI, enriched by chaos theory, provides powerful solutions for addressing complex structural and design challenges that traditional methods struggle to solve. Chaos-based AI techniques optimize complex structural and mechanical systems, enhance the design process, and provide insights into maintenance, reducing the computational burden typically required for these tasks [57]. Another notable application is in transportation, where chaos-based AI methods optimize traffic flow in urban areas and improve the efficiency of logistics networks. These methods can be used to simulate transportation systems, helping to address congestion issues, enhance route planning, and improve overall transportation efficiency, offering significant improvements over traditional optimization methods, [89–91].

3.3.6 Environment, climate modeling, and energy

Chaos-based AI methods have revolutionized weather and climate forecasting by enhancing the modeling of complex, nonlinear atmospheric dynamics. These methods enable more reliable forecasting of extreme weather events, such as storms and droughts, while also improving environmental monitoring for air quality and ecosystem changes [92,93].

In addition to forecasting, chaos-based AI plays a key role in optimizing energy systems and environmental management. By applying chaos theory to power grids, AI models help improve energy distribution efficiency, predict demands, and stabilize systems that rely on fluctuating renewable sources such as solar and wind [94,95]. These advancements also aid in predictive maintenance and fault detection, ensuring the resilience and sustainability of energy infrastructure while contributing to better resource management in the face of climate change [96,97].

4. Challenges and limitations of applying chaos theory in AI

While chaos-based AI techniques have demonstrated significant potential across domains, their development and practical deployment face several key challenges. One of the primary issues is the inherent sensitivity of chaotic systems to initial conditions. While this sensitivity enables the modeling of complex, nonlinear behaviors, it can also lead to instability during training and make outcomes highly dependent on parameter tuning. As a result, achieving reproducible and reliable results often requires extensive experimentation and domain-specific adjustments.

Another challenge involves the lack of standardized methodologies and theoretical frameworks for integrating chaos into AI models. Unlike well-established neural network architectures or optimization frameworks, chaos-based methods are still in their developmental phase, with limited consensus on best practices. This complicates benchmarking, comparison, and replication of results across studies. Additionally, many chaos-based models are computationally intensive, particularly when simulating high-dimensional systems or when chaotic behavior is embedded in deep neural networks.

Interpretability and explainability also present significant obstacles. The nonlinear and dynamic nature of chaotic models can obscure the decision-making process, particularly in safety-critical applications such as medicine or autonomous systems. Finally, data quality and availability remain concerns; chaotic systems typically require high-resolution, continuous data to model accurately, which is not always accessible or feasible in real-world settings.

The AI models can introduce ethical and safety concerns, particularly in high-stakes domains such as healthcare, criminal justice, and national security. In these fields, the use of models that exhibit unpredictable or opaque behaviors could have serious and far-reaching consequences, from incorrect medical diagnoses to biased legal decisions or security vulnerabilities.

5. Future directions

The future of chaos-based AI lies in building more robust, scalable, and interpretable systems that can be seamlessly integrated into real-world applications. A crucial step forward involves developing hybrid architectures that combine chaos-based dynamics with stable learning frameworks. These integrations can harness the exploratory benefits of chaos while mitigating instability and improving learning consistency.

Another promising direction is the incorporation of domain knowledge into chaos-driven models. For instance, physics-informed learning or symbolic regression could be paired with chaos-based systems to guide learning with theoretical constraints, improving both generalization and trustworthiness. Research into adaptive control mechanisms may also offer better convergence and performance across tasks.

Emerging computational paradigms such as quantum computing and neuromorphic engineering present new frontiers for chaos-based AI. Quantum chaos, in particular, could lead to novel optimization and forecasting models capable of solving previously intractable problems. Furthermore, integrating chaos-based AI into edge and distributed systems could enhance real-time responsiveness in areas such as smart cities, energy networks, and environmental monitoring.

Ongoing interdisciplinary collaboration between mathematicians, engineers, computer scientists, and domain experts will be vital to overcoming existing limitations and fully harnessing the potential of chaos-enhanced AI. Establishing shared benchmarks, open-source tools, and clearer theoretical foundations will accelerate innovation and facilitate broader adoption across disciplines.

6. Conclusion

Chaos-based AI represents a compelling promising research direction in the design and application of intelligent systems. By embracing the inherent unpredictability and complexity of chaotic dynamics, researchers can push beyond the limitations of traditional deterministic models. As demonstrated across domains such as climate modeling, engineering optimization, and economic forecasting, the synergy between chaos theory and AI unlocks new capabilities for learning from complex, nonlinear systems.

Chaos based optimization methods harness the sensitivity and ergodicity of chaotic maps to improve global search capabilities and escape local optima, offering significant advantages over conventional algorithms. These methods have shown effectiveness in solving high-dimensional and multimodal problems, especially where traditional heuristics fall short. Their adaptability and robustness make them suitable for a wide range of engineering and scientific challenges.

Chaos-based neural networks also offer significant improvements over traditional architectures by embedding chaotic dynamics into both the structure and learning process. These enhancements contribute to better generalization, faster convergence, and increased resilience to overfitting and local minima. As research progresses, such models are expected to have profound impacts in areas demanding high adaptability and precision, such as biomedical engineering, robotics, and complex system modeling.

While the integration of chaos theory into AI offers substantial potential, it is accompanied by several technical and practical challenges. Issues related to interpretability, reproducibility, computational demands, and integration with conventional AI frameworks require careful attention. The lack of standardized evaluation benchmarks, along with ethical concerns surrounding unpredictable behavior—particularly in high-stakes domains—further underscores the need for responsible development and deployment.

Looking ahead, continued research must balance innovation with rigor—advancing new methodologies while addressing current limitations. Interdisciplinary collaboration, ethical foresight, and technical refinement will be key to translating the theoretical potential of chaos-based AI into reliable, impactful solutions. As the field matures, it is poised to reshape how we understand and engineer intelligence in uncertain and dynamic environments.

References

[1] P. Hamet, J. Tremblay, Artificial intelligence in medicine, Metabolism 69 (2017) S36–S40.

[2] S. Ahmed, M.M. Alshater, A. El Ammari, H. Hammami, Artificial intelligence and machine learning in finance: A bibliometric review, Res. Int. Bus. Finance 61 (2022) 101646.

[3] M. Soori, B. Arezoo, R. Dastres, Artificial intelligence, machine learning and deep learning in advanced robotics, a review, Cogn. Robot. 3 (2023) 54–70.

[4] H. Wang, T. Fu, Y. Du, W. Gao, K. Huang, Z. Liu, P. Chandak, S. Liu, P. Van Katwyk, A. Deac, Scientific discovery in the age of artificial intelligence, Nature 620 (2023) 47–60.

[5] D. Rickles, P. Hawe, A. Shiell, A simple guide to chaos and complexity, J. Epidemiol. Community 61 (2007) 933–937.

[6] D. Guegan, Chaos in economics and finance, Annu. Rev. Control 33 (2009) 89–93.

[7] Schöll, E. & Schuster, H. G. 2008. Handbook of chaos control.

[8] E. Ferrara, The butterfly effect in artificial intelligence systems: Implications for AI bias and fairness, Machine Learning with Applications 15 (2024) 100525.

[9] G. Quaranta, W. Lacarbonara, S.F. Masri, A review on computational intelligence for identification of nonlinear dynamical systems, Nonlinear Dyn. 99 (2020) 1709–1761.

[10] B. Ramadevi, K. Bingi, Chaotic time series forecasting approaches using machine learning techniques: A review, Symmetry 14 (2022) 955.

[11] R. Senkerik, I. Zelinka, M. Pluhacek, Chaos-based optimization-a review, J. Adv. Eng. Comput. 1 (2017) 68–79.

[12] A. Osama, S.I. Gadallah, L.A. Said, A.G. Radwan, M.E. Fouda, Chaotic neural network quantization and its robustness against adversarial attacks, Knowl. Base Syst. 286 (2024) 111319.

[13] Y. Horio, Chaotic neural network reservoir, in: 2019 International Joint Conference on Neural Networks (IJCNN), IEEE, 2019, pp. 1–5.

[14] G. Furquim, G. Pessin, B.S. Faiçal, E.M. Mendiondo, J. Ueyama, Improving the accuracy of a flood forecasting model by means of machine learning and chaos theory: A case study involving a real wireless sensor network deployment in Brazil, Neural Comput. Appl. 27 (2016) 1129–1141.

[15] X. Yang, X. Chen, X. Fang, S. Chi, M. Zhu, Improved mining subsidence prediction model for high water level area using machine learning and chaos theory, Energy Explor. Exploit. 40 (2022) 1668–1685.

[16] A.D. Hall, R.E. Fagen, Definition of system, in: Systems Research for Behavioral Science, Routledge, 2017.

[17] A. Backlund, The definition of system, Kybernetes 29 (2000) 444–451.

[18] M. Brin, G. Stuck, Introduction to Dynamical Systems, Cambridge university press, 2002.

[19] D.K. Arrowsmith, C.M. Place, An Introduction to Dynamical Systems, Cambridge university press, 1990.

[20] G.M. Moatimid, T. Amer, Analytical solution for the motion of a pendulum with rolling wheel: Stability analysis, Sci. Rep. 12 (2022) 12628.

[21] K.A. Harper, M.D. Berkemeier, S. Grace, Modeling the dynamics of spring-driven oscillating-foil propulsion, IEEE J. Ocean. Eng. 23 (1998) 285–296.

[22] J.M. Montoya, S.L. Pimm, R.V. Solé, Ecological networks and their fragility, Nature 442 (2006) 259–264.

[23] C.E. Walters, M.M. Meslé, I.M. Hall, Modelling the global spread of diseases: A review of current practice and capability, Epidemics 25 (2018) 1–8.

[24] M. Callon, F. Muniesa, Peripheral vision: Economic markets as calculative collective devices, Organ. Stud. 26 (2005) 1229–1250.

[25] S. Sternberg, Dynamical Systems, Courier Corporation, 2010.

[26] T. Kailath, Linear Systems, Prentice-Hall, Englewood Cliffs, NJ, 1980.

[27] M. Vidyasagar, Nonlinear Systems Analysis, SIAM, 2002.

[28] Q. Din, Dynamics of a discrete lotka-volterra model, Adv. Differ. Equ. 2013 (2013) 1–13.

[29] A. Big-Alabo, V. Ossia, Conservative systems, Progress in relativity 235 (2020).

[30] J.K. Moser, Lectures on Hamiltonian Systems. Hamiltonian Dynamical Systems, CRC Press, 2020.

[31] B. Brogliato, R. Lozano, B. Maschke, O. Egeland, Dissipative systems analysis and control, Theory and Applications 2 (2007) 2–5.

[32] H. Dekker, Classical and quantum mechanics of the damped harmonic oscillator, Phys. Rep. 80 (1981) 1–110.

[33] E. Zeeman, Stability of dynamical systems, Nonlinearity 1 (1988) 115.
[34] C. Pukdeboon, A review of fundamentals of lyapunov theory, J. Appl. Sci. 10 (2011) 55–61.
[35] P. Lancaster, Stability of linear gyroscopic systems: A review, Lin. Algebra Appl. 439 (2013) 686–706.
[36] P. Andreani, A. Bevilacqua, Harmonic oscillators in CMOS—A tutorial overview, IEEE Open Journal of the Solid-State Circuits Society 1 (2021) 2–17.
[37] A. Varga, P. Van Dooren, Computational methods for periodic systems-an overview, IFAC Proc. Vol. 34 (2001) 167–172.
[38] J.A. Burns, The four hundred years of planetary science since galileo and kepler, Nature 466 (2010) 575–584.
[39] K. Tsiganis, Dynamics of small bodies in the solar system, Eur. Phys. J. Spec. Top. 186 (2010) 67–89.
[40] P. Morasso, M. Casadio, D. De Santis, T. Nomura, F. Rea, J. Zenzeri, Stabilization strategies for unstable dynamics, J. Electromyogr. Kinesiol. 24 (2014) 803–814.
[41] H. Yang, B. Jiang, V. Cocquempot, A survey of results and perspectives on stabilization of switched nonlinear systems with unstable modes, Nonlinear Anal. Hybrid Syst 13 (2014) 45–60.
[42] A. Algaba, M.C. Domínguez-Moreno, M. Merino, A.J. Rodríguez-Luis, A review on some bifurcations in the lorenz system, Nonlinear Systems, Vol. 1: Mathematical Theory and Computational Methods 1 (2018) 3–36.
[43] D. Park, Continuous Systems, Classical Dynamics and Its Quantum Analogues, 1979, pp. 302–335.
[44] R. Doerner, B. Hübinger, H. Heng, W. Martienssen, Approaching nonlinear dynamics by studying the motion of a pendulum II: Analyzing chaotic motion, Int. J. Bifurcation Chaos 4 (1994) 761–771.
[45] S.V. Ershkov, E.Y. Prosviryakov, N.V. Burmasheva, V. Christianto, Towards understanding the algorithms for solving the navier–stokes equations, Fluid Dyn. Res. 53 (2021) 044501.
[46] P. Ballard, A. Charles, An overview of the formulation, existence and uniqueness issues for the initial value problem raised by the dynamics of discrete systems with unilateral contact and dry friction, C. R. Mec. 346 (2018) 222–236.
[47] L. Moysis, M. Lawnik, M.S. Baptista, C. Volos, G.F. Fragulis, A review of chaotification techniques for discrete-time systems, Nonlinear Dyn. 113 (2025) 1–17.
[48] Weisstein, E. W. 2001. Logistic map. https://mathworld.wolfram.com/.
[49] R.P. Murphy, Chaos Theory, Ludwig von Mises Institute, 2010.
[50] E.N. Lorenz, Deterministic Nonperiodic Flow 1. *Universality in Chaos*, second ed., Routledge, 2017.
[51] Meta, A. 2016. An overview for chaos fractals and applications.
[52] J.B. Kim, Implementation of artificial intelligence system and traditional system: A comparative study, Journal of System and Management Sciences 9 (2019) 135–146.
[53] Elsevier. 2025. Scopus [Online]. Available: https://www.scopus.com [Accessed 03/04/2025 2025].
[54] M. Toloo, S. Talatahari, I. Rahimi, Multi-Objective Combinatorial Optimization Problems and Solution Methods, Academic Press, 2022.
[55] A. Kaveh, S. Talatahari, A general model for meta-heuristic algorithms using the concept of fields of forces, Acta Mech. 221 (2011) 99–118.
[56] A. Kaveh, R. Sheikholeslami, S. Talatahari, M. Keshvari-Ilkhichi, Chaotic swarming of particles: A new method for size optimization of truss structures, Adv. Eng. Software 67 (2014) 136–147.
[57] X.-S. Yang, S. Talatahari, A.H. Alavi, Metaheuristic Applications in Structures and Infrastructures, Newnes, 2013.
[58] M. Pourbaba, S. Talatahari, R. Sheikholeslami, A chaotic imperialist competitive algorithm for optimum cost design of cantilever retaining walls, KSCE J. Civ. Eng. 17 (2013) 972–979.
[59] B. Nouhi, S. Talatahari, H. Kheiri, Chaos embedded charged system search for practical optimization problems, Int. J. Optimiz. Civ. Eng 3 (2013) 23–36.
[60] S. Talatahari, M. Azizi, Chaos game optimization: A novel metaheuristic algorithm, Artif. Intell. Rev. 54 (2021) 917–1004.
[61] V. Goodarzimehr, S. Talatahari, S. Shojaee, S. Hamzehei-Javaran, P. Sareh, Structural design with dynamic constraints using weighted chaos game optimization, J. Comput. Des. Eng. 9 (2022) 2271–2296.
[62] S. Talatahari, M. Azizi, Optimization of constrained mathematical and engineering design problems using chaos game optimization, Comput. Ind Eng. 145 (2020) 106560.
[63] H. Salimi, Stochastic fractal search: A powerful metaheuristic algorithm, Knowl. Base Syst. 75 (2015) 1–18.
[64] J. Feng, J. Zhang, X. Zhu, W. Lian, A novel chaos optimization algorithm, Multimed. Tool. Appl. 76 (2017) 17405–17436.
[65] A.H. Gandomi, G.J. Yun, X. S. Yang, S. Talatahari, Chaos enhanced accelerated particle swarm optimization, Commun. Nonlinear Sci. Numer. Simulat. 18 (2013b) 327–340.
[66] L.-Y. Chuang, C.-J. Hsiao, C.-H. Yang, Chaotic particle swarm optimization for data clustering, Expert Syst. Appl. 38 (2011) 14555–14563.
[67] A.H. Gandomi, X.-S. Yang, S. Talatahari, A.H. Alavi, Firefly algorithm with chaos, Commun. Nonlinear Sci. Numer. Simulat. 18 (2013a) 89–98.
[68] S. Talatahari, B.F. Azar, R. Sheikholeslami, A. Gandomi, Imperialist competitive algorithm combined with chaos for global optimization, Commun. Nonlinear Sci. Numer. Simulat. 17 (2012) 1312–1319.
[69] S. Talatahari, A. Kaveh, R. Sheikholeslami, An efficient charged system search using chaos for global optimization problems, Int J Optim Civil Eng 1 (2011) 305–325.
[70] Y. Lecun, Y. Bengio, G. Hinton, Deep learning, Nature 521 (2015) 436–444.
[71] K. Aihara, T. Takabe, M. Toyoda, Chaotic neural networks, Phys. Lett. 144 (1990) 333–340.
[72] K. Qin, On chaotic neural network design: A new framework, Neural Process. Lett. 45 (2017) 243–261.

[73] Q. Deng, C. Wang, H. Lin, Chaotic dynamical system of hopfield neural network influenced by neuron activation threshold and its image encryption, Nonlinear Dyn. 112 (2024) 6629–6646.

[74] K. Bertels, L. Neuberg, S. Vassiliadis, D. Pechanek, On chaos and neural networks: The backpropagation paradigm, Artif. Intell. Rev. 15 (2001) 165–187.

[75] F. Fazayeli, L. Wang, W. Liu, Back-propagation with chaos, in: 2008 International Conference on Neural Networks and Signal Processing, IEEE, 2008, pp. 5–8.

[76] M. Islam, M.R. Rana, S.U. Ahmed, A.E. Kabir, M. Shahjahan, Training neural network with chaotic learning rate, in: 2011 International Conference on Emerging Trends in Electrical and Computer Technology, IEEE, 2011, pp. 781–785.

[77] S.S. Pati, U. Subudhi, Robust-momentum-learning-rate-based adaptive fractional-order least mean squares approach for power system frequency estimation using chaotic harris hawks optimization, Front. Energy Res. 12 (2024) 1467637.

[78] V. De Bortoli, A. Durmus, X. Fontaine, U. Simsekli, Quantitative propagation of chaos for Sgd in wide neural networks, Adv. Neural Inf. Process. Syst. 33 (2020) 278–288.

[79] Z.A. Khan, S. Zubair, H. Alquhayz, M. Azeem, A. Ditta, Design of momentum fractional stochastic gradient descent for recommender systems, IEEE Access 7 (2019) 179575–179590.

[80] D.M. Durairaj, B.K. Mohan, A convolutional neural network based approach to financial time series prediction, Neural Comput. Appl. 34 (2022) 13319–13337.

[81] Y. Sun, L. Zhang, M. Yao, Chaotic time series prediction of nonlinear systems based on various neural network models, Chaos Solitons Fractals 175 (2023) 113971.

[82] B. Jia, H. Wu, K. Guo, Chaos theory meets deep learning: A new approach to time series forecasting, Expert Syst. Appl. 255 (2024) 124533.

[83] Z. Man, J. Li, X. Di, Y. Sheng, Z. Liu, Double image encryption algorithm based on neural network and chaos, Chaos Solitons Fractals 152 (2021) 111318.

[84] J. Jiangtao, X. Zifei, L. Chun, M. Weipao, Z. Wanfu, L. Gen, Application of convolutional neural network and chaos theory in fault diagnosis of rolling bearings, J. Mech. Strength 44 (2022) 287–293.

[85] M.U. Rehman, A. Shafique, Y.Y. Ghadi, W. Boulila, S.U. Jan, T.R. Gadekallu, M. Driss, J. Ahmad, A novel chaos-based privacy-preserving deep learning model for cancer diagnosis, IEEE Trans. Network Sci. Eng. 9 (2022) 4322–4337.

[86] M. Dridi, M.A. Hajjaji, B. Bouallegue, A. Mtibaa, Cryptography of medical images based on a combination between chaotic and neural network, IET Image Process. 10 (2016) 830–839.

[87] A. Mabrouk, A. Dahou, M.A. Elaziz, R.P. Díaz Redondo, M. Kayed, Medical image classification using transfer learning and chaos game optimization on the internet of medical things, Comput. Intell. Neurosci. 2022 (2022) 9112634.

[88] Y. Song, Z. Chen, Z. Yuan, New chaotic PSO-Based neural network predictive control for nonlinear process, IEEE Trans. Neural Network. 18 (2007) 595–601.

[89] G.R. Thoms, R. Muresan, A. Al-Dweik, Chaotic encryption algorithm with key controlled neural networks for intelligent transportation systems, IEEE Access 7 (2019) 158697–158709.

[90] W.-C. Hong, Traffic flow forecasting by seasonal svr with chaotic simulated annealing algorithm, Neurocomputing 74 (2011) 2096–2107.

[91] A. Ait-Saadi, Y. Meraihi, A. Soukane, A. Ramdane-Cherif, A.B. Gabis, A novel hybrid chaotic aquila optimization algorithm with simulated annealing for unmanned aerial vehicles path planning, Comput. Electr. Eng. 104 (2022) 108461.

[92] J. Zhou, G. Qi, C. Liu, A chaotic parallel artificial fish swarm algorithm for water quality monitoring sensor networks 3D coverage optimization, J. Sens. 2021 (2021) 5529527.

[93] J. Liang, Y. Du, Y. Xu, B. Xie, W. Li, Z. Lu, R. Li, H. Bal, Using adaptive chaotic grey wolf optimization for the daily streamflow prediction, Expert Syst. Appl. 237 (2024) 121113.

[94] E.O.-N. Jnr, Y.Y. Ziggah, M.J. Rodrigues, S. Relvas, A hybrid chaotic-based discrete wavelet transform and aquila optimisation tuned-artificial neural network approach for wind speed prediction, Results Eng. 14 (2022) 100399.

[95] J. Duan, H. Zuo, Y. Bai, M. Chang, X. Chen, W. Wang, L. Ma, B. Chen, A multistep short-term solar radiation forecasting model using fully convolutional neural networks and chaotic aquila optimization combining WRF-solar model results, Energy 271 (2023) 126980.

[96] J. Cai, X. Ma, Q. Li, L. Li, H. Peng, A multi-objective chaotic particle swarm optimization for environmental/economic dispatch, Energy Convers. Manag. 50 (2009) 1318–1325.

[97] W. Jia, M. Liu, J. Zhou, Adaptive chaotic ant colony optimization for energy optimization in smart sensor networks, J. Sens. 2021 (2021) 5051863.

Chapter 19

Integrating artificial intelligence and generative AI in structural engineering: A survey of methods and applications

Siamak Talatahari[1, 2, 3], Behnaz Nouhi[1], Amin Beheshti[2], Fang Chen[1] and Amir H. Gandomi[1, 4]

[1]*Data Science Institute, Faculty of Engineering & Information Technology, University of Technology Sydney, Ultimo, NSW, Australia;* [2]*School of Computing, Macquarie University, Sydney, NSW, Australia;* [3]*Department of Computer Science, Khazar University, Baku, Azerbaijan;* [4]*University Research and Innovation Center (EKIK), Óbuda University, Budapest, Hungary*

1. Introduction

Artificial Intelligence (AI) has emerged as a transformative force in various engineering fields, and structural engineering is no exception [1–3]. Traditionally, structural engineering has relied on deterministic methods, mathematical models, and expert judgment for design, analysis, and maintenance [4,5]. However, as the complexity of modern structures and the volume of data generated by sensors and monitoring systems grow, traditional methods can become insufficient in addressing these challenges. This is where AI and specially Machine Learning (ML) offers significant promise by enabling data-driven approaches that can enhance decision-making [6], optimize analyzes and designs [7], and predict structural performance [8] more accurately.

Machine learning techniques, ranging from supervised learning to deep neural networks, have the potential to revolutionize the way engineers approach structural problems. By analyzing large datasets from various sources, including sensors, historical performance records, and simulation models, ML algorithms can uncover hidden patterns, make predictions, and automate tasks that were previously time-consuming and error-prone [9]. These advancements can lead to more efficient designs, improve safety standards, and reduce costs over the lifecycle of structures.

This review explores the integration of AI methods into structural engineering, focusing on both the methodologies and real-world applications. We will examine the various AI and ML techniques commonly used in the field, including supervised learning, unsupervised learning, reinforcement learning, and deep learning, and highlight their contributions to structural health monitoring, design optimization, predictive modeling, and more. Additionally, this review will discuss the challenges faced by practitioners in incorporating these technologies into existing workflows and the barriers that need to be overcome for broader adoption. Generative AI (GenAI), as a recent advancement in AI, will also be briefly investigated.

In the following sections, we present an overview of machine learning methods commonly applied in structural engineering, starting with the fundamentals of ML techniques in Section 2. This section introduces key concepts, such as supervised, unsupervised, reinforcement and deep learning, to provide a foundational understanding. In Section 3, we explore how these methods are applied to various structural engineering challenges, from structural health monitoring to sustainability. In Section 4, we explore the emergence of Generative AI (GenAI) in structural engineering and highlight several potential domains within the field that stand to benefit from its capabilities. Section 5 outlines the current challenges and limitations associated with integrating AI into structural engineering, while also identifying future research directions and development opportunities that could drive continued growth. Finally, Section 6 concludes the chapter with a summary of key findings and reflections on the evolving role of machine learning and AI in shaping the future of structural engineering.

Advanced Intelligence Methods for Data Science and Optimization. https://doi.org/10.1016/B978-0-443-28940-8.00011-7

2. Fundamentals of machine learning

Machine learning (ML), a subset of AI, enables systems to learn patterns from data and improve their performance on tasks without being explicitly programmed [9]. In structural engineering, ML provides a powerful framework for analyzing large volumes of complex data, making predictions, automating routine processes, and enhancing both the design and assessment of structures. It allows engineers to move beyond traditional rule-based methods and leverage data-driven approaches for more adaptive and optimized decision-making. To fully appreciate the transformative potential of ML in this field, it is important to understand the core types and techniques that underpin it. Fig. 19.1 presents a conceptual map of machine learning and its key branches. The following subsections will explore these concept in greater depth, emphasizing how they contribute to smarter, safer, and more efficient structural systems.

2.1 Supervised learning

Supervised learning is widely used in structural engineering due to its ability to model complex relationships between inputs and outputs based on labeled training data. The process begins by feeding the model a dataset consisting of input–output pairs [10], where the input represents features such as material properties [11], load conditions [12], or geometric characteristics of a structure [13], and the output corresponds to a desired prediction, such as stress, strain, or the structural element's condition [7]. Once the model has been trained on this data, it can generalize to make predictions on new, unseen inputs, which is particularly valuable in real-time monitoring and predictive maintenance.

In the context of structural engineering, regression techniques are often applied when predicting continuous values, such as the deformation or load-bearing capacity of structural components. For instance, regression models can help predict the stress or strain in beams [14] and columns [15] based on varying conditions such as material type, temperature, and loading. On the other hand, classification techniques are useful when dealing with categorical outputs [16]. For

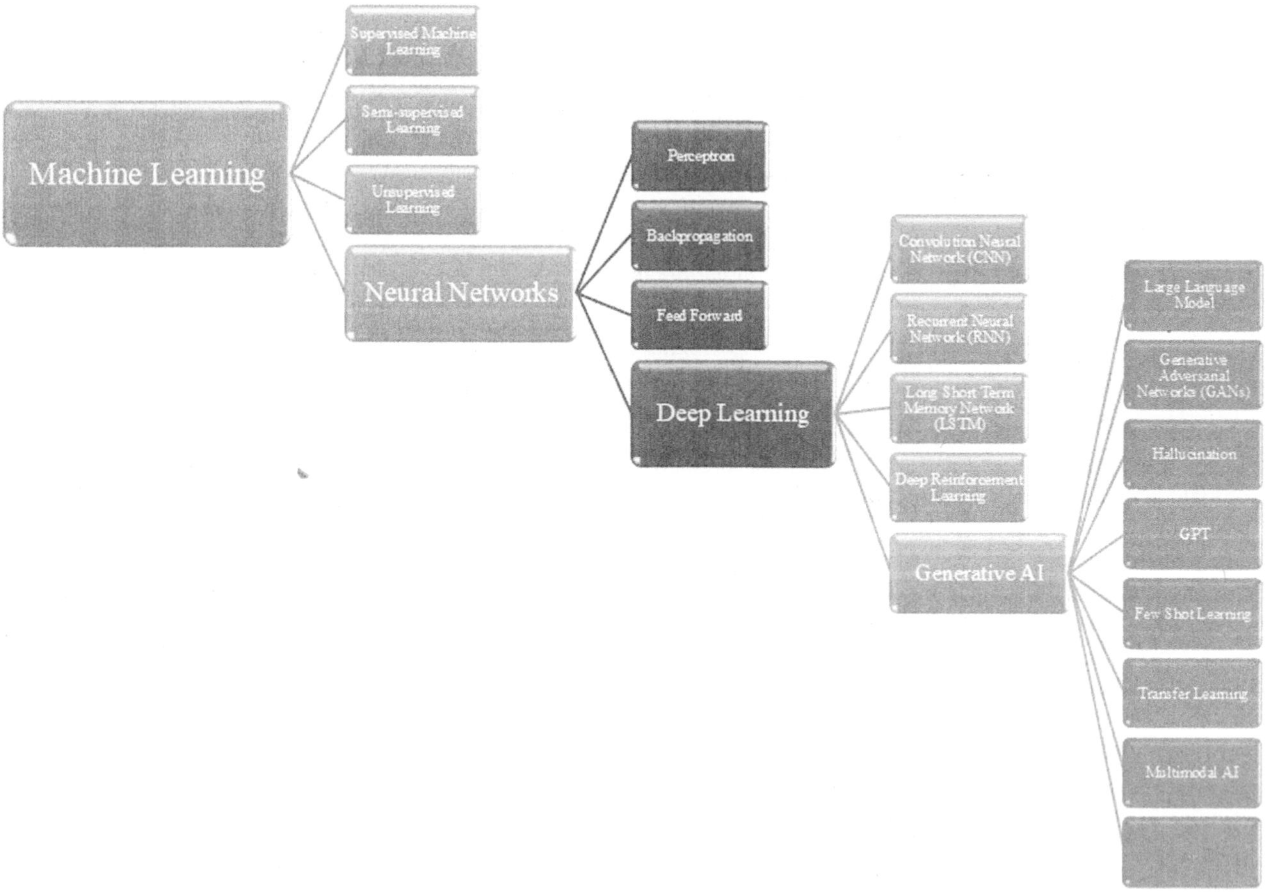

FIGURE 19.1 Overview of machine learning concepts and architectures.

example, sensor data from structures can be classified into different categories [17] such as "safe," "damaged," or "needs inspection," enabling quick decision-making and prioritization of maintenance activities [18]. These predictions can guide engineers in identifying high-risk elements, preventing potential failures, and ensuring the safety and integrity of structures over time [19].

2.2 Unsupervised learning

In unsupervised learning, the model is provided with input data that lacks labeled outputs. The primary goal is to discover hidden patterns or inherent structures within the data without predefined categories [20]. Unlike supervised learning, where the model is explicitly trained to predict a specific outcome, unsupervised learning algorithms aim to find natural groupings, associations, or data representations based on similarities and differences among the input features. This is especially valuable in structural engineering, where the data may be complex and unlabeled, such as sensor readings or large sets of environmental conditions [21].

The most common techniques in unsupervised learning are clustering and dimensionality reduction. In structural engineering, clustering can be applied to categorize different parts of a structure based on sensor data, which can help identify structural anomalies or segments with similar behaviors [22,23]. Dimensionality reduction techniques, such as principal component analysis (PCA), help reduce the number of input variables while preserving key information, making it easier to visualize complex data and uncover trends. For example, in the context of structural health monitoring, PCA can help identify the most significant features affecting the performance of a structure, reducing data complexity and improving the effectiveness of subsequent analysis or monitoring tasks [24]. These unsupervised learning methods are crucial in uncovering hidden insights that guide engineers in decision-making processes, particularly in the absence of labeled training data.

2.3 Reinforcement learning

Reinforcement learning (RL) is a type of machine learning where an agent learns to make decisions by interacting with an environment and receiving feedback in the form of rewards or penalties. In contrast to supervised and unsupervised learning, where the model learns from data directly, RL focuses on learning optimal actions through trial and error. The agent's objective is to maximize cumulative rewards by choosing actions that lead to favorable outcomes [25]. In structural engineering, RL is particularly useful for dynamic systems where the environment changes over time and decisions need to be made in response to those changes [26].

In structural engineering, RL can be applied in several areas, such as adaptive control systems [27], smart buildings [28,29], and real-time structural health monitoring [30,31]. For example, in the case of a smart building, RL can be used to optimize energy usage [32] by adjusting heating, cooling, and lighting systems based on real-time environmental conditions and occupant behavior. Similarly, in structural health monitoring, an RL agent can learn to adjust sensors' placement [33] or sensitivity to maximize the detection of potential damage [34] while minimizing the cost or number of sensors required. Additionally, RL can be applied to structural design optimization [35,36], where it explores design parameters iteratively, improving the structure's performance over time based on feedback about its strength, stability, or safety.

2.4 Deep learning

Deep learning utilizes neural networks with multiple layers to learn hierarchical representations of complex data [37]. These networks are capable of automatically extracting features from raw data, making them particularly effective in tasks such as image analyzes and visual recognition [38]. In structural engineering [39,40], deep learning techniques, such as Convolutional Neural Networks (CNNs) [41] and Recurrent Neural Networks (RNNs) [42], are increasingly used for applications such as structural analyses [43] or structural health monitoring [44], where sensor data or images of infrastructure are processed to detect damage.

For instance, CNNs have been widely applied in damage detection and visual inspection [45], where they can analyze images or videos of structural components (such as bridges or buildings) to identify cracks or other types of damage. Similarly, RNNs and Long Short-Term Memory (LSTM) networks are used to model sequential data, such as time-series data from sensors, to predict the future behavior of structures under different loading conditions [46,47]. These deep learning models are particularly powerful when handling large datasets and can significantly improve the accuracy and efficiency of damage detection and predictive maintenance systems. In addition, deep learning can be integrated with other optimization and design processes, allowing for adaptive designs and predictive models that improve over time [48,49]. For example, deep reinforcement method, which combines deep learning and Reinforcement learning [50], has been utilized as a shape optimization scheme for aerodynamic mitigation of wind-sensitive structures.

2.5 The importance of data in machine learning

The success of ML models fundamentally depends on the quality, quantity, and relevance of the data used for training and validation [51]. In structural engineering, data serves as the foundation for training predictive models that assist in evaluating structural performance, identifying damage or failure risks, and optimizing design configurations.

Data in this field can originate from a wide array of sources, including:

- Sensor networks embedded in buildings [52], bridges [53], and other civil infrastructure [54],
- Historical performance records and failure reports [55–57],
- Finite element analysis (FEA) and simulation models [58,59],
- Experimental test results from laboratory settings [8],
- Manual inspections and condition assessment reports [2],
- Environmental and usage data, such as wind speed, temperature, and traffic loads [60–62].

High-quality, well-labeled datasets are especially critical for supervised learning tasks, where models learn to associate inputs with specific outcomes, such as predicting failure modes, classifying structural health states, or estimating load-bearing capacity. In contrast, unsupervised learning can benefit from large unlabeled datasets to discover hidden patterns, such as clustering similar structural behaviors or identifying anomalies in real-time monitoring data. However, several challenges persist [62–64]:

- Data quality issues, such as noise, redundancy, missing values, and inconsistencies, can hinder model performance.
- Unstructured data (e.g., textual inspection reports or visual images) require specialized preprocessing techniques such as natural language processing or computer vision.
- Data sparsity in rare-event scenarios (e.g., extreme seismic loads) may lead to biased models unless synthetic data augmentation or simulation-based generation is applied.
- Domain-specific feature engineering is essential to transform raw data into formats that ML models can understand and effectively use.

To address these challenges, data preprocessing techniques such as cleaning, outlier detection, normalization, dimensionality reduction, and feature selection or extraction are crucial. Moreover, data fusion from heterogeneous sources (e.g., combining sensor data with simulation outputs) enhances the model's ability to generalize and improves its robustness across varied scenarios [2].

Incorporating real-time data streams from digital twins or structural health monitoring (SHM) systems allows for adaptive learning models that update predictions and decisions dynamically [65]. This continuous feedback loop is particularly valuable for critical infrastructure where performance can evolve due to aging, accumulated damage, or changing environmental and operational conditions. By integrating these real-time inputs, ML models can perform online learning, continuously refining their predictive accuracy and enabling proactive maintenance strategies. For example, a bridge outfitted with vibration and displacement sensors can feed continuous data into a trained model that alerts engineers to potential fatigue damage before it becomes critical, thereby enhancing both safety and cost-efficiency [66].

Moreover, the synergy between simulation data (e.g., from finite element models) and real-time measured data facilitates the development of hybrid physics-informed machine learning frameworks [67,68]. These models are capable of capturing both physical laws and empirical behavior, resulting in more robust and interpretable predictions. In this context, digital twins act as dynamic virtual replicas of physical assets, offering a platform where machine learning algorithms and domain knowledge converge to simulate, monitor, and optimize infrastructure performance throughout its lifecycle.

Additionally, privacy, data governance, and standardization issues must be considered, especially when dealing with infrastructure data shared across stakeholders such as construction firms, government bodies, consultants, and maintenance teams [69]. Without clear protocols for data ownership, access rights, and usage boundaries, the deployment of AI-driven solutions may encounter institutional resistance or legal obstacles. To ensure trustworthiness and compliance, it is critical to implement secure data pipelines, anonymization techniques, and compliance frameworks aligned with standards such as ISO 19650 [70] or regional data protection regulations [71].

3. Impacts of AI advancements in structural engineering

In this section, we explore the transformative impacts of AI on structural engineering, focusing on seven key areas where AI is reshaping the field, as shown in Fig. 19.2. We begin by examining how AI enhances structural health monitoring through real-time data processing, anomaly detection, and predictive maintenance. Next, we discuss AI's growing role in structural analyzes, design and optimization, enabling more efficient, cost-effective, and sustainable solutions. The application of AI in Building Information Modeling (BIM)-based construction automation is also highlighted, with an emphasis on process planning and resource management. The integration of smart materials and adaptive systems, empowered by machine learning, is also explored, along with AI's role in promoting sustainability in structural engineering workflows. Furthermore, we delve into AI-driven strategies for predictive maintenance and lifecycle management, as well as its contributions to risk assessment and improving structural safety.

The increasing academic interest in applying AI to structural engineering is vividly demonstrated in Fig. 19.3, which visualizes the number of publications across seven thematic areas based on data retrieved from the Scopus database [72]. While the growth trajectory differs among these areas, all exhibit a notable surge in research activity, particularly since the early 2010s. This upward trend reflects a broader paradigm shift in structural engineering, where data-driven approaches are becoming foundational to innovation and efficiency.

Among these domains, Materials and Systems Integration combined with ML has experienced the most dramatic rise. The number of publications in this area has increased from just 6 papers per year in 2010 to over 1300 publications in 2024, indicating explosive growth. Other key areas—such as Structural Health Monitoring, Risk Assessment and Safety, and Sustainability—have also seen significant increases. For example, publications in Structural Health Monitoring grew from 9 in 2010 to 602 in 2024, while Sustainability-related works rose from only 3 to 873 in the same period.

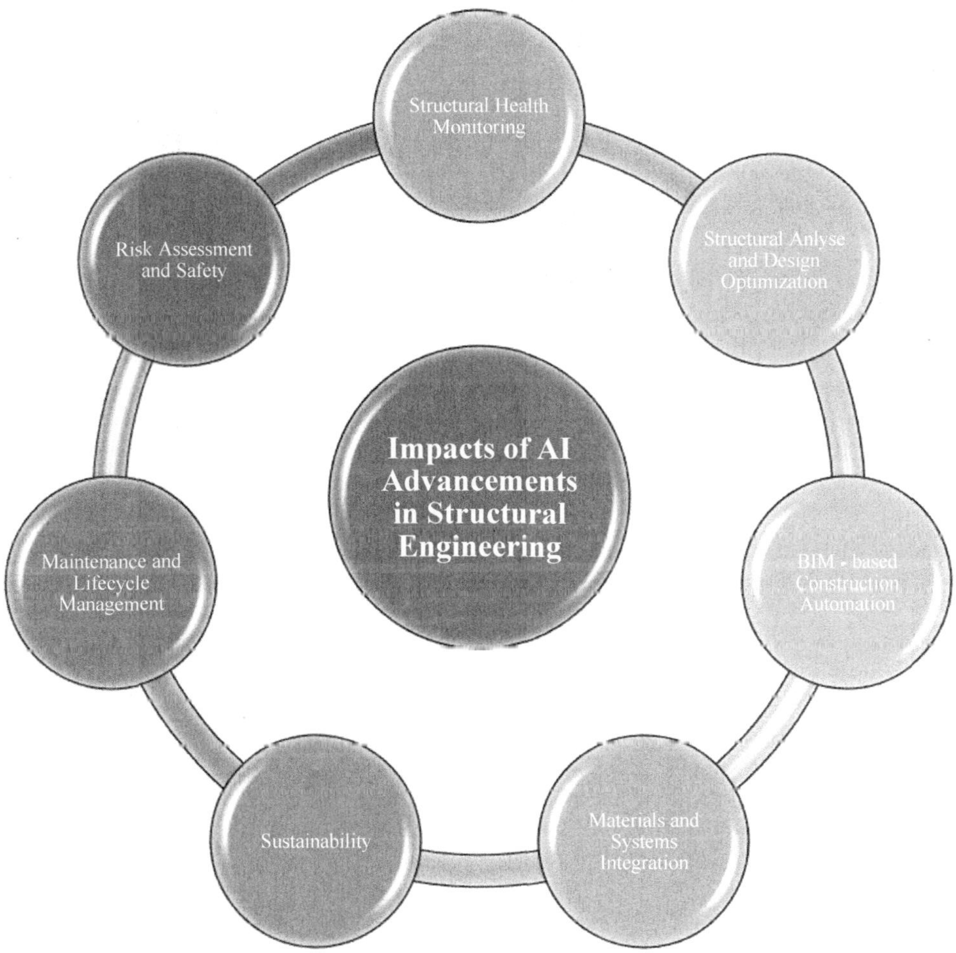

FIGURE 19.2 Key areas of AI application in structural engineering.

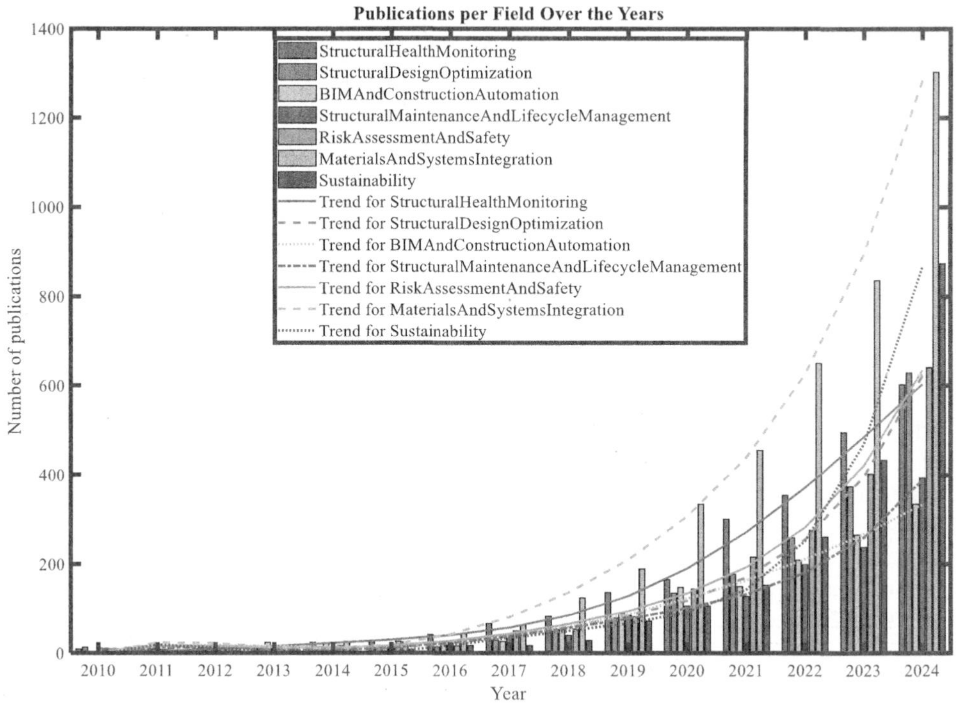

FIGURE 19.3 Number of publications in each key area of AI application in structural engineering.

This consistent and rapid growth across all categories highlights a major transformation in the structural engineering landscape. The integration of AI is no longer a speculative or emerging trend—it has become a defining feature of contemporary practice and research. These tools are now central to tackling long-standing challenges such as optimizing resource usage, reducing life-cycle costs, improving resilience against natural hazards, and designing structures that respond adaptively to their environments.

3.1 Structural Health Monitoring (SHM)

Structural Health Monitoring (SHM) plays a vital role in ensuring the safety, durability, and operational efficiency of infrastructure systems. Traditionally, SHM has relied on periodic manual inspections and threshold-based techniques, which, while widely used, are often labor-intensive, time-consuming, and prone to human error. The integration of AI, particularly ML, has revolutionized this field by enabling the shift from reactive maintenance strategies to proactive and even predictive maintenance frameworks [30]. Through real-time data processing, anomaly detection, and pattern recognition, AI facilitates continuous and automated monitoring, thus enhancing the early identification of structural issues and supporting more timely and effective decision-making.

Numerous studies have underscored the transformative impact of AI in SHM, as evidenced by the growing body of literature reviewed by Refs. [30,33,44,73–76]. The increasing scholarly attention is further highlighted in Fig. 19.4 (generated by VOSviewer [77]), which depicts the distribution of 2595 publications retrieved from the Scopus database [72] using a combination of keywords such as "structural health monitoring," "machine learning," "artificial intelligence," and some other related terminologies.

The bibliometric analysis reveals that the majority of these studies center around the integration of ML techniques into SHM systems, particularly for tasks such as damage and fault detection, modal and vibration analysis, computational modeling, optimization, and data-driven diagnostics. Among the most frequently associated terms in the literature are "damage & fault detection" (675 sources), "computational tools" (369 sources), and "ML or AI" (1569), which collectively underscore the centrality of intelligent algorithms in modern SHM paradigms.

In terms of domain-specific applications, bridge engineering emerges as a dominant field, with keywords such as "bridges" (128 occurrences), "bridge maintenance" (10), and "cable-stayed bridges" (12) highlighting the prominence of

FIGURE 19.4 Bibliometric keyword distribution of AI applications in structural health monitoring.

AI-powered SHM in the management of large-scale, safety-critical infrastructure. This is consistent with the practical challenges bridges pose—long spans, variable loading, and environmental exposure—which make them ideal candidates for continuous, intelligent monitoring systems.

The distribution of keywords also reflects the technological evolution of SHM methodologies. Techniques such as "deep convolutional neural networks" (DCNNs), "long short-term memory" (LSTM), and "graph neural networks" (GNNs) are gaining traction, with average normalized citation scores ranging from 1.3 to nearly 2.0, indicating both academic relevance and impact. Notably, "adaboost" and "extreme gradient boosting" also appear with relatively high citation scores, revealing the community's interest in ensemble-based learning for robust performance in noisy, real-world SHM datasets. Beyond conventional ML, new frontiers such as "explainable machine learning" and "meta-learning" have emerged to address the challenges of interpretability and model generalization, respectively.

From a sensor and systems perspective, "accelerometers" and "fiber Bragg grating sensors" are still integral to SHM, while emerging concepts such as "IoT" (Internet of Things) and "digital transformation" are reshaping the infrastructure monitoring landscape. "Infrastructure health" and "infrastructure monitoring" also show high citation metrics and strong link strength in the network, pointing to their central role in discussions around smart cities and resilient engineering systems.

As mentioned, one of the most valuable contributions of AI in SHM is its ability to detect subtle anomalies that precede visible damage. By recognizing early warning signs, such as changes in vibration frequency or localized strain increases, AI systems can flag emerging issues in real time. This early detection capability is crucial for critical infrastructure such as bridges, tunnels, and dams, where timely maintenance can prevent costly failures and enhance public safety [34]. In addition to detecting damage, AI helps optimize inspection and maintenance schedules [78]. Predictive models can forecast the future condition of structural components based on historical trends, environmental exposure, and loading conditions. For example, ML models can be used for condition assessment and life-cycle prediction in bridges, allowing for better inspection planning and resource allocation [79]. Such capabilities reduce downtime, prevent over-maintenance, and extend infrastructure lifespan.

The integration of AI with the Internet of Things (IoT) has further revolutionized SHM [80]. IoT-enabled smart sensors provide continuous, distributed data acquisition across large or hard-to-access structures. When combined with real-time AI analytics, this system enables engineers to monitor infrastructure performance dynamically and make informed decisions faster [81].

3.2 AI in structural analyzes and design optimization

AI is revolutionizing structural design by enabling engineers to automate complex design tasks and optimize both performance and processes. Traditionally, structural design relied on manual computations and iterative trial-and-error approaches to identify suitable configurations. However, recent advancements in AI, particularly in ML and metaheuristic optimization, have transformed this workflow, allowing the handling of vast variable spaces, nonlinearities, and multi-objective constraints with greater speed and precision [7,82–84].

Fig. 19.5 presents the keyword analysis results using VOSviewer [77], highlighting the most relevant and frequently occurring terms in recent literature on AI-driven structural analysis and design optimization [72]. In this visualization, the size of each node indicates keyword frequency, the link strength reflects cooccurrence relationships, and color represents clusters of thematically related terms.

Prominent terms such as "design optimization," "multiobjective optimization," "generative design," and "data-driven design" underscore their strong presence and ongoing relevance in the field. The clustering and proximity of these terms suggest thematic groupings, reflecting the increasing integration of AI, computational techniques, and performance-driven methodologies in structural engineering. Notably, terms such as "design optimization" (score: 1.0043, average publication year: 2023), "multiobjective optimization" (score: 0.9377, average publication year: 2022), "generative design" (score: 1.911, average publication year: 2023), and "data-driven design" (score: 1.4489, average publication year: 2023) highlight a growing emphasis on computationally enhanced, intelligent, and adaptive approaches in structural design. The relevance

FIGURE 19.5 Bibliometric keyword distribution of AI applications in structural analyze and design optimization.

score of each term reflects its centrality in the dataset, with higher scores representing more influential or frequently cooccurring concepts. The average publication year, on the other hand, provides insight into the recency of these terms in the academic discourse. For example, the average year of 2023 for "design optimization" suggests it is an ongoing and active area of research, while terms such as "generative design" and "data-driven design," also from 2023, show a trend toward newer, innovative approaches.

Clusters centered around optimization and modeling (notably linked with high cooccurrence strength) and those focused on ML and AI illustrate the highly interdisciplinary nature of current research in structural engineering. These clusters bridge traditionally distinct domains—civil engineering, computer science, and data analytics—demonstrating how complex structural challenges increasingly rely on computational intelligence and data-driven methodologies. The strong connectivity within and between these clusters highlights the growing convergence of algorithmic design, predictive modeling, and performance optimization in both academic and practical contexts.

Moreover, the emergence of keywords such as explainable AI, hyperparameter optimization, and surrogate modeling signals a meaningful evolution in research priorities—from merely achieving optimal performance to ensuring transparency, interpretability, and reliability in the design process. These concepts are particularly significant in safety-critical applications such as structural engineering, where decisions must be auditable and justifiable. Explainable AI techniques allow engineers to understand and validate model behavior, reducing the "black-box" nature of complex systems. Hyperparameter optimization enhances model efficiency and generalizability, while surrogate modeling enables computationally efficient approximations of complex simulations, which is especially valuable in iterative design process and real-time decision-making. Together, these developments reflect a shift toward trustworthy AI in structural design—where performance, interpretability, and computational efficiency are cooptimized to support more informed, robust, and accountable engineering practices.

3.3 AI for BIM-based construction automation

Building Information Modeling (BIM) has become a cornerstone in modern construction automation, transforming the way buildings and infrastructures are designed, constructed, and maintained [85]. Historically, construction processes were characterized by disjointed workflows, poor communication, and inefficiencies. However, the incorporation of AI and automation technologies into BIM has greatly improved the design, planning, and execution phases of construction projects [63,85–87]. These advancements facilitate the automation of tasks such as project scheduling, cost estimation, and quality control, reducing human error and enhancing project outcomes. Furthermore, the fusion of AI-driven design tools with BIM enables real-time optimization and monitoring, improving decision-making and resource allocation.

Fig. 19.6 presents a keyword analysis derived from recent research on BIM-based construction automation [72], using VOSviewer [77] to examine prominent terms and trends within this developing area. The visualization emphasizes the prominence and cooccurrence of key terms such as "construction automation," "BIM," "digital twins," "AI in construction," and "robotic construction." Significant keywords such as "construction automation" (score: 1.024, average publication year: 2023), "digital twins" (score: 1.205, average publication year: 2023), and "robotic construction" (score: 1.321, average publication year: 2023) highlight a growing emphasis on digital technologies that optimize construction automation. These trends reflect the increasing influence of AI and data analytics in enhancing efficiency and safety within the construction industry.

The clustering of terms related to digital construction technologies focused on automation and AI-driven design tools highlight the shift toward intelligent, real-time decision-making systems in construction. As BIM integrates with robotic systems and AI, construction projects may achieve better precision, shorter delivery times, and reduced waste, when AI-BIM workflows are properly validated and integrated. This synergy between BIM and automation is reshaping construction methodologies, enabling greater scalability, efficiency, and sustainability across diverse projects.

Emerging keywords such as "Augmented Reality (AR)," "AI-powered simulation," and "predictive analytics" signal the next wave of advancements in BIM-based automation. These technologies enable real-time monitoring and visualization of construction sites, allowing engineers to simulate and optimize building performance before construction even begins. AR and predictive analytics further support decision-making by providing intuitive, data-driven insights into construction workflows. The integration of these technologies with BIM frameworks helps address critical issues such as resource management, site safety, and quality control, leading to more efficient and cost-effective construction processes.

AI and BIM are also increasingly pivotal in advancing smart construction and prefabrication methods, where building components are manufactured off-site and later assembled on-site [88,89]. In this context, AI-driven BIM systems enhance the precision and efficiency of prefabricated designs by ensuring that components are optimally produced for seamless integration during assembly. This synergy minimizes material waste, reduces construction costs, and

FIGURE 19.6 Bibliometric keyword distribution of AI applications in BIM-based construction automation.

significantly shortens project timelines. In addition, automation tools powered by AI contribute to improved planning and coordination by optimizing task scheduling and sequencing [90]. By leveraging data from BIM models alongside historical project information, these systems can generate efficient timelines and allocate resources more effectively. Furthermore, they can anticipate potential disruptions or delays, offering data-informed strategies to address them before they impact the construction workflow [91].

3.4 AI for smart structural materials and systems

AI plays a key role in the integration of smart materials and adaptive systems into structural engineering, paving the way for more responsive and resilient structures. Smart materials, such as self-healing concrete [92] and shape-memory alloys [93], have the ability to change their properties in response to external stimuli such as temperature, stress, or moisture. These materials can repair themselves when damaged or adapt to changing environmental conditions, offering significant benefits in terms of durability and cost-effectiveness. AI is crucial in optimizing the performance of these materials by predicting their behavior, monitoring their condition in real time, and adjusting system parameters to ensure optimal functionality [94–97].

In addition to smart materials, AI enables the development of adaptive systems that can respond to dynamic changes in a structure's environment. For example, adaptive facades in buildings can adjust their transparency based on light levels, reducing energy consumption for heating and cooling [98,99]. Seismic dampers and other structural elements can also adjust to mitigate the effects of earthquakes [100,101]. AI algorithms continuously monitor environmental conditions and structural responses, ensuring that these systems function efficiently and effectively.

As shown in Fig. 19.7 generated by VOSviewer [77], recent trends in the literature reflect (based on the data of [72]) the increasing prominence of themes such as "damage & fault detection," "composite materials," "materials informatics," "mechanical properties," and "material design," which collectively indicate a growing research focus on smart materials, AI-driven diagnostics, and structural optimization. For instance, keywords such as "materials informatics" and "machine learning method" (Cluster 2 and 8 respectively) are positioned centrally in the network, suggesting their integrative roles across multiple domains. High citation scores for terms such as "mechanical property" (1.8062), "metal-organic frameworks" (1.7909), and "material design" (1.5267) indicate their relevance and impact within this evolving interdisciplinary field.

These developments underscore how AI is not only supporting the design and analysis of innovative materials but also enhancing real-time adaptability and long-term resilience in structural systems. For example, In recent years, ML has been widely applied across various domains of civil engineering, with notable success in concrete mix design [97,102,103]. This data-driven approach represents a significant advancement compared with traditional methods. These models can reduce the time and cost involved in mix design while enhancing the reliability and performance of concrete.

As another example beyond mix design, ML is increasingly being utilized in the discovery and development of novel structural materials. Researchers have used ML to model and predict mechanical, thermal, and durability properties of advanced materials, including fiber-reinforced composites, geopolymer concretes, and high-performance self-healing materials [96,104,105]. Such applications enable rapid screening of potential materials under varying environmental and load conditions, facilitating innovative engineering solutions that were previously difficult to achieve through conventional experimental methods alone.

Additionally, ML-driven techniques have been instrumental in investigating complex material behaviors, such as shrinkage, creep, corrosion resistance, and microcrack propagation [106–109]. By leveraging large datasets from

FIGURE 19.7 Bibliometric keyword distribution of AI applications in smart structural materials and systems.

experimental tests and simulations, ML models can uncover hidden patterns and provide insights into the long-term performance and failure mechanisms of construction materials. These insights not only contribute to the optimization of existing materials but also support the development of sustainable alternatives aligned with modern construction demands and environmental considerations.

In parallel with advancements in ML for material design, the development of smart structural systems represents another transformative trend in structural engineering. These systems incorporate AI, ML, and sensor technologies to create adaptive, responsive, and self-monitoring infrastructure. Key components of smart systems include SHM, Adaptive Control Systems, and Energy Harvesting Systems. SHM systems utilize networks of embedded sensors to continuously track parameters such as strain, vibration, and temperature as discussed in Section 3.1. Adaptive control systems further enhance resilience by adjusting the structure's behavior in real time in response to environmental changes such as wind or seismic activity [110]. For example, intelligent facades and damping systems can autonomously respond to dynamic loads, enhancing stability and energy efficiency. Moreover, AI-enabled energy harvesting systems are increasingly being integrated into infrastructure to capture ambient energy, contributing to sustainable and self-powered structural solutions [111]. Together, these technologies are pushing the boundaries of how structures are designed, monitored, and maintained, moving the field toward truly intelligent and resilient built environments.

3.5 Additional AI applications in structural engineering

3.5.1 Sustainability

AI is increasingly recognized as a transformative force in promoting sustainability within structural engineering. It enhances early design stages by evaluating environmental impact, energy efficiency, and material performance, enabling engineers to create resource-efficient structures with minimized waste. Studies such as those by Refs. [79,111,112] demonstrate how AI-driven optimization and life-cycle assessment tools support greener material choices and configurations that reduce energy consumption and carbon emissions throughout a structure's lifespan.

These themes are echoed in recent bibliometric trends [72]. As shown in Fig. 19.8 (generated by VOSviewer [77]), keywords such as "energy efficiency," "energy consumption," "life cycle assessment," and "environmental impact" occupy central positions in the knowledge network, with high average publication years (e.g., 2022–24) and substantial normalized citation scores (e.g., "life cycle assessment": 1.4992; "carbon emissions": 0.9668; "environmental impact": 1.0375), reflecting their increasing relevance. Particularly notable is "computational tools" (score: 1.0396 with 108 occurrences), which highlights the widespread adoption of AI-based decision-making in sustainable structural practices. Moreover, concepts such as "IoT" (Internet of Things) and "energy management" emphasize the role of AI in operational sustainability, as smart structures dynamically regulate their systems based on real-time sensor data.

3.5.2 Structural maintenance and lifecycle management

One of the most significant contributions of AI to structural engineering is its role in predictive maintenance and lifecycle management [91]. By leveraging ML algorithms, particularly ensemble methods such as extreme gradient boosting and hybrid models and integrating them with sensor data and IoT technologies, AI can forecast structural deterioration before it becomes critical.

When "structural maintenance" or "lifecycle management" is combined with "machine learning" or "artificial intelligence" as keywords in a Scopus search (title, abstract, or keywords), the literature increasingly highlights a shift from traditional fixed-interval inspections to intelligent, data-driven monitoring (Fig. 19.9, generated from Scopus data [72]). AI systems now analyze real-time data to detect early signs of structural issues—such as vibrations in bridges, foundation cracks, or material fatigue—enabling proactive maintenance. Notably, the term "bridges" features prominently in recent publications (44 occurrences, average publication year: 2022), frequently associated with "damage and fault detection" (214 occurrences). This trend underscores a growing emphasis on enhancing infrastructure safety through AI-enabled structural health monitoring.

These predictive capabilities translate into condition-based maintenance, optimizing both cost and safety. AI not only enables early detection but also assists in prioritizing maintenance tasks and extending the useful life of critical structures, as highlighted by the rising interest in "lifecycle management" keywords such as "buildings & infrastructure" (67 occurrences, Avg. Citations 29.73), and "inspection" (35.6 avg citations).

Furthermore, the emergence of terms such as "explainable machine learning" (Avg. year 2023, Avg. Norm. Citations 1.25) and "interpretability" (Avg. year 2023, 8 occurrences) underscores a shift toward transparent AI in this field, enabling stakeholders to trust and act on AI-driven insights.

FIGURE 19.8 Bibliometric keyword distribution of AI applications in sustainability.

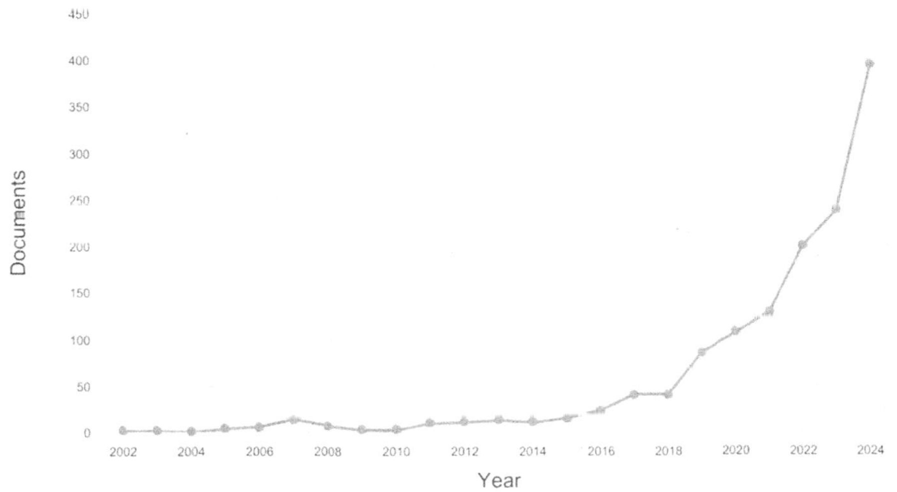

FIGURE 19.9 Number of publications over time of research on AI for structural maintenance and lifecycle management [72].

3.5.3 *AI for structural risk assessment and safety improvement*

AI has been applied widely for structural risk assessment and safety enhancement, reshaping how engineers monitor and manage the health of infrastructure—particularly in aging systems and in contexts requiring disaster resilience [113,114].

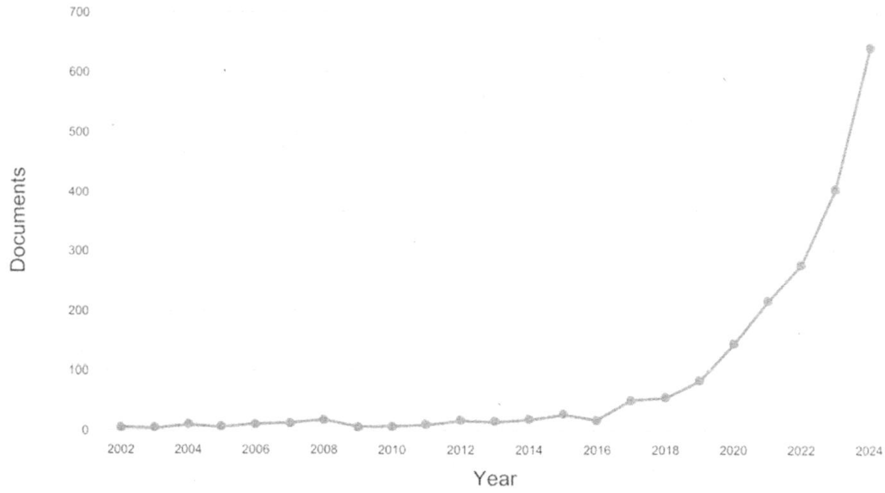

FIGURE 19.10 Number of publications over time of research on AI for structural risk assessment and safety improvement [72].

Traditional methods often rely on static models and limited data, whereas AI-driven systems provide real-time, adaptive analysis of complex structures.

Fig. 19.10 (provided by Ref. [72]) illustrates the growth in the number of publications over time on AI and ML applications in structural safety and risk assessment. The data are based on a comprehensive review of approximately 2500 articles identified using key terms such as machine learning, artificial intelligence, risk assessment, safety, and related ones.

AI-powered simulations are now routinely used to model disaster scenarios—such as earthquakes, floods, and hurricanes—to evaluate structural response under extreme conditions. During construction phases, computer vision algorithms—often integrated with BIM platforms—are employed to detect safety violations, ensure compliance, and ultimately foster a stronger safety culture and improve operational efficiency. Furthermore, AI applications in monitoring aging infrastructure have become critical in addressing concerns about long-term durability and performance, particularly for essential assets such as bridges, tunnels, and high-rise buildings. As ML and AI technologies continue to expand across the infrastructure sector, they are becoming central to building safer, more resilient, and smarter built environments [115].

4. Generative AI in structural engineering

Generative AI (GenAI) encompasses a cutting-edge class of artificial intelligence models, including large language models (LLMs) and multimodal systems, that are capable of generating new data, designs, and predictions by learning from a limited number of examples or prompt-based instructions [116,117]. While GenAI has rapidly gained traction across domains such as creative arts, software engineering, and healthcare, its application in structural engineering is a very recent and largely unexplored development. Nevertheless, it is beginning to attract attention for its potential to transform a field long dominated by deterministic rules and rigid design workflows.

Therefore, in structural engineering, GenAIs methods are beginning to reshape how engineers conceptualize, design, and evaluate structures. These advanced models enable unprecedented levels of automation and optimization throughout the design lifecycle—from generating innovative structural configurations to simulating material behavior and adapting to dynamic environmental conditions [118]. Unlike conventional engineering and traditional ML methods, which often depend on predefined constraints and require large amounts of data, GenAI leverages foundation models and vast unstructured datasets to produce creative, adaptive solutions—even in low-data environments (known as few-shot learning).

What sets GenAI apart is not just its flexibility and creativity, but its immense potential for the future. Thanks to its ability to model complex interactions, generalize across tasks, and assist with design, documentation, and analysis, GenAI may complement traditional ML and engineering tools, but its performance and reliability must be demonstrated through domain-specific validation. As the technology continues to mature, its integration into engineering workflows could lead to a fundamental shift by accelerating innovation, reducing development time, and unlocking new possibilities in the design and maintenance of structures. The following subsection highlights some key areas within structural engineering where GenAI's potential can be most effectively realized.

4.1 GenAI in design documentation and code generation

Large Language Models (LLMs), such as Generative Pretrained Transformers (GPT), represent a prominent example of GenAI with significant potential in structural engineering. These models can generate code, automate documentation, and enhance reporting tasks [119]. When supported by suitable training data or retrieval systems, LLMs can assist with technical manuals, engineering standards, and building codes.

For large-scale projects that demand extensive paperwork, LLMs reduce the burden of routine documentation, freeing engineers to focus on analytical and creative tasks. They can extract relevant information from existing designs and generate tailored outputs aligned with project-specific requirements. Their ability to interpret and contextualize complex documents also accelerates knowledge retrieval and decision-making. Furthermore, these models can be embedded into collaborative platforms to provide real-time assistance—answering questions, clarifying code provisions, or suggesting improvements. In doing so, LLMs foster better communication among project stakeholders and improve workflow efficiency across the design, approval, and construction phases.

4.2 Generative design through GenAI-Driven conceptualization

GenAI is particularly transformative in the early stages of structural design, where engineers explore multiple alternatives to meet structural, environmental, and economic objectives [120]. Traditional conceptual design often involves trial-and-error processes. In contrast, GenAIs introduce a fundamentally different paradigm: rather than merely optimizing existing designs, they autonomously generate entirely new structural configurations based on limited input prompts or design constraints. These models can explore a wide design space, balancing multiple factors and often uncovering unconventional yet feasible solutions.

Unlike conventional AI that typically predicts outcomes or classifies data, GenAI can leverage large-scale training on structural blueprints, simulation data, and contextual information to create novel designs that may not exist in current datasets. For example, a GenAI model exposed to thousands of structural forms can generate unique layout proposals or innovative material strategies that conform to safety codes while offering creative architectural expressions. By integrating with physics-informed simulations and real-time sensor inputs, these models not only suggest what has worked in the past, but also what could work in the future by bridging engineering functionality with design exploration.

4.3 AI-generated structural simulations and performance predictions

GenAI extends beyond conventional predictive modeling by generating synthetic simulations and performance scenarios for structural systems under diverse conditions, ranging from everyday loads to extreme events such as earthquakes, high winds, and temperature fluctuations. Unlike traditional AI models that often require predefined input–output pairs, GenAI can learn from vast and varied datasets to create entirely new performance predictions based on limited prompts or partially defined design parameters.

By using historical structural data, sensor outputs, and simulation results, GenAI can forecast how novel or altered designs might perform in unseen scenarios. This is particularly beneficial during early design stages where physical prototyping or high-fidelity finite element simulations are too time-consuming or costly.

Moreover, GenAI's use of deep learning and probabilistic reasoning enables the identification of failure modes, estimation of safety margins, and proposal of optimized structural components while accounting for uncertainties and nonlinear interactions. These generative simulations should be treated as aids to traditional analysis, not replacements for verified structural assessment.

5. Challenges, limitations, and future directions

5.1 Current challenges in AI integration

The integration of AI, particularly GenAI, into structural engineering faces several significant challenges. One of the most pressing issues is the lack of high-quality, domain-specific data. Structural engineering problems often require detailed datasets encompassing material properties, environmental conditions, construction methods, and historical performance records that are often fragmented, inconsistent, or proprietary. Without access to such rich datasets, AI models may fail to generalize effectively or produce reliable outputs in real-world scenarios. Additionally, the black-box nature of many AI models, especially deep learning-based approaches, presents concerns in safety-critical applications where transparency and interpretability are essential for validation and regulatory approval.

5.2 Technical and organizational limitations

Another key limitation is the gap between AI capabilities and practical engineering requirements. While AI models can assist in simulations or optimization tasks, they often lack the physical reasoning and domain constraints that experienced engineers routinely apply. Integrating AI outputs into established design codes, safety standards, and engineering workflows is still an evolving challenge. Furthermore, organizational resistance to adopting new technologies driven by concerns over reliability, skill gaps, or regulatory compliance can slow down AI adoption in practice. Many firms may also lack the computational infrastructure or in-house expertise to implement AI solutions at scale.

5.3 Future research opportunities

To address these challenges, future research should focus on the development of hybrid modeling approaches that integrate data-driven AI with physics-informed and domain-specific models. These hybrid systems can leverage the strengths of both worlds: the pattern recognition and adaptability of AI with the rigor, transparency, and consistency of physical laws. By embedding engineering principles directly into AI architectures, researchers can improve the accuracy, robustness, and interpretability of predictions which is essential for applications in safety-critical structural systems.

Furthermore, there is a growing need for the creation of large, open-access, and standardized datasets specifically tailored to structural engineering problems. These datasets can serve as benchmarks for evaluating and comparing models, fostering reproducibility and accelerating innovation across the field. They should include not only sensor data and performance logs but also metadata related to materials, loading conditions, design constraints, and failure modes.

To fully realize the potential of AI and GenAI in structural engineering, interdisciplinary collaboration will be key. Close cooperation among structural engineers, data scientists, computer scientists, and domain experts can ensure that models are not only technically sound but also aligned with practical needs, regulatory standards, and ethical considerations. Collaborative research environments can also help address issues of model trust, generalizability, and explainability, which are central to wider adoption in real-world engineering workflows.

Finally, researchers should explore adaptive learning frameworks, in which AI models continue to improve post-deployment by incorporating new data and feedback from real-world performance. This will support the development of intelligent systems capable of evolving with infrastructure demands offering a pathway toward resilient, efficient, and sustainable structural solutions in the era of smart cities and climate-aware engineering.

5.4 Toward scalable and explainable AI integration

As AI technologies mature, the path forward must prioritize scalability, explainability, and regulatory alignment to ensure their effective and trustworthy integration into structural engineering practice. The growing reliance on AI for tasks that directly impact safety, resilience, and economic efficiency makes transparency and interpretability not just desirable, but essential. Future AI systems must embed explainable AI (XAI) methods that enable engineers to understand the rationale behind AI-generated recommendations, predictions, or optimizations. This interpretability is particularly important in high-stakes decisions such as load-bearing assessments or retrofitting strategies, where opaque "black-box" models may raise safety and liability concerns.

Scalability is another critical factor for mainstream adoption. Current AI applications are often tailored to specific use cases or datasets, limiting their broader applicability. To overcome this, future systems should be designed with modular, interoperable architectures that can be integrated into various structural engineering workflows, from early-stage design to long-term infrastructure management. The adoption of cloud-based AI platforms, edge computing, and automated data pipelines can help scale these solutions to projects of different sizes and complexities.

Another significant frontier is the integration of AI into digital ecosystems, such as BIM, Digital Twins, and Cyber-Physical Systems (CPS). Embedding AI within these platforms enables dynamic, real-time decision-making by linking AI models with continuous data flows from sensors, simulations, and user interactions. This would allow for continuous performance monitoring, predictive maintenance, and rapid adaptation to changing environmental or usage conditions, leading to more responsive and intelligent infrastructure systems.

To ensure that AI aligns with existing engineering codes, ethics, and public accountability, regulatory frameworks must also evolve. AI development for structural engineering must include compliance with safety standards, data governance protocols, and model validation practices that are transparent and auditable. Standardized testing environments and third-party certification could become essential tools to evaluate the reliability and safety of AI models in engineering contexts.

Finally, the success of AI integration hinges on human capacity-building. The engineering workforce must be empowered through targeted education, upskilling programs, and cross-disciplinary training that introduces core concepts in AI, data science, and computational modeling. Integrating AI literacy into engineering curricula, licensing exams, and continuous professional development programs will equip current and future engineers with the tools needed to leverage AI responsibly and effectively. Moreover, fostering interdisciplinary collaboration among civil engineers, AI researchers, software developers, and domain experts, will be essential for designing AI systems that are technically sound, practically useful, and aligned with real-world engineering challenges.

6. Conclusion

This chapter reviewed the current state of AI in structural engineering, examining both traditional AI techniques and the emerging potential of GenAI. The integration of AI, including ML and deep learning, has already shown significant promise in enhancing the design, analysis, and maintenance of structures. By enabling data-driven decision-making, improving safety assessments, and optimizing designs, AI is transforming traditional engineering practices.

GenAI, in particular, holds immense potential for the future of structural engineering. Its ability to autonomously generate design alternatives, simulate structural performance, and optimize material use offers unique advantages in comparison to traditional methods. While GenAI's ability to generate innovative solutions from limited data has garnered increasing attention, AI as a whole continues to play a critical role in improving the efficiency and accuracy of structural engineering workflows.

Despite its transformative capabilities, the integration of AI into structural engineering faces several challenges, including data quality, model interpretability, and the high computational costs associated with training complex AI models. Moreover, the industry must overcome barriers related to regulatory frameworks, standardization, and the integration of AI with existing engineering tools. As these obstacles are addressed, the potential for AI in structural engineering will continue to grow, leading to safer, more efficient, and cost-effective infrastructure.

Future research and development should focus on overcoming these challenges while expanding the application of AI across various stages of the engineering lifecycle. Key areas for future exploration include hybrid AI-physics models, real-time monitoring integration, and the further integration of AI with Building Information Modeling systems. As AI technologies, particularly GenAI, continue to advance, they are poised to play an increasingly pivotal role in shaping the future of structural engineering, driving innovation, and optimizing the design and maintenance of the built environment.

References

[1] H. Salehi, R. Burgueño, Emerging artificial intelligence methods in structural engineering, Eng. Struct. 171 (2018) 170–189.

[2] H.-T. Thai, Machine learning for structural engineering: A state-of-the-art review, in: Structures, Elsevier, 2022.

[3] A. Chitkeshwar, Revolutionizing structural engineering: Applications of machine learning for enhanced performance and safety, Arch. Comput. Methods Eng. 31 (8) (2024) 4617–4632.

[4] J.S. Przemieniecki, Theory of Matrix Structural Analysis, Courier Corporation, 1985.

[5] W.-F. Chen, E.M. Lui, Handbook of Structural Engineering, CRC press, 2005.

[6] A. Waqar, Intelligent decision support systems in construction engineering: An artificial intelligence and machine learning approaches, Expert Syst. Appl. 249 (2024) 123503.

[7] S. Talatahari, et al., Developing a robust machine learning framework for predicting the behavior of large-scale structure, J. Build. Eng. (2025) 112204.

[8] H. Sun, et al., Machine learning applications for building structural design and performance assessment: State-of-the-art review, J. Build. Eng. 33 (2021) 101816.

[9] B. Mahesh, Machine learning algorithms-a review, Int. J. Sci. Res. 9 (1) (2020) 381–386.

[10] T. Hastie, et al., Overview of supervised learning, in: The Elements of Statistical Learning: Data Mining, Inference, and Prediction, 2009, pp. 9–41.

[11] T.D. Sparks, et al., Machine learning for structural materials, Annu. Rev. Mater. Res. 50 (1) (2020) 27–48.

[12] R. Davoudi, et al., Data-driven vision-based inspection for reinforced concrete beams and slabs: Quantitative damage and load estimation, Autom. ConStruct. 96 (2018) 292–309.

[13] A. Sóbester, A.J. Keane, Supervised learning approach to parametric computer-aided design geometry repair, AIAA J. 44 (2) (2006) 282–289.
[14] M.S. Sandeep, et al., Shear strength prediction of reinforced concrete beams using machine learning, in: Structures, Elsevier, 2023.
[15] K. Megahed, et al., Application of machine learning models in the capacity prediction of RCFST columns, Sci. Rep. 13 (1) (2023) 20878.
[16] A. Entezami, et al., Condition assessment of civil structures for structural health monitoring using supervised learning classification methods, Iran. J. Sci. Technol. Trans. Civil Eng. 44 (Suppl. 1) (2020) 51–66.
[17] M.H. Chegeni, et al., New supervised learning classifiers for structural damage diagnosis using time series features from a new feature extraction technique, Earthq. Eng. Eng. Vib. 21 (1) (2022) 169–191.
[18] O. Alshboul, et al., Empirical exploration of predictive maintenance in concrete manufacturing: Harnessing machine learning for enhanced equipment reliability in construction project management, Comput. Ind. Eng. 190 (2024) 110046.
[19] X. Wang, et al., Machine learning for risk and resilience assessment in structural engineering: Progress and future trends, J. Struct. Eng. 148 (8) (2022) 03122003.
[20] H.B. Barlow, Unsupervised learning, Neural Comput. 1 (3) (1989) 295–311.
[21] M.H. Daneshvar, H. Sarmadi, Unsupervised learning-based damage assessment of full-scale civil structures under long-term and short-term monitoring, Eng. Struct. 256 (2022) 114059.
[22] E. Akintunde, et al., Unsupervised machine learning for robust bridge damage detection: Full-scale experimental validation, Eng. Struct. 249 (2021) 113250.
[23] K.A. Eltouny, X. Liang, Bayesian-optimized unsupervised learning approach for structural damage detection, Comput. Aided Civ. Infrastruct. Eng. 36 (10) (2021) 1249–1269.
[24] D.A. Tibaduiza, et al., Structural damage detection using principal component analysis and damage indices, J. Intell. Mater. Syst. Struct. 27 (2) (2016) 233–248.
[25] A.K. Shakya, et al., Reinforcement learning algorithms: A brief survey, Expert Syst. Appl. 231 (2023) 120495.
[26] V. Asghari, et al., Reinforcement learning in construction engineering and management: A review, J. Construct. Eng. Manag. 148 (11) (2022) 03122009.
[27] S.G. Khan, et al., Reinforcement learning and optimal adaptive control: An overview and implementation examples, Annu. Rev. Control 36 (1) (2012) 42–59.
[28] L. Yu, et al., A review of deep reinforcement learning for smart building energy management, IEEE Internet Things J. 8 (15) (2021) 12046–12063.
[29] R. Panchalingam, K.C. Chan, A state-of-the-art review on artificial intelligence for smart buildings, Intell. Build. Int. 13 (4) (2021) 203–226.
[30] M. Flah, et al., Machine learning algorithms in civil structural health monitoring: A systematic review, Arch. Comput. Methods Eng. 28 (4) (2021) 2621–2643.
[31] A.D. Eslamlou, S. Huang, Reinforcement learning for multi-objective AutoML in vision-based structural health monitoring, Autom. ConStruct. 166 (2024) 105593.
[32] R. Jia, et al., Advanced building control via deep reinforcement learning, Energy Proc. 158 (2019) 6158–6163.
[33] W. Ostachowicz, et al., Optimization of sensor placement for structural health monitoring: A review, Struct. Health Monit. 18 (3) (2019) 963–988.
[34] S. Khazaeli, J.-A. Goulet, Damage detection for structural health monitoring using reinforcement and imitation learning, Struct. Infrastruct. Eng. (2024) 1–18.
[35] K. Hayashi, M. Ohsaki, Reinforcement learning for optimum design of a plane frame under static loads, Eng. Comput. 37 (3) (2021) 1999–2011.
[36] J.H. Jeong, H. Jo, Deep reinforcement learning for automated design of reinforced concrete structures, Comput. Aided Civ. Infrastruct. Eng. 36 (12) (2021) 1508–1529.
[37] Y. LeCun, et al., Deep learning, Nature 521 (7553) (2015) 436–444.
[38] Y. Guo, et al., Deep learning for visual understanding: A review, Neurocomputing 187 (2016) 27–48.
[39] H. Adeli, Neural networks in civil engineering: 1989–2000, Comput. Aided Civ. Infrastruct. Eng. 16 (2) (2001) 126–142.
[40] S. Lee, et al., Background information of deep learning for structural engineering, Arch. Comput. Methods Eng. 25 (2018) 121–129.
[41] S. Sony, et al., A systematic review of convolutional neural network-based structural condition assessment techniques, Eng. Struct. 226 (2021) 111347.
[42] K.A. Eltouny, X. Liang, Large-scale structural health monitoring using composite recurrent neural networks and grid environments, Comput. Aided Civ. Infrastruct. Eng. 38 (3) (2023) 271–287.
[43] C. Wang, et al., End-to-End structural analysis in civil engineering based on deep learning, Autom. ConStruct. 138 (2022) 104255.
[44] Y.-J. Cha, et al., Deep learning-based structural health monitoring, Autom. ConStruct. 161 (2024) 105328.
[45] F. Nex, et al., Structural building damage detection with deep learning: Assessment of a state-of-the-art CNN in operational conditions, Remote Sens. 11 (23) (2019) 2765.
[46] R. Zhang, et al., Deep long short-term memory networks for nonlinear structural seismic response prediction, Comput. Struct. 220 (2019) 55–68.
[47] S. Sharma, S. Sen, Real-time structural damage assessment using LSTM networks: Regression and classification approaches, Neural Comput. Appl. 35 (1) (2023) 557–572.
[48] Y. Yu, et al., Deep learning for determining a near-optimal topological design without any iteration, Struct. Multidiscip. Optim. 59 (3) (2019) 787–799.
[49] C. Xiang, et al., Accelerated topology optimization design of 3D structures based on deep learning, Struct. Multidiscip. Optim. 65 (3) (2022) 99.

[50] S. Li, et al., A knowledge-enhanced deep reinforcement learning-based shape optimizer for aerodynamic mitigation of wind-sensitive structures, Comput. Aided Civ. Infrastruct. Eng. 36 (6) (2021) 733–746.
[51] S. Gupta, A. Gupta, Dealing with noise problem in machine learning data-sets: A systematic review, Procedia Comput. Sci. 161 (2019) 466–474.
[52] A. Sofi, et al., Structural health monitoring using wireless smart sensor network–An overview, Mech. Syst. Signal Process. 163 (2022) 108113.
[53] P. Rizzo, A. Enshaeian, Challenges in bridge health monitoring: A review, Sensors 21 (13) (2021) 4336.
[54] F. Li, et al., Machine learning and remote sensing integration for leveraging urban sustainability: A review and framework, Sustain. Cities Soc. 96 (2023) 104653.
[55] S.S. Afshari, et al., Machine learning-based methods in structural reliability analysis: A review, Reliab. Eng. Syst. Saf. 219 (2022) 108223.
[56] E. Figueiredo, J. Brownjohn, Three decades of statistical pattern recognition paradigm for SHM of bridges, Struct. Health Monit. 21 (6) (2022) 3018–3054.
[57] M.M. Azad, et al., Intelligent computational methods for damage detection of laminated composite structures for mobility applications: A comprehensive review, Arch. Comput. Methods Eng. 32 (1) (2025) 441–469.
[58] P. Vurtur Badarinath, et al., A machine learning approach as a surrogate for a finite element analysis: Status of research and application to one dimensional systems, Sensors 21 (5) (2021) 1654.
[59] D. Nath, et al., Application of machine learning and deep learning in finite element analysis: A comprehensive review, Arch. Comput. Methods Eng. 31 (5) (2024) 2945–2984.
[60] X. Liu, et al., A multi-step predictive deep reinforcement learning algorithm for HVAC control systems in smart buildings, Energy 259 (2022) 124857.
[61] A. Shahraki, et al., A comparative study on online machine learning techniques for network traffic streams analysis, Comput. Netw. 207 (2022) 108836.
[62] T. Wu, R. Snaiki, Applications of machine learning to wind engineering, Front. Built Environ. 8 (2022) 811460.
[63] A. Zabin, et al., Applications of machine learning to BIM: A systematic literature review, Adv. Eng. Inform. 51 (2022) 101474.
[64] A.T.G. Tapeh, M. Naser, Artificial intelligence, machine learning, and deep learning in structural engineering: A scientometrics review of trends and best practices, Arch. Comput. Methods Eng. 30 (1) (2023) 115–159.
[65] I.A. Nhamage, et al., Strategies for maximising the value of digital twins for bridge management and structural monitoring: A systematic review, Arch. Comput. Methods Eng. (2025) 1–32.
[66] A.Z.a.O. Al-Hijazeen, et al., Implementation of digital twin and support vector machine in structural health monitoring of bridges, Arch. Civ. Eng. (2023), 31-47-31-47.
[67] S.R. Vadyala, et al., A review of physics-based machine learning in civil engineering, Results Eng. 13 (2022) 100316.
[68] S.H.M. Rizvi, M. Abbas, From data to insight, enhancing structural health monitoring using physics-informed machine learning and advanced data collection methods, Eng. Res. Express 5 (3) (2023) 032003.
[69] K. Ahmad, et al., What's up with requirements engineering for artificial intelligence systems?, in: 2021 IEEE 29th International Requirements Engineering Conference (RE), IEEE, 2021.
[70] X. Pan, et al., BIM adoption in sustainability, energy modelling and implementing using ISO 19650: A review, Ain Shams Eng. J. 15 (1) (2024) 102252.
[71] M. Chatsuwan, et al., A Review of BIM Maturity in Standards and Guidelines across Asia, In Proceedings of the 41st International Conference of CIB W, Vol. 78 (2024).
[72] Elsevier. "Scopus." Retrieved 14/04/2025, 2025, from https://www.scopus.com.
[73] V.R. Gharehbaghi, et al., A critical review on structural health monitoring: Definitions, methods, and perspectives, Arch. Comput. Methods Eng. 29 (4) (2022) 2209–2235.
[74] R. Zinno, et al., Artificial intelligence and structural health monitoring of bridges: A review of the state-of-the-art, IEEE Access 10 (2022) 88058–88078.
[75] P.S. Chakurkar, et al., Data-driven approach for AI-based crack detection: Techniques, challenges, and future scope, Front. Sustain. Cities 5 (2023) 1253627.
[76] P. Ghannadi, et al., A review of the application of the simulated annealing algorithm in structural health monitoring (1995-2021), Fractur. Struct. Integr. 17 (64) (2023) 51–76.
[77] N. Van Eck, L. Waltman, Software survey: VOSviewer, a computer program for bibliometric mapping, Scientometrics 84 (2) (2010) 523–538.
[78] W. Fan, et al., Machine learning applied to the design and inspection of reinforced concrete bridges: Resilient methods and emerging applications, in: Structures, Elsevier, 2021.
[79] J.G. Xu, et al., Data-driven rapid damage evaluation for life-cycle seismic assessment of regional reinforced concrete bridges, Earthq. Eng. Struct. Dynam. 51 (11) (2022) 2730–2751.
[80] C.A. Tokognon, et al., Structural health monitoring framework based on internet of things: A survey, IEEE Internet Things J. 4 (3) (2017) 619–635.
[81] T.J. Saravanan, et al., Internet of things (IoT)-based structural health monitoring of laboratory-scale civil engineering structures, Innov. Infrastruct. Solut. 9 (4) (2024) 110.
[82] P. Motamedi, et al., Ethnic groups chaos game optimization algorithm for optimal design of steel structures considering seismic risk, Eng. Optim. 55 (11) (2023) 1886–1904.

[83] E. Asadi, et al., A TSK fuzzy model optimization with meta-heuristic algorithms for seismic response prediction of nonlinear steel moment-resisting frames, Struct. Eng. Mech. 90 (2) (2024) 189–208.

[84] S. Khodadoost, et al., Optimal design of fractional-order proportional integral derivative controllers for structural vibration suppression, Sci. Rep. 14 (1) (2024) 17207.

[85] A. Heidari, et al., A systematic review of the BIM in construction: From smart building management to interoperability of BIM & AI, Archit. Sci. Rev. 67 (3) (2024) 237–254.

[86] Y. Pan, L. Zhang, Integrating BIM and AI for smart construction management: Current status and future directions, Arch. Comput. Methods Eng. 30 (2) (2023) 1081–1110.

[87] L. Yang, A comprehensive review of artificial intelligence applications in Building Information Modeling (BIM) and future perspectives, J. Comput. Technol. Appl. Math. 2 (2) (2025) 1–10.

[88] Y. Ma, E. Qiao, Visualized management system of prefabricated construction and installation engineering based on BIM and machine learning, in: 2021 IEEE International Conference on Industrial Application of Artificial Intelligence (IAAI), IEEE, 2021.

[89] M. Awe, et al., Towards 4D BIM: A systematic literature review on challenges, strategies and tools in leveraging AI with BIM, Buildings 15 (7) (2025) 1072.

[90] K. Li, et al., Automated generative design and prefabrication of precast buildings using integrated BIM and graph convolutional neural network, Dev. Built Environ. 18 (2024) 100418.

[91] J. Lai, et al., Applying artificial intelligence in construction management: A scoping review, J. Internet Technol. 26 (1) (2025) 1–12.

[92] N. De Belie, et al., A review of self-healing concrete for damage management of structures, Adv. Mater. Interfac. 5 (17) (2018) 1800074.

[93] A. Tabrizikahou, et al., Application and modelling of shape-memory alloys for structural vibration control: State-of-the-art review, Constr. Build. Mater. 342 (2022) 127975.

[94] P. Jiao, A.H. Alavi, Artificial intelligence-enabled smart mechanical metamaterials: Advent and future trends, Int. Mater. Rev. 66 (6) (2021) 365–393.

[95] G.U. Alaneme, et al., Critical review on the application of artificial intelligence techniques in the production of geopolymer-concrete, SN Appl. Sci. 5 (8) (2023) 217.

[96] T. Ali, et al., A systematic literature review of AI-based prediction methods for self-compacting, geopolymer, and other eco-friendly concrete types: Advancing sustainable concrete, Constr. Build. Mater. 440 (2024) 137370.

[97] Q. Tian, et al., Building the future: Smart concrete as a key element in next-generation construction, Constr. Build. Mater. 429 (2024) 136364.

[98] N. Heidari Matin, A. Eydgahi, Technologies used in responsive facade systems: A comparative study, Intell. Build. Int. 14 (1) (2022) 54–73.

[99] R. Özlük, et al., Artificial intelligence algorithms, simulation tools and software for optimization of adaptive facades: A systematic literature review, J. Build. Eng. (2025) 112566.

[100] F. Raeesi, et al., An inverse TSK model of MR damper for vibration control of nonlinear structures using an improved grasshopper optimization algorithm, in: Structures, Elsevier, 2020.

[101] S. Talatahari, et al., System identification of dampers using chaotic accelerated particle swarm optimization, Chin. J. Artif. Intell. 1 (1) (2022) E200521193450.

[102] B. Chen, et al., Optimization of high-performance concrete mix ratio design using machine learning, Eng. Appl. Artif. Intell. 122 (2023) 106047.

[103] M. Sifan, et al., Efficient mix design method for lightweight high strength concrete: A machine learning approach, in: Structures, Elsevier, 2023.

[104] A.H. Gandomi, et al., New design equations for elastic modulus of concrete using multi expression programming, J. Civ. Eng. Manag. 21 (6) (2015) 761–774.

[105] M. Rathnayaka, et al., Machine learning approaches to predict compressive strength of fly ash-based geopolymer concrete: A comprehensive review, Constr. Build. Mater. 419 (2024) 135519.

[106] H. Jia, et al., Machine learning algorithms in the environmental corrosion evaluation of reinforced concrete structures-A review, Cement Concr. Compos. 133 (2022) 104725.

[107] K.R. Shadbad, et al., The effects of nanoparticle additives on thermophysical properties of concrete mixtures, Open J. Civ. Eng. 12 (4) (2022) 587–614.

[108] K. Aghaee, A. Roshan, Predicting time to cracking of concrete composites subjected to restrained shrinkage: A review with insights from statistical analysis and ensemble machine learning approaches, J. Build. Eng. (2024) 110856.

[109] B. Ni, et al., A review on properties and multi-objective performance predictions of concrete based on machine learning models, Mater. Today Commun. (2025) 112017.

[110] O. Gheibi, et al., Applying machine learning in self-adaptive systems: A systematic literature review, ACM Trans. Autonom. Adapt. Syst. 15 (3) (2021) 1–37.

[111] T. Kucova, et al., Thermoelectric energy harvesting for internet of things devices using machine learning: A review, CAAI Trans. Intell. Technol. 8 (3) (2023) 680–700.

[112] Z. Yao, et al., Machine learning for a sustainable energy future, Nat. Rev. Mater. 8 (3) (2023) 202–215.

[113] A. Bajwa, AI-Based Emergency Response Systems: A Systematic Literature Review on Smart Infrastructure Safety, 2025. Available at: SSRN 5171521.

[114] G. Borah, Emerging trends in smart green building technologies, in: Heat Transfer Enhancement Techniques: Thermal Performance, Optimization and Applications, 2025, pp. 391–415.

[115] S. Arora, P. Khare, AI/ML-enabled optimization of edge infrastructure: Enhancing performance and security, Sensors 4 (2) (2024).

[116] M. Shahabikargar, et al., Generative AI-Enabled Knowledge Base Fine-tuning: Enhancing Feature Engineering for Customer Churn, 2024.
[117] K.-B. Ooi, et al., The potential of generative artificial intelligence across disciplines: Perspectives and future directions, J. Comput. Inf. Syst. 65 (1) (2025) 76–107.
[118] N. Rane, Transforming structural engineering through ChatGPT and similar generative artificial intelligence: Roles, challenges, and opportunities, Chall. Opport. (2023) (September 20, 2023).
[119] S. Kähkönen, Improving Software Development Workflows Using Generative AI, 2024.
[120] W. Liao, et al., Generative AI design for building structures, Autom. ConStruct. 157 (2024) 105187.

Chapter 20

An introduction to essential methods for uncertainty quantification in neural networks

Hassan Gharoun[1], Mohammad Sadegh Khorshidi[1], Fang Chen[1] and Amir H. Gandomi[1, 2]

[1]*Faculty of Engineering & Information Technology, University of Technology Sydney, Ultimo, NSW, Australia;* [2]*University Research and Innovation Center (EKIK), Óbuda University, Budapest, Hungary*

1. Introduction

In machine learning (ML), specifically neural networks, it is generally assumed that the distribution of the data used to train a model (source domain) and the data used during inference (target domain) should be identical or very similar. When there is a mismatch between these distributions—referred to as a distribution shift—the model's predictions can vary significantly, leading to inconsistent performance. This inconsistent performance can often be attributed to the model's architecture and configuration not being optimized for the new, unseen distribution. Even in the absence of distribution shift, such variability in predictions may occur due to inherent noise in the data. This variability or inconsistency in a model's predictions is known as uncertainty, which reflects the model's lack of knowledge about its predictions. Confidence should be interpreted as a calibrated estimate of predictive reliability. This definition is crucial as highlights a common misconception: the numerical probability values output by neural networks—and also most ML models do not necessarily reflect the model's true level of confidence [1]. These numerical probability values are generally normalized values via the Softmax function representing class probabilities and even with a high softmax output, a model's predictions may still lack robust confidence [1].

To put it plainly, sources of uncertainty are classified into two main categories:

- Aleatoric uncertainty: also named data uncertainty, stems from multi-modality, noise, complexity, and in general lack of knowledge of ambient conditions. Aleatoric uncertainty is not reducible as depends on the input distributions.
- Epistemic uncertainty: also known as parametric uncertainty, refers to uncertainty arising from model choices, such as parameter values, model structure, and incomplete knowledge of the model's components. Epistemic uncertainty is reducible.

The predictive models' uncertainty is the summation of aleatoric uncertainty and epistemic uncertainty. While the uncertainty in predictions may arise from various distinct sources of uncertainty, most ML models, including neural networks make predictions without assessing the uncertainty of those predictions. This can lead to the risk of guiding a human operator—or worse, an automated system—toward incorrect decisions [2]. The following two examples may arguably be among the most talked-about instances in recent years that have sparked discussions concerning model uncertainty. In 2016, a severe accident occurred when a driver-assistance system misinterpreted the white side of a trailer as open sky [3]. In a separate incident, concerns about racial prejudice emerged when a visual recognition tool mistakenly categorized two human individuals as nonhuman primates [4]. In light of such lapses in ML/DLs outcomes, there's a surging necessity to concentrate on quantifying and interpreting models' uncertainties. This clarity not only enhances the user experience but also encourages wider adoption of the model [5].

Advanced Intelligence Methods for Data Science and Optimization. https://doi.org/10.1016/B978-0-443-28940-8.00012-9

Accordingly, this chapter introduces the fundamental concepts of uncertainty quantification (UQ) and highlights the most widely used UQ techniques. The objective is not to compare the performance of various methods but rather to provide clear definitions and essential techniques, enabling readers with no prior knowledge to grasp the core principles of UQ.

2. Preliminary

Neural networks, inspired by the intricate neural structures of the human brain, have emerged as a cornerstone in the realm of computational intelligence. These networks, often multilayered, are designed to recognize patterns, make predictions, and classify data through a series of interconnected nodes, commonly referred to as "neurons." Followings delve into the mathematical underpinnings that govern the operation of these networks, providing a foundational understanding of their structure and functionality [6].

The initial step in a neural network's operation involves a linear transformation of the input data. Let's consider an input vector $\mathbf{x}$ of dimensionality D. This vector undergoes a transformation using a weight matrix $\mathbf{W}_1$ and an added bias term $\mathbf{b}$, resulting in a transformed vector, mathematically represented as $\mathbf{W}_1\mathbf{x} + \mathbf{b}$.

Following this linear transformation, the data is subjected to a nonlinear activation function. The activation function serves as a bridge, smoothly transitioning values between 0 and 1 (or another range, depending on the function used), making it particularly useful for tasks that require binary outputs or probabilities. Such a function forms the foundation of a basic computational unit in neural networks, often referred to as a neuron or perceptron.

Building upon the concept of the perceptron, neural networks extend this idea by organizing multiple perceptrons into layers. These networks are typically structured in layers, with each layer comprising a set of neurons. Data flows sequentially through these layers, undergoing transformations at each stage. The output from one layer acts as the input for the subsequent layer, creating a cascading flow of information. This layered structure allows for the modeling of complex patterns and relationships in the data.

For a neural network with three hidden layers, the process begins with an input vector $\mathbf{x}$. This vector undergoes a series of transformations as it progresses through the layers. In the first layer, the input is transformed using a weight matrix $\mathbf{W}_1$ and a bias vector $\mathbf{b}_1$. Mathematically, this can be represented as:

$$\mathbf{a}_1 = \sigma(\mathbf{W}_1\mathbf{x} + \mathbf{b}_1) \tag{20.1}$$

where σ is the activation function.

The output $\mathbf{a}_1$ then serves as the input for the second layer, undergoing another transformation:

$$\mathbf{a}_2 = \sigma(\mathbf{W}_2\mathbf{a}_1 + \mathbf{b}_2) \tag{20.2}$$

Similarly, the third layer processes $\mathbf{a}_2$ as:

$$\mathbf{a}_3 = \sigma(\mathbf{W}_3\mathbf{a}_2 + \mathbf{b}_3) \tag{20.3}$$

Here, $\mathbf{W}_i$ represents the weight matrix and $\mathbf{b}_i$ is the bias vector for the ith layer. The dimensionality of each $\mathbf{W}_i$ and $\mathbf{b}_i$ is determined by the number of neurons in the respective layers.

Upon propagation to the output layer, which receives input from the final hidden layer, the network endeavors to formulate its predictions. Consider the classification tasks. The output of the third hidden layer, $\mathbf{a}_3$, is passed through the softmax function to yield a probability distribution over potential classes. Formally, the softmax function is articulated as:

$$\text{softmax}(a_{3i}) = \frac{\exp(a_{3i})}{\sum_j \exp(a_{3j})} \tag{20.4}$$

This resulting vector encapsulates the predicted probabilities for each class. To assess the fidelity of these predictions, the cross-entropy loss function is predominantly utilized as the training objective for classification. It quantifies the divergence between the predicted probabilities and the true class labels. Given the true label y and the predicted probability $\widehat{y}$ from the softmax function, the cross-entropy loss is delineated as:

$$L(W_1, W_2, W_3, B) = -\sum_i y_i \log(\widehat{y}_i) \tag{20.5}$$

In this formulation, y_i represents the true label for the ith class, while $\widehat{y}_i$ denotes the network's predicted probability for that class. The training phase's objective revolves around refining the weights W_1, W_2, W_3 and biases B to minimize this loss, typically employing iterative optimization techniques like gradient descent.

With these transformations in place, the neural network is set up to process input data and produce outputs. However, the accuracy of these outputs is contingent upon the optimization of the network's weights and biases. To achieve this refinement, the training process is initiated. This involves the iterative adjustment of weights and biases using optimization techniques like gradient descent. As the network undergoes training, it progressively refines its predictions to align more closely with the actual data labels. However, the optimized weights are deterministic point estimates and do not explicitly capture the uncertainty inherent in the model's parameters and predictions. In other words, while the network may provide output probabilities, these represent a form of "best guess" rather than a true measure of how confident the model is in its predictions, particularly in terms of model uncertainty (or variability) in unseen data.

To capture this uncertainty, it's essential to place probability distributions over the model parameters (epistemic uncertainty) and over the model's outputs (aleatoric uncertainty). This probabilistic approach allows us to quantify the variability in the model's predictions, offering insights into both the model's internal confidence and the inherent unpredictability of the data. Methods for UQ can be broadly divided into two main categories: Bayesian and non-Bayesian approaches. In the following sections, the Bayesian perspective on UQ will be examined.

3. A Bayesian perspective on uncertainty quantification

In the following discourse, the foundations of Bayesian neural networks (BNNs) are elucidated [7]. Consider the classification task and let $\mathscr{D}_{\text{tr}} = \{\mathbf{X}, \mathbf{Y}\}$, where each input $\mathbf{x}_i$ is in $\mathbb{R}^d$ and the corresponding output $\mathbf{y}_i$ belongs to one of the classes in the set $\{1, \ldots, \mathrm{C}\}$. Given a neural network with N hidden layers, the preactivated output $h_{[j]}$ of each layer $j\{j$ from 1 to $N+1\}$ is formulated as:

$$h_{[j]} = f_{[j]}^{\omega[j]}\left(h_{[j-1]}\right) = \omega_{[j]} \cdot \eta\left(h_{[j-1]}\right]) \tag{20.6}$$

where $\omega_{[j]} \in \mathbb{R}^{d_j \times d_{j-1}}$ denotes the weight matrix for the jth layer, and η is an element-wise nonlinear function. It's noteworthy that $\mathbf{x} = h[0]$ and the dimensionality d is represented as d_0.

By successively applying transformations across layers, the neural network can be conceptualized as a transformation function f parameterized by ω-which is a concatenation of vectorized weight matrices from all layers—that maps $\mathbf{X}$ to $\mathbf{Y}$, i.e., $\mathbf{Y} = f^{\omega}(\mathbf{X})$ where:

$$f^{\omega}(\mathbf{X}) = f_{[N+1]}^{\omega[N+1]}\left(f_{[N]}^{\omega[N]}\left(\cdots f_{[1]}^{\omega[1]}(X)\right)\right) \tag{20.7}$$

To optimize the neural network's parameters, i.e., ω, the Bayesian framework treats the weights of the network as random variables, rather than fixed values. This probabilistic perspective introduces a distribution over potential weight values, encapsulating the inherent uncertainty about them. Before observing any data, a prior belief about the possible weight values is established, represented by a prior distribution.

Upon observing the data, the aim is to update this prior belief to form a posterior distribution over the weights. This posterior encapsulates the updated beliefs about the probable weight values after considering the observed data.

Thus, Eq. (20.4) can be reformulated as follows:

$$p(y = c|x, \omega) = \frac{\exp\left(f_{\omega}^{c}(x)\right)}{\sum\limits_{c_i} \exp\left(f_{\omega}^{c_i}(x)\right)} \tag{20.8}$$

In the Bayesian paradigm, a prior distribution $p(\omega)$ is imposed on the parameter vector ω. This leads to the posterior distribution:

$$p(\omega|X, Y) = \frac{\prod\limits_{i=1}^{N} p(\mathbf{y}_i|\mathbf{x}_i, \omega)p(\omega)}{p(Y|X)} \tag{20.9}$$

where $p(w|X, Y)$ represents the posterior distribution given the dataset in terms of w, while $p(w)$ signifies the prior distribution associated with w.

For any new input x^* and its corresponding output y^*, the predictive distribution is given by:

$$p(y^*|x^*, X, Y) = \int_{\omega} p(y|x, \omega)p(\omega|X, Y)d\omega \tag{20.10}$$

Computing an exact posterior inference $p(\omega|\mathscr{D})$ is challenging since is often computationally intensive due to the necessity of integrating over the entire parameter space ω [7]. However, approximations are feasible and numerous methodologies have been proposed to address this. These approaches will be discussed in subsequent sections.

3.1 Markov Chain Monte Carlo

Employing Bayesian techniques lies in the deployment of a prior distribution, an endeavor that can often be intricate [8]. A frequently adopted assumption in prior distribution is the utilization of the "uniform distribution," implying an equal likelihood for all potential outcomes. However, evidence suggests that this seemingly equitable assumption can lead to erroneous interpretations, particularly in intricate scenarios [9]. While deterministic methods for shaping posterior distributions in probabilistic inverse problems are computationally efficient, they necessitate rigid assumptions about the posterior's form [10]. Such assumptions can be misleading, particularly when the actual posterior distribution exhibits characteristics like skewness or multiple modes [11]. To circumvent the need for strict parametric assumptions regarding the shape of the posterior distribution, Markov Chain Monte Carlo (MCMC) is frequently employed [12].

A Markov chain is defined by a series of random variables, denoted as $X_1, X_2, \ldots, X_n$. The intrinsic property of this series is that its current state is the sole determinant of its future, uninfluenced by preceding states. This relationship is mathematically captured as [13]:

$$\text{Prob}(X_{n+1} = x|X_1 = x_1, X_2 = x_2, \ldots, X_n = xn) = \text{Prob}(X_{n+1} = x|X_n = xn) \tag{20.11}$$

This signifies that the probabilistic distribution of the subsequent state, X_{n+1}, hinges entirely on its current state, X_n. To navigate through these states and determine the progression of the chain, a transition operator is employed. This operator essentially dictates the rules or probabilities for the chain's movement from one state to another. In simpler terms, it describes how likely it is for the system to transition from its current state to any other possible state [14]. For discrete systems, this is often represented as a matrix, where each entry indicates the probability of moving from one specific state to another. In continuous systems, it's represented by a function detailing the likelihood of such transitions.

In the realm of BNNs, this concept finds a specific application. The inferential step in BNN, referenced by Eq. (20.10), can be expressed as [15]:

$$p(y^*, x^*|X, Y) = \int_{\omega} p(y|x, \omega)p(\omega|X, Y)d\omega \approx \frac{1}{N}\sum_{i=1}^{N} p(y^*|x^*, \omega_i) \tag{20.12}$$

In this context, each ω_i is a sample extracted from the posterior distribution, facilitated by MCMC techniques. These methods produce a series of samples within a state space, where the generation of every sample is predominantly influenced by the one immediately before it. The rules governing this sampling process are defined by a proposal distribution, $T(\omega'|\omega)$, which delineates the probability of transitioning from a current sample, ω, to the next, ω' [15].

The transition operator is applied iteratively for T iterations. As this process unfolds, the resulting sequence of random variables, under appropriate conditions, will converge to the desired posterior distribution, however, it's indeterminate how many iterations are required [16].

Among the foundational techniques in MCMC methodologies, the Metropolis–Hastings algorithm, Gibbs sampling, and Metropolis within Gibbs stand out as both well-established and widely recognized. While all three aim to generate samples from a desired probability distribution, they differ notably in their approaches. The Metropolis-Hastings algorithm is versatile, proposing new states from a chosen distribution and accepting them based on a calculated ratio. In contrast, Gibbs sampling operates by sequentially updating variables, directly drawing from their full conditional distributions. The hybrid method, Metropolis within Gibbs, merges these strategies: while it updates variables akin to Gibbs sampling, it employs a Metropolis-Hastings (MH) step for variables with challenging conditional distributions [13].

After introducing the foundational techniques of MCMC methodologies, it's crucial to understand their real-world applications and their advancements. In a seminal work by Ref. [17], MCMC was applied in Bayesian Probabilistic Matrix Factorization, targeting the Netflix dataset, which contains ratings given by users to movies. Their primary goal was to predict unobserved ratings. This Bayesian approach not only enhanced predictive accuracy but also provided a more robust measure of uncertainty in movie rating predictions, outperforming traditional MAP-based methods.

While the aforementioned MCMC methodologies have been pivotal in various applications, it's also essential to delve into the challenges and advancements in related techniques. One such technique that has garnered attention is the Hamiltonian Monte Carlo (HMC). Traditional HMC methods, while effective, can sometimes be inefficient in exploring the state space, particularly when compared to methods using random-walk proposals. The computational challenge intensifies with large datasets, as the standard HMC approach necessitates evaluating the gradient over the entire dataset. Ref. [18] introduced the Stochastic Gradient HMC as a novel approach to address the challenges of large datasets in sampling. When stochastic gradients are directly incorporated into HMC, they introduce noise. This noise can disrupt the dynamics of the system and lead to inaccuracies in the sampling process. Implementing HMC with stochastic gradients often necessitates frequent MH correction steps, which can be computationally expensive. To address this challenge, they innovatively incorporated a friction term. This term acts as a counterbalance to the inherent noise from stochastic estimates, creating a synergy reminiscent of Stochastic Gradient Descent with momentum, thus ensuring more efficient and accurate exploration of the state space.

Transitioning from HMC, there are also innovative frameworks designed to tackle data-scarce scenarios. In the quest to address these challenges, particularly in domains where data acquisition is costly, Ref. [19] introduces the Icebreaker framework. The Icebreaker framework integrates advanced Bayesian modeling techniques with the power of MCMC. Furthermore, Icebreaker introduces the concept of Partial Amortized Inference. This technique amalgamates the efficiency of amortized inference, which uses neural networks to estimate variational distributions, with the precision of sampling-based methods for global latent weights. By doing so, it ensures that the computational cost remains manageable, especially when dealing with large datasets. The partial amortization specifically addresses the challenge of missing data, allowing the model to infer latent variables based on partial observations, thereby enhancing the model's adaptability and robustness in real-world scenarios with incomplete data.

Furthering the discussion on optimizing Bayesian reasoning, Ref. [20] introduces an advanced methodology to accelerate Bayesian reasoning in neural networks, specifically focusing on the Stochastic Gradient Markov Chain Monte Carlo (SG-MCMC) framework. Traditional MCMC methods, like HMC, are computationally intensive, especially with large datasets. To address this, the authors propose a parallelized version of SG-MCMC. In this approach, multiple compute cores (workers) run separate SG-MCMC chains, enhancing the exploration of the parameter space. To efficiently manage communication between these workers and a central core (master), two periodic communication protocols, namely downpour and elastic, are introduced. This methodology aims to significantly reduce training times, ensuring faster and efficient Bayesian learning in neural networks without compromising accuracy.

While many MCMC methods have been developed, addressing the challenges posed by modern neural networks remains crucial. The conventional MCMC approaches often grapple with the intricate, multimodal landscapes inherent to these networks. The cyclical SG-MCMC [21] elegantly addresses this by implementing a cyclical stepsize schedule, oscillating between expansive exploration phases and intensive sampling phases. This dual-phase approach ensures a comprehensive sweep of the solution space while also permitting a granular examination of promising regions. The method's theoretical foundation, underscored by its proven nonasymptotic convergence, offers a compelling case for its efficacy.

The Thermostat-Assisted Continuously Tempered Hamiltonian Monte-Carlo (TACT-HMC) [22] method is an advanced approach designed to enhance the capabilities of the traditional MCMC in Bayesian learning. MCMC is pivotal for sampling from intricate distributions, but it often falters when faced with multi-peaked distributions or vast datasets. TACT-HMC addresses these challenges by integrating the HMC with continuous tempering, which modulates the system's "temperature" to facilitate easier exploration across energy barriers between distribution peaks. Additionally, to stabilize the sampling process against the noise introduced by using mini-batches from large datasets, the method incorporates Nosé-Hoover thermostats. Furthermore, the Adaptive Biasing Force (ABF) is employed to ensure that the tempering variable can effectively traverse its entire range by counterbalancing any restrictive forces. In essence, TACT-HMC refines the traditional HMC, promising efficient sampling from complex distributions, especially in scenarios inundated with large datasets.

Lastly, addressing the unique challenges posed by discrete parameters in HMC, [23] introduces the Dropout HMC method. HMC struggles when faced with these discrete parameters, such as those introduced by Dropout. By combining these two techniques, the researchers aim to harness the regularization benefits of Dropout while still leveraging the efficient sampling capabilities of HMC. The proposed method modifies the direction and rate of change used in HMC to account for the randomness of Dropout. The paper also touches on Stochastic Gradient HMC, which uses noisy updates and, when combined with Dropout, acts as a safeguard against overfitting. This fusion allows for better estimation of predictive uncertainty in models, ensuring more reliable and robust predictions, especially in complex tasks like image classification.

3.2 Variational inference

For many years, MCMC has been the prevailing methodology for performing approximate inference [24]. However, MCMC techniques generally demand substantial computational resources as they necessitate the retention of all sampled parameters from a posterior at every step of the training iteration. Thus this method can be computationally prohibitive and may lead to inefficiencies when implemented in highly complex deep neural networks (DNNs) [7]. Variational inference (VI) was introduced as an alternative strategy to the MCMC [25]. The inference procedure for BNNs, introduced in Eq. (20.10), is hereby revisited:

$$p(y^*, x^*|X, Y) = \int_{\omega} p(y|x, \omega)p(\omega|X, Y)d\omega \tag{20.13}$$

The principle underlying VI is to approximate the distribution $p(\omega|X, Y)$ in a manner that is congruent with the posterior distribution [16,26,27]. This approximation is realized by invoking a more manageable distribution—termed the variational distribution, denoted as $q_\theta(\omega)$. When considering two distributions, $p(\omega|X, Y)$ and $q_\theta(\omega)$, this method strives to minimize the divergence, denoted as $D(q_\theta(\omega)\|p(\omega|X, Y))$.

For this minimization, the Kullback–Leibler divergence is most frequently employed [16]:

$$\mathrm{KL}(q_\theta(\omega)\|p(\omega|X, Y)) = \int q_\theta(\omega)\log\left(\frac{q_\theta(\omega)}{p(\omega|X, Y)}\right)d\omega \tag{20.14}$$

By minimizing the Kullback–Leibler divergence, an approximation of the predictive distribution can be obtained as follows [16]:

$$p(y^*|x^*, X, Y) \approx \int p(y^*|x^*, \omega)q_\theta^*(\omega)d\omega := q_\theta^*(y^*, x^*) \tag{20.15}$$

In this methodology, the variational distribution, $q_\theta(\omega)$, serves as a simpler, more tractable approximation to the true posterior, allowing for effective inference in complex models.

Minimizing Eq. (20.13) directly is challenging since it incorporates $p(\omega|X, Y)$. Nonetheless, it is established that the minimization of Eq. (20.13) can be achieved through the maximization of the Evidence Lower Bound (ELBO) [16,28,29]:

$$\mathscr{L}_{\mathrm{VI}}(\theta) := \int q_\theta(\omega)\log p(Y|X, \omega)d\omega - \mathrm{KL}(q_\theta(\omega)\|p(\omega)) \tag{20.16}$$

Here, $q_\theta(\omega)$ is optimized to adequately represent the data by maximizing the initial term, while it also seeks to closely align with the prior by minimizing the latter term. This technique is referred to as VI.

Reducing the Kullback–Leibler divergence to its minimal value, zero, would theoretically ensure a perfect alignment between the variational distribution and the true posterior distribution. Nevertheless, achieving such exact alignment is seldom feasible in real-world applications. This is primarily due to the variational distribution often is characterized by a lower degree of parameterization and, consequently, lacks the flexibility required to model the comprehensive characteristics and complexities of the true posterior distribution [26].

Building upon the challenges of approximating the true posterior distribution, Ref. [30] proposes a novel approach. Instead of approximating the uncertainty of every weight in a neural network, they introduce uncertainty at the layer level, making the model more efficient. To ensure the model can be trained using gradient descent, they employ the reparameterization trick, expressing random weights and biases in terms of deterministic variables and noise. A key component of their approach is the Kullback–Leibler divergence, which measures the difference between the approximated distribution and the true posterior, used as a regularization term. While traditional methods might use complex distributions for better theoretical approximations, the authors argue for a simpler distribution, noting that it provides a more reliable approximation in practice, especially for deep architectures. They implement their approach in the popular Caffe deep learning (DL) framework, ensuring the model is updated correctly during training.

While the idea of introducing uncertainty at the layer level offers a fresh perspective, it's also essential to understand the foundational principles of BNNs. In the context of BNNs and VI, the weights of the network are represented by probability distributions rather than fixed values. One common way to represent these distributions is using Gaussian (or Normal) distributions, which are defined by their mean and covariance.

Expanding on the representation of weights in BNNs, Ref. [31] delve into the optimization of BNNs using an advanced form of VI. Traditionally, BNNs with VI employ diagonal covariance matrices, which assume that network weights are independent of each other. However, this work introduces a significant enhancement by replacing these diagonal matrices with full covariance matrices. This change allows the network parameters to exhibit correlations, capturing more intricate relationships in the data. By permitting these correlations, the model can express richer uncertainties and potentially achieve better generalization. This extension of VI, while computationally more demanding, offers a more comprehensive representation of the underlying problem, showcasing the trade-off between computational complexity and model expressiveness.

While the aforementioned methods focus on the intricacies of weight representation and optimization, there are also efforts to enhance the efficiency of the VI process itself. MOPED [32] is a method designed to improve the efficiency of VI in Bayesian DNNs. Instead of starting the Bayesian process from scratch, MOPED uses the weights from a previously trained regular DNN as initial beliefs or "priors." This approach leverages the knowledge already gained from the trained DNN, giving the Bayesian process a head start. By doing so, MOPED ensures that the VI process converges faster, provides reliable uncertainty estimates, and maintains the accuracy of the model, effectively extending VI by incorporating prior knowledge from deterministic DNNs. In continuation of their foundational work on MOPED, Ref. [33] further extend the methodology in their subsequent research. While the original MOPED method leveraged weights from a pretrained deterministic DNN as initial beliefs or "priors," the new extension delves deeper into refining this process. The advanced MOPED approach not only uses point-estimates from pretrained standard DNNs to set informed priors but also optimizes the model using Mean Field Variational Inference with a full-scale Kullback–Leibler divergence term in the ELBO. This nuanced approach ensures a more informed and adaptive Bayesian process.

Traditional VI with continuous latent variables faces computational challenges due to the intractability of the variational lower bound. In "Auto-Encoding Variational Bayes" by Ref. [34], the authors introduce the Stochastic Gradient Variational Bayes (SGVB) estimator to tackle this issue. SGVB employs a reparameterization trick, expressing latent variables as deterministic functions of random noise. This transformation allows the variational lower bound to be differentiated and optimized using standard stochastic gradient methods. As a result, the method offers a scalable and efficient solution to the longstanding challenge of approximate inference in complex models with continuous latent variables.

Traditional VI often employs simplistic posterior forms, such as Gaussian distributions, potentially overlooking the true intricacies of the distribution. Addressing this, normalizing flows were introduced, offering a sequence of invertible transformations that refine a basic initial distribution into a more sophisticated one. A notable advancement in this domain is the Multiplicative Normalizing Flows (MNFs), as presented by Ref. [35]. MNFs, characterized by their multiplicative transformations, enhance the expressiveness of the variational posterior in BNNs. Crucially, MNFs achieve this without a substantial computational burden, striking a balance between precision and efficiency.

BNNs and VI have been at the forefront of addressing uncertainties in DL. However, a persistent challenge has been to efficiently capture both model and parameter uncertainties. Ref. [36] introduces a novel approach to this issue by proposing a stochastic VI method tailored for BNNs. This paper introduces latent binary variables associated with each weight in the neural network, determining the inclusion or exclusion of specific weights. This innovative approach allows for the exploration of various model architectures, effectively capturing model uncertainty by discerning essential from nonessential network connections. To address parameter uncertainty, the authors assign variational distributions to the weights of the included connections, representing the uncertainty about each weight's exact value. The paper employs stochastic VI, a departure from traditional deterministic methods. This stochastic approach facilitates efficient exploration of the model and parameter space by sampling from the variational distributions during optimization. Crucially, the authors' methodology jointly optimizes over both the binary latent variables and the neural network weights, ensuring a harmonized exploration of architecture and weight values.

In a notable advancement to VI, Ref. [37] seamlessly integrated Graph Neural Networks with BNNs and VI, enhancing the precision and interpretability of molecular property predictions.

Ref. [38] innovatively enhanced VI by integrating Gaussian mean-field approximations and introducing a low-rank factorization of variational parameters. The Gaussian mean-field simplifies the approximation by assuming parameter independence. The low-rank factorization, akin to data compression, offers a compact representation of parameters, reducing computational demands and potentially mitigating overfitting. Additionally, the study addresses the challenge of noisy gradient estimates in VI by improving the Signal-to-Noise Ratio (SNR) of the Stochastic Gradient. This ensures more reliable gradient updates, crucial for VI convergence.

Ref. [39] address the uncertainty estimation in DNNs, particularly in the presence of out-of-distribution (OOD) data, by introducing Intermediate Layer VI (ILVI). To better capture prediction uncertainties, a latent layer was incorporated within the network's architecture using ILVI. To further refine this uncertainty estimation, they proposed a loss function that integrates Dirichlet distributions, a multivariate generalization of the beta distribution, which is especially suitable for multi-class problems. VI was employed to approximate the posterior distribution of the latent variables in the DNN. By synergizing VI with Dirichlet distributions, the research aimed to provide a more calibrated and reliable uncertainty measure, particularly for OOD scenarios. The results indicate that this combined approach can produce dependable uncertainty estimates without undermining the DNN's primary performance in tasks such as segmentation.

In the realm of BNNs, one prevailing challenge is the overparametrization, where networks remain densely populated with weights, potentially leading to inefficiencies and overfitting. Addressing this, Ref. [40] propose a novel Bayesian approach that simultaneously considers both structural and parameter uncertainties. Their method introduces "on-off switches" for each weight, determining its inclusion or exclusion in the network. Guiding these switches are "spike-and-slab priors": the spike promotes weights to be zero, effectively turning them "off," while the slab allows for varied non-zero values when weights are "on." This technique aims to discern essential weights from redundant ones, fostering a more streamlined and precise BNN. Through this, the authors present a promising avenue for enhancing the efficiency and accuracy of BNNs.

3.3 Monte Carlo dropout

The effective implementation of VI predominantly relies on the choice of an appropriate variational distribution. Undertaking evaluations, exemplified by Eq. (20.13), frequently proves challenging for intricate distributions, potentially inducing biases when simpler ones are employed [28]. Moreover, performing evaluations involving extensive datasets can lead to significant computational burdens [28]. Given the inherent complexities and complications, the practical deployment of VI in BNNs has been notably challenging. To address this, Gal and Ghahramani [1] have proposed an innovative method, remarkable in its simplicity, aimed at approximating posterior inference.

But, first, what is dropout? Dropout serves as a prevalent regularization strategy, frequently employed in neural networks with the objective of mitigating overfitting and enhancing generalization [41]. It operates by intermittently omitting a subset of the neurons in a layer during the training phase, assigning them a value of zero. Through the employment of this mechanism, different subsets of neurons undergo activation or deactivation within each training iteration. This allows the network to learn unique features, aiding in the prevention of overfitting by encouraging more versatile and generalized learning. The most prevalent method of implementing dropout is by deactivating neurons using Bernoulli variables during the training phase. However, other strategies have also been introduced, such as Dropconnect and the incorporation of Gaussian weights. Dropconnect, unlike neuron dropout, independently drops connections between neurons during training by assigning a Bernoulli variable to each weight, allowing for a more diversified and generalized model. Gaussian weights, on the other hand, assume a Gaussian distribution for the weights [42] (Fig. 20.1).

Now, what is a Monte Carlo dropout (MCD)? In simple words, dropout, originally, is reserved for the training period of the model; however, MCD extends this functionality to the inference period. MCD advances the original dropout technique by extending its use to the model's inference phase, not just the training phase. By generating and then averaging predictions for each data point, the model can then capture the variability in its predictions by averaging these outputs.

But how can this simple method serve as a substitute for VI in estimating posterior inference? A complete proof is beyond the scope of this chapter, and interested readers can refer to Ref. [1]. Herein, a succinct overview of operational mechanics is provided (adapted from Ref. [28]):

In the MCD approach, each layer i of the neural network has an approximating distribution for its weights, represented as $q_\theta(W_i)$. This is mathematically expressed as:

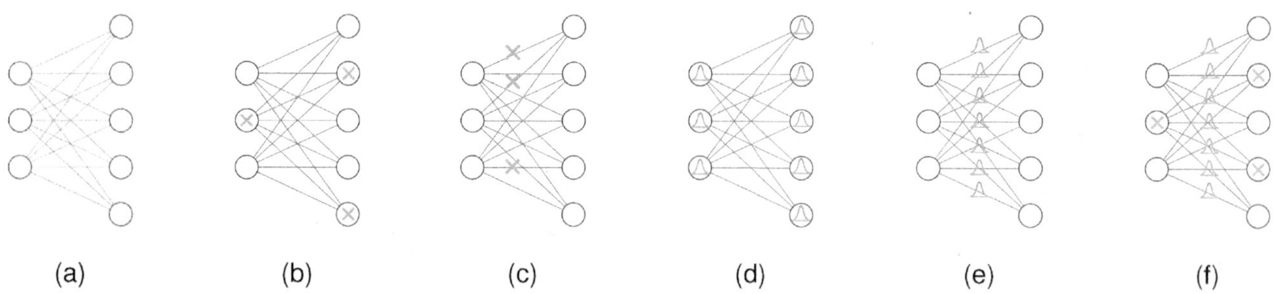

FIGURE 20.1 Different variational distributions by dropout. (A) simple neural network—No dropout; (B) Bernoulli dropout; (C) Bernoulli DropConnect; (D) Gaussian dropout; (E) Gaussian DropConnect; (F) spike-and-slab dropout. *Source: P. McClure, N. Kriegeskorte, Representing Inferential Uncertainty in Deep Neural Networks Through Sampling (2016).*

$$\begin{aligned} W_i &= M_i \cdot \text{diag}\left(\left[Z_{i,j}\right]_{j=1}^{K_i}\right) \\ Z_{i,j} &\sim \text{Bernoulli}(p_i) \text{ for } i = 1, \ldots, L, \text{ and } j = 1, \ldots, K_{i-1} \end{aligned} \tag{20.17}$$

Here, each $Z_{i,j}$ signifies a Bernoulli random variable which decides whether the connected input should be retained, with p_i representing the probability of retaining the input, counterintuitively opposite to the conventional dropout rate.

This method grapples with the complication of directly computing the integral in Eq. (20.15) with $q_\theta(W)$. Significant revelations by Gal and Ghahramani [1] propose that the integral in Eq. (20.15) can be approximated. This approximation enables the formulation of an unbiased estimator for $L_{\text{VI}}(\theta)$ by minimizing standard loss functions, combined with L_2 regularization, a method widely recognized in training neural network models:

$$L_{\text{dropout}} = \frac{1}{N}\sum_{i=1}^{N} E(y_i, \hat{y}_i) + \lambda \sum_{i=1}^{L} \left(\|W_i\|_2^2 + \|b_i\|_2^2\right) \tag{20.18}$$

Here, $E(y_i, \hat{y}_i)$ denotes loss functions such as the softmax loss or mean squared error loss. This VI is analogous to a Gaussian Process approximation of a neural network, facilitating the derivation of an approximate predictive posterior, along with its mean and variance, illustrated as follows:

$$\begin{aligned} P(y^*|x^*, D) &= \mathcal{N}\left(y^*; f_W(x^*), \tau^{-1}I\right) \\ E_{q_\theta(y^*|x^*)}(y^*) &\approx \frac{1}{T}\sum_{t=1}^{T} f_W(x^*) \\ \text{Var}_{q_\theta(y^*|x^*)}(y^*) &\approx \tau^{-1}ID + \frac{1}{T}\sum_{t=1}^{T} \left(f_W(x^*)\right)^T f_W(x^*) - \left(E_{q_\theta(y^*|x^*)}(y^*)\right)^T E_{q_\theta(y^*|x^*)}(y^*) \end{aligned} \tag{20.19}$$

In this approach, T test predictions from the network, trained using Eq. (20.18), are averaged to conclude the model's inference process.

Numerous researches have employed MCD as a tool for UQ estimation. Ref. [43] employ MCD to discern the inherent uncertainty in their neural network model, aiming to craft more potent universal adversarial perturbations. By maximizing the activation of convolutional neurons using MCD, they identify the most uncertain or activated neurons. The hypothesis is that by targeting these neurons, the perturbations crafted will be more effective. This chapter emphasizes the significance of understanding model uncertainty, positing that recognizing areas of uncertainty allows for the exploitation of these vulnerabilities to create perturbations that the model is more susceptible to. A key concept introduced is the virtual Epistemic uncertainty, which pertains to the uncertainty in the model parameters. Through MCD, the authors simulate multiple model variations by randomly deactivating neurons, examining the output variance across these models to gauge epistemic uncertainty. Furthermore, the research meticulously analyzes the impact of different sampling probabilities and the number of samplings on the efficacy of their perturbation methodology. The overarching premise of the paper is that a deeper comprehension of a model's uncertainty, achieved using MCD, can lead to the creation of more robust and universal adversarial perturbations.

MCD demonstrates notable behaviors in uncertainty estimation within DNNs, as it introduces an inherent bias in the network's expected output and exhibits a variance influenced by the dropout rate and model size. Interestingly, the uncertainty estimates provided by MCD do not hinge on the quantity or variance of training data. Furthermore, the method's effectiveness is intricately tied to the network architecture and training procedure choices, necessitating meticulous calibration and understanding of MCD's behavior, especially in applications where precise uncertainty estimation is pivotal [44]. However, [45] highlights that standard MCD predictions are not always well-calibrated. To tackle this, the authors propose two novel loss functions, integrating Expected Calibration Error and Predictive Entropy (PE) with cross-entropy, enhancing the calibration of MCD for classification tasks.

Ref. [46] innovatively employs MCD within a 3D Convolutional Neural Network to capture uncertainties in medical image segmentation. This approach addresses a critical need in medical imaging: understanding the confidence level of automated predictions, which can significantly influence clinical decisions. The authors introduce four distinct uncertainty measures derived from MDC: predictive variance, variance of MC samples, PE, and mutual information (MI). Predictive variance offers insights into the model's inherent noise, while the variance of MC samples gauges the spread of predictions across multiple model runs. PE measures the information content in the model's predictive density function, and MI captures the relationship between the model's posterior density and the prediction density. By integrating these measures, the authors provide a comprehensive view of model uncertainty, enhancing the reliability and potential clinical adoption of DL models in medical imaging.

Neural networks, while powerful, often operate as black boxes, making their decision-making processes opaque. A key challenge has been not only identifying which input features (like image pixels) influence a network's decision but also gauging the network's certainty about this influence. To address this, [47] introduces Monte Carlo Relevance Propagation (MCRP). This method integrates MCD with Layer-wise Relevance Propagation. By keeping dropout activated during inference, the network's decisions are sampled multiple times, yielding varied importance scores for input features. This sampling, enabled by MCD, allows the estimation of both the average importance and its uncertainty for each feature. In essence, MCRP enhances traditional feature importance techniques with a measure of confidence, offering a more nuanced understanding of neural network decisions.

In the realm of DL, a pervasive challenge arises when models are trained on data with "noisy labels." Such incorrect annotations can lead to the undesirable phenomenon where models memorize these inaccuracies, subsequently compromising their performance on novel, untainted data. Ref. [48] introduces MCD as a promising countermeasure to this issue. At its core, MCD leverages the regularization effect inherent to dropout techniques, which prevent overfitting by intermittently deactivating certain neurons during the training phase. Uniquely, MCD extends this principle to the inference stage, engendering multiple "thinned" network versions. This ensemble-esque strategy curtails the model's propensity to exude undue confidence in its predictions, particularly when confronted with noisy labels. Furthermore, MCD exhibits a "prolonged memorization effect," mitigating the model's inclination to internalize the noise, thereby fostering enhanced generalization capabilities. The research also underscores MCD contribution to network sparsity, positing that it engenders neural networks with a preponderance of inactive neurons. This sparsity translates to fewer adjustable parameters, further reducing the risk of overfitting. Notably, despite its multifaceted advantages, MCD imposes negligible computational overhead during training and only a minimal increment during inference. This efficiency, combined with its robustness against noisy labels, underscores MCD's potential as a pragmatic solution for real-world scenarios riddled with label inaccuracies.

Perhaps one of the domains where confidence holds particular significance is the healthcare sector. In medical image analysis, traditional DL models often grapple with repeatability issues, leading to inconsistent predictions for slightly varied inputs. Such inconsistencies can have profound clinical implications. Addressing this challenge, MCD has been identified as a pivotal tool. Research indicates that by leveraging MCD, models exhibit enhanced repeatability, particularly at class boundaries where traditional models are most vulnerable [49]. Ref. [50] used test-time augmentation in combination with MCD to estimate aleatoric uncertainty in medical image segmentation. This method extends the structure-wise uncertainty estimation by generating MC samples using both test-time dropout and test-time augmentation. In the expanding landscape of MCD applications, its utility for anomaly detection has been notably explored. Ref. [51] extends MCD by introducing a postprocessing step aimed at refining the detection process. After the neural network, equipped with MCD, generates its predictions, data points that fall outside the established uncertainty bounds of MCD are identified as potential anomalies. Crucially, this method doesn't merely focus on individual anomalous points. Instead, it emphasizes the identification of sequences or clusters of dependent anomalous points within time series data. This nuanced approach recognizes the inherent temporal dependencies in time series data, ensuring a more robust and fewer false positives in anomaly detection. MCD has also been applied to scene understanding tasks. Ref. [52] employed MCD sampling to qualitatively understand the model uncertainty in deep convolutional encoder–decoder architectures for scene understanding. This approach allows for a better understanding of the uncertainty associated with the model's predictions.

DL models, when utilizing variational Bayesian inference, often exhibit miscalibrated uncertainty, leading to discrepancies between predicted uncertainties and actual model errors. MCD emerges as a solution [53], approximating epistemic uncertainty by enabling multiple stochastic forward passes during inference. By averaging these outputs, MCD refines the model's uncertainty estimates. Ref. [53] further introduces temperature scaling, a postprocessing technique that adjusts the model's confidence estimates. By re-scaling the softmax outputs using a calibrated temperature value, temperature scaling ensures that the model's uncertainty aligns more closely with its true error, thereby addressing the prevalent miscalibration issue.

3.4 Bayes by backprop

In the pursuit of advancing computational methodologies, a novel and efficacious approach has been developed to approximate the posterior distribution, known as Bayes by Backprop. Bayes by Backprop is a technique designed for training neural networks with weights characterized by probability, facilitating the estimation of uncertainty in the predictions made by the model. It employs a form of VI to approximate the posterior distribution of the neural network's weights.

The procedure initiates by defining a prior distribution over the weights, generally a Gaussian distribution. The goal during training is to identify the posterior distribution that most accurately represents the observed data by minimizing the Kullback Leibler divergence between the true posterior and an approximating distribution, usually selected as a factorized Gaussian distribution.

The technique utilizes a reparameterization trick to calculate the gradients required for backpropagation. Rather than sampling directly from the approximating distribution, samples are drawn from a standard Gaussian distribution and undergo a deterministic transformation to acquire samples from the approximating distribution, enabling efficient gradient computation through backpropagation.

Throughout the training phase, Bayes by Backprop minimizes a loss function in Eq. (20.22), composed of two components: the negative log-likelihood of the observed data and the Kullback–Leibler divergence between the approximating and the prior distributions [25]. The negative log-likelihood component ensures model adherence to the training data, while the Kullback–Leibler divergence component serves as a regularization term, promoting weight adherence to the prior distribution.

$$F(\mathscr{D},\boldsymbol{\theta}) = \mathrm{KL}[q(\mathbf{w}|\boldsymbol{\theta})\|P(\mathbf{w})] - \mathbb{E}_{q(\mathbf{w},\boldsymbol{\theta})}[\log P(\mathscr{D}|\mathbf{w})] \tag{20.20}$$

Training neural networks with Bayes by Backprop allows for the derivation of a distribution over the weights as opposed to a singular point estimate, enabling the estimation of uncertainty in the model's predictions, such as the derivation of confidence intervals or predictive variances.

Building upon the above foundational principles, Ref. [54] have tailored Bayes by Backprop for Recurrent Neural Networks (RNNs). Recognizing the inherent challenges posed by RNNs, such as the temporal dependencies and the potential for exploding or vanishing gradients, the authors ingeniously integrated Bayesian techniques to instill uncertainty and regularization directly into the RNN architecture. Their methodology claims a significant reduction in the number of parameters, by as much as 80%, while simultaneously enhancing the quality of uncertainty estimates. A salient feature of their approach is the introduction of a novel posterior approximation that harnesses local gradient information, refining it based on current batch statistics. This innovation ensures that the approximation is not only more accurate but also versatile, with potential applications extending beyond RNNs. Empirical results presented in their work further corroborate the superiority of Bayesian RNNs over traditional RNNs in tasks such as language modeling and image captioning.

In the realm of continual learning, the Uncertainty-guided Continual Bayesian Neural Networks (UCB) approach stands out as a significant advancement that leverages the principles of Bayes by Backprop. This methodology, as detailed by Ref. [55], employs BNNs to naturally account for uncertainty in parameter estimates. Each parameter is represented by a distribution defined by a mean and variance, with the UCB utilizing this to determine parameter importance. The core innovation lies in defining importance based on the well-established uncertainty in the parameters' distribution. Two primary variants of UCB are introduced: one that dynamically adjusts learning rates based on current uncertainty and another that employs the SNR to determine parameter importance, pruning the least important ones. Rooted in Bayes by Backprop principles, UCB showcases the potential of BNNs in continual learning scenarios, offering flexibility without the need for additional memory or task-specific information during testing.

Bayes by Backprop was evaluated for its performance in cardiac MRI segmentation alongside other methods [56]. While Deep Ensembles generally showed superior performance in terms of segmentation accuracy and probability calibration, Bayes by Backprop demonstrated notable strengths under specific conditions. Specifically, Bayes by Backprop exhibited superior performance on images with noise distortions. The study also highlighted the potential of leveraging uncertainty measures to make manual review for segmentation quality control more efficient. In this context, Bayes by Backprop's performance under noise distortions suggests its utility in certain challenging imaging scenarios.

3.5 Bayesian active learning

Bayesian Active Learning (BAL) is a synergistic framework that integrates Bayesian inference and active learning principles to strategically select data points that are rich in information for labeling, with the objective of enhancing the efficacy of ML models.

Within the BAL framework, an initial prior distribution is defined over the model parameters, representing preliminary beliefs about these parameters prior to the assimilation of any data. With the acquisition of labeled data points, the posterior distribution of the parameters is refined via Bayes' theorem, amalgamating the prior distribution and the likelihood of the newly observed data.

The essence of active learning is manifested in the strategic selection of data points for labeling. Contrary to random selection of unlabeled data, active learning strategies aspire to identify and prioritize data points that are anticipated to significantly diminish the model's predictive uncertainty. This is generally achieved by evaluating the uncertainty or informativeness of each unlabeled data point and prioritizing those with maximal uncertainty or anticipated information gain [57].

Through the iterative identification and labeling of information-rich data points, BAL optimizes the utilization of labeled data, mitigating the necessity for extensive labeled datasets [58]. This is especially advantageous in contexts where data labeling is resource-intensive or cumbersome.

To provide a more concrete illustration, consider a practical scenario wherein a model is being developed to classify images into categories of cats and dogs. Initially, the model exhibits a high degree of uncertainty regarding the classification of numerous images. In such a situation, the model, adhering to the principles of BAL, strategically selects the images about which it harbors the most uncertainty and seeks their respective labels (cat or dog). Upon the acquisition of these labels, the model undergoes a refinement in its knowledge base, subsequently enhancing its confidence and accuracy in the classification of analogous images. This procedure is iterative, with the model persistently opting for images that are perceived as most uncertain and informative, thereby facilitating continuous learning and adaptation.

One of the seminal contributions to the introduction of model uncertainty measurement in active learning proposed by Ref. [57]. This research adeptly bridges the gap between Bayesian DL and the active learning paradigm. By introducing a mechanism that inherently captures and quantifies model uncertainty, it addresses a significant challenge in the realm of DL. A standout feature of their methodology is the innovative use of dropout as a means for approximate Bayesian inference within Bayesian Convolutional Neural Networks. This approach not only facilitates a pragmatic estimation of uncertainty but also ensures that the intrinsic architecture of standard DL models remains largely unaltered. The authors further enrich their discourse by delving into a comparative analysis of various acquisition functions, placing a special emphasis on those that effectively harness model uncertainty. This comprehensive exploration offers a nuanced understanding of uncertainty sampling in the context of active learning.

Ref. [59] extended active learning by proposing a novel UQ method using BNNs to estimate the expected error of labels in unlabeled samples. This Bayesian approach, combined with dropout, offers a robust mechanism for uncertainty estimation in DL. Furthermore, they introduce a self-paced learning strategy, designed to minimize noise in pseudo-labeled samples. Through iterative training, this method ensures the inclusion of only the most reliable samples, leveraging the negative 11-norm regularizer. The proposed algorithm seamlessly integrates both active and self-paced learning. Starting with a minimal set of labeled data, the algorithm employs self-paced learning on the unlabeled dataset. Upon reaching optimal performance, the active learning component, an extended emphasis of the study, selects the most informative samples for labeling. This iterative process guarantees efficient and robust model training.

Ref. [60] critiques traditional active learning methods like Expected Loss Reduction and Mean Objective Cost of Uncertainty (MOCU) for their limitations in long-term performance. Such methods can become stagnant and fail to identify the true model's optimal classifier. To combat this, the authors present Soft MOCU, an acquisition function derived from a concave approximation of MOCU. Soft MOCU promises theoretical convergence in BAL by continuously adapting to model uncertainty. The paper substantiates its claims with mathematical proofs, demonstrating Soft MOCU's strictly concave nature and its assurance of convergence to the genuine optimal classifier. Empirical results further showcase Soft MOCU's superior performance against other methods across various datasets.

Ref. [61] delves into the realm of active learning, presenting a detailed exploration into the role of Bayesian layers in capturing model uncertainty using the MNIST dataset. Within this active learning framework, the authors experimented with eight different architectures, adjusting the position and number of Bayesian layers. Their acquisition functions, integral to the active learning process, encompassed Random, Max Entropy, and Variation Ratios, with comprehensive training details provided. A standout result was the superior performance of networks with a few Bayesian layers near the output in capturing uncertainty, challenging the conventional need for fully Bayesian networks. This innovative finding suggests a potential reduction in computational cost and training time for Bayesian networks. The paper's strength lies in its comprehensive approach, offering a nuanced understanding of the effectiveness of Bayesian layers in an active learning context. However, the primary use of the MNIST dataset, known for its simplicity, is a limitation. It raises questions about the methodology's performance on more intricate datasets or in real-world scenarios.

Ref. [62] critically examines the limitations of current batch data acquisition methods in BAL, highlighting their propensity to select redundant data points, which in some instances, even underperform when compared to random data acquisition. To address this, they introduce BatchBALD, a novel approach that offers a tractable approximation to the MI between a batch of points and the model parameters. Notably, BatchBALD is designed to account for dependencies within an acquisition batch, ensuring that the data points chosen are not only informative but also diverse. Recognizing the combinatorial complexities of scoring subsets of points, the authors propose a greedy algorithm that boasts a $1 - \frac{1}{e}$-approximation, positioning it as both efficient and apt for real-world applications. Furthermore, the authors have taken commendable steps to bolster the computational feasibility of their method, introducing techniques that significantly reduce computational demands through the factorization of certain probabilities and the employment of batch matrix multiplication. Their commitment to validating their approach is evident in the extensive experimental results provided. These experiments, conducted on a range of datasets such as MNIST, EMNIST, and CINIC-10, reveal that BatchBALD consistently surpasses the traditional BALD method, particularly in situations characterized by repeated or near-identical data points.

Ref. [63] introduces the Expected Posterior Information Gain (EPIG) as a notable advancement in BAL, positioning it as an alternative to the established BALD (Bayesian Active Learning by Disagreement). EPIG is designed to optimize the learning process by maximizing the expected information gain in the posterior distribution upon acquiring new data. Defined in terms of the expected generalization error under a cross-entropy loss, EPIG quantifies the anticipated enhancement in model understanding after observing a new data point. The authors' empirical evaluation spans synthetic data, UCI datasets, and MNIST data, showcasing EPIG's efficacy across diverse scenarios. When juxtaposed with BALD, EPIG's strengths become evident, marking it as a promising tool in active learning.

Ref. [64] addresses the observed lack of diversity in data acquisition during the active learning process, attributing this challenge to the phenomenon known as mode collapse. To counteract this issue, they propose an innovative solution: employing an ensemble of MC-Dropout models. Each member of this ensemble is characterized by distinct weights, ensuring diverse representations. The ensemble is then conceptualized as a mixture model, with predictions averaged across both ensemble members and multiple MC-Dropout forward passes. Through rigorous empirical analysis, the authors convincingly demonstrate the superiority of their methodology over traditional BAL methods. However, while the ensemble approach offers enhanced performance, it may introduce additional computational overhead, which could pose challenges in scalability and real-time applications.

3.6 Variational autoencoders

Autoencoders [65] are conceived as neural networks with the primary objective of learning an "informative" representation of data in an unsupervised manner by endeavoring to reconstruct their input [66]. To grasp the essence of autoencoders, let's take a closer look at their architecture illustrated in Fig. 20.2. The principal components of autoencoders are categorized into three distinct elements: an encoder, a latent variable (or feature representation), and a decoder. The encoder and the decoder are fundamentally functions (mostly neural networks), whereas the term "latent variable" is a term to denote a tensor of real numbers represented by z [67].

Let's formalize the above concept (adapted from Ref. [67]): suppose there exists a vector of latent variables, z, residing in a high-dimensional space, Z, from which sampling can be readily performed according to a predefined probability density function, $P(z)$, applicable over Z. Subsequently, assume the presence of a set of deterministic functions, $f(z;\omega)$, characterized by a vector ω within a space ω, with $f: Z \times \omega \rightarrow X$. While f is deterministic, if z is random and θ is constant, then $f(z;\theta)$ becomes a random variable within the space X. The goal is to optimize ω so that when z is sampled from $P(z)$, $f(z;\omega)$ will, with substantial likelihood, resemble the X's in the dataset.

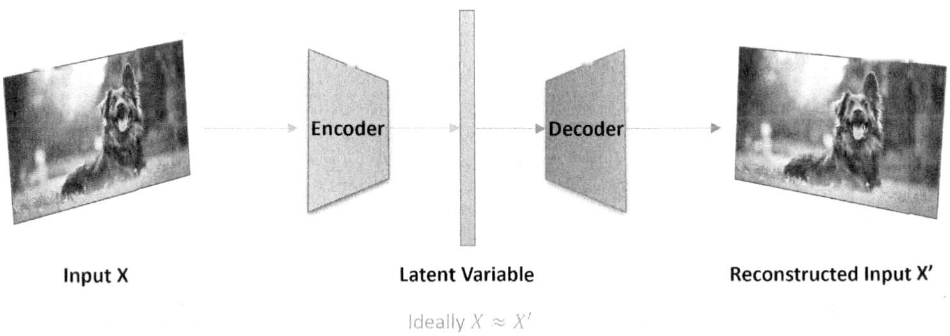

FIGURE 20.2 General structure of autoencoders.

To articulate this concept with mathematical precision, the objective is to augment the likelihood of each X in the training dataset under the comprehensive generative procedure, as expressed by:

$$P(X) = \int P(X|z;\omega)P(z)dz \tag{20.21}$$

In this equation, $f(z;\omega)$ is substituted by a distribution $P(X|z;\omega)$, enabling the explicit representation of the dependence of X on z through the application of the law of total probability.

A pivotal advancement in autoencoders by Ref. [34] led to the advent of Variational Autoencoders (VAEs) serve as proficient techniques for modeling the posterior distribution.

VAE postulated that there exists an approximate posterior distribution over the latent variable z_i given a data point x_i acting as a probabilistic encoder and regulated by the parameters ϕ. Additionally, a prior distribution for the latent variables z_i is presumed, represented by $p_\theta(z_i)$. In contrast to autoencoders, where the encoder produces z (a probability distribution that symbolizes the latent embeddings), the encoders in VAEs yield μ and $\log(\sigma^2)$ and create ϵ from $\mathcal{N}(0,I)$. Subsequently, z is sampled utilizing a reparameterization trick from these values. This variable z is then supplied as input to the decoder [68]. The variable z is subsequently used as input for the decoder, whose role is to attempt the reconstruction of x; z is articulated as [68]:

$$z = g(\epsilon,\phi,x) = \mu + \sigma \odot \epsilon \tag{20.22}$$

Here, $\odot$ denotes the operation of elementwise multiplication, and z is a probability distribution that encapsulates the pertinent features derived from the input x. Given that $z \sim \mathcal{N}(\mu,\sigma^2)$, z can be reparameterized as [68]:

$$z = \mu + \sigma\epsilon, \epsilon \sim p(\epsilon) = \mathcal{N}(0,1) \tag{20.23}$$

The general schema of VAE is illustrated in Fig. 20.3.

The parameters θ and ϕ are undetermined and must be learned from the data. The observed latent variables z_i are construed as a code provided by the recognition model $q_\phi(z|x)$.

The marginal log-likelihood is articulated as an aggregate over the individual data points as:

$$\log p_\theta(x_1,x_2,\ldots,x_N) = \sum_{i=1}^{N} \log p_\theta(x_i) \tag{20.24}$$

and each point can be reformulated as:

$$\log p_\theta(x_i) = DKL(q_\phi(z|x_i)\|p_\theta(z|x_i)) + L(\theta,\phi;x_i) \tag{20.25}$$

where the initial term is the Kullback–Leibler divergence of the approximate recognition model from the true posterior, and the subsequent term is termed the variational lower bound on the marginal likelihood, defined as:

$$L(\theta,\phi;x_i) \equiv E_{q_\phi(z|x_i)}[-\log q_\phi(z|x) + \log p_\theta(x,z)] \tag{20.26}$$

Given the nonnegativity of the Kullback–Leibler divergence, $L(\theta,\phi;x_i)$ serves as a lower bound on the marginal log-likelihood. Since the marginal log-likelihood is uninfluenced by the parameters θ and ϕ, enhancing the lower bound refines our approximation of the posterior concerning the Kullback–Leibler divergence.

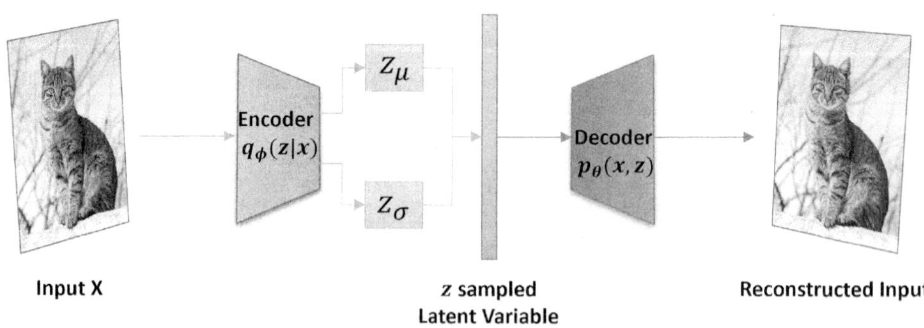

FIGURE 20.3 General structure of VAEs.

The variational lower bound can be elaborated further as:

$$L(\theta, \phi; x_i) = -DKL\left(q_\phi(z|x_i)\middle\|p_\theta(z)\right) + E_{q_\phi(z|x_i)}[\log p_\theta(x_i|z)] \tag{20.27}$$

The process of VI is realized by optimizing $L(\theta, \phi; x_i)$ for all data points concerning θ and ϕ. A variety of probability distribution functions can serve as the posterior distribution; however, it is predominantly presumed to be a multivariate Gaussian denoted as $P(X|z;\theta) = \mathcal{N}\left(X\middle|f(z;\theta), \sigma^2 \cdot I\right)$.

VAEs exhibit a versatile applicability that extends beyond UQ, as evidenced by numerous studies that have adeptly tailored VAEs to a diverse array of domains, such as prognostic health management [69], speech modeling [70], and text classification [71]. Focusing on the application of VAEs in UQ, Ref. [72] delves into the intricacies of UQ in MRI image recovery using DL models, with a particular emphasis on the utilization of VAEs. By ingeniously leveraging VAEs, the researchers have crafted a probabilistic reconstruction scheme that encapsulates acquisition uncertainty within a latent code. This latent representation subsequently facilitates the generation of pixel variance maps via Monte Carlo sampling. A noteworthy methodological advancement is the incorporation of Stein's Unbiased Risk Estimator as an alternative to the traditional mean-squared-error, enhancing the accuracy of risk prediction. The findings underscore the dichotomy of adversarial losses, which, while aiding in the retrieval of high-frequencies, simultaneously introduce heightened uncertainty. Conversely, the adoption of recurrent unrolled networks emerges as a promising avenue, demonstrating a marked reduction in prediction uncertainty and risk. The study's methodological refinements to the VAE framework offer significant potential for advancing the domain of MRI reconstruction.

Ref. [73] tailored VAEs for image reconstruction from corrupted data to map high-dimensional data to a lower-dimensional latent space, addressing challenges in prior selection and UQ. They innovatively reformulate the inverse problem in terms of latent variables, ensuring a Gaussian prior for tractability. Notably, the paper introduces the EL2O method to analyze the posterior, which offers advantages over traditional methods like MCMC, especially in multi-modal contexts. The integration of a normalizing flow to improve the VAE's latent space distribution is a commendable addition. Their empirical results on the MNIST dataset demonstrate the efficacy of their approach in handling various data corruptions. This work offers significant advancements in UQ using VAEs, providing a robust alternative to existing methodologies.

Ref. [74] present a novel approach to UQ using VAEs. They introduce a hierarchical prior structure, replacing the traditional Gaussian prior with a Gaussian Mixture Model. This modification allows for a more nuanced representation of data distributions. Additionally, the inclusion of a Wasserstein distance term in the ELBO objective not only stabilizes the training process but also enhances the quality of generated samples, marking a significant improvement in VAE methodologies.

Ref. [75] innovatively integrates the Just-in-Time learning framework with a VAE to address soft sensor modeling in nonlinear processes. The methodology hinges on the VAE's capability to transform high-dimensional process data into latent variables, with the extracted features characterized as Gaussian distributed variables. A significant mathematical refinement is the application of the Kullback–Leibler divergence to ascertain the similarity between historical data and a new query sample. This divergence offers a robust measure of relevance, especially in the context of UQ. Furthermore, the Gaussian Process Regression is adeptly employed to construct a local model using pertinent historical samples. The approach demonstrates promise in tackling challenges like nonlinearity, data redundancy, and inherent uncertainties, offering a sophisticated enhancement to the traditional VAE framework.

4. Non-Bayesian perspective for quantifying uncertainty: Ensemble approaches

The strategy of employing ensemble learning is highly influential in the realms of ML and DL, as it combines several models to enhance the accuracy of predictions. This methodology has undergone extensive research and implementation across diverse fields. An extensive review of ensemble learning by Ref. [76] underscores its superiority in enhancing predictive accuracy when contrasted with singular models.

In a typical ensemble of models, each individual model renders its own prediction for a given input. When these models are diverse, meaning they are constructed with different architectures, parameters, or trained on different subsets of the data, their predictions can vary significantly for the same input. The variance or dispersion of these predictions across different models in the ensemble provides a measure of epistemic uncertainty, which is indicative of the model's uncertainty due to lack of knowledge or lack of training data. A high variance in predictions implies higher uncertainty, reflecting a lack of consensus among the constituent models, whereas lower variance implies greater certainty about the prediction.

In addition to variance, many ensemble methods can yield probabilistic outputs, producing a distribution of possible outcomes rather than a single point estimate. For example, each model in the ensemble can estimate the probability distribution of a class label in classification tasks. By averaging or combining these probabilistic predictions from all models in the ensemble, one can extract both the expected prediction (i.e., the mean of the distribution) and the uncertainty associated with it (i.e., the variance or entropy of the distribution). This form of uncertainty, often termed aleatoric uncertainty, quantifies the inherent noise or randomness in the observed data.

In the specific context of an ensemble of neural networks, the combination of multiple networks each with distinct initializations, structures, or training processes allows for the incorporation of different inductive biases and learning trajectories, thereby contributing to the diversity of predictions. The quantification of uncertainty in this scenario is crucially facilitated by the divergence in the predictions or by the generated probabilistic outputs from each network, enabling more robust and reliable uncertainty estimates that can be vital for informed decision-making in various applications, from medical diagnoses to autonomous vehicles.

Recent literature emphasizes the distinction between aleatoric and epistemic uncertainties in ML. Addressing the challenges posed by traditional methods, an innovative approach to ensemble construction has been proposed by Ref. [77] using MCD. Instead of the conventional method of training multiple models, this technique leverages dropout, a regularization strategy, in a unique manner. By performing multiple forward passes with varied dropout activations within a single neural network, MCD simulates a MC sampling. Each distinct dropout pattern during these passes effectively crafts a "thinned" version of the network, thereby creating an ensemble of models. This ensemble adeptly captures both the inherent data randomness (aleatoric) and the model uncertainty (epistemic), offering a more comprehensive UQ.

Ref. [78] introduces an ensemble-based approach using U-statistics to estimate uncertainty. By training neural networks on subsamples of data, the ensemble's variance provides insight into the point estimates' uncertainty. This ensemble method, rooted in the U-statistic framework, offers confidence intervals for mean point estimates derived from neural network ensembles. Addressing this issue, MCD is an alternative ensemble-based technique that promotes model UQ. By randomly dropping out neurons during training and prediction, MCD can be interpreted as producing an implicit ensemble through stochastic forward passes, providing a distribution of outputs.

One notable approach that extends the ensemble methodology for UQ is the Ensemble Multi-Quantiles (EMQ) approach [79]. At its core, EMQ is an ensemble learning approach that predicts multiple quantiles of the conditional distribution $p(y|X = x)$. The method starts with an initial assumption of a Gaussian distribution for $p(y|X = x)$. This Gaussian assumption serves as the first step in the ensemble, providing a baseline prediction. Subsequent steps in the ensemble aim to refine this prediction by adaptively adjusting the quantiles. The ensemble steps are designed to strike a balance between maintaining the structural integrity of the Gaussian distribution and introducing flexibility to better fit real data. EMQ is designed to depart from the Gaussian assumption gradually, allowing it to discover an optimal conditional distribution during the boosting process. This adaptiveness ensures that the method can capture complex data patterns, such as multi-modality or long tails, which a simple Gaussian might miss. The paper introduces various regularization strategies, including an "adaptive T strategy," which determines the number of ensemble steps based on performance on a validation set. This strategy helps in preventing overfitting and ensures that the model finds an optimal balance between flexibility and structural integrity.

Ref. [80] investigates the calibration challenges of overparametrized DL models, particularly in situations with limited data. It critically assesses the relationship between data-augmentation, ensembling, and postprocessing calibration, three pivotal techniques in DL. The research reveals that while ensembling can enhance accuracy, it doesn't always improve calibration. In fact, when combined with certain data-augmentation techniques like mixup regularization, it can lead to less calibrated models. The paper also introduces the "Pool-Then-Calibrate" strategy, emphasizing the sequence in which model aggregation and calibration are executed. This approach, when applied in data-scarce scenarios, can notably reduce calibration errors. Furthermore, the paper touches upon Bayesian perspectives on ensembling, presenting deep ensembles as practical alternatives to BNNs. The research underscores the need for a nuanced understanding of these techniques to achieve reliable UQ in DL.

Ref. [81] addresses the challenge of UQ in DNNs, emphasizing that traditional neural networks don't inherently capture uncertainty. They introduce AutoDEUQ, an automated approach for creating an ensemble of DNNs. This method combines both neural architecture and hyperparameter search to generate diverse ensembles. The ensemble's predictive variance is then decomposed into two types of uncertainties: aleatoric (data-driven) and epistemic (model-driven). The paper demonstrates that AutoDEUQ surpasses several existing methods in regression benchmarks. The ensemble's strength lies in its diversity and consistent high performance across models, ensuring robust UQ. The study underscores the importance of ensemble methods in capturing and quantifying uncertainties in DL predictions.

Ref. [82] critically examines the traditional ensemble modeling approach in climate science, where each model is given equal weight. The authors argue that this "model democracy" often overlooks significant biases in some models. Instead, they propose a refined weighting scheme based on three criteria: the model's performance against observed data, its independence from other models, and its alignment with established scientific knowledge. This nuanced approach aims to enhance the robustness and confidence in model projections. The paper underscores the need for a systematic method to determine model robustness, emphasizing the potential of improving ensemble modeling not just for climate predictions but across various fields where UQ is essential.

DL has revolutionized feature extraction in imaging, rapidly converting data into spatial arrays of features. However, when applied to experimental imaging, like atom-resolved electron microscopy, DL faces challenges due to out-of-distribution drift, where a model trained for one condition falters under another. Addressing this, Ref. [83] introduces a combined approach of ensemble learning and iterative training. This method not only improves feature detection but also quantifies uncertainty in DL analysis, adapting to changing imaging conditions without human intervention. By training an ensemble of models on simulated data and applying them to experimental data, they found significant prediction variations across models. Through iterative training, they refined these models for better accuracy. Their approach, demonstrated on cases like 2D graphene systems, offers a promising solution to DL challenges in atom-resolved electron microscopy.

Ref. [84] delves into the significance of UQ in DNNs, particularly focusing on out-of-distribution (OOD) data. A standout method introduced is "Deep Ensembles," which employs multiple DNNs trained on the same data. By averaging their predictions, it not only enhances accuracy but also serves as a non-Bayesian uncertainty estimator. In evaluations, Deep Ensembles consistently outperformed other methods, showcasing its robustness in detecting OOD samples with minimal accuracy loss. This underscores the potential of ensemble-based approaches in ensuring reliable predictions, especially in safety-critical applications. The study offers valuable insights into the evolving role of ensemble methods in improving the reliability and interpretability of DNN predictions.

Ref. [85] tackles the challenge of UQ in 3D medical image segmentation using DL models. Recognizing the limitations of traditional methods, which often produce overconfident predictions, the authors introduce a novel approach to calibrate ensembles of DL models to better approximate classification probabilities. Instead of relying on identical models with different random seeds, their method trains models with varying sensitivities and precisions by adjusting the loss function weights. This calibrated ensemble is shown to outperform established methods in approximating classification probabilities. The paper further demonstrates the potential applications of their method in active learning, creating pseudo-labels for training on unlabeled datasets, and enhancing human–machine collaboration. The authors' approach offers a promising direction for improving the reliability and interpretability of DL predictions in medical imaging.

5. Prediction entropy: Measuring epistemic and aleatoric uncertainty

Particularly in classification tasks, where a model's output is a conditional probability distribution over a set of discrete labels Y a simple uncertainty metric is the entropy of the predicted distribution:

$$H[P(y|x)] = -\sum_{y \in Y} P(y|x) \log P(y|x) \tag{20.28}$$

However, this entropy of the predictive distribution doesn't separate epistemic and aleatoric uncertainties. A more sophisticated uncertainty metric, capable of differentiating between the two types of uncertainty, is the information gain between the model parameters and the observed data, expressed by MI. The concept of MI between two stochastic variables, X and Y, is represented as:

$$MI(X, Y) = H[P(X)] - E_{P(y)}[H[P(X|Y)]] = H[P(Y)] - E_{P(x)}[H[P(Y|X)]] \tag{20.29}$$

In a ML model, the MI can be approximated using Bayesian interpretations and can be dissected into PE and expected entropy. Let's denote the posterior distribution $p(\omega|X, Y)$ as $p(\omega|D)$ for brevity, where D represents the dataset comprising both X and Y. In this refined context, the MI for a specific test instance, x^*, and its corresponding label, y^*, within the posterior distribution can be articulated by modifying Eq. (20.29) as:

$$I[y^*, \omega|x^*, D] = \underbrace{H[P(y^*|x^*, \omega)]}_{\text{Predictive Entropy}} - \underbrace{E_{p(\omega|D)} H[P(y^*|x^*, \omega)]}_{\text{Expected Entropy}} \tag{20.30}$$

In the structure outlined in Eq. (20.30), an approximation is readily available via the Bayesian interpretation of dropout. Utilizing dropout inference and adhering to Eqs. (20.19)–(20.21), approximations of the predictive distribution, entropy, and MI are efficiently achieved as outlined by Ref. [1]. Here, the predictive distribution is approximated as [86]:

$$p(y|D,x) \approx \frac{1}{T}\sum_{i=1}^{T} p(y|\omega_i,x) \tag{20.31}$$

This is equivalently denoted as:

$$: = p_{\text{MC}}(y|x)$$

The entropy of the predictive distribution is approximated in a similar fashion:

$$H[p(y|D,x)] \approx H[p_{\text{MC}}(y|D,x)] \tag{20.32}$$

The MI is calculated as follows:

$$MI(\omega,y|D,x) \approx H[p_{\text{MC}}(y|D,x)] - \frac{1}{T}\sum_{i=1}^{T} H[p(y|\omega_i,x)] \tag{20.33}$$

Here, ω_i are samples drawn from the dropout distribution.

6. Overview, challenges, and future directions

Having delved into the intricacies of various methodologies for UQ in preceding sections, it is now pertinent to succinctly encapsulate the limitations inherent to each. MCMC techniques, while formidable, face computational challenges, especially in high-dimensional scenarios, and often grapple with issues like slow convergence and susceptibility to local modes. MCD requires multiple forward passes during testing, increasing computational demands. VI can sometimes produce overconfident uncertainty estimates due to the constraints of the chosen approximating family and the nonconvex nature of the ELBO. BAL is computationally demanding and relies heavily on a model's ability to produce uncertainty estimates. Bayes by Backprop necessitates augmented memory for storing gradients for both weights and variational parameters, and its scalability remains a concern. VAEs might yield indistinct samples, and balancing the reconstruction loss and Kullback–Leibler divergence can be challenging. Ensemble Methods, despite their efficacy, are computationally intensive due to the need to train multiple models, and storage requirements increase with the number of models. If models within the ensemble are highly correlated, the uncertainty estimates might be overly confident [16].

Building on this understanding, it's essential to underscore a pivotal distinction. While the aforementioned methods offer insights into model uncertainty, they don't inherently bolster a model's confidence or predictive accuracy. Specifically, while Bayesian approaches, such as MCMC, VI, Bayes by Backprop, and VAEs, primarily focus on capturing the posterior distribution to quantify model uncertainty, they don't necessarily enhance the model's confidence. Among the discussed methods, only BAL with its active learning paradigm, which selects the most uncertain samples, might aid in improving model confidence. However, the overarching goal of these techniques is to provide a nuanced understanding of uncertainty rather than directly augmenting model performance.

References

[1] Y. Gal, Z. Ghahramani, Dropout as a Bayesian approximation: Representing model uncertainty in deep learning, in: International Conference on Machine Learning, PMLR, 2016, pp. 1050–1059.

[2] L. Kaplan, F. Cerutti, M. Sensoy, A. Preece, P. Sullivan, Uncertainty Aware AI ML: Why and How, arXiv preprint arXiv:1809.07882 (2018).

[3] National Highway Traffic Safety Administration, Tesla Crash Preliminary Evaluation Report, Technical Report PE 16-007, U.S. Department of Transportation, National Highway Traffic Safety Administration, January 2017.

[4] J. Guynn, Google photos labeled black people "gorillas" (July 2015). https://www.usatoday.com/story/tech/2015/07/01/google-apologizes-after-photos-identify-black-people-as-gorillas/29567465/.

[5] M. Habibpour, H. Gharoun, A. Tajally, A. Shamsi, H. Asgharnezhad, A. Khosravi, S. Nahavandi, An Uncertainty-Aware Deep Learning Framework for Defect Detection in Casting Products (2021). arXiv:2107.11643.

[6] C.F. Higham, D.J. Higham, Deep learning: An introduction for applied mathematicians, SIAM Rev. 61 (4) (2019) 860–891.
[7] Y. Kwon, J.-H. Won, B.J. Kim, M.C. Paik, Uncertainty quantification using Bayesian neural networks in classification: Application to biomedical image segmentation, Comput. Stat. Data Anal. 142 (2020) 106816.
[8] J.A. Scales, R. Snieder, To bayes or not to bayes? Geophysics 62 (4) (1997) 1045–1046.
[9] J.A. Scales, L. Tenorio, Prior information and uncertainty in inverse problems, Geophysics 66 (2) (2001) 389–397.
[10] K. Mosegaard, A. Tarantola, et al., Probabilistic approach to inverse problems, Int. Geophys. Ser. 81 (A) (2002) 237–268.
[11] G.K. Stuart, S.E. Minkoff, F. Pereira, A two-stage Markov Chain Monte Carlo method for seismic inversion and uncertainty quantification, Geophysics 84 (6) (2019) R1003–R1020.
[12] D. Gamerman, H.F. Lopes, Markov Chain Monte Carlo: Stochastic Simulation for Bayesian Inference, CRC Press, 2006.
[13] S. Sharma, Markov Chain Monte Carlo methods for Bayesian data analysis in astronomy, Annu. Rev. Astron. Astrophys. 55 (2017) 213–259.
[14] F. Zucca, On some properties of transitions operators, arXiv preprint math/0103072 (2001).
[15] W. He, Z. Jiang, T. Xiao, Z. Xu, Y. Li, A survey on uncertainty quantification methods for deep learning, ACM Computing Surveys 58 (7) (2026) 1–35.
[16] M. Abdar, F. Pourpanah, S. Hussain, D. Rezazadegan, L. Liu, M. Ghavamzadeh, P. Fieguth, X. Cao, A. Khosravi, U.R. Acharya, et al., A review of uncertainty quantification in deep learning: Techniques, applications and challenges, Inf. Fusion 76 (2021) 243–297.
[17] R. Salakhutdinov, A. Mnih, Bayesian probabilistic matrix factorization using Markov Chain Monte Carlo, in: Proceedings of the 25th International Conference on Machine Learning, 2008, pp. 880–887.
[18] T. Chen, E. Fox, C. Guestrin, Stochastic gradient Hamiltonian Monte Carlo, in: International Conference on Machine Learning, PMLR, 2014, pp. 1683–1691.
[19] W. Gong, S. Tschiatschek, S. Nowozin, R.E. Turner, J.M. Hernández-Lobato, C. Zhang, Icebreaker: Element-wise efficient information acquisition with a Bayesian deep latent Gaussian model, Adv. Neural Inf. Process. Syst. 32 (2019).
[20] C. Li, C. Chen, Y. Pu, R. Henao, L. Carin, Communication-efficient stochastic gradient MCMC for neural networks, Proc. AAAI Conf. Artif. Intell. 33 (2019) 4173–4180.
[21] R. Zhang, C. Li, J. Zhang, C. Chen, A. G. Wilson, Cyclical stochastic gradient MCMC for Bayesian deep learning, arXiv preprint arXiv:1902.03932 (2019).
[22] R. Luo, J. Wang, Y. Yang, J. Wang, Z. Zhu, Thermostat-assisted continuously-tempered Hamiltonian Monte Carlo for Bayesian learning, Adv. Neural Inf. Process. Syst. 31 (2018).
[23] S. Hernández, D. Vergara, M. Valdenegro-Toro, F. Jorquera, Improving predictive uncertainty estimation using dropout-Hamiltonian Monte Carlo, Soft Comput. 24 (2020) 4307–4322.
[24] W. K. Hastings, Monte Carlo Sampling Methods Using Markov Chains and Their Applications (1970).
[25] C. Blundell, J. Cornebise, K. Kavukcuoglu, D. Wierstra, Weight uncertainty in neural network, in: International Conference on Machine Learning, PMLR, 2015, pp. 1613–1622.
[26] C. Zhang, J. Bütepage, H. Kjellström, S. Mandt, Advances in variational inference, IEEE Trans. Pattern Anal. Mach. Intell. 41 (8) (2018) 2008–2026.
[27] A. Graves, Practical variational inference for neural networks, Adv. Neural Inf. Process. Syst. 24 (2011).
[28] R. Seoh, Qualitative analysis of Monte Carlo dropout, arXiv preprint arXiv:2007.01720 (2020).
[29] D.M. Blei, A. Kucukelbir, J.D. McAuliffe, Variational inference: A review for statisticians, J. Am. Stat. Assoc. 112 (518) (2017) 859–877.
[30] K. Posch, J. Steinbrener, J. Pilz, Variational inference to measure model uncertainty in deep neural networks, arXiv preprint arXiv:1902.10189 (2019).
[31] K. Posch, J. Pilz, Correlated parameters to accurately measure uncertainty in deep neural networks, IEEE Transact. Neural Networks Learn. Syst. 32 (3) (2020) 1037–1051.
[32] R. Krishnan, M. Subedar, O. Tickoo, Efficient priors for scalable variational inference in Bayesian deep neural networks, in: Proceedings of the IEEE/CVF International Conference on Computer Vision Workshops, 2019.
[33] R. Krishnan, M. Subedar, O. Tickoo, Specifying weight priors in Bayesian deep neural networks with empirical bayes, in: Proceedings of the AAAI Conference on Artificial Intelligence 34, 2020, pp. 4477–4484.
[34] D. P. Kingma, M. Welling, Auto-encoding variational bayes, arXiv preprint arXiv:1312.6114 (2013).
[35] C. Louizos, M. Welling, Multiplicative normalizing flows for variational Bayesian neural networks, in: International Conference on Machine Learning, PMLR, 2017, pp. 2218–2227.
[36] A. Hubin, G. Storvik, Combining model and parameter uncertainty in Bayesian neural networks, arXiv preprint arXiv:1903.07594 (2019).
[37] S. Ryu, Y. Kwon, W.Y. Kim, A Bayesian graph convolutional network for reliable prediction of molecular properties with uncertainty quantification, Chem. Sci. 10 (36) (2019) 8438–8446.
[38] J. Swiatkowski, K. Roth, B. Veeling, L. Tran, J. Dillon, J. Snoek, S. Mandt, T. Salimans, R. Jenatton, S. Nowozin, The k-tied normal distribution: A compact parameterization of Gaussian mean field posteriors in Bayesian neural networks, in: International Conference on Machine Learning, PMLR, 2020, pp. 9289–9299.
[39] A. Hammam, F. Bonarens, S.E. Ghobadi, C. Stiller, Towards improved intermediate layer variational inference for uncertainty estimation, in: European Conference on Computer Vision, Springer, 2022, pp. 526–542.
[40] A. Hubin, G. Storvik, Variational inference for Bayesian neural networks under model and parameter uncertainty, arXiv Preprint arXiv:2305.00934 (2023).

[41] Z. Ma, A. Sattar, J. Zhou, Q. Chen, K. Su, Dropout with tabu strategy for regularizing deep neural networks, Comput. J. 63 (7) (2020) 1031–1038.

[42] P. McClure, N. Kriegeskorte, Representing inferential uncertainty in deep neural networks through sampling (2016).

[43] H. Liu, R. Ji, J. Li, B. Zhang, Y. Gao, Y. Wu, F. Huang, Universal adversarial perturbation via prior driven uncertainty approximation, in: Proceedings of the IEEE/CVF International Conference on Computer Vision, 2019, pp. 2941–2949.

[44] F. Verdoja, V. Kyrki, Notes on the behavior of mc dropout, arXiv preprint arXiv:2008.02627 (2020).

[45] A. Shamsi, H. Asgharnezhad, A. Tajally, S. Nahavandi, H. Leung, An uncertainty-aware loss function for training neural networks with calibrated predictions (2023). arXiv:2110.03260.

[46] T. Nair, D. Precup, D.L. Arnold, T. Arbel, Exploring uncertainty measures in deep networks for multiple sclerosis lesion detection and segmentation, Med. Image Anal. 59 (2020) 101557.

[47] K. Fabi, J. Schneider, On feature relevance uncertainty: A Monte Carlo dropout sampling approach, arXiv preprint arXiv:2008.01468 (2020).

[48] P. Goel, L. Chen, On the robustness of Monte Carlo dropout trained with noisy labels, in: Proceedings of the IEEE/CVF Conference on Computer Vision and Pattern Recognition, 2021, pp. 2219–2228.

[49] A. Lemay, K. Hoebel, C.P. Bridge, B. Befano, S. De Sanjosé, D. Egemen, A.C. Rodriguez, M. Schiffman, J.P. Campbell, J. Kalpathy-Cramer, Improving the repeatability of deep learning models with Monte Carlo dropout, Npj Digit. Med. 5 (1) (2022) 174.

[50] G. Wang, W. Li, M. Aertsen, J. Deprest, S. Ourselin, T. Vercauteren, Aleatoric uncertainty estimation with test-time augmentation for medical image segmentation with convolutional neural networks, Neurocomputing 338 (2019) 34–45.

[51] M.A.M. Sadr, Y. Zhu, P. Hu, An anomaly detection method for satellites using Monte Carlo dropout, IEEE Trans. Aero. Electron. Syst. 59 (2) (2022) 2044–2052.

[52] A. Kendall, V. Badrinarayanan, R. Cipolla, Bayesian segnet: model uncertainty in deep convolutional encoder-decoder architectures for scene understanding, in: Proceedings of the British Machine Vision Conference 2017, British Machine Vision Association, 2017.

[53] M.-H. Laves, S. Ihler, K.-P. Kortmann, T. Ortmaier, Well-calibrated model uncertainty with temperature scaling for dropout variational inference, arXiv preprint arXiv:1909.13550 (2019).

[54] M. Fortunato, C. Blundell, O. Vinyals, Bayesian recurrent neural networks, arXiv preprint arXiv:1704.02798 (2017).

[55] S. Ebrahimi, M. Elhoseiny, T. Darrell, M. Rohrbach, Uncertainty-guided continual learning with Bayesian neural networks, arXiv preprint arXiv:1906.02425 (2019).

[56] M. Ng, F. Guo, L. Biswas, S.E. Petersen, S.K. Piechnik, S. Neubauer, G. Wright, Estimating uncertainty in neural networks for cardiac MRI segmentation: a benchmark study, IEEE Trans. Biomed. Eng. 70 (6) (2022) 1955–1966.

[57] Y. Gal, R. Islam, Z. Ghahramani, Deep Bayesian active learning with image data, in: International Conference on Machine Learning, PMLR, 2017, pp. 1183–1192.

[58] S. Mohamadi, H. Amindavar, Deep Bayesian active learning, a brief survey on recent advances, arXiv preprint arXiv:2012.08044 (2020).

[59] Q. Wang, W. Wu, Y. Qi, Z. Xin, Combination of active learning and self-paced learning for deep answer selection with Bayesian neural network, in: ECAI 2020, IOS Press, 2020, pp. 1587–1594.

[60] G. Zhao, E. Dougherty, B.-J. Yoon, F.J. Alexander, X. Qian, Bayesian active learning by soft mean objective cost of uncertainty, in: International Conference on Artificial Intelligence and Statistics, PMLR, 2021, pp. 3970–3978.

[61] J. Zeng, A. Lesnikowski, J. M. Alvarez, The relevance of Bayesian layer positioning to model uncertainty in deep Bayesian active learning, arXiv preprint arXiv:1811.12535 (2018).

[62] A. Kirsch, J. Van Amersfoort, Y. Gal, Batchbald: Efficient and diverse batch acquisition for deep Bayesian active learning, Adv. Neural Inf. Process. Syst. 32 (2019).

[63] F.B. Smith, A. Kirsch, S. Farquhar, Y. Gal, A. Foster, T. Rainforth, Prediction-oriented Bayesian active learning, in: International Conference on Artificial Intelligence and Statistics, PMLR, 2023, pp. 7331–7348.

[64] R. Pop, P. Fulop, Deep ensemble Bayesian active learning: Addressing the mode collapse issue in Monte Carlo dropout via ensembles, arXiv preprint arXiv:1811.03897 (2018).

[65] D. E. Rumelhart, G. E. Hinton, R. J. Williams, et al., Learning internal representations by error propagation (1985).

[66] D. Bank, N. Koenigstein, R. Giryes, Autoencoders, Machine Learning for Data Science Handbook: Data Mining and Knowledge Discovery Handbook, 2023, pp. 353–374.

[67] U. Michelucci, An introduction to autoencoders, arXiv preprint arXiv:2201.03898 (2022).

[68] D. Addo, S. Zhou, J.K. Jackson, G.U. Nneji, H.N. Monday, K. Sarpong, R.A. Patamia, F. Ekong, C.A. Owusu-Agyei, Evae-net: An ensemble variational autoencoder deep learning network for covid-19 classification based on chest x-ray images, Diagnostics 12 (11) (2022) 2569.

[69] R. Zemouri, M. Lévesque, É. Boucher, M. Kirouac, F. Lafleur, S. Bernier, A. Merkhouf, Recent research and applications in variational autoencoders for industrial prognosis and health management: A survey, in: 2022 Prognostics and Health Management Conference, IEEE, PHM2022 London, 2022, pp. 193–203.

[70] X. Bie, L. Girin, S. Leglaive, T. Hueber, X. Alameda-Pineda, A benchmark of dynamical variational autoencoders applied to speech spectrogram modeling, arXiv preprint arXiv:2106.06500 (2021).

[71] X. Fu, Y. Wei, F. Xu, T. Wang, Y. Lu, J. Li, J.Z. Huang, Semi-supervised aspect-level sentiment classification model based on variational autoencoder, Knowl. Base Syst. 171 (2019) 81–92.

[72] V. Edupuganti, M. Mardani, S. Vasanawala, J. Pauly, Uncertainty quantification in deep MRI reconstruction, IEEE Trans. Med. Imag. 40 (1) (2020) 239–250.

[73] V. Böhm, F. Lanusse, U. Seljak, Uncertainty quantification with generative models, arXiv preprint arXiv:1910.10046 (2019).

[74] L. Jin, H. Lu, G. Wen, Fast uncertainty quantification of reservoir simulation with variational u-net, arXiv preprint arXiv:1907.00718 (2019).
[75] F. Guo, R. Xie, B. Huang, A deep learning just-in-time modeling approach for soft sensor based on variational autoencoder, Chemometr. Intell. Lab. Syst. 197 (2020) 103922.
[76] O. Sagi, L. Rokach, Ensemble learning: A survey, Wiley Interdiscip. Rev. Data Min. Knowl. Discovery 8 (4) (2018) e1249.
[77] M.H. Shaker, E. Hüllermeier, Ensemble-based uncertainty quantification: Bayesian versus credal inference, in: Proceedings 31 Workshop Computational Intelligence 25, 2021, p. 63.
[78] J. Schupbach, J.W. Sheppard, T. Forrester, Quantifying uncertainty in neural network ensembles using u-statistics, in: 2020 International Joint Conference on Neural Networks (IJCNN), IEEE, 2020, pp. 1–8.
[79] X. Yan, Y. Su, W. Ma, Ensemble multi-quantiles: adaptively flexible distribution prediction for uncertainty quantification, IEEE Trans. Pattern Anal. Mach. Intell. 45 (11) (2023) 13068–13082.
[80] R. Rahaman, et al., Uncertainty quantification and deep ensembles, Adv. Neural Inf. Process. Syst. 34 (2021) 2006320075.
[81] R. Egele, R. Maulik, K. Raghavan, B. Lusch, I. Guyon, P. Balaprakash, Autodeuq: Automated deep ensemble with uncertainty quantification, in: 2022 26th International Conference on Pattern Recognition (ICPR), IEEE, 2022, pp. 1908–1914.
[82] R. Knutti, C. Baumberger, G. Hirsch Hadorn, Uncertainty quantification using multiple models-prospects and challenges, in: Computer Simulation Validation: Fundamental Concepts, Methodological Frameworks, and Philosophical Perspectives, 2019, pp. 835–855.
[83] A. Ghosh, B. G. Sumpter, O. Dyck, S. V. Kalinin, M. Ziatdinov, Ensemble learning and iterative training (elit) machine learning: applications towards uncertainty quantification and automated experiment in atom-resolved microscopy, arXiv preprint arXiv:2101.08449 (2021).
[84] A. Schwaiger, P. Sinhamahapatra, J. Gansloser, K. Roscher, Is uncertainty quantification in deep learning sufficient for out-of-distribution detection? Aisafety@ijcai 54 (2020).
[85] T. Buddenkotte, L.E. Sanchez, M. Crispin-Ortuzar, R. Woitek, C. McCague, J.D. Brenton, O. Öktem, E. Sala, L. Rundo, Calibrating ensembles for scalable uncertainty quantification in deep learning-based medical image segmentation, Comput. Biol. Med. (2023) 107096.
[86] L. Smith, Structure and Uncertainty in Deep Learning, Ph.D. thesis, University of Oxford (2022).

Chapter 21

Equivariance and symmetry behind neural networks

Kia Ghods

Department of Computer Science, Princeton University, Princeton, NJ, United States

1. Introduction

The extraordinary success of deep learning has fundamentally transformed artificial intelligence, enabling remarkable advances in computer vision, natural language processing, and beyond. Yet beneath this empirical triumph lies a profound mathematical structure that is only beginning to be understood. While early neural networks achieved success through sheer computational power and large datasets, the most transformative architectures Convolutional Neural Networks (CNNs), Graph Neural Networks (GNNs), and Transformers–share a deeper organizing principle: the systematic exploitation of symmetry through equivariance.

The concept of symmetry has been central to scientific understanding since antiquity, from the crystallographic patterns studied by ancient mathematicians to the fundamental laws of physics that remain invariant under spatial and temporal transformations. In 1872, Felix Klein's Erlangen Program revolutionized geometry by proposing that different geometries could be unified through their underlying symmetry groups, establishing group theory as the mathematical language of symmetry [1]. This mathematical framework would eventually prove equally transformative for neural network design.

The emergence of CNNs in the 1980s and their spectacular success on ImageNet [2,3] demonstrated that architectural design choices profoundly impact learning performance. While the connection between CNNs and translational symmetry was implicit in their original design [2], it was the work of [4] that generalized this perspective into a systematic group-theoretic framework, formalizing equivariant neural networks for arbitrary discrete symmetry groups. This generalized framework reveals that CNNs succeed precisely because they respect the translational symmetry inherent in image data, automatically sharing parameters across spatial locations and generalizing learned features throughout the visual field—and that the same principle extends well beyond translation.

This discovery catalyzed the emergence of *Geometric Deep Learning*, a principled framework for designing neural architectures that explicitly encode domain-specific symmetries [5,6]. Rather than treating architectural innovations as isolated engineering advances, Geometric Deep Learning reveals deep connections between seemingly disparate methods: CNNs exploit translation symmetry, GNNs leverage permutation symmetry, and Transformers achieve equivariance through self-attention mechanisms before selectively breaking symmetry with positional encodings [7].

The implications extend far beyond individual architectures. When neural networks respect the natural symmetries of their input domains, they achieve superior data efficiency, enhanced generalization, and improved robustness compared with symmetry-agnostic alternatives [4,8]. This suggests that the path toward more capable AI systems may lie not merely in scaling computational resources, but in developing deeper mathematical understanding of the geometric and algebraic structures that govern learning.

This chapter provides a comprehensive mathematical foundation for understanding how symmetry principles govern neural network design. We begin by establishing the group-theoretic framework that formalizes symmetry. We then develop the concepts of equivariance and invariance, showing how these properties emerge as natural constraints on neural network architectures. Through rigorous analysis of CNNs, we demonstrate how discrete convolution implements

Advanced Intelligence Methods for Data Science and Optimization. https://doi.org/10.1016/B978-0-443-28940-8.00009-9

translational equivariance while pooling operations strategically introduce local invariance. Finally, we extend these principles to Graph Neural Networks and Transformers, revealing the universality of symmetry-aware design.

Our analysis positions these insights within the broader framework of Geometric Deep Learning, arguing that the most effective neural architectures are those that explicitly encode the inherent symmetries of their target domains. This symmetry-aware design philosophy offers a principled path toward more efficient, interpretable, and robust AI systems by leveraging mathematical structures rather than relying solely on increased data scale or computational power.

2. Mathematical foundations

2.1 Group theory fundamentals

To understand how symmetry governs the success of neural network architectures, we must first establish the mathematical framework that formalizes the concept of symmetry itself. Group theory provides this foundation, offering a precise language for describing and manipulating symmetric transformations.

2.1.1 Definitions and axioms

Definition 2.1. (Group). A group is an ordered pair $(G, \circ)$ consisting of a set G and a binary operation $\circ: G\times G \to G$ such that the following axioms are satisfied:

1. Closure: $\forall g_1, g_2 \in G$, we have $g_1 \circ g_2 \in G$.
2. Identity: $\exists e \in G$ such that $\forall g \in G$, $e \circ g = g \circ e = g$.
3. Associativity: $\forall g_1, g_2, g_3 \in G$, $(g_1 \circ g_2) \circ g_3 = g_1 \circ (g_2 \circ g_3)$.
4. Inverse: $\forall g \in G, \exists h \in G$ such that $g \circ h = h \circ g = e$.

2.1.2 Example: Dihedral group D_4

To ground these abstract concepts, we examine the dihedral group D_4, which encodes the symmetries of a square. This group serves as an ideal pedagogical example because its elements have clear geometric interpretations while exhibiting rich algebraic structure [4,6].

Definition 2.2. (Dihedral Group D_4). The dihedral group D_4 is the group of symmetries of a square, consisting of rotations and reflections that leave the square's geometric footprint unchanged. The group D_4 admits the following presentation:

$$D_4 = \langle r, f \,|\, r^4 = e, f^2 = e, rf = fr^{-1} \rangle$$

where

- r represents a 90° counterclockwise rotation
- f represents a reflection (e.g., about the vertical axis)
- e is the identity element (no transformation)

This presentation generates eight distinct elements:

$$D_4 = \{e, r, r^2, r^3, f, fr, fr^2, fr^3\}$$

The complete group structure is captured by group's multiplication table, or Cayley table (Table 21.1):
Verification of Group Axioms:

1. Closure: Every entry in the Cayley table belongs to D_4.
2. Identity: The row and column corresponding to e reproduce the group elements unchanged
3. Associativity: As the elements of D_4 are symmetries (bijections of the square), their composition behaves like function composition—which is associative.
4. Inverses: From the presentation, we can explicitly construct inverses: r^k has inverse r^{4-k} as $r^k \circ r^{4-k} = r^4 = e$, and fr^k has inverse fr^k as $(fr^k)(fr^k) = (r^{-k}f)fr^k = r^{-k}er^k = e$.

Notably, D_4 is non-Abelian, as demonstrated by the relation $rf \neq fr$ (equivalently, $rf = fr^{-1} = fr^3 \neq fr$).

TABLE 21.1 Cayley table for the dihedral group D_4.

$\circ$	e	r	r^2	r^3	f	fr	fr^2	fr^3
E	e	r	r^2	r^3	f	fr	fr^2	fr^3
r	r	r^2	r^3	e	fr^3	f	fr	fr^2
r^2	r^2	r^3	e	r	fr^2	fr^3	f	fr
r^3	r^3	e	r	r^2	fr	fr^2	fr^3	f
f	f	fr	fr^2	fr^3	e	r	r^2	r^3
fr	fr	fr^2	fr^3	f	r^3	e	r	r^2
fr^2	fr^2	fr^3	f	fr	r^2	r^3	e	r
fr^3	fr^3	f	fr	fr^2	r	r^2	r^3	e

2.2 Group actions on data

The power of group theory in machine learning emerges when groups act upon the data spaces that neural networks process. Group actions provide the formal mechanism by which abstract symmetries manifest as concrete transformations of images, graphs, or other structured data [4–6].

Definition 2.3. (Group Action). Let G be a group and X be a set (data space). A (left) group action of G on X is a function $\phi : G \times X \rightarrow X$, typically denoted as $\phi(g,x) = g{\cdot}x$, satisfying:

1. Identity: $e{\cdot}x = x$ for all $x \in X$.
2. Compatibility: $h{\cdot}(g{\cdot}x) = (h \circ g){\cdot}x$ for all $g, h \in G$ and $x \in X$.

These axioms ensure that the action respects the group structure, making the transformation of data algebraically consistent and predictable.

Example 2.1. (Action of D_4 on Images). Consider the action of D_4 on the space of square images $X = \mathbb{R}^{H \times W}$ where $H = W$. Each group element $g \in D_4$ acts by applying the corresponding geometric transformation:

- $e{\cdot}x = x$ (identity transformation)
- $r{\cdot}x$ rotates image x by 90° counterclockwise
- $f{\cdot}x$ reflects image x about the vertical axis
- $(r^2 f){\cdot}x$ applies reflection followed by 180° rotation

The compatibility axiom ensures that sequential transformations compose correctly: e.g., applying reflection f followed by rotation r yields the same result as applying the single transformation $fr^3 = rf$.

Lemma 2.1. (Orbit-Stabilizer). Let G be a finite group acting on a set X. For any point point $x \in X$, the orbit $\mathrm{Orb}(x) = \{g{\cdot}x : g \in G\}$ and stabilizer $\mathrm{Stab}(x) = \{g \in G | g{\cdot}x = x\}$ satisfy:

$$|\mathrm{Orb}(x)| \cdot |\mathrm{Stab}(x)| = |G|$$

Remark. For an arbitrary (possibly infinite) group G, the result generalizes to a bijection between the left cosets of $\mathrm{Stab}(x)$ in G and the elements of $\mathrm{Orb}(x)$, giving $[G : \mathrm{Stab}(x)] = |\mathrm{Orb}(x)|$, where $[G : H]$ denotes the index of subgroup H in G. This is the form needed when the acting group is infinite (e.g., the translation group $T \cong \mathbb{Z}^2$ of Section 4). This fundamental result will prove crucial for understanding how neural networks can leverage group structure for efficient learning and generalization.

3. Symmetry in machine learning

Now that we understand how a group action transforms data, we can ask a critical question: how should a function, such as a neural network layer, behave when its input is transformed? This brings us to the core concepts of equivariance and invariance.

3.1 Equivariance versus invariance

Definition 3.1. (Equivariant Function). Let G be a group acting on input space X and (possibly via a different representation) on output space Y. A function $f : X \rightarrow Y$ is G-equivariant if:

$$f(g \cdot x) = g \cdot f(x) \quad \forall g \in G, x \in X$$

We note that the dot on the left-hand side denotes the action of G on X, and the dot on the right-hand side denotes the action on Y; we use the same symbol for both, with the relevant action always clear from context.

That is, a function is equivariant if it doesn't matter whether we transform the input first and then apply the function, or apply the function first and then transform the output. The transformation and the function "commute." We note that this mathematical framework was formalized in the context of neural networks by Refs. [4,9].

Definition 3.2. (Invariant Function). A function $f : X \rightarrow Y$ is G invariant if:

$$f(g \cdot x) = f(x) \quad \forall g \in G, x \in X$$

Invariance is a special case of equivariance where the group acts trivially on the output space (i.e., $g \cdot y = y$ for all $\in G, y \in Y$). In other words, a function is invariant if its output is completely insensitive to transformations of the input.

3.1.1 Geometric interpretation

To understand these concepts intuitively, consider a function $\mathscr{F}_{\text{corner}}$ that detects the location of a specific corner in a square image. Under a 90° rotation $\in D_4$:

Equivariant behavior: If the corner was originally at position (i, j), after rotation it appears at the rotated position. The function output transforms predictably with the input transformation.

Invariant behavior: A classification function $\mathscr{F}_{\text{class}}$ that outputs "square" should return the same label regardless of the square's orientation.

3.1.2 Commutative diagram

Another way to understand equivariance is through the following commutative diagram. For an equivariant function $\mathscr{F} : X \rightarrow Y$, the following diagram commutes:

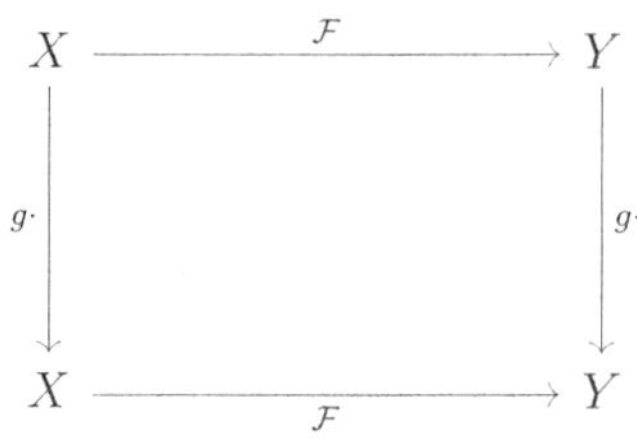

That is, both paths from the top-left X to the bottom-right Y yield identical results: $\mathscr{F} \circ g = g \circ \mathscr{F}$ when viewing group elements as transformation operators.

3.2 Inductive biases from symmetry

3.2.1 Inductive bias through architectural constraints

When we design neural networks to be equivariant to certain transformations, we embed powerful inductive biases into the model architecture. This has profound implications for learning efficiency and generalization.

Theorem 3.1. (Parameter Sharing in Equivariant Networks). If a neural network layer is designed to be G-equivariant, then parameters are automatically shared across all transformations in the group orbit of any input location.

Proof Sketch: Equivariance requires that the response to $g \cdot x$ equals g applied to the response to x. This constraint forces the same computational rule (and thus parameters) to apply at all locations related by group transformations.

This fundamental result explains the parameter sharing mechanism underlying CNN success [2,4]; moreover, parameter sharing has two critical benefits:

1. **Data Efficiency**: The model learns from effectively augmented data without requiring explicit augmentation. Each training example implicitly provides information about all its group transformations. This principle has been demonstrated across various domains [4,8].
2. **Generalization:** Patterns learned at one location automatically generalize to all locations reachable by group transformations, reducing overfitting and improving robustness.

4. Convolutional Neural Networks through the lens of symmetry

Convolutional Neural Networks represent one of the most successful applications of symmetry principles in deep learning. Their architecture directly implements translational equivariance through the convolution operation while achieving progressive invariance through pooling mechanisms. This section provides a rigorous mathematical analysis of how CNNs exploit translational symmetry.

4.1 The translation group and its action on images

Before analyzing convolution, we must formalize the symmetry that CNNs are designed to respect.

Definition 4.1. (Translation Group). The translation group in $\mathbb{Z}^2$ is:

$$T = \{t_{(a,b)} | (a,b) \in \mathbb{Z}^2\}$$

where $t_{(a,b)}$ represents translation by (a, b) pixels.

This group acts on discrete images $x \in \mathbb{R}^{H \times W}$ through:

$$(t_{(a,b)} \cdot x)[i,j] = x[i-a, j-b]$$

with appropriate boundary conditions (zero-padding, periodic, etc.). The mathematical formalization of translation symmetry in CNNs builds on foundational work [2,4].

Lemma 4.1. (Translation Group Properties). The translation group T satisfies:

1. **Closure:** $t_{(a,b)} \circ t_{(c,d)} = t_{(a+c,b+d)} \in T$.
2. **Identity:** $t_{(0,0)}$ is the identity element
3. **Associativity:** translation composition is associative
4. **Inverse:** $t^{-1}_{(a,b)} = t_{(-a,-b)}$.

Moreover, the group $(T, \circ)$ is isomorphic to $(\mathbb{Z}^2, +)$, making it an abelian group.

4.2 Convolution as equivariant operation

The fundamental insight underlying CNN success is that discrete convolution naturally implements translational equivariance.

Definition 4.2. (Discrete Convolution). For input $x \in \mathbb{R}^{H \times W}$ and kernel $k \in \mathbb{R}^{K \times K}$, the convolution operation is:

$$(x * k)[i,j] = \sum_{m=0}^{K-1} \sum_{n=0}^{K-1} x[i+m, j+n] \cdot k[m,n]$$

Remark on convention. Strictly speaking, the operation defined above is the cross-correlation of x with k; the mathematical convolution flips the kernel through the origin, giving $\sum_{m,n} x[i-m, j-n] \cdot k[m,n]$. We follow the universal convention in the deep learning literature [2], in which "convolution" refers to cross-correlation. The distinction is immaterial for our context, as both operations are translation-equivariant (Theorem 4.1), and since the kernel is learned, the two conventions are operationally equivalent, in that a kernel learned under one is the reflection through the origin of the kernel learned under the other.

Theorem 4.1. (Translation Equivariance of Convolution). The convolution operation is equivariant with respect to the translation group. Specifically:

$$t_{(a,b)} \cdot (x * k) = (t_{(a,b)} \cdot x) * k$$

Proof: We need to show that translating the output is equivalent to translating the input before convolution.
Left-hand side (translate output):

$$\left(t_{(a,b)}\cdot(x*k)\right)[i,j] = (x*k)[i-a,j-b]$$
$$= \sum_{m=0}^{K-1}\sum_{n=0}^{K-1} x[i-a+m,j-b+n]\cdot k[m,n]$$

Right-hand side (translate input):

$$\left((t_{(a,b)}\cdot x)*k\right)[i,j] = \sum_{m=0}^{K-1}\sum_{n=0}^{K-1}\left(t_{(a,b)}\cdot x\right)[i+m,j+n]\cdot k[m,n]$$
$$= \sum_{m=0}^{K-1}\sum_{n=0}^{K-1} x[i+m-a,j+n-b]\cdot k[m,n]$$

Both expressions are identical, completing the proof.□

This equivariance property was first rigorously analyzed in Ref. [4] and forms the theoretical foundation for CNN effectiveness [2,3].

Corollary 4.1. (Multichannel Equivariance). For multichannel convolution with input $x \in \mathbb{R}^{C_{\text{in}}\times H\times W}$ and kernels $K \in \mathbb{R}^{C_{\text{out}}\times C_{\text{in}}\times K_H\times K_W}$, translation equivariance is preserved:

$$t_{(a,b)}\cdot(x*K) = \left(t_{(a,b)}\cdot x\right)*K$$

4.2.1 Parameter sharing through equivariance

The equivariance property directly explains the parameter sharing mechanism in CNNs.

Proposition 4.1. (Spatial Parameter Sharing). Translation equivariance requires that the same kernel parameters be applied at every spatial location.

Proof: Suppose different parameters were used at different locations. Then, translating an input would require different computations at each translated position, violating equivariance. Therefore, identical parameters must be shared across all spatial positions. □

This mathematical constraint provides the theoretical foundation for CNN's computational efficiency and generalization ability.

4.3 Pooling and the introduction of invariance

While convolution preserves translational structure through equivariance, pooling operations strategically break this symmetry to achieve local invariance [2,4].

Definition 4.3. (Max Pooling). For input feature map $x \in \mathbb{R}^{H\times W}$ and pooling window size $p\times p$, max pooling is:

$$\text{MaxPool}_p(x)[i,j] = \max_{0\le m,n<p} x[pi+m,pj+n]$$

Theorem 4.2 (Pooling and Translation). Let MaxPool_p denote non-overlapping max pooling with window size p applied to a feature map $x \in \mathbb{R}^{H\times W}$. (i) Equivariance modulo subsampling. For any translation by an integer multiple of the stride, MaxPool_p is exactly equivariant: $\text{MaxPool}_p\left(t_{(pa,pb)}\cdot x\right) = t_{(a,b)}\cdot\text{MaxPool}_p(x)$ for all $(a,b)\in\mathbb{Z}^2$. (ii) Approximate local invariance. For a translation $t_{(a,b)}$ with $|a|,|b|<p$, the pooling output at position (i,j) is computed over a shifted window $[pi-a,pi-a+p)\times[pj-b,pj-b+p)$ which overlaps the original window in a $(p-|a|)\times(p-|b|)$ region. The output is exactly unchanged whenever the argmax of x over the original window lies in this overlap and remains the maximum over the shifted window. In typical CNN feature maps, where activations are spatially concentrated and pool windows are small relative to the scale of feature variation, this condition holds for most positions, yielding approximation (rather than exact) invariance to sub-window translations. *Proof of (i).* By definition, $\text{MaxPool}_p\left(t_{(pa,pb)}\cdot x\right)[i,j] = \max_{0\le m,n<p} x[pi+m-pa,pj+n-pb] = \text{MaxPool}_p(x)[i-a,j-b] = \left(t_{(a,b)}\right)\cdot\text{MaxPool}_p(x)[i,j]$. *Proof of (ii).* Direct from hypothesis: if some position (i^*,j^*) attains the max over both the original and shifted windows, both pooling outputs equal $x[i^*,j^*]$.

4.3.1 The equivariance-invariance hierarchy

CNNs implement a carefully designed progression from equivariance to invariance.

1. **Convolutional Layers**: Maintain strict translation equivariance, preserving spatial relationships while detecting features
2. **Pooling Layers:** Introduce controlled local invariance, reducing sensitivity to precise feature locations
3. **Global Pooling/Flattening:** Achieve complete translation invariance for final classification

Theorem 4.3 (Hierarchical Invariance). Consider a CNN $f = f_{\text{global}} \circ f_L \circ \cdots \circ f_1$ in which each convolutional block is translation-equivariant in the sense of Theorem 4.1 (with pooling components contributing equivariance modulo subsampling, Theorem 4.2 (i)), and f_{global} is global average pooling, $f_{\text{global}}(y) = (HW)^{-1}\sum_{i,j} y[i,j]$. Let $s \in \mathbb{Z}_{>0}$ denote the cumulative subsampling factor of the feature extractor $F := f_L \circ \cdots \circ f_1$.
On inputs defined on the full integer lattice $\mathbb{Z}^2$, f is invariant to all translations byinteger multiples of s

$$f\left(t_{(sa,sb)} \cdot x\right) = f(x) \quad \forall (a,b) \in \mathbb{Z}^2, x$$

On finite inputs with zero-padding, the same identity holds up to boundary effects, which are negligible when feature activations are spatially concentrated away from the image border.

4.4 Mathematical analysis of CNN architecture

4.4.1 Formal CNN definition

Definition 4.4. (Convolutional Neural Network). A CNN is a function composition:

$$f = f_{\text{global}} \circ f_L \circ \cdots \circ f_1$$

where each f_i is a convolutional block:

$$f_i(x) = \sigma(\text{Pool}(x * K_i + b_i))$$

with σ a nonlinear activation, K_i learnable kernels, and b_i bias terms.

4.4.2 Receptive field and group orbits

Definition 4.5. (Receptive Field). The receptive field of a neuron at position (i,j) in layer ℓ is the set of input positions that influence that neuron's activation.

Proposition 4.2. (Receptive Field Symmetry). Due to translation equivariance, all neurons at the same layer have identically sized and shaped receptive fields, differing only by a translation.

This property ensures that the same feature detection capability exists at every spatial location, embodying the translation symmetry principle.

4.4.3 Feature map transformations

Lemma 4.2. (Feature Map Equivariance). For a feature map $F^{(\ell)} \in \mathbb{R}^{C \times H \times W}$ at layer ℓ:

$$F^{(\ell)}(t_{(a,b)} \cdot x) = t_{(a',b')} \cdot F^{(\ell)}(x)$$

where (a', b') represents the translation in the feature space coordinates, accounting for stride and pooling effects.

This result shows that the hierarchical feature representations in CNNs maintain predictable geometric relationships under input transformations.

4.5 Implications for learning and generalization

The mathematical structure of CNNs provides several key advantages.

1. **Sample Efficiency:** Each training example effectively provides information about all its translated versions
2. **Parameter Efficiency:** Shared parameters across spatial locations reduce model complexity
3. **Generalization:** Features learned at one location automatically apply everywhere
4. **Robustness:** Local invariance through pooling provides tolerance to small spatial variations

These benefits arise directly from the principled application of group theory to neural network design, demonstrating the power of symmetry-aware architectures.

The next section extends these principles beyond translation symmetry to explore how other symmetries are exploited in modern deep learning architectures.

5. Extensions and applications

The principles of symmetry and equivariance extend far beyond the translational symmetry of images. Modern deep learning's most successful architectures across diverse domains—from graph neural networks to transformers—can be understood through the same mathematical lens. This section demonstrates the universality of symmetry-aware design principles.

5.1 Graph Neural Networks and permutation symmetry

Graphs represent relationships between entities without inherent ordering, making them naturally symmetric under permutations of node labels. Graph Neural Networks (GNNs) are specifically designed to respect this fundamental symmetry.

5.1.1 The Permutation Group and graph symmetry

Definition 5.1. (Permutation Group). The symmetric group S_n is the group of all permutations of n elements:

$$S_n = \{\pi: \{1,2,\ldots,n\} \to \{1,2,\ldots,n\} | \pi \text{ is bijective }\}$$

For a graph $G = (V,E)$ with $|V| = n$, any permutation $\pi \in S_n$ acts on the graph by relabeling vertices:

$$\pi \cdot G = (V, \{(\pi(u), \pi(v)) : (u,v) \in E\})$$

Graph neural networks exploit permutation symmetry to process graph structured data [10–13].

Lemma 5.1. (Graph Isomorphism and Permutation). Two graphs are isomorphic if and only if one can be obtained from the other by a permutation of vertex labels.

By Lemma 5.1, it follows that any meaningful function on graphs must be invariant to vertex relabeling–equivalent to permutation symmetry.

5.1.2 Message-passing as permutation-equivariant operation

Definition 5.2. (Message-Passing Neural Network). A message-passing GNN updates node representations through:

$$h_v^{(t+1)} = \text{UPDATE}^{(t)}\left(h_v^{(t)}, \text{AGGREGATE}^{(t)}\left(\{h_u^{(t)} : u \in \mathcal{N}(v)\}\right)\right)$$

where $\mathcal{N}(v)$ denotes the neighbors of node v.

Theorem 5.1. (Permutation Equivariance of Message-Passing). If the AGGREGATE function is permutation-invariant (e.g., sum, mean, max), then the message-passing operation is permutation-equivariant.

We note that this fundamental result was established in Ref. [13a] and forms the basis for understanding GNN expressivity.

Let $\pi \in S_n$. For a graph with feature matrix $H = [h_1, \ldots, h_n]^\top$ and adjacency A, the action of π pushes features and adjacency forward: we define $(\pi \cdot H)\{\pi(v)\} := h_v$ and $(\pi \cdot A)\{\pi(u), \pi(v)\} := A_{u,v}$ for all $u, v \in V$. Under this convention, the feature at node $\pi(v)$ of the permuted graph $(\pi \cdot H, \pi \cdot A)$ is h_v, and the neighbors of $\pi(v)$ are $\pi(u) : u \in N(v)$ with features $\{h_u : u \in N(v)\}$. The message-passing update at node $\pi(v)$ of the permuted graph is therefore $[\text{MP}(\pi \cdot H^{(t)}, \pi \cdot A)]\{\pi(v)\} = \text{UPDATE}^{(t)}(h_v^{(t)}, \text{AGGREGATE}^{(t)}(h\pi(u)^{(t)} : u \in N(v)))$. The aggregation argument is a multiset listing of the features $\{h_u^{(t)}\}$ (just under relabeled indices), and since $\text{AGGREGATE}^{(t)}$ depends on its input only as a multiset, its value equals $\text{AGGREGATE}^{(t)}(\{h_u^{(t)} : u \in N(v)\})$. Substituting, $[\text{MP}(\pi \cdot H^{(t)}, \pi \cdot A)]\{\pi(v)\} = \text{UPDATE}^{(t)}(h_v^{(t)}, \text{AGGREGATE}(\{h_u^{(t)} : u \in N(v)\})) = h_v^{(t+1)} = [\pi \cdot \text{MP}(H^{(t)}, A)]\{\pi(v)\}$. Since this holds for every $v \in V$, $\text{MP}(\pi \cdot H^{(t)}, \pi \cdot A) = \pi \cdot \text{MP}(H^{(t)}, A)$.

Corollary 5.1. (Graph-Level Invariance). By composing permutation equivariant layers with a permutation-invariant readout function (e.g., sum over all nodes), GNNs achieve permutation invariance for graph-level tasks.

5.2 Transformers and attention mechanisms

Transformers [7] demonstrate a fascinating approach to symmetry: they begin with complete permutation equivariance and selectively break it through positional encodings when sequence order matters.

5.2.1 Self-attention as permutation-equivariant operation

Definition 5.3. (Self-Attention). For input sequence $X \in \mathbb{R}^{n\times d}$, selfattention computes:

$$\text{Attention}(Q,K,V) = \text{softmax}\left(\frac{QK^\top}{\sqrt{d_k}}\right)V$$

where $Q = XW_Q, K = XW_K, V = XW_V$ are query, key, and value matrices.

Theorem 5.3. (Permutation Equivariance of Self-Attention). Self-attention without positional encodings is permutation-equivariant.

Interestingly, this equivariance property was noted in Ref. [7] and explains why positional encodings are necessary.

Proof: Let $\pi \in S_n$ be a permutation acting on sequences by reordering rows. We represent this as left-multiplication by the permutation matrix P_π. For input $X \in \mathbb{R}^{n\times d}$, the permuted input is $\pi\cdot X = P_\pi X$.

For the attention computation:

- $Q' = (\pi\cdot X)W_Q = \pi\cdot(XW_Q) = \pi\cdot Q = P_\pi Q$
- $K' = (\pi\cdot X)W_K = \pi\cdot K = P_\pi K$
- $V' = (\pi\cdot X)W_V = \pi\cdot V = P_\pi V$

And thus, the attention weights become:

$$A' = \text{softmax}\left(\frac{Q'(K')^\top}{\sqrt{d_k}}\right) = \text{softmax}\left(\frac{(P_\pi Q)(P_\pi K)^\top}{\sqrt{d_k}}\right)$$

As $(P_\pi K)^\top = K^\top P_\pi^\top$ and $P_\pi^\top = P_\pi^{-1}$ for permutation matrices:

$$A' = \text{softmax}\left(\frac{P_\pi QK^\top P_\pi^{-1}}{\sqrt{d_k}}\right)$$

Observe that for permutation matrices, $P_\pi QK^\top P_\pi^{-1}$ is exactly the matrix $QK^\top$ with both rows and columns permuted by π. The softmax operation applies row-wise, so:

$$\text{softmax}\left(P_\pi MP_\pi^{-1}\right) = P_\pi\text{softmax}(M)P_\pi^{-1}$$

where $M = QK^\top/\sqrt{d_k}$ Thus, $A' = P_\pi AP_\pi^{-1}$ where $A = \text{softmax}\left(QK^\top/\sqrt{d_k}\right)$.

Hence, we have that

$$\begin{aligned}\text{Attention}(\pi\cdot X) = A'V' &= \left(P_\pi AP_\pi^{-1}\right)(P_\pi V) = P_\pi AV\\ &= P_\pi\ \text{Attention}\ (X) = \pi\cdot\ \text{Attention}\ (\text{X})\end{aligned}$$

This establishes permutation equivariance. □

5.2.2 Positional encodings: Controlled Symmetry Breaking

Definition 5.4. (Positional Encoding). Positional encodings add position-dependent information to break permutation symmetry:

$$\widetilde{X} = X + PE$$

where $PE \in \mathbb{R}^{n\times d}$ encodes positional information.

Proposition 5.1. (Symmetry Breaking). With positional encodings, transformers are no longer permutation-equivariant, enabling sequence order sensitivity.

This design choice illustrates a key principle: start with maximal symmetry, then break it selectively where domain knowledge requires it.

5.2.3 Comparison with CNNs: Built-in versus additive geometry

The contrast between CNNs and Transformers reveals two approaches to handling geometric structure [2,6,7]:

CNNs: Geometry is built into the architecture through convolution's spatial structure. Translation equivariance is fundamental and cannot be removed.

Transformers: Begin with no geometric assumptions (permutation equivariance), then add geometric information through positional encodings. This modularity allows the same architecture to handle sequences, images, or graphs.

6. Conclusion

This chapter has demonstrated that the remarkable success of modern deep learning architectures can be understood through the lens of symmetry and group theory. Far from being merely empirical engineering advances, Convolutional Neural Networks, Graph Neural Networks, and Transformers represent systematic applications of profound mathematical principles that have governed scientific understanding for over a century.

Our analysis reveals several key insights. First, the effectiveness of CNNs stems directly from their implementation of translational equivariance through discrete convolution, with parameter sharing emerging as a natural mathematical consequence rather than an ad hoc design choice. Second, the progression from equivariant feature extraction to invariant classification through pooling operations reflects a principled hierarchy that balances information preservation with task-specific requirements. Third, this same mathematical framework extends seamlessly to other domains: GNNs exploit permutation symmetry to process graph-structured data [10,11], while Transformers achieve permutation equivariance through self-attention before selectively breaking symmetry with positional encodings [7].

These findings support the central thesis of Geometric Deep Learning: that the most effective neural architectures are those that explicitly encode the natural symmetries of their input domains [6]. This

perspective transforms neural architecture design from an art into a science, providing principled guidelines for developing models that are simultaneously more efficient, more interpretable, and more robust.

6.1 Future directions and emerging paradigms

The mathematical foundations established in this chapter point toward several promising research directions that extend beyond traditional symmetry considerations.

Higher-Order Symmetries and Gauge Theories: Recent work has begun exploring more sophisticated symmetries, including gauge equivariance [14] and coordinate-independent representations [15]. These approaches promise to handle more complex geometric transformations while maintaining computational tractability.

Topological Data Analysis in Neural Networks: An exciting frontier lies at the intersection of neural networks and topological data analysis (TDA). Persistent homology and other topological tools are beginning to provide new insights into neural network behavior, from analyzing decision boundaries to understanding representational geometry [16]. TDA offers a natural extension of symmetry-based analysis by capturing global structural properties that persist across multiple scales, potentially revealing why certain architectures excel at specific tasks.

Learned and Adaptive Symmetries: Rather than hard-coding symmetries into architectures, emerging approaches seek to learn relevant symmetries directly from data [17]. This includes discovering unknown symmetries in scientific datasets, adapting symmetry constraints during training, and developing architectures that can selectively break symmetries when beneficial for specific tasks.

The mathematical framework developed in this chapter—connecting abstract algebra to practical neural network design—represents more than theoretical insight. It offers a roadmap for the systematic development of AI systems that are grounded in deep mathematical principles rather than empirical trial and error. As we continue to push the boundaries of artificial intelligence, this principled approach to architectural design will likely prove essential for creating systems that are not only more powerful, but also more reliable, interpretable, and aligned with the fundamental structures that govern our world.

The story of symmetry in neural networks is far from complete. Just as Klein's Erlangen Program unified seemingly disparate geometries through group theory, the geometric deep learning framework promises to unify our understanding of neural architectures through their underlying symmetries. This mathematical lens not only explains past successes but illuminates the path toward future breakthroughs in artificial intelligence.

References

[1] M. Artin, Algebra, Pearson Prentice Hall, 2011.

[2] Y. Lecun, L. Bottou, Y. Bengio, P. Haffner, Gradient-based learning applied to document recognition, Proc. IEEE 86 (1998) 2278–2324, https://doi.org/10.1109/5.726791.

[3] A. Krizhevsky, I. Sutskever, G.E. Hinton, ImageNet classification with deep convolutional neural networks, in: Advances in Neural Information Processing Systems (NeurIPS), 2012, pp. 1097–1105.

[4] T.S. Cohen, M. Welling, Group equivariant convolutional networks, in: International Conference on Machine Learning (ICML), PMLR, 2016, pp. 2990–2999.

[5] M.M. Bronstein, J. Bruna, Y. LeCun, A. Szlam, P. Vandergheynst, Geometric deep learning: going beyond Euclidean data, IEEE Signal Process. Mag. 34 (2017) 18–42, https://doi.org/10.1109/MSP.2017.2693418.

[6] M.M. Bronstein, J. Bruna, T. Cohen, P. Veličković, Geometric Deep Learning: Grids, Groups, Graphs, Geodesics, and Gauges, 2021 arXiv:2104.13478.

[7] A. Vaswani, N. Shazeer, N. Parmar, J. Uszkoreit, L. Jones, A.N. Gomez, L. Kaiser, I. Polosukhin, Attention is all you need, in: Advances in Neural Information Processing Systems (NeurIPS), 2017, pp. 5998–6008.

[8] S. Dieleman, J.D. Fauw, K. Kavukcuoglu, Exploiting cyclic symmetry in convolutional neural networks, in: International Conference on Machine Learning (ICML), PMLR, 2016, pp. 1889–1898.

[9] R. Kondor, S. Trivedi, On the generalization of equivariance and convolution in neural networks to the action of compact groups, in: International Conference on Machine Learning (ICML), 2018, pp. 2747–2755.

[10] K. Xu, W. Hu, J. Leskovec, S. Jegelka, How powerful are graph neural networks? in: International Conference on Learning Representations (ICLR), 2019.

[11] T.S. Cohen, M. Welling, Steerable CNNs. International Conference on Learning Representations (ICLR), 2017.

[12] W.L. Hamilton, R. Ying, J. Leskovec, Inductive representation learning on large graphs, in: I. Guyon, U.V. Luxburg, S. Bengio, H. Wallach, R. Fergus, S. Vishwanathan, R. Garnett (Eds.), Advances in Neural Information Processing Systems (NeurIPS), 2017, pp. 1024–1034.

[13] P. Veličković, G. Cucurull, A. Casanova, A. Romero, P. Liò, Y. Bengio, Graph attention networks, in: International Conference on Learning Representations (ICLR), 2018.

[13a] T.N. Kipf, M. Welling, Semi-supervised classification with graph convolutional networks, in: International Conference on Learning Representations (ICLR), 2017.

[14] T.S. Cohen, M. Weiler, B. Kicanaoglu, M. Welling, Gauge equivariant convolutional networks and the icosahedral CNN, in: International Conference on Machine Learning (ICML), PMLR, 2019, pp. 1321–1330.

[15] Weiler, M., Cesa, G., General E(2)-Equivariant Steerable CNNs, in: Advances in Neural Information Processing Systems (NeurIPS), 2019, pp. 14334–14345.

[16] S. Watanabe, H. Yamana, Topological measurement of deep neural networks using persistent homology, Ann. Math. Artif. Intell. 90 (2022) 75–92, https://doi.org/10.1007/s10472-021-09761-3.

[17] A. Perin, S. Deny, On the ability of deep networks to learn symmetries from data: a neural Kernel theory, J. Mach. Learn. Res. (JMLR) 26 (2025) 1–70.

Index

'*Note:* Page numbers followed by "f" indicate figures and "t" indicate tables.'

E

F

T

U

V

9780443289408